THE PLAYBOY INTERVIEW II

The PLAYBOY INTERVIEW

VOLUME II

edited by G. Barry Golson

A WIDEVIEW/PERIGEE BOOK

Perigee Books
are published by
The Putnam Publishing Group
200 Madison Avenue
New York, New York 10016

Published simultaneously in Canada by General Publishing
Co. Limited, Toronto.

Library of Congress Cataloging in Publication Data

Main entry under title:

The Playboy interview II.

1. Biography—20th century. 2. Interviews.
3. Interviewing (Journalism) I. Golson, G. Barry.
II. Playboy. III. Title: Playboy interview 2.
IV. Title: Playboy interview two.
CT120.P554 1983 081 82-19071
ISBN 0-399-50768-X
ISBN 0-399-50769-8 (pbk.)

First Perigee printing, 1983.
Printed in the United States of America.
1 2 3 4 5 6 7 8 9

CONTENTS

FOREWORD

While the public and critical reception given to the first volume of *The Playboy Interview* has been a source of pride to the journalists and editors involved, it is particularly satisfying to issue this second volume. Now, it's true that anyone who has ever had to justify a sequel inevitably comes up with reasons to insist the second work is as important as the first. But if the reader will be patient . . .

First, a brief recap of what this feature is and how it came to be. (For a more detailed account, please see the Foreword in Volume I.) In 1962, at the urging of editor-publisher Hugh M. Hefner, PLAYBOY editor Murray Fisher fashioned the magazine's first Q-and-A out of a series of conversations between writer Alex Haley and jazz musician Miles Davis. Unlike the celebrity profiles that were a staple of magazine journalism then, Fisher insisted on a breadth, a thoroughness, and a candor that were unprecedented. In subsequent interviews, both journalist and subject would persist until something close to the goal—a verbal autobiography—had been achieved. The standards set by Fisher; the look of the feature, designed by art director Art Paul; and the roster of subjects interviewed combined to produce one of the most widely imitated and ultimately most widely respected journalistic forums in the world.

I began supervising the interviews in 1974, under the editorship of Arthur Kretchmer. Together, we added a strong sense of news and topicality to the interviews so that by the end of the decade their visibility was very high. It was at that time that we decided to collect the most memorable pieces in an anthology issued in 1981. It was that selection process—I chose thirty-one interviews out of over two hundred—that produced, understandably, a bias toward the "classics"—those giants such as Martin Luther King, Jr., Fidel Castro, Albert Schweitzer, Jimmy Carter, which loomed most strongly in the memory. Many fascinating interviews with people in a variety of professions thus had to be omitted from the first volume.

In this volume we can take the time to know historian Arnold Toynbee, racist Robert Shelton, religious deprogrammer Ted Patrick, Vietnam turncoat Robert Garwood; their names may be less familiar, but their ideas and experiences, as drawn from them by their interrogators, affected our lives and times. Entertainers such as Robert Redford or Johnny Carson are not only surprisingly thoughtful and articulate on a wide variety of subjects, but may well have had a wider impact in the world of ideas than expected. Finally, this volume affords the opportunity to include some people who simply were passed over for space reasons—Ayn Rand, Salvador Dali, William Buckley—and whom it is a pleasure to introduce at last. Together, the two collections reflect accurately a full cross section of PLAYBOY's "candid conversations."

Because these interviews appeared in a certain context of time and events, I have provided brief introductions to each piece to remind the reader of what was happening then, and why the editors made the selections they did. Where appropriate, I have also provided some background on how the interview was conducted. (Where I played some role, I refer to myself in the third person for consistency.)

For space reasons as well as readability I have greatly condensed the biographical data that accompanied the interviews, and in some cases I have trimmed the interviews themselves. This has been done only to shorten now-familiar accounts of events or to reduce material that is irrelevant today—plugs for upcoming books and movies, for instance. In no case has more than 10 percent of an interview been edited.

A few words on technique (also recalling the Foreword in Volume I): As originated by editor Fisher, the procedure, following anywhere from six to twenty-five hours of tape-recorded conversations, was to refine the raw verbiage of a tape transcript into a linear, continuous conversation. The refining did not mean that liberties were taken with the spoken words, but rather that the material was distilled of repetitions and meanderings for the sake of the printed page—which listeners can mentally edit out, but readers cannot. That the technique is successful is supported by the fact that many of the interviewees later said publicly that no other interview had ever reported so faithfully what they said—even though no PLAYBOY interview was ever published verbatim. And although the conversation is sometimes published as if there were no breaks between topics, it has always been made clear to the reader that a PLAYBOY interview is the melding of several or many conversations between subject and journalist.

Since the publication of Volume I, another tradition has continued just as vigorously: timeliness, often unexplainable in terms of PLAYBOY's long lead time. Volume I concluded with the tragic death of John Lennon as his interview was being read by PLAYBOY subscribers. Since then, Robert Garwood's interview appeared just as his Marine court-martial wound up; Henry Fonda's as infirmity and an Oscar caught up with him; Lech Walesa's on the very week that martial law was declared in Poland; and Edward Koch's days after his unexpected bid for the governorship of New York State. Appearing in a magazine whose interview subjects are selected six months in advance, these occurrences can only be explained as fitting into a certain rhythm and tradition of newsworthiness, and not necessarily as the logical outcome of editorial acumen, alas.

Since the interviews are the product of individual work and care, this is the place to thank and acknowledge such veterans of Volume I as Larry Dubois, Larry Grobel, Sam Merrill, PLAYBOY senior editor Gretchen McNeese, and Robert Scheer, and to add to the list such continuing contributors as Flo Conway and Jim Siegelman, Winston Groom, Anya and Kristina Bittenek, and Peter Manso. There are others whose work is deeply appreciated, but goes unmentioned in this collection—no doubt awaiting inclusion in another volume in the years to come. Finally, thanks to Thia Golson and Laura MacKenzie for help and advice in preparing both volumes.

G. BARRY GOLSON
Executive Editor
PLAYBOY
New York, 1982

THE PLAYBOY INTERVIEW II

AYN RAND

March 1964

Interviewer: Alvin Toffler

Ayn Rand is a particularly appropriate first selection for this volume. The conversation that follows appeared just six years after the publication of *Atlas Shrugged,* Rand's romantic (and hefty) novel about the individual triumphing over collectivism. Just a few months earlier, President John F. Kennedy had been assassinated, and in the trauma and confusion that followed, it must have been invigorating and comforting to read opinions by someone who was so *certain* of her values, with every thing and every idea in its place. In sum, Rand was an early cult figure, especially among the young, with powerful attraction on intelligent adolescent minds.

For PLAYBOY readers there were particular themes in Rand's ideas that would reappear in future interviews: strong feelings against censorship, puritanism, religion, oppression. This was also an extremely early exploration of feminism—early for *any* mass publication—which was a topic that PLAYBOY was to live with uneasily in the future. ("What is proper for a man is proper for a woman," Rand told PLAYBOY. "There is no particular work which is specifically feminine. Women can choose their work according to their own purpose and premises in the same manner as men do.") This, at a time when women's magazines were publishing recipes and the general magazines were reviewing Betty Friedan with alarm and condescension.

Stylistically, the Rand conversation was also a harbinger of interviews to come. For instance, at one point the interviewer cites a quote Rand allegedly made, and the author snaps back: "I never said that. . . . That is cheap nonsense, and please leave this in your copy." Magazines of the era were self-protective by tradition, "cleaning up" their copy and publishing in an omniscient, infallible voice. It was something new to let the reader into the process, to show the magazine being corrected by Rand, to reveal character at the expense of institutional dignity.

The interviewer, Alvin Toffler, boned up on Rand's philosophy for several months before confronting the formidable lady in her Manhattan apartment for this interview. Later in the decade he wrote *Future Shock* (though no cause and effect is implied). Ayn Rand died early in 1982, her obituaries respectful and her books still being widely read.

Ayn Rand is among the most outspoken—and important—intellectual voices in America today. She is the author of what is perhaps the most fiercely damned and admired best-seller of the decade: Atlas Shrugged, *which has become one of the most-talked-about novels in the country. Ayn Rand discussion clubs dot college campuses. Professors debate her ideas in their classrooms. And sales of her previous best-seller,* The Fountainhead, *continue to climb.*

That any novel should set off such a chain reaction is unusual; that Atlas Shrugged *has done so is astonishing. For the book, a panoramic novel about what happens when the "men of the mind" go on strike, is 1,168 pages long. It is filled with lengthy, sometimes complex philosophical passages; and it is brimming with as many explosively unpopular ideas as Ayn Rand herself. Despite this success, the literary establishment considers her an outsider. Almost to a man, critics have either ignored or denounced the book. She is an exile among philosophers, too, although* Atlas *is as much a work of philosophy as it is a novel. Liberals glower at the very mention of her name; but conservatives, too, swallow hard when she begins to speak. For Ayn Rand, whether anyone likes it or not, is sui generis: indubitably, irrevocably, intransigently individual.*

She detests the drift of modern American society: She doesn't like its politics, its economics, its attitudes toward sex, women, business, art, or religion. In short, she declares, with unblinking immodesty, "I am challenging the cultural tradition of two-and-a-half-thousand years." She means it.

A dark-haired woman with penetrating brown eyes and a computer-quick mind, Ayn (rhymes with mine) Rand was born to the family of a small businessman in St. Petersburg, Russia, where she lived through the Soviet Revolution. She attended the University of Leningrad, loathing communism and its philosophy. In 1926 she managed to leave the USSR, stayed for a few months with distant relatives in Chicago, then moved on to Hollywood. She had always wanted to be a writer. Since her command of English was somewhat less than adequate for writing fiction, she found a job preparing outlines for silent movies, as she went about mastering her new language. Between bouts of unemployment, she worked as a movie extra, waitress, newspaper subscription salesgirl, and studio wardrobe-department clerk.

Then in 1936, she completed her first novel, We the Living*—an attack on totalitarianism, set in Soviet Russia—which drew little notice. Two years later she finished* Anthem, *a short novel about a society in which the word "I" has been extirpated in favor of the collectivist "we." It was not until five years and twelve publishers' rejections later that her first commercially successful book,* The Fountainhead, *appeared; the story of an architect's battle for his own individuality, it became a national best-seller, and was later made into a movie.*

For nearly a decade after that, Miss Rand struggled to write Atlas Shrugged, *which she views not merely as a novel, but as the crystallization of a philosophy aimed at nothing less than reversing the entire direction of change in America—turning society toward a state of pure laissez-faire capitalism, even purer than that which existed during the nineteenth century. But her philosophy—which she calls "Objectivism"—encompasses more than economics or politics: Primarily, it sets forth a new kind of ethics which she defines as a morality of rational self-interest.*

In a series of intellectually electric conversations with PLAYBOY'S *interviewer, Alvin Toffler, Miss Rand spoke clearly and urgently about her work and her views. Answering question after question with a clipped, even delivery, her deep voice edged with a Russian accent, she paused only long enough between words to puff on cigarettes held in a blue-and-silver holder (a gift from admirers) engraved with her initials, the names of the three heroes of* Atlas Shrugged, *and a number of diminutive dollar signs. The dollar sign, in* Atlas Shrugged, *is the symbol of "free trade and, therefore, of a free mind."*

PLAYBOY: Miss Rand, your novels and essays, especially your controversial best-seller, *Atlas Shrugged,* present a carefully engineered, internally consistent world view. They are, in effect the expression of an all-encompassing philosophical system. What do you seek to accomplish with this new philosophy?
RAND: I seek to provide men—or those who care to think—with an integrated, consistent and rational view of life.
PLAYBOY: What are the basic premises of Objectivism? Where does it begin?
RAND: It begins with the axiom that existence exists, which means that an objective reality exists independent of any perceiver or of the perceiver's emotions, feelings, wishes, hopes or fears. Objectivism holds that reason is man's only means of perceiving reality and his only guide to action. By reason, I mean the faculty which identifies and integrates the material provided by man's senses.
PLAYBOY: In *Atlas Shrugged* your hero, John Galt, declares, "I swear—by my life and my love of it—that I will never live for the sake of another man, nor ask another man to live for mine." How is this related to your basic principles?
RAND: Galt's statement is a dramatized summation of the Objectivist ethics. Any system of ethics is based on and derived, implicitly or explicitly, from a metaphysics. The ethic derived from the metaphysical base of Objectivism holds that, since reason is man's basic tool of survival, rationality is his highest virtue. To use his mind, to perceive reality and to act accordingly, is man's moral imperative. The standard of value of the Objectivist ethics is: man's life—man's survival qua man—or that which the nature of a rational being requires for his proper survival. The Objectivist ethics, in essence, hold that man exists for his own sake, that the pursuit of his own happiness is his highest moral purpose, that he must not sacrifice himself to others, nor sacrifice others to himself. It is this last that Galt's statement summarizes.
PLAYBOY: What kind of morality derives from this, in terms of the individual's behavior?
RAND: This is presented in detail in *Atlas Shrugged.*
PLAYBOY: The heroine of *Atlas Shrugged* was, in your words, "completely incapable of experiencing a feeling of fundamental guilt." Is any system of morality possible without guilt?
RAND: The important word in the statement you quoted is "fundamental." Fundamental guilt does not mean the ability to judge one's own actions and regret a wrong action, if one commits it. Fundamental guilt means that man is evil and guilty by nature.
PLAYBOY: You mean original sin?
RAND: Exactly. It is the concept of original sin that my heroine, or I, or any Objectivist, is incapable of accepting or of ever experiencing emotionally. It is the concept of original sin that negates morality. If man is guilty by nature, he has no choice about it. If he has no choice, the issue does not belong in the field of morality. Morality pertains only to the sphere of man's free will—only to those actions which are open to his choice. To consider man guilty by nature is a contradiction in terms. My heroine would be capable of experiencing guilt about a specific action. Only, being a woman of high moral stature and self-esteem, she would see to it that she never earned any guilt by her actions. She would act in a totally moral manner and, therefore, would not accept an unearned guilt.
PLAYBOY: In *Atlas Shrugged,* one of your leading characters is asked, "What's the most depraved type of human being?" His reply is surprising: He doesn't say a sadist or a murderer or a sex maniac or a dictator; he says, "The man without a purpose."

Yet most people seem to go through their lives without a clearly defined purpose. Do you regard them as depraved?
RAND: Yes, to a certain extent.
PLAYBOY: Why?
RAND: Because that aspect of their character lies at the root of and causes all the evils which you mentioned in your question. Sadism, dictatorship, any form of evil, is the consequence of a man's evasion of reality. A consequence of his failure to think. The man without a purpose is a man who drifts at the mercy of random feelings or unidentified urges and is capable of any evil, because he is totally out of control of his own life. In order to be in control of your life, you have to have a purpose—a productive purpose.
PLAYBOY: Weren't Hitler and Stalin, to name two tyrants, in control of their own lives, and didn't they have a clear purpose?
RAND: Certainly not. Observe that both of them ended as literal psychotics. They were men who lacked self-esteem and, therefore, hated all of existence. Their psychology, in effect, is summarized in *Atlas Shrugged* by the character of James Taggart. The man who has no purpose, but has to act, acts to destroy others. That is not the same thing as a productive or creative purpose.
PLAYBOY: If a person organizes his life around a single, neatly defined purpose, isn't he in danger of becoming extremely narrow in his horizons?
RAND: Quite the contrary. A central purpose serves to integrate all the other concerns of a man's life. It establishes the hierarchy, the relative importance, of his values, it saves him from pointless inner conflicts, it permits him to enjoy life on a wide scale and to carry that enjoyment into any area open to his mind; whereas a man without a purpose is lost in chaos. He does not know what his values are. He does not know how to judge. He cannot tell what is or is not important to him, and, therefore, he drifts helplessly at the mercy of any chance stimulus or any whim of the moment. He can enjoy nothing. He spends his life searching for some value which he will never find.
PLAYBOY: Couldn't the attempt to rule whim out of life, to act in a totally rational fashion, be viewed as conducive to a juiceless, joyless kind of existence?
RAND: I truly must say that I don't know what you are talking about. Let's define our terms. Reason is man's tool of knowledge, the faculty that enables him to perceive the facts of reality. To act rationally means to act in accordance with the facts of reality. Emotions are not tools of cognition. What you feel tells you nothing abut the facts; it merely tells you something about your estimate of the facts. Emotions are the result of your value judgments; they are caused by your basic premises, which you may hold consciously or subconsciously, which may be right or wrong. A whim is an emotion whose cause you neither know nor care to discover. Now what does it mean, to act on whim? It means that a man acts like a zombie, without any knowledge of what he deals with, what he wants to accomplish, or what motivates him. It means that a man acts in a state of temporary insanity. Is this what you call juicy or colorful? I think the only juice that can come out of such a situation is blood. To act against the facts of reality can result only in destruction.
PLAYBOY: Should one ignore emotions altogether, rule them out of one's life entirely?
RAND: Of course not. One should merely keep them in their place. An emotion is an automatic response, an automatic effect of man's value premises. An effect, not a cause. There is no necessary clash, no dichotomy between man's reason and his emo-

tions—provided he observes their proper relationship. A rational man knows—or makes it a point to discover—the source of his emotions, the basic premises from which they come; if his premises are wrong, he corrects them. He never acts on emotions for which he cannot account, the meaning of which he does not understand. In appraising a situation, he knows why he reacts as he does and whether he is right. He has no inner conflicts, his mind and his emotions are integrated, his consciousness is in perfect harmony. His emotions are not his enemies, they are his means of enjoying life. But they are not his guide; the guide is his mind. This relationship cannot be reversed, however. If a man takes his emotions as the cause and his mind as their passive effect, if he is guided by his emotions and uses his mind only to rationalize or justify them somehow—*then* he is acting immorally, he is condemning himself to misery, failure, defeat, and he will achieve nothing but destruction—his own and that of others.

PLAYBOY: According to your philosophy, work and achievement are the highest goals of life. Do you regard as immoral those who find greater fulfillment in the warmth of friendship and family ties?

RAND: If they place such things as friendship and family ties above their own productive work, yes, then they are immoral. Friendship, family life and human relationships are not primary in a man's life. A man who places others first, above his own creative work, is an emotional parasite; whereas, if he places his work first, there is no conflict between his work and his enjoyment of human relationships.

PLAYBOY: Do you believe that women as well as men should organize their lives around work—and if so, what kind of work?

RAND: Of course. I believe that women are human beings. What is proper for a man is proper for a woman. The basic principles are the same. I would not attempt to prescribe what kind of work a man should do, and I would not attempt it in regard to women. There is no particular work which is specifically feminine. Women can choose their work according to their own purpose and premises in the same manner as men do.

PLAYBOY: In your opinion, is a woman immoral who chooses to devote herself to home and family instead of a career?

RAND: Not immoral—I would say she is impractical, because a home cannot be a full-time occupation, except when her children are young. However, if she wants a family and wants to make that her career, at least for a while, it would be proper—if she approaches it as a career, that is, if she studies the subject, if she defines the rules and principles by which she wants to bring up her children, if she approaches her task in an intellectual manner. It is a very responsible task and a very important one, but only when treated as a science, not as a mere emotional indulgence.

PLAYBOY: Where, would you say, should romantic love fit into the life of a rational person whose single driving passion is work?

RAND: It is his greatest reward. The only man capable of experiencing a profound romantic love is the man driven by passion for his work—because love is an expression of self-esteem, of the deepest values in a man's or a woman's character. One falls in love with the person who shares these values. If a man has no clearly defined values, and no moral character, he is not able to appreciate another person. In this respect, I would like to quote from *The Fountainhead,* in which the hero utters a line that has often been quoted by readers: "To say 'I love you' one must know first how to say the I.' "

PLAYBOY: You hold that one's own happiness is the highest end, and that self-sacrifice is immoral. Does this apply to love as well as work?

RAND: To love more than to anything else. When you are in love, it means that the person you love is of great personal, selfish importance to you and to your life. If you were selfless, it would have to mean that you derive no personal pleasure or happiness from the company and the existence of the person you love, and that you are motivated only be self-sacrificial pity for that person's need of you. I don't have to point out to you that no one would be flattered by, nor would accept, a concept of that kind. Love is not self-sacrifice, but the most profound assertion of your own needs and values. It is for your *own* happiness that you need the person you love, and that is the greatest compliment, the greatest tribute you can pay to that person.

PLAYBOY: You have denounced the puritan notion that physical love is ugly or evil; yet you have written that "Indiscriminate desire and unselective indulgence are possible only to those who regard sex and themselves as evil." Would you say that discriminate and selective indulgence in sex *is* moral?

RAND: I would say that a selective and discriminate sex life is not an indulgence. The term *indulgence* implies that it is an action taken lightly and casually. I say that sex is one of the most important aspects of man's life and, therefore, must never be approached lightly or casually. A sexual relationship is proper only on the ground of the highest values one can find in a human being. Sex must not be anything other than a response to values. And that is why I consider promiscuity immoral. Not because sex is evil, but because sex is too good and too important.

PLAYBOY: Does this mean, in your view, that sex should involve only married partners?

RAND: Not necessarily. What sex should involve is a very serious relationship. Whether that relationship should or should not become a marriage is a question which depends on the circumstances and the context of the two persons' lives. I consider marriage a very important institution, but it is important *when* and *if* two people have found the person with whom they wish to spend the rest of their lives—a question of which no man or woman can be automatically certain. When one is certain that one's choice is final, then marriage is, of course, a desirable state. But this does *not* mean that any relationship based on less than total certainty is improper. I think the question of an affair or a marriage depends on the knowledge and the position of the two persons involved and should be left up to them. Either is moral, provided only that both parties take the relationship seriously and that it is based on values.

PLAYBOY: As one who champions the cause of enlightened self-interest, how do you feel about dedicating one's life to hedonistic self-gratification?

RAND: I am profoundly opposed to the philosophy of hedonism. Hedonism is the doctrine which holds that the good is whatever gives you pleasure and therefore, pleasure is the standard of morality. Objectivism holds that the good must be defined by a rational standard of value, that pleasure is not a first cause, but only a consequence, that only the pleasure which proceeds from a rational value judgment can be regarded as moral, that pleasure, as such, is not a guide to action nor a standard of morality. To say that pleasure should be the standard of morality simply means that whichever values you happen to have chosen consciously or subconsciously, rationally or irrationally, are right and moral. This means that you are to be guided by chance feelings, emotions and whims, not by your mind. My philosophy is the opposite of hedonism. I hold that one cannot achieve happiness by random, arbitrary or subjective means. One can achieve happiness only on the basis of rational values. By rational values, I do not mean anything that a man may arbitrarily or blindly declare to be rational. It is the province of morality, of the science of ethics, to define for men what is a rational standard and what are the rational values to pursue.

PLAYBOY: You have said that the kind of man who spends his time running after women is a man who "despises himself." Would you elaborate?

RAND: This type of man is reversing cause and effect in regard to sex. Sex is an expression of a man's self-esteem, of his own self-value. But the man who does not value himself tries to reverse this process. He tries to derive his self-esteem from his sexual conquests, which cannot be done. He cannot acquire his own value from the number of women who regard him as valuable. Yet that is the hopeless thing which he attempts.

PLAYBOY: You attack the idea that sex is "impervious to reason." But isn't sex a nonrational biological instinct?

RAND: No. To begin with, man does not possess *any* instincts. Physically, sex is merely a capacity. But how a man will exercise this capacity and whom he will find attractive depends on his standard of value. It depends on his premises, which he may hold consciously or subconsciously, and which determine his choices. It is in this manner that his philosophy directs his sex life.

PLAYBOY: Isn't the individual equipped with powerful, nonrational biological drives?

RAND: He is not. A man is equipped with a certain kind of physical mechanism and certain needs, but without any knowledge of how to fulfill them. For instance, man needs food. He experiences hunger. But, unless he learns first to identify this hunger, then to know that he needs food and how to obtain it, he will starve. The need, the hunger, will not tell him how to satisfy it. Man is born with certain physical and psychological needs, but he can neither discover them nor satisfy them without the use of his mind. Man has to discover what is right or wrong for him as a rational being. His so-called urges will not tell him what to do.

PLAYBOY: In *Atlas Shrugged* you wrote, "There are two sides to every issue. One side is right and the other is wrong, but the middle is always evil." Isn't this a rather black-and-white set of values?

RAND: It most certainly is. I most emphatically advocate a black-and-white view of the world. Let us define this. What is meant by the expression "black and white"? It means good and evil. Before you can identify anything as gray, as middle of the road, you have to know what is black and what is white, because gray is merely a mixture of the two. And when you have established that one alternative is good and the other is evil, there is no justification ever for choosing any part of what you know to be evil.

PLAYBOY: Then you believe in absolutes?

RAND: I do.

PLAYBOY: Can't Objectivism, then, be called a dogma?

RAND: No. A dogma is a set of beliefs accepted on faith; that is, without rational justification or against rational evidence. A dogma is a matter of blind faith. Objectivism is the exact opposite. Objectivism tells you that you must not accept any idea or conviction unless you can demonstrate its truth by means of reason.

PLAYBOY: If widely accepted, couldn't Objectivism harden into a dogma?

RAND: No. I have found that Objectivism is its own protection against people who might attempt to use it as a dogma. Since Objectivism requires the use of one's mind, those who attempt to take broad principles and apply them unthinkingly and indiscriminately to the concretes of their own existence find that it cannot be done. They are then compelled either to reject Objectivism or to apply it. When I say apply, I mean that they have to use their own mind, their own thinking, in order to know how to apply Objectivist principles to the specific problems of their own lives.

PLAYBOY: You have said you are opposed to faith. Do you believe in God?

RAND: Certainly not.

PLAYBOY: You've been quoted as saying "The cross is the symbol of torture, of the sacrifice of the ideal to the nonideal. I prefer the dollar sign." Do you truly feel that two thousand years of Christianity can be summed up with the word *torture*?

RAND: To begin with, I never said that. It's not my style. Neither literarily nor intellectually. I don't say I prefer the dollar sign—that is cheap nonsense, and please leave this in your copy. I don't know the origin of that particular quote, but the meaning of the dollar sign is made clear in *Atlas Shrugged.* It is the symbol, clearly explained in the story, of free trade and, therefore, of a free mind. A free mind and a free economy are corollaries. One can't exist without the other. The dollar sign, as the symbol of the currency of a free country, *is* the symbol of the free mind. More than that, as to the historical origin of the dollar sign, although it has never been proved, one very likely hypothesis is that it stands for the initials of the United States. So much for the dollar sign.

Now you want me to speak about the cross. What is correct is that I do regard the cross as the symbol of the sacrifice of the ideal to the nonideal. Isn't that what it does mean? Christ, in terms of Christian philosophy, is the human ideal. He personifies that which men should strive to emulate. Yet, according to the Christian mythology, he died on the cross not for his own sins but for the sins of the nonideal people. In other words, a man of perfect value was sacrificed for men who are vicious and who are expected or supposed to accept that sacrifice. If I were a Christian, nothing could make me more indignant than that: the notion of sacrificing the ideal to the nonideal, or virtue to vice. And it is in the name of that symbol that men are asked to sacrifice themselves for their inferiors. That is precisely how the symbolism is used. That is torture.

PLAYBOY: Has no religion, in your estimation, ever offered anything of constructive value to human life?

RAND: Qua religion, no—in the sense of blind belief, belief unsupported by, or contrary to, the facts of reality and the conclusions of reason. Faith, as such, is extremely detrimental to human life: It is the negation of reason. But you must remember that religion is an early form of philosophy, that the first attempts to explain the universe, to give a coherent frame of reference to man's life and a code of moral values, were made by religion, before men graduated or developed enough to have philosophy. And, as philosophies, some religions have very valuable moral points. They may have a good influence or proper principles to inculcate, but in a very contradictory context and, on a very—how should I say it?—dangerous or malevolent base: on the ground of faith.

PLAYBOY: Then you would say that if you had to choose between the symbol of the cross and the symbol of the dollar, you would choose the dollar?

RAND: I wouldn't accept such a choice. Put it another way: If I had to choose between faith and reason, I wouldn't consider the choice even conceivable. As a human being, one chooses reason.

PLAYBOY: Do you consider wealthy businessmen like the Fords and the Rockefellers immoral because they use their wealth to support charity?

RAND: No. That is their privilege, if they want to. My views on charity are very simple. I do not consider it a major virtue and, above all, I do not consider it a moral duty. There is nothing wrong in helping people, if and when they are worthy of the help and you can afford to help them. I regard charity as a marginal issue. What I am fighting is the idea that charity is a moral duty and a primary virtue.

PLAYBOY: What is the place of compassion in your philosophical system?

RAND: I regard compassion as proper *only* toward those who are innocent victims, but not toward those who are morally guilty. If one feels compassion for the victims of a concentration camp, one cannot feel it for the torturers. If one does feel compassion for the torturers, it is an act of moral treason toward the victims.

PLAYBOY: Would it be against the principles of Objectivism for anyone to sacrifice himself by stepping in front of a bullet to protect another person?

RAND: No. It depends on the circumstances. I would step in the way of a bullet if it were aimed at my husband. It is not self-sacrifice to die protecting that which you value: If the value is great enough, you do not care to exist without it. This applies to any alleged sacrifice for those one loves.

PLAYBOY: Would you be willing to die for your cause, and should your followers be willing to die for it? And for the truly nonsacrificial Objectivists, is *any* cause worth dying for?

RAND: The answer to this is made plain in my book. In *Atlas Shrugged* I explain that a man has to live for, and when necessary, fight for, his values—because the whole process of living consists of the achievement of values. Man does not survive automatically. He must live like a rational being and accept nothing less. He cannot survive as a brute. Even the simplest value, such as food, has to be produced. The same is true of his more interesting, more important achievements. All values have to be gained and kept by man, and if they are threatened, he has to be willing to fight and die, if necessary, for his right to live like a rational being. You ask me, would I be willing to die for Objectivism? I would. But what is more important, I am willing to *live* for it—which is much more difficult.

PLAYBOY: In your emphasis on reason, you are in philosophical conflict with contemporary writers, novelists and poets—many of whom are self-admitted mystics, or irrationlists, as they have been called. Why is this so?

RAND: Because art has a philosophical base, and the dominant philosophical trends of today are a form of neomysticism. Art is a projection of the artist's fundamental view of man and of existence. Since most artists do not develop an independent philosophy of their own, they absorb, consciously or subconsciously, the dominant philosophical influences of their time. Most of today's literature is a faithful reflection of today's philosophy—and look at it!

PLAYBOY: But shouldn't a writer reflect his time?

RAND: No. A writer should be an active intellectual leader of his time, not a passive follower riding any current. A writer should shape the values of his culture, he should project and concretize the value goals of man's life. This is the essence of the Romantic school of literature, which has all but vanished from today's scene.

PLAYBOY: Leaving us where, literarily speaking?

RAND: At the dead end of Naturalism. Naturalism holds that a writer must be a passive photographer or reporter who must transcribe uncritically whatever he happens to observe around him. Romanticism holds that a writer must present things, not as they are at any given moment, but, to quote Aristotle, "as they might be and ought to be."

PLAYBOY: Would you say that you are the last of the Romanticists?
RAND: Or the first of their return—to quote one of my own characters in *Atlas Shrugged.*
PLAYBOY: What is your appraisal of contemporary literature in general?
RAND: Philosophically, immoral. Aesthetically, it bores me to death. It is degenerating into a sewer, devoted exclusively to studies of depravity. And there's nothing as boring as depravity.
PLAYBOY: Are there any novelists whom you admire?
RAND: Yes. Victor Hugo.
PLAYBOY: What about modern novelists?
RAND: No, there is no one that I could say I admire among the so-called serious writers. I prefer the popular literature of today, which is today's remnant of Romanticism. My favorite is Mickey Spillane.
PLAYBOY: Why do you like him?
RAND: Because he is primarily a moralist. In a primitive form, the form of a detective novel, he presents the conflict of good and evil, in terms of black and white. He does not present a nasty gray mixture of indistinguishable scoundrels on both sides. He presents an uncompromising conflict. As a writer, he is brilliantly expert at the aspect of literature which I consider most important: plot structure.
PLAYBOY: What do you think of Faulkner?
RAND: Not very much. He is a good stylist, but practically unreadable in content—so I've read very little of him.
PLAYBOY: What about Nabokov?
RAND: I have read only one book of his and a half—the half was *Lolita,* which I couldn't finish. He is a brilliant stylist, he writes beautifully, but his subjects, his sense of life, his view of man, are so evil that no amount of artistic skill can justify them.
PLAYBOY: As a novelist, do you regard philosophy as the primary purpose of your writing?
RAND: No. My primary purpose is the projection of an ideal man, of man "as he might be and ought to be." Philosophy is the necessary means to that end.
PLAYBOY: In your early novel, *Anthem,* your protagonist declares, "It is my will which chooses, and the choice of my will is the only edict I respect." Isn't this anarchism? Is one's own desire or will the *only* law one must respect?
RAND: Not one's own will. This is, more less, a poetic expression made clear by the total context of the story in *Anthem.* One's own rational judgment. You see, I use the term *free will* in a totally different sense from the one usually attached to it. Free will consists of man's ability to think or not to think. The act of thinking is man's primary act of choice. A rational man will never be guided by desires or whims, only by values based on his rational judgment. That is the only authority he can recognize. This does not mean anarchy, because, if a man wants to live in a free, civilized society, he would, in reason, have to choose to observe the laws, when those laws are objective, rational and valid. I have written an article on this subject for *The Objectivist Newsletter*—on the need and proper function of a government.
PLAYBOY: What, in your view, *is* the proper function of a government?
RAND: Basically, there is really only one proper function: the protection of individual rights. Since rights can be violated only by physical force, and by certain derivatives of physical force, the proper function of government is to protect men from those who initiate the use of physical force: from those who are criminals. Force, in a free soci-

ety, may be used only in retaliation and only against those who initiate its use. This is the proper task of government: to serve as a policeman who protects men from the use of force.
PLAYBOY: If force may be used only in retaliation against force, does the government have the right to use force to collect taxes, for example, or to draft soldiers?
RAND: In principle, I believe that taxation should be voluntary, like everything else. But how one would implement this is a very complex question. I can only suggest certain methods, but I would not attempt to insist on them as a definitive answer. A government lottery, for instance, used in many countries in Europe, is one good method of voluntary taxation. There are others. Taxes should be voluntary contributions for the proper governmental services which people do need and therefore would be and should be willing to pay for—as they pay for insurance. But, of course, this is a problem for a distant future, for the time when men will establish a fully free social system. It would be the last, *not* the first, reform to advocate. As to the draft, it is improper and unconstitutional. It is a violation of fundamental rights, of a man's right to his own life. No man has the right to send another man to fight and die for his, the sender's, cause. A country has no right to force men into involuntary servitude. Armies should be strictly voluntary; and, as military authorities will tell you, volunteer armies are the best armies.
PLAYBOY: What about other public needs? Do you consider the post office, for example, a legitimate function of government?
RAND: Now let's get this straight. My position is fully consistent. Not only the post office, but streets, roads, and above all, schools, should all be privately owned and privately run. I advocate the separation of state and economics. The government should be concerned only with those issues which involve the use of force. This means: the police, the armed services, and the law courts to settle disputes among men. Nothing else. Everything else should be privately run and would be much better run.
PLAYBOY: Would you create any new government departments or agencies?
RAND: No, and I truly cannot discuss things that way. I am not a government planner nor do I spend my time inventing Utopias. I'm talking about principles whose practical applications are clear. If I have said that I am opposed to the initiation of force, what else has to be discussed?
PLAYBOY: What about force in foreign policy? You have said that any free nation had the right to invade Nazi Germany during World War II . . .
RAND: Certainly.
PLAYBOY: . . . And that any free nation today has the moral right—though not the duty—to invade Soviet Russia, Cuba, or any other "slave pen." Correct?
RAND: Correct. A dictatorship—a country that violates the rights of its own citizens—is an outlaw and can claim no rights.
PLAYBOY: Would you actively advocate that the United States invade Cuba or the Soviet Union?
RAND: Not at present. I don't think it's necessary. I would advocate that which the Soviet Union fears above all else: economic boycott. I would advocate a blockade of Cuba and an economic boycott of Soviet Russia; and you would see both those regimes collapse without the loss of a single American life.
PLAYBOY: Would you favor U.S. withdrawal from the United Nations?
RAND: Yes. I do not sanction the grotesque pretense of an organization allegedly devoted to world peace and human rights, which includes Soviet Russia, the worst aggressor and bloodiest butcher in history, as one of its members. The notion of pro-

tecting rights, with Soviet Russia among the protectors, is an insult to the concept of rights and to the intelligence of any man who is asked to endorse or sanction such an organization. I do not believe that an individual should cooperate with criminals, and, for all the same reasons, I do not believe that free countries should cooperate with dictatorships.

PLAYBOY: Would you advocate severing diplomatic relations with Russia?

RAND: Yes.

PLAYBOY: How do you feel about the test-ban treaty which was recently signed?

RAND: I agree with Barry Goldwater's speech on this subject on the Senate floor. The best military authorities, and above all, the best scientific authority, Dr. Teller, the author of the hydrogen bomb, have stated that this treaty is not merely meaningless but positively dangerous to America's defense.

PLAYBOY: If Senator Goldwater is nominated as the Republican presidential candidate this July, would you vote for him?

RAND: At present, yes. When I say "at present," I mean the date when this interview is being recorded. I disagree with him on a great many things, but I do agree, predominantly, with his foreign policy. Of any candidates available today, I regard Barry Goldwater as the best. I would vote for him, if he offers us a plausible, or at least semiconsistent, platform.

PLAYBOY: How about Richard Nixon?

RAND: I'm opposed to him. I'm opposed to any compromiser or me-tooer, and Mr. Nixon is probably the champion in this regard.

PLAYBOY: What about President Johnson?

RAND: I have no particular opinion about him.

PLAYBOY: You are a declared anticommunist, antisocialist and antiliberal. Yet you reject the notion that you are a conservative. In fact, you have reserved some of your angriest criticism for conservatives. Where *do* you stand politically?

RAND: Correction. I never describe my position in terms of negatives. I am an advocate of *laissez-faire* capitalism, of individual rights—there are no others—of individual freedom. It is on this ground that I oppose any doctrine which proposes the sacrifice of the individual to the collective, such as communism, socialism, the welfare state, fascism, Nazism and modern liberalism. I oppose the conservatives on the same ground. The conservatives are advocates of a mixed economy and of a welfare state. Their difference from the liberals is only one of degree, not of principle.

PLAYBOY: You have charged that America suffers from intellectual bankruptcy. Do you include in this condemnation such right-wing publications as the *National Review*? Isn't that magazine a powerful voice against all the things you regard as "statism"?

RAND: I consider *National Review* the worst and most dangerous magazine in America. The kind of defense that it offers to capitalism results in nothing except the discrediting and destruction of capitalism. Do you want me to tell you why?

PLAYBOY: Yes, please.

RAND: Because it ties capitalism to religion. The ideological position of *National Review* amounts, in effect, to the following: In order to accept freedom and capitalism, one has to believe in God or in some form of religion, some form of supernatural mysticism. Which means that there are no rational grounds on which one can defend capitalism. Which amounts to an admission that reason is on the side of capitalism's enemies, that a slave society or a dictatorship is a rational system, and that only on the ground of mystic faith can one believe in freedom. Nothing more derogatory to capitalism could ever be alleged, and the exact opposite is true. Capitalism is the only system that can be defended and validated by reason.

PLAYBOY: You have attacked Governor Nelson Rockefeller for "lumping all opponents of the welfare state with actual crackpots." It was clear from his remarks that among others, he was aiming his criticism at the John Birch Society. Do you resent being lumped with the John Birchers? Do you consider them "crackpots" or a force for good?

RAND: I resent being lumped with anyone. I resent the modern method of never defining ideas, and lumping totally different people into a collective by means of smears and derogatory terms. I resent Governor Rockefeller's smear tactics: his refusal to identify specifically whom and what he meant. As far as I'm concerned, I repeat, I don't want to be lumped with anyone, and certainly not with the John Birch Society. Do I consider them crackpots? No, not necessarily. What is wrong with them is that they don't seem to have any specific, clearly defined political philosophy. Therefore, some of them may be crackpots, others may be very well-meaning citizens. I consider the Birch Society futile, because they are not *for* capitalism, but merely *against* communism. I gather they believe that the disastrous state of today's world is caused by a communist conspiracy. This is childishly naïve and superficial. No country can be destroyed by a mere conspiracy, it can be destroyed only by *ideas*. The Birchers seem to be either nonintellectual or anti-intellectual. They do not attach importance to ideas. They do not realize that the great battle in the world today is a philosophical, ideological conflict.

PLAYBOY: Are there any political groups in the United States today of which you approve?

RAND: Political groups, as such—no. Is there any political group today which is fully consistent? Such groups today are guided by or advocate blatant contradictions.

PLAYBOY: Do you have any personal political aspirations yourself? Have you ever considered running for office?

RAND: Certainly not. And I trust that you don't hate me enough to wish such a thing on me.

PLAYBOY: But you are interested in politics, or at least in political theory, aren't you?

RAND: Let me answer you this way: When I came here from Soviet Russia, I was interested in politics for only one reason—to reach the day when I would not have to be interested in politics. I wanted to secure a society in which I would be free to pursue my own concerns and goals, knowing that the government would not interfere to wreck them, knowing that my life, my work, my future were not at the mercy of the state or of a dictator's whim. This is still my attitude today. Only today I know that such a society is an ideal not yet achieved, that I cannot expect others to achieve it for me, and that I, like every other responsible citizen, must do everything possible to achieve it. In other words, I an interested in politics only in order to secure and protect freedom.

PLAYBOY: Throughout your work you argue that the way in which the contemporary world is organized, even in the capitalist countries, submerges the individual and stifles initiative. In *Atlas Shrugged*, John Galt leads a strike of the men of the mind—which results in the collapse of the collectivist society around them. Do you think the time has come for the artists, intellectuals and creative businessmen of today to withdraw their talents from society in this way?

RAND: No, not yet. But before I explain, I must correct one part of your question.

What we have today is not a capitalist society, but a mixed economy—that is, a mixture of freedom and controls, which, by the presently dominant trend, is moving toward dictatorship. The action in *Atlas Shrugged* takes place at a time when society has reached the stage of dictatorship. When and if this happens, that will be the time to go on strike, but not until then.

PLAYBOY: What do you mean by dictatorship? How would you define it?

RAD: A dictatorship is a country that does not recognize individual rights, whose government holds total, unlimited power over men.

PLAYBOY: What is the dividing line, by your definition, between a mixed economy and a dictatorship?

RAND: A dictatorship has four characteristics: one-party rule, executions without trial for political offenses, expropriation or nationalization of private property, and censorship. Above all, this last. So long as men can speak and write freely, so long as there is no censorship, they still have a chance to reform their society or to put it on a better road. When censorship is imposed, *that* is the sign that men should go on strike intellectually, by which I mean, should not cooperate with the social system in any way whatever.

PLAYBOY: Short of such a strike, what do you believe ought to be done to bring about the societal changes you deem desirable?

RAND: It is *ideas* that determine social trends, that create or destroy social systems. Therefore, the right ideas, the right philosophy, should be advocated and spread. The disasters of the modern world, including the destruction of capitalism, were caused by the altruist-collectivist philosophy. It is altruism that men should reject.

PLAYBOY: And how would you define altruism?

RAND: It is a moral system which holds that man has no right to exist for his own sake, that service to others is the sole justification of his existence, and that self-sacrifice is his highest moral duty, value and virtue. This is the moral base of collectivism, of all dictatorships. In order to seek freedom and capitalism, men need a nonmystical, nonaltruistic, *rational* code of ethics—a morality which holds that man is not a sacrificial animal, that he has the right to exist for his own sake, neither sacrificing himself to others, nor others to himself. In other words, what is desperately needed today is the ethics of Objectivism.

PLAYBOY: Then what you are saying is that to achieve these changes one must use essentially educational or propagandistic methods?

RAND: Yes, of course.

PLAYBOY: What do you think of your antagonists' contention that the moral and political principles of Objectivism place you outside the mainstream of American thought?

RAND: I don't acknowledge or recognize such a concept as a "mainstream of *thought.*" That might be appropriate to a dictatorship, to a collectivist society in which thought is controlled and in which there exists a collective mainstream—of slogans, not of thought. There is no such thing in America. There never was. However, I have heard that expression used for the purpose of barring from public communication any innovator, any nonconformist, anyone who has anything original to offer. I am an innovator. This is a term of distinction, a term of honor, rather than something to hide or apologize for. Anyone who has new or valuable ideas to offer stands outside the intellectual *status quo.* But the *status quo* is not a stream, let alone a "mainstream." It is a stagnant swamp. It is the innovators who carry mankind forward.

PLAYBOY: Do you believe that Objectivism as a philosophy will eventually sweep the world?
RAND: Nobody can answer a question of that kind. Men have free will. There is no guarantee that they will choose to be rational, at any one time or in any one generation. Nor is it necessary for a philosophy to "sweep the world." If you ask the question in a somewhat different form, if you say, do I think that Objectivism will be the philosophy of the future, I would say yes, but with this qualification: If men turn to reason, if they are not destroyed by dictatorship and precipitated into another Dark Ages, if men remain free long enough to have time to think, then Objectivism is the philosophy they will accept.
PLAYBOY: Why?
RAND: In any historical period when men were free, it has always been the most rational philosophy that won. It is from this perspective that I would say, yes, Objectivism will win. But there is no guarantee, no predetermined necessity about it.
PLAYBOY: You are sharply critical of the world as you see it today, and your books offer radical proposals for changing not merely the shape of society, but the very way in which most men work, think and love. Are you optimistic about man's future?
RAND: Yes, I am optimistic. Collectivism, as an intellectual power and a moral ideal, is dead. But freedom and individualism, and their political expression, capitalism, have not yet been discovered. I think men *will* have time to discover them. It is significant that the dying collectivist philosophy of today has produced nothing but a cult of depravity, impotence and despair. Look at modern art and literature with their image of man as a helpless, mindless creature doomed to failure, frustration and destruction. This may be the collectivists' psychological confession, but it is not an image of man. If it were, we would never have risen from the cave. But we did. Look around you and look at history. You will see the achievements of man's mind. You will see man's unlimited potentiality for greatness, and the faculty that makes it possible. You will see that man is not a helpless monster by nature, but he becomes one when he discards that faculty: his mind. And if you ask me, what is greatness?—I will answer, it is the capacity to live by the three fundamental values of John Galt: reason, purpose, self-esteem.

SALVADOR DALI

June 1964

Interviewer: Sterling McIlany

If, in 1964, anyone represented in the public mind a successor to the Van Gogh tradition of the artist living just this side of madness, it was surely Salvador Dali. His mustachioed flamboyance and theatrical eccentricities (especially when there were reporters or cameras present) had made him the most visible painter of his time. His work was also still taken seriously by many.

Critical appreciation of artists varies with the season (and Dali's work has been derided for several seasons past), but no matter where his reputation eventually rests, Dali's conversation holds up wonderfully—sometimes as genuinely hilarious banter. Whether he is mock-seriously linking his paintings of limp watches to the discovery of DNA, or explaining why rhinoceroses give him cosmic gooseflesh (while regretting that Madame Dali will not let him keep one as a New York apartment pet), he showed himself to be a maestro of the put-on.

As interrogated by journalist Sterling McIlany in the library of Manhattan's St. Regis Hotel, Dali was also refreshingly frank about having sold out for money. ("In New York it is possible to catch a tremendous amount of money all the time.") In the process, he also made some interesting points about the use of one's art for popular and commercial purposes that prefigured Warhol and others.

To art buff and art historian alike, Salvador Felipe y Jacinto Dali is one of the most compelling and paradoxical figures of our time. As the most famous living exponent of surrealism, he has been hailed by one critic as "chief cartographer of the mind's hidden country, and perhaps its chief custodian." His seemingly inexhaustible flood of netherworldly images—drawn, he says, from dreams, nightmares and paranoiac visions—has left its mark, for good or ill, on almost every field of the contemporary graphic arts. He has been a fountainhead of avant-garde designs for jewelry, stage sets, automobiles, ballet costumes, restaurants, store windows, magazine covers, prototypal pop-art sculpture and experimental films. In 1929, with fellow Spaniard Luis Buñuel, he filmed Le Chien Andalou, *a surrealistic classic that still startles art-film audiences with a gory sequence in which an eyeball is slit open with a straight razor. Though his grotesque and hallucinatory subject matter—ranging from limp watches and fur-lined bathtubs to rhinoceros horns and flaming giraffes—has been denounced as "diseased and disgusting," his technical brilliance as a painter has been compared by some to that of the Flemish masters, with whose works many of his own hang in museums around the world.*

Dali's most conspicuous claim to fame, however, is a bizarre and highly publicized private life, played at stage center for most of his sixty years, which has annoyed his detractors almost as much as it has amused the public. The flamboyant trademarks of his carefully cultivated public personalty—brocade vest, silverheaded cane, scimitar mustaches and outrageous exhibitionism—have inspired such epithets as "sensation-seeking charlatan," "the noisiest artist of our generation" and "a great talent corrupted and devoured by a sickness that forces him to impersonate a clown." Dali remains impervious to such slings and arrows—and unswervable in his sense of "divine destiny." In his autobiography, The Secret Life of Salvador Dali, *he declares that at the age of seven "I wanted to be Napoleon. And my ambition has been growing steadily ever since."*

The son of a notary, Dali was born in Figueras in the Spanish province of Upper Catalonia, a land whose people have been known since medieval times for their fierce spirit of independence. True to this heritage, he wasted no time in alienating his elders—and presaging his future: He was expelled from elementary school for incorrigibility, and after five stormy years as an art student, was thrown out of college (Madrid's prestigious Escuela Nacional de Bellas Artes de San Fernando) for mil-

itant nonconformity. Drawn to Paris in search of artistic succor and self-determination, Dali took root and grew swiftly. His first one-man show there was a sensation—news of which preceded his first visit to America in 1934. By the time of his return in 1940, both he and his limp watches had become fashionable fixtures in the elegant salons and drawing rooms of Manhattan, where he has remained ever since, parlaying eccentricity and egocentrism into worldwide fame and considerable fortune. Still stylish, still surrealistic and still enormously successful, he was on hand when one of his more recent canvases, The Discovery of America by Christopher Columbus, *was added to the permanent collection at Huntington Hartford's newly opened Gallery of Modern Art, and another (jawbreakingly entitled* Galacidalacideoxyribonucleicacid) *was placed on display in the Spanish Pavilion at the New York World's Fair.*

When we approached the artist late this spring with our request for an exclusive interview, Dali was busy preparing to leave his baroque apartment in Manhattan's St. Regis Hotel for his home in Port-Lligat, a fishing village on the northeast coast of Spain, where he and his wife spend the summer and autumn months each year. Nevertheless, confessing an inability "to resist the opportunity to talk about myself," he readily consented to take time out for a few hours with PLAYBOY.

PLAYBOY: In your autobiography, *The Secret Life of Salvador Dali,* you begin the account of your life by stating that your first recollections are of the womb. Would you restate them for us?

DALI: Mostly it was like fried eggs but with no frying pan. In my prenatal vision, the yellow part of these eggs, the yolk, is almost normal—but with plenty of viscosity and reflections—while the whites are completely divine because they are full of iridescent colors. Everything is soft, everything is dark; it isn't necessary to be troubled about reality. It is the best thing we ever know. In the moment when we are born, we lose paradise. Suddenly there is too much light and everything becomes too dry. It is violence—the trauma of being. Almost everyone has these prenatal influences, but not in the way of Dali.

PLAYBOY: Speaking of prenatal influences, do you feel that there may be some connection between your own intrauterine vision of fried eggs and the recurrent image of limp watches in your paintings?

DALI: In a way, yes. The symbol of the limp watches, like all of my symbols, has many meanings—though I never know what they mean when I first use them. Only after years appears an explanation—sometimes three or four explanations. In the beginning, when I first made the limp watches in Paris, I believed they were only an illustration of the anguish of time and space. I had just finished eating a slice of camembert cheese one evening and I became obsessed with its softness, with the nature of softness itself; so I added the soft watches to a landscape of Port-Lligat in Spain that I had already begun. I never believed the painting was so important. But now I am sure that this painting is also an exact prophecy of the discovery of DNA, deoxyribonucleic acid, the hereditary code of life found in the nucleus of the cell, which was described by the scientists Watson and Crick in 1953—the most important scientific event of our time, thirty years after Dali's painting. This is really fantastic, because this is the painting that everybody believes is the craziest, the most irrational and the most incomprehensible of Dali.

PLAYBOY: That *is* fantastic. But you said that the limp watches have *many* meanings. What else do they represent?

DALI: The limp watches are also a prefiguration of Christ, because they resemble the soft cheese that obsessed me, and Dali has discovered that the body of Jesus is the same as cheese. This is not only Dali; the first man who talked about this was Saint Augustine, who once compared the body of Christ to mountains of cheese. So Dali has merely reintroduced the concept of cheese back into the body of Christ. In the communion, there have always been the bread and the wine for the body and blood. In the same way, the soft watches, like soft cheese, are the presence of the body of Christ in my painting.

PLAYBOY: Of course. Crutches are another prominent prop in many of your paintings. Is their symbolism equally complex?

DALI: When I was very small, I discovered a pair of crutches in an attic storeroom. They became for me the symbol of death and resurrection. But contrarily, they are also related to an impotence complex—something to hold something up. In my early life, you see, I believed that I was impotent. Since then, of course, I learn that this is not true. But I continue to use the crutches in my painting, only now it is sublimation.

PLAYBOY: What does the rhinoceros—another familiar subject—represent to you?

DALI: It is for me the symbol of cosmic gooseflesh. Its skin has plenty of granulations. I like this. Already I have received as gifts two living rhinoceroses. But Madame Dali did not accept them, because they are too much trouble to keep in my New York apartment.

PLAYBOY: The unicorn horn is another of your favorite symbols. Isn't it phallic?

DALI: The horn of the unicorn is at once phallic and a symbol of chastity, as in the most paradoxical of my paintings, *Young Virgin Autosodomized by Her Own Chastity.* I'm sorry to say that I have not yet received as gift a living unicorn. Perhaps one of your readers would offer one as a token of esteem for Dali.

PLAYBOY: Madame Dali might raise the same objection she did to the rhinoceroses.

DALI: I withdraw the request.

PLAYBOY: To return to your symbolism—in another of your most famous, and to many, most perplexing, paintings, *A Giraffe Aflame,* is a figure of a woman bristling with what appear to be dresser drawers emerging from her body. What did you intend to convey with this image?

DALI: The same as in an earlier painting of the *Venus de Milo,* which I made the same size as the Greek original in the Louvre, but with the improvement of many drawers. In the Greek civilization, you see, there exists no introspection, no Freud, no Christianity. With the addition of drawers it is possible to look inside the body of the *Venus de Milo* to the soul: Thus Dali creates a Freudian and Christian appearance in the Greek civilization.

PLAYBOY: How does the inspiration for these symbolic images actually come to you?

DALI: Dali every morning wakes at six o'clock to make pee pee, and in this pee-pee moment I understand everything with tremendous lucidity. This is the most divine moment for knowing everything most clearly. One morning while I make pee pee I am absolutely sure that Dali's machine for thinking—a rocking chair from which hang on strings many little goblets filled with hot milk—foreshadows the invention of cybernetics. The next day I check and discover that Norbert Wiener's manifesto on cybernetics was written fifteen years after Dali constructed his thinking machine. But my machine is never manufactured because I am not at all concerned with electronics, and it is only a crazy idea.

PLAYBOY: The word *crazy* has occasionally been used by others to describe *you* as well as your ideas. Are you really as eccentric as your paintings and public personality have led many to believe—or, as some suspect, have you merely employed eccentricity as a calculated device of self-advertisement?

DALI: I am not actually crazy. A psychiatrist in Paris worked for seven years to determine whether Dali is crazy or not. After many conversations he decided that Dali possesses one of the best organized brains he had ever encountered. He said that my brain contains the characteristics of paranoiac delusion structure; but paranoiac delusion, of course, is absolutely creative, the best kind of crazy. The whole difference between a crazy man and Dali is that Dali is not pathological. But even in true pathologic paranoiac delirium there exists some contact with reality. For instance, a good example of pathologic delirium: A man feels that his family is against him and that they want to poison his food. He begins to look around very closely at his family and discovers many things about them that are absolutely true. His fundamental assumption, of course, is wrong: Nobody wants to kill him. This is delirium and is crazy. But from this obsessional idea comes a marvelous quantity of perceptions of truth. He discovers many real things, thousands of insights and relationships that are unavailable to the average person, that usual people never perceive. Because I have this power of discernment, I discover things that other people could not possibly suspect exist.

PLAYBOY: For example?

DALI: Look at the mouth of the girl in that painting on the wall, and at this lamp on the table, and at your hand on the recording machine. Most people see no connection between these things. But Dali, on the contrary, establishes immediately a complete system of interpretation relating these objects. The difference between Dali's paranoiac delusion and the other kinds of craziness is his ability to communicate his visions of delirium to other people. This is the ability to see clearly, which is at the basis of every artist. The clearest such vision was that of Leonardo da Vinci, who could create, for example, an entire battle scene just by looking at random water spots on a damp wall—sometimes for an hour or more. This is the true paranoiac phenomenon, because if you can see something in this way, it is possible for you to tell other people "This is the nose of a man," for example—and they will see it exactly the same as you. In the other kind of crazy it is the contrary: You may have a vision or a dream, but after it passes, you cannot communicate it to other people, because it is not systematic or organized. The most important thing in my life is this ability to organize systematically the most complex elements of my environment; to create a cosmos.

PLAYBOY: Lucid visions such as you describe—even to the creation of a private cosmos—have been reported by many of those who have experimented with such hallucinogenic drugs as mescaline and LSD 25. Have you ever tried them?

DALI: No, no, no, because I am not courageous at all—and I don't need drugs to make the visions. There are many other methods to stimulate the vision. I now work with Dr. Jayle of Marseilles on contact lenses to create the dream in Technicolor.

PLAYBOY: In Technicolor?

DALI: Exactly. The eye never experiences total darkness. There are always little patterns. These patterns are the origin of the images you see before you go to sleep. You are completely awake, but you close your eyes and you see many extraordinary vivid images and abstract shapes, which are called hypnagogic images. They are the product of residual retinal patterns. In the dream state they become concrete patterns. Dr. Jayle is making contact lenses to irritate these images, to make more of these patterns and more vivid ones. And here is my all-time crazy idea which I tell Dr. Jayle for the quick approach to create hypnagogic images: Between two lenses you place living flies. And on the back of every fly is one drop of phosphorus. You put on the lenses and close your eyes and watch the flies jumping and romping in every direction: an abstract movie inside your eyelids, much better than mescaline or LSD 25.

PLAYBOY: What was Dr. Jayle's reaction to the idea?

DALI: Dr. Jayle says this is genius. But, of course, it is not practical to put flies in your eyes every day.

PLAYBOY: Some critics feel that your artistic gifts have been eclipsed by your devotion to such fanciful notions as this, and by your predilection for bizarre acts of exhibitionism. To recall only a few: Dressed in a gold space suit, you once arrived by ship in New York in a transparent plastic egg symbolic of your intrauterine "paradise." In Paris you pulled up to the Sorbonne in a white Rolls-Royce filled with a thousand white cauliflowers—to deliver a lecture on "Vermeer and the Rhinoceros." And just last year in New York you held up traffic by appearing in the window of a Fifth Avenue bookshop in a hospital bed, wearing a golden leather dressing gown while your pulse was being recorded for public view on an electrocardiograph. . . . Why do you do these things?

DALI: Dr. Rumaguere of Paris, whom I told you about—the one who proved Dali is not crazy—explains this need for everybody to pay attention to Dali. He says Dali possesses a sublime complex, a Dioscuri complex: Castor and Pollux. In Greek mythology Zeus was transformed into a swan and he made love with Leda. From this lovemaking Leda produced two eggs, one divine and the other an ordinary egg. In the divine egg are twins, Pollux and Helen. This doctor discovered that Pollux and Helen are Dali and Madame Dali. In the other egg are two usual, mortal people. Clytemnestra and Castor. Castor, the mortal brother of Pollux, is the mortal effigy of Dali, actually my brother, who died of meningitis at the age of seven, three years before Dali was born.

His name was also Salvador, and the family called me, the next child, Salvador, too. For me this is the trauma, the greatest tragedy of my life, but also the greatest good. After I was born my family told me every day, every moment about the other Salvador. They never talked about me, but about him. It became a tremendous obsession. I believed that my flesh and my soul were a part of the dead brother, the mortal Salvador. And this was the beginning of the eccentricities of my life, the source of my exhibitionism. It is necessary for Dali constantly to prove to everybody that the real Salvador is not the other, the dead brother. I must put bread on my head, grow a mustache, everything to create a hyperexhibitionism, to make everybody pay attention to Dali, to prove that I am alive. From this exhibitionism I become, like Pollux, immortal, while the other Salvador becomes dead, finished. This is why the egg is so important as a symbol in my life. In my house in Spain there is a room in the shape of an egg.

PLAYBOY: You say you need public attention. But do you genuinely enjoy making a spectacle of yourself?

DALI: Very much. At this moment when you catch me with the tape recorder I like very much; this is very good. But the most fantastically happy day in my life was when two photographers from *Paris Match* came to see me in London. They want one complete day of Dali, every detail. The next day we begin. Even while I eat in a restaurant they take the pictures. I lift a little piece of camembert to my mouth and "pop" with the camera. Every single moment is absolutely extraordinary. But the next day is a thousand times better. When I receive the contact prints I look again all day long and I relive exactly every little moment of this day. It is like Proust writing his autobiography. My life is like millions of people watching me on television, every moment, every second. This is the most divine thing.

PLAYBOY: Whom do you consider the world's greatest living artist?

DALI: In all the arts today, the only good is Dali—but for conception, not for realization. There is no time to realize good paintings. I am afraid to create something good, a masterpiece, because if I do the next year I will be dead—creatively, at least. For everybody it is the same. Raphael after painting something marvelous and Vermeer after painting his *View of Delft* found it impossible to do more. The same is true for Mozart. For Leonardo every painting was a disaster, but he kept painting, because he felt that perhaps the next year he would achieve something marvelous. I feel so, too.

PLAYBOY: Most art historians regard Picasso rather than Dali as the greatest living artist. Do you rank him second?

DALI: He is a genius, but he is destructive, anarchistic. He works in an ugly way, in caricature. He destroys beauty. For me the most important thing is the classic beauty of Raphael, Velázquez, Goya and Vermeer. This classical ideal, with its exacting disciplines of technique, is the most essential thing for a painter to study; but the painter cannot learn it today, and this is a most tragic thing. The best abstract painters today commit suicide because they do not have a classical background. Now the figure is again returning to art, but for most artists this is impossible because they have no knowledge of drawing. And so they involve themselves with extrapictorial ideas such as pop art, which is concerned with the common object—the soup can, the comic strips. The actual painting of these objects is less important than the idea of the utilization of these objects.

PLAYBOY: Couldn't many of your own early surrealist works, which were assembled from the same kind of throwaway items—old shoes, bottles, pieces of furniture—be called forerunners of contemporary pop art?

DALI: Yes, yes, I wish to tell everyone of the Dalinian antecedents of pop art. Most important were the symbolic mechanisms which I created with Albertto Giacometti. In 1936 I constructed a surrealistic object using an old slipper of Madame Dali's, which contained a glass of warm milk. Above this was suspended one lump of sugar which disintegrates in the milk. There is also in this assemblage a little piece of excrement and an extra lump of sugar containing several of my pubic hairs, which float around in the milk when the sugar dissolves. At this same time I created another fantastic object from a chair given to me by a friend. The leather place where you sit down I replaced with one of chocolate that turns white with age. Under one leg of the chair I placed a doorknob, and another leg I plunged into a big glass of beer. All of which creates a very unstable equilibrium and causes the chair to lean far over and topple easily. I call this antecedent of pop art Dali's *Atmospheric Chair*.

PLAYBOY: That's very interesting, but—

DALI: Let me tell you also about my *Hypnagogic Clock*. This is beautiful. It is formed by one enormous piece of French bread set on a pedestal. I made holes in the bread into which I put one dozen bottles of ink, each holding a pen. On the bottom of this bread were sixty little strings from which I suspended little cards with sixty little watercolor pictures of the ink bottles and pens. And once I exhibited a mannequin with a very long loaf of bread on her head; on her face were many ants. But Picasso, destroyer of beauty, destroyed this, too—his dog jumped up and ate the bread. You can see that I am preoccupied with the symbolism of bread.

In Paris I had the idea for a Dalinian secret society to create a new movement of spiritual value in every nation. The idea was to bake a loaf of bread fifty feet long—it is necessary, of course, to build a special oven long enough to bake it in—which would be placed one night in the gardens of the Palais Royal. It would have a highly demoralizing effect on its discoverers. The bread would be examined for explosives and poisons. it would become the subject of conversation and newspapers. Who had done it? Why? And then another loaf of bread sixty-five feet long would suddenly appear in the courtyard at Versailles. And on the same day loaves of bread one hundred feet long would appear in all the capitals of Europe, in America, in Shanghai, everywhere. Everyone would think this is the work of a dangerous international conspiracy.

PLAYBOY: You're probably right, but—

DALI: I must tell also about the truly fantastic siphon which I create for a soda-dispenser bottle. It has a plunger twenty-five feet long. Everything else is normal. It was exhibited in the Julien Levy Gallery in New York, one of my first exhibits in this country. But nobody notices it at all. The people came and looked at this object and nobody paid any attention because it creates an insuperable problem: out of reality to create a completely irrational object. Nobody cared. But now with pop art everybody makes a tremendous reputation with these things.

PLAYBOY: Why, in your opinion?

DALI: Because pop art is part of the healthy trend away from abstract expressionism—which has become a caricature—back to the maximum of visual reality with no modifications, back to painting everything exactly as it appears with no changes. Such objective copying is not new. Vermeer, in the seventeenth century, was more pop art than the best-known modern pop artists, like Lichtenstein. Lichtenstein is subjective, a romantic. He paints an ice-cream soda in a kind of old-fashioned glass that no longer exists in the drugstore. He does this because he remembers an ice-cream soda as a nostalgic memory of a happy childhood, a Proustian kind of art, a remembrance of things past. But Vermeer, no; Vermeer is not sentimental or romantic at all. He is completely objective, completely classical. When he painted his *View of Delft,* he changed absolutely nothing. No optical instrument could give a clearer, truer picture. The great masters of art never changed the visual appearance, they did not distort. Even with the Greeks, such as Praxiteles, this was true. The finest art is always the most photographic.

PLAYBOY: Do you feel that your belief in the central role of science in shaping the art of the future is shared by other contemporary artists?

DALI: Some painters of today are concerned about the developments of science. But most work in a perfectly intuitional manner, reflecting the cosmology of today with no real scientific knowledge of it. But this is not important. Sensible people know that it is not necessary to learn from books, but from sensitivity and intuition. In the case of Dali, of course, painting is but one single small mode of expressing his own original cosmology, which enables him, through his genius and his paranoia, to create a synthesis of nature impossible even for the scientist, because the scientist is too much involved in his specialization. The important thing for Dali is everything: the painting, the pop art, the lenses, the French bread—a complete cosmology, a single Dalinian continuity in every field—in morals, in philosophy, in religion, in science.

PLAYBOY: How does the Dalinian cosmology reconcile the traditional incompatibility between science and religion?
DALI: Dali reached religion because of his study of science. In the beginning of my life, I was very atheistic, because my father was a freethinker, very much influenced by the anticlericalism, the rationalism of the French Revolution. He would not let me go to Christian schools when I was a child. The real start of my interest in religion were the days beginning with my interest in nuclear physics—the discoveries in quantum physics of the nature of energy, that matter becomes energy, a state of dematerialization. I realized that science is moving toward a spiritual state. It is absolutely astonishing the mystical approach of the most eminent scientists: the declarations of Max Planck and the views of Pierre Teilhard de Chardin, the great Jesuit scientist: that man in his constant evolution is coming closer and closer to a oneness with God. And now the announcement of Watson and Crick about DNA. This is for me the real proof of the existence of God. All of my knowledge, of both science *and* religion, I incorporate into the classical tradition of my painting.
PLAYBOY: With all of your extrapictorial interests, how much time do you have left to devote to your painting?
DALI: About six months a year, which is the time I spend at my home in Port-Lligat. I awake with the sun and work until it sets.
PLAYBOY: How do you spend the six months a year in New York?
DALI: In New York I sleep mostly.
PLAYBOY: For six months?
DALI: Yes, yes, yes, I sleep all the time. When the hour came for this interview I was in bed.
PLAYBOY: Is that why you chose New York as your second home?
DALI: That, and other reasons. Also I like New York because there are more ideas here than anywhere else—a fantastic quantity of ideas. But more importantly, after Madame Dali, I most love money. In New York it is possible to catch a tremendous quantity of money all the time. The origin of this joy of money is my Spanish mysticism. In the Middle Ages the alchemists wanted everything they touched to turn to gold. This transmutation of material things is the best kind of spiritualization.
PLAYBOY: You mentioned your love for Madame Dali. In contrast to many famous figures in the arts, you have maintained a quiet and continuous history of married life with the same woman.
DALI: For thirty years, or something like that. A very remarkable marriage in every way—from the very beginning, when we were married with only a civil rite, not a religious ceremony, because the first husband of Madame Dali is Paul Éluard, the poet. It is not possible in Catholic countries to remarry in a church. But after Éluard is dead, in that moment we perform a Catholic marriage in a little church with an archbishop. And I love so tremendously the organ, the trumpet, the bishop, all the ceremony, that I wanted to be married again immediately. I would like all of my life to become a ritual. But there is only one archbishop in Port-Lligat, so we can't be married again. But the archbishop tells me it is possible to marry the lady again in a Coptic ceremony, the most beautiful of all. It doesn't improve anything, but it also doesn't take away anything. So we had three ceremonies: civil, Catholic and Coptic. I absolutely love this idea. Dali is the contrary of everybody because everybody makes divorce over and over, while I marry my wife again and again. Also another curious thing: I never make love except with Madame Dali.

PLAYBOY: Not even during your student days in Madrid?
DALI: In my whole life never before I met my wife, because I was fantastically afraid about sex, even though there were tremendous opportunities. I was afraid that I was impotent, because I read an erotic book in Spain which discussed in the very brutal Spanish manner how to make love—not in the front but only in the back—and it says the girl produces a noise as if you had broken a watermelon. I felt that for me to cause such a noise was impossible, and this created a complex of impotence. But later, as I told you before, I discover that I am not impotent.
PLAYBOY: Do you plan on having any children?
DALI: I don't like the child. I don't like the dog, the cat, nothing small. Only the flounder—and only in my dreams, where the flounder is living in the carpet and not in the sea. But I am nevertheless tremendously interested in everything erotic. Everything in my painting and everything in religion is very erotic. There is a religious book proving that all the great Spanish mystics, Saint Theresa and Saint John of the Cross, were completely chaste but they had erotic ecstasies like orgasms when they saw angels and most beautiful things. Erotic ecstasies and religious ecstasies are very close: One is mechanical, the other is spiritual. But my voice disappears. Madame Dali says I use my voice too much.
PLAYBOY: One final question, then. Would you tell us about any plans you may have for the future?
DALI: Yes, yes—but first I have thought of a tremendous idea for you, for a most beautiful pop-art cover for PLAYBOY: photograph of Dali's fantastic *Aphrodisiac Jacket*. It consists of one regular smoking jacket—but with plenty of little jigger glasses fastened onto the front. All of the glasses are filled with crème de menthe, and in every glass is a dead fly in the bottom. Very luxurious, very brilliant object. Only two days ago Dali discovers the real mathematical significance of this creation in the *Scientific American* magazine, about the smell of peppermint: It shows every kind of smell arranged mathematically, according to the constitutional geometry of its molecules, including the molecular arrangement of the smell of peppermint. So one of my greatest pop-art objects is now becoming completely scientific. Add to this creation plenty of straws, each in the middle of the green crème de menthe. Then put inside the jacket a nude model, showing the legs and the beginning of the bosoms; her sex is not showing, but almost, almost. It is possible instead of a coat hanger to show the girl's face—but not the whole face, just up to the mouth. But you decide. Perhaps it is best to use a smoking jacket of moire silk pattern. Some people tell me that in a shop for theatrical supplies you can get a "twist" jacket, which is more fancy and extraordinary than the usual ones—the kind twist boys like the Beatles would wear. Since the sexes of the Beatles is so ambiguous—nobody knows if it is boy or girl with the hair so long—the quintessence of ambiguity is this smoking jacket of Dalinian pop art. I propose that this is the most beautiful, the most fantastic cover for PLAYBOY.
PALYBOY: Thanks for the suggestion. We'll take it under advisement. Now will you tell us about your plans for the future?
DALI: Yes. In two years, I plan a tremendous agony: to cut off my mustache. I will do this because my hair collapse on top, and I wish to wear a wig. But it is not possible to have both a mustache and a wig—this is too much. So I must cut off my mustache. The ceremony will take place in Venice, and there will be television and everybody will come—a completely liturgical scene. I will then have not one but two wigs made—one gray for the daytime, one black for night; and with this gesture, the monarchy will arrive back in Europe. General Franco will decide to reestablish the

monarchy in Spain, and in this moment of the return of the monarchy, *everybody* will wear wigs again, and there will be a renaissance of ornamentation and plumes and tremendous quantities of little cakes and candles. Art and painting will flourish. And so will Dali.

HENRY MILLER

September 1964

Interviewer: Bernard Wolfe

No conversation with an author was more naturally anticipated or expected by the magazine's readers than the one with Henry Miller. As the pioneer of confessional literature and unexpurgated prose, the editors of PLAYBOY had an early affinity for Miller which was reciprocated. Following this in-depth interview, his unpublished stories were solicited and published and Miller remained, until his death in 1980, an avuncular figure for the magazine and its readers.

Novelist Bernard Wolfe, also a frequent contributor to PLAYBOY in its early years, conducted this interview at poolside in Miller's Pacific Palisades home. Wolfe had been a close friend, colleague, drinking buddy, and "brother iconoclast" of Miller's for nearly twenty-five years. Interestingly, PLAYBOY editor A. C. Spectorsky was then intent on keeping the "respectability" of this feature high, so the very words that Miller discusses as having been banned in his books are not referred to directly in the interview. The use of genuinely explicit language, although defended by PLAYBOY, would not appear in the magazine until a few years later.

We asked Bernard Wolfe to interview Henry Miller, the maverick of American letters. Here is his report:

"When the first copies of the first Paris edition of Tropic of Cancer *reached our shores in 1934, appetizingly camouflaged in the dust jackets of Escoffier and Brillat-Savarin cookbooks, mine were among the damp hands that reached for them. It was our good luck that the desultory hawkshaws of U.S. Customs never stopped to wonder at this surge of undergraduate passion for* l'haute cuisine; *for more than a few of us cut our literary eyeteeth on that contraband book. To us it was, as its author feistily proclaimed, a badly needed 'gob of spit in the face of Art,' as well as an incendiary demonstration of the napalm still latent in the English language.*

"We campus malcontents worked up a lively image of the berserker who concocted that paper-backed bombshell—and the equally explosive volumes that followed . . . We knew a giant when we read one; the deeper underground a book was driven, the taller grew its author.

"Years passed. World War II drove the wild man out of Europe, and when he showed up one day on the streets of New York, where some of us had settled with our typewriters and our distempers, we gaped. The Rimbaud of Myrtle Avenue, the Villon of the 14th Ward, was nowhere near as big or as loud or as rambunctious as we'd imagined him. He was slight and bone-thin. His voice was soft, mellifluous. The gray hair that fringed his bold bald pate was neatly crew-cut. His jowls were as clean-shaven as his nails were clean and manicured. He wore impeccably tailored Bond Street tweeds and a natty plaid ulster. He was kind, courteous, considerate, mild, modest, gentle, and all but old-worldly in his gallant manners with the womenfolk—the very antithesis of the capering, carousing cutup called Henry Miller in the books of Henry Miller. The rapacious desperado of Cancer *had turned out to be everybody's Dutch uncle. . . .*

"But with something added—something not exactly avuncular, some special clear unblinking light in the deceptively mild blue eyes half draped by slanty mandarin lids, some special husky vibrant sound in the misleadingly gentle voice that has never deviated from the flat Brooklyn tones of his birth.

"Henry went West. He holed up for a time in the Santa Monica hills. Later he settled in his aerie on the highest rise of the Big Sur mountains in northern California, to stay put for twenty years. Now bestsellingly U.S.-published, duly stamped with the Supreme Court seal of approval, and socially acceptable among all but ladies' auxiliary literary tea societies, he's back in the Los Angeles area, living in Pacific Palisades to be near his two teenage children by his third wife. Our paths cross often, and I am forever amazed at how little he's changed. At seventy-two he's still lean as an ax handle, with eye undimmed and Brooklyn drawl intact."

PLAYBOY: One critic has described your work as "toilet-wall scribbling." Just to set the record straight: Are you now, or have you ever been, a toilet-wall scribbler?
MILLER: No, never. But that reminds me of a story about the French *pissoirs* which might apply to me. A university professor was just coming out of the *pissoir* while another professor was entering. As they passed each other, the one entering noticed that the one leaving had a pencil in his hand. "Aha," he snickered. "So you're one of those who writes on toilet walls?" "Oh, no," said the departing gentleman, "I was just correcting grammar."
PLAYBOY: Your books have been widely branded—and banned—as pornography. What's your reaction to the charge?
MILLER: Well, I *can* be said to have written obscene things, but I don't think of myself as a pornographer. There's a big difference between obscenity and pornography. Pornography is a titillating thing, and the other is cleansing; it gives you a catharsis. It's not done just to tickle your nerve ends—though I would add parenthetically that I don't go along with those judicious-minded critics and intellectuals who try to pretend that when you write erotically, with obscene language and all that, the reader should be impeccably immune, never have a lustful thought. Why the hell *shouldn't* a reader have lustful thoughts? They're as legitimate as any other kind. I might also add that apparently I'm even capable of arousing *other* kinds of thoughts. I get many letters from readers who say, "We're not at all interested in your sexual writing; it's your philosophy we find stimulating."
PLAYBOY: Still, as far as stimulation is concerned wouldn't you say that most readers prefer your erotica to your philosophy?
MILLER: Perhaps so, but the importance of my work lies in my vision of life and of the

world, not in the free use of four-letter words. These banned books of mine fit in with the tradition of literature widely known and accepted in Europe for the last thousand years. Unfortunately, for the last three hundred years, English-language literature has been castrated, stifled; it's pallid, lacking integration and totality. Preceding this period, sex communication never had contained this shocking quality. There was a freedom of expression. There was no emphasis put upon sex. It fitted in naturally because it was and is a part of life. But the Anglo-Saxon people, in the past three centuries, have been terribly deprived—starved, literally speaking, for the natural and normal expression of sex which can counteract unnatural feelings of guilt. So now they leap on the sensational, and because they have found in me this missing element, they overemphasize it.

PLAYBOY: Hasn't it been said that *you* are the one who overemphasizes it?

MILLER: It might just as well be said that I overemphasize the subject of the freedom of the individual. I feel I have simply restored sex to its rightful place in literature, rescued the basic life factor from literary oblivion, as it were. Obscenity, like sex, has its natural, rightful place in literature as it does in life, and it will never be obliterated, no matter what laws are passed to smother it. Let me tell you about an incident that may give an indication of my point of view. My little son and I were walking in one of the great forests of northern California. All alone, not a sound, not a person around for miles. Suddenly he started looking frantically about, holding himself, you know. "What's wrong?" I asked him. "I have to go to the bathroom," he said. "Well, you can't," I replied. "There's no bathroom here. Do you mean you have to take a leak? Come on, do it right here near this big tree. Come on, I'll show you. You can't 'go to the bathroom' on a tree." And so there we stood, father and son in the beautiful forest, pissing on a tree. So you see, in life as in writing, I use common words to express myself because it is the only way for me. I haven't considered, chosen or selected. One might just as well ask why I've written the way I have about people, countries, streets, religion, and so on. I haven't singled out sex for special treatment, but I've given it the *full* treatment.

I had been writing for fifteen years and getting nowhere. Everything I had written was derivative, influenced by others. Then finally I decided to please *myself*. It was a great gamble, but finally I cut the umbilical cord, and in severing it I became an entity. I became *myself*, you see? When they speak of tradition in the literary world, they are speaking of men who are individualists, who are entities, who, in becoming themselves, become part of tradition. As for being obsessed with sex, *they* are the ones who are obsessed: they who make so much over the sexual content of what I have written. When people have been deprived, they make up for lost ground the moment the barriers are down. This is what is happening with the banned books. Other countries accepted them as a basic part of life. All over the world they think of us Americans as a people obsessed with the *idea* of sex but lacking a full and natural experience of sex. The English-speaking peoples are precisely the ones who understand the least what I've written and why.

PLAYBOY: Would you care to enlighten them now?

MILLER: I can try. I was sick to death of the lack of substance in English literature, with its portrayal of a truncated, partial man. I wanted a more substantial diet, the whole being, the round view you get in the paintings of Picasso, the works of Montaigne and Rabelais and others. So I rebelled, and perhaps overgenerously made up for this lack and weakness in the literature of my time.

PLAYBOY: One critic has alleged that your "overgenerous" depiction of sex—far from fascinating readers—has actually rendered the subject uninteresting as a literary topic. Do you think he may have a point?

MILLER: Naturally, anything done to excess becomes uninteresting. But I don't think we need worry about making sex uninteresting. All that was taken care of by the Creator when He created male and female. What is important is whether we have a healthy or a sick attitude toward sex or anything else.

PLAYBOY: Though willing to concede that you personally may not be obsessed with sex, another detractor has accused you of "using freedom of expression as the high-sounding cover-up for a cynically commercial effort to cash in on the sure-fire sales appeal of sex." Have you?

MILLER: I have never knowingly been cynical or insincere. And as for the commercial aspect, that was farthest from my mind. I was merely determined to write as I pleased, as I viewed life, do or die, without thought for the consequences.

PLAYBOY: Did you anticipate the worldwide storm of public protest, censorship and suppression that followed the publication of *Tropic of Cancer*?

MILLER: I was not concerned with this problem. I had had fifteen years of punishment and rejection before *Cancer* was published. It was something I had to do, and that was all there was to it.

PLAYBOY: What was the initial reaction of European critics to the *Tropics*?

MILLER: A very broad question. Shall I say "varied"? Critics are the same all over the world. They judge by what they are—which we won't get into. On the whole, however, I must say that whether for or against, their approach to my work was on a higher level than that of the Anglo-Saxon critics, who, now that these books are being published here, are saying, after condemning them—and reading them under the counter—for nearly thirty years, "It's about time" or "So America is really growing up at last."

PLAYBOY: Do you agree with them, at least, that popular acceptance of the *Tropics* in the U.S. means that "America is really growing up at last"?

MILLER: Times *have* changed—but whether in the direction of more freedom or less is difficult to say. There is still a great gap between the accepted behavior of individuals, as regards sex, and the freedom to express this in words. I don't delude myself that the world suddenly sees eye to eye with me on the subject of sex—or any other subject, for that matter. Only the Scandinavian countries, Sweden and Denmark, seem to me to be truly liberated in this sense.

PLAYBOY: Still, don't you view the American publication of the *Tropics*, and the Supreme Court decision upholding it, as a kind of personal vindication?

MILLER: I had my victory, if you wish to call it that, long before this American success, if you wish to call *it* that. In the countries where my books circulated freely, I was, if not a popular writer, certainly an accepted writer. I had my reward in being accepted and acknowledged by many of the foremost writers and thinkers in Europe. One is truly accepted or understood only by one's peers.

PLAYBOY: In addition to literary admirers, you've acquired, along with a controversial reputation, a coterie of disciples so worshipful that it has been called a cult. Are you flattered by this sort of idolatry?

MILLER: Of course not! The most devastating thing about achieving any success as a writer is to meet the people who rave about your work. It makes you wonder about yourself.

PLAYBOY: Though many critics share the admiration of your fans for the vitality of your work, others have used the following adjectives to describe you as a writer:

"undisciplined," "chaotic," "confused," "self-contradictory" and "overemotional." What's your reply?

MILLER: Isn't it enough to *write* books without being obliged to answer for them? It's the function of the critic to criticize. He's like the fifth wheel on a wagon. Oh, well—by conventional standards, I suppose I *am* an undisciplined, chaotic, disorganized writer. But some of us, fortunately, pay no heed to standards. Undoubtedly I'm as muddled as the next man. but look at the great philosophers—are they so clean and clear? Kant—my God, what murky, cloudy thinking that is! Or take Aristotle—I can't read Aristotle, it's a jungle of nonsense to me. I like Plato much better. But I can get lost with Plato, too. I'll tell you, it may be because of my eclecticism that I'm misunderstood. One time I'm talking this way, another time that way. Naturally, I contradict myself now and then. Who doesn't? One would have to be stagnant not to do so. But I contend that I'm always driving at truth. One has to approach reality from all directions—there's no one way to go at it. The more avenues you open up, the clearer the ultimate thing should be. I'm antisystem and antistructure, yes. But that's hardly confusion.

PLAYBOY: It's also been said that you suffer from "verbal diarrhea," that your "billowing, undisciplined, rough-hewn prose urgently requires the attention of a sharp blue pencil." What do you have to say about this?

MILLER: I've never pretended to be a careful, inch-by-inch writer, like Hemingway was—but neither am I one of those careless, sprawling writers who feel that the slag belongs with the ore, that it's all one, part and parcel of the same thing. I must confess there's a great joy, for me, in cutting a thing down, in taking the ax to my words and destroying what I thought was so wonderful in the heat of the first writing. You think when you spew the words out that they're imperishable, and a year later they seem trivial or flat. The ax-wielding is as much a part of the creative process as the first volcanic gush. But this editing, at least for me, is not aimed at achieving flawlessness. I believe that defects in a writer's work, as in a person's character, are no less important than his virtues. You need flaws; that's what I'm trying to say. Otherwise you're a nonentity.

PLAYBOY: Nevertheless, in recent criticism of you work, novelist Lawrence Durrell, a longtime friend of yours, has taken you to task for these very flaws—and for excusing them in yourself. Have his remarks affected the cordiality of your relationship?

MILLER: Not at all—as you'd know if you'd read my answer to his criticism of my later books. You'd see that I took it all in good part. He could have said much worse than he did, and it wouldn't have altered my feelings toward him.

PLAYBOY: Which are?

MILLER: As a man, I still like and admire him. As a writer, I could make the same criticism of him that's made of me: that the big passages, the panoramic frescoes, really grip you—his wonderfully descriptive purple passages, majestically done, marvelously elaborate and intricate, which exist in and of themselves—whereas the philosophical sections, presenting his thoughts on art and aesthetics, seem drab by comparison—at least to me. Durrell, you see, is first and foremost a poet. He's in love with language itself. Some people find him too ornate, but I love his excesses—they reveal the artist in him.

PLAYBOY: Which other contemporary writers do you regard as artists?

MILLER: I don't think I really keep up, but let me think. O'Casey and Beckett and Ionesco I admire very much. But some of our better-known American playwrights leave me cold. I don't get any kick, any lift out of them. I can't read Nabokov. He's not for me; he's too literary a man, too engrossed in the art of writing—all that display of virtuosity. I do like Kerouac—I think he has a marvelous natural verbal facility, though it could stand a bit of disciplining. Such a wealth of feeling—and when it comes to nature, superb. Burroughs, whom I recognize as a man of talent, great talent, can turn my stomach. It strikes me, however, that he's faithful to the Emersonian idea of autobiography, that he's concerned with putting down only what he has experienced and felt. He's a literary man whose style is unliterary. As for Saul Bellow, I've read only one of his books, *Henderson, the Rain King*, and I must say, I was infatuated with it. I wish I could write something in that vein. For a while I was interested in Ray Bradbury; he seemed to have opened a new vein. But I think he's shot his bolt. There are still startling ideas in his books now and then, wonderful flashes; one senses an inventive mind at work. But it's all in an area that doesn't excite me too much. Science fiction just isn't rich enough.

PLAYBOY: As one whose writing is strongly sexual in flavor, are you as interested in, and influenced by, Freudian psychology as some of the writers you've mentioned?

MILLER: When I first read Freud thirty or thirty-five years ago, I found him extremely stimulating. He influenced everybody, myself included. But today, he doesn't interest me at all. I think it's fine for a writer to roam about wherever he wants; anything that's of deep import to an artist must certainly nourish him. But the whole subject of Freudianism and analysis bores me almost as much as talking to analysts, whom I find deadly dull and single-tracked.

PLAYBOY: What's your objection to analysis itself?

MILLER: Let's put it this way—the analyst is sitting there as an intermediary, father-confessor, protector; he's there to awaken his patient and give him greater strength to endure whatever he has to endure. Well, I say that experience itself, whatever it be—brutal, sorrowful or whatever—is the only teacher. We don't need priests and we don't need analysts; we don't need mental crutches of any sort. More than anything, what I criticize is their efforts to restore the maladapted person to a society whose way of life *caused* him to be maladapted in the first place. They want us to accept things as they are. But things as they are are wrong.

PLAYBOY: But you've often insisted that people are really self-determined, that it's really a dodge to blame society for our troubles. Isn't that a contradiction of what you've just said?

MILLER: It seems contradictory, but to me it isn't. Look, when you develop the proper strength, you can live in *any* society. You can achieve a certain immunity—not a total one, certainly, but enough not to become sick, not to be paralyzed. I say if there's strength to be gotten, where else would you look for it than inside yourself? Now it may be that some of us are doomed, some won't have the strength, and will go down—but that's an inescapable fact of life. Some can rise up to meet it and others can't. But to say that we can catch those who are sick and sinking, and buoy them up through analysis—I don't believe it.

PLAYBOY: You were quoted recently as saying that the American approach to things sexual, particularly in plays, movies and television, is becoming increasingly "cute." Do you regard this trend as psychologically sick—and how significant do you feel it is?

MILLER: Of course it's sick—and it could be significant. Cuteness has its part, like anything else, but playing around with sex, on this teasing level, the look-but-don't-touch sort of thing, could make the American male perpetually dissatisfied with his wife or girl. It's another version of this phony misleading drive of Americans to coat everything with glamour—creating a glamorous world of illusion and then trying to live in it. It doesn't work. I think the cute approach to sex is about on a par with a cute approach to the atom bomb. But it *is* nice for men to be fussed over and titillated; they need that. It's a part of their basic nature, regardless of the fact that they may be in love with their own wives or girls. Take the geisha in Japan: She is an important part of a man's life. American women should be educated in school, taught as the Japanese are taught how to treat a husband or lover. There wouldn't be so many marriages that fail. In the Western world, a couple gets married in a romantic mood, but then there's nothing to show them how to go on increasing and nurturing their love. Instead of waiting until they turn out the lights, why not learn how to make a man happy at the dinner table or just sitting about reading? Why don't they wear something flimsy, keep acting out the love role as they did in the beginning? It might make the difference. But it's like churchgoers who run to church on Sundays and then forget religion the rest of the week.

PLAYBOY: Who do you feel is responsible for this situation?

MILLER: I blame most of this unhappy sexual situation on the men. They don't behave as men, as the boss, the dominant head of the family. They allow the women to jockey with them for equality, to become their rivals. This does not make for the ideal sexual climate. In Europe the man is still the boss. He even slaps his woman around a bit, but the woman is happier in this subordinate role.

PLAYBOY: In view of what you indicate is their more feminine, less competitive role, do you feel that European women are more exciting sexually than American women?

MILLER: Any *real* woman, European or otherwise, is exciting. Frankly, I know of only one sexual type: Either she has *it* or she doesn't.

PLAYBOY: Will you describe "it"?

MILLER: Everyone of any sensitivity knows when he is in the presence of a great person or a saint. The same applies to a woman with *it*. She exudes *it*. She neither shrinks from sex nor juts forward unnaturally when the subject arises. American women seem to have to prove themselves. They wear sex on the surface of their beings like a patina. But the natural ones *feel* it, as a part of their very being. Sophia Loren is an example. She is *living* it. She is all woman. Most of your American sex symbols of the cinema, on the other hand, are just wearing it. It's all on the outside. They feel nothing, really—so neither do you.

PLAYBOY: Would you be willing to tell us what kind of sexual relationship you've found most gratifying—with whatever nationality of woman?

MILLER: I prefer to keep that information to myself. It's nobody's business but my own. Even an author has *some* rights! But I will say that the atmosphere of hazard, peril or danger of embarrassment is most exciting—the encounter with someone, even a stranger, in an alleyway, a dark hall or doorway, maybe even a telephone booth.

PLAYBOY: Why?

MILLER: Well, I suppose it's because it's the opposite of our everyday experience. The element of surprise is what makes it so intriguing—you aren't set, you have no stand one way or the other. I must amplify: I feel that I'm a man to whom things happen. I seldom deliberately set out to bring things about. I'm always sort of open and vulnerable, waiting for something to come about—which actually *permits* things to happen much more frequently, don't you see? If I set out to have an experience, a sexual or love experience, it would have a totally different tonality to it, it seems to me—probably in a lower key.

PLAYBOY: You've said that the "hero" of *Cancer* is a man who initiates nothing, who merely accepts things as they come to him. Isn't that a Buddhist view?
MILLER: Perhaps. I make no secret of the fact that I have been much influenced by Taoistic writing and Oriental philosophy in general. I think we all take from others. I don't think there's such a thing as an original artist. We all show influences and derivations. We can't avoid using or being used. When it comes time to express yourself, what you put forth should be done unconsciously, without thought of influences. But all this is in your blood already, in the very stream of your being. I've come to believe that I'm at my best, I express myself best, when I'm following the philosophy of the East, but I wouldn't propose it as the one way. I think each one has to find his own unique route.
PLAYBOY: Does this imply that you incline toward the role of observer rather than protagonist?
MILLER: No. I think the peculiar quality of an artist is that he's both participant and observer at the same time. He's playing a dual role always. I mean, I don't go through life as a writer who's always making notes in a mental diary, though I *am* aware of making note of things for future use. I can't help it; it's my nature. But I don't enter into things in a spirit of detached research. When I participate, I do so as a human being; I'm simply more aware than most men of what's actually happening.
PLAYBOY: You just referred autobiographically to the role of the "artist." Yet you've called *Tropic of Cancer* "a gob of spit in the face of Art." Do you see any contradiction between this scorn for "Art" and your self-identification as an artist?
MILLER: No. I think that only a man who has been steeped in art, who is truly inoculated, as it were, with culture, can see the defect in it. This is a double-edged thing. One has to be an artist in order to speak against art. Coming from a layman, it has no validity. Only someone immersed in art could renounce it. I mean that one should lop off all that is stupid, nonsensical, unimportant—all that goes with capital letters when one invokes the words *Culture* and *Art*. We have an analogy in what happened to the philosophy of Zen when it was brought from India to China. What did the Chinese do? They took Buddhism as the Hindus had known it and they lopped off the superstructure; they brought it down to earth and made it viable, livable, I would say. My purpose, when referring to art in this denigrating way, is to bring it closer to life. Art has a tendency to detach itself from life. One has to bring it back again, like a gardener taking care of a plant—cut away the overgrowth, give the roots a chance to breathe.
PLAYBOY: Do you feel that you've done this in your own writing?
MILLER: I hope so, in my own small way. What I've strived to do is to get away from the fictive and down to the reality about oneself, embrace every aspect of one's being, look at it all clearly, boldly. That's the whole purpose of writing, isn't it, to reveal as many sides of yourself as possible? Though I've done all sorts of short-term things, books of the moment, offshoots without any consistent note running through them, there has also been the long-term job, the record I want to make of my life, no matter how long it takes or how many volumes. That is a planned work: *The Rosy Crucifixion* is the master title. Though I haven't thought about it every minute, it has always been in the back of my head.
PLAYBOY: When did you decide to write it?
MILLER: I laid it out way back in 1927, in about thirty-five pages of telegraphic notes, and I'm still working from them, from the very last pages. *Sexus* and *Plexus* both

came out of these notes, and now the concluding volume of *Nexus*, which I've nearly completed.

PLAYBOY: Would you read us a sample of those notes?

MILLER: Well, if you insist. Here are a couple of pages I used as raw material in writing *Plexus* and *Nexus*. They begin like this: "L. decides to make puppets and sell them. Also death masks. At dawn I go out and steal milk bottles and rolls that are left in vestibules. Panhandling along Broadway outside the burlesque shows and movies. Incident at Borough Hall when the guy throws money at me in the gutter. I begin to paint the walls myself and hang up crazy charts. S. arrives and looks on, nodding his approval of the disruption. Reminiscences of childhood. Relations with L. are improving. Sleeping three abed. J. now jealous. Working this to death. More gold digging on a grand scale, only now it's a burlesque. The two of them look like freaks. L. hiring herself out for experiments of all kinds. I get the idea of selling my blood. Begin visiting the hospitals. Must eat better food, drink milk, red wine, and so one. The jujitsu expert at Hubert's Cafeteria bringing the rent to us while we are in bed, slipping it under the door. The German savant—a ticket chopper on the elevated station. The two sailors listening in to scenes from the shed outside of L.'s room and freezing to death. Drunks with B., the Cherokee Indian. The night of S.'s birthday. We go out to celebrate, I in a torn khaki shirt. The night club uptown. Drinking everything in sight. Then the line-up and search by thugs. S., in his crazy way, calmly palming off a bad check on them for $125. The scene in the vestibule of cloakroom when the ex-pugilist beats the piss out of the drunken customers. Returning at dawn to find L. sleeping in my place. Dragging her out of the bed by the scalp. Peeing over her on the floor. Then falling asleep in the bathtub, nearly drowned. Return to Paul and Joe's near 14th Street. Waiting at the Bridge Plaza to see if J. is coming over the bridge in a taxi. Finding her home in bed, paralyzed with drink. Next day vomiting begins. Continues for three or four days, night and morning. The story of rape by jujitsu doctor. J.'s explanation. Go in search of wrestling doctor, murder in heart. Returning silently and listening to their conversation on the stairs. Suddenly the explosion in Jersey City and discovery of L. standing on stairs. Last confrontation. Dragging her along in the snow despite protestations and denials. I leave for the West . . ."

PLAYBOY: You see to have led a rather violent life in those days.

MILLER: I was a pretty turbulent character, all right—and not a very agreeable one, either. Though I never failed to make friends, I was always in hot water, always arguing and disputing. I was an obnoxious sort of chap who had to get his ideas across, who was forever buttonholing people and bludgeoning them with words. I made a pest of myself. I was an idealist and a rebel—but an unpleasant one. As I've grown older, I've become even more rebellious—but also more adapted, at least to myself. Maybe I've become more skillful in the art of dealing with people and circumstances, so that I don't blow my top so easily anymore. But I'm still entirely capable of violence. In fact, one fear I have about myself is that I may lose control one day and do something unthinkable. But of course, we're *all* incipient criminals. Most of us simply lack the courage to act out our criminal urges. I've been fortunate enough to find an escape valve in writing. I've been able to act out my antisocial urges, stir up trouble, deal out my shocks and jolts on paper; and thanks to the release of all this steam, I've slowly become—well, more human, let's say.

PLAYBOY: Do you find, with your lengthening emotional distance from the early expe-

riences recorded in your notes, that it has become easier to write about them?
MILLER: Technically, yes. But with time, of course, everything tends to grow cold. One has to blow on the embers. It's not easy to warm a thing up again, to put yourself back in the old positions, at the emotional pitches you once attained, to re-create the conversations—talk that lasted all night, ten hours, full of fight and struggle, going the whole gamut from personal trivia to literature and history and every damn thing. Today these things are easier to write about, yes, but they're almost impossible to recapture in their pristine fire and substance. You have to fall back on your imagination, to rely on your artistry.
PLAYBOY: But it's been said that in *Sexus* and *Plexus* you seem to show total recall of both emotions and events.
MILLER: I may give that illusion, but if you could compare my reconstructions with tape recordings of the original scenes, you'd find a tremendous disparity. Lately I've been inventing more freely than before, but always in conformity with the remembered feel of the thing. I never invent in the sense of disguising or altering; I always want to recapture, but not in the strictly photographic-phonographic sense. Also, of course, I've left a lot out. One can't put everything in, even if one lives to be a hundred.
PLAYBOY: You've been working on *The Rosy Crucifixion,* on and off, for some thirty-seven years now. Why has it taken so long?
MILLER: Well, you see, the more one writes about oneself, the less important it all seems. One writes to forget himself, or better said, to forget *the* self. When I started writing, especially the *Tropic*s, I thought: No one has suffered as much as I. I had to get it out—so many volumes, so many millions and millions of words. And now that it's almost finished, I don't want to write like that anymore, understand? But I find that I'm caught in my own web. Now that the *Tropic*s are socially acceptable, I've suddenly become fashionable, and people are hounding me from every direction to translate these books into plays, films, librettos. I can't do this! I can't change these books into something else. I thought once I'd finished writing them that that was the end. I wanted to forget them. But they're coming back to haunt me.
PLAYBOY: Don't you take some comfort in the very fact of this social acceptability, however belated, and in the royalties you've been reaping?
MILLER: It's sort of amusing, but also it's absurd and a bit of a headache. You see, in a way it's too late. The money should have been there in the beginning. Getting it now doesn't alter my life in the least. I continue to live on very little for myself. My problem now isn't how to get money, but how not to get too *much* of it. It frightens me. *Millions,* these movie people talk about! Can you believe it? Already I've given away to my friends and family over half of what I've received from *Cancer*. It's just too *much*. Having too much of anything worries me—especially money. It makes me uncomfortable. But I have to think of my children. They have to have their schooling and their living. Nowadays, at least, if they want to go someplace or do something special they dream up, I can give them a hundred dollars and it means nothing. But do you know I'm contributing to *three* families? Me and my divorces. I think I'll have an aspirin—maybe three. Would you care to join me?
PLAYBOY: No, thanks. But tell us: With all your extracurricular commitments, how do you find time for writing?
MILLER: Good question! The phone calls, the correspondence to answer, propositions to consider, contracts to decide on! Do you know it takes me a good four hours a day at least? I have hardly any time *left* for writing. I should have a secretary. Well, maybe

not, because if I did, naturally I would fall in love with her, and then I wouldn't get *any* writing done. You see, I couldn't possibly have an ugly old girl for a secretary, could I? She must be beautiful, attractive. And there I'd be—again. I fall in love so easily.

PLAYBOY: Still?

MILLER: It seems normal to me to fall in love over and over. Is it a sign of youth or of wisdom? It seems to me that most of us grow old long before our time. Being in love is the natural condition of the heart. I'm talking about loving someone *else,* of course, not yourself. But I was talking about work. The demands are never-ending. The moment one starts getting big money, he becomes involved with tax problems, lawyers, people who want money from you for a thousand causes—especially themselves. You have to suffer because of it. It's a challenge to your normal way of life. Time that should be spent working is taken up with all of these unvital, unpleasant things. I feel sometimes as if I may throw in the sponge and quit writing entirely.

PLAYBOY: Are you serious?

MILLER: Probably not—but if I decided tomorrow to take up some other pursuit, I'd certainly have no qualms about it. Sometimes I think it would be lovely to be a gardener or a nurseryman. That way nobody would get hurt, cheated, deceived or disillusioned; authors aren't the loveliest people in the world, you know. But if I don't stop writing, at least I want to start having some fun with it. I'm tired of doing those long, somber, serious things. Why shouldn't I have some fun now with writing?

PLAYBOY: Will sex be as big a factor in your future writings as it has been?

MILLER: I doubt it. Not because I have lost interest in sex, but because I have about come to the end of my autobiographical writing. As I said earlier, it seems to me that people have focused too strongly on this element in my work: they think it's—how shall I say it?—the dominant note of my writing because it has the quality of shock. At least it had for the early readers. Especially in America, many were too taken aback by the forthrightness of the *Tropic*s to see in them, as I do, a quality of lyricism. Though it may sound immodest, I'm forever amazed at the singing passages in them. They're not always pleasant, of course, but even when sordid and nihilistic, they are nevertheless poetic. Critics abroad have always pointed this out. But I think there's a range of thought and feeling that goes far beyond either of the *Tropic*s in some of my later work—in *The Books in My Life,* for instance, and such collected works as *The Wisdom of the Heart* and *Sunday After the War*, in which essays are mingled with stories.

PLAYBOY: Do you consider these your finest works?

MILLER: No. *The Colossus of Maroussi* is my own favorite, and I find it's coming more and more to be accepted by the public. I'd rather be known in the future by *The Colossus* than by any other effort. It shows me at my best—a man who's enjoying himself and appreciative of everything.

PLAYBOY: Was this change in style and attitude from the nihilism of the *Tropic*s the result of a change in your life?

MILLER: I would rather think so. One might say it was due to the feeling of exultation and exaltation that came over me in Greece. I wrote *Colossus* just after returning to the U.S. I wrote it hot, as it were.

PLAYBOY: But then you reverted to a more pessimistic tone in *The Air-Conditioned Nightmare,* a grim chronicle of your disenchantment with America. Why?

MILLER: It was the disparity between the two countries. I set out on a tour of America with hopes that I might write, maybe not an exalted report, but a book of appreciation

of my country after a long absence. But everywhere I went, I was let down. And I would be again, I think, if I took another look today. Perhaps even more so.
PLAYBOY: Why do you take such a dim view of your homeland?
MILLER: I've always felt that I'm *in* this country and not *of* it. I feel little connection with the things around me here. I'm not interested in political or social movements. I live my own restricted life, with my friends. What I read about the American way of life, about what goes on here, fills me with horror and dismay. It's become even more of an air-conditioned nightmare than it was when I wrote the book. I'm being corroborated, I feel, by events.
PLAYBOY: How do you mean?
MILLER: Well, it seems to me that in the seventy-two years I've lived, we've advanced—what, half a millimeter? Or have we gone back a few yards? This is how I look back on what we call our "progress." However civilized we seem to be, we're still just as ignorant, stupid, perverse and sadistic as savages. For seventy-two years I've been waiting to see some breakdown of the artificial barriers surrounding our educational system, our national borders, our homes, our inner being—a shattering of the wretched molds in which we're fixed—but it never happens. We have the dynamite but we don't set it off. I get sick of waiting. Despite the rosy dreams of the politicians and the so-called intellectuals of today, we're not going to bring about a better world peaceably and in an evolutionary manner, through piecemeal improvements; we progress, as we regress, in catastrophic jumps. And when I talk about the violent, explosive alteration of things, it's a wish as much as a prediciton of future events. To me it means a new chance, a new birth. I'm tired of history. I want to see everything swept away to clear the ground for something new. I want to get beyond civilization to what has been called the posthistoric state and see the new man who will live without all the restrictive, inhibiting barriers that hedge us in.
PLAYBOY: Do you think this is a realistic hope?
MILLER: How can we tell? If we knew what was coming—good or bad—we'd probably give up struggling to achieve it. It's true enough that the evidence of the past gives us little reason to believe that we ever will, for in the unfolding of history, the advances we have made have seemed to me illusory. We relapse time and time again. It can be argued that we always will, that man will always remain basically the same—that he's spiritually incurable. Well, maybe that's true about the majority of mankind, but there have been enough emancipated individuals throughout the course of history—prophets, religious leaders, innovators—to make me believe that we *can* break the old, suffocating molds, that we *can* somehow end forever the vicious and futile cycle of aspiration and disenchantment, transcend the age-old and recurring dilemmas, rid ourselves of the appurtenances of so-called civilization—jump clear of the clockwork, as someone put it. If we can, it's just barely possible that someday what's buried in us and longs to come out will find expression. I can't imagine what the form of that ideal future may take—but it will mean giving egress, however, belatedly, to the human spirit.
PLAYBOY: Do you feel that your own career has made any lasting and meaningful contribution toward that end?
MILLER: Who could dare to hope for that much? I'd say, undoubtedly, that I have brought about a tangible revolution which has won for English-language authors a certain degree of freedom from censorship—at least temporarily. I wonder, however, now that you put the question, what sort of effect I would *want* to have, were I capable of having one—I mean, in an *everlasting* way. But of course nothing is everlasting,

unless it be the endless cycle of creation and destruction on which you and I and each of us, for good or ill, leaves his own unique but infinitesimal mark. We are just men and women, after all. And the lowest is not so different from the highest. To be human, truly human, that is quite enough for me.

IAN FLEMING

December 1964

Interviewer: Ken Purdy

If James Bond books were merely a Sixties trend, they were a trend that outlived many others. That a fictional adventure hero should captivate everyone, from President John F. Kennedy to millions of readers worldwide (and many more millions of moviegoers later on), seems reason enough to include this light and painless look at James Bond's creator.

Several other reasons give this interview resonance, however. It is also a study in a way of life that has all but disappeared, as Ian Fleming describes a lazy afternoon at his home in Jamaica drinking rum punches—vestiges of the privileged colonialist before the sun set completely on their empire. It is also the only interview conducted by Ken Purdy, who became a great favorite with PLAYBOY readers in later years writing with elegance and expertise about automobiles. Finally, the interview takes on a poignancy when it is remembered that it appeared in December 1964, several months after Fleming's unexpected death at fifty-six of a heart attack, and is therefore something of a final testimony.

Since Edgar Allan Poe invented the modern detective story with The Murders in the Rue Morgue, *expert practitioners of the form have known huge audiences and heavy material rewards. In this procession, the late Ian Fleming, creator of James Bond, secret agent nonpareil, will long hold a prominent place. His publishers have sold thirty million copies of his twelve books in twelve years—give or take a couple of million. There are few literate communities in the world, from Hong Kong to Helsinki, in which he is not being read today. Even those who read only Yiddish or Siamese need not be deprived of the pleasure of his literary company—though Fleming himself, at the age of fifty-six, died of a heart attack late last summer, not the first he had had. He had known for some time that he had little prospect of a long life. Yet even in the four hours between the onset of the attack and his death in a Canterbury hospital, he managed to maintain the image of urbanity that distinguished him: En route to the emergency ward, he told the ambulance attendants that he was sorry to have had to trouble them. It was something that most Englishmen of his class would have said, almost pro forma, but it was also very James Bond. There is no doubt that his own character, and the one he had created, were intricately interleaved in Fleming's mind.*

Despite, or perhaps in part because of, his enormous popularity, the literary establishment took little notice of Fleming during his lifetime, and not much more at his death. In general, their judgment of his worth may prove to have been deficient, for he may still be read when novelists presently of some stature have been forgotten. He had an original view; he was an innovator. His central device, the wildly improbable story set against a meticulously detailed and somehow believable background, was vastly entertaining; and his redoubtable, implacable, indestructible protagonist, though some thought him strangely flat in character, may well be not so much the child of this century as of the next.

Several months before his death, Fleming consented to our request for an extended and exclusive interview. Our interviewer says of their meeting:

"He invited me to pick him up for lunch at his London office in Mitre Court, a byway between Fleet Street and the Inns of Court, which is to say, between the worlds of British law and journalism. The reception room was presided over by a pleasant and serene woman whose manner was not unlike M's Miss Moneypenny in the Bond books. She showed me into his inner office, a sedately elegant study draped and carpeted in wine red, neatly stacked with galley proofs and immaculately furnished with a gilt-framed mirror, brass penholder, ashtray, cigarette lighter and crimson letterboxes. A black homburg, a tightly furled umbrella and a dark-blue Burberry raincoat hung from hooks on the back of the door.

"As I entered, Fleming rose from behind a massive leather-topped desk to usher me to a chair—a tall man, lean, tending to be florid, wearing a navy-blue suit of typical British cut marked by one eccentricity: cuffs on the sleeves; light-blue shirt and black-and-white polka-dot bow tie, knotted with offhanded Churchillian looseness. We exchanged pleasantries. He was suave, amused, sardonic—but one sensed that he was kind. More than others, the Englishman reflects his station in life with his air, attitude and speech, and one versed in these matters could place Fleming instantly—and accurately—as Eton and Sandhurst, inherited money, government service, world travel, social assurance. He hadn't married until he was forty-three. Mrs. Fleming was Anne Geraldine Charteris, former wife of Lord O'Neill and of Lord Rothermere, owner of London's Daily Mail.

"After a few minutes of amenities, we left his office and repaired next door to El Vino's, a venerable Fleet Street grog shop where one may drink from the wood instead of the bottle. I felt like having a whiskey and water, but in deference to my companion's standing as a gourmet, decided instead on an amontillado. His own choice rather shook me: brandy and ginger ale. Afterward we went for lunch to the White Tower, a deservedly reputable London restaurant where we shared a superb meal with excellent wine, and talked of what came into our heads, for rapport; we were the last to leave the place, at around three o'clock. We declared our mutual ease and made another date for ten days hence in Mitre Court, where we concluded the interview."

PLAYBOY: It is the belief of some psychologists that neurosis is a necessary concomitant of the creative drive. As a creative writer, do you agree?

FLEMING: I think that's perfectly true. I think that to be a creative writer or a creative anything else, you've *got* to be neurotic. *I* certainly am in many respects. I'm not really quite certain how, but I am. I'm rather melancholic and probably slightly maniacal as well. It's rather an involved subject, and I'm afraid my interest in it does not go deeper than the realization that the premise does apply to myself. Possibly it all began with an overprivileged childhood.

PLAYBOY: According to published biographies, your well-to-do family had high hopes of launching you on a distinguished career in the military. After putting you through Britain's exclusive Sandhurst Academy they learned of your last-minute decision, upon receiving your commission, to "pack it in." What made you change your mind?

FLEMING: I didn't take up my commission after Sandhurst simply because they had suddenly decided to mechanize the army, and a lot of my pals and I decided that we didn't want to be glorified garage hands, and that the great days of the cavalry regiments were passing, or shortly would be ended forever—no more polo, no more pig-sticking and all that jazz. So a lot of us, having taken our commissions, just gave them up. I was born in 1908; this would have been around 1925, and disillusionment of that kind—and kinds more severe—was common then, as you know. My mother was infuriated. My father had been killed in the First War, and my mother felt responsible for imposing discipline on me and on my three brothers, who were all doing splendidly. She insisted that I must *do* something, something respectable, and so I opted for the Foreign Office. I went abroad to learn languages. I went to the University of Geneva and the University of Munich. I don't think of myself as a linguist, but I know French and German very well, because one must if one has any serious inclination toward the Foreign Office. You have to have French and German first-class and one other language partially, which in my case was Russian. My languages are all that remain to me of my original education.

PLAYBOY: Apart from enabling you to sprinkle your James Bond books with foreign terms and bits of conversation, have they proved valuable to you?

FLEMING: They are a tremendous extension of one's life generally, whereas all the other stuff I've learned—algebra and trigonometry and all that—I've completely forgotten, and as far as I know, none of it was ever of any use to me at all, in any case. But having languages is a tremendous help. You've got to live abroad for two years at least to learn a language. When I came home, I took the Foreign Office examination, but I passed seventh and there were only five vacancies, and that was that.

So I started looking around for work that would fit in with what talents and abilities I possessed. All I had done up to that time, aside from a great deal of studying, had been to begin collecting. I had decided, after concerning myself with first editions for a time, that I would collect books that signalized a right-angle turn in the world's thought on any particular subject, a book of permanent value in the history of the world.

PLAYBOY: You were saying you were looking for a job.

FLEMING: Yes—and finally I found one. Because a man called Sir Roderick Jones, who was chairman of Reuter's, was a friend of my mother's, I went into Reuter's, the great international news agency. I stayed with them for three years and had the most exciting time of my life, because in those days news-agency work was like a gigantic football match, and Reuter's and the Associated Press, of America, were a part of the Allied Agency group, and there were freebooters such as United Press and International News who were trying to break into our territories all around the world. We had some superb battles in Germany and Russia, and so on, and it was all highly enjoyable. It was in Reuter's that I learned to write fast and, above all, to be accurate, because in Reuter's if you weren't accurate you were fired, and that was the end of that.

PLAYBOY: What took you from journalism into Naval Intelligence?

FLEMING: Well, when I left Reuter's, I did a period in the City [London's business and financial district] as a partner in the firm of Rowe and Pitman's, one of the great English stockbroking firms, extremely nice fellows. It was a very pleasant sort of City club—they're still great friends of mine today—but I got rather fed up, and *The Times* gave me a special correspondent's job to go to Moscow on a trade mission. When I came back from that in about March or April of 1939, suddenly I began to hear funny little questions being asked about me; friends would tell me that so-and-so had been asking about where had I been, what did I know, and so on. This turned out to be a quiet casing for a job in Naval Intelligence; and the reason was that because, of all people, the governor of the Bank of England and the head of Baring Brothers, a very big merchant-banking firm in the City, had been asked to find a man of about my age with good languages and some knowledge of the City, which in fact I hadn't got at all. In any case, it ended with a luncheon at the Carlton Hotel, with the Director of Naval Intelligence, Admiral J. H. Godfrey, still my warm friend, and a couple of other very quiet characters in plain clothes, and I suddenly found myself in the Admiralty with an honorary rank of lieutenant in the Royal Naval Volunteer Reserve, and put down as Personal Assistant to the Director of Naval Intelligence. I stayed in that job throughout the war.

PLAYBOY: What were your duties?

FLEMING: My job got me right into the inside of everything, including all the most secret affairs. I couldn't possibly have had a more exciting or interesting war. Of course, it's my experience in Naval Intelligence, and what I learned about secret operations of one sort or another, that finally led me to write about them—in a highly bowdlerized way—with James Bond as the central figure.

PLAYBOY: Did you really settle on the name James Bond, as reported, because you'd been reading a book by a man of that name, and you thought it sounded "suitably flat and colorless"?

FLEMING: Yes, that's absolutely so. It was James Bond's *Birds of the West Indies,* a famous ornithological work, and I wanted my hero to be entirely an anonymous instrument and to let the action of the book carry him along. I didn't believe in the heroic Bulldog Drummond types. I mean, rather, I didn't believe they could any longer exist in literature. I wanted this man more or less to follow the pattern of Raymond Chandler's or Dashiell Hammett's heroes—believable people, believable heroes.

PLAYBOY: One reviewer has written of Bond, "He is the bad guy who smoulders in every good citizen." Do you agree?

FLEMING: I don't think that he is necessarily a good guy or a bad guy. Who is? He's got his vices and very few perceptible virtues except patriotism and courage, which are probably not virtues anyway. He's certainly got little in the way of politics, but I should think what politics he has are just a little bit left of center. And he's got little culture. He's a man of action, and he reads books on golf, and so on—when he reads anything. I quite agree that he's not a person of much social attractiveness. But then, I didn't *intend* for him to be a particularly likable person. He's a cipher, a blunt instrument in the hands of government.

PLAYBOY: You've been quoted as saying that you don't like Bond personally. Is that true?
FLEMING: Well, I've lived with him for about twelve years now, and we've been getting into deeper and deeper trouble together. So I've come to have a certain sympathy with what is going to happen to him, whatever that may be.
PLAYBOY: Do you sometimes feel that you are Bond, and Bond is Fleming?
FLEMING: No, Bond is a highly romanticized version of *anybody*, but certainly not I, and I certainly couldn't keep up with him; I couldn't have, even at his age, which is, and has always been, in the middle thirties. He's a sort of amalgam of romantic tough guys, dressed up in twentieth century clothes, using twentieth century language. I think he's slightly more true to the type of modern hero, to the commandos of the last war, and so on, and to some of the secret-service men I've met, than to any of the rather cardboardy heroes of the ancient thrillers.
PLAYBOY: Do you consider his sexual prowess, and his ruthless way with women, to be true to life—even among commandos and secret-service men?
FLEMING: Naturally not; but we live in a violent age. Seduction has, to a marked extent, replaced courtship. The direct, flat approach is not the exception; it is the standard. James Bond is a healthy, violent, noncerebral man in his middle thirties, and a creature of his era. I wouldn't say he's particularly typical of our times, but he is certainly *of* the times. Bond's detached; he's disengaged. But he's a believable man—around whom I try to weave a great web of excitement and fantasy. In that, at least, we have very little in common. Of course, there *are* similarities, since one writes only of what one knows, and some of the quirks and characteristics that I give Bond are ones that I know about. When I make him smoke certain cigarettes, for example, it's because I do so myself, and I know what these things taste like, and I have no shame in giving them free advertising.
PLAYBOY: Including the gold-ringed cigarettes of Balkan and Turkish tobacco mixed for Bond by Morland's of Grosvenor Street?
FLEMING: Certainly. Why not?
PLAYBOY: Isn't that a rather injudiciously conspicuous brand for a secret agent to be smoking?
FLEMING: Of course it is. No self-respecting agent would use such things. He'd smoke Players or Chesterfields. But the readers enjoy such idiosyncrasies, and they accept them—because they don't stop to think about it. The secrecy of my secret agent is pretty transparent, if you think about it even briefly. But the pace, the pace of the narrative gets one by these nasty little corners. It's a sleight-of-hand operation. It's overpowering the reader. You take him along at such a rate, you interest him so deeply in the narrative that he isn't jolted by these incongruities. I suppose I do it to demonstrate that I *can* do it.
PLAYBOY: Why do you pay so much attention to minutiae in your books?
FLEMING: The main reason is that these things excite and interest me. I'm observant, I think, and when I walk down the street or when I go into a room, I observe things and remember them very accurately. It amuses me to use my powers of observation in my books and at the same time to tell people what my favorite objects are, and my favorite foods and liquors and scents, and so on. Exact details of individual private lives and private tastes are extremely interesting to me. I think that even the way in which a man shaves in the morning is well worth recording. The more we have of this kind of detailed stuff laid down around a character, the more interested we are in him.

I make notes of such details constantly; I write down my thoughts and comments and I note menus, and so forth. I've just written down something I picked up in Istanbul the other day: "Now there is no more shade." This is a Turkish expression, used when a great sultan, like Mustafa Kemal, dies. The general cry of the people was "Now there is no more shade," which is rather an expressive way of saying now there is nothing to protect us, now that the great man has gone. I write things like that down and often use them later on in my books.

PLAYBOY: Of course, you have research done for you as well.

FLEMING: Yes, but generally only after I've written the book. After I've finished a book I realize that I've been rather vague or thin on some topic or other, and then I go to the right man and try to get the true gen out of him and then rewrite that particular area.

PLAYBOY: Are you interested in the skills of individual specialists? Would you, for example, go out of your way to meet Chic Gaylord of New York, who makes custom-tailored revolver and pistol holsters for the New York City police and the FBI?

FLEMING: Quite honestly, the whole question of expertise in these matters bores me. Obviously, I want to know the facts. If a Gaylord holster is better than a Berns-Martin, I want to know about it, but there my interest rather ends. However, I'm not a bad shot; in fact, I shot for Sandhurst against West Point at one time. And just to see that my hand isn't trembling too much, I like to have a shot at a tin can or something now and again.

PLAYBOY: Speaking of firearms, does it amuse you that your imaginative device of Bond's permissive double-0 prefix—licensing him to kill—should be taken so seriously by your readers when, in fact, *any* intelligence agent may find it necessary to kill in the line of duty, and to that extent might be considered to have the right to do so?

FLEMING: Well, though this was purely a fictional device to make Bond's particular job more interesting, the double-0 prefix is not so entirely invented as all that. I pinched the idea from the fact that, in the Admiralty, at the beginning of the war all top-secret signals had the double-0 prefix. This was changed subsequently for the usual security reasons, but it stuck in my mind and I borrowed it for Bond and he got stuck with it.

PLAYBOY: Is there, in your opinion, any such thing as the proverbial perfect murder?

FLEMING: Well, no technique, I should think, is more deadly and efficient than that employed by the gunmen of what its proprietors so amusingly call the Cosa Nostra in America, where a man may be sent all the way from Detroit to kill another man sitting in a bar in New York and walk away with no demonstrable connection with him. That is a near-perfect type of killing—the sort of killing that the secret services do, particularly the Russians, who've been pretty keen on it in West Germany. Their latest gimmick, the cyanide-gas pistol, which is more or less a water pistol filled with liquid cyanide, is a particularly good stunt, because a man can be killed while, say, climbing stairs, and when he's found, the cyanide has dissipated and leaves no trace. It's natural to assume that he has had a heart failure climbing the stairs. But you've got to have a lot of nerve for that sort of thing, and whatever it is that enables a good killer to function also seems to defeat him in the end. The killer's spirit begins to fail, he gets the seed of death within himself. As I wrote in one of my books, *From Russia with Love,* the trouble with a lot of hired assassins such as the Russians use is that they feel rather badly when they've killed five or six people, and ultimately get soft or give themselves up, or they take to drugs or drink. It would be interesting to conduct an inquiry to determine who was the greatest assassin in history—who was, or who is. I have no particular candidate. But they all do grow a sort of bug inside them after a bit.

PLAYBOY: You've been criticized for being "obsessed" with violence in your books. Do you feel the charge is justified?

FLEMING: The simple fact is that, like all fictional heroes who find a tremendous popular acceptance, Bond must reflect his own time. We live in a violent era, perhaps the most violent man has known. In our last war, thirty million people were killed. Of these, some six million were simply slaughtered, and most brutally. I hear it said that I invent fiendish cruelties and tortures to which Bond is subjected. But no one who knows, as I know, the things that were done to captured secret agents in the last war says this. No one says it who knows what went on in Algeria.

PLAYBOY: You said a moment ago that professional assassins "grow a sort of bug inside them after a bit." Does that include Bond?

FLEMING: Yes, it does disturb Bond to kill people, even though he continues to get away with it—just as he continues to get away with driving conspicuous motorcars.

PLAYBOY: In recent books you've had him driving a supercharged Bentley. Why did you pick this particular car for him?

FLEMING: I probably chose the supercharged Bentley because Amherst Villiers was and is a great griend of mine, and I knew something about it from my friendship with him. I put Bond into a Bentley simply because I like him to use dashing, interesting things.

PLAYBOY: Do you share his taste for exotic cars?

FLEMING: Yes. I'd like to have a supercharged Bentley myself, but nowadays—I'm fifty-six, after all—I like a car I can leave out in the street all night and which will start at once in the morning and still go a hundred miles an hour when you want it to and yet give a fairly comfortable ride. I can't be bothered with a car that needs tuning, or one that will give me a lot of trouble and expenditure. So I've had a Thunderbird for six years, and it's done me very well.

PLAYBOY: Unlike Bond, you say you are bored by guns, and you don't drive an exotic vintage car. Do you share, at least, his passion for casino gambling?

FLEMING: I do like to gamble. I play bridge for what might be called serious stakes. I like *chemin de fer*. I play at clubs here in London, private clubs. And I may go to Le Touquet, places like that on the Continent. I like to think that I am reasonably competent at the gaming tables—we all think so, I suppose—but still, I win as much as I lose, or a bit more. I like that, which I suppose demonstrates that I am not a true compulsive gambler, because the compulsive gambler doesn't care much whether he wins or loses. He is interested primarily in the "action." I remember one occasion on which I very much wanted to win. I was on my way to America with the Director of Naval Intelligence, Admiral Godfrey. We were in Estoril in Portugal, and while we were waiting for transport, we killed some time in the casino. While there, I recognized some German agents, and I thought it would be a brilliant coup to play with them, break them, take their money. Instead, of course, they took mine. Most embarrassing. This incident appears in *Casino Royale,* my first book—but, of course, Bond does *not* lose. In fact, he totally and coldly vanquishes his opponent.

PLAYBOY: *Casino Royale,* and all of the other Bond books, have been written at your home in Jamaica. How did you happen to pick the West Indies as a creative hide-away?

FLEMING: I first went to Jamaica on a Naval Intelligence assignment around 1942 to meet with my American opposite numbers from the Office of Naval Intelligence to see if we could do something about the U-boat sinkings in the Caribbean. I stayed in the good old Myrtle Bank Hotel, and it poured every day—and I loved every minute of it. I'd never been in the tropics before and I thought they were wonderful, as I suppose any Scotsman would. I was determined that at the end of the war I'd come back and find a plot and build a house and live in it whenever I could. It's worked out like that. When I went back in 1946, I borrowed a car from a man called Sir William Stevenson, who was chief of our intelligence service in the States during the war; he had a house in Jamaica and I went round and finally I found this disused donkeys' racecourse by the sea. I bought the racecourse and I built on it a square of a house which I had designed while I was working in the Admiralty during the last two or three years of the war, looking forward to something more pleasant than the V-1s and V-2s. And I go there every year during January and February and a bit of March, and the whole thing's been a great success. It's by a little banana port called Oracabessa, and the house is called Goldeneye, a name I chose.

PLAYBOY: Why?

FLEMING: I had happened to be reading *Reflections in a Golden Eye* by Carson McCullers, and I'd been involved in an operation called Goldeneye during the war: the defense of Gibraltar, supposing that the Spaniards had decided to attack it; and I was deeply involved in the planning of countermeasures which would have been taken in that event. Anyway, I called my place Goldeneye. The alternative choice was Shamelady, which is the Jamaican name for the sensitive plant, the one which curls up when the leaves are touched. When I and a friend inspected the plot, we looked over the edge of the cliff, and there was the most beautiful naked Negress bathing in the waves, so I thought that Shamelady would be a good name for it—the whole thirty acres were covered with the plant—but it would have been a little bit too fancy. In any event, the house has been a great success. As you said, I have written all my books there.

PLAYBOY: Do you spend most of your time there at the typewriter?

FLEMING: By no means. I get up with the birds, which is about half-past seven, because they wake one up, and then I go and bathe in the ocean before breakfast. We don't have to wear a swimsuit there, because it's so private; my wife and I bathe and swim a hundred yards or so and come back and have a marvelous proper breakfast with some splendid scrambled eggs made by my housekeeper, who's particularly good at them, and then I sit out in the garden to get a sunburn until about ten. Only then do I set to work. I sit in my bedroom and type about fifteen hundred words straightaway, without looking back on what I wrote the day before. I have more or less thought out what I'm going to write, and, in any case, even if I make a lot of mistakes, I think, well, hell, when the book's finished I can change it all. I think the main thing is to write fast and cursively in order to get narrative speed.

Then, about quarter-past twelve, I chuck that and go down, with a snorkel and a spear, around the reefs looking for lobsters or whatever there may be, sometimes find them, sometimes don't, and then I come back, I have a couple of pink gins, and we have a very good lunch, ordinary Jamaican food, and I have a siesta from about half-past two until four. Then I sit again in the garden for about an hour or so, have another swim, and then I spend from six to seven—the dusk comes very suddenly in Jamaica; at six o'clock it suddenly gets very dark—doing another five hundred words. I then number the pages, of which by that time there are about seven, put them away in a folder, and have a couple of powerful drinks, then dinner, occasionally a game of Scrabble with my wife—at which she thinks she is very much better than I am, but I know I'm the best—and straight off to bed and into a dead sleep.

PLAYBOY: And you return to England in March with a completed manuscript?

FLEMING: Except for minor revisions, yes.

PLAYBOY: How do you spend the rest of the year?

FLEMING: Commuting between London—where we have a very nice little house—and the country, where I keep a small but comfortable flat on Pegwell Bay in Sandwich; that's in Kent. I work the "Fleming Two-Day Week," which means that I try to spend at least four days and five nights in the country and only two nights up in London, because I don't like big towns. Generally I come up on Monday night and I go down again to Sandwich on Thursday morning, with any luck.

PLAYBOY: What do you do with your time in the country?

FLEMING: Well, I get up late, about half-past eight or nine, have breakfast, coffee and a boiled egg—three and a half minutes, not three and two thirds, like James Bond. I read newspapers and deal with a certain amount of mail and then I go off to the golf course; the one I play on is in Sandwich—the Royal St. George—a course known to a great many Americans, and one that Bobby Jones and all the great men have played; Jack Nicklaus won the Gold Vase on that course three or four years ago. And I meet some friends there and we have a drink or two and lunch and then I go out and play a tough game of golf for fairly high stakes, foursomes generally, not American fourball, but each pair hitting the ball in turn. And we laugh a lot and it's great fun. Then I go back home in the evening and sit down and have a couple of very powerful bourbons and waters with ice and read awhile, and then I have whatever my wife has decided to cook for me and I go straight off to bed.

PLAYBOY: And when you're in London?

FLEMING: In London we have, as I said, a very nice little house—but it hasn't got any trees around it, which I would like, and I would prefer to live higher up, somewhere like Hampstead, on the heights above London, with birds and trees and a bit of garden. But my wife, who likes to entertain, feels that this would be too far from the House of Commons for our friends to come, and altogether too suburban. In any case, I get up in the morning about the same time as in the country, have the same breakfast, and at about half-past ten I drive to my office, where my secretary has the mail ready for me, which I cope with and then dictate a few letters. Then I correct some proofs or go over whatever I happen to be working on at the moment and have lunch with a friend—always a male friend; I don't like having lunch with women—and perhaps I go to my club, Boodles, or the Turf, where I sit by myself and read in that highly civilized privacy which is the great thing about some English clubs. In the afternoon I have more or less the same routine correcting proofs. I go home and have three large drinks and then we either stay in for dinner or have people in, or go out; but more often we have dinner together and go to bed.

PLAYBOY: Your books were often among those at the bedside of President Kennedy, who publicly declared himself an enthusiastic Bond fan. He was even said to have considered Bond his favorite fictional character. Did he ever tell you why?

FLEMING: No, he didn't. In any case, I don't think Bond *was* President Kennedy's favorite fictional character; I think he was his favorite *adventure* character. But I think perhaps that Bond's sort of patriotic derring-do was in keeping with the President's own concept of endurance and courage and grace under pressure, and so on. Strangely enough, *many* politicians seem to like my books. I think perhaps because politicians like solutions, with everything properly tied up at the end. Politicians always hope for neat solutions, you know, but so rarely can they find them.

PLAYBOY: Do you have other admirers among world figures of major stature?

FLEMING: I don't know, really. For one, I don't believe Mr. Khrushchev is one of my readers, and we haven't met. I do have among my memorabilia a short typewritten note from Joseph Stalin, signed in his hand and, I think, typed by him as well, saying that he is sorry, but he must decline to be interviewed.

PLAYBOY: It was Stalin who organized SMERSH, the Soviet counterpart of the Gestapo, which served as Bond's adversary in several of your earlier books. What made you decide to abandon it in *Thunderball* for the ideologically unaligned gang of international conspirators which you call SPECTRE?

FLEMING: I closed down SMERSH, although I was devoted to the good old *apparat*, because, first of all, Khrushchev did in fact disband SMERSH himself, although its operations are still carried out by a subsection of the K.G.B., the Russian secret service. But in that book—I think it was *Thunderball* that I was writing at the time of the proposed summit meeting—I thought, Well, it's no good going on if we're going to make friends with the Russians. I know them, I like them personally, as anyone would, as anyone would like the Chinese if he knew them. I thought, I don't want to go on ragging them like this. So I invented SPECTRE as an international crime organization which contained elements of SMERSH and the Gestapo and the Mafia—the cozy old Cosa Nostra—which, of course, is a much more elastic fictional device than SMERSH, which was no fictional device, but the real thing. But that was really the reason I did it, so as not to rag the Russians too much. But if they go on squeezing off cyanide pistols in people's faces, I may have to make them *cosa mia* again.

PLAYBOY: Mystery writer Raymond Chandler has said of you, "He writes more correctly, neatly, concisely and vividly than most of our 'serious' novelists." On the other hand, *New York Times* critic Anthony Boucher has said that in his view you write "monumentally badly." Do you have any comment on these contrasting appraisals?

FLEMING: I daresay Ray Chandler said that because he was a friend of mine. As for Anthony Boucher, he's never liked my books, and it shows what a good reviewer he is that he says so. Others, happily—such as Cyril Connolly—think otherwise. There is no doubt, however, that I—and even Anthony Boucher—should write better. There is no top limit to writing well. I try to write neatly and concisely and vividly because I think that's the way to write, but I think a large amount of that comes, as I said earlier, from my training as a fast-writing journalist, under circumstances in which you damned well *had* to be neat and correct and concise and vivid. I'm afraid I think Reuter's training was much more valuable to me than all the reading in English literature I did at Eton or in Geneva or wherever.

PLAYBOY: You have said that you write unashamedly for money. Is that true?

PLAYBOY: Yes, it is. I *do* write for money—but also for pleasure. I'm very glad that people say kind things about my books—because, naturally, if they didn't say so, I shouldn't make any money, and consequently I shouldn't enjoy the writing so much. I think that communicating enjoyment is certainly a very good achievement, even in the fairly modest seam of literature that comprises thriller writing. But it's true that I write below my ultimate capacity—or at least I *think* I probably do. If I really settled down and decided to write a *War and Peace* among thrillers, if I shut myself up and decided to do this and nothing else, I daresay I might bring it off, if such a thing is possible. There's a great deal of violence and sex in all great novels, so I daresay if I tried to do it in the modern vein I might conceivably succeed.

But I'm more interested in action than in cerebration, and I should think that the great *War and Peace* thriller would be more likely to be written by a man like Graham Greene or Georges Simenon, because either of them would do it more truthfully and accurately than I ever could. I enjoy exaggeration and things larger than life. It amuses me to have a villain with a great bulbous head, whereas, as you know, they're generally little people with nothing at all extraordinary-looking about them. Then, too, I'm afraid I shouldn't be able to write in sufficient depth to make this hypothetical thriller stand up as a classic.

PLAYBOY: Why not?

FLEMING: I'm too interested in surface things, and I'm too interested in maintaining a fast pace, in writing at speed. I'm afraid I shouldn't have the patience to delve into the necessary psychological introspection and historical background. But in the end, I must say, I'm very happy writing as I do. And I greatly enjoy knowing that other people, quite intelligent people, find my books amusing and entertaining. But I'm not really surprised, because they entertain and amuse me, too.

JEAN-PAUL SARTRE

May 1965

Interviewer: Maraleine Gobeil

The Sartre interview represented an early journalistic coup for PLAYBOY. During the two years leading up to this conversation, the pendulum of popular and critical opinion had swung against the author and philosopher, as his ideas came under attack and the French public wearied of Sartre's stubborn hammering at them with the same old accusations: "Your life is absurd. . . . There is no God. . . . Workers of the world should march to the barricades." This was a modern and prosperous France, and the new generation preferred to sit and watch the girls at the sidewalk cafés of Paris, not to debate concepts of reality.

It was therefore prescient of PLAYBOY editor Murray Fisher to assign a full-length interview with what appeared to be a fading cultural hero. Between the time Fisher got Sartre's approval to send over a journalist, and the appearance of the magazine on the newsstands, Sartre had been awarded, and had rejected, the Nobel Prize. This conversation with writer Maraleine Gobeil, conducted in French, was the only one granted by Sartre to an American publication that year.

To the surprise of many, there turned out to be more than *angst* and absurdity as central themes in Sartre's thought. He also ventured that a woman's looks were of embarrassingly great importance to him, and that as a rule, he preferred women's company to that of men. He found men boring, he said, because they have specialized sensibilities and talk shop.

*French writers have always had a gift for inciting wars of the spirit, but probably no French writer since Voltaire has given the civilized world a case of the jitters comparable to that inflicted upon it by a stocky, walleyed, fifty-nine-year-old ex-professor named Jean-Paul Sartre. As a philosopher (*Being and Nothingness, What Is Existentalism?*) novelist (*Nausea, The Age of Reason*) playwright (*The Flies, No Exit, The Respectful Prostitute*) essayist (*Situations, Saint Genet*), autobiographer (*The Words*), pamphleteer, editor, author of political petitions and demands, even as a writer of popular songs, he has let loose a torrent of words upon a groaning but responsive public. In his role as a resister, a denier, a ferocious and uncompromising visionary, he began by anatomizing the decay of French democracy between the two wars. The first great dramatic challenge of his life was the conquest and occupation of France by the Germans, which called forth both the most sordid and most heroic qualities of the French character. Sartre took his place, along with Albert Camus and François Mauriac, as one of the writer-heroes of the Resistance, at the risk of his life and the cost of his freedom; he was imprisoned by the Nazis. Later, atheist Sartre parted company violently with the Catholic Mauriac and the pantheist Camus, and proceeded after the Liberation to assume the role of writer as political leader—founder of parties, propagandist, struggler for causes, perpetual schismatic. His ambiguous relationship with the Communists, with sexual anarchists, with the oddballs and the woebegone and the nihilists, has given the Sartrean version of existentialism a kind of public influence that none of the milder, more university-oriented forms have ever enjoyed. Christian existentialism could not compete with the wild intellectual activists of the postwar chaos and reformation of Europe. Sartre's personal metabolism outraced the competition—at least in the struggle for the minds of the young.*

During the immediate postwar period, many Americans came to study, write, or discover themselves in the nervy, dangerous, angry Paris of those days. For many of them, Sartre's famous love affair with Simone de Beauvoir, his discovery of Juliette Greco and Jean Genet, his patronage of the Café de Flore and the Deux Magots and such nightclubs as the Tabou and the Rose Rouge, all were part of the living legend he had become. Sartre also founded a monthly magazine, Les Temps Modernes, *to expound his unconventional views on everything from China to the orgasm. Meanwhile, the existentialist vocabulary—words like* anguish, abandonment, despair *and* forlornness*—poured out of his overflowing heart in a manner that paradoxically suggested both a love of life and a mordant sense of pleasure. The pessimism of the philosopher seemed to free the man for joy and action.*

The bitter recriminations that followed the rupture of his friendship with Albert Camus caused many to turn their backs on Sartre. He took an intransigent position against France's efforts to keep its colonies, and probably only his world fame prevented his going to prison over Algeria. He was called a traitor. His apartment was bombed. He moved, but kept on writing. One of Paris' young intellectual lions said of him then, "Sartre? I remember him. Very funny man. Too serious."

And then, as if to prove that a writer cannot be considered dead until he is lowered into the grave, the seemingly spent bombshell burst once again. With the publication of the first volume of his autobiography, The Words, *Sartre was once more hailed as the high priest of French letters. Ideological opponents and personal enemies, with a rare and un-French generosity, admitted that the sly old boy had done it again—or perhaps had finally fulfilled his promise.*

It was entirely in character that the attempt of the Nobel Prize committee, last November, to bestow on Sartre its prestigious prize of some $53,000 was interpreted by its intended recipient as a kind of bribe from the literary establishment. He asked them not to offer him the prize; but they did anyway. Boris Pasternak had refused it in 1958 under pressure from the Soviet government, but Sartre became the first writer in history to spurn this supreme accolade of his own accord. Perhaps a clue to his refusal can be found in his play The Devil and the Good Lord, *at the moment when the demagogue Goetz seeks to prove his virtuousness by summoning a leper. As a crowd watches, the leper approaches. Then he sees that Goetz intends to use him by publicly kissing him. The leper raises his hand in disgust and says, "Not on the mouth!"*

Bespectacled and diminutive (only five feet four), he greeted us cordially in his modest two-room bachelor apartment on the tenth floor of a nondescript apartment building in Paris. Chainsmoking cigarettes before his open window, overlooking the rooftops of Montparnasse, he seemed at first a bit reluctant to speak freely because of our spinning tape recorder; but it was soon forgotten as he, and we, became absorbed in conversation.

PLAYBOY: At the end of World War Two, while you were propounding the austere philosophy of existentialism in essays, novels and plays, you were said to preside in Paris over an exuberant, worldly—and some say hedonistic—movement of bohemian singers, actors, musicians, dancers, political activists, journalists and students of every stripe. How do you explain these paradoxical stories about you?
SARTRE: The fact is that a few kids who played in orchestras also happened to like my books, and everyone promptly started thinking that this had something to do with my personal philosophy. They used to say I was responsible for a whole generation of young people wearing dirty check shirts from American PXs. What nonsense!
PLAYBOY: Wasn't your philosophy of "anguish" and "despair" thought to be responsible for many of the suicides that took place in France during these years?
SARTRE: Yes, that's so. And a journal called *Samedi Soir* was full of the tallest possible tales about me. Here's one of them: A girl said I'd invited her to my bedroom quite in the manner of the professional seducer; that I opened a cupboard, took out an overripe camembert cheese and held it under her nose, saying, "Smell!" According to her, I then showed her the door and said, "Now you can go." But do you know why I'm really considered "scandalous"? It's because, ever since 1945, the press has made a point of describing me as dead and done for. Every paper has said the same thing, and so the rumor has spread. They haven't stopped announcing my death since I started writing; haven't stopped saying I was played out, in my grave. What infuriates people is that I'm doubly a "traitor." I'm a bourgeois and I speak harshly of the *bourgeoisie;* an oldster, and my contacts are mostly with young people. I get on well with them. They're my basic public. Men in their forties always disapprove of me, even if they liked me in their youth. So I'm twice a traitor—a traitor in the conflict of the generations, and a traitor in the class war. The 1945 generation thinks I've betrayed them because they got to know me through *No Exit* and *Nausea*, written at a time when I hadn't yet worked out the Marxist implications of my ideas. Marxism

just didn't interest me up to that time. I was young, of good family, and had the impression that the world could be mine without having to undergo the compulsions of want and work. And so I struggled on as best I could.

PLAYBOY: Did you know yet what you wanted to do with your life?

SARTRE: I was beginning to. At sixteen, you see, I wanted to be a novelist. But I had to study philosophy in order to enroll in the École Normale Supérieure. My ambition was to become a professor of literature. Then I came across a book by Henri Bergson in which he describes in a concrete way how time is experienced in one's mind. I recognized the truth of this in myself. A little later, I discovered "phenomenology." That is, I learned that one could talk in a concrete way about any subject whatsoever; also that one could talk in a philosophical way, ranging further, and more scientifically even, than the language of philosophic textbooks. I had the idea of uniting literature and philosophy in a technique of concrete expression—with philosophy providing the method and the discipline, and literature supplying the words. What interested me was unraveling the curious and concrete relations between things and man, and later, between men and themselves.

PLAYBOY: In exploring these relations, you have written that you were influenced, during World War Two, by the German philosopher Martin Heidegger.

SARTRE: True. I was a prisoner of war and some priests in prison with me asked me to talk to them about philosophy. Heidegger was the only author the Germans allowed us. He argues that, in the last analysis, objects are *utensils*. In my first novel, *Nausea*, I looked at trees and tried to define just what they are by means of words, so as to get down to essences; in other words, I embarked on a perpetual questioning of things, of trying to ascertain what they *are*. What are objects? Why are we here and what are we up to? As Heidegger sees it, a tree is something that's cut down for firewood or for building; a tree is what it's *used* for—like a man. But a man is free to realize himself, to choose for himself and others. I can't examine the structure of a man's life without glimpsing, beneath it, all the other structures that bring us back to human needs—to work, to tools. Even when I make a cup of coffee I change the world. In *Existentialism and Humanism,* I explained that a man's every decision, in the smallest as well as the largest sense, makes him a legislator deciding for the whole of mankind. There must be a complete and profound responsibility.

PLAYBOY: You have written that "man is condemned to be free." What did you mean by that?

SARTRE: Condemned because he is thrown into the world responsible, without excuse. Abandoned by eternal values, we must create our own values.

PLAYBOY: How?

SARTRE: *Original choice* is the term I use to describe what happens at the moment—a protracted moment, covering a certain span of time—in which one makes something of oneself, of that self which so far has been made by others. We start by being made by others, and then we remake ourselves, starting out from what others have made of us. But at the moment when we remake ourselves, a dialectic comes into play: We find ourselves very different from what we expected and what others expected of us. This is freedom, but it is not a cheerful thing. That's why I use the expression *condemned to be free.*

PLAYBOY: In your play *The Flies* you wrote: "Once freedom has lit its beacon in a man's heart, the gods are powerless against him." But in asserting that "the gods are powerless," aren't you—who profess to be an atheist—acknowledging that God exists?

SARTRE: If I have this theory of freedom, it's precisely because I do *not* believe in God. On several occasions I have drawn attention to a very interesting aspect of Christianity. According to the fathers of the Church, Augustine in particular, God had a respect for human freedom. God created man free, so as to respect this freedom. So God isn't there to call the Christian to account for his decisions. He is alone. It's too easy to fall back on God's commandments. Actually, then, the Christian is alone—like me, like Genet, like anyone else. There is, of course, the theory of grace. But in practice there are several such theories, and even when grace is operative, there still comes a moment when you are alone, facing up to God. God had nothing to say, for example, about the Algerian war. There were priests who behaved like decent folk and others who behaved like swine—either with an eye to true morality or with an eye to the interests of the established Church.

PLAYBOY: Carrying your personal theology a step further, would you explain the statement in *No Exit* that "Hell is other people!"?

SARTRE: Other people are hell insofar as you are plunged from birth into a situation to which you are obliged to submit. You are born the son of a rich man, or an Algerian, or a doctor, or an American. Then you have a cut-and-dried future mapped out, a future made for you by others. They haven't created it directly, but they are part of a social order that makes you what you are. If you're a peasant's son, the social order obliges you to move to the city where machines await you, machines that need fellows like you to keep them going. So it's your fate to be a certain type of worker, a country kid who has been driven away from the country by a certain type of capitalist pressure. Now the factory is a function of your being. What exactly *is* your "being"? It is the job you're doing, a job that masters you completely because it wears you down—along with your pay, which classifies you exactly by your standard of living. All this has been thrust on you by other people. Hell is the proper description for that kind of existence. Or take a child who was born in Algeria in 1930 or 1935. He was doomed to an explosion into death and the tortures that were his destiny. That, too, is hell.

PLAYBOY: Is there no hope, "no exit" from this destiny?

SARTRE: Certainly there is. You can take action against what people have made of you and transform yourself. That Algerian child, though predestined to torture or to death, is living out his revolt today; it's he who makes that revolution.

PLAYBOY: You speak of artists and revolutionaries. Do you think there are many others in the world who are capable of changing their fate?

SARTRE: It takes a lot to change a destiny. That destiny has got to be intolerable. And when it's tolerable, it's really worse. This is what I call "alienation." In our social order a man is always dominated by material things, and these things are themselves produced, created and exploited by others. These others do not confront him face to face. No. They impinge on him through the agency of objects. You, for example, have separated yourself from me—alienated me—with this tape recorder. We put all of modern civilization between us. Thus we *ourselves* become things. A crowd of other things intervene, from the maker of this gadget of yours to the magazine that you represent.

PLAYBOY: Your critics have taken you to task for dwelling fatalistically on such themes: on the "alienation," "anguish" and "despair" of modern life, while at the same time preaching freedom as an attainable goal—yet without proposing a concrete or affirmative means of achieving it.

SARTRE: People think that one fine morning, when he's pulling on his socks, a man can decide: "Hmm, today I shall invent a moral code." But a moral code can't be "invented." It must be something that already exists in some way. We must not confuse the moralist with the founder of a religion. Mohammed utilized existing religions; as you know, all that's basic to the Koran was the work of Jews. The Koran is a transformation of Judaism, carried out by some Semitic tribes. Mohammed, however, claimed to be directly inspired by Allah: "Here is what Allah says we must do." But a true moralist—that's something very different. A system of morality that dictates its own laws, without taking into account existing moral laws—though amending them, of course—would not really be a system of morals. It would merely reflect the ideas of the social group to which the man preaching it belonged.

Here's an example: André Gide says: "Don't search for God elsewhere than everywhere." And he goes on to preach "fervor," "thirst," "surrender to sensual joys," and so on. Do you think Gide's code makes sense for a factory worker, or even for an engineer, or for a doctor who has a waiting room crowded with patients? All it means is this: "I, Gide, belong to the upper-middle class and have the special sensitivity cultivated in that class. That's why I have been able to devote myself to literary work. This literary work shows that I have a sensibility adaptable to every variety of experience." Here we have the moral code of an upper-middle-class writer. It is acceptable to other writers belonging to the same class. I can understand it, though I'm not a member of that class by birth. I can wonder if it wouldn't be rewarding to act like Gide's character. But advice of that sort is lost on a worker who does eight hours on an assembly line. He's tired out. How can one tell him to go out and ransack the universe for sensations when he has been stupefied by a day of brain-deadening, brutalizing labor?

PLAYBOY: But do *you* have a meaningful moral code, some tangible means of attaining freedom, to offer this worker?

SARTRE: His problem is not to keep his freedom but to *win* it. And we must help him do this. No true moral system exists today, because the conditions of a moral code worthy of the name are not present. Men are not visible to one another. Too many machines and social structures, as I was saying, block the view. It's impossible to speak of any true moral system today; only of moral codes applying to certain classes and reflecting specific habits and interests. The basic conditions enabling men to be available for a new social order are lacking. In a society such as ours, it's inevitable that the mass of social structures—not to mention the personal compulsions, private destinies—form barriers to mutual understanding. Thus you trot along with your personal destiny and you meet a Negro, an Arab, a Cuban, each with his own destiny, and any real relationship proves extremely difficult. Or else you must belong to a "movement" in which you make a total break with everything outside it and associate yourself with, say, the Cuban struggle or the Algerian struggle. Yet even then—with the best intentions—you will not achieve complete solidarity. The man whom you contact won't be *completely* a man for you; he'll be a "thing." For the American, for example, the Cuban is "sugar"—a reminder that there is trouble over sugar.

PLAYBOY: Or communism.

SARTRE: Yes—or some kind of propaganda. Today, to establish fellowship among men, we must struggle against the order of things. That's the worthwhile moral imperative. As to what people will make of their freedom, if and when they win it, it's not for us who are completely isolated—alienated—to predict. But to treat a man as a man, as a human being, is a matter of principle, a principle we must never abandon.

PLAYBOY: Though you are a Marxist, you have never joined the Communist Party and, despite your many trips to the USSR, the French Communist Party doesn't approve of you. You are not on the side of the bourgeoisie, yet you aren't wholeheartedly with the Communists, either. Just where *do* you stand ideologically?
SARTRE: I'm an intellectual, not a politician. But as a citizen, I can join pressure groups. That explains why I was wholeheartedly with the Algerians. These are the duties of a citizen. Since my skills are intellectual, I can serve as a citizen by writing. My duty as an intellectual is to think, to think without restriction, even at the risk of blundering. I must set no limits within myself, and I must let no limits be set *for* me. As for my relations with the Communist Party, Marxism can work out its full possibilities only if it has "fellow travelers"—that is, friends of the Communists who do not fetter themselves politically and try to study Marxism objectively from within.
PLAYBOY: Do the Communists *permit* objective study of Marxism from within?
SARTRE: Right now it's a problem that's being faced openly almost everywhere in Eastern Europe. It's the problem of the relation between political discipline and the demands of intellectual life—not intellectual life practiced in isolation, but *revolutionary* intellectual life. The liberation demanded by the intellectuals of the East is not to reinstate a sort of bourgeois eclecticism, but the freedom to continue the revolution through intellectual means.
PLAYBOY: You speak of agitating for revolution—presumably by the proletariat against the capitalists. But isn't it true that the working class in Western Europe, certainly including France, is enjoying a period of unprecedented prosperity, that the conditions of economic oppression which breed revolution, therefore, just don't exist any longer? Your critics ask that you stop visiting the revolutionary countries: Cuba, Algeria, China, the USSR, and see France as it really is.
SARTRE: The France I see today is not so beautiful that I should spend that much time in consecration of her. It's a France riddled with lies. When I hear talk of an "affluent society," I think we're being hoodwinked. The fact is that about half the French population lives at the bare subsistence level. The government camouflages the facts. Just now a kind of spurious optimism prevails in France. They want to transform us into a society of consumers. By harping on this idea of affluence, they try to make us think that the demand for wage increases is no longer due to exploitation of the workers—a monstrous travesty of the facts! Next, starting out from that notion of affluence, they are trying to condition *us* by conditioning our purchases. They want to create the organization man—in other words, to build up a sort of twofold technocratic slavery, and at the same time create the consumer-minded man; that is, a man whose desires are molded by the desires of others. All these things are taking place today and link up with capitalism's attempts to hold its ground.

We, the French, are trying everywhere we can—in the French Congo, for example—to transform capitalism into neocapitalism. We keep in power, as our accomplices, a black bourgeoisie, thanks to which investments can still be made. Thus we retain an economic hold on a country we have ceased to rule by repression. In Algeria, on the other hand, French financial aid is being given to a socialist government capable of sharing this aid with the workers.
PLAYBOY: Then you approve of De Gaulle's economic policy in Algeria?
SARTRE: It was simply in De Gaulle's interest that it couldn't be said that Algeria, ceasing to be a colony, became a land where people died of hunger. This, of course, was in the interests of "the system." But it's above all in our own interest, the interest

of the French people in general, to carry on our aid to, and retain our link with, Algeria. What's good about this aid is that we are assisting not a class but a government. That's the big difference.

PLAYBOY: How do you feel in general about De Gaulle's foreign policy?

SARTRE: De Gaulle's foreign policy seems to me entirely bound up with nothing more than the need to *have* a foreign policy of some sort. It has no real substance. But in a way it's good, since it tends to loosen the ties within alliances.

PLAYBOY: Such as NATO?

SARTRE: I was thinking of the consequences of his decision to recognize Communist China. When Algeria was freed, De Gaulle decided to support an underdeveloped country—Red China—against the USA and the USSR, thus claiming that he, as the leader of a developed capitalist country, was championing the cause of the underdeveloped peoples. This, of course, was preposterous. France simply hasn't the means to give effective help to the underdeveloped countries. Moreover, when we compare what the Americans *could* do, but do not do, with what the Russians *are* doing—at Aswan, for instance—we can see that the underdeveloped countries have no special interest in linking themselves to France, given the structure of present-day France. Thus this policy has no real foundation. But it's very important for the Chinese, because it gives them one more ally at the UN. As regards France, it represents only the fanciful efforts of a man who, in point of fact, is just attempting to dream up a foreign policy.

PLAYBOY: One of the keystones of De Gaulle's foreign policy is his atomic *force de frappe*, with which he hopes to enforce France's claim as "a third power" between East and West. How do you feel about it?

SARTRE: It's a terrible risk, not because of our poor little bomb, with which we'll never do anything, but simply because Germany and every other country will now have a right to make its own bomb. Two notions are suggested by this *force de frappe:* on the one hand, the ideas of "grandeur" and "splendid isolation" for which De Gaulle stands; and, on the other, the impossibility for France to have a leftist foreign policy—that of a world in which individual nations are not crushed into a conglomerate mass. While De Gaulle tries to work out a foreign policy in solitary grandeur, we find, alas, that we are being invaded by American culture and American social mores. I fight against this because I think that all forms of independence should be preserved, but in another fashion than De Gaulle's. Only the left can bring about this freedom. But the Americans are wrong to worry about De Gaulle's occasional gestures of independence. At the least hint of real outside danger, things would resume their usual course, and France would retreat under America's nuclear umbrella.

PLAYBOY: Don't you share the concern of most Americans about the dangers of nuclear power in the hands of several nations?

SARTRE: No, because I'm French and we French seem to have a complete light-headedness about the bomb. I remember a cartoon showing a café in which Americans, British and Frenchmen are sitting. The Anglo-Americans are reading papers headlined THE BOMB, but the French are reading papers headlined THE PRICE OF MILK HAS GONE UP. We French display an amazing lack of interest in the bomb and even regard our indifference as a slight superiority. The last twelve years of colonial warfare have swamped all our powers of attention on this issue. We were too much taken up with the Algerian war to worry about the production of atomic armament. Fascism is what the Frenchman is afraid of. But he's blind to what is *really* threatening us: as I said earlier, a form of technocratic organization which is weakening men's political awareness and slowly but surely reducing them to the servile state.

PLAYBOY: Do you feel that this is true of French letters as well as French society?

SARTRE: I'm afraid so. There are no great writers in France today. The practitioners of the "New Novel" are talented, and viewed as experiments in form, their books are interesting. But they bring us absolutely nothing except a justification of our technocratic, politically sterile French social order. Literature should be the work of clear-eyed men who take into account the totality of mankind. Literature has got to realize that it exists in a world where children die of hunger. Literature has got to realize that it lies within our power, as writers and as human beings, to do something for others. And others can do something for us.

PLAYBOY: Yet you wrote in your last book, *The Words*, that "I am disillusioned. . . . I no longer know what to make of my life."

SARTRE: When I said that, I meant that I had cured myself of my youthful illusions.

PLAYBOY: What illusions?

SARTRE: The illusion that a bourgeois writer is bound to be pessimistic, that he is condemned to solitude by the fact of his taking arms against society. In *The Words*, I describe how I have come to realize that I am a *member* of society—a society in motion. And because I have now broken free from the illusions of youth, I believe I've become an optimist.

PLAYBOY: If that's so, why did you write that you no longer know what to make of your life?

SARTRE: When I said that, I meant that with one's liberation from illusion comes a curious feeling of detachment, of being at loose ends—in my case, not because I can think of nothing worth doing, but because there remain so *many* tasks for me to embark on: keeping in touch with the world, with the social order, perhaps even indulging in Camus' "sensual raptures." But let me illustrate further what I mean when I say that I no longer know what to make of my life. Any man feels that way when he's suddenly cured of a grand passion—for a woman, say. When it's over, one asks oneself, "Why did I love that woman?"—and can't even remember just who she was. Once you had a compulsion to see this woman, to hear her voice, think about her, spy on her. All that is ended. You are cured of a monomaniacal obsession and you feel a relief, because this kind of passion for a woman is not an ideal state—and yet you also feel at loose ends, detached.

PLAYBOY: You speak, obviously from experience, about emotional involvement with women; yet you seldom write about it in your books. Why?

SARTRE: I simply have other things to write about. That doesn't mean I don't have, and haven't had, my share of emotional involvements; as a matter of fact, women play a rather *large* role in my life—but a small one in my books. Those raptures—I know them well, but I feel a distaste for writing about them, because underlying them is the idea that one can actually be a *man* today, when in fact it's impossible. Camus can say, "We must uphold man's right to be happy." That's quite right, but he thinks it can and must be upheld *immediately*; in other words, that the conditions of happiness can be achieved *today*. It would be very agreeable, of course, if one could share one's sensual raptures with everybody by writing about them—but enjoying them alone means shutting oneself off from certain relations with our fellow human beings. When I was in Algeria, it was hard to indulge in joys of that kind when just beside me was a child whose eye was eaten out by flies. I'm not saying it was impossible; only that it would have made me feel embarrassed. Then, too, as a writer, I feel I should deal with what I'm best fitted for—what others cannot say better than I can. I often think that someday I'll write about my joys, but then I remind myself that this side of my life isn't really worth holding up as an example.

PLAYBOY: Aren't you being modest? We're told that in public you're almost constantly surrounded by admiring and attractive women.

SARTRE: It's true that I have always tried to surround myself with women who are at least agreeable to look at. Feminine ugliness is offensive to me. I admit this and I'm ashamed of it. But the reason is simple. Even at its most formal level, even when there's complete indifference, the association of a man with a woman always has sexual implications. An ugly woman evokes, like all women, that special pleasure we get from being in a woman's company, but she spoils it by her ugliness. Alas. When you have the man-woman relation interfered with by ugliness—provoked and denied, well, it's a very awkward business.

But the main reason I surround myself with women is simply that I prefer their company to that of men. As a rule I find men boring. They have specialized sensibilities and they talk shop. But there are qualities in woman that derive from the female predicament, from the fact that she is both a slave and an accomplice. That's why her sensibility ranges so much wider than a man's. She is available. For instance, one cannot sit in a café and talk with a man about the people passing by. He gets bored with this and goes back to his professional worries, or else to intellectual gymnastics. But intellectual gymnastics are something I can quite adequately indulge in all by myself. In fact, it's more rewarding to wrestle with one's words and problems alone. Discussions with men never much entertain me; the conversation always sinks. But from a woman you get the sensibility of a different being, an intelligence perhaps superior to a man's, and not hampered by the same preoccupations.

Similarly, what I particularly appreciate in my Jewish friends is a gentleness and subtlety that is certainly an outcome of anti-Semitism. That's why we are always race-conscious, even if we disapprove of racialism. I like the Jews as they have been made by persecution. In my opinion, they stand for one of the values of the present-day world, just because of the way they have been shaped by persecution. A Jew, of course, might retort: "That's racial prejudice. It's up to you to like us as men, or as a religious community, but you shouldn't indulge in satisfactions of your sensibility or intellect just because we have managed to win through after starting with an intolerable handicap imposed on us by others." To come back to women, I think I must have a feminine side to my mind which pleases them. And like Simone de Beauvoir, I'm in favor of total feminine emancipation. But when the day comes, of course, the special qualities of sensibility for which I prefer the company of women will be due purely to chance; sometimes a woman will have them, sometimes a man. They'll cease being a feminine prerogative.

PLAYBOY: Let's turn to the subject of your preferences in literature, if we may. Some years ago you said that you regarded John Dos Passos as "the great writer of our time." Why did you think so? And do you still feel that way?

SARTRE: I found his books, and those of Faulkner, most interesting. He invented certain journalistic techniques, certain cinematic techniques, and simultaneity. This was new at the time. I especially liked his *Manhattan Transfer* and *The 42nd Parallel.* But he didn't continue.

PLAYBOY: Have you read any other American books you've liked in recent years?

SARTRE: Very few.
PLAYBOY: For instance?
SARTRE: Well, I've liked most *The Organization Man* by Whyte, *The Exurbanites* by Spectorsky, and all the books of C. Wright Mills, my late and dear friend.
PLAYBOY: Let's talk about your own work. Several of your plays have been adapted for the screen; have you liked any of them?
SARTRE: The movie versions of my plays have all been very bad—except for *The Respectful Prostitute.*
PLAYBOY: Still, haven't you earned a good deal in royalties from these films? Besides, you are a continual best-seller.
SARTRE: True; I have quite *large* sums of money to spend, as a matter of fact. But I also have many obligations. And the fact is that I hate to possess. It seems to me that *we* are possessed by the things we possess—whether it be money or the things it buys. When I like an object, I always want to give it to someone. It isn't generosity—it's only because I want *others* to be enslaved by objects, not me. And I get pleasure from the thought that someone will like an object I give him.
PLAYBOY: You eschew wealth—but how about fame? Are you pleased with the world-wide eminence you've attained, or rather regained, in recent years?
SARTRE: In some ways, perhaps—but I don't want to become the prisoner of my status, whatever it may be at the moment. Always the here and now is a condition I regard as temporary and wish to leave behind. I persist in a childish illusion: the illusion that a man can always better himself. I warn myself that I've written some books, but if I feel it my duty to defend the ideas expressed in these books, even if things change, then I am no longer myself. I would become the victim of my own books. I don't think that one should make a point, as Gide did, of systematically breaking with one's past; but I want always to be accessible to change. I don't feel bound by anything I've written. Nevertheless, I don't disown a word of it, either.

[The following exchange took place several months later, immediately after Sartre's refusal of the 1964 Nobel Prize for Literature.]
PLAYBOY: One final question: Why did you reject the Nobel Prize?
SARTRE: I'd rather not talk about it.
PLAYBOY: Why not?
SARTRE: Because I don't think that an academy or a prize has anything to do with me. I consider that the greatest honor I can have is to be read.

ROBERT SHELTON

August 1965

Interviewer: Bern Keating

If a swing from the philosophy of a Nobel Prize winner to the arguments of a semiliterate "imperial wizard" of the Ku Klux Klan seems abrupt, consider what it must have been like for PLAYBOY readers of the day. In the full flush of the civil-rights movement, shortly after the murder of activist Viola Liuzzo and the bombing of four little black girls, this interview had a powerful effect.

In that atmosphere, a bigot solemnly intoning, "Our research and studies have found that there is more stirring and movement of the nigra when they have a full moon; they show a higher increase in the rate of crime and sex," made its own point more dramatically than a spokesman for the black cause might have. Editor Fisher sent Southern-born journalist Bern Keating to Alabama to speak with the most prominent Klan member at the time, a former air-conditioner salesman who styled himself the head of the United Klans. When Fisher called from Chicago to set up the appointment, Shelton replied: "You're the magazine that published that nigger pinup last March. Well, I talk with most anybody as part of my job, so I guess I'll even talk to you." As a note preceding the interview warned, PLAYBOY'S editors decided not to correct Shelton's syntax or pronunciation for self-evident reasons.

Overlapping loyalties among splinter groups of the notorious Ku Klux Klan, unwritten alliances among certain Klan federations—and violent hostility among others—have confused reporters trying to make sense of the turbulent renascence of the hooded order of white, Anglo-Saxon, native-born Protestant superpatriots.

Out of the kaleidoscopic shifting of Klan liaisons, however, one leader has emerged as the most notorious, and the most powerful, of the lot: Robert Shelton of Tuscaloosa, Alabama, Imperial Wizard of the United Klans of America, whose federation, rightly or wrongly, is blamed for nearly every Klan outrage from Florida to Texas. Because the KKK is a secret society, no one outside the Klan knows just who and how many belong to Shelton's group, but the best informed observers in the FBI and the Southern press estimate his membership—mostly in the Carolinas, Georgia, Alabama and Tennessee—at about 10,000.

Little more is known for certain about Shelton himself, or his ascendancy to Klan leadership, for he refuses to discuss either his past or his private life. But investigators have been able to ascertain a few solid facts about his personal background: Born thirty-six years ago in Tuscaloosa, he was educated in public schools there, dropped out of the Univesity of Alabama after taking a few courses, then attended a vocational trade school where he studied automobile mechanics. After serving as a sergeant in the army from 1949 to 1951, he went to work as a factory hand for the

B. F. Goodrich Company in Tuscaloosa, but was fired for refusing to give up his extracurricular Klan activities. For a year he managed a local tire store, which he quit to supervise public relations for a trucking company; after another year he quit again, this time to become an air-conditioner salesman. Then, about nine months ago—having served as Imperial Wizard of the United Klans since 1961—he abandoned all outside work to devote his full energies to the KKK.

In the interests of finding out more about Shelton, his Klan and his racist convictions, we obtained his unlisted Tuscaloosa office phone number from a knowledgeable Southern newspaperman (who made us promise not to reveal where we got it) and called the Imperial Wizard with our request for an exclusive interview.

Arriving in Tuscaloosa a week later, we drove to the address he gave us—a ramshackle downtown office building—spied the United Klan office door at the end of a dingy hall, walked in and found ourself in a room overflowing with untidy piles of newspapers, unopened mail and mimeographed press releases. A pleasant secretary ushered us into the inner office, where Shelton himself greeted us unsmilingly with a cold handshake from behind a desk flanked by American and Confederate flags.

Ascetically thin and hawk-faced, he was totally unlike the stereotype of the hot-eyed fanatic. His speech was curiously flat, toneless and unpunctuated, and except for a solitary mirthless smile, when he commented that the Johnson-Humphrey ticket had not been on the ballot in Alabama last November, his face was inscrutably masklike and expressionless throughout our four-hour conversation. Nattily bedecked—not in his familiar Klan robes, but in an Ivy League houndstooth sports jacket, black knit tie, black slacks and an enormous diamond ring on his little finger—Shelton bypassed the amenities, making no secret of his antipathy toward the press, and instructed us to get right down to business. We did.

PLAYBOY: What are the aims of the Ku Klux Klan?

SHELTON: To protect this great country and oppose mongrelization of the races. It is obligatory upon the nigra to recognize they are living in the land of the white race by courtesy of the white race.

PLAYBOY: America's twenty million native-born Negroes would undoubtedly take issue with that statement.

SHELTON: That's just why the Klan exists. White people cannot be expected to surrender control to any other race.

PLAYBOY: They're not being asked to.

SHELTON: On the contrary, they are being *made* to do so. The white man is being defranchised as our forefathers were in the Reconstruction era.

PLAYBOY: By Negroes?

SHELTON: By the Civil Rights Act, which is nothing but legislation for the nigra. This dastardly, infameous piece of legislation is designed solely to bring about turmoil.

PLAYBOY: Why can't whites keep every right they now have and still extend rights to Negroes?

SHELTON: The Jewish race as well as the Catholics and other religious faiths have their rights, but this does not give them the right to destroy the faith of a settled race on this continent. Don't force something we don't want in our faith.

PLAYBOY: How are Jews and Catholics forcing their beliefs on you?

SHELTON: With this liberalism, this civil rights. It's understandable that the Jew and the Catholic, being a minority themselves, would be sympathetic with the nigra. They have in the past contributed financially, morally and physically to the civil-rights struggle. But now they are changing. They are beginning to see that the nigra thinks he is the all-power controlling factor. Many other people, too, that had been inclined to show partiality to the nigra in his struggle are reverting to the segregationist side because of the outside interference and because they have had an opportunity to see the low morals and the inner workings of the civil-rights movement.

PLAYBOY: If this alleged drift from sympathy for Negroes continues among Jews and Catholics, would they be welcomed into the Klan?

SHELTON: No. Only white, gentile, Protestant, native-born Americans can take the Klan oath. The Knights of the Ku Klux Klan is a fraternal order of real men who are 100-percent American. But the Jew or Catholic might be welcomed into the Klan if he qualified.

PLAYBOY: What would he have to do to qualify?

SHELTON: Give up his religion.

PLAYBOY: What is the purpose of the Klan's concealing robes and hoods?

SHELTON: The robes are in memorandum of our forefathers and are used in ritualistic work. We wear hoods, but this organization does not use masks. We do not hide our identity. Our meetings are public.

PLAYBOY: What is the symbolism of the burning cross at all Klan gatherings?

SHELTON: The cross has been used by crusaders for the last nineteen centuries.

PLAYBOY: There weren't any crusaders until the eleventh century.

SHELTON: Today we use the cross as a rallying point to meet oppression and to establish Christianity.

PLAYBOY: Christianity was established 1,965 years ago. But why do you burn the cross?

SHELTON: Lighting the cross signifies that this is to light the way of Christ and to show light of truth to the world. We use it to rally Christians and to meet the oncoming tide.

PLAYBOY: What tide?

SHELTON: The tide of world communism.

PLAYBOY: Are you attempting to stem that tide when you burn crosses on the lawns of civil-rights sympathizers?

SHELTON: This organization does not participate in burning crosses of intimidation. When we have a problem to discuss with any individual, a committee of one, two or three Klansmen in street clothes will approach this person to discuss any grievances we may have with him, to give him our point of view, to persuade him to see things our way.

PLAYBOY: This technique seems to be effective. In January of this year, Klan threats forced the cancellation of a speech in Bogalusa, Louisiana, by Brooks Hays, a Southern moderate political leader. How do you justify such violations of the right to free speech and assembly?

SHELTON: This is not a one-sided sword. The FBI and the Justice Department has harassed members of this Klan and other right-wing organizations, causing them to lose their jobs. They have harassed Klansmen at work though the Klansmen asked them not to come to the job but to their homes if they wanted to discuss anything. And that's just part of the story of economic intimidation, reprisals and harassments that individuals receive when they become known as Klansmen—from employers who fire Klansmen, from the FBI and the Justice Department.

PLAYBOY: Isn't the Klan under federal surveillance and investigation because of its own intimidation and brutalization of civil-rights workers?
SHELTON: We do not believe in violence.
PLAYBOY: If that's true, why do the Justice Department and many local police officials, including secret infiltrators of the Klan, blame the KKK—in the ten years since its revival in 1954—for thirty-two bombings in Alabama, thirty-four bombings in Georgia, ten racial killings in Alabama, thirty Negro church burnings in Mississippi, the ambush killing of Colonel Lemuel Penn, the castration of an elderly Negro in Birmingham, the murders of Reverend James Reeb and Mrs. Anthony Liuzzo in Alabama, plus many floggings of civil-rights workers and labor leaders?
SHELTON: This is a prejudice of the misinformed public and harassment by this FBI and Justice Department that don't know what they are talking about. I would like to point out that no Klansman has ever been convicted of those crimes, and I think it would be only fair to not blame the Klan for things that hasn't been proved. Not one conviction. As I said, we do not believe in violence—despite that certain individuals have committed acts of violence under cover of darkness, shielded by masks and robes resembling the official regalia of the Knights of the Ku Klux Klan. "Ballots, not bullets" is our motto.
PLAYBOY: How do you reconcile that statement with the testimony of eyewitnesses that Dr. Robert Hayling, a Negro civil-rights leader in St. Augustine, Florida, was caught spying on a recent Klan meeting and publicly beaten?
SHELTON: We do not believe in violence.
PLAYBOY: In Pike County, Mississippi, sheriff's records show two Negro floggings, four Negro churches burned and one bombed, along with thirteen Negro homes, a Negro store and a Negro barbershop—all during the summer of 1964. One of the eleven men convicted of the bombings carried a card signed by you. Can you explain that?
SHELTON: That was merely a card that I have given to thousands of people. It is just a form of pocket card for advertising, with a calendar on the back side and the insignia of the Klan on the front side, along with my name and address, in case anybody wants to reach me.
PLAYBOY: Then how do you explain the case of Paul Dewey Wilson, who was arrested last year in McComb, Mississippi, while wearing a deputy sheriff's badge and hauling four rifles, a pistol, eight wooden clubs, a blackjack, brass knuckles and a hypodermic syringe in his car—and carrying a membership card in the United Klan signed by you?
SHELTON: We don't have membership cards. The card he had was the card I described—just a business card.
PLAYBOY: He also had a black leatherette apron and black hood, which are allegedly the Klan executioner's garb. Are they?
SHELTON: No—not in our organization.
PLAYBOY: Even segregationist Governor Paul Johnson of Mississippi has said, "The Klan claims it does not indulge in violence. Its activities, however, indicate otherwise." Any comment?
SHELTON: He is entitled to his opinion. We are against violence.
PLAYBOY: So you've said.
SHELTON: There is several Klans, you know. That is the trouble of throwing every nut in the same bag and saying it's all the same kind of nuts.

PLAYBOY: That's an aptly chosen metaphor. But all of those arrested for recent racial murders—those of Lemuel Penn, Reverend Reeb and Mrs. Liuzzo—have been members of your own United Klan.
SHELTON: There are many Klans. The FBI has arrested people without any proof whatsoever.
PLAYBOY: Are you claiming that the men arrested for these murders are not members of your United Klan?
SHELTON: I'm not saying they were and I'm not saying they're not. It would be a violation of my sacred Klan oath to identify members of the Klan. But speaking of violating oaths, we are finding many cases where the Federal Bureau of Investigation is purging witnesses with attempts to bribe.
PLAYBOY: Don't you mean *suborning* witnesses?
SHELTON: I mean they are offering money to get them to make statements on promises of giving them land, relocating their family, giving them money.
PLAYBOY: Can you cite a case?
SHELTON: I certainly can: that pimp Gary Rowe, the FBI informer in this Luziano case.
PLAYBOY: You mean Liuzzo?
SHELTON: Even the FBI admits they gave him three thousand dollars and we have reason to think it was more.
PLAYBOY: You call Rowe a pimp. What do you mean by that?
SHELTON: There are three kinds of undercover agents. There is the spy; there is the inside informer; and there is the pimp. By that I mean the kind of fellow who eggs along, who urges on his cohorts to do his dastardly deeds and then reports them. And this man is one of those—a pimp.
PLAYBOY: You mean he urged the three Klansmen to murder Mrs. Liuzzo?
SHELTON: He is a pimp and I have told you what a pimp is.
PLAYBOY: Is Collie Leroy Wilkins, who was tried for the murder of Mrs. Liuzzo, a United Klansman?
SHELTON: That's only speculation. I'm not saying yes or no.
PLAYBOY: If he isn't, we find it odd that he was defended with Klan funds by a Klan lawyer, and that you sat throughout most of the trial beside Wilkins at the defense counsel's table. Were there any Klansmen on the jury?
SHELTON: That is what is irksome to me. The prosecutor asked every juryman if he was a member of a secret order. But I notice he did not ask if they were Knights of Columbus, just Klansmen.
PLAYBOY: But it was an accused Klansman on trial, not a Knight of Columbus.
SHELTON: Well, there was no Klansman on that jury, that much I can tell you flatly. The prosecutor made sure of that.
PLAYBOY: In any event, the case ended in a mistrial when the jurors failed to agree on a verdict. Do you feel that justice was served?
SHELTON: No, I do not. After the President's accusiations on television, it was impossible for Wilkins to have an impartial trial. In the first place, the government had no evidence whatsoever to submit at the pretrial hearing to show cause to hold these individuals. They were no witnesses presented, yet the bond was established at fifty thousand dollars each. We immediately requested a hearing before a federal judge to appeal for a more reasonable bond; but he had already prejudged the cases—evidently he had heard the President make the accusiation on national television and he refused to even discuss setting a lower bond for the murderers of the woman from

Detroit. It shows the unfairness of prejudging, as the President did in this case.
PLAYBOY: Haven't you just prejudged them yourself by calling them "the murderers of the woman from Detroit?"
SHELTON: Oh, I meant to say "the *accused* murderers," of course. But as I was saying, it set a low presency for the highest executive of this land to go before the general citizenry to establish himself as a megalomaniac. Meaningly, that he places himself above God to be the judge on an individual's guilt by judging him without any evidence being submitted whatsoever. Had it not been for the President's intrusions, Wilkins would have been acquitted on the first ballot.
PLAYBOY: As part of his summation to the jury, the Klan's attorney, Matt Murphy, said: "I never thought I'd see the day when Communists and niggers and Jews were flying around under the banner of the United Nations, not the American flag of the country we fought for, not the flag of the country we are in, and I am proud to be white and I stand here as a white man and I say we are never going to mongrelize the race with nigger blood and the Martin Luther Kings, the white niggers, the Jews, the Zionists who run that bunch of niggers, the white people are not going to run before them. Jim Clark says 'Never.' I say 'Never' myself. . . . I urge you as patriotic Americans not to find this young man guilty." Are those also your own sentiments?
SHELTON: Certainly. Those beatniks, tennis-shoe wearers, sex perverts at Selma were carrying the United Nations flag for anybody to see.
PLAYBOY: Well, it's not a crime to carry a UN flag, of course. But even if your description of the Selma marchers were accurate, how is it relevant to the innocence or guilt of the Klansmen accused of Mrs. Liuzzo's murder?
SHELTON: It is further evidence of the pressure of the influx of these outsiders, of the federal government, of the whole international conspiracy to break the back of the Klan. They will stoop to any level. They were offering only the word of a pimp, Gary Rowe. He is not a real informer; he is a political prostitute. I have letters from relatives of his in Savannah, Georgia, saying he is the lowest scum on earth. Why, just two days before the shooting, he pistol-whipped a man in Birmingham, beat him senseless to the ground with the butt of his pistol.
PLAYBOY: What was the man's name?
SHELTON: That man was a religious member of a sect that doesn't permit violence, so he just held his arms to his sides while this pimp pistol-whipped him.
PLAYBOY: What was the man's name?
SHELTON: Rowe did the same thing a month previous.
PLAYBOY: Can you prove these charges?
SHELTON: It is on the police docket in Birmingham. Look it up. He said and kept hollering while he hit that man that nobody could touch him because he was protected by the federal government. When the FBI stoops to using people that low, we have come a long way downhill and it is time to stop and take a look around to see what is happening to us.

[Subsequent investigation of Shelton's charges revealed that Rowe was tried for assault and battery in Birmingham Court on March 15, 1965, but the case was dismissed on the grounds of insufficient evidence. The other incident took place in Fultondale, Alabama, not Birmingham; the charge was public drunkenness, not assault; and the man charged, and tried on March 23, 1965, was not Rowe but a man named Charles Powell. According to the town's mayor, in fact, it was Rowe who brought the charges against Powell.]

PLAYBOY: Let's move on, if we may—

SHELTON: Before you change the subject, I would like to call your attention to a few facts in connection with this Luziano case.

PLAYBOY: Liuzzo.

SHELTON: From medical records which was called into this office and to my lawyer from one of the institutions in Detroit, we find that she has been an in-and-out patient in a mental hospital there in Detroit. We also find at the time she was killed she was on probation from courts in Detroit. There is even some doubt as to whether or not her and her husband were actually living together for the last three months.

[Mr. Liuzzo's attorney states she was never a patient in a mental hospital and that she was indeed living with Mr. Liuzzo up to the moment of her departure for Selma. It is true that she was on probation—as the result of having refused to send her children to school, to call attention to the Michigan legislature's refusal to raise the compulsory school age from sixteen to eighteen.]

PLAYBOY: Even if your charges were true, do you consider this a justification for killing her?

SHELTON: I am violently opposed to death by violence. But if Mrs. Liuzzo had been at home with her family, this incident wouldn't never have happened. She should have stayed home and not come to Selma.

PLAYBOY: Why? Didn't she and the other out-of-state demonstrators at Selma have every constitutional right to go to Alabama or any other part of the United States they chose?

SHELTON: We're not going to Detroit to demonstrate demanding that they take nigras off registration. Let the people of Detroit clean up their own back yard and tend to their own confounded business and leave us alone. When you bring in outside agitators who are misfits in other societies, it brings resentment from all people.

PLAYBOY: Not *all* people. Nor do most Americans consider civil-rights workers misfits. But speaking of Detroit back yards, a Klan-type cross was burned in the back yard of Mrs. Liuzzo's Detroit home shortly after her funeral. Does your Klan have a klavern in Detroit?

SHELTON: I'm not going to be specific in the location of any unit.

PLAYBOY: A reporter quoted an unidentified Klansman at a rally in Morganton, North Carolina, as saying that Mrs. Liuzzo "got what she deserved." Do you agree?

SHELTON: I am not for any person's life being taken through violence. I am saying, however, that she was out of her rightful place at home; a married woman and a mother, she was off involved in immoral surroundings.

PLAYBOY: Speaking of immoral surroundings, Anthony Liuzzo said after his wife's death, "They should put a ninety-foot fence around Alabama and let those segregationists live with themselves." Any comment?

SHELTON: The only necessity of putting a fence around Alabama is to keep some of the misfits and sex perverts out.

PLAYBOY: Does that include Mrs. Liuzzo and Reverend Reeb?

SHELTON: If they had stayed home, this would never have happened.

PLAYBOY: At a press conference after Mrs. Liuzzo's death, you said that the Klan "Bureau of Investigation" was looking into her background for "possible Communist connections." Do you claim to have found any?

SHELTON: No, but we are certainly checking her background.

PLAYBOY: Mrs. Liuzzo was a Roman Catholic. Communism is atheistic. Do you think she could be both a Catholic and a Communist?
SHELTON: Perhaps she was a Communist dupe rather than a conscious agent. However, there was numbers of priests and nuns at Selma, and one Catholic that viewed the march on television told me it was uncommon to see a nun in high-heeled shoes or a priest in his regalia of the Church with suede shoes on.
PLAYBOY: Why is it that none of the several hundred members of the press on the march reported seeing this?
SHELTON: Well, this Catholic friend of mine saw it and he told me about it.
PLAYBOY: What is his name?
SHELTON: I can't violate his confidence.
PLAYBOY: Then let's change the subject. At a recent Klan rally in Hemingway, South Carolina, you called President Johnson "a conniving, misgiving fool." What did you mean by that?
SHELTON: I did not say that. That is a misinterpretation. I only called him a megalomaniac.
PLAYBOY: We're sorry to contradict you, but that rally was televised nationally on ABC, and you were clearly heard by millions of viewers to say and we quote you: "If LBJ thinks that he is going to run the Klan underground or break our backs by using us as a fish bait to his liberal element, the demands to investigate the United Klans of America by the House Inactivities Committee, he is a conniving, misgiving fool." In that same speech, you also said of the President, "If he continues with his yakking, he will be one of the greatest organizers the Klan has ever had." Would you elaborate?
SHELTON: I may make him an honorary Klansman, he has done us so much good with his yakking. You can see from the unopened mail deliveries on my desk, consisting of up to thirty-three thousand letters [our estimate: about three hundred], that the ratio is running about 99 to 1 in favor.
PLAYBOY: How do you know the sentiment of an unopened letter?
SHELTON: Well, the two or three I have had the time to open was certainly in favor. The people are saying if the President is going to be on the side of Martin Luther King, they want to be on the side of the Ku Klux Klan.
PLAYBOY: At the time of his announcement that the FBI had arrested four Klansmen for the murder of Mrs. Liuzzo, the President warned Klansmen to resign "before it is too late." What do you think he was threatening to those who did not get out?
SHELTON: The President of the United States thinks he can force a Klansman to choose his associations and his fraternal organization for his "New Society."
PLAYBOY: Great Society.
SHELTON: Whatever you call it, if this society he is advocating with the civil rights struggle is composed of sex perverts, beatniks, pinkos, Communists, the lowest misfits from all over the country that are participating in all of these sex orgies openly, in defiance of the public eye, of indecent exposure, I want no part of it.
PLAYBOY: Are you referring to the fornication that allegedly took place—according to segregationist "eyewitnesses"—on the march from Selma to Montgomery?
SHELTON: I am—and it did.
PLAYBOY: Hundreds of clergymen, newsmen and press photographers accompanied the marchers; yet none of them reported the slightest breach of propriety en route.
SHELTON: Either they were blind or covering up. There has been a compiled listing of

pictures and films showing these fornifications. I have over five thousand photographs—pictures of the charges that have been made of fornification. They will be shown at a later date.

PLAYBOY: Pictures of the charges or pictures of the fornication?

SHELTON: Of the fornification.

PLAYBOY: Why haven't you made them public?

SHELTON: At the proper time they will be presented.

PLAYBOY: When?

SHELTON: In due time and to the proper investigation authorities.

PLAYBOY: Did you have Klan secret agents among the marchers?

SHELTON: I'm not saying. But I don't think we could hardly have gotten all the photographs but what we have sources of getting information.

PLAYBOY: In a telegram you sent to the President after his televised denunciation of the Klan, you said you wanted to confer with him privately about "sex perverts in government and Communist agents in the civil-rights movement." Would you elaborate?

SHELTON: When the President first went into the White House and went around turning out all the lights, I was puzzled what he was up to. Then the Jenkins case came along and I understood.

PLAYBOY: How about Communist agents in the civil-rights movement? Would you name some?

SHELTON: There have been definite indications in investigations in this area.

PLAYBOY: Conducted by whom?

SHELTON: By the Klan Bureau of Investigation, among others.

PLAYBOY: You'll forgive us if we don't accept its findings as documentary fact.

SHELTON: Don't take our word for it. Counteragents working with the federal government have also signed notarized statements saying there are *many* active Communists in the civil-rights struggle.

PLAYBOY: Can you show us these statements?

SHELTON: I have them in my files.

PLAYBOY: The FBI has reported that there are a few Communists active in some of the more militant civil-rights groups, but Attorney General Nicholas Katzenbach has said that their numbers are insignificant and that the Communist Party cannot be said to exert any influence whatever over the civil-rights movement or its leaders.

SHELTON: He is ignorant of the conspiracy. He knows better.

PLAYBOY: How can he be ignorant and yet also know better?

SHELTON: I have pictures implicating many known Communists.

PLAYBOY: Can you show us the pictures, cite specific names, tell us to whom, apart from you, they are "known" as Communists?

SHELTON: I am not privileged to divulge that information at this time.

PLAYBOY: On several occasions you have called for a House Un-American Activities Committee investigation of CORE, SNCC and the NAACP for possible Communist infiltration. Would you be as willing to submit to a congressional investigation of the Klan?

SHELTON: Certainly. Why not? What's good for the goose is good for the gander. If the civil-rights groups were being investigated, we would gladly open our doors to the same scrutiny.

PLAYBOY: The Attorney General has said that the Klan has been infiltrated by many FBI agents. Did this come as a surprise to you?

SHELTON: No. We know we have infiltration. However, it's not necessary for them to infiltrate. If they fill out an application, they can do so and we'll welcome them into the Klan and have fraternal unionism.
PLAYBOY: Have you spotted any of the FBI spies in your own Klan?
SHELTON: Absolutely.
PLAYBOY: Do you have them under countersurveillance?
SHELTON: No. Because we have nothing to hide. In some cases, these informers are actually turning the money they get for informing to the FBI back to the Klan itself.
PLAYBOY: What do you mean?
SHELTON: These so-called informers are sometimes more loyal to the Klan than the FBI knows.
PLAYBOY: As you know, several Klansmen besides Gary Rowe have promised to reveal Klan secrets to the Un-American Activities Committee. What's your reaction?
SHELTON: Any individual who would reveal secrets of the Klan would be violating his oath to his God and to his fellow Klansmen.
PLAYBOY: If you were subpoenaed to testify before the House Un-American Activities Committee, would you do so?
SHELTON: No. I would not. The same law that applies to the NAACP, the Communist Party, SNCC and CORE would also have to apply to us.
PLAYBOY: You mean the Fifth Amendment, which empowers a witness to avoid self-incrimination by refusing to testify?
SHELTON: That's correct.
PLAYBOY: But if you have nothing to hide, why would you refuse to testify?
SHELTON: Well, if I did not have to violate my sacred oath by divulging Klan secrets, I might testify—provided the committee was carrying out its purpose of investigating for infiltration of communism and of individuals and groups advocating the overthrow of the American government. But if it is for the purpose of left-wing elements using the Klan as the bait to destroy the committee itself because of its Southern membership, then I am opposed to any type of investigation, and I wouild refuse to testify. The FBI has already slandered the Klan by calling it a subversive organization, which is an outrageous lie.
PLAYBOY: Four Klan groups are cited on the subversive list.
SHELTON: This Klan is not on the list. The four Klan groups cited are not the United Klan. Of course, the Attorney General at a stroke of a pen can put any group he wishes on the subversive list.
PLAYBOY: Any group? How about the Boy Scouts?
SHELTON: Perhaps not, but I am surprised he hasn't already done it to us, since he is of the liberal mind himself.
PLAYBOY: President Johnson said of the Klan, "I know their loyalty is not to the United States but to a hooded society." Is that true?
SHELTON: That was the remark that I called him a liar for. Better than 70 percent of the Klan are veterans of World War One, World War Two and the Korean conflict. The Grand Dragon of Tennesse has sent the President a telegram telling him what to do with the two Silver Stars, the two bronze medals, the two Purple Hearts and the left arm he left in Korea. Practically all of the leadership of the Klan are veterans that received medals.
PLAYBOY: Victor Riesel, the labor columnist, recently wrote that the majority of

Klansmen are "the unlettered, the semiliterate, the unskilled." Do you disagree?
SHELTON: Absolutely. I don't know what script he is reading from. We have many people in the Klan—doctors, lawyers, veterans. We have all phases of the everyday life of the people.
PLAYBOY: Are there Klansmen in police and sheriff's departments?
SHELTON: Yes. We have Klans people in all walks of life.
PLAYBOY: Calvin Craig of Georgia, your second-in-command, has said the United Klan has members holding high-ranking federal jobs. Which jobs?
SHELTON: We have Klansmen in all walks of life, but I don't care to be more exact. I would be violating my Klan oath. If they want to reveal themselves as members, of course, that is their business.
PLAYBOY: Do these federal officeholders report to the Klan and take Klan orders?
SHELTON: We have loyal members in all walks of life.
PLAYBOY: Does the Klan have connections with other conservative groups, such as the John Birch Society, the Minute Men and the Christian Crusade?
SHELTON: We are not associated with any other patriot group. However, we are not opposing.
PLAYBOY: Do you endorse the views and objectives of the Birch Society?
SHELTON: Which views?
PLAYBOY: What is your attitude on the fluoridation of water, a "Communist-inspired" bugaboo of the John Birch Society?
SHELTON: It is establishing socialized medicine. I am not against any individual that has a desire for his child to receive fluoride for preventing tooth decay, which I am told it does, but I am opposed to forcing or for establishing socialized medicine, which certainly injecting fluoride is—especially a *chemical* fluoride, which they are using to prevent tooth decay. It is not generally known that the fluoride used in water systems is a by-product of aluminum-alloy shavings, which is a deadly poison.
PLAYBOY: Dental authorities assert that the fluoride used to prevent tooth decay does not cause harmful side effects. Do you share the view of the Birch Society that fluoridation is part of a conspiracy to poison Americans through the pretense of preventing tooth decay?
SHELTON: Well, it can be used in a conspiracy. Very definitely the Russians used fluoride effectively on their prisoners in the concentration camps in Russia.
PLAYBOY: For what purpose?
SHELTON: To break down their resistance to propaganda, to help brainwash them. It has the effect to accumulate. The body absorbs small doses and there is no method of the body casting this out as it does other chemicals.
PLAYBOY: Laboratory researchers have found no evidence whatever of such bizarre mental side effects from the use of sodium fluoride. But let's move on to another Birch Society *cause célèbre*: the nuclear-test-ban treaty, which it violently opposes. How do you feel about it?
SHELTON: I am against making any agreement on a disarmament program, of which this would be a first step.
PLAYBOY: Why?
SHELTON: The United Nations disarmament program will leave the individual citizen disarmed in his own home.
PLAYBOY: The nuclear-test-ban treaty was signed to prevent further contamination of the atmosphere with radioactive fallout. What possible connection could this have with the control of private firearms?

SHELTON: It's the opening wedge, the start of this three-stage disarmament plot. In the event of a revolution, as is predicted by many people, America might find itself unarmed.

PLAYBOY: What revolution? Waged by whom and against what?

SHELTON: From the evidence we have in regards to the civil-rights struggle in Selma, Montgomery, Marion and Birmingham, the tone of speech being used in the riots in Harlem, New York, many of the nigra leaders are strong advocates of a bloody revolution. We witnessed them on television call for a hundred volunteers to go out into the street.

PLAYBOY: Who made this appeal? The only speeches we have heard called for peaceful demonstrations.

SHELTON: We have witnessed these nigras in Selma making speeches saying: "If it's war the Southerner wants, we will burn Jim Crowism and any other opposition as Sherman burned the South to the ground in the Civil War. We will march through Dixie and leave a bloodbath. There is no other way out."

PLAYBOY: Who made that speech?

SHELTON: Well, King was one.

PLAYBOY: That isn't true.

SHELTON: Well, there is violence everywhere he goes.

PLAYBOY: But the violence is directed *against* Dr. King and his followers by white segregationists. He does not initiate it. In the event of a Negro rebellion such as you predict, however, don't you think the U.S. Army or the National Guard would be adequate to put down the revolt—especially since Negroes as well as white Southerners would presumably be disarmed?

SHELTON: Eventual execution of the disarmament program will place us under the protection of a One World police force from the United Nations; we could not be under the jurisdiction of the U.S. Army or our own troops.

PLAYBOY: Where did you get that extraordinary idea? It's not in the American Constitution, the United Nations Charter, or in any legislative or executive program of the American government.

SHELTON: You can see it plainly, the drift to One-Worldism. If revolution was to take place and we had troops down here from the Congo or Leopoldville or some Asian country, you can realize the dangers of oppression to white Americans. We would be under a worse heel of tyranny than we are under now.

PLAYBOY: What sort of tyranny?

SHELTON: I can see you've been soft-soaped like most of the unsuspecting American public. It's all part of the One World conspiracy to internationalize this country with its One World court, its One World race—even its One World language, which will probably be some mumbo jumbo from the dark jungles of Africa. This international conspiracy has as its purpose the complete undermining of the American way of life.

PLAYBOY: By whom is this "conspiracy" being engineered?

SHELTON: The key individuals involved in this international conspiracy are those who are speaking out against the segregationists of the South, against the John Birch Society, against the Minute Men and the Klan.

PLAYBOY: That includes most of the American public. Are they *all* in on the conspiracy?

SHELTON: In the first place, don't be too sure the American public is all that much against us. It is later than you think. We've got to realize when we refer to Russia and

the Communist state, this is not where the financial structure was that brought about the revolution of the Bolsheviks against the czar. The money was supplied and many men was supplied from New York City.
PLAYBOY: By whom?
SHELTON: By the international banking concern of Kuhn and Loeb.
PLAYBOY: Do you mean the Wall Street investment banking house?
SHELTON: Yes, this international banking concern—with a network of confederate banking interests in England, Switzerland, and so forth—is not only the moneybags but the brain trust of the international Communist conspiracy.
PLAYBOY: Are you saying, in other words, that the secret headquarters of world communism is New York rather than Moscow or Peking, and that Kosygin, Brezhnev and Mao Tse-tung take their orders from a group of international banking firms headed by Kuhn, Loeb and Company?
SHELTON: Absolutely right.
PLAYBOY: That will come as news not only to political scientists but also to Kosygin, Brezhnev and Mao, not to mention Kuhn and Loeb. How did you come by this fascinating bit of intelligence?
SHELTON: I have my sources. I cannot name them for fear of reprisal against them by the conspiracy.
PLAYBOY: Can you tell us the names of those who head the conspiracy?
SHELTON: I told you—Kuhn and Loeb, and a group of other international financiers.
PLAYBOY: Are these financiers Jewish, by any chance?
SHELTON: All of them, to my knowledge. They are financial wizards, and they head an international cartel that already owns our monetary system and controls the economy of this country.
PLAYBOY: How, exactly?
SHELTON: By keeping us drained through taxation and by executing their liberal spending policies abroad.
PLAYBOY: Perhaps you didn't know that tax laws are passed by the Congress, and that the nation's spending policies are determined by the President and the Bureau of the Budget.
SHELTON: Don't you believe it. Not only does this international cartel control the economy, but it is financing a Bolshevik revolution right here in the United States, just as it did in Russia in 1917. This conspiracy existed even at the time of the War Between the States.
PLAYBOY: Kuhn, Loeb and Company, which you called the brain trust of the conspiracy, wasn't founded until 1867, after the war was over. Who was in charge of it in 1861?
SHELTON: The House of Rothschild. This was their method of maneuvering the country into civil strife to divide in order to conquer.
PLAYBOY: Has this remarkable conspiracy been going on ever since then?
SHELTON: Indeed it has.
PLAYBOY: Do you believe that Jewish financiers were also responsible for, say, World War One?
SHELTON: Absolutely. And when Hitler was gaining his power, he had the financing of Jews. Then he more or less double-crossed them. You know, of course, that Hitler's grandmother was Jewish. The *Police Gazette* had an article showing gravestones and saying that some of his forebears were Jewish.

PLAYBOY: Most scholars do not consider the *Police Gazette* an unimpeachable source. But tell us? Did you approve of Hitler's actions against the Jews?
SHELTON: I don't approve of the destruction and death of any person.
PLAYBOY: Was the Jewish conspiracy also reponsible for the Depression, in your opinion?
SHELTON: Absolutely. Herbert Hoover has gotten the blame for it, but he was placed in leadership when this country was already at its lowest ebb because of the conspiracy engineered by these international financiers.
PLAYBOY: Actually, the Depression didn't begin until after Hoover had been President for several months. In any case, it hardly seems likely that these international financiers would have conspired to create a monetary crisis that would result in their own bankruptcy—which happened in many cases. What's your opinion of Franklin D. Roosevelt's New Deal, which many credit with rescuing the country from the Depression?
SHELTON: Roosevelt did more than any other President to liberalize, to socialize and to bring this country into the social revolution we are experiencing today.
PLAYBOY: Are you saying that he was a conscious agent of the conspiracy?
SHELTON: Either that or he allowed himself to be duped.
PLAYBOY: Was Harry Truman a dupe, too?
SHELTON: He was a fair President, but too many of the conspirators had already infiltrated the government, so that he had no choice but to follow their conspiratorial policy.
PLAYBOY: How about Eisenhower?
SHELTON: If he had had the initiative to take the steps his conscience told him he should, he could have reversed this trend to communism.
PLAYBOY: But he didn't?
SHELTON: No.
PLAYBOY: Did John F. Kennedy?
SHELTON: President Kennedy had realized he was being guided into the deep-blue end of the stream. He was struggling to get back on dry land, and this was the reason of the assassination.
PLAYBOY: He was assassinated because he was resisting the international financiers' conspiracy?
SHELTON: He was trying desperately to pull away. That was the reason of the assassination.
PLAYBOY: Oswald was not an independent agent?
SHELTON: Absolutely not. He was a Marxist assassin acting on orders. The Warren Commission was nothing but a Sunday-coating dress-up to suppress the facts.
PLAYBOY: Are you saying that the assassination, and this alleged suppression of "the facts," were engineered by the international Jewish financiers' conspiracy?
SHELTON: Absolutely.
PLAYBOY: And Jack Ruby, of course, being Jewish . . .
SHELTON: Absolutely. Hired to silence Oswald.
PLAYBOY: Is President Johnson, too, in on the conspiracy?
SHELTON: Clearly. President Johnson is a power-hungry politician. In statements he made in the Senate, he was opposed to civil rights as being unconstitutional, saying that he hoped he would never see anything so drastic as the Civil Rights Bill being brought forth. Now we see a complete reversal. It reminds me of LBJ *vs.* LBJ in a lawsuit.

PLAYBOY: Governor Wallace has denounced the press for its "leftist bias" in reporting about the civil-rights movement—particularly about racial incidents in Alabama. Do you agree with him?
SHELTON: Absolutely. The vast majority of the press is in on the conspiracy. The local reporter is usually all right; he has to make a living for his family. It is in the editorial head offices that you find the distortion directed by this conspiratorially controlled press. The national news medias creates anything that is sensational, that will sell copy. They go out of their way to grasp anything that appears sensational in racial demonstrations to sell news.
PLAYBOY: Such as the Reeb and Liuzzo killings, and the deaths of the four Negro girls in the Birmingham church bombing?
SHELTON: The Klan can be made a sensational issue by reaching into the past pedestals of history and trying to place the Klan of today in the same category as the Klan of the Reconstruction era. But this Klan is definitely not the Klan of our forefathers, because this is a different time.
PLAYBOY: All the murders we mentioned have been committed during your administration as Imperial Wizard of the United Klans.
SHELTON: As I said before, we had nothing to do with any of them. We do not believe in violence.
PLAYBOY: Let's change the subject. How do you feel about mixing the races?
SHELTON: I would say race mixture is definitely harmful.
PLAYBOY: Why?
SHELTON: There are various hereditary diseases that certainly would bring about withholding of advancement. For example, the nigra has a dread disease called sickle-cell anemia that is only found in the nigra. It is not found in the white race unless there is mixing of the blood.
PLAYBOY: A national survey conducted some years back reported that almost one in five "white" Americans had some Negro blood. Do you accept those figures?
SHELTON: It is possible.
PLAYBOY: Would you consider someone of, say, 1/32 Negro ancestry to be white?
SHELTON: If you're breeding animals for registration and you don't have the full breed, you don't get your papers. For maintaining the heritage of the race, we've got to maintain a pure race.
PLAYBOY: Why?
SHELTON: To maintain the power to govern for future generations. Only the pure race have to the highest degree the power to govern. You cannot show me any nation in history that did not crumble once they allowed their races to become amalgamated and thus lost their moral foundations.
PLAYBOY: Can you name one that did?
SHELTON: The Roman Empire, for instance, fell after their morals collapsed.
PLAYBOY: The Roman Empire was at its height during the reigns of its pagan emperors and did not collapse till after its emperors and most Romans had been Christians for more than a hundred years. Since you profess to be a Christian yourself, can you tell us where it says in the Bible that segregation is morally right?
SHELTON: There are many verses in the Bible that verify and maintain this.
PLAYBOY: Name one.
SHELTON: Well, *Acts,* seventeenth chapter, twenty-sixth verse, for instance.
PLAYBOY: Let's look it up in this Bible on your desk . . . . The opening words of that verse are "God hath made of one blood all nations of men . . ."

SHELTON: Many so-called students of the Bible attempt to use partial phrases of the Scripture as you just did to justify intermingling of the races, to create a false image of the fatherhood under God and the brotherhood of man.
PLAYBOY: There's no such thing as the brotherhood of man?
SHELTON: Only of white, native-born, gentile, Protestant Americans. I don't have to accept a nigra into my home, and if I refuse him this hospitality, I am not a sinful person.
PLAYBOY: The purpose of the civil-rights movement is not to force anyone to accept Negroes into his home, but to win for Negroes the same fundamental human rights enjoyed by whites—the vote, adequate housing and schooling anywhere they choose, equal job opportunities, equal access to public accommodations.
SHELTON: Asking me to take a nigra into my home is the same as a minister of the Gospel being forced to accept a criminal, or a bootlegger, or a gambler into his home on a social basis.
PLAYBOY: Are you equating Negroes with criminals, bootleggers and gamblers?
SHELTON: Certainly not. Not in all cases. But if it is distasteful to me for nigras to be in my house, it is my right not to have them in my house.
PLAYBOY: That is your privilege as a private citizen. Federal law clearly states, however, that it is not your privilege to refuse the use of *public* facilities—including churches—to anyone on the basis of skin color, no matter how distasteful it may be to you personally. Recognizing this fact, the national governing body of the Methodist Church, to which you belong, has urged racial integration of its member chuches. Has yours complied?
SHELTON: No, sir, it certainly has not.
PLAYBOY: What would you do if it did?
SHELTON: I would leave the church. Many people would leave the church. I have no desire to meet the nigra. I don't want him forcing himself on my society.
PLAYBOY: Do you know any Negroes personally?
SHELTON: Certainly. How could you avoid it?
PLAYBOY: Do you have any Negro friends?
SHELTON: I do not. I don't want the nigra forcing himself socially.
PLAYBOY: Do you have any white friends?
SHELTON: Those who feel as I do—and there are many of them. But about these churches and integration. The Southern Baptists and also the so-called Methodists have went to the extent of recommending such books as James Baldwin's *Another Country* and Martin Luther King's books. In these books are nothing but the utmost of filth.
PLAYBOY: Filth in Dr. King's books? Where?
SHELTON: You have to read them for yourself.
PLAYBOY: We have, and we don't find any in them.
SHELTON: For any church that calls itself a church to recommend this type of literature for the age group of fourteen to nineteen is beyond anything I can say. The beginning of *Another Country* is a sex orgy of interracial participation. Definition of sexual feelings and desires and how they are animally carried out.
PLAYBOY: How can you place Baldwin's erotic novel—which has received wide critical acclaim—in the same category with the writings of Martin Luther King?
SHELTON: I have just given you two examples. I could name countless others. The newsstands are flooded with filth.
PLAYBOY: Magazines as well as books?

SHELTON: All kinds of publications are going overboard in trying to create a sexual desire, a lust for sexual latitude in this country. When you create a lustful desire in the younger generation, you break down the morality of the country, and once you do that the country itself will tumble.
PLAYBOY: Can you give us the titles of a few magazines that you feel are generating this moral decay?
SHELTON: PLAYBOY is one of them. Why, you even had a nude nigra model in the March issue, who incidentally comes from Tuscaloosa.
PLAYBOY: You sound a strange note of civic pride. Do you think movies are obscene, too?
SHELTON: Absolutely, many of them. They should be cleaned up. There should even be a cleaning up of television programs.
PLAYBOY: Which programs?
SHELTON: It's not exactly what they say, but the motions that's carried out on the programs. [Shelton stood up and did an animated imitation of a belly dance.]
PLAYBOY: What show did you see that on?
SHELTON: I am too busy to be memorizing the names of television shows. I am too busy combating the civil-rights phase of this international conspiracy to demoralize our children and adults, to weaken our moral strength and introduce debauchery so as to make the eventual takeover easier.
PLAYBOY: Do you subscribe to the common segregationist belief that Negroes have lower standards of sexual morality than whites?
SHELTON: I do.
PLAYBOY: Do you base that belief on firsthand knowledge?
SHELTON: Certainly not. But scientific texts I have read show this clearly.
PLAYBOY: What texts?
SHELTON: I can't name them offhand.
PLAYBOY: You announced in a speech not long ago that Negroes are "responsive to the phases of the moon." Just what did you mean by that?
SHELTON: Our research and studies have found that there is more stirring and movement of the nigra when they have a full moon; they show a higher increase in the rate of crime and sex during the full moon.
PLAYBOY: Can you name the scientific sources on which this "research" was based?
SHELTON: Not right off.
PLAYBOY: Do you believe that Negro men yearn after white women in preference to Negro women?
SHELTON: Why else do we see so many attacks being made in New York and Chicago, where the nigra thinks he is strong with his civil-rights movement? Why do we see all of these assaults and rapes being committed against white women? There is a psychological reason why they have eliminated the practice of describing rapists in Northern newspapers as being nigra.
PLAYBOY: A study of nationwide police records by an NBC investigating team found that only an insignificant percentage of rape cases are interracial. The vast majority are rapes of black by black and white by white. In Philadelphia, to name one Northern city, the number of whites raped by blacks is almost identical to the number of blacks raped by whites.
SHELTON: Well, all I can say is, let the nigra have his enjoyments with his own race, but meantime don't interfere with the same activity of the white.

PLAYBOY: Do you think that so-called "unconventional" sex practices are more common among Negroes than among whites?
SHELTON: From some of the whites that I witnessed participating in this civil-rights struggle—these sex perverts and beatniks and pinkos, tennis-shoe wearers and all—these whites that have been involved in the civil-rights movement here in Alabama are mistfits and in all probability are perverts just as oddball as some nigras.
PLAYBOY: You have been quoted as saying if the police cannot stop civil-rights demonstrations, the Klan will. You said you will use "whatever means are necessary." Would those means include the use of firearms?
SHELTON: That is a misquote. I said if it reached the point the police could not stop the nigra invasion of private property and the protection of the home, then the Klan would take whatever steps were necessary.
PLAYBOY: Would those steps include the use of firearms?
SHELTON: An individual must maintain the power to protect his home. His home is his castle, or it was till the advocates of civil rights, as at Selma, denied the right of a man to his private property by walking up on his porch and asking to use the rest room and when refused exposing themselves off the front porch and into the front yard.
PLAYBOY: Can you document these charges?
SHELTON: When a case such as this occurs, an individual should have the right to protect his property and I am certainly going to protect mine.
PLAYBOY: What would you do if Martin Luther King were to launch a Negro voter-registration drive in Tuscaloosa?
SHELTON: The Klan has never had any objections to a nigra qualifying to vote if he is qualified. However, we are opposed to nigra or white who are not qualified to register and vote.
PLAYBOY: Do you think the voting test in Alabama has been honestly run?
SHELTON: There might have been some discrepancies because of the nigras' intimidations and demands for massive demonstrations instead of coming up as individuals. The Klan has never had any objections to a nigra qualifying to vote if he can qualify. But there must be some type of aptitude test on the national level.
PLAYBOY: But the Klan has protested that they did not want the federal government intruding in the state's control of its own voting requirements.
SHELTON: You have to screen out the unqualified. But the majority of the nigras have never had a desire to vote, anyway.
PLAYBOY: How do you know?
SHELTON: They have never even requested the vote on many occasions. But they have never been denied this right to the extent that the news medias make an issue of it. The only time that we see a collection of nigras is when an individual like Martin Luther King or some such professional agitators and promoters come into town and, through the superstitional belief of religion, they whip the local nigras into a frenzy so that they can just about guide them into the streets and do anything else they want to. But once they leave, then you see the nigra going back to his daily routine of life. They do not have and have not shown the initiative to have any mass voter-registration drives in the past.
PLAYBOY: The mass march from Selma to Montgomery to demand those voting rights was led by Nobel Prize winner Dr. Martin Luther King. Doesn't this honor indicate that world opinion is with the Negro rather than with the Klan?
SHELTON: It was a pathetic thing to give King the Nobel Peace Prize. He has done

more than any other individual to create turmoil and tension and to divide the races, white and black.

PLAYBOY: Many would feel that is a curious statement coming from one of the nation's leading exponents of racial segregation. But speaking of dividing the races, many of your views are shared by the Black Muslims, the segregationist Negro religious sect headed by Elijah Muhammad. What do you think of their proposal to gather the nation's twenty million Negroes into black enclaves from which all whites would be excluded?

SHELTON: It would be a workable solution, whether in the United States or in north Brazil or in South America.

PLAYBOY: Brazil *or* South America?

SHELTON: Or wherever. It might be Africa.

PLAYBOY: The Muslims have suggested that Negroes might take over a whole state. How about Alabama.

SHELTON: Why not New York instead? I know what you are trying to get me to say. You want me to agree with the Black Muslims.

PLAYBOY: You just did when you said that the Muslims' segregated resettlement plan was "a workable solution."

SHELTON: Well, I have never associated with the Black Muslims. I have never met with any Black Muslim and I have no desire to meet one. Jim Venable, the head of the so-called National Klans, used to be associated with me till I heard of him defending a Black Muslim in Shreveport. That was the last I cared to have to do with him.

PLAYBOY: Several reporters who covered a recent United Klan rally in Atlanta said that Jeremiah X, the Atlanta Muslim leader, attended and was favorably referred to by the speakers.

SHELTON: Not by me.

PLAYBOY: What was your reaction to Malcolm X's statement, shortly before his death, that he was going to present evidence in court that the Black Muslims have received financial and moral support from the Klan?

SHELTON: This Klan does not have money to give to the Black Muslims or anybody else.

PLAYBOY: Malcolm was murdered by Muslim assassins before he could testify. You have said Martin Luther King will also be assassinated. By a Klansman?

SHELTON: Certainly not. No, it will be by one of his own people. There is a power struggle within the movement. They all want to sit in the King's seat. And that seat they want is in the best restaurant in town.

PLAYBOY: Do you have any plans to thwart the public-accommodations section of the Civil Rights Act? How are you going to prevent integration of schools, lunchrooms, hotels, swimming pools, playgrounds and golf courses?

SHELTON: We shall borrow a page from the North and resort to *de facto* segregation. And eventually, when the Negroes realize we will never give in or give up, both races will go back to peaceful segregation by the natural grouping of races in different residential neighborhoods and in their own places of worship, schooling and recreation.

PLAYBOY: In view of the quickening pace at which integration is proceeding throughout the South, and the determination of the administration to enforce it, your prediction would seem to be wishful thinking. There is every indication that most Southerners are beginning to realize that integration cannot be stopped. Do you seriously believe that the Klan can hold it back forever?

SHELTON: Certainly. That is the purpose of my life. The Klan can hold back any massive movement for right now. Then a cycle or revolution is going to come to pass and it is going to revert back. Then one day we are going to witness a stronger, even more segregated society than we have ever before witnessed in the past.
PLAYBOY: We hope and believe, Mr. Shelton, that you couldn't be more wrong.

ARNOLD TOYNBEE

April 1967

Interviewer: Norman MacKenzie

It was early 1967, the war in Vietnam was raging, the debate over U.S. conduct in the war was almost as fierce, students were demanding "relevance"—and PLAYBOY, the most widely read publication among both servicemen and students, appeared carrying an interview with a British historian whose specialty was ancient Babylon and Rome. Some relevance. Just how "relevant" was PLAYBOY?

Consider, then, the points that Arnold Toynbee made in this interview at a time that most large-circulation magazines were generally supportive of the war: that the Vietcong and North Vietnam represented the only hope of unifying Vietnam; that Ho Chi Minh would win (and later astonish the Chinese by his ingratitude); that China, despite its internal convulsions, was in the process of moderating its foreign policy. To thoughtful Americans seeking some perspective, Toynbee's ability to link the aspirations of nationalism with the forces of history was an astonishing change from such cant as "Hell, no, we won't go" or "America, love it or leave it." If PLAYBOY influenced its readers politically during the Sixties, this interview was one reason.

As to its readability today, the reader may want to consider these other points that Toynbee also makes: that nuclear weapons *must* be reduced; that U.S. support of totalitarian states will eventually hurt it; that the Palestinian Arabs have a right to their own state; and that the greatest disservice America has done to Western civilization is its "fanatical attitude toward communism."

Hailed by many scholars as the greatest historian of the century, Arnold Joseph Toynbee, at seventy-seven, is one of the most brilliant, distinguished and controversial of living Englishmen. Best known as the author of A Study of History*—a prodigious attempt, which occupied him for twenty-seven years and fills a dozen weighty volumes, to chronicle and assess nothing less than the entire recorded history of mankind—Toynbee is also an acknowledged authority on contemporary international relations and a contentious critic of American foreign policy in particular. He was a member of British delegations to peace conferences after both world wars, and for* *much of his working life has supervised the annual survey published by the Royal Institute of International Affairs in London.*

Although Toynbee's eminence and accomplishments are beyond dispute (he is a Companion of Honor, a title granted by the queen for outstanding literary achievement or public service, and bears honorary degrees from Princeton, Columbia, Cambridge and his own university, Oxford), other historians have assailed him for what they consider an obsession with dead rather than living civilizations, and for his insistence that the Western world may collapse unless it rediscovers a sense of spiritual purpose.

Toynbee, however, credits his classical background with giving him "a mental standing ground outside the time and place into which I happen to have been born" and "a lifelong conviction that human affairs do not become intelligible until they are seen as a whole."

Western civilization can escape the fate of Babylon and Rome, Toynbee believes, if the people of the West accept his thesis that "our choice is going to be not between a whole world and a shredded-up world, but between one world and no world." He prophesies "that the human race is going to choose life and good, not death and evil. I therefore believe in the imminence of one world, and I believe that, in the twenty-first century, human life is going to be a unity again in all its aspects and activities." Among the obstacles to such a unity, Toynbee has often singled out nationalism as a prime cause of war and social disintegration, Zionism—which he considers a nationalistic perversion of Judaism, a religion he professes to admire—has been one of his most frequent targets. "All the far-flung ghettos of the world are to be gathered into one patch of soil in Palestine to create a single consolidated ghetto there," he once wrote. S. O. Liptzin, Chairman of the American Jewish Congress Commission on Jewish Affairs, considers Toynbee's dubious distinction between Judaism and Zionism "insulting and dishonest." Another critic has called Toynbee "an outright, if highly sophisticated anti-Semite." Toynbee himself claims he is neither an enemy of the Jews nor an advocate for the Arabs; but while visiting the Arab countries, he has chosen to bypass Israel—which he invariably refers to as "Palestine"; he has also publicly denounced "the Jewish massacre of Arabs in 1948." His questionable attitude toward the Jews, like the other controversial issues that have evolved out of his search for a "total" view of mankind, will continue to be debated as long as his works are read.

As he spoke in a gentle but emphatic voice, Toynbee sat passively, relying on subtle idiosyncrasies of expression—especially a trick of squinting, and a habit of lifting his eyebrows in mock surprise—to dramatize his statements. We began our conversations by asking him to amplify some of his well-publicized criticisms of the United States.

PLAYBOY: A few years ago you wrote that America is "the leader of a worldwide counterrevolutionary movement in defense of vested interests. She now stands for what Rome stood for. Rome consistently supported the rich against the poor." Do you still feel that way?

TOYNBEE: More than ever, I'm afraid. The U.S. government and the American people used to sympathize with and encourage liberation movements all over the world, such as the Spanish-American struggle against Spain, the Irish and Indian movements against Britian, the Italian *Risorgimento* against Austria, and the Polish movement against Austria, Prussia and Russia. But today, America is making it her business to oppose and defeat so-called wars of liberation wherever they break out, and in some cases she has actively supported reactionary and unrepresentative regimes in other countries. She has even practiced countersubversion, as in Guatemala a few years ago. I think this policy is immoral; it is also bound to bring its own retribution. In resisting subversive left-wing practices to which she objects, America has in some cases fallen into adopting the same practices herself. The occasion of this big—and, as I see it, unfortunate—change in American attitudes and policy was the Bolshevik revolution of 1917. The deeper cause of the change, I should say, is that America has become immensely rich, and therefore has become defensive-minded. She suspects other people of wanting to take her wealth from her, and this has made her militantly antiliberal.

PLAYBOY: Is this view what led you to make such extreme statements as your remark that "Madison Avenue is more danger to the West than communism"?

TOYNBEE: That *is* an extreme statement, but I believe it is a correct one. Communism is a threat to the West from outside, but not a very serious one. No Western country seems likely to be converted to communism. Most Western countries, including the U.S., are becoming welfare states, which is a form of inoculation against communism. Madison Avenue, however, is a threat from the *inside,* and we are betrayed by what is false within. Pushing sales by advertising is propagating what Plato called "the lie in the soul." It is substituting the "image" of things for the truth about them. It is, in fact, a campaign of subversion against intellectual honesty and moral integrity—and these are the indispensable foundations of decent civilized life.

PLAYBOY: You seem to be implying that America should be more concerned with its domestic integrity than with what the government construes as a moral responsibility to protect the free world from falling under Communist control.

TOYNBEE: If, at any time between 1914 and 1946, you had told me that one day I should wish to see America return to isolationism, I should not have believed you. Of course, I still do not really wish to see America go isolationist. The world has now become a unity, and we must all, therefore, become world-minded—especially America, because she is at present the most powerful country in the world. I do not want to see communism spread, but neither do I want to see the system of capitalist "free enterprise" spread. I should like to see communism, capitalism and other ways of life—the ways of the majority of mankind—that are neither Communist nor capitalist, finding means to coexist with one another. That is why I think America's policy of opposing communism by force is misconceived. It defeats its own object. The only effective means of preventing the spread of communism—or any other way of life, for that matter—is to make some different way of life more attractive on the test of its results. In Europe, the U.S. is helping Europeans to do things that the Europeans themselves believe to be good for them. In Asia, the U.S. is trying to impose on Asians things that the U.S. feels to be good for Asians—or to be good for American interests in Asia. The Americans and the Northwest Europeans have the same way of life; Asians, however, have their own ways, which are neither Communist nor capitalist.

PLAYBOY: In this context, you have said: "In refusing to recognize that the Vietcong represents a national liberation movement made by the South Vietnamese themselves, and in attributing the war wholly to Communist intervention from the outside, the United States is unintentionally making herself the heir of European colonialism in Asia." Do you stand by that statement?

TOYNBEE: I certainly do. I arrived at this conclusion as a result of a number of meetings and discussions with people in different parts of the United States in the fall of

1964 and the spring of 1965. To my mind, the most alarming thing about the American attitude toward Vietnam—and this applies to the administration as well as to the general public—is that, as I see it, the American attitude is so unrealistic. I think America wants to play the role of Saint George on a world scale, and therefore needs a worldwide dragon: monolithic world communism. I happen to think it is an *imaginary* dragon that she is hugging, that the U.S. will not look at the realities. As I see it, the motive that makes the Vietcong and North Vietnam fight this colossus of the United States at tremendous cost to themselves is one that is very well known. What they want is national liberation from foreign domination, and then national reunification. They wanted to get rid of the French, and now they want to get rid of the Americans. They want to be reunited again. This is a perfectly understandable motive; it is one that inspires people to fight wars of liberation. But the U.S. goes on insisting that this is part of a world Communist conspiracy. Until the Americans get down to looking at the realities, without prejudice, they won't begin to solve their difficulties in Vietnam.

PLAYBOY: Some commentators feel that the Chinese are willing to see the United States drawn more and more deeply into Vietnam, because it offers them a chance to demonstrate to the world that the U.S. is an imperialist power. Do you think this is the case?

TOYNBEE: I think that some such motive is probably present. After all, the Chinese are causing America odium and expense in lives and money. Vietnam is costly, after all. But, of course, the Chinese might miscalculate; the risk in this policy is that the war with the U.S. might in the end make Vietnam turn against China. China is not being a very handsome partner to Vietnam. So the Chinese can't go all the way in this policy. I also think we should recognize that the Chinese have a strong motive for wishing to get America farther removed from their own doorstep in Vietnam, in Taiwan, in Korea. They would like to see her farther off. I think that is a genuine anxiety on their part.

PLAYBOY: Are you suggesting that the U.S. withdraw completely from Southeast Asia, in order to cease causing China anxiety?

TOYNBEE: I believe the right policy for America would be to try to get a Southeast Asia that wasn't dominated either politically or militarily by any major power, either by herself or by China. Americans might say: "Well, if we go out, China will come in." But what is the priority of Chinese motives? I think China's paramount motive in Southeast Asia is to get America out. As I said, America is uncomfortably close to China's doorstep, from China's point of view. The safeguard, from the American point of view, would be that, if China did then think of encroaching on Southeast Asia, there would always be the deterrent that this might provoke the U.S. to return. A really neutral Southeast Asia could well receive aid from both America and China. Both these countries, I believe, have a common interest in ensuring that Southeast Asia shall be politically and militarily independent.

PLAYBOY: Yet you have suggested that the U.S. should "stand aside and allow self-determination in Vietnam . . . even if this leads, as it most certainly will lead, to . . . a Communist regime."

TOYNBEE: I think it is desirable that there should be a regime in Vietnam that will be genuinely independent and neutral and that will therefore form a kind of insulator between the United States and China. I think this is desirable from the point of view of Vietnam itself, and from the point of view of China and America, too. The only Vietnamese regime I can think of that would be capable of doing this is a united

Vietnam under Ho Chi Minh. That is what we would get if we had self-determination in Vietnam—and that, to my mind, is very desirable, even at the cost of this being a Communist regime. Ho Chi Minh is a Communist, after all, only because the French and the Americans forced him to turn to communism as a means of organizing the movement for independence. He started as a nationalist. He is still a nationalist first. All Communists or capitalists are nationalists first and foremost. Any other ideology always comes second, I think, to nationalism. I believe the North Vietnamese hate having been thrust into China's arms by France and being firmly kept there now by America. As I see it, America is playing China's game, not America's and Russia's game, by making war in Vietnam. If America withdrew and allowed the two forcibly separated halves of Vietnam to reunite under Ho Chi Minh, I believe a reunited Vietnam would be as effective a barrier to China's expansion as Yugoslavia is to Russia's.

PLAYBOY: Do you see Ho playing a Tito-ist role in the Far East?

TOYNBEE: Yes, and astonishing China by his ingratitude, just as Austria astonished Russia by her ingratitude at the time of the Crimean War.

PLAYBOY: Do you think the United States would accept a Communist regime in Vietnam?

TOYNBEE: They have accepted a Communist regime in Yugoslavia, haven't they? They have recognized that from their point of view, Tito is as good a thing as they can get—in that part of the world, anyway. My hope would be that they would come to see that Ho Chi Minh was as good a thing as they could get in Southeast Asia. But there is a serious psychological obstacle. America first has to admit that she has made a mistake—a big one.

PLAYBOY: Many of those opposed to U.S. withdrawal from Vietnam argue that to do so would open the door to Communist takeovers in Laos, Cambodia and even Thailand. How do you feel about this "domino theory"?

TOYNBEE: The domino theory depends on the dogma that communism or anticommunism is the capital question in everybody's mind. I entirely disbelieve in this. I think communism is a very secondary thing, and that capitalism is also a very secondary thing at present, compared with nationalism. I think Cambodia and Laos and Thailand will follow their national interests—whatever they think these are. If they think their interest is to go Communist, they will go Communist. But I don't think the fact of Vietnam's going Communist will necessarily lead to the neighboring countries' going Communist, too. As a matter of fact, they are very anxious *not* to fall under Chinese control. For about two thousand years, all the people of Southeast Asia have been afraid of falling under Chinese domination, and sometimes they have temporarily fallen under it. I think that if the American presence were removed, then the whole national effort of these countries would go back to resisting being taken over by China instead of America. In Vietnam, in particular, there would be some hope of stabilizing the regime on this basis of independence, because the Vietnamese people have a stronger national consciousness; I think they are the most upstanding of all these peoples. After all, they have resisted China for two thousand years; they resisted the French; and now they are resisting the Americans.

PLAYBOY: You have expressed a great deal of hostility toward nationalism in many of your writings. How do you reconcile your support of self-determination in Vietnam with your low regard for nationalism?

TOYNBEE: Nationalism is the big enemy of the human race in present conditions, because technology has made the world one, while the habit of nationalism tries to keep it apart. Technology can be used to better mankind; but if we can't get over nationalism, technology will be used to smash up mankind, I think. Though I dislike all nationalism, however, I dislike an aggressive nationalism more than I dislike a defensive nationalism. It seems to me that before you can get over nationalism, you have to satisfy the nationalism of people who have been subject to foreign rule—like so many peoples in Asia and Africa, including the Vietnamese. The only desirable long-term policy is that all nationalism should be subordinated to some kind of general government of the human race. We are a long way off from that; but unless we can get there, now that we are in the atomic age, our future is pretty black.

PLAYBOY: China can now make nuclear weapons, and will soon have rockets to carry them. How do you think this will change the nuclear "balance of terror"?

TOYNBEE: For the moment, atomic weapons are making China cautious in action—as distinct from her words—because her nuclear installations are hostages to fortune while they are in the embryonic stage. If and when China has stockpiled nuclear weapons and rockets on the American and Russian scale, America and Russia will have to treat China as an equal.

PLAYBOY: In view of the bellicosity of China's leaders, do you believe that they might be more ready than the Russians to risk the use of nuclear weapons against the West?

TOYNBEE: Their words would make us think so; but the more they have to lose, the more cautious they are likely to become.

PLAYBOY: The upsurgence of the warmongering Red Guard movement, with Mao Tse-tung's wholehearted support, would seem to give little evidence of a trend toward caution in Chinese foreign policy.

TOYNBEE: I think the Red Guard uprising is merely a still more violent form of the violent reaction in China against foreigners that began as long ago as the Boxer rebellion at the beginning of this century—nearly half a century before the Communist takeover. This constantly increasing Chinese militancy is, I believe, a reaction to China's century of humiliation, from 1839 to 1945, during which the Chinese were trampled on by Britain, France and Japan, in turn, and were treated as "natives," after having been the center and source of civilization in their half of the world for more than two thousand years. I think the Chinese have turned savage now because they want two things that cannot be combined. They want to get rid of everything Western and, at the same time, they want to have the material power and wealth that can be given only by a mastery of Western science and technology. As they acquire it, I expect China's policy to evolve in the way Russia's has evolved—toward coexistence with the West; and the West, as far as China is concerned, includes Russia. For the moment, I think the Chinese hate America and Russia equally.

PLAYBOY: Since the Soviet Union is now moving closer to what the Chinese consider heretical capitalist ideas such as wage incentives and the mass production of consumer goods, do you see industrialization leading to a withering away of Communist ideals in Russia?

TOYNBEE: No, I do not. I expect industrialization to lead, everywhere, to a mixture of free enterprise with socialism. The technological and economic forces that are at work on both sides of the Iron Curtain are identical, and they are going to produce uniform results. President Johnson's Great Society and Mr. Kosygin's post-Stalinist communism will be very like each other. The past conflicts between Protestants and Catholics, and between Moslems and Christians, throw light on what is likely to happen. After all, Christianity and Islam coexist in the world today, after thirteen centuries of war and hostility; both Protestantism and Catholicism have managed to survive in the same world, though for centuries after the Reformation each party swore that the world would be an impossible place to live in as long as the other party was on the map. The same thing is likely to happen to communism and capitalism. They are each going on swearing that they cannot coexist with the other, yet they are beginning to coexist more and more. And what is more, they are beginning to become less and less unlike each other. They keep their labels but change their contents. Eventually, I suspect, they will become practically indistinguishable from each other. For I think that the same thing is happening to Russia now as began to happen to America in 1917. Russia, in her turn, is ceasing to be revolutionary and is becoming conservative. For the moment, this makes a present to China of the prorevolutionary role in the world that was played by America until 1917 and by Russia after that date. But China, too, will surely become conservative in her turn, as she becomes more affluent. Traditionally, in their politics, the Chinese have been conservative and moderate.

PLAYBOY: Do you think that, as China catches up industrially and economically with Russia, their ideological differences will slowly disappear?

TOYNBEE: Probably so—but I think the ideological dispute between China and Russia is a screen for a deeper and perhaps more lasting conflict of national interests, and the heart of this conflict lies in China's determination to regain all the territories that were taken from her during the century 1839–1945. She has already regained Sinkiang, Manchuria, and Tibet. Till 1856–1860, the whole left-bank half of the Amur Basin, as well as the territory between the Ussuri River and the sea down to the site of Vladivostok, inclusive, was Chinese. The Chinese would like to recover these lost territories from Russia; but China is no match for Russia yet. Before many more years, however, she will be.

PLAYBOY: Would you say that this is one of the major anxieties underlying Russia's antagonism toward China today?

TOYNBEE: I should. Look at the length of the land frontier between Russia and China. After all, if America got tired of boxing with China, she could just pull her troops back across the Pacific and have half the world between her and China. But Russia can't disengage from China. Once, long ago, I traveled from Peking back to Ostend by train. The Russians and Chinese were fighting in Manchuria then, over the railway that the Russians had built on what the Chinese claimed to be their land. I can't forget the impression of coming out of that teeming country, China, into the empty expanse of Siberia. There they were, side by side. It was like two levels of water. When you have two very different levels of water, there is tremendous pressure to combine at the same level. Now, the Russians are conscious of this. They are trying to fill eastern Siberia and to industrialize it, but it is a race against time. I think they have great cause for anxiety.

PLAYBOY: Do you anticipate that this territorial dispute may lead to war between Russia and China?

TOYNBEE: I do not expect to see armed clashes between nuclear powers. But, of course, I may be too optimistic.

PLAYBOY: Do you think the differences beteween Moscow and Peking could be turned to the advantage of the West?

TOYNBEE: Yes, I do. If peace were to be reestablished in Vietnam, I think that Russia might seek insurance against Chinese nationalism by reaching an understanding with the United States. Russia, after all, is far more genuinely threatened by Chinese chauvinism than is the United States. But this new lineup would only continue the

Cold War while shifting the line of division between the opposing parties. I don't want to see a lineup of the West and Russia against China. But I do want to see a *rapprochement* between Russia and America—not necessarily *against* China but for a more positive purpose: to stabilize the world and put the world in order. Nothing can put the world in order except the combined action of the United States and the Soviet Union. Vietnam is the key, because while President Johnson goes on with the Vietnam War, and U.S. bombers smash up the country, Russia just can't afford to side with America. Nationalism may be more important than communism, but take another example. If a Moslem country were fighting a holy war against a Christian country, it would be difficult for another Christian country to collaborate with the Moslems who were fighting a holy war against its coreligionists. The same sort of thing applies here; we have to allow for the outward appearance of Communist solidarity. So I think that the Vietnam War is the key to relations between Moscow and Washington.

PLAYBOY: How do you see relations between the U.S. and China developing in the next ten years?

TOYNBEE: It very much depends upon the attitude of the U.S. toward China. As I see it, America has been busy since 1949 sticking pins into the tiger and then saying, "Look what a ferocious tiger it is—it reacts." The French have a saying: "This creature is very wicked; it defends itself when attacked." I think this sums up my view of American relations with China. America has been stirring up China; she has been as nasty to China as she can be. For instance, she has been lobbying to keep China out of the United Nations and has been urging other countries to stop trading with China. How can you expect China not to be nasty to America and to America's Western satellites? What I would try first is behaving to China as if she were an ordinary country with ordinary human rights, to see how she reacts to that.

For the present regime of China, as for the present regime in Russia, communism is an instrument of nationalism, not an end in itself. I always go back to the original struggle in Russia between Stalin and Trotsky. So far as I know, Trotsky was the only leading statesman in any Communist country who was genuinely prepared to sacrifice the national interest of his country in order to propagate the Communist world revolution. That's what Trotsky wanted to do with Russia. But Stalin wanted to exploit communism in Russia's national interests, and Stalin won. This is significant. I think the nationalist will always win over any other kind of ideologist. Therefore, I believe that what China wants with communism is to use it as an instrument for restoring China to her traditional position in the world. That may be a position of very great power and importance, but it is something quite different from expending China's national resources and well-being in order to convert the whole world to communism by force.

PLAYBOY: Can you see any way the U.S. could avoid supporting reactionary dictatorships as a bulwark against Communist takeovers?

TOYNBEE: By going back to her original tradition. If you go back 150 years, you will find passages in Metternich's dispatches in which he bewails the revolutionary subversive action of the United States in South America and Europe, very much the way in which Mr. Dulles bewailed the actions of the Soviet Union there. America started with a revolutionary tradition, but about the time of the Russian Revolution, she suddenly made this about-face and became the Metternich of the present day, trying to organize another Holy Alliance against revolution.

PLAYBOY: Do you think that racial or religious differences are as important historically as economic or class conflicts?

TOYNBEE: It is awfully hard to measure the relative importance. I think Marx was right to criticize the old-fashioned kind of history, which was in terms of politics and wars entirely—a history of kings and queens and battles and political revolutions. But Marx made no real progress by saying: "It is not politics; it is economics that counts. That is the key thing." I don't think there *is* any key thing; or if there is, it is probably the underlying religious feelings that people have. Religion gets down to the deepest layers of the human soul. On the whole, I should say that no aspect or activity of human life is the sole key to history. The old-fashioned political view of history, the view that politics is more important than economics, is borne out, against Marx, by the facts. When people have the choice between an economic interest and a political interest, they will nearly always sacrifice the economic interest for the political goal. One remarkable case is that of Trieste in recent times. Trieste was a very flourishing port for the whole Habsburg monarchy, but the population was mainly Italian. They had this choice: Did they wish to see the Austrian Empire broken up and themselves united with Italy at the cost of being ruined economically, or did they prefer to remain prosperous economically and remain Austrian subjects? They preferred to be Italians and be ruined—and I think this is rather characteristic. I can think of many other instances. Politics are more romantic than economics. You can appeal more powerfully to peoples' emotions on political or military issues than on economic matters. People are pretty silly about this.

PLAYBOY: Do you feel that the United Nations has been effective in arbitrating such political and military disputes on an international level?

TOYNBEE: Its history so far has been sadly like the history of the League of Nations. Its technical organizations, like those of the League of Nations, have been a great success; they have played a very valuable role in a world where we are trying to help the backward countries to get abreast of the more advanced countries. But that in itself will not keep the peace of the world. There will be no advance for anybody unless we can keep the world in order.

PLAYBOY: What do you think are the chances of putting the world in order?

TOYNBEE: Pretty good. I believe that the world *is* going to be put in order, and I also believe that mankind will fairly soon come to a point at which we shall be willing to buy order at a high cost in terms of liberty. We shall not like to give up our traditional liberty to go to war, to go on strike, to spend our earnings as we choose instead of paying them away in taxes for the public authorities to spend as *they* choose. But I believe that peace and affluence are what most people desire, and we cannot have these without order in the age of mechanization. I therefore believe that the human race would submit to a Russo-American—or a Russo-American-Chinese—dictatorship if it believed that, at this price, it could have affluence and peace. This was the state of mind of the peoples of the Mediterranean world in the first century B.C. That was why they welcomed Augustus' world dictatorship and, by welcoming it, made it possible.

If the 125 sovereign independent states of this atomic-age world remain sovereign and independent, they will destroy one another and the human race as well. The only hope of survival for these states lies in voluntarily subordinating themselves to a world government. The original thirteen North American states have survived because they have subordinated themselves to the Union. I should like to see the rudiments, anyway, of a world government for the crucial things, for life-and-death things like the control of atomic energy and the production and distribution of food—to take the two most urgent issues. I don't think we can get through without that. Treaties between individual governments will not be enough to ensure that atomic energy is not used either to blow the world up or to poison it, or to see that enough of the right kind of food is produced and is then distributed to the right places.

PLAYBOY: Would you like to see some kind of international peace-keeping force?

TOYNBEE: Yes, I would. Of course, it can only be of avail with the smaller powers. A peace-keeping force could deal with Rhodesia, perhaps; it might deal with India and Pakistan. It could even deal with powers the size of France and Britain. The mere fact that, in December 1956, Russia and America happened to have the same point of view was enough to stop Britain, France and Israel dead in their attack on Egypt. But a peace-keeping force couldn't deal with rows among America, China, and Russia. You would need the combined force of Russia and America backing some system of world government rather than just the moral force of treaties over such crucial matters as food and atomic weapons.

PLAYBOY: You have written that the invention of nuclear weapons has helped to keep the peace since the end of World War Two. How?

TOYNBEE: Let's suppose they hadn't been invented. It is hard to imagine that, in such circumstances, there wouldn't have been already a final war between Russia and America. That would have been the natural sequel, I think to the Second World War. One of the two surviving superpowers would have knocked the other out and would have established a world empire as the result of a third world war. But that can't happen in the nuclear age, because they would each knock the other out; there couldn't be a winner. No one would be left to organize the world as a conqueror. I think that has been a deterrent. I also think a nuclear club is extremely important. The proliferation of nuclear weapons is one of the great menaces in the world today. I should really like to see nuclear weapons confined to Russia and American and, I suppose, China. We cannot prevent China from having nuclear weapons now. But I should like to see Britain and Egypt give them up and I would like to see France somehow induced, after De Gaulle has departed, to give them up as well. Of course, if nuclear weapons were limited to Russia and America, there wouldn't be democratic government of the world. A Russo-American world government would probably be very authoritarian, but it would at least ensure the survival of the human race—and that is the first consideration, to my mind. I have eleven grandchildren, and I want them to survive; that comes first for me.

PLAYBOY: Are there any practical steps you think could be taken to achieve universal nuclear disarmament?

TOYNBEE: There are 123 states in the world besides Russia and America. If Russia and America were to have a nuclear monopoly, they would have to persuade the rest of the world that they were not going to misuse their power but were going to use it to preserve the human race, not to destroy it. They would also have to persuade the world that they were genuinely proposing to scale down their own nuclear weapons gradually to the vanishing point. If they could make people really believe those two things, then there might be some chance of persuading the world. What is at issue is the survival of the human race versus the self-destruction of the species; so we had better let the Russians and the Americans have this temporary monopoly, pending the complete abolition of nuclear weapons.

PLAYBOY: Are you suggesting that the great powers should use their nuclear stockpile as a means of discouraging the development of nuclear capacity or missile systems by lesser powers?

TOYNBEE: Yes—by giving a guarantee of nuclear protection to any power that is willing to renounce nuclear weapons.
PLAYBOY: Is it realistic to expect any nation to relinquish its atomic weapons voluntarily?
TOYNBEE: Weapons do tend to be idolized, don't they? They have a kind of ceremonial value—like swords. They survive as focuses of emotion long after they cease to have any practical value. It is possible that they will become a kind of status symbol, that people will keep nuclear weapons for this reason, though they are a little more expensive than even the most elaborate swords. But if war were really ruled out and if peace were preserved for many generations, I suppose a time might come when people would be rational enough to ask whether there was any point in keeping these nuclear weapons. But here we come up against a very irrational element in human affairs, especially concentrated on things like war and weapons. Each time a new weapon was invented in the past, people would say that it was so awful that they must not use it. But they did use it, and though it was awful, it didn't wipe out the human race. We have got something now, however, that could really extinguish life on this planet. Mankind has not been in this situation since toward the end of the Paleolithic Age. Toward the end of the Paleolithic Age, we got the better of lions and tigers and creatures like that, and from that time onward the survival of the human race was ensured. But in 1945 our survival again became uncertain, because we became our *own* lions and tigers, so to speak. The threat to the survival of the human race has actually been much greater since 1945 than it was during the first million years of human history, because man equipped with modern technology is much more formidable than any lion or tiger or microbe could be. So we are in a very dangerous situation, one that is really unique. On the other side of the balance sheet, however, is the fact that atoms for peace could give mankind an unheard-of material prosperity and power for constructive action. This is also something new. So the extreme possibilities are very far apart, with a choice between certain annihilation on one side and a kind of earthly paradise on the other.
PLAYBOY: Do you think any useful steps can be taken to restrict the extension of the arms race into space?
TOYNBEE: I think they could be. The recent Russo-American treaty for the demilitarization of outer space is a promising first step. As a start, you could get a minimum of mutual confidence established between America and Russia. Things are bad enough on this planet without our extending our differences to infinity. But all this concern with space may change our attitude on some things. Take this question of nationalism and national sovereignty. Until the other day, until a few hundred years ago anyway, the surface of this planet was infinite, as far as man knew; he hadn't explored all the unknown regions on earth, so the sovereign state then seemed a more sizable and respectable object compared with the size of the known universe than it seems now. I mean, to cut up one planet into 125 sovereign states, when our whole world has become just a dot among millions of galaxies—well, there is a kind of disproportion in doing that. People might realize the absurdity of this. I think it might have a quite important psychological effect, making people see that local sovereign states are ridiculous when set against the scale of the universe.
PLAYBOY: You have argued that, despite its technological prowess, the West may be in a process of decline comparable with that of Rome and Greece. Do you feel any inclination to revise that rather pessimistic judgment?

TOYNBEE: I have never been pessimistic, since I have never, like Spengler, thought of it as being predestined or fated that a civilization must break down after so many centuries. I have always thought that the future was open for every civilization, and that it wasn't necessary for the Greek civilization to break down. I think the Greeks could have taken a different line that would have enabled them to go on in perpetuity, and I think the same holds for our own civilization. I feel that its future is open. It depends on us—the living generation and the future generations—whether we crush it or whether we preserve it and improve it. But I am a pessimist in the sense that, on looking back over the past, I think we can see very clearly the ways in which people did wreck a number of civilizations, and how they have repeated the same unnecessary mistakes quite a number of times. This suggests that it is rather easy for people to go on making these mistakes.
PLAYBOY: Could you name some of these mistakes—particularly those you feel we are repeating today?
TOYNBEE: Going to war, above all. Also, trying to suppress opinions that one dislikes and trying to hold down subject peoples who are ripe for independence. In the past, war has been the immediate cause of breakdown, but wars are probably symptoms of something *else* that has gone wrong. Obviously, in our turn, we may bring the same thing on ourselves. The first thing to try to do about this is to make war impossible. In order to do this, we must get back *behind* war to social justice. I think there are two hopeful signs. People are rather historical-minded now; they are aware of the mistakes made in the past. And the best safeguard against making the same mistakes again is to know what they were and what the consequences were. We might make other mistakes, but perhaps we shan't make those particular mistakes. I also think we are now much more sensitive in our consciences about social justice; privileged people are becoming, increasingly, throughout the world, more ready to concede social justice voluntarily and that, too, is a safeguard against destruction.
PLAYBOY: Are you thinking of the efforts now being made in the United States to solve the problems of poverty and civil rights?
TOYNBEE: Yes, and I would also note the change of heart among the wealthy people of this country, in my lifetime. I have lived to see, in Britain, a far-reaching redistribution of wealth and a recognition by the rich and the privileged that social injustice is hateful, even to themselves. They have shown a great deal of good humor in accepting the change, in bearing high taxation, and so on. The American rich, being more recently rich and much richer than the richest rich in Britain have ever been, are more surly and sulky about this. But I think they are coming round. I think President Johnson's idea of the Great Society is probably going to succeed in America, if everything isn't wrecked by the Vietnam War.
PLAYBOY: Speaking as a historian rather than as a critic of current U.S. foreign policy, do you feel that America has made a significant contribution to the health, wealth and happiness of mankind?
TOYNBEE: America has made a very significant contribution. Ever since the American colonies were founded, they have given a new opening and a new hope to people of all kinds who have in some sense been penalized in Europe. They were people who hadn't been given an economic opportunity, or who had been in political or religious trouble. They were able to make a new start in America. That planted deeply in American minds the idea that there is no ceiling on an individual and no limit to the progress of a family. In America a man can rise to any level. Now, this is something very good and very stimulating. It is what human life ought to be like. That's been a very great

American contribution to the welfare of mankind. I think this aspect of the American way of life sets an example to the rest of the world. It has awakened hope in other countries—hope that the same thing might be possible for them, too. Go to a place like India, where the social structure has been frozen for thousands of years, and where things are now stirring. The ordinary person in the villages of India now feels that life can perhaps be made better. I think this is ultimately due to the American example, although the Indian peasants may not be directly conscious of this.

PLAYBOY: Let us look at the other side of the ledger. What would you say has been America's greatest disservice to Western civilization?

TOYNBEE: Her fanatical attitude toward communism. This is the old intolerance of the sixteenth- and seventeenth-century wars of religion come to life again. What the twentieth century needs is eighteenth-century tolerance. When students become political-minded—as has begun to happen on American college campuses—this is usually a sign that something has gone gravely wrong with their country. I think this rising student revolt against the Vietnam War may be the first symptom of a coming general revolt in the U.S. against "the American way of life." My impression is that this way of life is unsatisfying and that it has made the Americans an unhappy people. Sooner or later, I believe there will be a strong reaction against it among Americans of all ages and all social classes.

PLAYBOY: How long do you think the United States will maintain its position as the leading world power?

TOYNBEE: Not long, because history is moving faster and faster. In the end, *the* Continent—that is, Asia plus its European peninsula—will become preponderant over the Americas, which, after all, are only a couple of large islands. Britain's predominance lasted for about one century; France's previous predominance lasted for about two centuries. Shall we give the U.S. fifty years?

PLAYBOY: Do you think that, judged against the perspective of history, communism is likely to rank with the other great ideological movements, such as Mohammedanism or Buddhism or Christianity?

TOYNBEE: I don't expect it to have the long-term hold on people's hearts that Buddhism, Christianity and Islam have had. If you look at those other three religions, you will see that they all offer very direct practical counsel and aid to the individual human being in this personal life, in the problems he faces in his passage through life. This is what gives them their hold on human hearts. Now, communism is all for the collective welfare of mankind, not for the individual's welfare. It assumes that the individual is going to take a stoic line and say that his individual life is unimportant so long as the community prospers. But human beings are egotistic. An ideology that gives nothing to the individual ego, either in this world or in another world, isn't, in the end, going to be able to compete on equal terms. This is a weak point of communism in a competition for converting the world, for it fails to recognize that human affairs are a network of relations between individuals, that all action and all choice comes out of some individual personality. If one has ever tried to get teamwork done in the intellectual field, one realizes that a committee can't write a poem, and I doubt whether they can even write a report. All real action and real thought comes out of individual minds. So in one sense, I rate the importance of the individual very high. But I think that a great man can't actualize his greatness unless the environment is favorable for him; in that sense, he is beholden to his environment. But there are also situations in which, if a great man does not turn up, a society can't solve the problems that confront it. I think a good example of this is Churchill and Britain in 1940. If there had been no Churchill, would Britain have held out? Perhaps not. On the other hand, if Churchill had been prime minister of France instead of Britain, would Churchill's personality have been able to make France stay in the war? Perhaps so.

PLAYBOY: Do you think President Kennedy was a great man?

TOYNBEE: President Kennedy was great in truly caring for the welfare of the whole human race. He will be remembered as the first American President who was mankind's president, too.

PLAYBOY: Probably more than any other living historian, you have studied the lives of great men. Do you see any pattern in their character or behavior?

TOYNBEE: There is one characteristic that, though far from being general, has been common to a number of great men. That is, some of the greatest men have been people who have had a broken career; they have started off on some ordinary, conventional line; they have come to grief in that; and then they've withdrawn from the world and come back in some new capacity. Saint Paul started off as a fanatical orthodox Pharisee. He had a religious experience, withdrew into the desert for several years and then came back as a Christian missionary, which was obviously going to be his true career. He wouldn't be remembered now if he had never been anything but a persecutor. Thucydides is another case. He started out as a minor naval commander, and he had a reverse and he was exiled; he came back as a writer of the history of the war in which he had not been a military success himself. This is a rather significant and important pattern, but it is by no means universal; many great men have gone steadily through without this great withdrawal.

PLAYBOY: Could this pattern of withdrawal and return be related to what Jung called the "forty-year-old success"?

TOYNBEE: There does appear to be a psychological law operating here—a law that people who somehow got on the wrong path recover themselves in the middle of life. They are twice born; and they are different from the once-born. The twice-born often get farther; it's like a rocket that has a second boost.

PLAYBOY: Several fellow historians have pointed out the similarity of your views and those of Jung. How much influence did Jung actually have on you?

TOYNBEE: He had a latish influence. I can't remember when I first read Jung; it must have been about halfway through the 1930s or a bit later, I suppose. I read his book on psychological types first. There were an awful lot of new ideas for me in that, and so he had a very strong influence. But it came about three-quarters of the way through the writing of my own book. What fascinated me was the way he assembled his evidence. He would take one of his own clinical cases, a piece of Greek mythology, some historical event, something out of astrology, and he would show you that these were all expressions of some identical primordial image deep down in the psyche, which was coming out in all these different ways. He saw a psychological unity at the bottom of human nature. This seemed to me to throw a lot of light on things in history that interested me enormously.

PLAYBOY: Are you referring to Jung's idea of a collective unconscious for the human race?

TOYNBEE: Yes. It fits in, you see, with my notion that there is a fairly constant, fixed human nature. Before, we knew a little about the surface world of the intellect; but now—thanks to the insights of men like Jung—the psychological world, the vast continent of the subconscious, has been immensely expanded. This gives a huge new dimension to all studies of human affairs, I think.

PLAYBOY: Did Freud influence your thinking as much as Jung?
TOYNBEE: No, and I think I can see why. It was because his theories were more strait-laced, more narrowly geared. I don't believe in sex being at the bottom of everything, even if one takes the word *sex* in the very esoteric sense in which Freud uses it—or came to use it by the end. I don't believe in this or any other single key to human affairs. It is just one explanation among a number; I feel that we ought to have a wider horizon, that's all.
PLAYBOY: There are some religious moralists who associate the breakdown of a civilization with a period of spiritual decline and sexual decadence. They feel that we're living in such a time today. Do you think there is any historical justification for this view?
TOYNBEE: It is very hard to say; the sexual manners and customs of various societies are so different. What seems horrible to some people seems quite all right to another lot. The early Christians were, of course, in revolt against the sexual manner of the Greek and Roman world. Under the early Roman Empire, from the Christian point of view, sexual morals were bad; but I don't know that they were any worse at the time when Rome was obviously in decline than they had been when Rome was flourishing. I am thinking of things like homosexuality, like looseness in marriage relations, and so on. So I am a bit skeptical about this kind of pious argument about morals. One must not simplify too much. As I said before, I don't believe sex or economics or politics or even religion is the sole key explanation of anything in human life.
PLAYBOY: Yet you've been accused by one critic of believing that "civilization exists for the sake of religion." Is he wrong?
TOYNBEE: As I said, one must not simplify too much. Though I do believe in the great and fundamental importance of religion, I am very unorthodox from the point of view of any religion, and I don't think religion is the only thing in life. Go to India, and you will find that economics are certainly no less important in that exceedingly and perhaps excessively religious country. But I don't mean that Hinduism is not acceptable, while my own ancestral religion is. Certainly not. I regard Christianity as being one among half a dozen approaches to the central mystery of the universe. I think each of these different approaches—Christian, Jewish, Moslem, Hindu, Buddhist, and so on—has something in it that the others don't have. Therefore, I value them all—but I couldn't swallow any one of them whole.
PLAYBOY: Could you give a name to your own spiritual beliefs?
TOYNBEE: Yes. Religious-minded agnosticism.
PLAYBOY: Would you elaborate?
TOYNBEE: I believe in the reality of a spiritual presence behind the universe, but this may not be a personality—that is, not God as conceived by Jews, Christians and Moslems. I am an agnostic in the sense that I think we ought not to shirk facing up to our ignorance of the answers to the questions that are of the greatest importance to human beings.
PLAYBOY: Would you call yourself a humanist then?
TOYNBEE: Certainly not. It would be ludicrous to imagine, as humanists do, that human beings are the highest form of spiritual life in existence. When human beings worship themselves as gods, they always quickly come to grief.
PLAYBOY: As a student of Christianity, how do you feel about the ecumenical trend toward unity among the churches.
TOYNBEE: I find this very surprising, very welcome and very encouraging. It seems to have arisen in both the Protestant and the Catholic churches since the end of the

Second World War. It is one of the good and hopeful things in the present-day world, and it isn't limited to the Christian churches. About ten years ago, I was in a number of Buddhist countries—Ceylon, Burma, Thailand, Japan and also in that part of India where Buddhism started. I noticed then a corresponding movement in that part of the world. I saw that the northern and southern Buddhists are getting together again and that the Hindus are welcoming the Buddhist pilgrims to the scene of the Buddha's enlightenment and making things agreeable for them—feeling that, after all, Hindus and Buddhists have a common past. It seems to me to be a worldwide phenomenon, and to be one of the positive and encouraging trends in the world today. Certain leading figures, like Pope John, have furthered this movement very much, but there must be some very strong answering feeling among the members of the churches to have made this remarkable success possible.

PLAYBOY: Is it on this sort of evidence that you base your belief that the twenty-first century will be a period of human unity?

TOYNBEE: It is one of the things, yes. There are persuasive forces like religion; and there are compulsive forces like technology. Technology faces us with a choice between unity and destruction, I think. Because it is a compulsive force, we may be very unwilling to be driven by it. But religion may lead us toward the same goal in a happier way.

PLAYBOY: You don't seem to feel that way about Judaism. The Jewish faith, you've written, has become an instrument of "Zionist nationalism"—which like all nationalism, you regard as a divisive and destructive force. Because of this view, one critic has called you "an outright, if highly sophisticated, anti-Semite." Do you feel that your attitude toward the Jews has been misrepresented?

TOYNBEE: Yes, I do. What makes Judaism what it has been since the Romans evicted the Jews from Palestine has been that the Jews have found a way of living without a country of their own in which they are in the majority—living as a minority in the midst of other people, taking part in other people's life in many ways, making a living and contributing to the economic life of other people's countries. At the same time, the Jews have kept their continuity and have remained a self-conscious community, largely thanks to their special religious organization and religious law, religious manners and customs. Zionism, on the other hand, is an attempt to turn Judaism, and the Jewish community, away from its traditional form, into just one more example of the local nationalisms of the present-day world. As it is doing this at the expense of the people who lived in the country before, I think this is perverse. Thus, I distinguish entirely between my attitude toward the Jewish people and the Jewish religion on the one hand and my attitude toward the Zionist movement on the other, just as I distinguish between my attitude toward English-speaking people in general and my attitude toward Mr. Smith and his Rhodesian colleagues at the present moment. I am 110 percent against what seems to me to be colonialism—I mean the exploitation and ill-treatment of weaker peoples. But I am not for that reason against the nation or the race that does these things; they can always stop doing them. I am not against them in themselves and I am not against those elements in that nation who are not guilty of colonialism. So I distinguish very sharply between my feelings about the Jews and about Zionism. I feel what all decent persons feel about the extermination of the European Jews by the Nazis, but I also have a very strong feeling about the eviction of the Arabs from their homes in Palestine. The Arabic-speaking people of Palestine have been there since the Romans evicted the Jews in the first and second centuries of the Christian era. The Palestinian Arabs have a right to their homes, and I feel that

Zionism, by evicting them, has become guilty of colonialism. The Zionists seem to be obsessed with the idea that having their own country will somehow prevent the Germans or someone else from doing again what has been done to the Jews in Europe in the past. I think that they are thereby exposing their descendants to the risk of suffering the same sort of thing in the Arab world. It seems to me to be a retrogressive step. Nationalism, anyway, is a retrogressive movement. The Jews have hitherto been cosmopolitan, and I think it is a pity that they should fall into nationalism now. This is what I am against. I value the Jewish religious contribution to the Western world; it is a most desirable element in our Western civilization. But I believe that the future of the Jews, the Jewish religion and the Jewish culture lies in the Western world, particularly in the United States. It does not lie in Israel.

PLAYBOY: Are you suggesting that the Jews should be evicted from Israel and emigrate to the United States?

TOYNBEE: Jews in Palestine are obviously in much greater peril than Jews in Western countries outside Germany. On the whole, I don't expect—and I do not want—to see the Jews now in Palestine evicted, as the Crusaders were. I want to see the minimum of suffering for the maximum number of people. Modern technology, applied to distillation of seawater, could provide subsistence in Palestine *both* for its evicted Arab population *and* for the present Jewish settlers there. I want to work for a solution on these lines, however great the psychological and political difficultes may be.

PLAYBOY: If a substantial number of Arab refugees could return to Israel, would this remove your objections to Zionism and to Israel?

TOYNBEE: If they could return to Israel under decent conditions, not necessarily having just the same farms or patches of land that they had originally, and could then become first-class citizens of the state of Israel, yes, that would remove a great many of my objections. There are people in Israel and Jews in other parts of the world who want this solution, but they are in a minority at present. Again nationalism is the enemy both of the Jews and of the Arabs.

PLAYBOY: You have visited most of the Middle Eastern countries at one time or another in your life. Why have you not been to Israel since its foundation?

TOYNBEE: You have to make a choice. I wanted to see the Arab countries, and I want to go on visiting them. But, as a matter of fact, I have seen the whole of Israel, looking either across the frontier or from the air. I think that if I visited Israel on the ground, I should much admire the material economic progress that Israel has made. I think I should admire the kibbutzim particularly. But, then, I might also have admired what the Nazis would have done economically in Poland if they had kept possession of that country. Yet that would not have made me think it was a good thing that they should have conquered and annexed Poland.

PLAYBOY: Speaking of conquest and annexation, how do you feel about President Nasser's expansionist policy in North Africa and the Middle East—in Yemen and other Arab states?

TOYNBEE: Insofar as the United Arab Republic's policy is one of expanding its own power, as distinct from serving the interests of its sister Arab countries, its policy will arouse resistance. I hope to see the Arab countries unite with one another on a footing of equality. Inevitably, Egypt—with its central position, big population and advanced civilization—will be the nucleus of any Arab union.

PLAYBOY: Do you feel that Arab nationalism is less reprehensible than Zionist nationalism?

TOYNBEE: Well, it's a defensive nationalism. The Arabs are only saying: "We want to be free in the countries we inhabit, and we don't want our countries to be taken from us." But I'm not unreservedly a supporter of the Arabs. For instance, there is one case of Arab nationalism that I deplore as strongly as I deplore Zionism—the nationalism of the Arabs of the Northern Sudan against the non-Arab Africans of the Southern Sudan. The Northern Sudan Arabs seem to me to be flagrant colonialists trying to impose themselves, their rule, their religion, language and culture on a non-Arab African people that wants to be itself and does not want to be dominated. Now, when I find Sudanese Arabs doing that, or when I find Iraqi Arabs trying to sit on the heads of the Kurds in Iraq, I am just as much against that as I am against the white racialists in Rhodesia or the Zionists in Palestine. I think I am consistent in this.

PLAYBOY: Your views on Zionism are not the only ones that have stirred controversy in the course of your career. The Dutch historian Pieter Geyl, for example, has attacked you for "fallacious arguments and spurious demonstrations." He has also said that your books contain a "maddening profusion of vastly learned examples, stated in an attractive or impressive but frequently slipshod fashion and proving exactly nothing." What is your reaction to this criticism?

TOYNBEE: We all suffer from built-in limitations of the working of the human mind. We have to work by setting up hypotheses and looking for illustrations that may or may not prove our point. Human minds cannot work in any other way. Yet even the scientists cannot guarantee that his test cases are fair samples. The important point, I think, is to make sure of being scrupulously honest, always ready to discard a hypothesis if it is disproved by a test case. I hope I am ready to do that, but you know that everyone falls in love with his own hypotheses and finds it hard to discard them. I may well be a sinner and not up to the scientific standard. But I think in a sense Geyl is unfair. He implies that he himself is not subject to these common human limitations. I should like to ask him how he sets about doing his thinking work himself.

PLAYBOY: Have you enjoyed your many disagreements with other historians?

TOYNBEE: It depends with whom. I have thoroughly enjoyed Geyl's criticism, because he is a jolly man, though a very pugnacious man. But I think it depends on the critic's motive. If somebody is out to argue with you because he wants to get nearer to the truth, then it is an exhilarating experience, however severe. It starts your mind ticking again. But if somebody is just out to kill you personally, then it's rather unfruitful, melancholy, really, not much use to you or to anyone else.

PLAYBOY: How do you feel about British historian A. J. P. Taylor's characterization of you as "an expatriate, a rootless man . . . at home only among the ruins"?

TOYNBEE: It is a historian's business to make himself at home in other times and places besides his own, in order to bring those other times and places to life again for his contemporaries.

PLAYBOY: For much of your life you have been simultaneously involved in studying current affairs and the great events of history. How have these two careers fitted into each other?

TOYNBEE: I don't think I could have thought of following either of the two careers without following the other one at the same time. I came, I suppose, to take a comprehensive view of history because I had one foot in current history and the other in the past. It was an accident, really. I was educated in Greek and Roman history, and from that I came to be interested in the present-day Near East. I had gone there on a visit to look at things I had learned about in studying ancient Greek history. That was in 1911. If you are studying recent history, the great difficulty is to see it in perspective; you can get that perspective only from the study of less recent history. Conversely, the only way you can get into the lives and feelings and thoughts of dead people is by an analogy with living people whom you know. The only time in which you can catch people alive is the present time, when you are alive yourself. The English historian Gibbon said that a captaincy in the Hampshire Militia was not without its lessons for the historian of the Roman Empire. Take another example—Plato's complaint about Homer, which is really a testimonial: Homer, Plato complains, had just a taste of a carpenter's job or an armorer's job or a peasant's job, but he wrote as if he had spent a lifetime being a carpenter, an armorer or a peasant, or whatever it might be. Just that little taste of practical life illuminates a tremendous amount of history.

PLAYBOY: Which do you think has had the greater impact on your thinking—classical education on your view of the modern world, or your firsthand knowledge about the modern world in studying the patterns of past civilizations?

TOYNBEE: That is a very difficult question, because the interaction has been so great. Many people would say that I have falsified my view of the ancient world by importing modern analogies into it, and vice versa—that I have seen the modern world too much in Greek or Roman terms. The Russian historian Rostovtzeff was much criticized for his book on the social and economic history of the Roman Empire. He was accused of importing the Russian Revolution of 1917 into the history of Rome in the third century A.D. Maybe he did import it, but it is also possible that he wouldn't have been able to see into the inwardness of the Roman revolution except by analogy with the experiences that he himself had gone through.

PLAYBOY: You once described a moment early in your life when you were walking along a street in London and suddenly found yourself "in communion not just with this or that episode in history but with all that had been and was to come . . . aware of the passage of history flowing through me in a mighty current, and of my own life welling like a wave on the flow of this vast tide." Would you tell us more about this experience?

TOYNBEE: What I experienced at that moment was something that I don't think I have experienced before or since. At that moment it felt—how shall I put it?—as if the walls of my ego were breaking down, as if I was *solidaire,* identical, at one, with the universe as a whole. I think this is a very difficult thing for anyone who has been brought up in our modern Western culture to understand, because our culture emphasizes the individual, the individual consciousness, individual freedom and liberty, individual responsibility, individual economic interest. In the West, one is conditioned to be separate from one's environment, to be up against it, in opposition to and in tension with it. But there are many cultures—the Hindu culture is one of these—in which this experience is such a common one that nobody would notice it.

PLAYBOY: Those who take hallucinogenic drugs have reported transcendental epiphanies of oneness and eternity. Was your own experience anything like that?

TOYNBEE: Yes, I think it was. This is part of the makeup of religious experience. I think that part of the essence of religious experience is to feel the unity of the universe. A further element of religious experience is that you feel the universe to be centered on some—what shall we call it? I mustn't use the word *God*, because it won't do for Hinduism or Buddhism, so I will say—centered on some spiritual presence or power. But you can't feel that unless you feel the unity of the universe first, unless you sense the interrelation of human events in all times and places.

PLAYBOY: You had this experience shortly before you began to write your *Study of History*. Did it have anything to do with your decision to undertake this monumental work?

TOYNBEE: Yes. The thing was turning in my head at that time and I was casting about to find my way into the subject. In August 1914, I was teaching Greek and Roman history as a don at Oxford, and I was very much interested in Thucydides—in his account of the great war in which he fought and about which he wrote his famous history. As I read his work, it seemed to me that this was, as Thucydides believed, a turning point in Greek history, quite unlike anything that had happened before, and that would be well worth my while to spend my life studying what happened then. But I still thought that it was an old story, something that could happen to the Greeks, perhaps, but not to our modern world. Suddenly, in 1914, my point of view was altered; a great war had now broken out in *my* world, too, and the things that Thucydides had described were happening to me and my contemporaries. Over two thousand years had passed since Thucydides had lived through those events, yet somehow he had had much the same experiences as those that Westerners were about to face in 1914. It was a strange feeling. Measured by the calendar, Thucydides' experience was all old stuff; but I began to see that a simple chronological standpoint was not the only way of looking at history—that, in a psychological sense, past and present events might be regarded as being contemporary with each other. That gave me the idea of setting Greek and Roman history side by side with Western history, and seeing them not just as ancient and modern history but as two instances of the same historical experience, instances that could be compared with each other. Then, of course, having found one such parallel, I wanted to go on to find as many other parallels of this kind as I could. The result has been my *Study of History*.

PLAYBOY: In the memoir you published at the age of seventy-five, you described yourself as Janus, the mythological figure who faces both backward and forward. As you stand now, facing the past and the future, as you have done all your life, do you feel detached from the current of history or do you feel some sense of involvement in the present?

TOYNBEE: I have always felt a sense of involvement. My wife and I worked together for thirty-four years on writing an annual survey of international affairs, and the assignment was to write a cold-blooded, objective, impersonal narrative of what was happening. But I found that, for myself—and I think for anybody, really—this is quite impossible. All I can do is to put my cards on the table and say: "I am a certain kind of person with a certain background, certain feelings—right or wrong—certain prejudices. So you must bear this in mind and discount it in reading what I write about controversial questions. I can't pretend that I am wholly detached." I couldn't be detached about, say, the Italian attack on Abyssinia or about the things that Hitler did. My commitment is pretty concrete; I have grandchildren and I want my grandchildren to have grandchildren who will have grandchildren. I want that very much. I want the human race to survive, and I very much admire what I have been told that Bertrand Russell said on his ninetieth birthday—that one ought to care very much about what is going to happen after one is dead.

PLAYBOY: If your unflagging work schedule is any evidence, that's not an imminent prospect.

TOYNBEE: Well, I've been blessed with both a long life and a robust constitution. But those are gifts of the gods, and the gods are unfair and capricious in the way they distribute these gifts—and withdraw them. I am very conscious of this, because about half of my generation were killed in the First World War. I escaped being killed because I got dysentery from walking about in Greece in 1911 and 1912, so I wasn't in the army in 1914 to 1918. The older I grow, and the more time I have to produce, the more I am conscious of the unproduced works of those dead contemporaries of mine, and the more painfully I feel the irrationality and senselessness of this aspect of human life—especially when people are arbitrarily killed in wars. Disease used to kill ever so many; but in that respect the expectation of life is much better than it used to be. The expectation of dying from war, however, may well be greater now than ever before. Anyway, I am conscious of this unearned gift—the length of time that I have been given to follow my calling as a historian. Time is enormously important for anyone studying human affairs. It's also a help if one's mind stays sharp. Some people begin to lose their wits, to lose the cutting edge of their mind, in their sixties; other people, like Bertrand Russell, seem to be as lively at ninety as when they were undergraduates. This is very unfair, but there it is.

PLAYBOY: Do *you* feel as lively at seventy-seven as you were in your youth?

TOYNBEE: As you get older, you find that you have to limit your marginal activities. Though you can still do the same things, it takes more out of you, and you take longer to recuperate. So it is wise to concentrate on what you want to do most.

PLAYBOY: What do you want to do most?

TOYNBEE: Well, I very much enjoy reading; but I regard reading as an indulgence, and my work is writing; so my reading must take care of itself and find its own time. If I know I am going to try to write about something, I think a year or two ahead, and I ask myself what I shall need to have read in order to be prepared by that time to write on the subject. Then, at such times as I find for reading, I will concentrate on that future point. But I give every morning, and usually after teatime, too, to writing. I don't wait for the mood; I write every morning, doggedly, whether I feel in the mood or not. What you write in your off mood will not be as good as what you write when you are in the right mood—but you can improve it afterward; you can bring it more or less up to standard. If you wait for the mood, you may wait forever—and then you won't accomplish much.

PLAYBOY: What do you feel you have accomplished?

TOYNBEE: Well, I have tried to present mankind's history as the unity that I believe it really is. This is the traditional Jewish, Christian and Moslem view of history. The current tendency in history, in the West generally and particularly in Britain, is to make mincemeat of history. This, in my opinion, makes nonsense of it.

PLAYBOY: In looking back over your career, do you feel you've completed the task you embarked upon so many years ago?

TOYNBEE: It's funny that you should ask that question, for I have always had a sort of agenda for my life. My first agenda, when I was a young don at Oxford, was to write a small history of Greece and then a rather large book on the social and economic consequences of the Hannibalic wars. I produced the first one some years ago, and then the other day I finished that agenda by publishing in two volumes the book on the second of the two subjects that I had set for myself so long ago. Meanwhile, I have written unforeseen things like the *Survey of International Affairs* and my *Study of History*. It is a rather queer feeling to find, after fifty years or more, that I have completed my agenda. It is the same sort of disconcerting sensation as when you find that your children have finished their education and grown up. When you have children growing up, it feels as if their childhood were stretching away into eternity; the various stages of their education seem interminable. Then, one day, with a bang, it is all finished. Now, with a bang, my agenda of intellectual work has been finished. I have discovered, though, that when one agenda is finished, another starts.

PLAYBOY: Can you say what your next agenda will be?

TOYNBEE: I have two permanent concerns. The first is to work for the unification of the world on all levels of life and activity. The second is to work for the recovery of the traditional unitary view of history. I have no doubt that these two concerns, which are obviously facets of the same single concern, can be counted on to produce new agendas for me as long as I live and also keep my wits.

JOHNNY CARSON

December 1967

Interviewer: Alex Haley

This was Alex Haley's last interview published by PLAYBOY (he was already researching a more personal project involving his African roots), and although there may be little more perishable than an entertainer such as Johnny Carson speaking about yesterday's television season, it is surprising how current much of this interview remains. The reason lies partly in the nature of Carson himself: He may be among the most familiar personalities in American life, but he has granted few interviews and even fewer glimpses into his inner life. And so, despite anachronisms (the discussions of hippies and generation gaps have nostalgic charm), the reclusive Carson responds here to Haley's gentle prodding and discusses his feelings, his success, his battles with the network, and makes it sound remarkably contemporary. As for Carson on sex, drugs, politics—it is not only contemporary; it is virtually the *only* time Carson shed his television armor to address those subjects naturally. It has been said many times that Carson sets America's agenda: When he comments on something during his nightly monologues, it means the topic is official and has entered the mainstream. When he ridicules someone, that person better reassess. Here, for a change, is a self-assessment.

Footnote: In 1977, when Haley was promoting *Roots,* he made an appearance on the Carson show. The two men talked and reminisced about the interview Haley had conducted for PLAYBOY a decade earlier. Then Haley brought out a surprise: a genealogical chart of the Carson family prepared by one of the firms that helped Haley trace his own family roots. A producer of the show later said it was the only time he had seen Carson at a loss for words—and in tears.

Carson's mastery of his craft is the polished product of almost three decades as an entertainer. At the age of fourteen, as "The Great Carsoni," Johnny was earning three dollars an engagement for entertaining the Elks and Rotarians of Norfolk,

Nebraska—his home town—with card tricks and other feats of magic; in high school, he was class historian—and an imaginative practical joker. After a two-year stint in the navy (he once entertained Secretary of the Navy James Forrestal for several hours with his card tricks), Johnny entered the University of Nebraska, where he earned money off-campus as a comedian and radio announcer; met his first wife, Jody Wolcott, and wrote a thesis on comedy. Following a year in Omaha, where he acquired local renown as an offbeat radio personality, he moved to Hollywood and hosted a Sunday-afternoon television show called Carson's Cellar. *In 1954, while writing gags for Red Skelton, he got his first major break: Called upon to substitute for his boss after Skelton was injured in a rehearsal, he won plaudits for his performance—and his own night-time TV show on CBS; but* The Johnny Carson Show *lasted only thirty-nine feverish weeks. The producer attributed its failure to Carson's lack of "power"; Johnny felt that too many people had been trying to give him advice.*

After this setback, Carson acquired a manager, Al Bruno, and was promptly hustled off to New York. In the course of the next five years, as host of a daytime quiz show, Who Do You Trust? *he learned to improvise risqué but socially acceptable double entendres and to coax humor out of lady wrestlers, snake charmers and the matrons who comprised the bulk of his viewers and guests. The rest of his time was filled with a heavy schedule of personal appearances on the Ed Sullivan, Perry Como and Dinah Shore shows, stints as a guest panelist on* What's My Line? *and* To Tell the Truth *and even feature acting roles on* Playhouse 90 *and* The U.S. Steel Hour. *When Jack Paar decided to step down as ringmaster of the grueling* Tonight Show *in 1962, he named Carson—who had successfully subbed for him on several occasions—as the only man who could fill his shoes. NBC agreed, but many observers wondered if the new man was really up to Paar. He was—and then some; since he took over* Tonight, *Carson has eclipsed his predecessor's popularity; the show is the biggest money-maker on television, with both advertisers and studio tickets SRO; and its host has become the biggest star in television.*

In the opinion of many, however, Carson's success has made him cocky; and his reputed high-handedness has led colleagues to refer to their boss only half-humorously as "The Prince."

Reporters, eager to capitalize on the irony that such a willing performer should be such a reluctant celebrity, have often characterized Carson as a withdrawn, unaffectionate, even hostile man. One Tonight Show *guest has bluntly called him a "cold fish." Even his old friend announcer Ed McMahon has said that he "packs a tight suitcase." Though others have risen to his defense—notably, Mrs. Carson, who explained to a writer at some length that Johnny cares very much about people but doesn't find it easy to verbalize his feelings—few succeed in glimpsing his private life, let alone in reaching him on a personal level.*

We decided to interview Carson early this fall, when he was riding high on the wave of public interest that followed his dispute with the network. Always wary of reporters, he regards the public's curiosity about him as a tiresome irritation that "just goes with the territory." But during his conversations with PLAYBOY *interviewer Alex Haley—which were conducted daily, over the course of a week, both at Carson's home and in his NBC office—he overcame his reticence and provided us with by far the most candid interview he has ever granted. "At first," Haley reported, "he was evasive, but by the end of our talks, I had come to like and respect him as a man with the guts to be stubborn about his convictions in a profession where the most common concern is to swing with the 'in' crowd, whatever the personal compromise." Haley opened the discussion by asking Carson about his offscreen image as a loner.*

PLAYBOY: Recent newspaper and magazine articles about you have focused on the contrast between your affable television image and what they claim is your dour, antisocial personality in private life. Writing in *TV Guide,* Edith Efron even went so far as to say that "Johnny Carson is a dual personality; pure sweetness and light on the screen—and offscreen, plunged into some Dostoievskyan murk." How do you feel about this kind of armchair psychoanalysis?
CARSON: I couldn't care less what anybody says about me. I live my life, especially my personal life, strictly for myself. I feel that is my right, and anybody who disagrees with that, that's his business. Whatever you do, you're going to be criticized. I feel the one sensible thing you can do is try to live in a way that pleases *you.* If you don't hurt anybody else, what you do is your own business.
PLAYBOY: Of course. But off the air—even to many of those who know you well—you seem withdrawn and even hostile. According to reports, longtime associates on the show say that you scarcely speak except as business demands, that you have almost no friends in or out of show business, that you hardly ever go out socially, that you shrink from your own public. Why?
CARSON: I think I owe one thing to my public—the best performance I can give. What else do they want from me? As for being sociable, I hate the phoniness in the showbiz world. I know this will be taken wrong, but I don't like clubs and organizations. I was never a joiner. I think most groups are hypocritical, restrictive and undemocratic. I don't run with anybody's herd. I don't like crowds. I don't like going to fancy places. I don't like the whole nightclub scene. Cocktail parties drive me mad. So I do my job and I stay away from the rest of it. Isn't that my right? Am I not entitled to prefer the enjoyment of my home? Am I not entitled to a private life? I can't go anywhere without being bugged by somebody. I'd love to just hike out down the street, or drop in a restaurant, or wander in the park, or take my kids somewhere without collecting a trail of people. But I can't. When you get successful, you just have to quit going out in public as often as you used to. Wherever you go, some clown grabs you and demands an autograph; it's a pain in the butt. I've had a guy in a *urinal* ask me for an autograph!
PLAYBOY: Don't all entertainers have to put up with that kind of thing?
CARSON: Of course. But it doesn't stop there. Everybody I meet in public seems to want to audition for me. If I ask a guy what time it is, he'll sing it to me. Everywhere I turn, there's somebody's niece who plays the kazoo or does ballet with skin-diving flippers. I'll never forget coming out of a restaurant one night, when this hand reaches from an alley and literally turns me completely around. It was this woman. "I want you to hear my son sing," she says. And out she shoves this kid—"Sing, Albert!" And he did—right there in the street. I've had cabdrivers pull over to the curb to tell me about some relative who ought to be on the show. That's why I've got cabophobia—the fear of being talked to death in an enclosed space. But you haven't heard the worst of it. One night, Ed McMahon and I dropped into a nightclub; we wanted to catch an act there. We had barely sat down when some drunken bruiser comes over and hauls me up by the arm. Right there, I was ready to rip into him; I didn't care how big he was—but I kept saying to myself: "Don't!" I could see the headlines if I did. He all but drags me to his table of maybe fifteen or twenty friends and he yells to the band to

stop so I can entertain them. I told him I was sorry, I was very busy. I had to get up early. Now he's insulted. "Come on—I promised my friends." Well, I walked away: Ed and I had to leave—and I'd made some enemies. You can't win. So you stay away from public situations.

PLAYBOY: Have you changed since you became a star, or have you always felt this strongly about guarding your privacy?

CARSON: In other words, has success spoiled Johnny Carson? No, I don't think so. I don't think it's *you* that changes with success—it's the people around you who change. Because of your new status, they change in relation to you. Let me give you an example. I loved the towns I grew up in as a boy, and after I became a celebrity, I went back several times. I would have had the time of my life seeing the old places and the old faces again, but the attitude of those same people was, "I guess you're so big we bore you now." What was I supposed to say to that? Agree with them? They'd be furious. But if I said I was enjoying myself, they'd say I was being condescending. You see what I mean?

There was a "Johnny Carson Day" for me at the last Nebraska Centennial in Columbus, Nebraska. I went, I enjoyed most of it. It was a real honor, and I sincerely mean that. But I have since decided not to go back home again. It's just too much of a strain. My folks will have to come to New York to see me. I guess people will find all kinds of things wrong with my saying that; they'll say I'm conceited and egocentric—but I'm just being honest.

PLAYBOY: To be honest, *are* you conceited and egocentric?

CARSON: Find me any performer anywhere who *isn't* egocentric. You'd better believe you're good, or you've got no business being out there. People are brought up to think, "It's nice to be modest. It's nice to hide your light under a bushel." Well, bullshit! I've never bought that. In my business, the only thing you've really got is your talent; it's the only thing you have to sell. If you want to call that conceit, go ahead. I don't know where you'll hear that word more than in show business—but it's often not conceit at all. Often it's a public compensation for shyness. That's certainly the case with me. From the time I was a little kid, I was always shy. Performing was when I was outgoing. So I guess I *am* a loner. I get claustrophobia if a lot of people are around. But there's a big difference between being a loner and being lonely. I'm far from lonely. My day is full of things I enjoy, starting with my show. Any time my work is going well and I have a relationship with a woman that's pretty solid, that does it for me.

PLAYBOY: Last April, you won a healthy pay raise by going on strike against NBC. Is that one of the reasons you say your work is going well?

CARSON: Since when has it been wrong to ask for a pay raise? Have you seen carved in stone anywhere that it's unfair to bargain for a better deal for yourself? It was made to look as if I'm Jack the Ripper. Some of the columnists figured I was too greedy for a nice, small-town Nebraska boy. Like one letter asked, "How can you *do* that with people in the world starving?" What in the hell is the logic of that? I explained, time and again, carefully, why I stayed out—but nobody wants to believe you when you take a personal stand about something. The whole thing got written and talked far out of proportion. Look—the reason was simple; at least to me it was. *Tonight* was and is the biggest money-making show NBC has. It brings in twenty-five million dollars a year, cold cash; but NBC treated *Tonight* like some bastard step-child. We had a ridiculous budget. I hadn't liked that setup long before the strike. But that still wasn't the specific issue with me. The specific issue was that NBC directly violated our contract during the strike: They used reruns of *The Tonight Show* without any effort at all to negotiate. My contract stated clearly that any reruns would be negotiated in advance in good faith to arrive at equitable fees. They knew why I stayed out. They sent me a check for the reruns and I sent the check right back. But finally, NBC and I came to terms. I'm satisfied. I think they are. The show's doing fine. That's that.

PLAYBOY: Not quite—if you don't mind our pursuing the subject a bit further. It's been reported that your new contract will earn you more than four million dollars in the next three years. is that true?

CARSON: I won't tell you—for two reasons. One is that a term in the new contract specifies that neither NBC nor I will make public the details of the contract; I intend to abide by that agreement. Another reason is that in Nebraska, I was raised to consider that it's not good manners to ask anyone, "How much money do you make?" All I will say is that the new contract calls for an increase in the monies that I receive for doing the show.

Look—do you know that Dean Martin makes a lot more, maybe half again, at least, than I do? But all that means nothing whatever to me. I have no use for eight houses, eighty-eight cars and five hundred suits. I can't eat but one steak at a time. I don't want but one woman. It's silly to have as one's sole object in life just making money, accumulating wealth. I work because I *enjoy* what I'm doing, and the fact that I make money at it—big money—is a fine-and-dandy side fact. Money gives me just one big thing that's really important, and that's the freedom of not having to worry about money. I'm concerned about *values*—moral, ethical, human values—my own, other people's, the country's, the world's values. Having money now gives me the freedom to worry about the things that really matter.

But I wouldn't call myself a great deal happier now than when I was earning $47.50 a week in Omaha. You could live on that in 1949 in Omaha. The guys at the station and I used to sit around and yak about how great it would be if we could earn $150 a week. We couldn't have *believed* what I make now. We couldn't have believed where I live now, the job I have—none of it. But I'm still sleeping in a bed; it cost a lot more, but I don't sleep any better than I did then. And I still like hamburgers—but in all of New York City, you cannot buy one as great as I used to buy at the Hamburger Hut in Norfolk, Nebraska. You see what I mean? Believe me, it's all relative.

PLAYBOY: During your year in Omaha, you often worked six and seven days a week almost around the clock. Doesn't it please you to be earning a great deal more than you did then, for a great deal less work?

CARSON: Maybe it looks easy to a lot of people, but sitting in that chair will take more out of you than if you were chopping down trees all day. I spend seven and a half hours on the air every week. I think anyone who does this show ought to get an Emmy just for showing up. I'm serious. It's not the physical strain; it's debilitating mentally. In fact, I'll tell you something: My biggest anxiety is about the day I'll know I've reached a point where I can't bring the show anything more that's new. I was forty-two this October, see? Physically, I have no concerns; but mentally, it's one of those shows where you're working from wake up in the morning until you go to bed, and then even in bed. The pressure is to keep it from getting dull. I believe we give more honest humor and entertainment in one week than most prime-time shows in a season. But think about trying to keep that up, five nights a week, and maybe you'll appreciate the strain. And that's just strain about the overall planning; then you add the strain of each show when you're on the air. When that red light goes off at the end, I get up from the chair already planning the show for the next night. If it looks easy, I'm doing my job. It both bugs me and pleases me when people tell me how relaxed I make the show look. Great! Maybe the public figures I'm getting well paid for it, but it's the toughest job in television. Listen—understand that I'm not complaining. I love the show; otherwise, I wouldn't be there. I'm just saying it's tough.

PLAYBOY: You said your workday begins when you wake up. Would you describe a typical day for us?

CARSON: Well, I get out of bed at nine or ten in the morning. And I'm not one of those who spring up yelling, "Yippee! Another day!" I'll grumble and sulk around a couple of hours, reading newspapers and trying to pick out an idea I might do something with on the show. But I don't really start functioning until noon or later; then about two I go to the studio and the pace begins to quicken. Planning the time slots for this guest, that guest, rehearsing the skits, trying to anticipate what could go wrong with some physical participation I want to do—like the time I dueled with a fencing master. Or the time I did a snake dance with Augie and Margo. Or when I try out gadgets or toys. Or the times I've done exercises with Debbie Drake. She's great fun. One of my good lines came with that. Debbie and I had just lain down on the exercise mats, side by side, and it popped into my head to ask her, "Would you like to leave a call?"

PLAYBOY: Are all of your ad libs spontaneous and unrehearsed?

CARSON: Very few of them are. Ad-libbing isn't very often the instant creation of a good line. More often it's remembering something you've used before and maybe making a quick switch to fit a fresh situation. Once I had Red Buttons on and he was getting into an involved analysis of politics, so I told him finally, "You're kind of a redheaded Dr. Schweitzer tonight, aren't you?" and Red started being his funny self again. Now, that's a situation bit I've used many times. Every comedian has a bag full of them. I remember once a woman on *Who Do You Trust?* telling me at great length, *too* great length, about a pregnant armadillo. She was about to bore the audience, so I asked her, "How come you know these things if you're not an armadillo?" They're usually old bits, but they work like brand-new if people laugh. Like the time we had this Latin Quarter showgirl on the show. She walked on in one of those poured-in dresses, with her hair done up in some exotic style. I said, "I suppose you're on your way to a 4-H Club meeting," and the audience cracked up. That's the humor of the ludicrous, of extreme contrast. I've used it many times before and I know I will many times again.

PLAYBOY: Apart from the skits and your participation bits and, in a sense, some of the ad libs, how much preparation is involved in each show?

CARSON: The minimum that's safely possible. That's part of the formula. I have little or no advance contact with guests, for instance, unless they're involved in some skit. And the writers prepare my opening bit—that first ten minutes after I walk on. But I edit what they give me until I'm entirely comfortable with it, using something topical I've found in the papers, if I can. Then the necessary staff people and I plan a rundown of the show. By the time all this is done, it's six P.M., and we start taping the show at 6:30. Then I'm on my own. So the objective is spontaneity within a planned framework; but for the most part, we're winging it. My job isn't to hog the show. Ideally, I'm the audience-identification figure, the catalyst. When I've got a guest who's going great on his own, I let him go. If he looks good, I look good. Sometimes, of course, the chemistry isn't right, or something will go wrong, and I'll have to change the pace or pull a switch during a commercial or a station break.

All too often, though, a guest will either clam up or be vapid and bland, and I'll have to cut it short and come on next with a bullwhip demonstration, or some skit I can do on a moment's notice, to wake us up—or wake up the audience. Sometimes I can get us going again by coming up with a good gag keyed to what a guest is talking about. Like once during the New York World's Fair, I got off one that the Moroccan Pavilion had a belly dancer, but the Fair's business was so bad she had a cobweb in her navel. Another time, Mr. Universe was on, explaining the importance of keeping yourself fit and trim. That sort of thing can get deadly dull, of course, and I was feeling for a good gag when he told me something like, "Remember, Mr. Carson, your body is the only home you will ever have." And I said, "Yeah, my home is pretty messy. But I have a woman come in once a week." Can you imagine the mail I got on that one? But nearly anything you say, you can't help offending somebody out there. If I say "naked," if I use the word *pregnant,* I'll get probably five hundred letters complaining that I'm hastening national immorality. A lot of them are from nuts—you can tell that—but many are from perfectly sincere people who happen to think that practically anything is immoral. Let me do a sketch about the President or about a rabbi and there'll be a storm of criticism.

PLAYBOY: Do you let this kind of reaction affect your choice of material?

CARSON: You can't afford to. The only time I pay attention to audience mail is when it contains something I find possible to use for the show's benefit. You can't let an audience run your show for you. If you do, soon you won't have any audience.

PLAYBOY: What's your reaction to Newton Minow's celebrated indictment of television as a vast wasteland?

CARSON: Sure, there's a *lot* of chaff on television. No doubt of it. But let's not forget a fundamental fact about this medium. It starts in the morning, about six A.M., and goes off anywhere from one to three A.M. Where are you going to find the people to write consistently fine material nineteen to twenty-one hours a day, 365 days a year? A Broadway play that's going to run for ninety minutes can take a year or more to get written, by the biggest playwrights in the business; then it can spend months and months on the road, being tested every night and changed daily; they can bring in the best script doctors in the country—and yet that play can still open on Broadway and bomb out the first night. How can you expect television to do any better—or even as well when it's showing more in a week than appears on Broadway all year? I'm not defending the medium just because I'm in it; I'm just trying to explain that television has an impossible task. Why should it be the job of television to educate or edify or uplift people? This is an entertainment medium. I have never seen it chiseled in stone tablets that TV is philanthropic. Is it television's job to improve people's minds—when the libraries are full of empty seats? Are we supposed to provide instant education?

There are lots of things I'll knock the industry for—including the fact that there's too much junk on the air. But there are a lot of fine programs, too. And I think television is steadily working to improve its programming: the competition is so hot, it guarantees that. Another thing people so often entirely overlook when they're criticizing is that this still is a very young industry. My first TV broadcast was when I was at the University of Nebraska. I was playing a milkman in a documentary called, believe it or not, *The Story of Undulant Fever.* You know what the broadcast range of that show was? The cameras were in the university theater's basement and the screen was up in the auditorium—and that was the first television at the university. And that was in 1949; *that's* how young television is. So I don't go for this general rapping of the television industry. How long, how much longer, have the newspapers and the magazines and the movies been around? Does television offer any more junk than they do? Does television feed its viewers anything *like* as much rape and lurid details? Yet television is always being knocked in newspaper and magazine editorials. I'm not against the press, but that sort of attack is not only unfair but hypocritical.

PLAYBOY: For most TV sponsors, the fate of a show is decided by its popularity rather than its quality, by means of rating systems that have been widely attacked not only for their life-or-death importance to network programmers but for the inadequacy and inaccuracy of their audience samplings. How much stock do you place in them?

CARSON: I'm reminded of the story about this gambler in a small-town saloon who is taken aside and told that the wheel he's playing is crooked. He says, "I know, but it's the only wheel in town." The industry seems to want a yardstick, and I guess the ratings are the only one they can find. I don't know how accurate they are, but I'd hate to think that a random sampling of twelve hundred viewers gives a true national picture. I'm certain that people aren't watching what they tell the pollsters they watch. People often want to project themselves as some kind of intellectuals, so they'll say they watched the news, or some forum, or the National Educational Network show, when, in fact, they watched *Bonanza* or *The Flying Nun*. You know? One thing I'm sure of: Ratings certainly don't indicate if people are buying the sponsor's product. But I'm glad I have the ratings I get—accurate or not. Anybody would be. I don't concern myself too much about them, though, because one show will be up, another one down. If you start worrying about a particular show, chances are you'll do worse the next. What really counts is how your ratings average out over, say, six months. I never worry about an individual program after it's over. That was yesterday; what's tomorrow?

PLAYBOY: *The Tonight Show,* under your control, has been criticized for deliberately *avoiding* controversy. Is there any truth to that?

CARSON: Well, bullshit! That's my answer. I just don't feel that Johnny Carson should become a social commentator. Jack Paar got into that, being an expert on everything happening. So did Dave Garroway and Steve Allen and Godfrey. Who cares what entertainers on the air think about international affairs? Who would want to hear me about Vietnam? They can hear all they want from people with reason to be respected as knowledgeable. Controversy just isn't what this show is for. My number-one concern, and the concern of NBC, is a successful *Tonight* show. I'm not the host of *Meet the Press*. I think it would be a fatal mistake to use my show as a platform for controversial issues. I'm an entertainer, not a commentator. If you're a comedian, your job is to make people laugh. You cannot be both serious and funny. One negates the other. Personally, I want to be a successful comedian. Audiences have proved time and again that they don't want a steady diet of any entertainer airing his social views—especially if he's a comedian. When a comic becomes enamored with his own views and foists them off on the public in a polemic way, he loses not only his sense of humor but his value as a humorist. When the public starts classifying you as thoughtful, someone given to serious issues, you find yourself declassified as a humorist. That's what happened to Mort Sahl. He was one of the brightest when he began; then he began commenting humorlessly on the social scene in his shows. How many shows has Mort lost now? I think he realizes this now—and he's starting to get funny again. Like most people, of course, I have strong personal opinions. I might even be better informed than the average person, just because it's my business to keep up on what's happening. But that doesn't mean I should use the show to impose my personal views on millions of people. We *have* dealt with controvesial subjects on the show—sex, religion, Vietnam, narcotics. They've all been discussed, by qualified guests, and I've taken stands myself. But it's only when the subject rises naturally. I won't purposely inject controversy just for the sake of controversy. It would be easy, if that's what I wanted. I could get in the headlines any day by attacking a major public figure like Bobby Kennedy or by coming out in favor of birth control or abortion. But I just don't see it, and I don't play it that way. I won't make this show a forum for my own political views.

PLAYBOY: Isn't it possible for you to air your social and political views without abandoning your role as a comedian? Can't you comment humorously and satirically rather than seriously on current issues?

CARSON: It should be—because that's the essence of comedy at its best—but that's not the way it works in practice, at least not on television. Americans, too many of them, take themselves too seriously. You're going to get rapped—by the viewers, by the sponsors and by the network brass—if you joke about doctors, lawyers, dentists, scientists, bus drivers, I don't care who. You can't make a joke about Catholics, Negroes, Jews, Italians, politicians, dogs or cats. In fact, politicians, dogs and cats are the most sacred institutions in America. I remember once somebody stole the car of Mickey Cohen, the racketeer, with Cohen's dog inside, and I said on Steve Allen's show that the police had recovered the dog while it was holding up a liquor store. Well, the next day this joker telephoned and said, "I don't want you should joke about Mickey Cohen," and I told him the joke was about his dog. "That compounds the felony," this character said. "You just better watch your step." Look—a comic has got to tread on some toes to be funny, but he's got to be careful how *many* toes he steps on, and who they belong to. I think the biggest rap mail I ever got was once when a girl said on the show that we should send Elvis Presley to Russia to improve our Soviet Union relations, and I said, "I don't know about Russia, but it might improve relations here." Presley fans tore me up. You can't say anything about practically anything that can be considered someone's vested interest. Once I planned to air a joke about how the government ought to be run like Madison Avenue would run it. Write ads like, "You can be *sure* if it's the White House." But I was told, "No, can't kid the government." Well, why *not?* Another time I was intending to kid the phone company a bit, and I couldn't—because the *Bell Telephone Hour* was on the same network. If you plan to stay in television, you just have to adjust to these taboos, however ridiculous they are. But I must say that the timidity of the censors really floors me sometimes. For instance, it's touchy, touchy if you say "damn" on TV. Once, in 1964, somebody brought a dog on my show that actually said "Hello." It stunned me so that I blurted, "The damn thing talks!" Well, that word got blooped from the soundtrack before the show was aired. I say that any adult who gets offended at hearing "damn" or "hell" ought not to be watching television—or reading books. These same people, interestingly enough, seem to have no similar objection to the amount of violence on TV; otherwise, you wouldn't see so much of it. I've come to the conclusion that it's OK to kill somebody on television as long as you don't say "damn!" as you strike your victim down.

PLAYBOY: In its recent cover story about you, *Time* magazine clucked editorially about what it felt was your taste for bathroom humor. Do you feel that's a justified criticism?

CARSON: That's one of the two things in that whole article that I resented. The other line I didn't like was that I had divorced my first wife. I didn't; she divorced me. I didn't initiate it. The way they put it made it sound like I was the kind of guy who made it big and then got rid of the one who had stuck with him all the way. Anyway, about that bathroom-humor bit. I think the writer didn't use the word he intended; I think he meant double-entendre jokes—because toilet humor I don't like at all, not from me or from my guests.

PLAYBOY: Then you do indulge in double entendres?

CARSON: Occasionally, yes—but without striving for it and without violating what I consider good taste.

PLAYBOY: The rap letters you've said you receive from viewers imply otherwise.

CARSON: There's a lot of hypocrisy in audiences. I'd never dream of telling even on a nightclub stage, let alone my show, some of the jokes that are told in a lot of the living rooms from which we get those letters! If you can't talk about anything grown-up or sophisticated at midnight without being called immoral and dirty, then I think we're in trouble. After all, by the time we go on the air, the children are supposed to be in bed asleep. I can't just prattle about what I had for lunch and expect people to tune in every night. We'd be dead soon if we got dull enough *not* to get letters; we have to get in something now and then that's provocative. Take comics. You can't have Sam Levinson on all the time, talking about kids and school. You have to liven things up occasionally with somebody like Mel Brooks. Mel can get close to the line, on the line, or he'll edge beyond it; he may offend, but when he's going great, really winging, he's near a genius. There are some guests, of course, who make a fetish of blue material. But if I once feel that, you won't see them on my show again. Nor will I let a guest say something blue that I can sense in advance—especially if it's just to be blue. But I'm not going to worry about it if something happens to slip—and it can just as well be me as a guest. Even when no double meaning is intended, that pious bunch out there in the audience will make up its own and write in about it. That's more of a commentary about them, in my opinion, than it is about us.

PLAYBOY: Many of those same people, and their journalistic spokesmen, seem to feel that the sexual suggestiveness—and overt erotica—they perceive on television, in movies, magazines and books is evidence of a moral decline in society at large. What's your reaction?

CARSON: Well, if you're talking about sexual morality, I wouldn't agree that it's declining; but it's certainly changing. Young and old, we are very much in the process of taking a fresh look at the whole issue of morality. The only decline that's taking place—and it's about time—is in the old puritanical concept that sex is equated with sin. You hear the word *permissiveness* being thrown around; right away, in so many people's minds, that translates to *promiscuity*. But it just ain't so. You read about college administrators deploring the dangers of too much permissiveness on campus. The fact is that the biggest problems in this area are being experienced at colleges that are persisting in the old tight disciplines and trying to oversee every student activity that might hold any potential for sexual contact. It doesn't work, of course. At one school I know about, in the men's dorms, they're permitted to have female visitors only for one to two hours in the early evening. All that means is that if a couple wants to go to bed, they can't do it in the afternoon. On campuses with very little administrative supervision, there are no problems at all. Giving students latitude for personal freedom doesn't result in everybody jumping into the hay with everybody else. They're still just as selective about whom they have sex with. It's not promiscuity; it's just that private behavior is left up to the individual. I'm for that. Whether you agree or disagree with Madalyn Murray on the subject of atheism, you've got to admit she has a point when she said in her PLAYBOY interview, "Nobody's going to tell me I've got to get a license to screw." It's ludicrous to declare that it's wrong to have sex with anyone you're not married to. It's happening millions of times every day. If the laws against it were enforced, we'd have to build prisons to hold four-fifths of the population.

PLAYBOY: When you talk about the ludicrousness of laws and mores forbidding sex outside marriage, do you mean pre- or extramarital sex?

CARSON: Premarital. Some may consider it old-fashioned, but I feel that very few people can have sex elsewhere and still maintain a good marriage. It's tough enough to keep up a good, solid marital relationship even when both partners are completely faithful.

PLAYBOY: How do you feel about such groups as the Sexual Freedom League?

CARSON: For some, they seem to work; but for me, I pass. I simply couldn't imagine engaging in anything like that. At the same time, I recognize there are all kinds of sexual deviations in this world; they are real *needs* for a lot of people, or they wouldn't be doing whatever they do. As long as it's this way, I think we ought to come to grips with the fact that there never can be any successful legislation against private, non-exploitive sex. I don't want to start sounding like some boy philosopher, but our sex laws seem to be predicated on the puritanical assumption that all sex—especially any variations from the marital norm—is dirty and should be suppressed. At the same time, our national obsession with sex seems to be predicated on the belief that sex constitutes the entire substance of the relationship between man and woman—and that's just as sick as feeling that it should have *no* part in human relationships. It's a damn healthy *part* of a good relationship, that's for sure. But it's just a part, and we seem bound and determined to make it unhealthy.

PLAYBOY: How would you suggest we go about ridding society of these hang-ups?

CARSON: We need to start with the kids. We need to completely overhaul not only our own neurotic values but the abysmal sex education in our schools. When anthropologist Ashley Montagu was on my show not long ago, he said—and I couldn't have agreed with him more—that in any sexual relationship, adult or otherwise, married or unmarried, the key word is *responsibility*. We have to teach our young people to ask themselves, "Am I ready to assume the *responsibility* of a sexual relationship?" Even the clergy are openly saying this to youth now. They've quit, most of them, trying to sweep sex under the rug, as if it doesn't happen.

Like their parents, kids flock to see James Bond and Derek Flint movies—outrageously antiheroic heroes who break all the taboos, making attractive the very things the kids are told they shouldn't do themselves. Well, they're figuring "Why *can't* I?" and they're not buying the adult advice anymore. Why should they? They're seeing a war that nobody wants, and the frightening prospect of a world war three that would incinerate us all. If anybody is capable of doing that, it's the adults, not the young people. The vast majority of us don't want to face the fact that we're in the middle of a sweeping social revolution. In sex. In spiritual values. In opposition to wars no one wants. In opposition to government big-brotherhood. In civil rights. In basic human goals. They're all facets of a general upheaval.

PLAYBOY: One of the most conspicuous facets of that upheaval has been the exodus of thousands of young people out of society and into hippie communities. Do you feel they've chosen a viable alternative to the square society they find unlivable?

CARSON: No, I don't. They seem to be involved in some kind of search for identity, but I don't think they're going to find it—not in Haight-Ashbury, anyway. Most of them, to me, seem lost and floundering. They've removed themselves from society, yet we see that they continue to expect society to provide them with necessities like medical help and food.

PLAYBOY: The hippie movement is linked in the public mind with usage of psychedelic drugs. How do you feel about this trend?

CARSON: I think it's one of the most frightening things youth, or anybody else, could possibly get involved in. We just don't have enough authoritative information yet about how dangerous it is to tamper with the mind—but even what little we do know should be enough to give them pause. Don't they know about the high ratio of genetic defects—known already, *this* early? These drugs are so new that research has just barely scratched the surface of the damages they can cause. Already, we know about chromosome debilitation. We see hospital emergency wards filling with young people, some not yet twenty years old, completely wigged out! Nobody ever tells them the facts. All they hear about is how they can take these chemicals and *expand* themselves, *find* themselves. Bullshit! Who have we yet seen emerge from the drug culture with any great new truths? Timothy Leary? A brilliant man, obviously. But what's the philosophy he expounds? "Tune in, turn on, drop out." I wouldn't let him on my show. I wouldn't let him spout that nonsense.

PLAYBOY: In condemning the use of chemical turn-ons, do you classify marijuana along with LSD and the other psychedelics?

CARSON: No, I don't put marijuana in the same bag with LSD or any of the hard narcotics. People are wrong when they say marijuana isn't addicting, though. I've known people who use it, known them all my adult life, and I know they are at least psychologically addicted. But it's just a mild stimulant, actually. And I think that the laws against its use are repressive out of all proportion. But that doesn't mean I'd want to try it myself—or any of the other hallucinogens: it's tough enough to navigate in this world *without* drugs. It may not seem like *much* of a world to the kids, but it's the only one we've got, and dropping out of it isn't going to solve anything.

PLAYBOY: Many young people, of course, far from dropping out, have become activists in the student-protest movement, intent on changing society rather than abandoning it. How do you feel about this kind of rebellion?

CARSON: I feel that any of us has the right to dissent from what we don't like. But to what extreme do we wish to carry it? I think students ought to have the right to protest, but not to the point of anarchy—like that Berkeley situation. I got the impression that they often didn't know just what it was they were protesting against. Essentially, there was just a small, hard-core leadership throwing around words like *freedom!* and *rights!* What rights are they talking about? What about *other* people's rights? When they brandish four-letter placards and shout "Fuck!" at free-speech rallies, what the hell are they proving except how sophomoric they are? As for the burning of draft cards, I think it's stupid and pointless—though no more stupid and pointless than the war itself, it's unlike any war we were ever in. An undeclared war. An unpopular war. And it keeps going on and on. I'm a father with a boy coming out of high school next year, and I don't look forward to his marching off over there. I don't think anybody dissenting against this war has any business being called "un-American," but I still don't see burning draft cards. I'm all for the right to dissent: lots of things need to be changed. But I think we have to respect some boundaries, some limits, if we don't want to wreck the country. It can happen a lot quicker than people think if too many dissents and rebellions get out of perspective—and out of hand.

PLAYBOY: Do you think the Negro riots pose that kind of danger?

CARSON: They certainly do—if we don't do something to end them once and for all: and I don't mean with more tanks. The big thing on television now is show after show, special after special, about the reasons for the riots. Presidential commissions are formed, committees of mayors and police chiefs convene, to investigate the causes and the culprits. That's ridiculous. The *why* of the black revolution is no great mystery. What's sparked it all, of course, is *desperation;* and it's tragic that most whites can't seem to grasp that simple fact. Negroes saw the Civil Rights Act passed ten years ago—yet they haven't really seen much since then in the way of enforcement. Negro leaders call on the government to appropriate fifty billion dollars to "erase the ghettos"—but that's not going to solve anything, either, not by itself. You could gut Harlem today and rebuild it tomorrow—but unless we do something to uproot the injustices that *created* the ghetto, all we'll have built, at a cost of billions, is a nicer cage. This obsessive emphasis on money, money, money—just money—simply isn't the answer. And neither is this pressure that's being applied by civil-rights organizations, when a job is open for which a Negro and a white are equally qualified, to give that job automatically to the Negro, just *because* he's a Negro. Fundamentally, that's both condescending and subtly demeaning to that Negro. The problem isn't going to be solved by reverse favoritism any more than it is by giveaways. It comes down to just one basic word: *justice*—the same justice for *everyone*—in housing, in education, in employment and, most difficult of all, in human relations. And we're not going to accomplish that until all of us, black and white, begin to temper our passion with compassion, until we stop thinking in terms of more guns and more money and start listening to more realistic and responsible leaders—leaders who will begin, however belatedly, to practice what they preach: equality for all.

PLAYBOY: In the three years since President Johnson's reelection, a great deal has been said and written about the credibility gap—particularly in regard to the disparity between his professions of peaceful intentions in Vietnam and his continued escalation of the war. How do you feel about it?

CARSON: Well, I have to admit that at times I find myself with the very uncomfortable feeling that the public isn't getting all the information it ought to, that we're not being told what's really happening—but not just in Vietnam. I'd say it started, at least for me, with the U-2 incident. The government denied and denied and denied—and then the truth came out. The most recent instance, of course, was the revelation of CIA spying on college campuses by hiring students as undercover agents to report on so-called subversive activities. I get the feeling that George Orwell may have been right when he predicted that Big Brother might be watching all of us someday. It's not very reassuring about the ideals of those we entrust with the power to promote and protect the interests of this country.

PLAYBOY: On your show a few months ago, New York's Governor Rockefeller suggested that you consider running for Congress yourself—as a Republican candidate for the Senate against Bobby Kennedy. What do you think of the idea?

CARSON: No, thanks! Even if Governor Rockefeller hadn't been saying that with tongue in cheek, I wouldn't have the slightest interest in running for public office. I'd rather make jokes about politicians than become one of them. Once on the show, somebody asked me where tomorrow's *comedians* were coming from, and I told him, based upon my recent observations, from the Democratic and Republican parties.

PLAYBOY: Your own origins as a comedian could hardly be more unlike the familiar showbiz story that begins on the Lower East Side and ends on the great White Way, with stop-offs en route on the vaudeville-burlesque-Borscht Belt circuit. You've never talked much about your personal background on the air or off, other than to say that you're from the Midwest and that you were once an amateur magician. Would you like to fill us in on the rest?

CARSON: Well—I was born in Corning, Iowa. No cracks, please. I'm the product of a typical middle-class upbringing. My father was then a lineman for the power district; that means a guy who climbed up and down telephone poles. Later on, he became the power district's manager, and he has since retired. We moved around to different small towns—places like Clarinda, Shenandoah, Avoca. I started school in Avoca, Iowa. I think I was eight when we moved to Norfolk, Nebraska, a town of about ten thousand. I will never forget looking down on Main Street from a fourth-floor hotel window there, thinking how high up I was and marveling at so much traffic down in the street.

I think it was that same year I first realized I could make people laugh. I played Popeye in a school skit—you know, imitating him, with the funny voice. My sister Catherine and my brother Dick [now Carson's director] and I grew on up through high school there in Norfolk. We had a big frame house in town. It was a typical small-town Midwestern boyhood. Dick and I fished and skinny-dipped in the Elkhorn River, and summers the family would vacation at a lake in Minnesota. I was at a friend's home one day when I picked up an old book I saw: *Hoffman's Book of Magic*. It described all the standard tricks and how to make some of the equipment yourself, and there was an ad for a kit of stuff from a mail-order place in Chicago. So I sent away for it, and the stuff came, and I couldn't think about anything else but making things and working with the magic. I ordered every catalog advertised and read them from cover to cover, and spent every quarter I could get for more stuff. Finally, one Christmas I got this magician's table with a black-velvet cover. I have never since seen anything more beautiful than that was to me. The next thing was ventriloquism. I bought a mail-order course, also from Chicago, for fifteen dollars.

PLAYBOY: When did you first realize you wanted to be an entertainer?

CARSON: I just can't say I ever *wanted* to become an entertainer; I already *was* one, sort of—around our house, at school, doing my magic tricks, throwing my voice and doing the Popeye impersonations. People thought I was funny; so I kind of took entertaining for granted. I was full of card tricks, too. Around the house, I was always telling anybody I saw, "Take a card—any card." It was inevitable that I'd start giving little performances. My first one was for my mother's bridge club. They thought I was great; and I *felt* great, making my mother so proud, you know? And after that I went on to give shows at Sunday-school parties, church socials, anywhere they'd have me. I was fourteen when I earned my first fee for my act—three dollars from the Norfolk Rotary Club. Then I began to get a fee like that at picnics, county fairs, 4-H clubs, service clubs, chambers of commerce. I was billed as "The Great Carsoni," wearing a cape my mother had sewed for me.

By 1943, when I graduated from Norfolk High. I was making pretty fair pin money with my act. Funny thing, though, I still didn't have any intention of entertaining as a serious career. I was still very small town in my outlook. It would be another three or four years before I'd find out that the Catskills weren't a dance team. I was still playing with the idea of becoming a psychiatrist, an engineer or a journalist. And I had decided on engineering when I entered college. But the war was on, you know, and I was accepted for a V-12 program that would get me a naval air commission; but they sent me to Columbia University's midshipman school instead; there just weren't any flying training openings then. I got my ensign's commission and went to the Pacific on the battleship *Pennsylvania.* I had dragged a footlocker of gear for my act with me and I entertained the officers and men every chance I got. In the comedy bits, mostly, I'd knock officers; the enlisted men loved that. Later, when I was at Guam, I did the same thing there.

Finally, when I got out, I entered the University of Nebraska, this time trying journalism. I thought it would help me learn to write comedy. But that who-when-where-why-what bit couldn't have bored me more, so I switched to radio and speech. It was while I was at the university that I got my first radio job for ten dollars a week at the local station, WOW, for playing in a comedy Western called *Eddie Sosby and the Radio Rangers.* It came on three mornings a week and I had to get permission to be fifteen minutes late those mornings for my Spanish class. Then, in my senior year, I did a thesis on comedy. I analyzed the best comics then performing and taped excerpts of their performances to illustrate things like timing and sequence, building punch lines, recognition devices and running gags, things like that. Comedians like Fibber McGee and Molly, Jack and Mary Benny, Rochester, Ozzie and Harriet, Milton Berle and Bob Hope. When I got my A.B. degree in 1949, I went straight to my first job, fifty dollars a week for doing anything and everything at WOW. I did commercials, news, station breaks, weather reports, everything.

I guess the next thing was my first marriage—to Jody. We'd been going together several years. Soon my first son was born, Chris. Meanwhile, I got a radio show, *The Squirrel's Nest* I called it, and I picked up twenty-five dollars on the side for magic acts I'd do anywhere I could.

I was getting along well enough where I was, but at the same time, I knew that I could never go very far as long as I stayed in Nebraska. The action and the opportunities were all either in New York or California. So I got a cameraman friend to shoot a half-hour film of me doing a little bit of everything I could do. When a vacation came up, I packed the wife and kids in our beat-up Olds, with a U-Haul trailer, and we took off for California. When we arrived in San Francisco, I knocked at every radio and TV door; at most of them, I couldn't even get inside. They'd say, "No openings, sorry." So we went on into Los Angeles—looking like something out of *Grapes of Wrath* driving down Sunset Boulevard. Same kind of hearty welcome.

But finally, a childhood family friend, Bill Brennan, who had gone into radio sales in L.A., successfully recommended me for a staff-announcer job that had opened at KNXT, a local station. I went there and did everything except sweep out the place. When I could find the time, like on nights when I was disc-jockeying, while the record was playing, I was sitting there in the booth putting together an idea for a TV show. See, I had made an agreement with myself when I got to L.A.—that if I didn't have my own show after a year, I was going to move on to New York. I was never one who believed in "waiting for the breaks." I believe we make our own breaks. Well, the CBS people finally looked at my idea and gave me a spot they had open locally on Sunday afternoons. You won't believe the budget—for each show, twenty-five dollars! I wrote my own scripts, mimeographed them and acted in them—and got pretty fair newspaper notices. On one show, I had a friend rush past the camera on the air and I announced, "That was my guest today, Red Skelton." Well, Skelton heard about it and really did turn up for one of my shows. Then some others did, including Fred Allen. Skelton and I really got on well, and finally he offered me a job writing for his show. I grabbed it.

I guess you'd call it the proverbial big break when the telephone rang one day and somebody told me Skelton had been hurt in a rehearsal. He was supposed to walk through one of those breakaway doors, but the door hadn't broken and Red had been knocked cold about ninety minutes before showtime. I had always been doing bits and cracking gags around the office and they wanted to know if I could make it to the station and go on for Red. I don't know how I got there in time, but I did. And I made cracks about Red getting hurt and said, "The way I fell out here, I think Red's doctor ought to be doing this show." Well, it came off all right. I got good notices. And that got me my next job—*The Johnny Carson Show.* That was my first *big* lesson. It ran out its contracted thirty-nine weeks in 1955 and then folded. That's where I learned that if you get too many cooks involved, that if you don't keep control, you're going to bomb out, and there's nobody to blame but yourself.

PLAYBOY: Will you explain what you mean by that?

CARSON: I mean that it was primarily through my own naïveté that the show failed. I had built the show initially around a format of low-key skits and commentary on topical subjects—something rather like *The Tonight Show.* We got good reviews, but the network people felt the ratings should have been higher, and I let them start telling me what to do. "We've got to make the show *important,*" they told me. How would they go about doing that? With chorus girls? They were going to make me into Jackie Gleason! I'd come rushing on in a shower of balloons, with chorus girls yipping, "Here comes the *star* of the show, *Johnny Carson*!" And the rest followed in that vein. I let myself be a poor imitation, and that's sure, swift death for any entertainer. But I think if nobody ever fails, he never has success. The show flopped—but to me only in the sense that it went off the air after thirty-nine weeks. I learned the hard way that you have to go with your decisions.

PLAYBOY: Do you consider that show your greatest failure?

CARSON: Professionally it was. Personally, no. That was when I was divorced from my first wife. That's the lowest I've ever felt, the worst personal experience of my life. We'd been married ten years—since college, in fact. And children were involved—three sons. I think that's the worst guilt hang-up you can have, when children are involved. But divorce sometimes is the only answer. I think it's almost immoral to keep on with a marriage that's really bad.

PLAYBOY: After the low point you described, when *The Johnny Carson Show* went off the air, did things begin to improve professionally?

CARSON: Not by a long shot. I still had a lot more to learn—this time about the people who are supposed to give a performer so much *help* in this business. There I was: My show was closed. I was out of work. That kind of news flies throughout the show-business world with the speed of light. You're out.

This was about the time I dropped back financially until I had to borrow from my father. I decided I had to go to New York. I couldn't do any worse there and I might do better. So I borrowed more, from a bank that was good enough to let me have it. And in New York, finally I got the chance to go on *Who Do You Trust?* Now, do you want to guess what happened? When I get solid on that show, really doing all right, here come this agency's top guys. Big deal—old buddy-buddy, let bygones be bygones, no hard feelings, let's forget the past. "How about our representing you again? We've got it all figured out how to shoot you straight to the top." I listened until they finished their spiel and then I said, "Thank you, no gentlemen. Where were you when I needed you?" Anyway, I finally went with another agency, MCA, one of the giants. I was doing fine now, getting the treatment they call "servicing the client." I remember one day I was getting ready to leave their office to do the show, and this agency man makes moves to go with me. I asked him, "What are you doing?" He said, "Don't you want me to go to the show with you?" I told him I thought I could make it alone. What I *felt* like telling him was, "You want to do something for me? Iron my shirts." I don't even like to think about it. But now, I don't even have an agency. MCA dissolved, you know. I've got a lawyer who handles most of my affairs. I've *learned.* Agencies play the percentages. You make it, they'll take ten percent. When I needed 'em, nobody was there. I'll never forget it. I'm just telling it the way it is. If somebody wants to call that being a loner, if somebody wants to call that being vindictive, then so be it!

PLAYBOY: How did the break come from *Who Do You Trust?* to *The Tonight Show?*

CARSON: In my first four years on *Who Do You Trust?* I'd been offered all kinds of situation-comedy shows, but I had turned them down for one or another reason. And I had been doing guest spots, and I had filled in for Paar on *Tonight,* and I had done pretty well as his replacement. It was NBC that came up with the offer for me to replace Paar permanently. I turned it down, cold; not many people know that. I just wasn't sure I could cut it. I just didn't feel I could make that jump from a half-hour daily quiz show to doing an hour and forty-five minutes every night. I was doing fine in daytime TV; I was solid and secure. And I felt I'd be stupid to try to replace Jack Paar. But I kept sitting in for him. And then, some months later, NBC made their offer again; Jack was nearer to leaving the show. Somebody had to replace him. My manager got on me, insisting that I owed myself the opportunity of reaching the big night audience. And NBC said they would wait until I finished my contract on *Who Do You Trust?* While all this was going on, I was gradually building more confidence in myself—the more I thought about it. Nobody could tell me; I had to tell myself I could do it. And finally I did; I accepted the offer. Everyone I knew had some advice after that. One group told me I was nuts to try replacing Paar, but that made me all the more determined. Others became instant producers and told me, "Here's how to handle that show. . . ." That bugged me; I'd been through that in California and lost a good show because of it. I had cabdrivers, waiters, everybody giving me advice.

Two things were in the back of my head: One was that I wasn't going to be any imitation of Jack Paar; I was going to be Johnny Carson. The other thing was that I wanted the show to make the most of being the last area in television that the medium originally was supposed to be—live, immediate entertainment. I knew it wasn't going to be any sauntering in and sitting at a desk and that's all. The main thing in my mind that I had going for me was that I'd done nearly everything you could in the industry—but at the same time I knew that thinking that way was a danger. If I went out there with every critic waiting, and if I did everything I knew how to do, it would look like deliberate showing off, like trying to say, "Hey, look at me—I'm so versatile!" I had to fight that natural temptation to go out there and make some big impression. Finally, I decided that the best thing I could do was forget trying to do a lot of preplanning. I didn't want to come out with something that smacked of a month's preparation, because I wasn't going to be able to keep that up every night. It all boiled down to just going out there and being my natural self and seeing what would happen.

PLAYBOY: What happened, of course, was one of the most remarkable successes in television history. But you mentioned going out there and being your natural self. Do you, really?

CARSON: Are we back to that—my reputation for being cold and aloof, for being a loner and living in a shell and all that crap? Look, I'm an entertainer; I try to give the public what it wants while I'm on the screen, and I'm completely sincere about it. If I don't happen to be a laughing boy off the screen, that doesn't make me a hypocrite or a phony. In any case, what I am and what I do on my own, it seems to me, is nobody's business but mine. As long as I don't commit any crimes, you have no right to judge me except by my performance as a professional. On that level, you're welcome to think whatever you want about me. But there's only one critic whose opinion I really value, in the final analysis: Johnny Carson. I have never needed any entourage standing around bolstering my ego. I'm secure. I know exactly who and what I am. I don't need to be told. I make no apologies for being the way I am. I'm not going to run around crying that I'm misunderstood. I play my life straight—the way I see it. I'm grateful to audiences for watching me and for enjoying what I do—but I'm not one of those who believe that a successful entertainer is *made* by the public, as is so often said. You become successful, the way I see it, only if you're good enough to deliver what the public enjoys. If you're not, you won't have any audience; so the performer really has more to do with his success than the public does.

As for myself, I've worked ever since I was a kid with a two-bit kit of magic tricks trying to improve my skills at entertaining whatever public I had—and to make myself ready, whenever the breaks came, to entertain a wider and more demanding public. Entertainment is like any other major industry; it's cold, big business. The business end wants to know one thing: Can you do the job? If you can, you're in, you're *made*; if you can't, you're out.

I knock myself out for the public—five shows a week, ninety minutes a show; and most of every day goes to working on that ninety minutes. It takes more out of me than manual labor would, and I simply won't give any more of myself than that. I demand my right to a private life, just as I respect that right for everybody else. The *Tonight* staff knocks themselves out with me; then they go their way, I go mine, and we get along fine. I make the major decisions. That's my responsibility.

I'm doing the best I know how. I've put my whole life into whatever you see on that screen. But whenever the day comes that I think it's my time to go, I'll be the first to tell the network to get somebody else in that chair. And when I do, they'll be saying, "Who could follow Carson?"—just like they said, "Who could follow Paar?" Well, believe me, somebody can—and will. The public is fickle, and you can be replaced, no matter how good you are. Until that happens, I'm going to go on doing my best. I like my work and I hope you do, too—but if you don't, I really couldn't care less. Take me or leave me—but don't bug me. That's the way I am. That's me. That's it.

WILLIAM F. BUCKLEY, JR.

May 1970

Interviewer: David Butler

Although the PLAYBOY Interview, by 1970, was widely known as a forum for liberal thinking, it was a point of pride among the editors to give opposing—conservative—viewpoints their day, too. At that time, William F. Buckley was considered something of a right-wing gadfly (at a time when most of the media's attention was focused on the left), and this long, serious examination of his views was unusual. Of course, it is also interesting to read today Bill Buckley predicting that Red China would never be admitted to the United Nations, defending Spiro Agnew, and seeing a wonderful future for the government of South Vietnam. In fairness, though, it is Buckley at his most eloquent and silvery tongued. (Editor Fisher later said it was the only interview in which the taped transcripts needed virtually no work before being suitable for publication: the man speaks in perfectly parsed sentences.) Although even then it was no journalistic coup to have landed the ubiquitous Buckley for a chat, it was the most definitive interview of him done at the time—or so he told interviewer and PLAYBOY staffer David Butler.

"Hello, my learned friend. How goes the empire?" Recently returned from a fact-finding trip to Vietnam and in the midst of one of the several speaking tours he makes each year to spread the conservative word, William F. Buckley, Jr., is on the long-distance line with Henry Kissinger, President Nixon's top foreign policy adviser. The call is chatty, but Buckley assures him—by way of preamble to a debriefing session that will take place later in Washington—that "all the indices are good" over in Saigon. "As usual," he adds, "I think I've found the keys to the universe."

"As usual" is right. When he was six years old, Buckley wrote the King of England that it was high time for that country to get serious about repaying its World War One debt. At prep school, he crashed a faculty meeting to denounce a teacher for refusing to allow him to express his political views in class. And within forty-eight hours of his arrival at a San Antonio army base in 1946, he had written the commanding general that the post was mismanaged. An intermediary intercepted that letter—one of the few times cooler heads have prevented Buckley from expressing himself. "To the extent that one has confidence in one's intuitions," Buckley told an interviewer some years ago, "one wants to share them. I have great confidence in mine." During the past two decades, he has used every propaganda device except the teach-in to broadcast those intuitions and, in so doing, has found himself characterized as "an unprincipled, egocentric intellectual exhibitionist," "the most dangerous undergraduate Yale has seen in years" and "an urbane front man for the most primitive and vicious emotions in the land." But Buckley has also been called "a true liberal in the old, traditional sense of the word," "a brilliant journalist" and—by his

friend John Kenneth Galbraith—"the only reactionary I ever met with a sense of humor." In an insightful essay, "God's Right Hand," for last May's PLAYBOY, *George F. Gilder captured the prevalent Middle American attitude toward his subject: " 'He's so brilliant he frightens me,' " an unidentified middle-aged woman gushed. " 'But I love it.' "*

Buckley got his first big chance to give real offense at Yale, which he entered after his army service. There he learned how to fly, was tapped for the best clubs and accepted—while still an undergraduate—as a faculty member in the Spanish department. But all this was peripheral to his polemics: As a debater and chairman of the Yale Daily News, *he gave notice that at least one member of the Fifties' Silent Generation wasn't going to be. In 1951, the year after his graduation, Buckley leaped from the status of local irritant to national notoriety as the* bête noire *of liberal education with* God and Man at Yale—*a book that anticipated, in spades, the faculty critiques that so many of today's militant student bodies produce for themselves.*

But the deepest and most bitter liberal animosity toward Buckley dates from the appearance of McCarthy and his Enemies, *which Buckley and his brother-in-law L. Brent Bozell wrote in 1954. The two writers acknowledged some of the Wisconsin Senator's excesses—Buckley would insist that they acknowledged all of them—but maintained that "as long as McCarthyism fixes its goal with its present precision, it is a movement around which men of good will and stern morality can close ranks."*

Following the publication of McCarthy and His Enemies, *Buckley poured his energies—and his money—into* National Review, *America's only substantial right-of-center political journal. In the first issue of the magazine—which appeared in 1955 ten days before his thirtieth birthday—Buckley announced that its purpose was to "stand athwart history yelling 'Stop!' at a time when no one is inclined to do so, or to have much patience with those who urge it." In 1962, he began writing his syndicated newspaper column "On the Right," and in 1966, launched his television show* Firing Line.

It was in his magazine that Buckley refined his contempt for liberal Republicanism to the point where he felt obliged to oppose its most glamorous embodiment, John V. Lindsay, in New York's 1965 mayoral campaign. That adventure failed to get Buckley elected—which neither he nor anyone else ever considered a real possibility—but Buckley kept his cool through the campaign: He eschewed sidewalk politicking altogether, and the closest he got to venom was the crack "which fact should be obvious," in response to his Democratic opponent's boast of having been educated by the city of New York. But the famous Buckley sangfroid vanished in a flash three summers later, when he exchanged insults with fellow commentator Gore Vidal on ABC-TV during the course of the roughest night of the 1968 Democratic Convention in Chicago. "Not since George Sanders divorced Zsa Zsa Gabor has so much talent been wasted on such a nasty spat," Newsweek *said of the encounter, its subsequent magazine amplifications and resultant lawsuits.*

Associate editor David Butler, who conducted this interview with Buckley in locales as far-flung as Stockton, California, and Rougemont, Switzerland—Buckley's winter retreat—writes of his subject: "He exudes a personal charm that comes across in neither his lectures nor his writing and seldom in his television appearances. In a hotel, for example, the bellboys who bring him the several pots of coffee he drinks a day are treated to the kind of smiles and small talk that can issue only from a man who genuinely likes people, and the strangers who stop him on the street to say they watch Firing Line *every week are answered with a 'Nice to meet you' and a toothy smile that would shame Nelson Rockefeller.*

"The second remarkable thing about the man is his energy. 'God, I had a great day last week,' he told me when I arrived in Switzerland. 'I did a column on the train to Geneva in the morning, gave a talk there, came back here and skied all afternoon, went to a marvelous chamber-music concert that night and then got in a couple of hours' painting.' In New York, we talked one night until 2:30. Buckley then felt like singing, so we took our cognac and cigars into the living room for a half-hour of Cole Porter songs—Buckley is an accomplished pianist—and, finally, he insisted on driving me to my hotel on his Honda. When I arrived at his apartment later that same day, his gracious, almost equally energetic wife, Patricia, told me he had been up, making the day's first phone calls, at seven. Despite the pace, when Buckley folded himself into a chair for a taping session, it was as if no one else in the world had a claim on his time. His voice was less onorous than it is in public, but his answers were as erudite and intricately phrased as his writing. My first meeting with Buckley took place in mid-December, and it was with the imminent end of the decade that the questioning began."

PLAYBOY: It's already a cliché to say that the Sixties were a remarkable decade. Looking back, what event or development stands out in your mind as most important?

BUCKLEY: The philosophical acceptance of coexistence by the West.

PLAYBOY: Why "philosophical"?

BUCKLEY: Because a military acceptance of coexistence is one thing; that I understand. But since America is, for good reasons and bad, a moralistic power, the philosophical acceptance of coexistence ends us up in hot pursuit of *reasons* for that acceptance. We continue to find excuses for being cordial to the Soviet Union; our denunciations of that country's periodic barbarisms—as in Czechoslovakia—become purely perfunctory. This is a callousing experience; it is a lesion of our moral conscience, the historical effects of which cannot be calculated, but they will be bad.

PLAYBOY: Among the reasons cited for a détente with the Soviet Union is the fact that the money spent on continuing hot and cold wars with the Communist bloc would be better spent for domestic programs. With the 150 billion dollars we've spent in Vietnam since 1965, according to some estimates, we could have eliminated pollution throughout the country and rebuilt twenty-four major cities into what New York's Mayor Lindsay has said would be "paradises." Do you think our priorities are out of order?

BUCKLEY: When I find myself entertaining that possibility, I dismiss my thinking as puerile. But first let me register my objection to your figures: It's superficial to say that the Vietnam War has cost us 150 billion dollars. It has cost us X dollars in excess of what we would have spent on military or paramilitary enterprises even if there had been no war. That sum I have seen estimated at between eighteen and twenty-two billion dollars a year. Now, suppose I were to tell you that if Kerenski had prevailed in Russia in 1917, we would at this point have a budget excess sufficient to create the city of Oz in Harlem and everywhere else. The correct response to such a statement, for grownups, is twofold. First, we are not—unfortunately—in a position to dictate the activity of the enemy; we cannot ask him please to let down because we need money for Harlem. Second, there are no grounds for assuming that the American people would have consented to spending the kind of money we're spending on the Vietnam War for general-welfare projects. They might have said, "No, we'd rather keep the money and do what we want with it." I suspect they *would* have said just that, and with justification: The bulk of the progress that has been made in America has been made by the private sector.

PLAYBOY: With reference to the first part of your answer: At the strategic-arms-limitations talks, aren't we actually asking the Russians to let down their guard if we let ours down?

BUCKLEY: Yes, we are. And, ideally, there would be massive, universal disarmament. But we don't live in an ideal world. The fact is that the Soviet Union is prepared to make remarkable sacrifices at home in order to maintain its military muscle abroad. It is prepared to do so in a world that has seen the United States pull out from dozens of opportunities to imperialize. We have walked out of twenty-one countries—I think that's the accepted figure—that we've occupied in the past thirty years. The Soviet Union has walked only out of Austria, for very complicated reasons. Under the circumstances, one must assume that the arrant armament expenditures by the Soviet Union—for instance, twenty billion dollars to develop its ABM system and its MIRVs—have to do with the attraction of a first-strike capability. If the Soviets intended their MIRVs only as a deterrent to an American first strike, they would aim those missiles at American cities. But they aren't being fashioned that way. Now, I don't think the collective leadership of Russia would dream of making a first strike for so long as we are in a position to inflict insupportable damage in a second strike, whatever the urgings of their Dr. Strangeloves, who are not without influence. But, manifestly, America is not preparing for a first strike. If we were, we would be aiming our weapons not at Russia's population centers but at her military installations—and we're not.

PLAYBOY: MIT professor Leo Sartori, writing in *The Saturday Review,* implies that some of our ICBMs are aimed at Russia's missiles rather than at her cities. Doesn't this indicate that the U.S. is prepared—to the point of overkill—for a massive first strike against the Soviet Union?

BUCKLEY: Look. The intellectual, attempting to evaluate the military situation, tends to fasten on a frozen position. He says, "Assuming apocalypse were tomorrow, how would the two sides stand?" But it is the responsibility of the military to understand how military confrontations actually work—which means that you cannot prepare for Tuesday by being absolutely prepared for Monday. In a world in which it takes between four and eight years to develop what is actually intended as a first-strike *defensive* system, you may, in the course of preparing for that system, find yourself temporarily with a first-strike superiority. A caricature of what I'm talking about is the sudden apprehension by Darryl Zanuck when he was filming *The Longest Day*—on the Normandy invasion—that he actually found himself in command of the third largest military force in the world. Presumably, he would not have used it even to attack Otto Preminger. You need to ask yourself the subjective question: Do I know people in the United States whose hands are on the trigger, who are actually conspiring to opportunize on the temporary military advantage? It seems plain to me that the recent history of the United States ought to be sufficient to appease the doubts of the doubters. In fact, we have had such superiority even at moments when the enemy was at its most provocative—and yet we haven't used it.

PLAYBOY: Hasn't it been authoritatively asserted that U.S. superiority is overwhelmingly beyond the defensive or offensive necessity of any conceivable threat from another nuclear power?

BUCKLEY: That's a military judgment and I don't feel qualified to pronounce about it. I feel confident only to make an elementary philosophical point. I tend to believe that what the lawyers call "an excess of caution" is not something we should penalize the military for. I *want* an excess of caution, because I understand a mistake in that direction to be apocalyptic in its consequences. Now, if you say, "I can establish that we are spending money to develop a redundant weapon," my answer is: Go ahead and establish it. Meanwhile, I would rather side with the cautious, the prudent people. And here I find myself wondering how is is that Robert McNamara—who, for some reason, tends to be rather beloved by the liberals—how come *he* didn't object to the technological-military evolution that nowadays strikes so many people as untoward. And, again, why have we so drastically reversed our attitudes concerning what was for so long considered the liberal thing to do? During the Fifties, the great accent was on defense. The military-industrial complex—as you know—used to be called the "Arsenal of Democracy." Now, all of a sudden, when you talk about ABMs, the same people who encouraged us to spend fifty billion dollars—yes, fifty billion dollars—on defense during the Fifties object to spending an extra five billion dollars on defense in the Sixties.

PLAYBOY: You seem to delight in reminding people that liberals are capable of changing their minds in the light of changing circumstances. Why?

BUCKLEY: Quite apart from the fact that delightful pursuits are delightful, it is important for any ideological grouping to confront historical experience. For one thing, it makes the ideologists less arrogant; or it should. That ought to be a national objective, after we eliminate poverty.

PLAYBOY: Ten years ago, wasn't there more reason than there is now to believe that the Russians wanted to bury us, militarily as well as ideologically?

BUCKLEY: That is an exercise in ideological self-indulgence. How do you account for the anomalies? Such as the crash program the Soviet Union has developed in ABMs and MIRVs.

PLAYBOY: One can only repeat that the U.S. is developing these systems as furiously as Russia is; and many observers feel that the Soviets have, therefore, just as much reason to suspect our intentions as we do theirs. But we'd like to return to your observation that the United States has walked out of twenty-one countries in the past thirty years and ask this: Doesn't the fact that we've also walked *into* Vietnam and Santo Domingo, tried to walk into Cuba at the Bay of Pigs and attempted to control many other countries through quasi-military, CIA-type operations leave us open to the charge of imperialism you impute to the USSR?

BUCKLEY: Of course. But we are always at the mercy of the naïve. Imperialism suggests the domination of a country for the commercial or glorious benefit of oneself. The Soviet Union began its experience in imperialism not merely by jailing and executing people who disagreed with it but by systematic despoliation. In Czechoslovakia, for instance, they took one, two, three billion dollars' worth of capital goods and removed them physically to the Soviet Union. Far from doing anything of the sort, we did exactly the contrary; we sent our own capital goods to places like France and England and Spain and Latin America. I can't think of any country that we've "dominated" or "imperialized"—in the sense in which you use those words—that is worse off as a result of its experience with America than it would have been had we not entered into a temporary relationship with it.

PLAYBOY: One could argue that South Vietnam is such a country.

BUCKLEY: South Vietnam? My God! Above *all,* not South Vietnam. Not unless one is willing to say that South Vietnam would be better off satellized by North Vietnam—and derivatively by Asian communism—and consigned to perpetual tyranny. Put it this way: I will assent to the proposition that South Vietnam has been harmed by America's efforts during the past five years only to somebody who would say that France was harmed by the efforts of the Allied armies to liberate it during the Second World War.

PLAYBOY: We won't say that, but we will agree with the increasingly popular opinion that our adventure there has been a disaster—to us, as well as to South and North Vietnam—from the beginning. Yet you said recently that "the indices in Vietnam are good," which is something even McNamara and Westmoreland stopped saying three years ago. Why?

BUCKLEY: Because the indices *are* good, right down the line: First, there is the prestige of Thieu and our increased identification with him. A week or so after the 1968 Tet offensive, Professor J. Kenneth Galbraith gave it as the conventional wisdom that Thieu's government would fall within a matter of weeks. I predict that in the next election, he will get a significantly greater vote than he got the last time. Second, there is a lower rate of infiltration from the North. Third, the area controlled by the good guys is now much greater than it has ever been. The fourth positive index is the introduction in South Vietnam of a nonregular army, the equivalent of a militia, which makes it possible for people simultaneously to till their land during the day and yet be part of a large constabulary. Still another indication is the relative rise in South Vietnamese casualties and decrease in American casualties, which shows that they are beginning to shoulder even more of the human burden of the war.

PLAYBOY: How do you feel about Thieu's suppression of dissent among his political opposition—even moderate Buddhists and Catholics who have done nothing more subversive than suggest consideration of a postwar coalition government?

BUCKLEY: I am not in a position to judge whether Thieu suppresses more or fewer people than he should suppress in order to achieve his goals. I know that my own countrymen were prepared to take tens of thousands of innocent Japanese and throw them in jail during World War Two. And I know that moral-political revulsion over that act didn't come until years later—when we recognized that what we had done to the nisei was, in fact, historically unnecessary. But it remains that a man who was tempered by four centuries of parliamentary experience—Franklin D. Roosevelt—thought it an altogether appropriate thing to do. I am not, under the circumstances, confident that I can authoritatively advise Thieu what is the right kind of suppression to engage in during a civil war.

PLAYBOY: Then it *is* a civil war and not a case of Communist expansionism exported from Russia and China?

BUCKLEY: Yes, it is a civil war, provided one is prepared to define any war as a civil war if one finds a significant number of collaborationists within the indigenous population. There are South Vietnamese Communists, even as there were Norwegian quislings, Northern Copperheads and French appeasers. General Pétain was sentenced to death for obliging the Nazis less effusively than the Vietcong have done the northern imperialists. If the "civil" insurrection in Vietnam had depended on its own resources, it would have lasted about as long as the insurrection of the Huks in the Philippines.

PLAYBOY: You frequently use the fact that Thieu has fired twelve hundred civil servants to demonstrate what you consider his opposition to corruption. But weren't many of those firings really intended to get rid of his political opponents?

BUCKLEY: I didn't think to ask Thieu when I was over there. I assume it is because they were corrupt—at least the ones I'm talking about. I don't know how many he has fired for opposing his policies. I don't know how many officials Lyndon Johnson fired because they opposed *his* policies, or exactly how many FDR did—plenty, I assume. Incidentally, I thought John Roche made a rather good point when he said that the critics of Thieu fail to account for the fact that he moves about without any difficulty at all—without bodyguards or any other protection—throughout South Vietnam. And they fail to point out that he has done something no tyrant *ever* does, which is to arm the citizenry. The very first thing he did, when he became president, was to ask Westmoreland to increase the arming of the people. In Cuba, if you're caught with an unlicensed rifle, you're liable to be executed.

PLAYBOY: Your satisfaction with the relative rise in South Vietnamese casualties indicates that you believe in Vietnamization. If, as Presidents Johnson and Nixon have claimed, we have a moral and legal commitment to defend the South Vietnamese, why are we now disengaging?

BUCKLEY: We're not disengaging. We have a moral and legal commitment to give aid to the South Vietnamese in resisting aggression, pursuant to the protocol that extended the SEATO treaty to that area. We did not specify in SEATO the nature of the aid we would give. It is Nixon's strategy to arrive at a realistic formula: indigenous manpower and external material aid, precisely the way the Soviet Union and China have been handling the situation in behalf of North Vietnam. I advocated such a formula five years ago. Allowing for the cultural lag, it is time for its adoption.

PLAYBOY: Do you feel it was wrong, then, to send our troops in the first place?

BUCKLEY: No, we had to. The South Vietnamese were not prepared to defend themselves.

PLAYBOY: In other words, though it was right to send them in when we did, it's right to withdraw them now. Are you saying that everything we've done there has been correct?

BUCKLEY: Not at all—there are plenty of things we've done wrong. We shouldn't have stopped the bombing of the North and put the restrictions on it that we did. And, above all, I continue to believe that Japan is the key to that part of the world and that we may very well wish, before this decade is up, that she had the defensive nuclear weapons the nonproliferation treaty denies her.

PLAYBOY: Do you think that if America remains steadfast in Vietnam—with or without the support of our allies in Asia or Western Europe—the Communists will be less likely to test our commitments elsewhere in the world?

BUCKLEY: It's hard to say. In order to answer that question, you have to ask yourself: What is the point of view of the enemy? I have always maintained that the Soviet Union has been delighted over our experience in South Vietnam. It has cost them very little. But, at the same time, the Soviet Union has to reckon with the psychological realities. The psychological realities in the case of Vietnam are that America isn't prepared to do this sort of thing two or three times a decade. We did it in Korea and we're doing it in South Vietnam. If the Soviet Union decided to mount a challenge—let's say in the Mideast—it will probably have to reckon with the fact of a shortened

American temper. The shortened American temper could result in one of two things. It could result in isolationism, which would please the Soviet Union dearly and encourage it; or that shortened American temper could result in our saying, "Since we cannot afford protracted, graduated South Vietnam–type resistances, we're going to go back to another kind of resistance. We're going to knock the hell out of you."

PLAYBOY: Do you think that bellicose attitude *will* develop—and can you imagine it resulting in a nuclear strike by the U.S., say, over Berlin or in the Mideast?

BUCKLEY: Only if the Soviet Union is capable of a miscalculation on an order that is unimaginable, on the basis of our historical experience with a society that on the one hand is ideologically rabid but on the other appears to have a positively Rotarian instinct for survival.

PLAYBOY: Critics of the war point to the alleged massacre at My Lai to prove our indifference to the lives of Vietnamese civilians. How do you react to that incident, as it has emerged in the press?

BUCKLEY: If, indeed, there were no extenuating circumstances in the case—if everything that Captain Medina has said is proved wrong, for instance—then either we have a case of collective hysteria or we face the appalling alternative that what happened there expresses a trend within America. I find it extremely difficult to indulge that conclusion, for the reason that if it were so, we would have had many more such incidents.

PLAYBOY: In January 1967, ten Marines were court-martialed on charges resulting from the murders of a farmer, his mother, his sister, his three-year-old son and five-year-old niece and the gang rape of his wife. From the beginning of 1966 through October 1969, twenty-seven soldiers were convicted by U.S. courts-martial of murdering Vietnamese civilians; and since March 1965, twenty-one sailors and marines have been so convicted. The speculation is that most such crimes by U.S. military personnel against civilians in Vietnam go unreported. So it would seem that there *have* been many other such incidents, though perhaps on a smaller scale.

BUCKLEY: They are either so routine as to go unremarked—like, say, the incremental murder in Manhattan—or so spectacular as to be unbelievable. It took the most extraordinary coordination of ineptitudes to fail to bring the My Lai incident to light. Here we have a Pulitzer Prize–winning story—I predict that it will get the Pulitzer Prize—and yet the two newspaper people who had the story couldn't interest anybody in it for months. Editors wouldn't buy it precisely because they couldn't believe that kind of thing could have been committed on such a scale.

PLAYBOY: Do you see a moral difference between what is alleged to have happened at My Lai and the aerial bombardment of free-fire zones where, it's generally granted, some civilians almost always get killed?

BUCKLEY: Of course. It's a difference explicitly recognized in Thomistic doctrine, where the whole definition of a just war was arrived at. If, in order to achieve a military objective, someone gets killed, that is on one scale of morality—on the permissible scale in warfare. If, however, someone is killed simply for the sake of killing him, unrelated to any military objective, that's different. Nobody would have thought twice about My Lai if there had been a machine-gun nest there and we had plastered the village from the air, resulting in an identical loss of life.

PLAYBOY: But, of course, there wasn't a machine-gun nest there. Most critics of the war put little trust in those who decide which villages and which other targets are legitimate military objectives. Do you?

BUCKLEY: I trust that somewhere along the line there is a constant monitoring of the criteria that are used by people who have that kind of authority. In the specific case of Lyndon Johnson, I am informed that only he *personally* could authorize the bombing of certain targets where considerable civilian carnage might have resulted. I believe that he took that kind of meticulous concern not merely out of political considerations but because he was always very sensitive to the notion that he was an indiscriminate killer.

Let me digress at this point: A few months ago, in Hawaii, a professor informed my audience that we had dropped one and a half times as many bombs on a very small area of Vietnam as were dropped on Germany throughout World War Two. That statistic, he claimed, proves that we are committing genocide in Vietnam. I read the figures differently. It seems to me that if we have dropped that many bombs and killed as few people as we have—there are an awful lot of live Vietnamese left, no matter how you look at it—it must mean that an enormous effort is being made to drop bombs where people *aren't*.

PLAYBOY: According to official sources, several hundred thousand North and South Vietnamese civilians have been killed by American bombing raids. In view of those statistics, do you think the bombing has been justified?

BUCKLEY: It depends on whether there was an alternative, less bloody means of achieving the military objective. How many of those dead would be alive today if the North Vietnamese had desisted from infiltration as their principal technique? And if historical contexts interest you, bear in mind that we killed about as many German civilians in the course of a couple of raids over Dresden as we have killed Vietnamese in the five years in Vietnam.

PLAYBOY: For all our bombing—precise or indiscriminate—we have not yet won the war. Do you think North Vietnam could successfully have resisted the most powerful military nation on earth for this long if it didn't have the support of most Vietnamese, North and South?

BUCKLEY: There are both extensive and succinct ways to answer that. The succinct way is for me to ask you: Could Nazi Germany have triumphed over France without the overwhelming support of the French? My answer is—obviously—yes, Germany could, and did. The South Vietnamese situation is one in which the critical weapon was terror. I have great admiration for my countrymen, but I haven't the *least* idea whether or not we would have the stamina to resist an enemy that had strung up an equivalent number of our elite in the public squares. Roughly speaking, what the South Vietnamese suffered during the high period of terror from 1959 to 1963 would be the equivalent of, say, three million of our politicians, teachers, doctors, engineers and civil servants being executed. How we would behave under the circumstances I don't know. I tend to reject the ethnocentrically arrogant assumption that we Americans are uniquely valiant. I think it's not at all impossible that years from now, people will think of the South Vietnamese resistance through this entire period as one of the truly heroic historical efforts.

PLAYBOY: Weren't many of the South Vietnamese elite, during this same period, jailed or killed by the Diem regime?

BUCKLEY: What you're saying is: Did Diem and the rest of them go to lengths they needn't have gone in order to effect what they wanted to effect, which was the independence of Vietnam? My answer is—I don't know. A very good argument may be made that they didn't go to great-enough lengths. In fact, such an argument could appropriately be engraved on Diem's tombstone.

PLAYBOY: That sounds like an endorsement of political imprisonment and assassination.
BUCKLEY: In time of war? Of course. The detection and shooting down of Admiral Yamamoto was one of the triumphs of American intelligence during the Second World War, and it gets described at least once every ten years in the *Reader's Digest*. You do remember, don't you, how Walter Pidgeon almost assassinated Hitler at Berchtesgaden? Do you remember the political prosecutions during the Second World War, when the New Deal decided that [pro-Nazi authors] George Sylvester Viereck and Lawrence Dennis should be put behind bars, so that we could get on with the war? I think we overdid it. I hope the South Vietnamese aren't as jumpy as we were.
PLAYBOY: Is your claim that the leaders of South Vietnam have been motivated by a desire for independence consistent with their near-total reliance on the U.S.?
BUCKLEY: Of course they've depended on us. They are waging war not against an autarchic aggressor that is satisfied to use its own resources but against an aggressor that—from the very beginning—has been armed by great powers, namely, Red China and the Soviet Union. The South Vietnamese didn't have a *rifle factory* in 1954. As far as I know, neither do they now. And neither did the North Vietnamese.
PLAYBOY: Since you applaud the fact that we rushed to the assistance of the besieged South Vietnamese government, do you also think we should oppose any war of national liberation that happens to have Communist support?
BUCKLEY: No, I wouldn't be willing to make that generality. I'd want to know where it was, what the surrounding situation was, how important it was to either Russia or China at the moment—in short, what the consequences might be. I would like to note that neither of those countries has ever supported a *real* war of national liberation—in lower-case letters—that is, a war in which the objective really *was* national liberation. When the Communist powers get involved, the point is *never* national liberation, always satellization. Now, it seems to me that the United States position ought to be to support whatever elements in a particular country are heading in the better of the apparently available directions. John Stuart Mill says that despotism is excused as a temporary arrangement, provided the purpose of that despotism is to maximize rather than minimize freedom.
PLAYBOY: Isn't the idea of despotism maximizing freedom a contradiction in terms—at least in practice?
BUCKLEY: No. Lincoln put it well when he argued that it could not have been the intention of the framers of the Constitution to sacrifice all future prospects for freedom in order to celebrate constitutional punctilio.
PLAYBOY: Isn't it true that most indigenous Communist movements in Southeast Asia are motivated more by nationalism or by economic needs than by ideological communism?
BUCKLEY: No, it isn't. Most troops simply do what they are told. Intermediaries interpret the formulation that will most inspire a particular group of soldiers to act enthusiastically in obedience to orders—whether that's a matter of telling them that their kamikaze raids will instantly elevate them into the heavenly spheres, to live forever after in glory, or that they will become large landholders, or whatever. But the people who are directing the drives in that part of the world are, in my opinion, genuinely committed to a Communist vision. The general Western assumption has been that time erodes that vision; but it is, nevertheless, true that there is a fundamentalist

Marxism-communism rampant in China today. It may be inevitable that time will overcome that ideological pretension, but that is not the kind of thing around which one writes a foreign policy for the here and now.

PLAYBOY: Considering your hard-line view of China, how do you feel about Nixon's recent diplomatic overtures to Peking?

BUCKLEY: I don't really see why our attitude toward Red China ought to be different from our attitude toward the Soviet Union. The principal international leverage we have at this particular moment has to do with the Russian-Chinese feud. It strikes me as supremely intelligent to constantly advertise to the Soviet Union that, just as we were prepared to side with the Soviet Union in order to effect a victory over Hitler, so are we prepared to understand the potential desirability of a flirtation with Red China in order to contain the Soviet Union. Or the other way around. This strikes me as simply a return to traditional diplomacy.

PLAYBOY: Do you think that we should—and will—recognize Red China?

BUCKLEY: I think we should not recognize her—and that it is unlikely that we will. For one thing, it becomes increasingly apparent that all of the old arguments for recognition of Red China are meaningless. The old arguments were, first, "You can't ignore a nation of eight hundred million people." But it has gradually become manifest that we are hardly ignoring a country by failing to recognize it. As a matter of fact, we are sort of *super*recognizing it. The easy thing to do is to recognize; if you *don't* recognize, you're giving it a very special attention. Point two: The notion that if we recognize Red China, we would then be able to transact some differences with her—to talk about them—has been discredited by experience. We've had hundreds of meetings with Red China; we are probably having one tonight. So we go ahead and have the meetings anyway. Number three: We have discovered from the British experience that the mere fact of having an active consulate or an ambassador in Red China has no effect at all in terms of a thaw. The English have not been able to show that they've accomplished a single thing—even concerning the protection of their own citizens—that they might not have accomplished if they hadn't had their people there. Number four, and finally: It was Lyndon Johnson who said that he would agree to give passports to Americans who wanted to visit Red China—journalists and so on. What then happened, of course, was that Red China refused to grant visas. So that we are therefore left with no adverse practical consequences of a diplomatic nature having to do with the recognition of Red China, but purely with symbolic consequences. And those consequences, in my judgment, argue against recognition.

PLAYBOY: So far, you haven't disagreed with any aspect of President Nixon's foreign policy. One critic has suggested that you may feel a sense of obligation to him for appointing you to the advisory commission of the USIA.

BUCKLEY: Oh, for God's sake. The point is that when I look around the world today and ask myself what it is that I truly care about in international affairs that Nixon has let me down on, I don't come up with anything. On the other hand, I acknowledge that there may be a feeling of restraint deriving not from any appointment to the commission but from the fact that I have seen him once or twice privately. I have discovered a new sensual treat, which, appropriately, the readers of PLAYBOY should be the first to know about. It is to have the President of the United States take notes while you are speaking to him, even though you run the risk that he is scribbling, "Get this bore out of here." It's always a little bit more difficult to be rhetorically ruthless with somebody with whom you spend time. For example, I find it more difficult to be verbally ruthless with Hugh Hefner after meeting him as my guest on *Firing Line* and seeing

him on a couple of other occasions. Beyond that, if I'm kind to Nixon, it's also because I think he needs to be protected from that part of the right whose emphasis is unbalanced in the direction of the paradigm.
PLAYBOY: Is Nixon conservative enough for you?
BUCKLEY: My ideal conservative President would be one who would strike out for certain radical reforms that, in my judgment, would greatly benefit America and augment human freedom. But such a President cannot be elected—at this time—and couldn't get his programs through Congress. It is also true, I think, that the paramount need of this highly divided society at this particular moment is for conciliation; and Nixon—who is making gradual progress while attempting to fortify the bonds of common affection—is a good President from the conservative point of view.
PLAYBOY: Do you think that Vice-President Agnew served the purpose of conciliation when he referred to the leaders of last October's moratorium as "an effete corps of impudent snobs"?
BUCKLEY: No, he served other purposes. There *are* other purposes to be served, such as isolating the sources of discontent and the agitators and merchants of it. Some Presidents do that kind of thing adroitly, some don't. At a moment when we needed reconciliation after Pearl Harbor, I think it was wrong for FDR to call those who were against the war "the New Copperheads." But history appears to have forgiven him.
PLAYBOY: To many liberals, Agnew's attacks on the media late last fall brought to mind the Chinese emperors who executed messengers bringing bad news. Do you think that the press is as objective as it professes to be?
BUCKLEY: When Mr. Nixon in November said that North Vietnam cannot defeat or humiliate the United States, only Americans can do that, he meant that if the American people refuse to back an enterprise that—in the judgment of the men they elected to write their foreign policies—is essential to the good health of this country and of this century, then one must face two alternative explanations for their failure to do so. One is that they have run out of stamina. The other is that they have been constantly hectored into taking an erroneous position because they are insufficiently aware of the dimensions of the problem. He would obviously prefer the latter explanation to the former, as would I. He tends to feel that the majority of morally alert people in America have, for the most part, heard only a single side on the Vietnam issue—in the universities as well as in the press. He is absolutely correct. It is almost impossible, you know, to work your way through Yale or Harvard or Princeton and hear a pro-Vietnam speech. This is a pure caricature of academic freedom.
PLAYBOY: Aren't campus conservatives free to speak—and don't they, often and at length?
BUCKLEY: Well, you must mean students, because there are very few conservative professors. At Princeton, for example, sixty-five percent of the faculty voted for Humphrey in 1968, seven percent for Dick Gregory and seven percent for Nixon. And it's the professors I'm talking about; their capacity, at a college, is to instruct.
PLAYBOY: Then you're suggesting that the faculty allows its political bias to creep into every course.
BUCKLEY: Constantly. In any course in the humanities or social sciences. And not only in their teaching but in the books they assign. It seems to me that the entire academic community collaborated in the demonstration of academic bias when Walt Rostow and Dean Rusk went around looking for an academic post after they left Lyndon Johnson. What kind of a demonstration do you need beyond that? Here are two

people whose academic credentials are absolutely first-rate. But all of a sudden, you find MIT—that paragon of academic freedom and scientific devotion—saying that they assumed Walt Rostow had "forgotten" what he knew about economics as the result of his stay in government. That was one reason given by a senior faculty member; even James Reston made fun of it. You will notice nobody at Harvard went around saying that Galbraith "forgot" what he knew about economics as the result of his service for John Kennedy. Though I don't know. Maybe they hoped he had.

I think the health of any university is damaged by this monopoly of opinion. I spoke at the University of Minnesota a few months ago. A professor—a very distinguished historian—stood up and said that there are fifty professors of history at the university and one Republican, himself; that is, the ratio is fifty to one. Now, how much real political dialogue is the typical student at the University of Minnesota going to be exposed to, under the circumstances? And if he is *not* subjected to a true dialogue, then he tends to think dialogue is unnecessary, that what you need is asseveration. Placard justice: "Hey, hey, LBJ—how many kids did you kill today?"

PLAYBOY: Don't you think most students get the pro-Vietnam argument from their fathers?

BUCKLEY: That's unrealistic. Students are terrific snobs. I was one myself, though I had no right to be with my own father. The fact is that unless your father is right up with the academic vernacular—unless he's read Douglas Pike as recently as last week—you tend to feel that he's not equipped to discuss serious intellectual matters with you. In any case, I think that this hegemony of thought within the colleges is something that—perhaps without even knowing it—Agnew is scratching up against.

PLAYBOY: In his speech on TV news, the Vice-President's avowals of distaste for censorship, coupled with his allusions to the power of the FCC to withhold broadcasting licenses, struck many liberals as hypocrisy. How do you feel about it?

BUCKLEY: I think they were entitled to think of it as at least potentially hypocritical. I find absolutely mysterious the way in which the debate was ultimately joined. My devoted friend Frank Stanton, who emerged as the spokesman for the victims of this pogrom—or intended pogrom—didn't, for instance, pause to remark that Congress has *already* withheld total freedom from the industry. The whole equal-time provision is an effort by the Congress of the United States to say to the networks and television and radio stations, "Certain freedoms you don't have." The FCC finds as much in the fairness doctrine every year as the Supreme Court finds in the First Amendment.

PLAYBOY: So it was really unnecessary for Agnew to refer to licensing?

BUCKLEY: It may be that Agnew's speech will serve some sort of a maieutic function—that it will tease out of the system a public policy concerning the tendentious limits to which an individual station owner may go. Such a policy would be a refinement of the fairness doctrine, which was not only accepted but applauded by liberals as recently as four or five years ago. In any case, *I* would like to say: Let any radio or TV station owner do what he wants. If he wants to put only Benjamin Spock on from midnight to midnight, let him do it. But make it as hard as possible for him to achieve monopoly status—by licensing pay-TV, which is precisely the way to wed the individual eccentric with his individual network or station.

PLAYBOY: What was your reaction to the Vice-President's blast at the liberal *Washington Post* and *New York Times*?

BUCKLEY: If the press is so easily intimidated as to feel threatened by three speeches by the Vice-President of the United States—if all those effete snobs are moral pygmies after all—then I ought to be even more worried about the press than I am. Mr. Agnew is not Mussolini; for better or worse, he cannot close down *The New York Times*. To sum up: I think what Mr. Agnew was attempting to say to the American people was that, particularly in New York, the networks and the commentators tend to reflect a single point of view—they look and act like the Rockettes—and that it is necessary for people to escape from the assumption that that is the only point of view. I think he has done an extremely useful service. Of course, it isn't just Mr. Agnew who came to such a conclusion: The identical conclusion was arrived at a few weeks earlier by Theodore White, who is a renowned liberal, on my television program. Agnew was simply accenting the obvious: and the obvious, when it has been taboo to state it, tends to hurt. *Ce n'est que la vêritê qui blesse,* as Mr. Agnew would put it.

PLAYBOY: How would you feel if Agnew were to become President?

BUCKLEY: I have been persuaded for several years that the office of the President is so staggeringly complicated that nobody can, by conventional measurement, be "a good President." That is to say that nobody can conceivably oversee the range of activities that, technically, the President is responsible for overseeing. Under the circumstances, whereas it is widely supposed that the President needs to be a man of more and more complicated attainments, I tend to feel that he needs to be less and less a man of complicated attainments. A hundred years ago, a President really had to run the Post Office, among other things. Today, what one needs most from a President is good will, a working intelligence and sound character. The people who praise Harry Truman were willing to point this out at the time, incidentally, but were not willing to remember the thought when it looked as though Goldwater might be nominated by the Republican Party. Second, I do think that when a man becomes President, a transmogrification takes place: that which was theretofore inconceivable becomes somehow conceivable. Nobody could really imagine Harry Truman—even himself, as he subsequently confessed—as President. Allan Drury dwells on this in one of his books. On Monday, the man is just that vicious, sniping, polemical, Nixonite Vice-President: on Tuesday, he's inaugurated and suddenly things happen not only to his critics and to the people but also to him. In short, Agnew wouldn't sound like Agnew if he were President—and, in a sense, properly so.

PLAYBOY: When you list good will, a working intelligence and sound character as what we need most from a President, do you mean regardless of ideology?

BUCKLEY: A man can't have a working intelligence, as distinguished from an abstract intelligence, without a reasonably sound "ideology"—a word I don't use much.

PLAYBOY: By reasonably sound, you mean reasonably conservative.

BUCKLEY: Yes. Conservatism is the politics of reality.

PLAYBOY: Do you think the administration is using Agnew in an attempt to wrest away some of the support for George Wallace in the South?

BUCKLEY: I hope so. Anybody who can take nine million votes that went to George Wallace, baptise them and rededicate them to a hygienic conservatism certainly has my best wishes. It would be as though Adlai Stevenson had addressed the Communist Party and urged them to desert and follow the Democratic Party.

PLAYBOY: We note that in citing the West's acceptance of coexistence as the most significant development of the Sixties, you apparently downgrade the importance of the black revolution, which many consider the milestone of the decade. Why?

BUCKLEY: I think that the important philosophical fight in the area of American black-white relations was won by Abraham Lincoln, who insisted on the metaphysical fact of human equality. This was the great achievement of the American nineteenth century. The next milestone, as far as the Negroes are concerned, will come when whites turn to—and seek out—Negroes as a result of their individual achievements. This has come in some places and will come in others, but it is going to take time. It is certainly open to speculation whether all of the activities of the past fifteen years have significantly accelerated that emancipation.

PLAYBOY: Do you think the black struggle in the past fifteen years has *retarded* that emancipation?

BUCKLEY: America has, lately, given herself over to the promulgation of unrealizable goals, which dooms her to frustration, if not to despair. Voegelin calls it the immanentization of the eschaton—broadly speaking, consigning that which properly belongs to the end of life to the temporal order. That can lead only to grave dissatisfaction. The very idea of "Freedom now" was an invitation to frustration. *Now* means something or it means nothing. When months and then years went by and the kind of dream that Martin Luther King spoke about in 1963 in Washington didn't come true, a totally predictable frustration set in. It is one thing to engage in great ventures in amelioration; it is another to engage in great ventures in utopianization.

PLAYBOY: Couldn't it be argued that the career of Martin Luther King—even if it didn't create freedom—inspired a sense of dignity in the masses of black people?

BUCKLEY: It could. It could also be argued that the dignity was already there. What Dr. King inspired was more nearly self-assertion, which sometimes is and sometimes isn't the same as dignity.

PLAYBOY: Your belief that black Americans had dignity before the appearance of King strikes us as less important than the fact that millions of blacks themselves didn't think so.

BUCKLEY: Look. There was anti-black discrimination pre-King, there is anti-black discrimination post-King. If dignity is something that comes to you only after you succeed in putting an end to discrimination, then the blacks didn't have dignity then and don't have it now. If dignity is something that comes to you by transcending discrimination, then I say they had it then even as they have it now. What some blacks—and a lot of whites—now have, which is distinctive, is a greater tendency to self-assertion. I am trying to insist that that isn't the same as dignity.

PLAYBOY: In an *Atlantic* magazine interview on the occasion of your unsuccessful candidacy for membership in the Yale Corporation two years ago, you made the unluckily timed crack: "It was only a very few years ago that official Yale conferred a doctor of laws on Martin Luther King, who more clearly qualifies as a doctor of lawbreaking." A few weeks later, Dr. King was assassinated. Did you regret the publication of your quote? And do you think of Martin Luther King as a pernicious force in American history?

BUCKLEY: I regret but am philosophical about the fact that there is a lead time in journalism, so that you sometimes find yourself reading something that is inappropriate the day you read it, which, however, was altogether appropriate the day you wrote it. *Look* magazine's cover, after JFK's assassination, had on it, "Kennedy Could Lose." As regards what I wrote, I think it was correct. I wrote it a couple of days after Dr. King threatened massive civil disobedience if the forthcoming demands of his poverty marchers were not met. I don't want to answer your question about whether he will be seen as a good or a bad force in history, because I don't know. He was clearly a bad force on the matter of obeying the law. His attempt to sanctify civil disobedience is at least one of his legacies; if it emerges as his principal legacy, then he should certainly be remembered as a bad force. If, on the other hand, his principal legacy emerges—the wrinkles having been ironed out by the passage of time—as a spiritual leader of an oppressed people whom he urged on to great endeavors, then he will be a great historical force.

PLAYBOY: Could you yourself ever justify breaking a law?

BUCKLEY: Yes. I would justify the breaking of a law that, by more or less settled agreement on the separation of powers since the time of Christ, is ontologically outside the state's jurisdiction. For instance, when the government of Mexico, beginning a government or two after the overthrow of Diaz, forbade Mexicans to attend church, hundreds of thousands of them did so anyway, in underground churches. It seems to me that this is an excellent example of justified breaking of the law, against which there could be no reasonable recrimination.

PLAYBOY: Then it depends on the individual's idea of the character of the government as well as of the laws.

BUCKLEY: No, it doesn't. I didn't say the individual's idea and I didn't say the character of the government. I said the settled idea of the separation of powers and I said the character of the law, not of the government. Scholars, secular and religious, have agreed for two thousand years that the state has no business interfering in the traffic between man and his God; any attempt to do so breaks the legal bond that the government has over the individual. I assume, of course, that we are talking about free or relatively free societies. If we're talking about totalitarian societies, the essential relationship of the subject to the slavemaster ought to be mutinous.

PLAYBOY: Since you have referred to the religious justification for lawbreaking: Do you think a young man has the right to use the Fifth Commandment—thou shalt not kill—as justification for refusing induction into the Armed Forces?

BUCKLEY: The Fifth Commandment obviously is not a proscription against taking another man's life under any circumstances. Moses led a pretty robust army even after he came down from Mt. Sinai. The rendering should have been, "Thou shalt not murder." I am not correcting God—He had it right. The imprecision was King James'.

PLAYBOY: You said that the essential relationship of subject to slavemaster ought to be mutinous in totalitarian societies. Aren't there degrees of unfreedom—and isn't there a point at which the erosion of freedom must be resisted, perhaps by civil disobedience?

BUCKLEY: There is a point at which an individual citizen rejects his society. He has at that point several options. One is to leave. The society ought not to hinder his doing so. A second is to agitate for reform. The society ought to protect his right to do so. A third is drop out. The society ought to let him alone, to the extent it is possible to disengage reciprocating gears. A fourth is to disobey the laws or to revolutionize. In that event, the society ought to imprison, exile or execute him.

PLAYBOY: You've identified what you consider the utopianism of Martin Luther King's call for "Freedom now" as a negative aspect of the civil-rights revolution. Do you see any positive aspects to that revolution?

BUCKLEY: Yes, several. I supported Dr. King in Montgomery. I very much believe in voluntary boycotts. If Woolworth isn't going to let you sit down and buy a Coca-Cola, then goddamn it, don't patronize Woolworth. I certainly believe in equal access to public accommodations and I have always opposed the denial to anyone of any constitutionally specified right, by reason of race, color or creed.

PLAYBOY: Including the right to vote?

BUCKLEY: Yes.

PLAYBOY: But you have argued, haven't you, for limiting the franchise?
BUCKLEY: Yes. I think too many people are voting.
PLAYBOY: Whom would you exclude?
BUCKLEY: A while ago, George Gallup discovered that twenty-five percent or so of the American people had never heard of the United Nations. I think if we could find that twenty-five percent, they'd be reasonable candidates for temporary disfranchisement.
PLAYBOY: How would you find them?
BUCKLEY: Ask the Ford Foundation where they are. Incidentally, there's an interesting paradox here. I think that as power is centralized, one can make less of a case for extending the vote. In the ideal world, where power is decentralized—in my kind of a world—one wouldn't have to know what the United Nations was in order to assess intelligently the local situation and express yourself on it.
PLAYBOY: You didn't include the school-desegregation decision of the Supreme Court in your list of the beneficent results of the civil-rights movement. Why?
BUCKLEY: When *Brown vs. Board of Education* was passed, we at *National Review* called it "bad law and bad sociology." I continue to think it was lousy law, historically and analytically. There are, unfortunately, increased grounds for believing that it was also bad sociology. Coerced massive integration is simply not working at primary- and secondary-school levels, and I notice that, for instance in Harlem, the voters don't list integrated schooling as among their principal demands. What they want, and should have, is better education. The superstition that this automatically happens by checkerboarding the classroom is increasingly apparent to blacks as well as to whites. Meanwhile, in the total situation, you are taking very grave risks in jeopardizing the good nature of the white majority.
PLAYBOY: Could your concern for the good nature of the white majority be interpreted as acquiescence to their prejudice?
BUCKLEY: The word *prejudice* becomes a little strained, used in that way. Look, ninety-five percent of the white people who live in Washington are Democrats, political liberals who give speeches in favor of integration and vote for politicians who favor integration—and then take their children out of the public schools when Negroes enter those schools. If you call them prejudiced, they reply that that isn't it, but that they want for their children a better education than they will get at the public schools in Washington.
PLAYBOY: If every school in the country were integrated by law in the next two years, wouldn't you have a generation twenty years from now that was relatively free of race prejudice?
BUCKLEY: I fear not. There is still anti-Italian prejudice in Jewish sections of New York and anti-Jewish prejudice in Italian sections of New York, and they've been going to school together for more than twenty years. It may be, ages hence, when the final sociological report is stapled and submitted, that we will discover that it all had something to do with numbers. It may be that a school that has ten percent Negroes will be successful and a school that has thirty or forty percent Negroes won't make it; either the whites will pull out or racial antagonisms will disrupt the school. Meanwhile, the things to stress and restress are better education and better job opportunities for Negroes.
PLAYBOY: Beyond increasing job opportunities, what else can be done to eliminate poverty in America? Specifically, are you in favor of President Nixon's welfare-reform proposals?

BUCKLEY: We are eliminating poverty in this country faster than any society ever has. There is a downward-bound graph that begins with about fifty percent of the population poor at the turn of the century and dips to the present, where there are about nine percent poor, using the same indices. So my first comment is that I don't want anything to interfere with the direction of that graph, which the overhead costs and economic strategy of many social-welfare programs tend to do. Now, it may be that the curve is asymptotic, that it will never quite close. The residual poor will, of course, have to have some kind of a relief program, even as they do now. I myself would buy the Moynihan plan, or the Nixon plan, or the New Federalism—whatever you call it—as a substitute for all existing measures. It may well come down to a matter of American know-how moving in on a congeries of welfare systems to make welfarism both more manageable and an instrument that itself might break the so-called vicious cycle that everybody agrees has discredited the existing system.

PLAYBOY: What sort of program—if any—do you favor for eliminating hunger?

BUCKLEY: I'm attracted to the notion of giving out four basic food materials, free, to anybody who wants them. The cost, according to one economist, would come to about a billion dollars a year. The idea is that these ingredients would be available at food stores to anybody—you, me, Nelson Rockefeller—because it simply wouldn't be worthwhile trying to catch anyone who was taking the free food and didn't need it. With such a plan, you could officially and confidently say that the residual hunger in America was simply the result of people not knowing how to utilize these materials.

PLAYBOY: What are they?

BUCKLEY: Powdered skim milk, bulgur wheat, soybeans and a kind of lard. You can make very good bread out of them, for instance. This bulgur wheat, incidentally—which is a staple in the Mideast—is not much liked by Americans and yet Alice Roosevelt Longworth loves it, considers it a delicacy.

PLAYBOY: Do you agree with those analysts who feel that—in part because of the black revolution and because of federal "handout" programs—the general electorate is moving to the right?

BUCKLEY: There are all sorts of conflicting indices. The Moynihan plan that we just talked about is left by orthodox conservative standards; if it had been proposed by Franklin Delano Roosevelt in 1933, it might have gotten even *him* impeached—and yet the people seem willing to accept it. But looking at the broad indications, I do feel that there is a move to the right. I've always believed that conservatism is, as I said a while ago, the politics of reality and that reality ultimately asserts itself, in a reasonably free society, in behalf of the conservative position. An excellent example was the race riots of the mid-Sixties. Even the participants discovered that those Gadarene experiments were futile.

PLAYBOY: Mayor Daley's celebrated order to the Chicago police to maim looters in the rioting that followed the assassination of Martin Luther King confirmed the feeling of many young people—black and white—that American society places a higher value on property than on human life. Do you think looters should be shot?

BUCKLEY: I reject the notion that a property right is other than a human right—that is, it's not an animal right or a vegetable right. The commitment of the state to the individual is to protect the individual's freedom and property, property being one of the things that materialize from the exercise of freedom and, therefore, in many senses, are the fruits of freedom. So I elect a mayor to protect me and my property effectively, with graduated responses to various conditions. If theft is an aberration—

as it is, for instance, in the Scandinavian countries—I would consider a mayor who orders his men to shoot thieves to be absolutely barbaric. But if theft reaches near-epidemic conditions, a different response is indicated. I wish there were something in between simply shouting "Hey! Come back!" and shooting somebody in the leg. Unfortunately, I fear that when that in-between thing is discovered, liberals are going to come up with elaborate reasons for not using it—Mace being an excellent example.

PLAYBOY: Mayor Daley's shoot-to-maim order, and his handling of demonstrators at the Democratic Convention that same summer, struck many observers as proof of an authoritarian and ugly aspect of America's turn to the right. If you had been mayor of Chicago, would you have handled the protesters as he did?

BUCKLEY: No. I've been pretty well satisfied that it was a basic mistake not to open up Lincoln Park. You simply can't require people to evaporate—incorporealization not being a typical human skill. But with the exception of his ruling on the use of the park, and the workaday tactical errors, I think Daley's resoluteness was justified. Obviously, the excesses of his police were *not* justified, but a lot of Americans were glad the demonstrators got beat up. They were glad for the commonplace reason—there's a little sadism in all of us—but they were also glad because they knew goddamn well that the chances of the demonstrators' breaking the law with impunity were overwhelming. It was sort of a return to posse justice. If you knew absolutely that Abbie Hoffman and the boys were never going to spend a night in jail—which was a good guess at the time—then people figured, "What the hell, beat 'em up. At least get *that* satisfaction out of it."

PLAYBOY: Is that the way you felt?

BUCKLEY: No. But I understand the feeling.

PLAYBOY: This decade is opening with a widespread crackdown on such militant black groups as the Black Panthers. Do you think there is a campaign to exterminate the Panthers?

BUCKLEY: No, But I think there should be. I mean, obviously, to exterminate the *movement,* even as I favor the extermination of Ku Klux Klanism, though not necessarily Ku Kluxers.

PLAYBOY: Why?

BUCKLEY: Because I am persuaded that the Panthers have solemnly registered their basic goals, which are to rob people, by category, of their rights to life, to liberty, to freedom; and because they are arming themselves for that purpose. Any organization caught—as the Panthers have been caught time and time again—with caches of machine guns and grenades and Molotov cocktails is presumptively guilty of non-Platonic ambitions. Every state in the Union forbids that sort of stockpiling of arms.

PLAYBOY: Where have the Panthers indicated that their basic goal is to rob people of their rights?

BUCKLEY: In their literature. Read it. I don't carry it around. It is as thoroughly impregnated with genocidal anti-white racism as ever the Nazis' was with anti-Semitism. And it makes no difference to the Panthers where on the left-right spectrum the white politician stands. On the death of Bobby Kennedy, the Black Panthers' national newspaper ran a photograph of him lying in a pool of his own blood in the Ambassador Hotel with the head of a pig replacing the head of Mr. Kennedy. The rhetorical totalism suggested here, combined with the doctrinal genocidal passions, suggest to me that whatever was the appropriate attitude toward Goebbels in, say 1930, is appropriate, in 1970, toward the Black Panthers.

PLAYBOY: Doesn't the publication of such a picture, however repugnant, come under the protection of the First Amendment?

BUCKLEY: It does, formalistically; which is why I included actions—the Panthers' stockpiling of weapons—among the reasons why I think their extermination as a movement is desirable. But I would like to note that it is a naïve liberal assumption to think that the Bill of Rights protects every manner of written or spoken dissent. In the heyday of McCarthyism, Professor Samuel Stouffer from Harvard did one of those *Travels with Charley* bits around the country to discover the extent to which the Bill of Rights was an article of practical faith held by the American people. He found out that something like seventy-five percent of us didn't believe that members of the Communist Party should enjoy *any* rights. Needless to say, he wrote a horrified book about his findings. Now, it is extremely easy for people with an ideologized knowledge of American history to suppose that this is something new, let alone that it is impossible to compose a theoretical defense of it. But it is apparent to me that the profoundest studies of what, for instance, Thomas Jefferson or Abraham Lincoln meant by freedom was a freedom that was severely limited, even theoretically, in the right it absolutely granted to anyone to call for the persecution, let alone the liquidation, of others. When Jefferson said, "Those who wish to dissolve the Union or to change the republican form of government should stand undisturbed as monuments of the safety with which error of opinion may be tolerated where reason is left free to combat it," I am convinced by such scholars as Harry Jaffa that he meant not that we should grant freedom to the enemies of freedom because they are entitled to it but that we should grant freedom to the enemies of freedom because we can afford to *indulge* them that freedom. Accordingly, it becomes a practical rather than a theoretical consideration whether, at any given moment in American history, a particular group of dissenters whose dissent is based on the desire to rob other people of their freedom ought to be tolerated.

PLAYBOY: Are we at such a moment in history—when we can't afford that freedom to a few hundred out of two hundred million Americans?

BUCKLEY: Quite possibly. I don't think the Panthers are in a position to take over the country, any more than the Klan was. But the Klan deprived particular people in particular places of their effective freedom. So have the Panthers, by the use of the same weapons: intimidation and, it is now alleged by one or two grand juries, both murder and conspiracy to murder. So I say: Let's do to them what I wish we had done to the Klan fifty years ago.

PLAYBOY: When you say that we should not tolerate a group of dissenters such as the Panthers, what do you propose we do about them?

BUCKLEY: Society has three sanctions available for dealing with dissenters of this kind. There is the whole family of social sanctions; if they don't work, we then have legal sanctions; if the legal sanctions don't work, we are forced to use military sanctions. As an example of the social sanctions, I give you what has happened to Gerald L. K. Smith, the fierce anti-Semite. Would Smith be invited to join the sponsoring group of the Lincoln Center? If he gave a thousand-dollar contribution to the President's Club, would he be admitted as a member? No. Gerald L. K. Smith has been effectively isolated in America, and I'm glad that he has been. After such an experience as we have seen in the twentieth century of what happens—or what can happen—when people call for genocidal persecutions of other people, we have got to use whatever is the minimal resource available to society to keep that sort of thing from growing. If the social sanctions work, then you have the Jeffersonian situation, in which libertarian rodomontade is onanistically satisfying—a society in which the least possible force is the effective agent of that society's cohesiveness. I would like to see people like Bobby Seale and Eldridge Cleaver treated at least as badly as Gerald L. K. Smith has been. But no: They get applauded, they get invited to college campuses, they get listened to attentively on radio and on television—they are invited to Leonard Bernstein's *salons*—all of which makes rather glamorous a position that, in my judgment, ought to be execrated.

PLAYBOY: They also get jailed, exiled and even shot.

BUCKLEY: Cleaver was jailed for committing rape, which Gerald L. K. Smith hasn't done, so far as I know. And he was wounded after a shoot-out with Oakland police. Huey Newton was convicted of voluntary manslaughter. A gang of them are up now for murder and conspiracy to terrorize. Now, I'll grant you this: I have not been satisfied that the killing of Cleaver's buddy in that particular battle in Oakland—the young man who walked out of the house in his shorts and T-shirt—was justified. The policeman who killed him may have panicked, as others of us have done, with less tragic consequences, to be sure. But he wasn't acting on orders from J. Edgar Hoover, whose sins, if there are any, are explicit rather than implicit. But to return to my point, if I may, about the attention lavished on such people: The same, to a certain extent, was true of George Lincoln Rockwell, who got an extensive ventilation of his views in this magazine. For as long as that kind of thing happens, you encourage people to consider as tenable a position that in my judgment ought to be universally rejected as untenable. The whole idea of civilization is little by little to discard certain points of view as uncivilized; it is impossible to discover truths without discovering that their opposites are error. In a John Stuart Mill–type society—in which *any* view, for so long as it is held by so much as a single person, is considered as not yet confuted—you have total intellectual and social anarchy.

PLAYBOY: On the other hand, by publishing an interview with a George Lincoln Rockwell, one might encourage him to expose the untenability of his views and thus help discredit both himself and his philosophy, even among those who might previously have been sympathizers.

BUCKLEY: I acknowledge the abstract appeal of the argument, but I remind you that it can be used as an argument for evangelizing people in Nazism, racism or cannibalism, in order to fortify one's opposition to such doctrines. The trouble is that false doctrines *do* appeal to people. In my judgment, it would be a better world where nobody advocated tyranny; better than a world in which tyranny is advocated as an academic exercise intended to fortify the heroic little antibodies to tyranny.

PLAYBOY: If the evils of a particular doctrine are so apparent, what harm is there in allowing someone to preach that doctrine?

BUCKLEY: What is apparent to one man is not necessarily apparent to the majority. Hitler came to power democratically. It's a nineteenth-century myth to confide totally in the notion that the people won't be attracted to the wrong guy. George Wallace, not Nixon or Humphrey, got the highest TV ratings. Take, once more, the Panthers. There are, I am sure, hundreds of thousands of Americans who would like to hear a speech by Eldridge Cleaver. One reason they would like to do so is because they like the excitement. Another is that they like to show off. People like to show their audacity, their cavalier toleration of iconoclasm—it's the same kind of thing, in a way, as shouting "F--- Mayor Daley" in a loud voice in the middle of a park in Chicago. Moreover, the views expressed by Eldridge Cleaver, et al., have not been proscribed by settled intellectual opinion, because, thank God, we have not experienced in America the kind of holocaust that Caucasians visited against the Jews in Germany. I contend that it is a responsibility of the intellectual community to anticipate Dachau rather than to deplore it. The primary responsibility of people who fancy themselves morally sophisticated is to do what they can to exhibit their impatience with those who are prepared to welcome the assassination of Bobby Kennedy because that meant one less pig. Their failure to do that is, in my judgment, a sign of moral disintegration. If you have moral disintegration, you don't have left a case against Dachau. If you don't have that, what *do* you have? Make love not war? Why?

PLAYBOY: You referred to the moral disintegration of some Americans. Would you make that a general indictment—applicable not only to those who tolerate the Panthers but to most Americans?

BUCKLEY: Yes. The most conspicuous attribute of the twentieth-century American is his self-indulgence. In a marvelous book called *The Odyssey of the Self-Centered Self,* Robert Fitch traces the principal concerns of civilization through the past two or three hundred years; our concerns were, he says, first predominantly religious, then predominantly scientific, then humanistic—and today are essentially egocentric. I think that ours is an egocentric society. The popular notion is that there is no reciprocal obligation by the individual to the society, that one can accept whatever the patrimony gives us without any sense of obligation to replenish the common patrimony—that is, without doing what we can to advance the common good. This, I think, is what makes not only Americans but most Western peoples weak. It comforts me that that also was the finding of Ortega y Gasset.

PLAYBOY: How does the increasing social awareness and involvement of young people fit into your thesis?

BUCKLEY: I don't say that somebody who spends the summer in Mississippi trying to bring rights to black people is primarily self-centered, although such a case could be made concerning some young people and by using less intricate psychological arguments than, for instance, the liberals fling around to prove that we are all racist. I'm talking about the general disease of *anomie,* which is the result of people's, by and large, having become deracinated, suspended from any relationship to the supernatural and prescinded from the historical situation. A lot of them retreat and think about themselves, even *exclusively* about themselves—the drug people—the dropouts, formal and informal. Certain others venture into utopianism, which, as I've said, necessarily and obviously breeds frustration and despair, conditions that some of them prefer even to drugs. But the lot of them, I think, fail to come to terms with the world, fail to come to terms with the end of life. They have absolutely no eschatological vision, except a rhetorical sort of secular utopianism. A related phenomenon: When I was last on the Johnny Carson show, he announced to his mass audience, "Well, after all, the reason the Soviet Union arms is because *we* arm," the implicit axiom being that there is obviously no difference between them and us. What makes it possible for the man who has the largest regular audience of anybody in the United States—not excluding the President—to say blandly something like that is wave after wave in the intellectual offensive against epistemological optimism, against the notion that some things are better than others and that we can know what those thing are.

PLAYBOY: Do you think this moral relativism is at least partially a consequence of the decline in religious belief?

BUCKLEY: Yes. In orthodox religious belief. It's a commonplace that there is no such thing as an irreligious society. The need for religion being a part of the nature of man, people will continue to seek religion. You see the Beatles rushing off to listen to the platitudinous homilies of the Indian quack, Maharishi-what's-his-name, but they'd rather be caught dead than reading Saint Paul. Young people who have active minds tend to be dissatisfied with the ersatz religions they pick up, and yet so formal is the contemporary commitment to agnosticism—or even to atheism—that they absoutely refuse to plumb Christianity's extraordinary reservoirs of rationality. I doubt if you could get one of these kids, however desperately in search of religion—who will go to any guru, who will even talk to Joan *Baez* and attempt to get religion from *her*—to read *Orthodoxy* by Chesterton or any book by C. S. Lewis.

PLAYBOY: Perhaps orthodoxy—lower case—is at fault. Many young people would say they think Christ was a great man; they might even know a good deal about Him. But they are appalled by Saint Paul's horror of the body and of sex.

BUCKLEY: I'm sure that among the vast majority of students, the knowledge of Christ is superificial and that the *only* thing they know about Saint Paul is that he was "anti-sex." In fact, Saint Paul's anti-sexuality was, I think, a mode by which he expressed the joys of asceticism, the transcendent pleasure of the mortification of the flesh. By no means is this distinctive to Christianity. In fact, Christianity in its formal renunciation of Manichaeism took a position concerning the flesh that is far more joyful than for instance, that of the Buddhists or of a number of other religions.

PLAYBOY: One of the reasons many people have difficulty accepting your religion, Roman Catholicism, is that they have been convinced by experts that there are soon going to be more people on the globe than the earth can support, yet the Church does its not-inconsiderable best to prevent the spread of birth control information. Do you also take a serious view of the population problem?

BUCKLEY: Yes. I do. I think it is the second most important problem in the world, after ideological communism.

PLAYBOY: Then the Church's position on birth control distresses you?

BUCKLEY: No. It is not established by any means that the influence of the Church is very direct on the matter of the increase in population. It happens that the birth rate is the greatest where the Church has no influence: India, for instance, or Nigeria. It is impossible to establish a correlation between the birth rate in Latin America and the prevailing religion on that continent. The Catholic position on birth control is, therefore, something against which we agonize rather more theoretically than practically.

PLAYBOY: What do you think we can do, then, to keep the population down?

BUCKLEY: Get people to stop reading PLAYBOY.

PLAYBOY: What's the real answer?

BUCKLEY: Well, the real answer is to make sure that people who don't want more children and who have no religious scruples against the use of abortifacients or prophylactics are aware of how they can get and use them. My own assumption is that we are moving toward the discovery of a chemical that will prevent conception, that will be generally dispensed—perhaps in the water supply—and can be readily neutralized by any woman who desires to do so.

PLAYBOY: Should the U.S. volunteer birth control information and devices to such overpopulated nations as India?

BUCKLEY: They don't need any more information. They can get it from the *Encyclopaedia Britannica*. As to giving them the pill—sure, if they ask for it.

PLAYBOY: Do you have any other sexual opinions that might shock the bishop?
BUCKLEY: I didn't give you a "sexual" opinion. I don't know that giving free pills to India is heretical. Would American rabbis object to free pork for India? Heresy? I don't think so. I happen, for example, to favor the legalization of private homosexual acts committed between consenting adults and of prostitution. The second is the more important. Legalizing prostitution would provide a ready outlet for pubescent lust and greatly facilitate the hygienic problem, pending the domination of the appetite and the restoration of morality. Also, it would cut down the profits and power of the Mafia, the existence of which enrages me.
PLAYBOY: How else would you combat the Mafia?
BUCKLEY: By making gambling—but not gambling debts—legal.
PLAYBOY: Advocating the legalization of gambling, prostitution and homosexual acts between adults puts you in agreement with most liberals. Do you also agree with them in the area of censorship? Would you defend the right of the state to, say, stop performances by Lenny Bruce?
BUCKLEY: I'm troubled by that problem. By the way, do, please, try to remember that the conservative opposes unnecessary legislation. I've written about the censorship dilemma. Obviously, a perfectly consistent, schematic libertarianism would give you an easy answer—let anybody do anything. Including cocaine-vending machines. But a libertarianism written without reference to social universals isn't terribly useful. Here, I think, is where the science of sociology becomes useful. If sociology suggests that societies don't survive without the observance of certain common bonds, certain taboos, then we can maintain that in the long run, we diminish rather than increase freedom by protecting people who violate those taboos. Having said that, let me add that I'm perfectly well aware that this particular argument can be abused by people who want a narrow conformity. I don't think Lenny Bruce would be arrested today in New York, the movement having been in the direction of permissiveness in the past four or five years. The question really is: Do we—or do I, I guess—approve of the trend, and I'm not so sure that I do. A society that abandons all of its taboos abandons reverence.
PLAYBOY: Doesn't society abandon something even more precious by attempting to preserve that reverence by force?
BUCKLEY: Again, it depends on the situation. If you have a society that is corporately bent on a prolonged debauch—determined to wage iconoclasm *à outrance*—then you've got a society that you can't effectively repress. I mean, you have a prohibitive situation. But if you have a society—as I think we still do—in which the overwhelming majority of the people respect their own and others' taboos, the kind of society that, say, forbids a lawyer from referring to Judge Marshall as a nigger, or Judge Hoffman as a kike, then it isn't much of an exertion on the commonweal to implement such laws as have been on the books in New York for generations. My final answer to your entire line of questioning is ambiguous: If you ask simply: Does the individual have the absolute right to do anything he wants in private contract with another party? then my answer is: No, only the presumptive right. A sadist cannot contract to kill a masochist. John Stuart Mill reduces the matter of sovereignty to the individual's rights over himself. The state hasn't the right to protect you against yourself—which is a good argument against my being required to wear a helmet when I ride my Honda.
PLAYBOY: Doesn't Mill's dictum against the state's right to protect you from yourself also argue for the abolition of most drug laws?

BUCKLEY: Does it? Take heroin. Except under totally contrived circumstances, there is no such thing in America as a person inflicting purely on himself the consequences of taking heroin. If a man goes that route, he deserts his family—if he has any; he becomes an energumen who will ravish society to sustain the habit, and so on. Most important—as far as I'm concerned—he becomes a Typhoid Mary of sorts. I know that I'm using a metaphor, but I can defend the use of this particular metaphor. We know from serious studies that heroin users desire to communicate the habit to other people and often succeed in doing so.

PLAYBOY: Do the same arguments apply to marijuana?

BUCKLEY: Not really, or not so severely. The first and most obvious thing to say about marijuana is that the penalties for using it are preposterous. But I don't believe that it ought to be legalized yet; the consequences of its use have not been sufficiently studied. It seems crazy to me that in an age when the federal government has outlawed Tab, we are wondering whether we ought to legalize marijuana. Now, it may be that marijuana is harmless, although at this moment, I am persuaded by those scientists who emphatically believe the contrary. It may be that we would be much better off persuading everybody who now drinks whiskey to turn on instead. But we don't *know*. Some scientists say that middle-aged people who take marijuana risk special dangers because they have gradually concatenated their own quirks, latent and active, into a moderately well-adjusted human being. Psychotropic drugs can shatter that delicate equilibrium. Conversely, it is speculated that marijuana can keep some young people from making the individual adjustments they need to make. Some scientists claim that prolonged use of marijuana wages a kind of war against your psyche, the final results of which are not easy to trace.

PLAYBOY: Your attitude toward grass typifies your agreement with middle-class Americans on some issues. Are there any contemporary American middle-class values that you *dislike?*

BUCKLEY: You'd have to make me a list of them. If ostentatious forms of material achievement are a middle-class value, I don't much like them, though I wouldn't go out of my way to evangelize against them; we all have our little vanities. I am told that in certain big corporations, it is unseemly for the junior V.P. to own a more expensive car than the senior V.P., and absolutely *verboten* for his wife to have a mink coat if the wife of the senior V.P. doesn't have one. But who *does* approve of Babbittry? Not even Babbitt. He merely practiced Babbittry. The middle-class values I admire are husbandry, industry, loyalty, a sense of obligation to the community and a sense of obligation to one's patrimony. When Winston Churchill died, Rebecca West said that he was a great affront to the spirit of the modern age because he was manifestly superior. I said in introducing Clare Boothe Luce, when we did a TV program in Hawaii a few months ago, that her documented achievements are evidence of the lengths to which nature is prepared to go to demonstrate its addiction to inequality. It is a middle-class value to defer, without animosity, to people of superior learning, achievement, character, generosity.

PLAYBOY: To whom do you personally feel inferior?

BUCKLEY: Millions of people, living and dead.

PLAYBOY: Who among the living?

BUCKLEY: To begin with, anyone who knows more than I do, which would be millions of people—or hundreds of thousands of people—right there. I also feel inferior to people who regulate their lives more successfully than I do, to people who are less annoyed by some of the petty distractions that sometimes annoy me, to people who are more philosophical in their acceptance of things than I am.

PLAYBOY: Does that include Mrs. Luce?

BUCKLEY: She's much more talented than I am.

PLAYBOY: Norman Mailer?

BUCKLEY: Much more talented than I am. Now, there are certain things in which I am Mailer's manifest superior. Politically, he's an idiot. And he's botched his life and the lives of a lot more people than I've botched, I hope. On the other hand, he's a genius and I'm not.

PLAYBOY: Among other contemporaries, how about T. S. Eliot?

BUCKLEY: You're talking about birds of paradise now. Like Whittaker Chambers. I make it a point to seek the company—intellectually, above all—of people who are superior to me in any number of ways, and I very often succeed.

PLAYBOY: To whom do you feel superior—and why?

BUCKLEY: To those who believe that they are the very best judges of what is wrong and what is right.

PLAYBOY: Would you please name names?

BUCKLEY: Would you please expand your printing facilities?

PLAYBOY: As long as the discussion has become personal: To what extent has your feud with Gore Vidal developed into a publicity stunt from which you both have benefited?

BUCKLEY: In my case, at least, to no extent at all. I don't see how one profits *a*) from being publicly libeled or *b*) from walking into a situation in which one pays legal expenses several times the value of anything one earned after industrious work preparing for television programs or doing an article.

PLAYBOY: Would you care to add anything to what you said about him on the air during the 1968 Democratic Convention and in response to his subsequent comments about you?

BUCKLEY: No.

PLAYBOY: Why did you agree to appear with him in the first place?

BUCKLEY: I agreed to appear in November of 1967 because I thought I could use the forum effectively to advance the conservative viewpoint. I was informed in April that Vidal had been selected to appear opposite me. My alternatives then were to break my contract or to proceed. I decided not to break the contract, even though Vidal was the single person I had named as someone I would not gladly appear against.

PLAYBOY: You have been publicly active for nineteen years. How successful do you think you have been in advancing the conservative viewpoint?

BUCKLEY: Very successful. That success has come primarily through the instrumentality of *National Review*, which has the second-highest circulation of any journal of opinion in America. It repeatedly furnishes the reading public with the very best conservative position, causing many people to abandon—however unhappily—their resolution to dismiss the conservative alternative as anachronistic, superficial and inhuman. I don't say that *National Review*, or something like it, would not have been created had I not been around; it most certainly would have—in fact, I only midwifed it—but I'd say that the mere fact of having done so renders me, as midwife, very successful.

PLAYBOY: Which failures of the conservative movement of the past ten to twenty years most distress you? The fact that Goldwater didn't get more votes than he did?

BUCKLEY: No, not at all. It was a forgone conclusion that he wouldn't get many votes from the moment Kennedy was assassinated. It's very hard to explain to militant pro-Goldwaterites like myself that in a strange sort of way, an inscrutable sort of way, voting against Goldwater was explainable as a conservative thing to do. The reason I say that is because a nation convulsed in November of 1963 as ours was reached for balm, for conciliation, for peace, for tranquillity, for order. To have had three Presidents over a period of fourteen months would have been dislocative beyond the appetite of many conservatives. Now, this doesn't mean that I side with those conservatives who voted against him—I happen to be more adventurous than some conservatives—but I can respect their point of view. In any case, that was not by any means my idea of the great disappointment of the Sixties. That was the failure, on the whole, to verbalize more broadly, more convincingly, the conservative view of things. The conservative critque has been very well made, but it hasn't got through with sufficient force to the opinion makers. It is still hard as hell to find a young conservative with writing talent. That distresses me deeply. Most of the people who write the really finished essays in the college newspapers are liberals, New Leftists. I don't know exactly why and I'm vexed by it, but there were only a dozen—or fewer—conservatives in the Sixties who have become writers of some achievement.
PLAYBOY: Personally, what do you expect to do during the next five years? If there were a conservative administration in this country—say, if Ronald Reagan became President—would you be tempted to accept a high post in the Administration?
BUCKLEY: No. In the first place, I don't like it much. In the second place—
PLAYBOY: Don't like what much—Washington?
BUCKLEY: That's right.
PLAYBOY: Cabinet meetings?
BUCKLEY: I don't much like any kind of meetings. Besides, I have no reason for supposing that I'm a skillful administrator; I may be or I may very well not be. But the kind of thing that I am practiced in requires considerable freedom of expression, and freedom of expression is obviously something you need to be very continent about when the point of the thing is to advance the collective endeavor.
PLAYBOY: With or without your own involvement in an official capacity, are you optimistic about the conservative movement in America?
BUCKLEY: I am, mildly. There has been some encouraging deideologization of politics in the past twenty years. When I went to college, Henry Wallace was still able to grip a lot of people with hopped-up visions like the nationalization of the steel industry. We've watched the experience of England since then and studied nationalized industries elsewhere, and *no* one will go to that parade anymore, no one except the types who squat in the fever swamps of ideology. The collapse of the poverty program as a federal enterprise strikes me as significant. It strikes me as significant, too, that Patrick Moynihan got up at an A.D.A. meeting a year or so ago and said, Let's face it, gang, conservatives know something intuitively that it takes us liberals years of intellectualizing to come up with—namely, that the federal government can't do everything it wants to do. Peter Drucker, who is certainly not considered a conservative fanatic, says now that the only things the government has proved it can really do competently are wage war and inflate the currency.
PLAYBOY: Even if you don't intend to run for office again, do you plan to keep writing?
BUCKLEY: Yes. We've kept an alternative landing field in operation, you see. When the liberals fly in, thirsty, out of gas, they'll find it in full working order—radar OK, bar

open, Coca-Cola and coffee on the house. We know it's necessary to assimilate the experience of the modern age. Cardinal Newman said in a related contest—between the logical positivists and the conservatives—that one of our great challenges is constantly to incorporate new experience, so as not to leave ourselves with a piece of brittle lace, the touching of which would cause it to crumble.

PLAYBOY: Don't most dogmas, theological as well as ideological, crumble sooner or later?

BUCKLEY: Most, but not all.

PLAYBOY: How can you be so sure?

BUCKLEY: I know that my Redeemer liveth.

ROMAN POLANSKI

December 1971

Interviewer: Larry Dubois

Roman Polanski's interview is included in this anthology less because of his insights into filmmaking—though Polanski was, and remains, a gifted director—than because of the fact that it was here he first broke his silence on the Manson murders at his home. A morbid topic of worldwide fascination for more than two years, the murders of Polanski's wife, Sharon Tate, and her friends seemed to symbolize for many the worst aspects of a turbulent decade: sex, drugs, hippies, evil gurus, and Hollywood excess. Polanski's penchant for macabre themes in his movies and reportedly decadent life-style did little to quiet the whispers about him, so the interview, appearing when it did, was eagerly read.

Polanski agreed to do the interview with PLAYBOY because he and Playboy Productions were collaborating on a new movie, *Macbeth,* which turned out to be a critical success but a commercial failure. He had no intention of discussing the murders—ever, he said. But Larry Dubois, a young free-lance writer hired by editor Fisher, was a patient and sympathetic listener and awaited the inevitable outpouring. After several weeks of taping on various subjects, Polanski abruptly began talking about his wife and the tragedy—and a very different picture from the one that had been rumored began to emerge. As he spoke about this and other things, Dubois captured the essence of a brilliant, troubled mind—and something of the decade.

There was virtually no action, and the plot was starkly simple: A successful middle-aged Polish journalist, his restless wife and a young hitchhiker they have picked up spend a weekend on a yacht, with subtle, potentially murderous psychosexual tensions developing among them. But Knife in the Water, *Roman Polanski's first feature film (which he co-authored), won an Academy Award nomination for best for-*

eign film of 1963 and made its director internationally famous at the age of thirty.

All the violence in Knife *was in the characters' minds, but Polanski's next two films (which he also co-authored) revealed what some began to consider a morbid fascination with scenes of gruesome death. In* Repulsion, *the frenzied insanity of a beautiful young Belgian girl (Catherine Deneuve) drives her to murder her suitor, and* Cul-de-Sac *told a black-humor tale of two criminals who take refuge in the isolated island home of a weak transvestite and his tarty bride. Polanski kept some of his allies among the critics who had heaped praise on* Knife, *but others couldn't stomach his taste for the macabre.* Time *saw* Cul-de-Sac *as "a jittery, tittery comedy of terrors. . . . In frame after frame, the danger lurks just out of sight until the onlooker feels like a man cooped up with a cobra he can't really see." But Judith Crist complained that the film was entertaining only "for those who can laugh while fighting off nausea."*

After a mildly amusing side step in The Fearless Vampire Killers, *a harmless parody of old horror movies, Polanski pushed on to somewhere near the outer limits of suspense with* Rosemary's Baby, *his adaptation of Ira Levin's best-selling novel about a modern-day witchcraft cult in Manhattan. Starring Mia Farrow and John Cassavetes, the film was a spectacular success both with the critics and at the box office.*

Polanski's personal brushes with suspense and brutality in life began at an early age. When he was eight, his mother died in a Nazi concentration camp and not long after, he escaped from the infamous Jewish ghetto in Krakow and survived the war by shunting among various families willing to take him in. One day, he had to dash for cover as a German soldier decided on some casual target practice and whizzed a bullet over Polanski's head. Then, when he was sixteen, a thug nearly beat him to death.

After he was graduated from Poland's superlative State School of Filming in Lodz, Polanski scrabbled to make a living in Paris for a couple of years before the Polish government finally gave him a budget for his screenplay of Knife in the Water *and sent him on his way up in the world. He quickly established a reputation as one of the celebrity circuit's most successful bachelors; and in 1968 he married Sharon Tate, a beautiful young American actress. Moving at a fast pace between film sets and their homes in London and Los Angeles, they were known as a jet-set couple until the night of August 9, 1969, when Sharon and three friends—Voyteck Frykowski, men's hairstylist Jay Sebring, and coffee heiress Abigail Folger—plus an eighteen-year-old boy who was visiting the caretaker, were sadistically murdered at Polanski's rented house in Los Angeles. The press gave the case saturation publicity and made it one of the most sensational mass murders in the country's history.*

For months, the popular theory was that the murders were committed by someone from the "rich hippie" crowd in which Miss Tate and Polanski were such popular figures. Eventually, the theory proved false, when police apprehended Charles Manson and his bizarre "family" of young men and runaway girls who were living at an abandoned ranch a few miles outside L.A. After a long and widely reported trial, Manson and two of his followers were sentenced to death for the murders and Polanski's name dropped out of the news and the gossip columns. Now, three years after Rosemary's Baby *and two years after the murders, he has completed the filming of Shakespeare's* Macbeth, *adapted for the screen by Polanski and British author-critic (and contributing editor) Kenneth Tynan and produced by Playboy Productions. To explore Polanski's vision of himself, his films and his life today,* PLAYBOY *sent free-lance writer Larry DuBois to London for the first interview he's granted in more than two years. DuBois writes of his experiences:*

"Roman Polanski inspires strong, and often conflicting, feelings in people; and after you've been around his pals, women and professional associates for a while, you get used to a frustrating ambivalence about him that is most often expressed in remarks that go something like: 'God, how I like that little bastard.' I couldn't say it any better myself. During the extended course of this interview, there were moments when I'd have fought for Polanski, moments when I only wanted to fight with him—or with the editor responsible for the assignment—and moments when I passionately wished I'd never met either one of them. During most of two and a half months chasing Polanski to wrench from him the twenty-odd hours of taped conversation I finally acquired, my irritation deepened.

"My memory barely extends as far back as the beginning of this assignment, but I recall that from his films and the press after the murders of his wife and friends, I had the image of Polanski as a flaky, perhaps even macabre character. On the contrary. He is as cavalier about his work as an ambitious executive and about as macabre as a California beach boy. His disposition is cheery and optimistic. He is straightforward to the point of discomfiting bluntness. He tends to surround himself with intelligent, serious people and gets bored quickly with what he calls 'the aimless, futile individuals' he sometimes encounters in St. Tropez.

"His only genuine indulgence is women, which is what he does with most of whatever free time he has in St. Tropez and elsewhere; and in that, he lives up to his image. At least superficially, his seductive style is roughly that of a wily street urchin (he's five foot five) faced with rich tourists, disarming them with a kind of youthful enthusiasm and naïveté. It works. In his other personal habits, he is almost depressingly disciplined. He exercises diligently. His diet includes wheat germ, yoghurt and other health foods. He rarely drinks more than a glass of wine or beer and he is not above lecturing his friends about the evils of cigarette smoking.

"Now that the interview is over, only one of our many differences still bothers me: He is a most terrifying driver of automobiles. I find nothing endearing about having rocketed with him in an XK-E through the French holiday traffic around St. Tropez at 110–120 miles per hour. When I tried to explain my own concept of personal safety, he just said, 'You must understand: What seems like a risk to you may not seem like a risk to me.' The uninitiated might read all sorts of meanings into that about his background, and some hidden fatalism. But I dropped the subject, because I knew that, as usual, he meant exactly what he said and no more.

"Finally, I should note that there is one section of this interview that didn't require a struggle to extract. One Sunday evening, we sat on the porch of his farmhouse with nothing around for miles but the silent French countryside, and I hesitantly brought up the subject of Sharon and the murders. For two straight hours, without any further coaxing, he told his story, simply and with none of his usual interruptions. He obviously wanted to go through it all once, let it all out; and when he was finished, I think he felt better. For myself, I was unspeakably depressed. It was a couple of days before either of us mentioned the interview again. The transition from that subject to another was a difficult one then, as it is now. So just one last thing: All along, Polanski kept telling me, when the tape recorder was off, that it would be impossible to translate his personality onto paper, since he expresses so much of his

irresistibly high-spirited and playful nature through antics rather than words. He's like a movie, he said; he has to be seen to be appreciated. I think he was wrong. I think readers will be able to develop their own affectionate ambivalence about him."

PLAYBOY: Your films have earned you a reputation as a master of the macabre. How do you explain your fascination with it?

POLANSKI: I don't know why I like it. Why do some people like boxing, or writing? I'm a filmmaker; I make pictures. I don't like to talk about them and I don't think about why I make them. You're asking me to psychoanalyze myself and this is not something that interests me at all.

PLAYBOY: We're not really asking you to psychoanalyze yourself—just to tell us about the personal vision you convey in your films.

POLANSKI: All right. I'm not preoccupied with the macabre—I'm rather more interested in the behavior of people under stress, when they are no longer in comfortable, everyday situations where they can afford to respect the conventional rules and morals of society. You can really learn something about a person when he's put into circumstances in which civilized values place his own identity, even his very being, in jeopardy. In a way *Knife in the Water* was my minute example of this. I took three people and put them in a situation that subjected them to stress, due to their confinement on the yacht and the competition between the two males. In a way, *Cul-de-Sac* was the same situation, where the people could not react the way they were accustomed to. Before the death of my wife, I was working on a film about the Donner Pass group, which got stranded in the Sierra Nevada Mountains in 1847. It's an extremely interesting story, because besides being symptomatic of the problems the pioneers faced in the beginning of that country, it shows civilized people reduced to circumstances where they have to decide on the most drastic moral issues, like eating each other, in order to survive. I don't know what I would do in that situation. But I don't think I would eat your flesh. I think I would rather die. Not because I would think there was something morally wrong with eating you after you were dead. I simply don't think I would be willing to swallow your flesh. Would you swallow mine?

PLAYBOY: Who knows? Our cultural aversion to the idea would probably make us throw up, anyway.

POLANSKI: Only in the beginning, my friend.

PLAYBOY: Do you film characters under stress in order to find answers you're seeking for yourself or to force the audience to confront problems you think you already understand?

POLANSKI: Neither. It simply fascinates me. When something fascinates you, you talk about it, and making films is my way of talking about it.

PLAYBOY: Why are you more fascinated by characters under stress than by those who aren't?

POLANSKI: I sometimes surprise myself that I don't ask myself these questions, but I don't. Perhaps if I did, I would know the answers, but I don't feel any need for that. That's the way I am. Perhaps it's because as a child I had plenty of opportunities to see how people behave under stress. I often think: How would a friend with whom you've drunk a lot of vodka and had a lot of fun respond when one morning you plant yourself on his doorstep and say, "Hide me. I'm being chased by the Nazis." And now he has to decide whether or not to risk his life for your friendship. But it's difficult for me to judge how much part the war plays in what I create. I don't think I'm obsessed by what I lived through. I was a child during the war, and children are resilient. Whatever you create, it's an accumulation of millions of things in you, of what you go through as a boy, as a young man, of what you read, of what you see in the cinema, of the people you know. All these have affected my emotional life. I remember, for instance, that one of the profound experiences of my youth was seeing *Of Mice and Men.* That has stayed with me. I couldn't stop thinking about this big, lovely man and his friend, and their friendship, and I thought that if I were ever a filmmaker, I would certainly try to do something along those lines, something against injustice and intolerance and prejudice and superstition. And I have. These elements are weaved through my films.

PLAYBOY: Why, then, did you decide to make *Rosemary's Baby,* which could be said to have celebrated, or at least popularized, superstition?

POLANSKI: You don't have to be superstitious to enjoy a fantasy. If you are around me for long, you will see that I have no belief at all in the supernatural of any kind. It's just a fashionable distraction for people seeking easy explanations to certain phenomena they are otherwise incapable of understanding. Myself, I am down to earth in my philosophy of life, very rationally and materialistically oriented, with no interest in the occult. The only obsession that compelled me to make that film was my liking for good cinema. When Bob Evans, the head of production for Paramount, called me and asked me to read the galleys of the book before it was published, I found it fascinating material for a film, with a terrifically suspenseful plot.

PLAYBOY: Suspense is another of the hallmarks of your films. What makes it so important to you?

POLANSKI: I'm in the drama business, and suspense is the essence of drama. In my films, I'm concerned with the unexpected and with making what is unbelievable believable. *Life* is like that to me. We can never control what will happen out there. I don't live my life suspensefully, but in cinema I like the constant unexpected because that's what makes a story interesting. The essential is not to allow the audience to be able to anticipate what is going to happen next.

I remember when I was six, some friends and I made this skull out of clay and put these pieces of glass in it for eyes and hung it on the wall, thinking that anyone who walked by would be scared of it. I also remember making a mask of the devil with a red tongue made out of a candy wrapper, then putting a flashlight behind it. These are the things that intrigued me—but not for any supernatural or bizarre reasons, only because I already liked the show-business aspect of this mask making. My fondness for the dramatic and the unexpected has always been so obvious to me that I never stopped to ask why. I must have been born with it.

PLAYBOY: There's still the question of taste and finesse. Some critics have said that you've indulged in excessive violence on the screen.

POLANSKI: The way I've done it *is* with finesse. Others do it euphemistically. They are afraid to show what is essential to the story. I will never forget a growing tension in the churchyard scene of *Zorba the Greek,* which culminates with a throat cutting that unfortunately happens just below the bottom edge of the screen. That was the end of the movie for me, because the director had copped out. He showed his cowardice. If you tell a joke that requires the use of four-letter words, then you have to *say* them. It's not good to say, "He grabbed her and . . . dot, dot, dot, dot." It's better to tell another story. Showing the violence is an analogous situation, isn't it?

PLAYBOY: But critics might argue that the graphic portrayal of violence is analogous to pornography, not only with no redeeming social value but with harmful effects on those who see it.

POLANSKI: These people delude themselves that violence can be caused by what is on the screen. They should ask little children on the street what causes violence and they would become more enlightened. For me, when I see something violent happening on the screen, I react *against* it; I think this is most people's reaction. If there is violence on the screen that *can* make people act violently in their lives, it's the sterilized Hollywood conception of violence. It's the Western where the bad guy aggravates you so much for ninety minutes that finally, when the good guy gets rid of him in a tidy way, you feel relieved and happy. So what develops in young minds is that when somebody is bad enough, you can get rid of him—and without a mess. This is murder committed the "clean" way, murder that can be endorsed by movie-rating authorities who miss its real meaning. To me, *this* is immorality.

But if you show killing in an agonizing, realistic way, with the spurting of blood and people dying slowly and horribly, that is reality, because very rarely does a man die instantly, and to witness that on the screen can do nothing but repel you from engaging in it in real life. Look at literature. The Bible is enough to make you faint. And when Sholokhov tells you about the atrocities in Russia in *And Quiet Flows the Don,* he describes them with utmost detail and nobody would ever think of criticizing it, because that's how literature evolved, whereas cinema is something young, something much more commercial, and boundaries were forced upon it, at least in the Anglo-Saxon countries, so it couldn't evolve in the proper way. Instead, the cinema has tended to draw hypocritical, gilded pictures of life and death.

PLAYBOY: For the past two years, you've remained silent about the murder of your wife and friends, despite the enormous and lurid exposure it has received in the press. Are you wiling to tell your side of the story now?

POLANSKI: It's not something I talk about with friends, but I would like to go through it once from beginning to end. I have terrific difficulty in trying to reconstruct that period, but I have some definite things to say about it. I lost something most precious to me, and I'm sure that the people who were close to us feel the same way. But when it happened, the press said in unison, "Yes, of course, that's the way he lived, that's what he created in his films, and here is the result." That was the first outburst. *Time* magazine said, "It was a scene as grisly as anything in Polanski's film explorations of the dark and melancholy side of the human character." I was baffled, to say the least, by the cheapness and platitude of such writing, I remember their headline: "NOTHING BUT BODIES." It was sickening, the way the press sensationalized something that was already sensational.

This was a subject I knew more about than anybody else, a subject very near to my heart. I had long known that it was impossible for a journalist to convey a hundred percent of the truth, but I didn't realize to what extent the truth is distorted, both by the intentions of the journalist and by neglect. I don't mean just the interpretations of what happened; I also mean the facts. The reporting about Sharon and the murders was virtually criminal. Reading the papers, I could not believe my eyes. *I could not believe my eyes!* They blamed the victims for their own murders. I really *despise* the press. I didn't always. The press made me despise it.

Some of those articles! From *Pageant:* "Those Sharon Tate Orgies: Sex, Sadism, Celebrities." Incredible! Particularly in view of the fact that a woman eight and a half months pregnant has limited desires for orgies. It was like the press suddenly had a new dictionary, with words like *masochism, sadism, sodomy, suicide, witchcraft, rituals, drug abuse* and *necrophilia*. They put in everything they could imagine. One magazine ran a photograph of Sharon with the four other victims floating around behind her like champagne bubbles while she is dancing. God *damn* them! The victims were assassinated two times: once by the murderers, the second time by the press.

PLAYBOY: Why, do you think?

POLANSKI: I don't know. I really don't know. I think because of some resentment, some bitterness, some jealousy; and let me tell you, a lot of journalists and nonjournalists who wrote "personal" accounts of what they claimed to know made a lot of money off the case. I wonder to myself: Were the people who wrote those slanderous articles any better than the murderers? I don't think so. They just use different forms of expression. Tell me, what makes the press so fucking vituperative?

PLAYBOY: There's no question that certain elements of the press had a field day exploiting the murders, but the legitimate press made a more serious and responsible effort to find out if there was some connection between the victims and the murderers. Wasn't that both logical and understandable?

POLANSKI: Yes, I suppose. But they all groped for the "irony" in the murders, which was nonsense, and then turned my films into a metaphor for the murders. And they all believed there had to be a logical motive, so they slandered us with articles about "the wild parties that led to the massacre"—which is an exact title of one newspaper story—and the connections of Jay Sebring and Voyteck with certain anonymous drug dealers. These articles remind me of the story about the guy who says to his friend, "Imagine. *Pâtê de foie gras,* two-inch steak, with spinach and French fries, chocolate pudding and coffee, all for twenty-five cents," and his friend says, "That's impossible. Where?" And he answers, "I didn't say where. I said, 'Imagine.' "

There is a couple who live in Hollywood, Joe Hyams and Elke Sommer. He's supposed to be a writer and she's supposed to be an actress, yet they were both out there peddling articles saying that they knew the way we lived and the people we hung around with, and so they knew that tragedy would happen to us sooner or later. Astonishing! I met them once in my life. Once! But there is something magical about the printed word, so the average reader says, "Well, if they print it, it must be true," and the press was booming about this sort of thing so often and with such assurance that even some of our friends were affected by it. They would read something and say, "We didn't know about that." And I would say, "I didn't either."

What people read about us after the murders would make them ask one question: When did they have the time to work, between their orgies and rituals and drug taking? How did I have time to make four films in three and a half years? How did Sharon have the time to make even more? How did Jay Sebring run a business? Abigail Folger was a social worker who got up at six in the morning to go to Watts to work, then to a speed-reading class after work, and she would come back at eleven at night, utterly exhausted and hardly able to perform rituals and orgies before getting up at six again the next morning. And Voyteck was desperately trying to get something together in films. I had promised him a job on a film about dolphins I was preparing, and he was very excited about that and doing his own research on the subject. *Time* magazine said he had "sinister connections to which even the tolerant Polanski objected." Where do they get this stuff? I ask you. Where do they get it?

PLAYBOY: Perhaps from the reputation you and many of your friends had around Los Angeles for being sort of "rich hippies" whose life-style revolved around parties, drugs, casual sex and the like.

POLANSKI: All us sinful hedonists, eh? Should that have made the tragedy seem understandable to people? How could the press accept that as the explanation? These were all very good people, and this was a happy, blameless period of my life. There were lots of parties at people's houses, on the beach or in the mountains, and often Sharon would make dinner, and there was this magnificent group of friends who would come to our house, and we would sit outside where it was warm, with the sky full of stars, and listen to music or talk for hours—films, sex, politics or whatever. We all tried to help each other, we were all happy at each other's successes, and it was beautiful, and so new to me. I never knew life could be a luxury. It had always been hotel rooms and struggle, and now I loved this life, I loved the place, I loved the people, I loved my work. I was paying my maid over two hundred dollars a week, which is probably what a Polish worker earns in six months. I could not believe such affluence and comfort. Sharon and I had great prospects. We wanted to settle for good in Los Angeles. We had big plans. It seemed to be a kind of peculiar, happy dream. But there was nothing freaked out, sinister or immoral about it.

PLAYBOY: There were stories that Sebring and Frykowski were into a drug-dealing scene.

POLANSKI: Those stories were nonsense. The most they would ever do was buy pot from someone for their own use.

PLAYBOY: At the time, the press stressed that Frykowski and Abigail Folger had been living in your house for several months, even while you were away, and that Sebring always seemed to be around. The implication was that this was evidence of bizarre goings on.

POLANSKI: Jay was a frequent visitor, but he *never* stayed at the house. It seemed reasonable to have Voyteck and Gibby stay there to watch the house while we were gone, and when Sharon returned from London to Los Angeles before I did, we both felt better that she would have someone there with her. So it could hardly be considered some bizarre scene. You've seen how people come and go from my house in St. Tropez. You've also seen that it's pretty innocent, in a college-fraternity sort of way.

PLAYBOY: What about the occult rituals that stories said were taking place—stories that gained momentum from the fact that you had directed *Rosemary's Baby*?

POLANSKI: Do you want me to be rude with you? As I said before, not only do I not endorse the occult but it is something so foreign to my rational, materialistic philosophy of life that I protest against those implications. And Sharon—it was *fantastic* what they were attributing to her. In death, they made a monster out of her. A monster out of the sweetest, most innocent, lovable human being. She was kindness itself to everybody and everything around her—people, animals, everything. She just didn't have a bad bone in her body. She was a unique person. It's difficult to describe her character. She was just utterly good, the kindest human being I've ever met, with an extreme patience. To live with me was proof of her patience, because to be near me must be an ordeal. She never had a bad temper, she was never moody. She enjoyed being a wife. The press and the public knew of her physical beauty, but she also had a beautiful soul, and this is someting that only her friends knew about. Before I met Sharon in 1966, my love life, as opposed to my sex life, had been unsuccessful and painful and I guarded my freedom. My first marriage had been a very traumatic experience.

PLAYBOY: In what way?

POLANSKI: After I left Poland and was wandering around Paris in circles, young and full of enthusiasm, I was married briefly to a Polish actress but I really hate talking about it for some reason. Not because it's painful to talk about but because it's so futile. So let's not talk about it. OK?

PLAYBOY: OK. You were saying you met Sharon in 1966.

POLANSKI: While filming *The Fearless Vampire Killers,* in which she had a role. I was living what *you* would call the life of a playboy, and marriage was the last thing in my mind. Except for the few months of my first marriage, I had lived all my life like a nomad. I grew up sitting on suitcases in the midst of war. My mother was taken to the concentration camp when I was eight and my father was taken a few months later. I felt that any type of family tie, anything that means nest, ends in tragedy. But seeing Sharon more and more often, I knew a sentimental relationship was developing. At the beginning, I was afraid of this. But she was so extremely understanding, tactful and clever. Being around me, she still made me feel absolutely free, and she made it clear that she was not going to engulf me. I remember once her words, "I am not one of those ladies who swallow a man." And it was true. Finally, she moved to my house in London and we began to live together, and a new emotional adventure started. After two years, I realized that she would like to get married. She never asked me, never said a word about it. So finally I said, "I'm sure you would like to get married," and she said she would. So I said, "We'll get married, then," and we did. By that time, I wasn't nervous about it at all.

Sharon was the first woman in my life who really made me feel happy. I mean literally aware of being happy. That's a very rare state. Strangely enough, about a week or two before her death, I remember an instant when I was thinking of it, and I was actually thinking: "I am a happy man!" And it was a sentiment that I hadn't known before, because there had always been something missing from my happiness, some little thing that always needed adjusting. I also remember thinking—and here is my middle-European background, probably—I remember thinking: "This cannot possibly last. It's impossible to last." And I suddenly got scared. I was thinking that you can't maintain such a status quo. I didn't have anything tragic in mind, but I was afraid, being quite a realist, that such a state cannot last indefinitely.

PLAYBOY: How did the news of the murders come to you?

POLANSKI: I was in our house in London, working on a script for *The Day of the Dolphin,* with my friends Andy Braunsberg and Michael Brown. I was walking around the room talking about one scene and the phone rang. It was my agent in Los Angeles. He said, "Roman, there was a disaster in a house." I said. "Which house?" "Your house," and then quickly, in one go, he said, "Sharon is dead, and Voyteck and Jay and Abigail."

PLAYBOY: What then?

POLANSKI: I just kept saying, "No, no, no, no." My first reaction was that there must have been a hill slide, with the mountains sliding down or something. I said. "How?" He said, "I don't know, I don't know." He was crying on the other end of the line, and I was crying, and I just kept saying it was insane, and finally he told me they had been murdered. A little while later, another friend came to our house and we went out and walked the streets for a while. When we came back, they called a doctor, who gave me a shot, and I slept.

PLAYBOY: How did you happen to be in London just then, when Sharon was eight and a half months pregnant, rather than with her?

POLANSKI: I had been working on that script for several months, while Sharon was doing a film in London. She was quite pregnant but working until the last possible moment. We were planning that I could finish the script and we would return to Los Angeles together, but the script kept dragging on. By this time, Sharon couldn't fly anymore, because the airlines don't allow you to after a certain period of pregnancy, so she decided to take the boat home. I couldn't take the boat, because it took so long, so I was supposed to take a plane as soon as I finished the script, and this was to be just days after she arrived in Los Angeles.

When she left London, I took Sharon to the boat, the Q.E. II, and we had lunch. When they asked visitors to leave the boat came the moment when we had to say good-bye to each other—the saddest moment of my life, because we were seeing each other for the last time and didn't know it. I remember I called her on the ship later that afternoon. She was telling me the news about our new dog, named Prudence. She told me the dog was very happy on the boat because her rubber ball never stopped rolling around the cabin. After that, we talked daily on the phone. The bill was astronomical. On the last call, just ten hours before it happened—it was a Friday—she told me that they had found a wild kitten and they were trying to feed it with an eyedropper, and they were keeping him in the bathtub because he was absolutely wild, jumping on people, etc. Funny how life is weaved out of these little banal moments that make it worthwhile. At the end of that call, I said, "I'm coming Monday." I was annoyed that I had to say Monday, because she couldn't wait for me to come, and I couldn't wait to leave, but the goddamn script kept dragging on. So I told her, "I'm coming Monday, whether I'm through or not." That was our last conversation.

PLAYBOY: How long did it take you to accept the fact of her death?

POLANSKI: A long time. At first the reaction is panic. Completely disjointed, you can't concentrate, you can't put things together to realize what has actually happened. You can't believe. You can't conceive of the fact that she and the others are no longer alive. I could not grasp this very thin moment that separated their existence from nothingness. After that came a period of utter grief that lasted as long as the investigation. Somehow, those two things were parallel. For months, I thought of nothing else and then, all at once, when the crime was solved, my obsession stopped. Then came the period of dismissal, of withdrawal. I moved to Switzerland and started skiing myself silly with a bunch of friends, hedonists you would call them. They were wonderful to me. Kind and gentle and tactful, but I was able to do it all only for the dismissal.

And after the period of extensive skiing and social life, I decided to go back to work. Right after the murders, everyone kept patting me on the shoulder and saying I must go back to work, and work would make me forget, make my life worthwhile. But I couldn't even have tried to pull myself together at that point, and I remember talking to Stanley Kubrick and he said, "I'm sure that everybody tells you to work. You can't work in this state of mind, but there will come a moment when you feel suddenly, 'I have to go out and work.' " And that is exactly what happened after the period in Switzerland. I have worked for over a year on *Macbeth* and now, two years after it happened, you talk to me, ask me questions, and it seems as though it all happened two weeks ago. So it's a kind of trial for me.

PLAYBOY: Do you want to go through with it?

POLANSKI: Absolutely.

PLAYBOY: When your period of grief set in, how did you feel about not having been there that night?

POLANSKI: I had, and still have, a tremendous feeling of guilt, a feeling that if I had been there, it wouldn't have happened, contrary to what our friends thought. They thought if I had been there, I wouldn't be here now.

PLAYBOY: Do you think you could have defended Sharon and the others from the murderers?

POLANSKI: I think I would have been able to prevent it. I don't think I would let myself be intimidated or overcome by anybody. I think I could have prevented it.

PLAYBOY: During the investigation of the murders, were you questioned by the police?

POLANSKI: Extensively. I stayed in Los Angeles because I thought my presence could be useful to them. As a matter of fact, along with our friends, the cops were the best people of all in this situation. Unlike the press, the police were realistic, but human and with genuine feeling. They were devoted to their job and I had occasion to see all sides of their personalities and their own personal problems. They were great people. I think of them with a lot of sentiment.

PLAYBOY: How did you think you might be useful to them?

POLANSKI: I thought maybe there would be some minute clue they had overlooked. And I thought I could think of people, people who had come to our house, for instance, who wouldn't occur to the police. The press was writing so much about Jay and Voyteck being the probable motives, or essential persons, that I finally started to believe there could be someone I didn't know about. So I tried to establish step by step what everybody who knew us was doing at the time. It was quite difficult without seeming too obvious, and I didn't want anyone to know I was in constant touch with the police. I never believed it was some drug supplier of Jay's. I thought it was the work of some insane person, terribly jealous of one of us for some reason, but I couldn't give myself any plausible answer. I just kept listening and looking.

It's very difficult for me talk about it. There are things I'm not sure we should even talk about. I was under this tremendous illusion that by solving the crime, it would be easier on me, somehow. Only after months did I understand that I was just chasing rabbits, running around in circles, that finding the murderers wouldn't bring her back. And I had to explain this to Sharon's parents, who I felt were under the same illusion. Colonel Tate, Sharon's father, was also seeing the police every day, for the same reasons I was. Thank God, Sharon's parents never allowed themselves to believe the trash the press was printing about us.

PLAYBOY: You never felt the Tates somehow blamed you?

POLANSKI: No. They were with me all the time. They knew the people who were our friends and they knew the press was lying about the way we lived.

PLAYBOY: As it turned out, did you do anything during the investigation that now seems to have been helpful?

POLANSKI: How could I? No one I knew had anything to do with it. I remember, at the very beginning, Lieutenant Bob Helder told me about this group of hippies living at that ranch with this guy they called Jesus Christ. Bob said they were suspected of being involved in the killing of some musician and writing a note on his body, and there was a possibility that these people had something to do with it. I said, "Come on, Bob, you're prejudiced against hippies." And I remember his words: "You should suspect everyone. Don't dismiss it so easily." But I didn't think much about it, because I could see *no* connection and I had nothing instinctively against them as hippies. The hippies, with their "Make love, not war" philosophy, were sympathetic figures to me.

PLAYBOY: Before you knew who was guilty, didn't you fear for your own life?
POLANSKI: In such a state, you don't give a damn for your own life. I was *hoping* that he, or they, would show up. I was living on the beach with a dear friend of mine, Dick Sylbert, the art director of *Rosemary's Baby*. He was mother and father and brother—I won't say wife—to me for three months, with me being constantly preoccupied. Poor guy. The neighbors were all up in arms about me being there. They believed what they read in the papers and thought they might have a scandal, or a murder, in their neighborhood. But I was prepared to defend myself if anything happened.
PLAYBOY: Were you carrying a gun?
POLANSKI: I asked the police and they said I shouldn't, because if something happened and I used a weapon, there would be all sorts of trouble. I didn't really want a gun anyway. I felt I could take care of myself; and anyway, it didn't matter, because I was obsessed with finding who was responsible. Then suddenly, when the police announced to the press that they had the murderers, the press had to somehow pretend they had known it was something like this all along, something totally unconnected with us and with my films, and I remember the policemen laughing sarcastically about how the press had now decided that the victims were not actually the guilty ones after all. Suddenly, it was obvious to them that it had been a bunch of crazy hippies, and people like Mr. Elke Sommer promptly forgot that he "saw the murder coming." The victims were now dismissed within twenty-four hours and new things started appearing—phony interviews with me and quotes that I was "overjoyed" at the news. That word hardly describes my emotions. But at that moment, a strange thing happened to me: I was relieved. I lost all interest in what was going to happen.
PLAYBOY: Why?
POLANSKI: I finally realized that the only way to get over it was to dismiss it completely, and also I knew I couldn't change anything. It's like the only way to cope with the stress was to dismiss everything, to erase that part of the tape from my memory bank. It just disappeared in my head. I had no reason to follow what the press said about Manson, because I had no reason to believe they would be any more accurate about him than they were about Sharon and me, so I didn't read at all about him. All that I do know about Manson I knew from the police in those days before they broke the news to the press. For my own good, I completely ignored him and that trial, particularly because the press made a real circus out of it. The way they handled it was as deplorable as the way they handled the reporting of the murders. Before you ask how I know if I didn't read about it, I'll tell you: There are headlines you can't avoid, and the radio. You can't *escape* knowing certain things. I can't reconstruct the trial period for you at all, but I suspect that the ritualistic element of the crazy sect was grossly exaggerated by the press and that the assassins willingly capitalized on that, being aware that this aura would give him more chance of publicity, which would render the trial more complicated.
PLAYBOY: What makes you suspect that?
POLANSKI: One of the policemen told me about one of Manson's friends being in jail—this was before the murders—and Manson was trying to get the money somewhere to bail him out, and they went to Terry Melcher, who had been renting the house before we moved in. I don't know the details and I don't even know if this was ever brought up at the trial, but in any case, I think they were after money that night, and Manson was clever enough to know that if money came to be viewed as the

motive, he wouldn't seem such a mystifying figure, because materialistic motives are always regarded as more easily understandable, and therefore dismissed, than any kind of ideological motives. Even if the ideological motives are pure evil, people will pay much more attention to them than to robbery by an ordinary criminal, because then they have to contest the *ideology*. Manson knew if he was seen as a false god, not only would he get more attention but he would even force the middle-class hypocrites he hated so much to look at him more closely and compare his values with theirs. But his ideological, ritualistic motives for the murders were tremendously exaggerated.

PLAYBOY: From what you know of him, how would you analyze a man like Charles Manson?

POLANSKI: In any hippie area, you see sometimes an older guy, maybe even middle-aged, maybe with a fat stomach, who without the cover of hippiedom would only be a fat, perhaps pathetic man. But here he is with the long hair and wearing flowery shirts, and he seems to be an entirely different individual, and he enjoys the promiscuity of this type of life, and he becomes an attractive person to the hippies, who may be very naïve and ignorant. Now, this guy is basically the same as he was in straight society, with all the same impulses and motivations he had developed there, whatever those may be, but he becomes a part of the hippies, and masquerades as one of them. Christ, it's so difficult to explain what I mean. I'm not a verbalist. I express myself every way better than with words. I want to tell you a story that will perhaps explain what I mean.

PLAYBOY: Go ahead.

POLANSKI: When I was sixteen in Poland, and tremendously interested in bicycle racing, I met a guy in his twenties, and I hung around with him a little bit and kind of liked him. He was what you would call now a groovy guy. He offered to sell me a racing bicycle for a very cheap price and I got greedy. I had this appointment to meet him in an old German bunker near the park, and I went down to meet him and he got me alone and hit me on the head with a stone five times. I still have the scars on my scalp. I lost consciousness for a few seconds, and then I saw him standing above me asking where the money was. He took it and my watch and ran away. I couldn't understand why he had done that. A few minutes later, he was caught by some truck drivers, and a week later, the detectives came to the hospital to ask me for details. I said, "Will he get a long sentence?" They laughed at me. "He's going to be hanged," one of them said. "He killed three people before this."

It was the first time I was acquainted with this type of individual. People seem to dismiss the fact that Manson had a criminal track record, too. He spent a great deal of his life in prison. He had a record long before he tried to be a hippie. This man who hit me with the stone was another Manson, only Manson was lucky to live in a period when certain attributes are considered virtues: He could wear long hair and a beard for his hippie masquerade, while preaching a philosophy that was basically criminal. This other guy, who was trying to murder me, he was just a murderer, and no one would view him as anything but a criminal. No one would have mistaken *him* for a Jesus.

PLAYBOY: You mentioned earlier that the hippies were sympathetic figures for you. Are they still?

POLANSKI: Remember the first be-ins in Central Park, when they would throw flowers at the policemen? How blameless. I think these people were sincere at that time. But the hippies don't really exist anymore. The hippie movement has degenerated, but the degeneration came from the top, not from the bottom. When the kids began preaching new values, the government tried to beat their ideas out of them. The reaction, from Berkeley on, was only what you could expect: violence.

PLAYBOY: Critics feel that drugs were an integral part of the hippie philosophy and a principal reason for the psychological degeneration of some of them, including the girls who carried out Manson's orders.

POLANSKI: I don't have a professional knowledge about drugs to say anything really sound about it, but I do know that marijuana and the other hallucinogenic drugs are rather a source of indolence. They are dropout drugs. They make people passive. In this respect, you could say that these drugs make people more easily influenced; but, on the other hand, they would not incite you to take any action, any active enterprise, and they are certainly not murderous drugs. You know what marijuana does to people: They want to lay about and do nothing, smile and listen to music. So you have to decide which way you want it. You can't blame these drugs for making people indolent and also for inciting them to violent crime.

PLAYBOY: But weren't hallucinogenic drugs a part of the whole pathology that turned Manson from a common criminal into a Jesus Christ figure in the eyes of his followers—a pathology that would require a certain passivity on the part of those being manipulated?

POLANSKI: I think definitely that the people who are submitted to this kind of life are more vulnerable than regular members of society; but whatever the drugs do, they don't make you lose the ability to distinguish between right and wrong. Do you think you could commit a murder under the influence of drugs?

PLAYBOY: No. But we're talking now about those emotionally crippled young girls who, without exposure to a cult of mind-bending drugs, slavelike promiscuity and the rituals of a would-be Jesus Christ, would almost certainly never have been galvanized into committing murder.

POLANSKI: Don't forget that certain individuals have a talent to draw masses behind them. Hitler did the same thing with normal, straight, square German society.

PLAYBOY: Even given the historical fact of Hitler, aren't you willing to admit that drugs, which you accept or at least defend, played some role in what happened?

POLANSKI: No. Which drugs? I think there is nothing wrong with marijuana. There are millions of people smoking pot, but there is no parallel of Manson's story within any other group of people that I could speak of. I can think of more similarities between Manson and *In Cold Blood* than with the pot smokers of this world. People are just looking for an easy excuse, an easy explanation for the murders. Personally, I don't think it had anything to do with smoking marijuana.

PLAYBOY: What about LSD?

POLANSKI: I have never endorsed LSD. I took about three trips on acid several years ago, and they were all bad and I swore off. But that's still an answer that's too easy. How about those people in West Pakistan, who maybe in their ordinary lives were just quiet peasants or office clerks before they were sent off with the army on its binges of murder? How about the German soldier committing atrocities during the war, who might have been an ordinary man with a family and children? Were these people under the influence of LSD? How about Charles Whitman and Richard Speck? How about Lieutenant Calley? He seems to me a very straight person by conventional standards. I just think that certain people need very little excuse to commit criminal acts, and maybe the drugs were an excuse for Manson and these girls to vent their murderous instincts.

PLAYBOY: How did you react to the death sentences they received?
POLANSKI: In principle, I'm against capital punishment. I think the world would be a better place if it were abolished. I don't think capital punishment is moral, because we should not presume to terminate somebody's life.
PLAYBOY: Then you oppose the sentences?
POLANSKI: You're asking a very difficult question. A very difficult question. Because I really don't know. I feel very often a need for revenge. I suspect revenge may be one of the most important motives in human progress and in seeking justice. But it remains to be determined how the revenge should be performed. If the criminal kills eight people and is captured and tried, is it moral or immoral to take his life? I think it's immoral. Capital punishment is just another brutalizing aspect of modern life.

I don't know if I'm being clear. If you ask me should there be capital punishment, I say no. But if you ask me about a particular case of someone who engineered a murder—and remember, my emotional state is involved—in a jurisdiction where capital punishment exists within the system in which he was judged, then I would say to give him anything less than the maximum that exists is immoral. Who should be given more? I think Manson did the utmost, and within the set of rules that exists, he should be given the utmost sentence. He committed his crime while capital punishment was still the maximum sentence that could be handed out in Calfironia. At one point, I was asked to make the gesture of asking for clemency for him, and I said I wouldn't do that. I think that would be an act of hypocrisy on my part; but I do ask for abolition of capital punishment for everyone, not just for Manson.
PLAYBOY: Was it an act of hypocrisy for Ted Kennedy to ask clemency for Sirhan Sirhan?
POLANSKI: Yes, I think so. That's precisely what I was thinking of when I said I wouldn't be willing to do that. I wouldn't be against siding with Ted Kennedy, saying that we are against capital punishment as part of the system of law. But I think it's phony nobility to go to bat, as it were, for your "pet" murderer, the one who caused *you* so much suffering.
PLAYBOY: You said earlier that your experiences during the war had taught you that family ties end in tragedy. After a little more than two years since the murders, do you feel they were yet another lesson that one's happiness will always be snatched away?
POLANSKI: You mention the word *lesson*. Unfortunately, there is no lesson to be taken. There is just nothing. It's absolutely senseless, stupid, cruel and insane. I'm not sure it's even worth talking about. Sharon and the others are dead. I can't restore what was.
PLAYBOY: But has the experience changed your vision of life?
POLANSKI: I don't know. I wouldn't call myself a fatalist, because those are people who just sit and wait for whatever will happen to them, and I'm not like that. I have always been sentimental and not a cynic, and that hasn't changed, but these are wounds that don't leave you without scars. I think I was probably a better human being before. It's difficult to define, but I think I was more gentle with people before. I don't think my emotional state now would permit me to develop serious new emotional ties with anybody.
PLAYBOY: Yet you appear to have feeling for, and ties with, those around you.
POLANSKI: You don't change your character drastically. It's only a note that changes. There was more youth in my feeling for people, more naïveté. I don't even know if the change is visible to my friends. I think it is.

PLAYBOY: Yet you give the impression of having adjusted. You seem a happy enough man.
POLANSKI: How could you even suspect me of such a thing? How could I be happy? There must be something that *makes* you happy.
PLAYBOY: You seem to enjoy your friends, and your women, and your work.
POLANSKI: These are things that give me pleasure, even make me content. But there's nothing that really makes me *happy*. Not anymore.
PLAYBOY: Then what keeps you going?
POLANSKI: I'm asking myself that question. What is it in the human being that makes him overcome practically everything and keep going? I don't know. There are endless people with tragedies more atrocious than mine, and they keep plowing away, too. After a period of mourning, they somehow restore their way of life. But I tell you, I know myself and I feel there's something gone. I don't have the same desires, the same dreams I used to have. I don't know why. It's something that's troubled me for quite some time now. It must be connected somehow with the death of Sharon, but also I think it's partly the fact that I have already achieved what I always dreamed of.
PLAYBOY: You mean that having achieved major success as a filmmaker, you're not as driven as you once were?
POLANSKI: Precisely. Throughout the years, my basic engine was the desire to make films. I dreamed of doing films, and somehow I don't feel this overpowering urge anymore. I first noticed the symptoms of my loss of enthusiasm when I went to Hollywood to make *Rosemary's Baby*. The first day I went onstage with seventy people waiting for me, I remembered the day I had first gone on location to shoot *Knife in the Water*. Then, I'd had butterflies in my stomach and that incredible feeling of anticipation that prevents you from going to sleep the whole night before. Now, here I was in Hollywood, in the place that belonged more to my dreams than to my reality, at the threshold of where everything would be handed to me, and I felt absolutely no thrill. I felt I was just going to work for the day—work I loved doing, but there was no *thrill* in it. Do you understand?
PLAYBOY: Yes. But how, then, did you turn in your best work? Or did you?
POLANSKI: I did a good job, but not my best work. Maybe it's just pride in craft. Maybe that is the way to achieve the maximum in what you do. I care about what I make. It's a dear thing to me and I think it remains so because it's a part of human nature to want to do something durable. Who was the Pharaoh who built the biggest of the pyramids? He must have been quite persistent, making these people put one stone on top of another for years in order to create something that would last. I'm quite persistent myself, only lately I am asking myself sometimes: "Why bother?" Maybe it's just that I am more sure of myself and my abilities. Maybe that's it. Or maybe I'm just more relaxed. But on the other hand, a cow is relaxed. Maybe I should ask some maharishi. Maybe he would tell me that I have become wiser. I would hate to become wiser, but I think that, in a way, that's what has happened.
PLAYBOY: Why do you resist wisdom?
POLANSKI: Because wise people are boring and they usually lack the enthusiasm and spontaneity to make things come together. I'm afraid it's inevitable that the more experience you acquire, the more you lose your desires, your dreams, your fantasies. It's the same thing in sex. I just don't enjoy it as much as I used to. It's getting a bit repetitious. It's very much like making films; your wisdom and security and experience bring your craft up to a high standard, but you get less thrill out of it as an individual.

PLAYBOY: Maybe your ordained role is to serve as a craftsman, bringing pleasure to moviegoers and women.
POLANSKI: I like that idea. I wish it were true. They say that happiness is seeking the fulfillment of our desires, and usually people spend their lives seeking that fulfillment. But I am at a stage where I'm seeking the *desires*. Have you got any ideas? Help me. Tell me what is the problem here. If not for the sake of the interview, then at least maybe I'll get something out of it.
PLAYBOY: Perhaps you're just suffering from the onset of middle age.
POLANSKI: I do start feeling that now, and I'm very surprised, because I thought it would never happen. Being a born optimist, who never thinks he's going to fail in anything he undertakes, I'm caught off guard by it. But I don't think it's going to last long. It's just a passing stage that will go away as I grow younger.
PLAYBOY: In the meantime, you seem to be doing a successful, if not inspired, job of living the life of what you would call a hedonist.
POLANSKI: I don't know whether I'm a hedonist. It's just my reputation. If I am, I work harder than any other hedonist I've ever met. I'm quite spartan in some ways. I get up early, I exercise to keep myself in shape; I rather like the boy scout, sportive way of life. Yet I do love everything life has to offer; so I don't reject luxury if I can afford it, and I don't reject any source of joy that you can acquaint yourself with in your lifetime—particularly sex.
PLAYBOY: Would one be correct to attribute your refusal to deny yourself any of life's luxuries or pleasure to your childhood during the war, when you were deprived of them?
POLANSKI: No. What if I had had a marvelous childhood with rows of lackeys and nannies bringing me hot chocolate and chauffeurs driving me to the cinema? Then you would say I am this way because I *had* such a luxurious childhood. The truth is I am just this way. Period. But I will tell you, I did have sexual problems as a youth.
PLAYBOY: What kind?
POLANSKI: I had an absolute patent on masturbation when I was twelve. I thought I invented it. But it made me feel terrifically guilty, and each time I was doing it, I was promising myself it was the last time, definitely the last time I was touching it. Until the next morning. I didn't make it with a chick until I was seventeen and a half which I think is very late.
PLAYBOY: According to the press, you've certainly made up for lost time ever since.
POLANSKI: I found out I like sex. How about that? I like fucking. You remember Kafka's story about the man who fasts professionally in a circus? He was breaking his own records, fasting longer and longer, and finally he fasts so long that everybody forgets all about him. They even forget to mark on his little blackboard the number of days of his fast, which already was incredible. Finally, a cleaning man comes and finds him agonizing under a pile of straw, and he leans down and asks, "Why did you do it? Why?" And with his dry lips and his fading voice, the faster says, "I hated food!" It's beautiful. There was no other reason for fasting. I'm the opposite. I screw because I like screwing. That's all there is to it.
PLAYBOY: Do you concern yourself with the moral issues involved with sex?
POLANSKI: Of course. I don't want to sound pompous, but in a way, I'm actually a moralist. I cherish certain qualities of a civilized mind, qualities that are very difficult to measure or describe, because they have quite flimsy names like nobility, loyalty,

etc. This applies, for instance, to my friends. Friendship to me is a very Sicilian thing. It's a matter of life and death. I would do absolutely anything for my friends, and I demand the same in return. Because friendship is a form of love. I separate love from sex. For many people, fornication is immoral. Strangely enough, it seems supremely moral to me to have sex with a girl I've met in the harbor at St. Tropez. Sex is beautiful. No one gets hurt. Just the opposite. It's simple, isn't it? So if it's true that I'm a playboy, it's only in this respect. The rest of being a playboy doesn't have much attraction for me.

PLAYBOY: Does it ever bother you that some people are more interested in your image as a playboy than in your films?

POLANSKI: I think it's great.

PLAYBOY: Wouldn't you rather be known as a film director whose personal life is of little curiosity?

POLANSKI: Do you mean like Walt Disney? My only disappointment is that people created this conception of me as a decadent man of excess without my active participation. In the beginning, I resented it, but finally I thought, so what? People never know the truth about an individual, anyway. Among all the movies I've seen, I like *Citizen Kane* the most, not only for the way it's done but for what it says. It says that you never know the real truth about anyone. So who cares? The image of a hard worker laboring all day doesn't go well with me. It doesn't help me in my social life. People would get bored with me if I told them, "Hey, listen, guys, I really work very hard. I get up at seven in the morning and I rush from one place to another on business and I don't have a spare minute to take a holiday." I only tell people I'm a busy man when I want to get rid of them. Like a PLAYBOY interviewer, you understand? Otherwise, I prefer to seem frivolous, a guy who socializes all the time. For one thing, I realized that this reputation helps me in my relations with women. I've noticed that as my reputation grows worse, my success with women increases.

PLAYBOY: How do you account for this?

POLANSKI: When I meet a new girl, she's already prejudiced against me. She's put off by my image and she thinks, "I'll never make it with *him*!" She wants to prove something to herself. She doesn't want to lower herself to the level of, let's say, her predecessors. But she's intrigued and she wants to know me as an individual, and underneath there is something difficult to describe—a kind of curiosity about me. People are intrigued by the devil and attracted when they discover that on top of having horns and a tail, he's also charming. So you see, she meets me and she's tremendously surprised that I'm not at all the way she thought I was, and already she begins to switch her attitude. She's thrown off guard. I know all this talk about women sounds pretentious and arrogant and megalomaniac. Jesus, it begins to sound that way even to *me*.

PLAYBOY: Kenneth Tynan, your friend and co-writer of the screenplay for *Macbeth*, implied in a recent article that your attitude toward women approaches the feudalistic.

POLANSKI: Ken, who is a good friend, knows absolutely nothing about my emotional-sexual relationships with women. He is a left-wing intellectual who feels he must support liberation movements, including the one by women, so I very often tease him by saying something about how reactionary I am on the subject. This causes complete outrage on his part, so you shouldn't treat seriously what Ken says about my feelings toward women.

PLAYBOY: In what ways are you reactionary about them?

POLANSKI: Well, you must admit that most women one meets do not have the brain of Einstein. I have a very firm theory about male and female intelligence. It causes an absolute outrage if you say that women on the average are less intelligent than men, but it happens to be true. Since society is becoming more and more democratic about these things, though, we'd better not mention that.
PLAYBOY: That's a highly debatable allegation, but in any case, Tynan wrote that you also dislike *bright* women. His exact words, as we recall, were that Polanski feels the only two acceptable positions for a woman are sitting down and lying down.
POLANSKI: That's a marvelous line, but it's complete crap. First of all, my wife, although people may not know it, was an extremely bright person. But she would never be pushy about her intelligence in order to show people how clever she was. She knew it's feminine to not try to *compete* with men and seem dominating. But I must admit that I rarely find an intelligent female companion with whom I can get along, for the reason that most women who are smart try to compete with the man, and I can't stand the competition of a female.
PLAYBOY: Why?
POLANSKI: Because that brings our relationship onto the wrong level. It becomes like between a man and a man, a masculine relationship. I'm too sensitive about a woman's behavior, and there are too many things that can put me off. Sometimes the most beautiful woman can put me off completely by doing something ungraceful. I'm certain, by the way, that a sensitive woman feels the same toward men. I think even more so. Sometimes I'm charmed by the fact that there are women with whom you can discuss the molecular theory of light all evening and at the end, they will ask you what is your birth sign. But there is nothing more enjoyable than a genuinely brilliant female companion who doesn't turn the relationship into a contest of ego.
PLAYBOY: In short, you simply prefer to dominate them.
POLANSKI: I *do* dominate them. And they like it! I know, I know, this is regarded today as a Neanderthal attitude. But I know one women's lib leader who, friends tell me, is a great cocksucker. By the way, what exactly is the women's lib position on fellatio? That it's OK, but only on an equal-time basis? And why do women sometimes use words like, "He's a *real* man"? It doesn't mean that he knits well or that he looks after the kids well. It has always meant a man who is more creative, more aggressive than a woman, because these are the qualities that have always been essential for the survival of our kind.
PLAYBOY: Does it frustrate you, or offend your male ego, when you meet a woman you want who seems to take no interest in you? Or has that ever happened?
POLANSKI: Once, I think, it happened, many years ago. No, it doesn't bother me at all, as long as she doesn't try to play games with me.
PLAYBOY: For example.
POLANSKI: To give examples, for me, is more or less like the effort of writing a screenplay. I have to sit and think, but if I were doing a screenplay, people would pay me for it.
PLAYBOY: No deal. You were talking about games people play.
POLANSKI: Let's say I meet a girl and she tries to give me the impression that she desires to go to bed with me that same evening, although I can sense immediately that it's not her intention. That's what I call games, and it lasts about ten minutes. Then I simply lose interest. I don't mind if she doesn't want to have sexual relations with me. Here you must believe me, because most males say that. But I really *don't* mind as long as she states it clearly by her behavior.

PLAYBOY: Why do you see yourself as different from most males in that regard?

POLANSKI: Because I can't demand every female to want me. I'm just being realistic about it. Or maybe it's because enough of them *do* want me that I don't feel rejected in general.

PLAYBOY: Is there anything of the Napoleonic about you—of the short man proving himself?

POLANSKI: My height must have some effect on me, but again, I don't psychoanalyze myself to discover it. I actually look smaller than I am. How tall do you think I am?

PLAYBOY: Five feet, six?

POLANSKI: Incredible! You are the first *ever* to give me extra height. I am five feet, five, which is a good size for a female. Maybe I should have been born a girl. Newsmen usually describe me as even shorter than I am. I barely reach four feet in these articles they write. Little do they know that from my point of view, it doesn't seem that I'm small. In fact, it seems to me as if I'm a giant. The terrible thing is that if people didn't tell me I was short, I would never notice. I once had this Yorkshire terrier, a wonderful little dog, and an Irish wolfhound—the largest dog in captivity—and the Yorkshire absolutely terrorized the wolfhound. I'm quite sure the terrier didn't realize he was smaller.

PLAYBOY: You're also someting of a physical-fitness nut, with your exercises and karate kicks, and wheat germ and yoghurt. How did that begin?

POLANSKI: One day when I was fourteen, I looked at myself in the mirror and I said to myself, "Jesus, what is this?" So I took a pillowcase and went down to where they were building a road and filled it up with cobblestones and started exercising. I wanted to make something of myself, so I wanted to be strong. At the same time, I started bicycle racing and skiing. Any kind of individual competition. I was totally uninterested in any kind of team effort like football. I like the drama and the glory of racers. They are individuals, and dreamers. To me, an appealing character is Jackie Stewart, because he has a lust for glory and he fulfills it.

You see sometimes men in their twenties who have let their bodies deteriorate, and they look like they're forty, and they look extremely tired and bored. These are the people who probably never had dreams they believed could be fulfilled. As a representative of a capitalist society, you must forgive me for quoting Lenin, but he said that the essential quality of a revolutionary is to be able to fantasize. To create revolution, you must be able to imagine its success. The same is true of films, and I was always dreaming of making great films.

PLAYBOY: When you were a boy, you mean?

POLANSKI: Yes. Even as a child, I always loved cinema and was thrilled when my parents would take me before the war. Then we were put into the ghetto in Krakow and there was no cinema, but the Germans often showed newsreels to the people outside the ghetto, on a screen in the marketplace. And there was one particular corner where you could see the screen through the barbed wire. I remember watching with fascination, although all they were showing was the German army and German tanks, with occasional anti-Jewish slogans inserted on cards. When I escaped from the ghetto, the first thing I looked forward to was the cinema. It was very cheap, since the Germans wanted people to go see German films, and I made the ticket money selling newspapers. It was regarded as something very low to go to the cinema, and the audience was mostly youngsters who weren't aware of their patriotic duty not to go. You could read slogans on the Wall—ONLY PIGS GO TO MOVIES, etc. But I didn't really care too much about being called a pig as long as I could go.

PLAYBOY: How do you explain this fascination?
POLANSKI: I don't know why, but I just loved it. Maybe the liking for cinema is no more mysterious than my liking for suspense; the show business and drama of cinema thrilled me as much as the purely technical aspect of *lanterna magica*—being able to project a picture on the wall and make it move.
PLAYBOY: How did you set about getting started in films?
POLANSKI: Right after the war, I got a job broadcasting on the radio as a child actor and, through that, I got a lead in a successful play in the theater. It was kind of a big splash for a kid. Later, I tried to get into acting school, but I didn't make it. Some of the professors were actors who knew me, and they thought I was too cocky. Already I was quite different from a majority of the applicants, who were scared and running around the corridors of the drama school with diarrhea and showing all the symptoms of submission and humility. I didn't have any of those symptoms, so they thought I wouldn't be good material to mold, and, thank God, I wasn't, because I would have ended up in some provincial theater in Poland making two thousand zlotys a month. At the time, I wasn't seeing much future in films, because my father ran a small plastics company, which the government considered "private initiative." That meant my political background was not the best, so the State School of Filming in Lodz seemed an impossible dream, because there was a tremendous number of applicants, and your political background was terribly important.
PLAYBOY: The curriculum at Lodz required five years for a diploma. Was it worthwhile to spend that much time studying instead of getting on-the-job training?
POLANSKI: When you analyze it, you see how advantageous it is to study cinema for five years. Besides all the practical training, like editing, camera operating, etc., you had courses in the history of art, literature, history of music, optics, theory of film directing—if such a thing exists—and so forth. The first year was very general and theoretical, and you got to know intimately the techniques of still photography, which is essential, I think, for anyone who later wants to be an expert in cinematography. The second year, the students made two one-minute films of their own. The third year, a documentary of eight to fifteen minutes. The fourth year, a short fictional film of the same length; and then in the fifth year, you made your diploma film, which could go up to twenty minutes. Mine ran twenty-five minutes and was over budget; already they were screaming at me to dance faster. It was called *When Angels Fall*, a kind of fantasy about an old lady who is a public-toilet attendant. And on top of everything else at the school, we also saw an incredible number of films—and not only each other's.
PLAYBOY: Including films from the West?
POLANSKI: Almost anything. The school was tightly connected with the Polish film archives and we could see anything we wanted. An important part of our education was a baroque wooden stairway where we would sit for hours arguing about films, which sometimes we were screening all day and all night. Occasionally, the discussions became rather heated. In fact, I have a scar under my eye from one of them. There were schools of cinema within the school. My school was *Citizen Kane,* and the school of the older students, the ones who were about to graduate when I was a cocky beginner, was *The Bicycle Thief,* and the postgraduates who were still hanging around were the Soviet Socialist Realism school—films like *Potemkin.* It was a fantastic place and I left it with very firm aesthetic ideals about films.
PLAYBOY: Can you express them in words?
POLANSKI: I'll try. For me, a film has to have a definite dramatic and visual shape, as

opposed to a rather flimsy shape that a lot of films were being given by the *Nouvelle Vague,* for example, which happened in more or less the same period. It has to be something finished, like a sculpture, almost something you can touch, that you can roll on the floor. It has to be rigorous and disciplined—that's *Citizen Kane* vs. *The Bicycle Thief.*

PLAYBOY: When did you make *Knife in the Water?*

POLANSKI: In 1960. But it took a long time. After we wrote the screenplay, it was rejected by the government film bureau, so I went to France, and when I came back two years later, it was a better period politically, so I submitted it again and they accepted it and gave me a very limited budget—which I went over, of course.

PLAYBOY: *Knife in the Water* was an original, and unusual, screenplay. Where did you get the idea for it?

POLANSKI: It was the sum of several desires in me. I loved the lake area of Poland and I thought it would make a great setting for a film. I was thinking of a film with a limited number of people in it as a form of challenge. I hadn't ever seen a film with only three characters, where no one else even appeared in the background. The challenge was to make it in a way that the audience wouldn't be aware of the fact that no one else had appeared even in the background. As for the idea, all I had in mind when I began the script was a scene where two men were on a sailboat and one fell overboard. But that was a starting point, wouldn't you agree?

PLAYBOY: Certainly, but a strange one. Why were you thinking about a man falling out of a sailboat?

POLANSKI: There you go, asking me to shrink my head again. I don't *know* why. I was interested in creating a mood, an atmosphere, and after the film came out, a lot of critics found all sorts of symbols and hidden meanings in it that I hadn't even thought of. It made me sick.

PLAYBOY: You went back to Paris, and stayed on there for a couple of years—even after *Knife* had its big success in America. Why?

POLANSKI: The fact that the film was a success didn't make me in such great demand by American producers. But it did make me think that I should seek the Anglo-Saxon world rather than remain forever in France, where the film was a total flop. But those were good years in Paris. I was writing with my friend Gerard Brach, and we wrote *Repulsion* and *Cul-de-Sac* during this period, though we couldn't find anyone to produce them. In France, they aren't looking so much for new talent as for established figures. So Gerard and I were living in miserable conditions. I didn't make any money on *Knife in the Water* and we were penniless and living in little hotels and places like that. Once we were stuffed together in a broom-closet sort of room where in the eighteenth century, I think, they used to stash one domestic—because two wouldn't have fit. It was virtually a cupboard. But I think of those years with tremendous nostalgia. Whenever we got together one hundred francs, we were as happy as kings. The first thing was to run to the cinema to see a movie. The second thing was to have dinner in one of the little restaurants of St. Germain des Prés. And the third thing was to try to pull some girls. Whenever I return to those cafés and see the same characters sitting at the same tables in the identical positions—only much older—I have a very mixed sensation, and these are moments of fear, because I think, "Christ, *I* could have been sitting here still."

PLAYBOY: Was it more difficult for you to "pull" the girls then, before you had celebrity as well as notoriety, not to mention money?

POLANSKI: It was much harder, not only because of the lack of notoriety but also

because I didn't have the necessary experience. I wasn't so cool. I was too eager, and I think that's the case with every young man.
PLAYBOY: What made you decide to leave Paris and go to the U.S.?
POLANSKI: Events precipitated themselves suddenly. In late 1963, I was invited to the New York Film Festival, where *Knife in the Water* was being shown. The United States used to be a very popular country in Europe, so it was in my dreams to go there.
PLAYBOY: What was your first impression of New York?
POLANSKI: I had somehow imagined the streets of New York to be very wide, very clean, with a very even surface, and surrounded by bright, shiny buildings. I found it dense and dirty and not smooth at all. At the time, that felt familiar and stimulating. The theaters, the restaurants all seemed exciting, and a lot of the New York intellectuals, who didn't seem so left-wing and tiresome at the time, I found very exciting—maybe because I didn't speak a word of English. As you may have noticed, I still don't. I also found the constant competition—the rat race, you call it—very exciting. But now it's to an extreme that is unbearable. In those days, the rats were still eating each other; now they're eating themselves. That makes it less exciting. Anyway, not long after that trip, I was called by Gene Gutowski, later my business partner, and he suggested that I go to England to try something there. So I made *Repulsion* in London. It was quickly a financial and critical success. You know the rest.
PLAYBOY: You said *Cul-de-Sac* is your best work. Why do you think so?
POLANSKI: I think it is the most cinematic of all my films, and remember that in a way, I see myself as a technician, so that's very important to me. It's the most cinematic because it's a piece that's virtually untranslatable into any other medium. Popularity and reviews mean nothing in this judgment. The films that are considered masterpieces, like *Citizen Kane* or *L'Avventura* or *A Space Odyssey,* when you look back and start going through the reviews to find out how they were received at the time, you're often surprised to find that it was not that well. Somehow certain films make their reputation throughout the history of cinema *despite* the critics and often despite the public, and sometimes despite both. I think *Cul-de-Sac* is already on the way, from what I hear about it whenever I talk to young people or cinema buffs. *Cul-de-Sac* is going to be a very durable movie.
PLAYBOY: For all those who've panned you, there are some writers in the film journals, especially in Europe, who rank you among the handful of the world's great directors. Would you agree with them?
POLANSKI: Guess! There aren't very many great directors. I think about five or six, like Fellini, Kubrick—No, wait a minute. I can either say that I'm one of the five or six best directors without naming the rest or I can name my five or six favorites without telling you that I think I'm a part of this group, because to do that would seem too presumptous. Which do you prefer?
PLAYBOY: Both. Before we finish this interview, there's one subject we haven't even touched on: politics. Though you crossed the Iron Curtain to live and work in the capitalist West, nothing you've said has indicated even a passing interest in affairs of state.
POLANSKI: I vaguely follow politics, but I don't think a knowledge of it is essential to lead an intellectually satisfying life. You can be involved with society without being at all interested in politics. I used to be quite political, but I quit when I understood that I couldn't do much about the situation. I'll tell you exactly my motivations, because this one I know the answer to. You know already my character. You know that I'm

determined when I set out to do something, and when I'm determined, I do it. I set a goal and I desperately try to achieve it. When I'm not able to achieve what I want to, I become desperately angry and frustrated, and that's the feeling I have for politics. When I was in my twenties and living in Poland, I was concerned, and gradually I understood that all my efforts were so futile that I was reduced to some kind of mental masturbation. So I just stopped trying. I think that if I had chosen politics for a full-time career, I would certainly not only talk about it but I would do a lot about it. In general, though, I think that people who go into politics are a pretty stupid, uninspired race. I suspect that politics is quite easy, and the fact that the results are so poor everywhere is primarily because mostly second-rate people go into it. Really talented and ambitious people are usually interested in other fields of life.

My perceptions of this occurred about the same time I understood one other thing that I think also kept me away from politics, and that is the essential problem of human character, as explained so well by Oscar Hammerstein—that too many people are too early in their lives too certain of too many things. So they are ready to die or kill for these things. You gradually come to understand that whichever side they're on, it's only by accident. The same baby who grew up as a Protestant in Ireland could just as easily have grown up as a Catholic in Ireland, so this man is fighting against someone he could have very easily been himself. My point is that what fucks up the world is idealism. Idealism is usually associated with the good guys, but I'll tell you, whoever is the Imperial Wizard of the Ku Klux Klan is as much an idealist in his mind as anyone else who believes deeply in his convictions and is willing to die for them or have others killed for them. These people don't expose their prejudices to a healthy doubt.

PLAYBOY: You hardly seem one to criticize others for lack of self-doubt.

POLANSKI: My self-confidence has to do with creative activity, not political activity. These political idealists I'm talking about are the do-gooders who want to do their number for the best interests of other people, not themselves. I do it for myself, not for some ideal of what I think is best for other people and for future generations. There is a whole world of difference.

PLAYBOY: Before we leave the subject, can we persuade you to give us some general idea, using at least broad conventional labels, about whether you consider yourself on the left or the right?

POLANSKI: I definitely don't identify with the right wing in America, but that doesn't mean I have any nostalgia for communism. Come to think of it, I do know one certainty about politics: Communism is a system that doesn't work. Terrible things happen when you start going against human nature, and having lived under communism, I can say that this is exactly what it does. It's basically structured on the assumption that everybody will be performing according to good will, according to the needs of the society, which is absolutely divorced from any conception of human nature. The result is expressed in another contemporary Polish proverb: "*Czy sie stoi czy sie lezy 2000 sie nalezy*" which I'll bet is the first Polish sentence that PLAYBOY has ever published [It is.-*Ed.*]—so don't misspell it. It means: "Whether you're standing up or lying down, they still pay you your two thousand zlotys." Most people are lying down.

I'm more sympathetic to capitalism, because it's not an artificial system that was invented by a group of brilliant people. It's a stage to which people naturally evolved. It's not the ideal system. Far from it. Anyone with any feeling has to be outraged by things like Vietnam, but I don't think there is anything about it that's peculiar to

capitalism. I always hear that this war made America lose her virginity, but the truth is that this war buggered America. If the Soviet Union found herself in a similar situation, I can assure you she would deal with the problem the same way—only faster, as it happened in Hungary, Poland and Czechoslovakia. God, politics is so vague. I don't want to talk politics. I really only do it when it's thrust upon me, mostly by intellectual friends, and I end up spending my energy in unnecessary arguments. So let's talk about something else—or nothing else.
PLAYBOY: One more question: What are your plans, now that you've finished *Macbeth?*
POLANSKI: I don't like to make plans, I don't know what I'll be doing. I'll make another film, but I don't know what. There's only one thing for sure: There will be no castles, no crowd scenes, no special effects, no horses, no costumes—preferably no clothes at all. Just two people on the beach! And perhaps not so much dialogue as in this interview. As I told you, I'm not a man of words, and I've run completely out of them. I'm drained. Enough said, PLAYBOY. OK?
PLAYBOY: OK.

GROUCHO MARX

March 1974

Interviewer: Charlotte Chandler

About a year before this interview took place, Groucho Marx did a one-night stand at Carnegie Hall consisting of reminiscences, songs, and film clips to a capacity crowd. Many in the audience were teenagers wearing Groucho mustaches and glasses, ecstatic at getting the chance to see their idol—whom they'd known only in old movies or TV reruns—in the seventy-eight-year-old flesh. Groucho later said that he was astounded at the affection in which he was held by young people. It was the beginning of a prolonged farewell for Groucho as he entered a final phase of public appearances, interviews, and guest spots on television before his death in 1977.

Except for diehard Groucho buffs, who have read everything written about and by the comedian, there is something fresh for everyone in this interview. Although the jokes and stories and quips have probably appeared before in bits and pieces, Groucho himself seemed determined to make this conversation with Charlotte Chandler as all-encompassing as possible. He had a snarling fondness for PLAYBOY, often writing letters of mock protest to the magazine; and in this interview, knowing he was speaking out to his final generation, he even paused from time to time to make a serious point. Those readers who were not surprised to find that Groucho's mayhem in the movies, and his lines on *You Bet Your Life,* were carefully rehearsed will appreciate the admission that Groucho was given a chance to "check" his interview galleys—and they came back considerably funnier. The Groucho student will find everything from how he got his name to how he punched up his obituary at *The New York Times* in one conversation. Incidentally, writer Chandler took this material as the basis for a popular and equally comprehensive book on Groucho, *Hello, I Must Be Going.*

To get a genuine interview with the indefatigable man behind the mustache, PLAYBOY *sent writer Charlotte Chandler to interview him. She reports:*

"Groucho is still readily recognizable as his alter ego, Dr. Hugo Z. Hackenbush of A Day at the Races *infamy. His distinctive voice is little changed; his serious expression is punctuated occasionally by dramatic movements of the famous eyebrows. Still verbally nimble, always on the attack against pretentiousness or pretensions, never at a loss for a word—or several—he remains the maestro of the illogical, of the deflated platitude and of* reductio ad absurdum.

"Groucho is a gentleman, and a gentle man, yet he is the undisputed king of the sarcastic insult. He is a man of another time, but a man whose audience is now larger, younger and more enthusiastic than ever. The reputed chaser, always on the prowl for the not-so-elusive female, is in reality a staunch believer in the sanctity of marriage. Groucho has been married a total of forty-seven years—albeit to three women; he was divorced from all three.

"The interview took place over many weeks in varied locations, most often in Groucho's comfortable contemporary home in Beverly Hills—the house he built for his third wife, Eden. There he's surrounded by treasured possessions, including a 1915 playbill from the Orpheum Theater in Oakland; two framed Time *covers, one featuring the Marx Brothers and the other Groucho alone; a collage depicting Groucho as the 'Blue Boy,' 'Whistler's Mother' and others; an ancient hat rack festooned with berets, bowlers, straws and caps; the lectern he used in* You Bet Your Life*; the guitar that he still plays; and pictures of his parents, himself and his brothers as children.*

"Some evenings we'd dine at Groucho's; the fare might be an elaborate roast or an indoor picnic from Nate and Al's Delicatessen. Other times we'd move on to Chasen's or the Beverly Hills Hotel, where in Groucho's honor the management for the first time in its history served clam chowder on a Saturday. Our meetings continued in New York, where Zabar's provided the herring in sour cream, smoked salmon, cream cheese, celery tonic and pumpernickel. So important is pumpernickel to Groucho that he measures the financial state of the nation by its current price. We talked over soufflé of fruits de mer *and* côte de boeuf *at Lutèce. While watching the telecast of his taped appearance on the Bill Cosby show, Groucho fortified himself with chocolate cake from La Côte Basque. On occasion, we were joined by Erin Fleming, Groucho's attractive personal manager, who is also an actress specializing in Shakespeare and Shaw, but who could easily have played the Thelma Todd roles in the early Marx Brothers pictures. In real life, she plays Margaret Dumont to Groucho's Groucho. We also got together with Groucho's friend and intellectual ideal, CBS vice-president Goddard Lieberson, and with Marx Brothers superfan and Groucho's superfriend, Woody Allen.*

"For formal occasions, Groucho always wore a blue blazer over a turtleneck sweater in red, blue or white—and underneath that, a gray TELL 'EM GROUCHO SENT YOU *T-shirt. In his lapel buttonhole was the Commander of Arts and Letters medal recently bestowed upon him by the French government at the Cannes Film Festival. Ever present were the long cigars that have become his trademark; these he lit with*

one of his most-prized souvenirs, a lighter engraved SRO *to commemorate that sold-out concert at Carnegie Hall.*

"Talking to Groucho was a delight, even though from the beginning he persisted in taking over the interview—as you will see."

GROUCHO: I don't know what kind of an interview you're looking for. You want a silly interview? I don't know any jokes.
PLAYBOY: We could start by asking what question most interviewers ask you.
GROUCHO: "Could Harpo talk?"
PLAYBOY: Maybe we'll ask that later. Why don't we begin instead by asking you the very first thing you remember?
GROUCHO: You're asking me to remember almost a hundred years ago.
PLAYBOY: Well, then, what are your earliest childhood memories?
GROUCHO: I remember riding on the back of a moving van. Gummo and I were back there; we must have been pretty young, because we didn't have our piano yet. And I remember playing stickball, which was a great challenge, because we played without a ball. We couldn't afford one. Anyway, we were surrounded by three breweries where we lived in New York City—Ruppert's, Ringer's and another one; when I went to school as a kid, I could always smell the malt. We used to go over to Park Avenue, where old man Ruppert lived in a big house with a fruit orchard, and we'd steal his apples and pears. There was a spiked fence about eight feet high, and dogs. We might have been dog meat, but we were very young, and we sure liked those apples and pears. I also remember the iceman delivering ice; you'd holler out the window to tell him how much you wanted. We had no icebox; we were very poor. While the iceman was delivering the ice, we'd get in his wagon and break off some ice. Ever since then, I've been great at breaking the ice.
PLAYBOY: How poor were you?
GROUCHO: So poor that when somebody knocked on the door, we all hid. We were paying twenty-seven dollars a month rent and there were ten of us. The five brothers, my father and mother, my grandmother and grandfather and an adopted sister. There were ten of us and one toilet.
PLAYBOY: Did you want to be an actor when you were a kid?
GROUCHO: No, I wanted to be a writer. But I became an actor because we were very poor and there were four brothers so—
PLAYBOY: You said there were five of you.
GROUCHO: That's true, but what's the difference? Anyway, I decided to be in show business.
PLAYBOY: Why?
GROUCHO: Because I had an uncle in show business who was making two hundred dollars a week, and I wasn't making anything.
PLAYBOY: Did you want to be rich?
GROUCHO: I always wanted to be rich. I still want to be rich. Why, years ago, I came to Los Angeles without a nickel in my pocket. Now I *have* a nickel in my pocket. Unfortunately, the nickel today isn't worth what is used to be. Do you know what this country needs? A seven-cent nickel. We've been using the five-cent nickel since 1492. So why not give the seven-cent nickel a chance? If that works out, next year we could have a eight-cent nickel. And so on.
PLAYBOY: You should have been an economist.
GROUCHO: Then I wouldn't have been rich.

PLAYBOY: When you were still poor, what did you think being rich meant?
GROUCHO: I used to think being rich meant having a lot of money. Now I think it means having a *lot* of money.
PLAYBOY: Do you have a lot or a *lot?*
GROUCHO: Somewhere in between.
PLAYBOY: Does your money come just from income or have you also made some good investments?
GROUCHO: I've always watched the stock market. Especially when it's going up. Do you know property values have increased since 1929 one thousand percent?
PLAYBOY: No, we didn't. Were you hurt by the crash?
GROUCHO: Yeah, I was wiped out. I had two hundred thousand dollars, which I'd saved over a period of many years playing small-time vaudeville, and I lost it in two days when the market crashed. My old friend Max Gordon phoned me at my home in Great Neck. His real name is Saltpeter, but he calls himself Max Gordon. And he called me up one morning and he said, "Marx, the jig is up." And hung up. I don't take his calls anymore.
PLAYBOY: You mentioned an uncle in show business.
GROUCHO: Al Shean. He was an actor in vaudeville. He had originally been a pants presser on the East Side. I don't think he was a very good pants presser, because as soon as he got his job as a presser, he formed a singing quartet and the fellow who ran the factory threw all four of 'em out. He was always forming quartets and getting fired.
PLAYBOY: Tell us about your parents.
GROUCHO: Well, my mother came from Germany, my father came from France. When he met my mother, neither one could understand a word the other was saying, so they got married. They spoke German, because my mother was the stronger of the two. My father wasn't very well educated. Neither was my mother, but she was brighter. She lived long enough to see us successful on Broadway.
PLAYBOY: Was your mother as important as we've heard in influencing you to go on the stage?
GROUCHO: Of course. And as soon as she could, she got the others to go along. That's how we became the Marx Brothers. She used to book us herself. She thought she ought to look young, so she wore a corset and a blond wig when she went to see agents. She was probably around fifty then, and everybody knew it was a wig. When she was at somebody's house playing cards, she'd get tired of wearing the corset, take it off and wrap it up in a newspaper with the strings hanging out.
PLAYBOY: She was from a theatrical family, wasn't she?
GROUCHO: My grandmother played the harp and yodeled. My grandfather was a ventriloquist and a magician.
PLAYBOY: How about your father?
GROUCHO: He was a tailor from Strasbourg, the worst ever. All his customers were easily recognized: One trouser leg was shorter than the other.
PLAYBOY: Did your father ever fool around on your mother?
GROUCHO: He must have. There were five boys.
PLAYBOY: We mean with other women.
GROUCHO: Not until my mother died. Then he got himself another girl.
PLAYBOY: Right away?
GROUCHO: Well, not at the funeral.
PLAYBOY: Who were your idols when you were young?

GROUCHO: I used to have a girl in Montreal.
PLAYBOY: Was she an idol?
GROUCHO: She was idle a good deal, but she made a pretty good living anyway. Does that answer your question?
PLAYBOY: No, so let's put it another way? Who did you like when you went to the theater?
GROUCHO: President Roosevelt.
PLAYBOY: He wasn't on the stage.
GROUCHO: Who said anything about the stage?
PLAYBOY: Did you have any girlfriends while you were growing up in New York?
GROUCHO: Not until later, when we started traveling in small-time vaudeville. And even then, we really weren't in towns long enough to meet anybody.
PLAYBOY: So how did you meet girls?
GROUCHO: We'd go to hook shops. We were a big hit in the hook shops.
PLAYBOY: How so?
GROUCHO: We were entertainment!
PLAYBOY: You mean you'd go to a whorehouse and perform?
GROUCHO: You can say that again. We also did our act. Harpo and Chico played the piano and I sang. The girls used to come to watch us at the theater—the madam and the girls—and if they liked us, they'd send a note backstage: "If you're not doing anything tonight after the show, why don't you come over and see us?" Sometimes we stayed all night. We were always after girls. We'd get into a town, and there was a hotel, and they had a piano on the mezzanine floor. Chico would start playing and there would be twenty dames there. Chico would pick out girls for us, too.
PLAYBOY: Did you meet any "nice" girls that way?
GROUCHO: Gummo did once, in New Orleans; her father came up to him after the show and said, "You took my daughter out tonight. If you take her out again, you'll go back to New York in a box." Actors weren't very popular in those days. Except in hook shops.
PLAYBOY: What was your first physical relationship with a woman?
GROUCHO: Going to bed.
PLAYBOY: We're going to have to be more careful how we phrase things: How did you lose your virginity?
GROUCHO: In a hook shop in Montreal. I was sixteen years old and I didn't know anything about girls. Before I left town, I had gonorrhea.
PLAYBOY: How did Chico lose *his* virginity?
GROUCHO: To the first girl he met.
PLAYBOY: And Harpo?
GROUCHO: Oh, Harpo didn't fool around much. He had a few dames. But Harpo only had three girls in his life that he was really stuck on, and they were all named Fleming.
PLAYBOY: You're now dating a girl named Fleming. How do you explain this coincidence?
GROUCHO: It's no coincidence.
PLAYBOY: What kind of man was Harpo?
GROUCHO: He was a short man. Even shorter when he was sitting down, which he always was, playing the goddamn harp. I hated the harp. But he was very serious about it. He was also serious about playing cards. And also that other game that's popular now. . . .

PLAYBOY: Backgammon?
GROUCHO: Yes. He was very good at those games, although he wasn't educated. He used to make a lot of money. You know, he'd play with guys like George Kaufman and Alexander Woollcott and Herbert Swope, who ran the *New York World*, and people like that, and he usually won. He was a very smart card-player and good at all kinds of games.
PLAYBOY: He was also a great practical joker, wasn't he?
GROUCHO: I don't know whether he was *great*. But I remember a good one he pulled in front of Tiffany's in New York. He went to Woolworth's and bought five or six dollars' worth of fake jewelry, then walked over to Tiffany's. He said he'd like to look at the jewelry, and he took it out into the street to look at it in the sunlight, and he did a phony stumble, and all the fake jewelry from his pocket flew all over the sidewalk. The cops came running.
PLAYBOY: Didn't you get involved with the law yourself when you "held up" the Morgan Guarantee Trust Company?
GROUCHO: Oh, yeah. I was wearing a cap and I walked up to the . . . what to you call her?
PLAYBOY: Teller?
GROUCHO: No, I didn't. She was with her husband. Anyhow, I said to the broad, "This is a stick-up!" A lot of bells started ringing and inside of three minutes there were twenty uniformed policemen surrounding me. I pulled my cap off and said, "I'm Groucho Marx. Don't you know me?" Luckily, they did. Otherwise, I would've been shot.
PLAYBOY: There's a rumor that you and Harpo once went to a party naked.
GROUCHO: It was when we were playing in *I'll Say She Is* and we were invited to a bachelor party for a friend of ours who was getting married. So Harpo and I got into the elevator and took off all our clothes and put them in suitcases. We were stark-naked. But we got off at the wrong floor, where the bride was having a party for *her* friends. So we ran around naked until a waiter finally came with a couple of dish towels—or, in my case, a bath towel.
PLAYBOY: Was Harpo a practical joker in Hollywood, too?
GROUCHO: Yeah. He used to call up people and tell them the water tank was on the bum and they were gonna cut off all the water. He did it to me once.
PLAYBOY: Didn't you recognize his voice?
GROUCHO: No. I filled all the buckets and pans with water. Then I filled all the bathtubs. He told me to leave everything filled, because it was going to be two or three days before the repairs would be made.
PLAYBOY: How could he fool you, his own brother?
GROUCHO: I didn't usually recognize his voice, unless he asked me for money.
PLAYBOY: It used to be said that no girl was safe alone with your alter egos—Captain Jeffrey T. Spaulding, Rufus T. Firefly, Otis B. Driftwood or Hugo Z. Hackenbush. Is that still true?
PLAYBOY: You're too good for that crummy crowd, baby. If I were fifteen years younger, no good-looking dame would get out of here alive.
PLAYBOY: Would a girl be in any danger today?
GROUCHO: When a guy is eighty-three, he should forget the whole thing. I know if I do it, it's going to be lousy, so why cheapen myself?
PLAYBOY: Doesn't this depress you?
GROUCHO: No, it doesn't depress me. I don't miss sex. I know I can't do it properly

anymore; if I could, I'd still be doing it. I've talked to a lot of guys who are seventy-eight, seventy-nine, and they *all* say it's hopeless. When you can't get it up anymore, you should quit. When a guy is eighty years old or thereabouts, he should read a book.

PLAYBOY: How do you account for your reputation as a lecher back when you were in your prime—at sixty-five or seventy?

GROUCHO: I was seething with charm. When my brothers and I were young, we were all looking for dames we could go to bed with. Nothing wrong with that. That's what they're for.

PLAYBOY: Don't you think they're good for anything else?

GROUCHO: Yes. A lot of them can cook and a lot of them can take care of a house.

PLAYBOY: You don't seem to be a devout believer in women's liberation.

GROUCHO: Well, I feel this way about it: I think if there's a war and a husband is enlisted, his wife should take a Service job, too, not necessarily in the front lines shooting at the enemy, but there are so many things that a woman can do in an army. Since the man is risking his life, why shouldn't the woman be doing something? But I think they should have the same salary advantages as men.

PLAYBOY: Have you met any liberated women lately?

GROUCHO: Erin Fleming. Erin is my idol. I told her if she ever quit me, I'd quit show business.

PLAYBOY: In what way is she liberated?

GROUCHO: She does as she pleases. I don't follow her around. I wouldn't give a damn if she met a guy and wanted to go to bed with him. I'd say, "Go."

PLAYBOY: Would you want her to tell you about it?

GROUCHO: In my particular case, I wouldn't care if she did. Because, like I say, I'm not interested in sex anymore.

PLAYBOY: When you still were, did you consider yourself a user of women?

GROUCHO: God, no. I think a woman can be a wonderful companion. I *like* women! After all, my mother was one. I didn't find that out until a couple of years ago.

PLAYBOY: You said your father was faithful to your mother. Do you believe in monogamy yourself?

GROUCHO: I don't think man is basically a monogamous creature. It's natural for a married man to be interested in other women.

PLAYBOY: Isn't it just as natural for a married woman to be interested in other men?

GROUCHO: Having affairs? It's not gonna be much of a marriage.

PLAYBOY: But it's all right for a man?

GROUCHO: The man is the chaser of the two. The woman is subconsciously a chaser, but the man is—a man is a man. And if there's an attractive girl, he'll make a play for her. I think that's wonderful.

PLAYBOY: But not for a married woman?

GROUCHO: I don't think it comes out even that way. I think the average woman, if she's married to a man she likes, won't necessarily cheat.

PLAYBOY: But if she did?

GROUCHO: She should get a divorce and pay alimony.

PLAYBOY: Why couldn't they both keep the relationship going and have extra-marital affairs as well?

GROUCHO: Well, then they shouldn't get married.

PLAYBOY: Why not, if they love each other?
GROUCHO: How can he love her if they're both after other people? It would be better for two people like that to live together and not get married.
PLAYBOY: Feeling as you do, why did *you* get married?
GROUCHO: With one of my wives, I asked myself that question for sixteen years. But you know something? I didn't cheat on her once.
PLAYBOY: Why not?
GROUCHO: I couldn't stop with just one.
PLAYBOY: Did you ever date rich women?
GROUCHO: I could've married one and owned the biggest department store in Portland.
PLAYBOY: Why didn't you?
GROUCHO: I didn't like her behavior in bed.
PLAYBOY: Was she too cold? Or inhibited?
GROUCHO: On the contrary. She always wanted to go to bed. I think she was a nymph.
PLAYBOY: You're complaining?
GROUCHO: I don't want a woman who knows more tricks than I do.
PLAYBOY: According to friends, you've never been romantically involved with a Jewish girl. Are you anti-Semitic?
GROUCHO: No, it just always seemed to me that making love to a Jewish girl would be like making love to your sister.
PLAYBOY: Have you ever been a *victim* of anti-Semiticism?
GROUCHO: Oh, sure. Years ago, I decided to join a beach club on Long Island and we drove out to a place called the Sands Point Bath and Sun Club. I filled out the application and the head cheese of the place came over and told me we couldn't join because I was Jewish. So I said, "My son's only *half* Jewish. Would it be all right if he went in the water up to his knees?"
PLAYBOY: Getting back to women—
GROUCHO: I've been trying to for years.
PLAYBOY: Have you ever had an interracial affair?
GROUCHO: The whole first part of my life was spent sleeping with colored girls. They were chambermaids in the hotels we used to stay in. In those days, all hotels had black chambermaids. You'd give her a couple of bucks and take her in your room and lay her. That was very common.
PLAYBOY: How were they?
GROUCHO: No different than a white girl. No, that's not true; some of 'em were even better. We couldn't get a white girl when we were in small-time vaudeville. They were afraid of actors. A lot of girls had been raped by actors. So we took what we could get, which was black chambermaids. But I remember doing a big act once with W. C. Fields and we had twenty girls in the show. They were all white and they were all friendly. I knew them by number rather than by name.
PLAYBOY: Who wrote your material when you started out?
GROUCHO: I did. Except for Harpo, who didn't say anything.
PLAYBOY: Did you write for Zeppo, too?
GROUCHO: I didn't have to. He was the funniest one of us. But he wasn't in the act that much. He was in more than Gummo, though, who went in the army during the First World War.

PLAYBOY: Why didn't he rejoin the act after the war?
GROUCHO: He didn't want to be an actor. He went into the garment industry. I remember Gummo had a son named Bobby, and Bobby came home from school one day and his father said to him, "How was it in school today?" And Bobby said, "Well, the teacher asked all of us who our fathers were, and I told her, 'Groucho Marx.' " And Gummo said, "Why did you say that?" And Bobby said, "Who knows *you?*"
PLAYBOY: You said you didn't have to write lines for Harpo, since he didn't say anything. Did Harpo *ever* talk in a Marx Brothers act?
GROUCHO: He talked a lot in a school act we used to do in vaudeville; he played a boy called Patsy Brannigan. In those days, if you did a school act, you usually had a Patsy Brannigan in the act. Patsy Brannigan was a kid with red hair and a funny nose. That's where Harpo got the idea for his wig. A fella had taught him a speech with a lot of big words in it and sometimes Harpo would dumbfound the audience by making this speech with all those big words. He didn't understand most of them, but he loved the speech.
PLAYBOY: What did Chico do in that act?
GROUCHO: He helped Harpo. Harpo used to wear a funny hat. And I would say to Harpo, "Take dat ding off." I was a German comedian. Harpo would take the "ding" off and give it to Chico and Chico would pass it to the guy who played a fag. Well, you asked; it was a pretty lousy act.
PLAYBOY: Did you get any laughs in those days?
GROUCHO: Now and then. Especially when Zeppo came onstage and said, "Dad, the garbage man is here," and I said, "Tell him we don't want any." Another time Chico shook hands with me and said, "I would like to say good-bye to your wife," and I said, "Who wouldn't?"
PLAYBOY: How did you create the Groucho character?
GROUCHO: When we were playing small-time vaudeville, I would try a line and if it got a laugh, I'd leave it in. If it didn't get a laugh, I'd take it out and write another line. Pretty soon I had a character.
PLAYBOY: How did the mustache originate?
GROUCHO: The mustache came about while we were doing a show called *Home Again* at Keith's Flushing. My wife was having a baby at the time and I used to spend a lot of time in the hospital with her. One night I stayed too long and by the time I got to the theater, it was too late to paste on my mustache, so I just smeared on some grease paint. The audience didn't seem to mind, so I stuck with it. Or got stuck with it. Or got sticky with it.
PLAYBOY: How did you develop the Groucho walk?
GROUCHO: I was just kidding around one day and I started to walk funny. The audience liked it, so I kept it in.
PLAYBOY: Did you always feel you were going to make the big time?
GROUCHO: No. Chico did, and he did the least work in the act. He said, "We won't always be playing these dumps." And Chico got a guy who owned a coal mine and a pretzel factory to put up the money for us to become big time. Chico was a smooth character. He would be talking long distance on the phone to one dame and having his hat blown by another at the same time.
PLAYBOY: What was your first big success?
GROUCHO: A play called *I'll Say She Is*. The money for it was put up by the pretzel-factory owner, who later got stuck on one of the girls in the chorus. It so happened

that Harpo was laying this same girl at the time, but fortunately, he didn't find out. Anyway, the play was a smash in Philadelphia. It was a real stinker, but when we took it to New York, Alexander Woollcott gave it a good review.

PLAYBOY: What did your childhood friends think of your success on Broadway?

GROUCHO: I had a friend in New York who lived on Ninety-third Street, where we lived. We always figured he was gonna be a Supreme Court Justice or something. Well, he became a lawyer, and he came to see *Animal Crackers* one day. He came to my dressing room afterward and he didn't mention anything about the show. So I said, "How'd you like it?" He said, "Don't you think you're kinda old to be jumping over furniture and making a fool of yourself in front of an audience?"

PLAYBOY: What was your reply?

GROUCHO: I pointed out that I was making a thousand dollars a week to make a fool of myself and that he was doing it for $150, and I asked him to empty the garbage on his way out.

PLAYBOY: You were soon making a lot more than a thousand a week in Hollywood. Did all that money—and your newfound fame in movies—attract a lot of women?

GROUCHO: Well, it helped my brother Chico—who didn't need any help along those lines. But if *I* wanted to go to bed with a girl, I had to *marry* her.

PLAYBOY: Which stars would you have liked to make it with but didn't?

GROUCHO: I'd have liked to have gone to bed with Jean Harlow. She was a beautiful broad. The fellow who married her was impotent and he killed himself. I would have done the same thing.

PLAYBOY: How about Carole Lombard?

GROUCHO: She was a great dame. I loved Lombard. She was married to Gable at one time, you know. I met her on the street one day—I did a whole series of shows with her—and I said, "How are you and Gable getting along?" and she said, "He's the lousiest lay I ever had." That's the way she talked—the way a lot of men do. Very sexy dame. She was also a hell of an actress. She did a picture with Jack Benny, which Lubitsch directed. Benny was wonderful in it. It was called *To Be or Not to Be*. Lubitsch was the best director, I guess, in this country. There was nobody to equal him. He wanted to do a movie with us.

PLAYBOY: Why didn't you do it?

GROUCHO: Well, we were tied up with Paramount making those five turkeys. I remember Lubitsch had an opening line that he tried out on me one day. It went like this: "You haf a girl in your betroom and she iss married. And her husband come home unexpectedly, just as a streetcar iss going through the betroom." And I said, "What's the joke?" My next line, he said, was, "Believe it or not, I was waiting for a streetcar." And then I was supposed to step out of a closet and onto the streetcar. He was a genius.

PLAYBOY: Speaking of geniuses, aren't you a friend of Orson Welles's?

GROUCHO: Well, I've done a lot of shows with him. Comedy shows. He's a great straight man. He's also a great round man.

PLAYBOY: Weren't you also a friend of Humphrey Bogart's?

GROUCHO: I was at his house all the time. He was a wonderful host. He'd have two or three shots of booze and get on his yacht to get away from Lauren Bacall. Not that he didn't like her. He just wanted to be around men. When I was around, could you blame him?

PLAYBOY: The Marx Brothers have also had a number of literary friends. Didn't you correspond with T. S. Eliot?

GROUCHO: He wrote to me first. He said he was an admirer of mine and he would like a picture of me. So I sent him a picture. And he sent it back. He said, "I want a picture of you smoking a cigar." So I sent him one. Later he told me there were only three people he cared about: William Butler Yeats, Paul Valery and Groucho Marx. He had those three pictures in his private office. When I went to visit him, I thought he wanted to talk about all those fancy books he had written, like *Murder in the Cathedral*. But he wanted to talk about the Marx Brothers. So naturally we became close friends and had a lot of correspondence. I spoke at his funeral.

PLAYBOY: What other writers have you known?

GROUCHO: Ring Lardner used to come to my house in Great Neck and get drunk. If I had been him, I would have gotten drunk, too. He had four boys at home and couldn't get any writing done, so he used to go to the Pennsylvania Hotel in New York and take a room and pull the shades down, because there might have been somebody in another room across the alley from where his room was—and that's the only way he could write. He would stay there for a week or two and then he'd go back to Great Neck, where his four sons were.

PLAYBOY: How about F. Scott Fitzgerald?

GROUCHO: *He* wasn't one of Lardner's sons.

PLAYBOY: Thanks for the information. We were wondering how well you knew him.

GROUCHO: I knew him very well, because he was stuck on a dame named Sheilah Graham, who used to play a little tennis at my house.

PLAYBOY: You're not going to make any jokes about playing a love game with her, are you?

GROUCHO: No, her serve was too big for me.

PLAYBOY: Who was the wittiest man you ever knew?

GROUCHO: George S. Kaufman. I remember once he went to Philadelphia to see the tryout of a play one of the Bloomingdales was backing. They were the department-store people. After he saw the play, he said, "Close the play and keep the store open nights."

PLAYBOY: Why are theater and movies more serious today—or at least less funny—than they used to be?

GROUCHO: There are no comedians left. Chaplin doesn't work anymore—he's too old and can't. Mae West isn't too old, but won't. Buster Keaton is dead. W. C. Fields is dead. Laurel and Hardy are dead. And Jerry Lewis hasn't made me laugh since he left Dean Martin. One of the reasons there are no comedians is that there's no more vaudeville. There is no place to train a comedian today. There's no place to be funny anymore. You've got just a few TV shows and nightclubs. There's no place for a comic to polish his act. That's what vaudeville provided.

PLAYBOY: You and Chaplin got together while he was over here for the 1972 Academy Awards. What did you talk about?

GROUCHO: He just kept saying, "Keep warm. Keep warm." I think he's one year older than I am. He was worried that I wasn't keeping warm enough. I was saying, "Hi ya, Charlie, how are ya?" And all he said was, "Keep warm."

PLAYBOY: How did you and Chaplin first meet?

GROUCHO: Well, my brothers and I were playing in Canada, and so was Chaplin. He was doing an act called *A Night at the Club*. It was a very funny act. I remember he had a big dowager in the act who used to sing, and while she was singing, Chaplin was chewing on an apple and spitting the seeds in her face. This is the kind of comedy they had sixty years ago. Anyway, when we were in Winnipeg one day, my brothers went off in search of a poolroom to kill three hours before leaving for the Coast. Since I didn't play pool, and I don't play cards, and I don't gamble, and I only smoke occasionally—just enough to cough—I took a walk and I passed this dump theater, the Sullivan-Considine. I heard the most tremendous roar of laughter, and I paid my ten cents and went in and there was a little guy on the stage, and he was walking around kinda funny. It was Chaplin. It was the greatest act I'd ever seen. All pantomime. He had a shirt that he wore for the whole six weeks, 'cause he was only getting twenty-five dollars a week and he didn't want to spend any money getting a clean shirt.

I went back to the hotel and told my brothers what a real comedian was, and I walked around funny like Chaplin, you know. Then the following week, I went backstage to visit him and tell him how wonderful he was, and that's how we got acquainted. Each week we would be in the same towns in Canada; I can't remember all the towns; this was a hell of a long time ago. We used to go to the whorehouses together, because there was no place for an actor to go in those towns, except if you were lucky, maybe you'd pick up a girl, but as a rule, you'd have to go to a hook shop. And then Chaplin and I got *very* well acquainted. Not together! I mean, I wasn't with him! I was *with* him, but not with a girl, I mean—

PLAYBOY: We understand. Had he made a movie yet?

GROUCHO: No. He hadn't made anything. He was just doing this act.

PLAYBOY: Did he ever mention wanting to make movies?

GROUCHO: No. It never occurred to him. He was a big hit in his act. Then, when we got to Seattle, there was Mack Sennett, who saw Chaplin in *A Night at the Club* and offered to sign him up. I talked to Chaplin afterward and I said, "I understand you were offered a job with Sennett and he offered you two hundred dollars a week." And he says, "I turned it down." I says, "You must be crazy! You turned down two hundred a week for this lousy vaudeville act you're doing?" He says, "Nobody could be that good, so I turned him down." Chaplin went back to England after that. He was afraid.

PLAYBOY: Would *you* have accepted an offer from Sennett?

GROUCHO: No. I was working with my brothers and they were busy shooting pool.

PLAYBOY: Seriously, do you think you would have been funny in silent films?

GROUCHO: No. In the first place, Harpo didn't talk at all in the act. And Chico didn't talk if he could find a dame. So the only one that really talked was me. Anyway, I really wanted to be on Broadway at that time. Broadway was bigger than pictures in those days. Audiences paid ten dollars a ticket for *Cocoanuts* and *Animal Crackers* for the entire run. Anyway, getting back to Chaplin, six years passed, and we were now playing the Orpheum circuit, and we got an invitation from Chaplin. He had bought the Mary Pickford home, he was so rich by this time from making pictures. So he invited us over for dinner. There was a butler in back of each chair, and there were solid-gold plates, and we had the most magnificent meal. He was a bigger star then than we were. Hell, he was the greatest thing in pictures.

PLAYBOY: How did you meet W. C. Fields?

GROUCHO: We were on the bill together in Toledo. He was a tough guy. He was doing his juggling act, and there was a pool table on the stage, because he used to do funny stuff with a pool table, and Ed Wynn was also on the show. So Wynn used to get under the pool table, and while Fields was doing his stuff, Wynn would stick his head out and make funny faces. One day Fields caught him doing this and when Wynn stuck his head out from under the table, Fields was standing there with a pool cue and he hit Wynn on the head and knocked him unconscious. He was a funny guy, but he didn't want anybody to interfere with his act. Or to upstage him.

When we were playing together in Toledo, he walked off our show. He told the manager of the theater that he had "humpers on the carumpers." They were just words he was making up, but that's the way he was: He didn't want to follow us on the show. We did a big act with thirty people, and he was standing there alone on the stage with a cigar box, singing "Yankee-Doodle went to town," and the audience was walking out of the theater. So Fields quit the show and took the next train for New York. I knew him years later, when he worked in Hollywood. He used to hide in the bushes in front of his house and shoot at tourists with his BB gun.

PLAYBOY: Tell us about some of the other great comics you knew. How about Buster Keaton?

GROUCHO: He used to put in gags for Harpo when we were at MGM.

PLAYBOY: In which films?

GROUCHO: *A Night at the Opera, A Day at the Races, Go West.* He was washed up by then, but he was good for Harpo. Harpo was always looking for a good piece of business. He didn't talk, he didn't need lines, but he did need good business, and Keaton was a hell of a comic in silent films.

PLAYBOY: What kind of man was Keaton?

GROUCHO: He was kind of eccentric. Near the end of his life, he bought a trailer and he would drive around Beverly Hills, stop the trailer, turn off the engine, take out a bridge table and have dinner in front of somebody's house. I guess everybody recognized it was Keaton, because nobody minded his eating his dinner in front of their house. It was a beautiful trailer.

PLAYBOY: It's common knowledge that you never got along well with Louis B. Mayer of MGM. Why?

GROUCHO: Mayer took things too seriously. Nobody else took us seriously in Hollywood—just Mayer. One day he was having a conference with the censor about Lana Turner showing too much cleavage in her last film and Mayer was trying to convince the censor that MGM was a highly moral studio. So Harpo hired a stripper for the afternoon and chased her around the room while Mayer was talking to the censor. Another time we were sitting in Mayer's waiting room and after hours of waiting, we started a bonfire in his outer office. We'd done that to Thalberg years before. But Mayer didn't think it was funny.

PLAYBOY: We can't imagine why. Was he vindictive about it?

GROUCHO: I think he wanted us to bomb. He didn't want us to take road tours and he refused to hire the best directors and writers; he gave us a lot of *schleppers* to work with, like the two German immigrants who wrote the ending to *A Day at the Races.* Mayer was cutting off his nose to spite his face. Now that I think about his nose, his face would have been better without it.

PLAYBOY: Do you have a favorite Marx Brothers film among those you did at MGM?

GROUCHO: I liked *Duck Soup* and *Horse Feathers* and I liked parts of *Animal Crackers.* But I guess my favorite is *A Night at the Opera.*

PLAYBOY: Why?

GROUCHO: It just has great scenes in it—great funny scenes. Like the scene in the stateroom where I'm meeting this lady, Mrs. Claypool, played by Margaret Dumont; I'm having a rendezvous with her. And when she arrives at my room, fourteen people come out. I enjoyed *all* my romantic scenes with Margaret Dumont. She was a wonderful woman. She was the same off the stage as she was on it—always the stuffy, dignified matron. And the funny thing about her was she never understood the jokes. Seriously, she never knew what was going on. At the end of *Duck Soup,* we're alone in a small cottage and there's a war going on outside and Margaret says to me, "What are you doing, Rufus?" And I say, "I'm fighting for your honor, which is more than you ever did." Later she asked me what I meant by that.

PLAYBOY: After *A Night in Casablanca,* you made three pictures in a row without your brothers. They're not considered your best efforts, are they?

GROUCHO: No, and neither are the pictures. After *Casablanca,* I made *Copacabana, A Girl in Every Port* and then *Double Dynamite.* That one was such a bomb it almost ruined the studio.

PLAYBOY: Which studio was it?

GROUCHO: RKO. A fellow named Howard Hughes was running it then, and he's the one who came up with the title *Double Dynamite.* That was supposed to be a clever description of Jane Russell's breasts. With thinking like that, it's no wonder Hughes is a billionaire. He'd *have* to be a billionaire; otherwise, how could he make a living?

PLAYBOY: The last Marx Brothers film, *Love Happy,* was made in 1950, and that same year you began a whole new career with the television quiz show *You Bet Your Life.* Did you like doing that series?

GROUCHO: You bet your life I did. It was some of the best stuff I ever did. I really had to think. I never worked so hard.

PLAYBOY: What was the meaning of the duck on your TV show and in your films?

GROUCHO: Well, it's easier to crack a joke about a duck than an elephant.

PLAYBOY: Didn't you once appear in a television production of *The Mikado*?

GROUCHO: Yes. I played Coco in *The Mikado* for NBC. That's how I got rid of my first wife.

PLAYBOY: By playing in *The Mikado?*

GROUCHO: Yeah. Well, it's Gilbert and Sullivan, you know, and I love Gilbert and Sullivan, so I kept playing it at home, and she didn't quite understand it. She wasn't educated. Until I married her, I don't think she'd ever heard of Gilbert and Sullivan.

PLAYBOY: Where did *you* first hear of them?

GROUCHO: When I was doing *Cocoanuts,* we had a fellow in the act who was what you'd call a straight man. His name was Basil Ruysdael. He had been in Gilbert and Sullivan operettas himself, and whenever we were backstage getting ready for a scene or something, he would start singing, "My object all sublime, I shall not . . . uh . . . to let the punishment fit the crime, the punishment fit the crime. And let each prisoner repent and willingly represent, a song of innocent merriment, of innocent merriment." I asked him, "What's that you're singing all the time?" "That's Gilbert and Sullivan," he told me. And I said, "Who the hell are they? A vaudeville team?" He said, "They were the greatest writers in England." That's how I got interested in them, and that's why I accepted that part in *The Mikado* when NBC offered it to me.

PLAYBOY: Are you sorry television has taken over so much of the movie industry?

GROUCHO: No, because most of the movies today are lousy. I saw Barbra Streisand in *Up the Sandbox* recently. I thought it was terrible. They tell me there was some kind of symbolism, fantasy, in it, but by that time, I was in the toilet smoking a cigar. As people get older, they don't want to get in their car and go to a theater and stand in line to see it—even if it's a good picture. The average person hasn't got that much

taste, either, so most people just turn on the television. It's much easier to just put on your bathrobe and look at a couple of lousy TV shows.
PLAYBOY: What was Hollywood like when you came out here?
GROUCHO: Well, I was much younger.
PLAYBOY: We assumed that. When did you move out here?
GROUCHO: We arrived here in 1930 from New York and immediately signed up with Paramount and did twelve pictures here.
PLAYBOY: Did you have wild times?
GROUCHO: Not that I can remember, unfortunately.
PLAYBOY: From the newspapers of that time, it looks like the Marx Brothers tore the town apart.
GROUCHO: We had fun. We were young. But I don't think the town has changed too much, except that there are fewer studios, because of television.
PLAYBOY: Would you be interested in playing in any more movies?
GROUCHO: No. Not unless it was a great part and the hours were short and they held up cards so I wouldn't have to memorize everything.
PLAYBOY: John Cassavetes has said that you are the greatest actor who ever lived.
GROUCHO: He was drunk.
PLAYBOY: Well, a lot of young, established actors admire the way you're able to play yourself on the screen.
GROUCHO: I play *with* myself, too, but mostly off screen.
PLAYBOY: What would you do if you retired completely?
GROUCHO: I'd get a message occasionally and shave and take a walk. But I'm not gonna retire. I'd like to die right onstage. But I don't plan on dying at all.
PLAYBOY: Do you turn down many jobs?
GROUCHO: Depends on the money. If a guy is worth almost a billion dollars—I'm talking about Bob Hope—and he offers me a thousand dollars to go on his show, I consider it an insult. I wouldn't unwrap a cigar for a thousand dollars. When I did a show down here a couple of weeks ago, I got ten thousand. For that kind of money, I not only unwrap a cigar but light it up and take a few puffs.
PLAYBOY: Would you ever do a show for free?
GROUCHO: Yes. I'd do a show with the baseball announcer Vin Sculley, because he's given me so much enjoyment all my life listening to him describe baseball.
PLAYBOY: Who are your closest friends?
GROUCHO: Nunnally Johnson, who was one of the top movie writers in this town; I knew him when I lived in Great Neck, and we've been friends ever since. And a fellow named Sheekman, who used to do a column for the Chicago *Times*. When I played Chicago, I offered to write a column for him because he had to do one every day. And when he came out here, I invited him to become one of the writers on our movies. Mostly, my friends are all roughly my age.
PLAYBOY: Who are your younger friends?
GROUCHO: Well, there's Woody Allen, and Erin, and Goddard Lieberson, and Goody Ace. There are a few others that keep in touch with me, like Dick Cavett, Jack Nicholson and Elliott Gould. I have lunch with them occasionally, provided they pick up the check.
PLAYBOY: A friend of yours told us you sleep with your bedroom door locked. Why?
GROUCHO: He's no friend of mine. But if you must know, I lock it when I'm all alone in the house.

PLAYBOY: Could that be because of your years in vaudeville, when you stayed in cheap hotels and locked your door so nobody would steal your money?
GROUCHO: Could be. I remember in those days how I used to put the bureau up against the door. That was also during a phase of my life when I wanted to jump out the window. We were doing well in vaudeville by then, living in good hotels like the Statler in Cleveland or Detroit, but I was always afraid of jumping out the window.
PLAYBOY: Why?
GROUCHO: I don't know. I guess it was a kind of nervous point in my life.
PLAYBOY: Were you depressed?
GROUCHO: No. I'd seen some Boris Karloff movies and I was scared. I was very young then. I saw one Karloff picture and I took sleeping pills every night for about a month after that. It was the only way I could get to sleep.
PLAYBOY: Did you see a psychiatrist about it?
GROUCHO: Yeah, but he said I was crazy, so I bit his leg and walked out.
PLAYBOY: What's your opinion of psychoanalysis?
GROUCHO: It won't get it up if you're eighty-three years old, so what's the point of it?
PLAYBOY: But back then, you felt you were going a little crazy?
GROUCHO: I was working very hard and I was single. And I had a wife who drank.
PLAYBOY: You were single and you had a wife?
GROUCHO: So I'm a liar.
PLAYBOY: You were married to your first wife during your years in vaudeville, weren't you?
GROUCHO: For part of them. We were married twenty-one years. She was so beautiful when I married her. She weighed about 109 then. The last time I saw her, she must have weighed 250.
PLAYBOY: This obviously wouldn't include marriage, but what's the most satisfying thing you've ever done?
GROUCHO: I went to Germany, and while I was there, they showed me Hitler's grave and I danced on it. I was never that much of a dancer, but I was great that day!
PLAYBOY: How do you feel about being eighty-three?
GROUCHO: I'm still alive. That's about it. I can tell I'm still alive because I wake up in the morning. If I don't wake up, that means I'm dead. But talking about not knowing whether you're alive or dead, I remember once when I visited the offices of *The New York Times,* they showed me my obituary. It wasn't very good. I offered to punch it up for them, but they turned me down.
PLAYBOY: Have you observed any special diet over the years?
GROUCHO: Well, since I turned eighty, I've tried to limit my eating exclusively to food.
PLAYBOY: Do you drink?
GROUCHO: The only drink I used to like is bourbon. Now I don't drink at all, except for an occasional shot of Maalox.
PLAYBOY: Have you ever tried marijuana?
GROUCHO: One cigarette that Garson Kanin gave me. I took six puffs and I couldn't get to the other side of the room.
PLAYBOY: Do you think it should be legalized?

GROUCHO: No, and I don't believe in booze, either. I didn't even have a drink until Prohibition. Then my father made wine in the cellar and killed all the rats.
PLAYBOY: What kind of cigars do you smoke?
GROUCHO: This one comes from Havana. It costs four dollars. *Real* Havana, not from the Canary Islands.
PLAYBOY: What's it called?
GROUCHO: Charley. Actually, this is the only cigar I have left that's genuine Havana. Bill Cosby gave them to me. Very few people can afford this cigar. Cosby can. I did a TV show for Cosby. It was all ad-libbed. We had a few cards to hold up, but they kept mixing them up. Cosby paid me off in cigars.
PLAYBOY: You've also made some talk-show appearances over the past couple of years.
GROUCHO: Yeah. You get so little for being on a talk show, you're lucky if you can afford a five-pack of White Owls.
PLAYBOY: We remember, on at least one Cavett show, hearing you speak out against the amount of sex in movies today. Do you approve of film censorship?
GROUCHO: Yes, I do. There are lots of children who go to movies. Besides, I don't like dirty pictures. I'm glad nobody took their clothes off in our movies. Can you imagine how ridiculous I'd have looked walking around naked with a cigar in my mouth?
PLAYBOY: There's a lot of explicitness on the stage these days, too. Have you seen any of the recent productions?
GROUCHO: No, I wouldn't even go to see *Oh! Calcutta!* I had tickets to the opening night from Kenneth Tynan and I said, "I don't want to see it. I understand that what they're doing on the stage is what a lot of people do in bed."
PLAYBOY: Sleeping?
GROUCHO: That's what I would have done in my seat if I'd have gone to see it.
PLAYBOY: Did you see *Hair?*
GROUCHO: I saw half of it and walked out. Dick Cavett asked me if I'd seen it and I said no, and he wanted to know why not. I told him, "Well, I was gonna go see it, and then I called up the theater and I said, 'How much are the tickets?' They said the tickets were eleven dollars apiece. I told them I'd call back, went in my bathroom, took off all my clothes and looked at myself in the full-length mirror. Then I called the theater and said, 'Forget it.' "
PLAYBOY: You said you saw half of it, and then you said you didn't see it at all. Which version are we to believe?
GROUCHO: Both. I told you I'm a liar.
PLAYBOY: They say good liars make great storytellers. What's your favorite story?
GROUCHO: Clean or dirty?
PLAYBOY: Just funny.
GROUCHO: Well, a hooker picks up a guy. No. A married woman picks up a guy, takes him to her apartment and they go to bed. While they're doing it, the man says, "I've never had a woman like you. You're the most extraordinary woman in bed that I've ever heard of. You know, I'm not a religious man, but when I die, if there's such a thing as a hereafter, I'm going to come back and find you, no matter where you are in the whole world." And she says to him, "Well, if you do come back, try to come in the afternoons."
PLAYBOY: Do you have any more jokes?
GROUCHO: No, except for this cheap cigar that Bill Cosby gave me. I'm suffocating.

PLAYBOY: Apart from cheap cigars, what annoys you most?
GROUCHO: This interview.
PLAYBOY: Hang on, it's just about finished. Have you any regrets?
GROUCHO: The fact that I *agreed* to this interview.
PLAYBOY: One last question: What would you do if you had your life to live all over again?
GROUCHO: Try more positions.

JANE FONDA AND TOM HAYDEN

April 1974

Interviewer: Ron Ridenour

Considering the other antiwar activists who were interviewed by PLAYBOY in the late Sixties and early Seventies, it was perhaps surprising the magazine didn't get around to Tom Hayden and Jane Fonda until 1974. By that time, events gave this Q-and-A an unusual perspective: Nixon was embroiled in Watergate, the POWs were coming home, and Kissinger's peace agreement between South and North Vietnam seemed to be holding. An interesting moment to talk with a founder of SDS and a member of the Chicago Seven, and his actress wife, a woman reviled for traveling to North Vietnam during the height of the war. Most of what the world had heard from them before this had been of the fire-and-brimstone variety. But with much of their early agenda now a political reality, the embattled couple was ready to take a breather, sit down and reflect on the past decade.

Ron Ridenour, a writer and publicist for the American Civil Liberties Union, conducted the intereview (although PLAYBOY staffer Douglas Bauer assisted with some follow-up questions) on the understanding that Fonda be allowed to explain why she had at first resisted doing a PLAYBOY interview. In a previous issue PLAYBOY had run a photograph of a nude Jane Fonda from her sex-kitten days in Paris, and the actress had taken offense. She tells her version of the incident in the interview, as well as some further thoughts on nudity, PLAYBOY, and feminism.

Late last year, Jane Fonda called reporters to the Los Angeles Press Club and told them she was suing the President. During the press conference, she held a bulging FBI file, a gift from columnist Jack Anderson, filled with memos discussing her personal finances, children, travels—all sorts of gossipy information she claimed was gathered illegally. Furthermore, said Fonda, there was a clear line of responsi-

bility for the file that was traceable to the man on Pennsylvania Avenue with the faulty tape machine.

Nobody attending the press conference seemed too surprised by the announcement, a measure of how Jane Fonda—and the nation—has changed. Less than ten years ago, the news would have sounded like some improbable studio publicity stunt. She was living luxuriously in France at the time and gaining simultaneous reputations as an actress of genuine talent and a tough, bright lady who took life on unconventional terms. But there was not yet any politics in the fabric of her life, and her style then seemed at least understandable, considering her rare parentage and bittersweet beginning years. Born to one of America's most esteemed actors and his second wife, socialite Frances Seymour Brokaw, Jane spent a childhood (in New England and Beverly Hills) marked by the trauma of her mother's suicide and a fierce adoration for her father that she felt was indifferently returned.

After two listless years at Vassar, she moved to Paris, where she studied painting and lived a free Left Bank life for a while. Back in the States at twenty-one she agreed, at a friend's persistent urging, to consider acting and went to one of Lee Strasberg's classes. He said she was good, and Fonda dived into a career, getting the starring role—with a little help from her father's good friend director Joshua Logan—in a fluffy romance called Tall Story. *Soon after, she showed the first real flashes of her emerging talent as a serious actress in* Walk on the Wild Side *and* Period of Adjustment, *while continuing to do innocent romps such as* Sunday in New York *and* Barefoot in the Park. *In between, she had returned to Europe, this time with a new sense of purpose. French cinema was moving in new directions, thanks to small budgets and the large visions of a bold, brilliant group of directors—among them, Truffaut, Chabrol and Vadim—and Jane, weary of Hollywood, wanted to participate. She did, becoming an international sex star and marrying Vadim. For more than six years, she sank roots, meticulously refurbishing her sprawling French farmhouse, giving birth to a daughter, Vanessa, and making films for her husband and others.*

It began to turn around for her, she says, while watching newsclips on French television of American war planes dropping bombs on villages, schools and hospitals in Indochina, and her decision to return to the U.S. was further solidified when she viewed films of that brutal night in 1968 when the Chicago police decided to pound the shit out of anything hairy that moved. "I felt a need to find out, to look for answers to what was happening to my own country," she has since explained. "I felt remote and very curious about the mood that could have produced what I was watching." So she returned to America, got in a car and started across the country looking for answers, stopping frequently to help local groups work against the war, poverty and many other problems she'd never faced personally before. Instead of finding answers, however, she saw only more to question and began to issue often shrill statements combining her own honest outrage with the rhetoric of others. "News people kept demanding comments from me, asking me what I thought about this or that: the condition of Indians, the black ghettos, what I had learned from the GIs in the coffeehouses, and I simply didn't know what I thought. After I realized what was happening, I decided to do some concentrated studying."

One of the leftist writers she read most avidly was Tom Hayden, a founder of Students for a Democratic Society, a leading radical of the Sixties and one of the foremost heads among those Fonda saw being pounded that night at the corner of Michigan and Balbo. It's hard to imagine two paths less likely to cross than Fonda's and Hayden's. Raised in a working-class section of Detroit, and educated in local Catholic schools, Hayden developed his radical sensibility at the University of Michigan and, in 1962, with a group of fellow students from across the country, drafted the Port Huron Statement, creating SDS and prophesying much of the decade's social and political upheaval.

After Port Huron, Hayden immersed himself in causes, working for civil rights in Mississippi, organizing for three years in the slums of Newark, writing several books and helping construct a plan for demonstrations at the 1968 Democratic Convention, which he and fellow radicals hoped would generate a protest so thunderous that the nation, no matter how deaf, could not help but hear. It certainly heard—and watched, recoiling from the grisly street theater—but the result of it all for Hayden was arrest and trial, the infamous Chicago Seven Conspiracy case, one of the most bizarre criminal proceedings ever played out in a courtroom, from which he was finally acquitted of all charges not long ago, more than three years after the circus had closed.

By the late Sixties, Hayden had become disillusioned with arguing radical factions and retreated from leadership to a Berkeley commune, where he continued to write prolifically—both books and articles—and to work against the war. He traveled several times to Hanoi, served as broker for the release of some POWs and eventually—somewhere between her headline-making "drug" arrest in Cleveland (for carrying what turned out to be vitamin pills) and her equally well-reported trip to North Vietnam in 1972—met fellow radical Jane Fonda. They began to see a good deal of each other, worked together preparing antiwar graphic exhibitions and shows, and soon after Fonda returned from that controversial visit to Indochina, they decided to have a baby—and got married.

They now spend most of their time lecturing and participating in the organizational efforts of their Indochina Peace Campaign, an organization of movement activists with offices in twenty-five states. But Jane has never gotten too involved in politics to find time for the acting work she sees as a vehicle to advance the causes she believes in—and uses to finance them. At the top of her craft, she was called America's finest actress after her Oscar-winning performance in Klute *and most recently starred in Joseph Losey's brilliant adaptation of* A Doll House. *But Tom and Jane's primary profession is Indochina (Hayden has taught Indochinese history at two Los Angeles colleges) and they frequently leave their Santa Monica house for extended tours to remind the world that the war, like some indestructible Frankenstein monster, is still alive.*

Since their personal travel calendar resembles the arrival-departure schedule at O'Hare, and because they often head out in opposite directions as their day-to-day work demands, it seemed we would have to find an interviewer with superhuman stamina. We decided, instead, to simply outnumber them, and assigned Leroy F. Aarons, West Coast bureau chief of The Washington Post *and Ron Ridenour, public-relations director of the Southern California ACLU, who—with backup help from* PLAYBOY *associate editor Douglas Bauer—managed to keep them seated long enough for several taping sessions. Aarons had met Hayden while covering various stories in which the radical leader played some part, and Ridenour, as a longtime civil libertarian himself, was acquainted with Fonda and with her politics. They report: "Wadsworth Avenue in Santa Monica, where Tom and Jane own an old two-story home, looks like a street from a neighborhood in Queens or Chicago's West Side that has been lifted intact and relocated next to the ocean. It's very nar-*

row, lined with old cars and battered vans, and its frame houses feature enclosed porches and roofs sagging from age.

"Since the first floor of their house was noisy with people working and talking, we usually proceeded upstairs, where Jane and Tom occupy five rooms painted various pastel shades. A large mattress is sprawled across the floor of their bedroom–living room, the most dominant piece of furniture in the place. Any lingering suspicion that they live in secret luxury from Jane's wealth is quickly erased.

"One additional Hayden, their new son, Troy, was present at some time during most of the later sessions. While we talked, about some aspect of movement politics or a particular Indochina horror, Jane would breast-feed Troy, then hand him over to Tom for burping. Meanwhile, their phones were constantly ringing and various friends came upstairs for coffee or just to say hello or goodbye.

"Since they had recently returned from a cross-country tour—attempting to arouse fresh indignation over the continuing Indochina war and to assess the potential for rebirth in the shards of the New Left—we began by asking them if they'd found much support this time around."

PLAYBOY: With the war in Vietnam all but over—at least as a major issue in this country—many observers consider the protest movement moribund. In your travels around the nation, have you found it more difficult than you used to to arouse and recruit support?

HAYDEN: We've found that, just as the "generation of peace" in American foreign policy hasn't happened, neither has the "cooling of America." Just as the '72 election was very depressing, the Watergate hearings have been very invigorating. Partly *because* of Watergate, I find political curiosity and reawakening, especially on the campuses. People can still be moved—even around the question of the war. You could wish that kids didn't have to be concerned any longer with Vietnam, but it's the reality of Vietnam that they *do.*

We cannot conclude that peace with honor has been achieved, that the war is over, when the greatest bombing offensive in history has ended, only to be replaced by the biggest police state in the world, funded ninety percent by American tax dollars. American handcuffs made by Smith & Weston chain General Thieu's political prisoners, confined in prisons often built by the American RMK-BRJ construction combine; his system of political surveillance and control has been developed or serviced by Computer Sciences Corporation of Los Angeles, which is teaching the Vietnamese to develop political dossiers on eleven and a half million South Vietnamese—the entire adult population. South Vietnam isn't even a country or a government; it's a war machine, and it's *still* an American responsibility.

FONDA: During our last trip around the country, the media frequently said to us, "Are you kidding? The American people don't care about Vietnam anymore. They care more about the price of meat." And yet our experience, time and time again, was that this is simply not true. People came to our presentations in as large numbers as they did last year. Granted that, frequently, they would come to see a celebrity. But most everyone sat through a very long program and a majority stayed to ask questions afterward. And the percentage of people who would then write their name down on a piece of paper indicating that they wanted to work for peace was one out of five.

PLAYBOY: Surely the peace agreement has had *some* deterrent effect on the antiwar movement.

HAYDEN: I think the peace agreement was the *fruit* of the antiwar movement.

PLAYBOY: Yes, but what about the situation since the peace agreement?

HAYDEN: Well, on the negative side, people in the middle who depend solely on the media for their information are more or less convinced that the war is over. And a lot of radicals took the peace agreement as their opportunity to go on to other things.

But the fact is that the peace agreement is not being honored. The U.S. government and its client Thieu are opposed to the agreement's political provisions, which call for democratic liberties and a free election in the south. How can we say there's no war in Vietnam when more than fifty thousand South Vietnamese died in combat in 1973—and the number is increasing? Our organization, the Indochina Peace Campaign, is demanding that the peace agreement be honored. America has a history of broken treaties, beginning with the ones we signed with the Indians. This one ought to be different.

FONDA: But I think the present climate in this country is such that popular change can come from places that would have never been dreamed of in the Sixties. I'm thinking specifically of the very real possibility that Nixon will be impeached by the Congress of the United States.

PLAYBOY: That may be true, but do you think the radical left will be successful in getting itself back together?

HAYDEN: I'm not sure how, but organizational attempts will be made. Maybe even quite major attempts—like a political party or an electoral coalition. It's interesting to think about new campus movements in comparison with the way it was in the early Sixties, when we began. Certainly there were disadvantages to starting with a pretty blank political environment in 1960—not having a sense of history, not knowing how to do even the simplest things, like running an office. But there were also advantages. There was no political jungle; there weren't a lot of factions as there are today.

Another advantage of the New Left of the Sixties, was, I think, that it took the administration and the CIA by surprise. I don't think there was any basis to anticipate that a radical movement would arise from the privileged campuses, and when it did, it wasn't immediately seen as subversive to the established order. It would be now. If a group of people said they were going to form a successor to the Students for a Democratic Society today and hold a convention in Port Huron, things would be made extremely difficult for them. But it's inevitable that new forms will arise.

PLAYBOY: Do you see any of these new groups as militant, with a philosophy that would advocate forced overthrow of government?

HAYDEN: Ninety percent of the struggle is political and cultural, not military. It's not a question of our forcibly overthrowing the established order; it's a question of people getting organized to work *within* the system to a point where the majority of the people are at least sympathetic to fundamental change. If at that point violent repression starts, as it often does, I would rather deal with it politically than resort to counterviolence. If a policeman shoots someone, instead of shooting back, you might put out forty thousand leaflets about the victim who was shot, and that would have a more devastating effect.

PLAYBOY: But can you conceive of ever picking up a gun to participate in a revolution?

HAYDEN: The question seems prosecutorial. It's so hypothetical. There *are* certain circumstances where there's a need for armed security. But that's in self-defense against police or vigilante attacks, and that's different from picking up a gun as part of a revolution. I think under conditions of severe repression, as has been the case with the Black Panther Party, for example, blacks would be justified in defending themselves. If the Watergate conspiracy had succeeded and a police state had been established, there would be a need for self-defense for *us,* too.

But the general answer to your question is no, I can't conceive of picking up a gun except in extreme cases of self-defense, because I visualize *political* success. I visualize the actual election of a progressive government in this country in the next generation. I can imagine two Kennedy terms followed by two Julian Bond terms. That evolution would politicize the American people in the direction of peace, justice and economic reform. It would foster a legitimate left opposition, no matter how hypocritical the Presidents themselves were. *Then* the test would be whether or not the kind of people involved in Watergate would accept the legitimacy of such a government or whether they'd try to overthrow it from the right. That would be the time to consider the question of weapons.

FONDA: I agree with Tom. I don't think I'll have to face such a choice in my lifetime either. But I'm not a pacifist. I understand why the Vietnamese are fighting. I understand why peole in Chile took up arms in the streets to oppose the junta, and if I can support that kind of struggle for other people in other parts of the world, obviously I would support it for us, if the same situation existed here.

PLAYBOY: Tom, how much of the blueprint for radical change that you laid out in the early Sixties has come to fruition?

HAYDEN: A lot of issues that we raised then—one man, one vote, poverty and unemployment, opposition to the war, rule by a power elite—have become mass issues, popular issues, and the concepts of organizing have become widespread.

PLAYBOY: In other words, much of what was formerly radical thought has been absorbed by the system. But doesn't piecemeal change, while keeping the system intact, blunt the main thrust of radicalism, which is to replace the system?

HAYDEN: The New Left was born politically suspicious of reforms, because the earlier left seemed to run into the problem of being co-opted into the New Deal; but the reforms of the Sixties—the eighteen-year-old vote, the poverty program, voter rights and equal-rights amendments—haven't co-opted people. You can't have your faith in the system restored by the right to vote when Watergate shows you what kind of political system we really have. Watergate was no surprise to us. We've been talking about things like that since 1962, since the Bay of Pigs and the Kennedy assassination, and people have always said, "You're paranoid." A lot of people who thought we were talking hysterically will now have to reconsider. People will also have to ask: Who were the real traitors to the Constitution and who were the truly democratic forces? Weren't the young people in the streets, standing for freedom, far more democratic than the men behind the White House curtains with American-flag pins in their lapels and thugs on call? I think the answer's obvious.

PLAYBOY: The fact that most people abhor Watergate doesn't mean they've changed their minds about the movement.

HAYDEN: I don't agree with your assessment. After traveling around the country and talking not just with college audiences but with newspaper editors, and so forth, I find a sympathy and an acknowledgment that we weren't so wrong after all. The roots of Watergate lie in the roots of the early Cold War, when people like Hunt and McCord—and Nixon—rose either in the clandestine services of the CIA or in the political anti-communist crusade. Most of the administration officials involved in Watergate—Magruder, Chapin, Mitchell—are ideologically committed conservatives who were involved in trying to stop protests throughout the Sixties.

Look at the characters. Tom Charles Huston, the aide who proposed the super-intelligence group to go over the head of J. Edgar Hoover, was an early leader of Young Americans for Freedom, the conservative counterpart to SDS. So was Douglas Caddy, the lawyer who brought bail money for the Watergate conspirators the night they were caught. Liddy had been an active prosecutor against the drug culture and the youth culture and is an extreme anti-Communist. Hunt, Barker and the Cuban exiles were violent CIA adventurers. Barker and Hunt were involved in attempting to overthrow the Cuban government in 1961. Robert Mardian administered six thousand draft-resistance cases and was an ardent wiretap advocate. Magruder and Dean were in charge of dealing with antiwar demonstrators. These were the bureaucrats who carried out the policies preferred by the big defense corporations that gave Maurice Stans most of the sixty million dollars for Nixon's 1972 campaign.

PLAYBOY: What made them resort to acts of repression in the pursuit of their convictions?

HAYDEN: They were frustrated by the protest movements that have grown to great magnitude in this decade, and they were even more frustrated by Vietnam. According to the public statements of Daniel Ellsberg—and, as far as I know, also according to Senate subcommittee hearings—after the 1968 election of Nixon, there was a secret decision made to escalate the military pressure on North Vietnam by secretly invading Laos, bombing Cambodia and sending navy frogmen into Haiphong Harbor so the North Vietnamese could see that the harbor was threatened. Having made that decision for escalation, there was one problem remaining: The American people, who had been sold the idea that the Vietnam engagement was about to end. That's what made a policy of repression necessary, and, specifically, that's what led to the super-safeguards that evolved into "the plumbers," because we know now that in May 1969, when *The New York Times* broke the story that Cambodia was being bombed, the Nixon administration became obsessed with leaks.

FONDA: Now that we know the facts of Watergate, we can see that Nixon's victory in 1972 was the product of his deceptions. He should be impeached—not simply because of these criminal activities but also because his first administration was responsible for six million people being killed, wounded or made refugees in Indochina, according to the Senate Subcommittee on Refugees. If we are to implement the democracy we speak of, the elections should be held over again. One of the lessons Watergate has taught us is that free elections aren't necessarily a reflection of reality if the public hasn't been given all the facts.

PLAYBOY: Were you generally pleased with the hearings and with the conduct of the inquiry?

HAYDEN: Senator Ervin, in particular, and his staff were very courageous. I think the hearings have given the American people a lesson about our rights against arbitrary authority and have revealed the White House power structure in a way unlike anything in American history. On the other hand, the areas of inquiry were very carefully circumscribed. There were many questions the senators avoided. You heard Jeb Stuart Magruder say that he worked for three years on the antiwar movement, but not one senator asked what he did. You heard that Liddy presented plans to mug and even kidnap demonstrators, but you didn't hear whether or not any part of his plans was implemented by secret police.

FONDA: The things that disturbs me most about the hearings was what wasn't explored in terms of a grand conspiracy that might have been responsible for the assassinations of the Sixties and that may be traceable to people working for the Committee to Re-Elect the President. There is evidence that should be taken seriously by more people that John Kennedy wasn't shot by just some maverick. Who killed him? Who killed Martin Luther King? Who killed Bobby Kennedy? Who killed Malcolm X? Who tried to kill Wallace? We already know that the Committee to Re-Elect the President was trying to stop Wallace. We also know how Nixon benefited from Wallace's being shot. And what about Mrs. Hunt carrying all that money on the plane that crashed? These are things that aren't being investigated at all. All those events were used by the right to foster an atmosphere to turn the people against the left.

HAYDEN: John Kennedy was shot right out of office. Bobby Kennedy might have defeated Nixon in 1968. Malcolm X might have unified the black community. Wallace might have drawn enough votes from Nixon to defeat him in a race against Muskie.

FONDA: King was beginning to talk about the relationship between the black movement and the war. He was starting to make links—between racism in this country and racism as acted out by our white leaders sending blacks to kill yellow people—that hadn't been made before.

HAYDEN: I've always doubted the notion that the assassinations of King and Malcolm and the Kennedys were the work of lone assassins, and I've always thought that groups of conspirators were involved, in some cases with official knowledge. But I think it's important for people like myself not to make assertions beyond what can be factually proved. So all I can say is that the Watergate investigation should have led to a reinvestigation of the assassinations of the Sixties.

What Jane's talking about are underlying questions such as: What did Hunt and McCord *do* in the CIA for twenty years before they shifted to the Nixon campaign? I mean, how many governments did Hunt conspire to overthrow? How many times was he successful? How many were Bay of Pigs fiascoes? This is what the public was right on the precipice of discovering.

PLAYBOY: Wasn't the Ervin committee charged only with getting to the bottom of 1972 campaign improprieties?

HAYDEN: Well, a few of the senators made grand speeches to the contrary. Senator Baker, for instance, and Senator Ervin spoke of the committee's mandate not only to get at the immediate specifics but also to deal with the general and philosophical. And all they seemed to be asking was how these boys with neatly combed hair could have consciously committed crimes. But at the edges of what they were pursuing were the most amazing questions. Did any of the witnesses have personal knowledge of or informed opinions about any of the major assassinations in the Sixties?

Doesn't every average person believe that the answer to that question is yes? Not that these men participated in any particular assassination, but that they may have some direct knowledge of who did. Why was Colson involved in the creation of falsified cables about the assassination of Diem in 1963? Does that shed any new doubts on the validity of the Pentagon Papers? Who were the protest leaders who were going to be kidnaped and taken outside the United States? What would have happened if Watergate hadn't been uncovered in June of 1972? What would have happened if that night watchman hadn't walked by. What were their next plans?

PLAYBOY: Still, do you see the fact that the system was able to "flush out" Watergate as an indication that it might, in some way, work?

HAYDEN: It needs a little more Drano. What has really amused me for a long time is how every time a scandal, a bribery, an assassination is exposed and dealt with publicly, even if it's a genocidal barbarism like My Lai, the system congratulates itself for having had the capacity to reveal it, as if it should be a matter of pride to learn that we're afflicted with corruption, exploitation and genocide.

If you think the way I do—that Watergate was not a temporary fit of extremism by some overzealous campaign aides in the 1972 election; if you see it as a part of developments that began in the Sixties, starting with the Bay of Pigs—then it's definitely the development of an antidemocratic force that has suffered failures before, suffered humiliation before, suffered the loss of personnel before. The Bay of Pigs was as big a catastrophe as Watergate, but the antidemocratic forces rebuilt very swiftly.

PLAYBOY: When you talk about antidemocratic forces, do you mean organized right-wing groups such as the John Birch Society?

HAYDEN: Yes. And the Young Americans for Freedom, the Secret Army Organization and other paramilitary groups.

PLAYBOY: Are these groups Nixon supporters?

HAYDEN: People in these groups have been divided over the last ten years about whether to work within the system or not. Many of them worked for Nixon from 1965 on, and when he was planning his 1968 campaign. Now that his administration has led to this Watergate debacle, I think the conclusion they can fairly draw is that it's quite difficult to establish an unconstitutional system under the cloak of the Constitution.

PLAYBOY: Jane, you recently sued many of these people—including the President—for what you've described as police-state tactics. What's the basis of your suit?

FONDA: About a year and a half ago, I read in Jack Anderson's column that he had a partial copy of my FBI dossier. He expressed shock that this kind of surveillance had been carried out against someone who was obviously not charged with a crime, and never violated the law, did not even have a misdemeanor on record. So when other things began to happen, when the enemies list was made public and it became clear that certain things that had happened over a period of time were in fact part of an organized effort to—in the words of John Dean—"screw" me, I decided that we should look into it further and that we should sue. So at that point, my attorney, Leonard Weinglass, asked Anderson for the dossier.

PLAYBOY: According to the file, what has the FBI discovered about you?

FONDA: They copied my entire address book, which was taken from me at the Cleveland airport when I was arrested in 1970 for allegedly smuggling drugs, which were later proved to be vitamin pills. They Xeroxed it and it appears as part of the FBI dossier. Also, two banks, the Morgan Guaranty Trust Company of New York and the City National Bank of Los Angeles, turned over—without subpoena—my bank accounts. So my financial statements are part of the FBI file.

Other appalling things appear. There's a whole section of the file, for example, devoted to my daughter, Vanessa, who went to a nursery school in Berkeley a few years ago that was run by people active in the movement. The file says things like, "The fifth informant said that he once saw children marching across the street carrying antiwar posters." So, according to this file, the FBI has people spying on a kindergarten! It goes from that kind of thing to transcripts of speeches I've made and the itinerary of the Free the Army troupe. There's another portion that relates to a time I talked to some soldiers in a coffeehouse on an army base. After I left, the FBI went in and interviewed some of the soldiers I talked with; they also talked to a chaplain's assistant—who turned out to be an informant for the FBI. The file indicates very clearly that I haven't committed any violation of the law whatsoever. I think most Americans would be very upset to know that their tax money is being used for this sort of domestic spying.

PLAYBOY: Does the file contain anything having to do with your Hanoi radio broadcasts?
FONDA: No. Every entry I have preceded my trip to Hanoi.
PLAYBOY: There have been subsequent charges that you made those broadcasts to undermine troop morale. What *were* your intentions?
FONDA: The GIs didn't need *me* to undermine their morale. I was simply giving an eyewitness account of what I, as an American woman, was seeing. Now, I assumed that most people in the air force—pilots who dropped bombs and didn't see their destruction close up—weren't going to desert or mutiny. But there were some who said, "I just can't do it anymore"—especially during the last months of the bombing. So I at least *hoped,* if a pilot had access to new information about the war, that as a human being he would eventually say, "I can't bomb anymore."
PLAYBOY: How about the accusation that your broadcasts prolonged the killing and, together with other protest activities, made negotiations more difficult?
FONDA: The only thing that forced the negotiations to take place, and forced an end to the killing, besides the Vietnamese resistance, was pressure by the antiwar movement, which got out information that the government wanted suppressed and mobilized public opinion that affected Congress and made it impossible for Nixon to continue, just as earlier it had forced Johnson to retire.
PLAYBOY: Would you explain your statements in Hanoi that many Vietnamese were victims of American antipersonnel weapons?
FONDA: The U.S. has an arsenal of weapons that are illegal under international law. Fragmentation grenades, spider mines, dragontooth mines and gravel mines. They are described by the corporations that made them—Honeywell, for example—so you know what they do to the body. When you see a woman whose body has maybe five hundred small holes in it, you know that probably comes from a guava or a pineapple bomb. If you see hundreds of children with their feet and hands blown off, chances are it was caused by a gravel mine, because that's what gravel mines are designed to do. They have no effect against anything except flesh. A gravel mine can't even blow a hole in the tire of an army truck. It can blow a child's foot off, and that's about all it can do. Toward that end, they are often designed to look like toys. The Pentagon describes them as "psychological-impact weapons."
PLAYBOY: You also charged that we were bombing cities in the North. Did you *see* the bombing?
FONDA: The cities I saw—Nam Dinh, south of Hanoi, for example—were eighty percent rubble. I saw bomb damage that had occurred the night before I arrived in a place. You see, there are certain areas where the dikes are strategic—where, for example, a lot of rivers converge and the dike wall holds back the water. If that particular portion of dike were destroyed, the waters would flood huge sections of the Red River delta, bringing the threat of death to millions of people. The bombs invariably hit the most strategic points of the dike and were dropped during times when the waters were highest. As it happened, the rains weren't so heavy in 1972. If the flooding had been what it was in 1971, we would have been responsible for one of the worst massacres in the history of the world, and this would have happened while Nixon was telling us the war was winding down. People are told the bombing of dikes was accidental, yet the Pentagon Papers tell us that this was being considered as an option during Johnson's administration.

I didn't go to Vietnam with any intention of talking on the radio, but after I was there about two days, I had seen more destruction to the hospitals, churches, villages, schools and cities than I care to think about. I asked the Vietnamese, my hosts and hostesses, if I could make tape recordings for the radio. I said I would like to do it every morning to describe what I was seeing.

PLAYBOY: How did the taping sessions proceed?

FONDA: Every morning a man would come to the hotel with a Sony tape recorder. I would sit down in a room alone with him and talk extemporaneously. I said, "Yesterday I saw children with their hands and feet blown off, and this is the kind of weapon that did it. Perhaps you're not aware of what's in the bombs you're dropping." I would talk about what it felt like to be an American seeing what our government was doing to these people. I read some excerpts from the Pentagon Papers over the radio. I talked about how the United States had prevented the reunification of Vietnam in 1956 and how we had installed a series of dictatorships in South Vietnam. In fact, I said essentially what I say when I speak in the United States. I said that we'd been lied to, and that I didn't think it was possible to continue, either as civilians having the war waged in our names or as pilots pushing buttons and pulling levers, without its destroying us as human beings. I said we really had to think about what we were doing, that we couldn't allow ourselves to be turned into robots.

PLAYBOY: Weren't you implicitly encouraging soldiers to desert?

FONDA: I never asked soldiers to desert or defect. I have very strong feelings about that. I don't feel that any civilian has any right to ask someone in the military to do something that could get him in trouble. I'm not the one who would have to stand court-martial or get sent to a stockade.

PLAYBOY: You say you would never ask anyone in the military to do something that could get him in trouble, but if soldiers had refused to fight, as you hoped they would after listening to your broadcasts, they *could* have been court-martialed.

FONDA: I hoped that, as human beings and as Americans who apparently cherish the concepts of democracy and independence, they wouldn't want to continue fighting if they knew facts about the war that the Pentagon has tried to keep from us. Making facts available, however, is different from advising someone to break a law.

PLAYBOY: What do you think your broadcasts accomplished?

FONDA: What speaking out always accomplishes. It may instill an idea, a new thought in the minds of even a few people. As far as I was concerned, if there was one pilot who was already having second thoughts about what he was doing and I could help him clarify his thoughts about it, it would be useful.

The controversy that was created about my trip—my charges that the U.S. was bombing dikes, the films I had showing the damage—became very important to the administration. Don't forget that Nixon was trying to get elected as a man who was winding down the war. He didn't want Vietnam to be an issue in the elections. My trip, Ramsey Clark's trip, everything that helped call attention to what was, in fact, an escalating air war, was very crucial. That's why there were all the shouts of treason. It was a Nixon tactic he's used since the Fifties to discredit his critics.

PLAYBOY: William Loeb editorialized in the Manchester *Union Leader* that "Miss Fonda should either be refused readmittance to the United States or, immediately following her return, be tried for treason. She should be shot if a verdict of guilty comes in." Why do you think you arouse such hatred?

FONDA: My impression is that most of the venom is from organized right-wing groups like the Veterans of Foreign Wars, Young Americans for Freedom and others connected with the Committee to Re-Elect the President.

PLAYBOY: Is that just an informed guess on your part or do you have evidence to substantiate it?
FONDA: We've seen it firsthand. I remember a time in Harrisburg, Pennsylvania, for example, when a man disrupted a press conference we were having about the war. He conducted a long, loud harangue against me, then admitted later that he worked for CREEP. Young Americans for Freedom has been the organizer of several widely publicized attacks against me in L.A. It's made to look like spontaneous Americana, but its roots are in Watergate.
PLAYBOY: Whoever incited it, the hostility against you is very strong. Why?
FONDA: A POW I know, a guy who was a prisoner for five years, explained it to me this way: "A lot of guys in prison were big fans of yours. They had seen a lot of your movies and they will never forgive you for betraying their dreams." I think that's the basis for a lot of it. I'm an actress, I'm famous, I come from a position in society that, given our culture, is enviable. I suppose some people also think I'm not acting "feminine." I'm saying that there are things wrong with our society and I'm going to speak out about them. I'm no longer going to accept the image of a mindless Barbarella floating through space. I'm no longer afraid to indicate that I have a mind, and I'm going to speak out.

But times have changed. We've toured the country to tell people about the U.S.-created police state in South Vietnam; we went to all parts of the country, including Texas and Arizona, and I encountered almost none of the venom you've mentioned. Hardly anyone even raised the issue of my statement about the North Vietnamese not torturing their POWs. I think Watergate has played a large role in changing people's heads.
PLAYBOY: Have you seen any signs of a boycott of your work from those within the film industry?
FONDA: No. I occasionally get letters from a few chapters of Veterans of Foreign Wars telling me they've organized a boycott, and some of Agnew's cronies in the Maryland legislature say they don't want my films shown; but, frankly, as long as Hollywood can make a buck off me, I'll get work.
HAYDEN: All this kind of activity simply points up one fact: Jane is a significant political figure who commands enormous respect in the movement. That's why she is the target of the American right, including the lunatic fringe, which has weapons and legal bases of power. In their view of the world, it's the outside agitator, the inspirational figure, who's the cause of the problem, not the product of the problem. They believe that if you cut off a movement at its head, then it's weakened. How else do you explain the assassinations of the Sixties?
PLAYBOY: Jane, do you feel you could be a target for assassination?
FONDA: I just assume that anybody who is critical, and is part of an organized movement, is a target for repression and possibly death. Look what we're dealing with. Look who the people are.
PLAYBOY: What precautions are you taking?
HAYDEN: Well, we're taking the problem seriously. In the Maryland legislature, one elected official actually got some publicity by advocating that Jane's tongue be cut out. Another said she should be executed. But the most serious threat, I think, comes from the right-wing groups that are so hysterical about mass leaders and outside agitators, and what we've tried to do is neutralize their ability to continue their political attacks. In the California legislature, for example, we found it relatively easy,

through the lobbying efforts of our Indochina Peace Campaign, to overturn a proposed resolution of censure.

PLAYBOY: But how does all this pressure make you feel?

HAYDEN: Unless such actions are stopped—whether they be assassinations or just underhanded attempts to discredit leaders of the movement—there's no possibility for peaceful, democratic politics in this country. We have a very good letter from a congressman whose name I can't mention; he clipped an article from the paper saying how Scott Nearing, the elderly Socialist who's a columnist for *Monthly Review* and who was once pilloried and hounded and discredited for his politics, had just been given an honorary degree at some university on something like his ninety-second birthday. This congressman sincerely sent this to Jane as a sign of how she'll someday be remembered. But of what value is it to be destroyed until you're ninety-two and then be remembered? That's what people typically do with reform leaders. If they're not dead, they get discredited; then, in later years, people say, "Well, she wasn't so bad."

PLAYBOY: How do you live with your fear for Jane's safety?

HAYDEN: I'm well prepared by what I've been through. She isn't the first person I've known who's in this situation. I've felt close to several who died, and been to enough funerals.

PLAYBOY: Jane, are you afraid?

FONDA: I think fear and hatred are both immobilizing emotions. I find the weight of people's hostility very depressing. But I've seen too many people change to get depressed or cynical for long.

HAYDEN: I've seen the same very strong feelings—love and hate and excitement—generated toward Jane that have been generated toward only a few other mass figures in my lifetime. And those figures were Martin Luther King, the Kennedys and Malcolm X.

PLAYBOY: Do you believe Jane is as influential a figure as they were?

HAYDEN: No, I didn't mean to compare influence. It's just that there is a very special role that's played by those who have mass followings. And in the Sixties, most of these figures were cut down by bullets.

PLAYBOY: It's been said—even by those who basically agree with you, Jane—that you've used whatever influence you have to distort and oversimplify many of the issues you've raised, particularly in connection with the war in Vietnam. Wouldn't your message be more effective if, for example, while denouncing the iniquity of the Saigon regime, you acknowledged that the Vietcong and the North Vietnamese haven't been entirely innocent of cruelty and repression?

FONDA: I'm very weary of the thinking that says there are two sides to every question. There aren't. Hitler, for example, was wrong. The question shouldn't be whether or not the North Vietnamese or the Provisional Revolutionary Government commits atrocities in the course of the war. The *real* question is: Who is ultimately responsible for the war? For those who don't already know the answer, I suggest they read the Pentagon Papers, which reveal that the United States has always been the aggressor in Vietnam. The idea that we were defending the south from a Communist invasion from North Vietnam was and continues to be a lie, designed to justify *our* invasion. The papers reveal that the forces we have been told are the enemy are the *popular* forces in Vietnam, analogous to the American revolutionaries here two hundred years ago. The Vietnamese are fighting a guerrilla war, and guerrilla warfare can be waged only if there is popular support. The Vietnamese have been successfully waging a guerrilla war against foreigners for thirty years.

I don't want to cater to our need to feel better about our government by saying that the other guy is bad, too. It doesn't help. As far as Saigon is concerned, I have no good words for the government we're supporting. I can't believe that Americans, if they really knew what the Saigon government was doing, would have anything good to say about it. It is a total betrayal of everything we cherish in this country. Democratic rights are being denied to the people, people are being murdered, there's no freedom of the press, there are hundreds of thousands of people in prisons in the most terrible conditions. And we are responsible. We pay for it with our taxes. Taxes for torture.

PLAYBOY: Do you want to give the impression that none of the conditions you just mentioned apply to North Vietnam?

FONDA: I think that's irrelevant. We aren't *responsible* for what happens there. We don't front the North Vietnamese government. We front Saigon. But I am not an apologist for North Vietnam. No way.

PLAYBOY: Wouldn't you concede, then, that North Vietnam as well as South Vietnam has suppressed dissent and imprisoned its political enemies?

FONDA: I don't know. I don't think so. But I was there only two weeks. I didn't see everything. I didn't see prisons. I don't pretend to know everything about the situation in North Vietnam. I can only tell you what I felt. The reason I say I don't believe they have political prisoners is because of the atmosphere. I've been in a Communist country where the atmosphere is such that it could *well* be that there are people who are being persecuted. It didn't feel the same in North Vietnam

PLAYBOY: Where was that?

FONDA: Russia. I felt great unhappiness, frustration; I sensed that the people were unfulfilled. Much the same as what I feel in this country. In North Vietnam, I didn't feel those things. I felt an incredible unity between the people and their government.

PLAYBOY: Give us an example.

FONDA: I walked the streets with the foreign minister of the North Vietnamese government. Now, in the streets of Hanoi, a number of people had guns, automatic weapons, because virtually everyone—men, women and children—was prepared to try to shoot down planes that were bombing their cities. And I walked down the street with this high government official, yet he had no bodyguards, no weapon, he wasn't in a bulletproof limousine and his house wasn't surrounded by electronic surveillance. When I expressed surprise at all this, my guide said to me, "Our government and our people are one." He said, "We don't have political assassinations here."

Now, those could be just words, but there was also an atmosphere I felt and there were things I saw that gave that feeling of unity. What I saw in the streets were not unhappy people. I saw people helping each other, caring for each other, touching each other. People who really seemed to be living to the utmost. Truly fulfilled people, which is remarkable, because they're so poor.

HAYDEN: I agree with the point Jane made earlier that our moral concern should be focused on our *own* country, but I think it's also necessary to know something about the Vietnamese. America killed 600,000 or 700,000 people there, wounded twice as many and made refugees of ten times as many. If you know nothing about them, what's the difference between you and a mad killer who knows not what he does?

When history is truthfully written, we'll realize that we lost a half-million guys there for nothing. When I say lost, I don't mean just dead, but also badly wounded—physically or psychically maimed. We invested, according to Senator Fulbright, somewhere over two hundred billion dollars in that war. And the consequences are going to be as severe as the cost. They're going to be with us for a long time. So to not know Vietnam is to not know America.

FONDA: It would help, in order to understand what we can learn from the killing, to talk about the attitudes found in the armed forces, the people who began—within the military—to say, "We don't want this anymore. We don't believe the Vietnamese are our enemies." Of course, official military propaganda consistently denied it, but there was a virtual collapse of morale within the American armed forces.

PLAYBOY: You challenged another official statement when you said that the army lied in asserting that it was North Vietnamese policy to torture POWs. How do you know it wasn't?

FONDA: The Pentagon carefully chose a small group of army lifers, the most biased and conservative officers in the military, to participate in a public-relations campaign that would create the impression that torture was the routine experience of our 566 POWs. I think many POWs said they were tortured in order to excuse their circumstances of capture or their statements and actions opposing the war.

HAYDEN: Sergeant Daniel Pitzer, a Green Beret released in '67, told me, when I was escorting him home, that it was standard operating procedure to collaborate with the Vietnamese as much as necessary and then repudiate the action by claiming torture when you got home.

FONDA: With only one exception, as far as we've been able to find through the research of the Indochina Peace Campaign, no one claims to have been tortured after '69. So right there you have the men themselves refuting the story the Pentagon was encouraging—that ninety-five percent of the men were tortured. The one exception is of special interest to me. David Hoffman claims that the North Vietnamese pulled his already-broken arm out of its socket to coerce him into seeing Ramsey Clark and me. Yet his copilot and prison roommate, Norris Charles, said he never heard of nor saw any torture in the camp. Neither did POWs Walter Wilber and Mark Gartley, who were in the same compound. Wilber was even quoted in his home-town newspaper as saying, about my visit, "She could see that we were all healthy and hadn't been tortured."

I think we should ask ourselves why Nixon made heroes of the POWs. Why not the vets, the ground troops who've come back legless and jobless? Why not the fifty thousand who died there? Could it be that paraplegics don't make good spokesmen for Nixon, that voices from the grave can't congratulate the President on achieving peace with honor?

HAYDEN: We have just visited about thirty-five cities around the country, and a POW named Bob Chenoweth, who spent five and a half years in North Vietnam, traveled with us. He lived, at different times, with a total of 108 POWs. That's about one-fifth, almost twenty percent of all of them, and he never heard anyone say that they were tortured. More and more POWs are coming to terms with their feelings about the war; but when many of them were first released, they came home to families who were still hawkish. So a good number of the POWs found themselves in limbo, not knowing where to turn. It's taken time.

PLAYBOY: That's somewhat the same lack of direction you expressed privately a decade ago, Jane—long before people began calling you radical—when you left the United States to live in Europe. Tell us why you went.

FONDA: I went because in the early Sixties, Europe seemed to be the place where things were happening. There was the New Wave in the cinema. I was trying to get back to what I had felt in the beginning, when I began acting. I missed the excitement of working in the theater in New York and the real contact I felt I had lost when I went to California. I didn't know how to deal with the values I found here in Hollywood.

PLAYBOY: You hadn't always wanted to be an actress, had you?

FONDA: No, at first I resisted the idea of acting very much. But I was out of school and I had no idea what to do with my life. I didn't want to get married. I remember as a freshman in college I had seen my girlfriends fall—engagement, bridal magazine, wedding ring, marriage. I said to myself, if I can get past my sophomore year without feeling that I should have a ring on my finger or there's something wrong with me, if I can get by that, then I'm saved. And I got by it. But I didn't know what I *did* want to do, and it's a terrifying feeling. I mean, I understand so well what kids feel now. They just don't know what they want their future to be.

Anyway, when I was twenty-one I began studying at Lee Strasberg's Actors Studio in New York and from then on, that was it. I mean, I ate and dreamed and lived acting twenty-four hours a day. And I think the reason I loved it so much was that it offered me a way of getting behind a mask and revealing things that I, as an uptight middle-class woman, had always been told I should not show.

PLAYBOY: So you found yourself in love with acting but disenchanted with Hollywood. Did you discover what you were looking for in Europe?

FONDA: What I was very impressed with there was the existence of filmmaking as an art, as opposed to filmmaking as big business. When you make a movie with a major studio in Hollywood, you deal with a vast bureaucracy. The content of the film, right down to what the actress may wear, can often be controlled by the heads of the studios or the bankers in New York. There's also usually a great deal of alienation between the workers and the final product. I'm talking about the grips, the technicians, the rank and file of the studios, who are mostly quite old—because young people can't get into the unions here—and jaded.

PLAYBOY: And you found things different in Europe?

FONDA: In Europe, films can be made more cheaply, more risks can be taken. Many, many more independent productions were being made while I was there. I would say generally that the workers were much more liberal and involved in the creation of a film. The man I was later to marry, Roger Vadim, was the first very young, absolutely unknown filmmaker to have made what was called a New Wave film on a very low budget. It was a huge success and, as a result, it opened the doors to all of the young directors who came later: Godard, Truffaut and all the rest. It was the beginning of the New Wave.

PLAYBOY: You're talking about Vadim's *And God Created Woman?*

FONDA: That's right.

PLAYBOY: Interestingly enough, the movie was predicated on the idea of the female as a sex object.

FONDA: One thing that was true of his films, however, was that the women were always strong. They were always the central characters, always the winners. She may have been portrayed as a beautiful object, but Brigitte Bardot ruled the roost. She kicked out any man she was tired of and invited in any man she wanted. She lived *like* a man in Vadim's films. I think the reason *And God Created Woman* was such a success was that it was the first time you saw a beautiful female creature behave exactly like a man, and it was a very liberating experience for a lot of women to watch her on the screen. Of course, there's the other side of the coin: Sex was the determining factor; woman objectified as sex object. But I think it's facile to dismiss that film as simply a sexy exploitation film. I think it was much more.

PLAYBOY: What about *Barbarella?* It would certainly be surprising to hear you refer to it as anything other than sexist.

FONDA: The trouble with Barbarella was that she wasn't Superwoman. Instead of being a great female, she was a sexy *girl.* Again, sex was the determining factor in who had the power. Besides that, I don't like making the kind of movies where you have to wait four hours because the dry ice isn't steaming or the birds that are supposed to be eating you are dying.

PLAYBOY: Which of your more serious films has given you some satisfaction?

FONDA: I'll always like *They Shoot Horses, Don't They?* I guess because it's one of the few movies I've done that says something truthful, that isn't just silly or prototyped. I don't feel very close to my character in the movie, who is cynical and fatalistic, but I think the metaphor of the marathon dance fits our society: people being manipulated by a few who reap the benefits.

PLAYBOY: For your performance in that film and several others, some critics have called you America's finest actress. How do you feel about that?

FONDA: I don't like any sort of rating or comparison, because it just exacerbates a tendency—which is exaggerated enough in my profession—for everyone to compete with one another.

PLAYBOY: You accepted an Oscar, which is certainly a competitive award, for your performance in *Klute.*

FONDA: I thought about that a whole lot, and there was one period when I had decided I wouldn't accept the Oscar if I won. Then I began to think I *should* accept it, because it does come from the people in my industry and *is* a vote of confidence from the people I work with and whose opinion I respect. I also feel that the Oscar means something to the American people.

PLAYBOY: Do you disagree, then, with the way Marlon Brando handled *his* award?

FONDA: I respect very much what he did. I think his gesture of having an Indian woman raise the issue of racism in Hollywood was fine and I applaud him for it.

PLAYBOY: Do you still have your own Oscar?

FONDA: It's holding up books on the bookcase downstairs—and the gold is flaking.

PLAYBOY: You've been quoted as saying you fought a lot with Vadim about his films, which you didn't particularly like.

FONDA: I don't want to talk about Vadim. He is a kind and gentle but very, very complex human being. And attempts that people make to categorize him and write him off as a male-chauvinist pig are inaccurate and do him injustice. Yes, he *does* put too much emphasis on the way women look. That's absolutely true. And I think that attitude took its toll on me; I don't mean to pretend that it didn't. But I don't regret the time I spent in France.

PLAYBOY: Are you still friends?

FONDA: Yes. We're still friends and he's the father of my daughter. He's a wonderful father and I'm very glad he *is* her father. There is just one more thing I'd like to say about my filmmaking experiences with Vadim, and then I don't want to talk about it any further. There was something that happened during the time I was working with Vadim that made it very hard for me to agree to be interviewed by PLAYBOY.

I was doing a movie with him called *La Curée,* which was based on a novel by Emile Zola, and there was a scene in it where I'm swimming with the man who is my lover in a sort of hothouse swimming pool, and we're naked. In fact, in the film you didn't see that we were; you only *sense* that we were naked. But you don't really see our bodies. I requested, when the time came to shoot the scene, that all the crew leave the set. The only people there, I thought, were the actor, my husband and the cameraman, who was a very close friend of ours.

OK, several months go by and PLAYBOY comes out and I see a whole layout of photographs of myself getting in and out of the pool naked. The shots were obviously taken by someone who was up on the studio catwalk, on the scaffolding, with a telephoto lens. Well, we checked and discovered that there was a French or Italian photographer who had sneaked illegally onto the closed set and had taken those pictures without my permission and sold them to PLAYBOY. PLAYBOY didn't ask permission to publish them, and I was outraged. It seemed that PLAYBOY couldn't see the difference between something that I had decided to do as an actress, when I knew exactly what was going to appear on the screen and could say, "That will have to be cut out," and the violation of an unknown cameraman who sneaked in, took pictures of me naked and sold them.

I tried to sue. Unfortunately, when you're famous, you have absolutely no right to privacy. Someone can do practically anything to you and there is no way that you can win an invasion-of-privacy suit. So it was dropped and PLAYBOY wrote me a private letter of apology that said they felt they had been taken advantage of by the photographer, too, and it ended there. Except that it didn't end in terms of the embarrassment I felt. So it was—and still is—with some difficulty that I agreed to do this interview. I just want to set the record straight.

PLAYBOY: What made you decide to do it?

FONDA: Well, I thought a lot about it, and at first I refused. You know, there are two things going on in PLAYBOY. On the one hand, it has some of the most important interviews that are being published today, since most of the other magazines that used to do them have closed down. They also run some very important articles, and I recognize them as such. On the other hand, I think the magazine is bought, essentially, for the centerfold. It's the purchase of naked women. I don't like the way PLAYBOY exploits women's bodies. I think it only titillates men's sexual fantasies.

PLAYBOY: It's a debatable premise that publishing nude pictures of the human body is exploitive; but if PLAYBOY's appeal is based primarily on its sexual content, why don't the girlie magazines, which publish many more—and nuder—pictures, outsell PLAYBOY? Our circulation began rising most rapidly when we began to publish not nuder pictures but articles and interviews such as the ones you mention.

FONDA: That may be true, but the fact is that because of those naked women, PLAYBOY has become the symbol of what is the enemy for women.

PLAYBOY: You don't believe it really *is,* do you?

FONDA: You're going to tell me how PLAYBOY has supported the women's movement by joining the fight for abortion reform. Well, that's fine, but it doesn't change certain basic things about the magazine. Before I agreed to be interviewed, I talked to a number of women I work with and am close to and I asked them what they felt I should do. Generally the feeling was that it's not often one is given room to speak, and with the climate as it is today, I felt it was important to be able to have space to say some things I felt were important. So that consideration overrode my reluctance.

PLAYBOY: What's your opinion of magazines such as *Viva* and *Playgirl,* which publish photos of nude men? Do you think they exploit *men's* bodies?

FONDA: Yes, I do, and I don't read them.

PLAYBOY: Fair enough. Let's change the subject. You were still in France when your own exploitation as a sex star was at its height. What occurred during that time to politicize you?

FONDA: What happened was that I was living there when people in this country were beginning to change. Essentially, I was away during the civil-rights movement. I was away during the beginning of the antiwar movement and felt the turmoil of that time only indirectly. When a Frenchman said to me that the United States air force had bombed a village, razed it "in order to save it," I told him he was lying, that it wasn't true. I said Americans don't do things like that. The first specific thing I can remember was watching television when there was a march of half a million people on the Pentagon and seeing people getting bludgeoned to the ground. I watched women leading marches. I watched women walking up to the bayonets that were surrounding the Pentagon, and they were not afraid. The soldiers were the ones who were afraid. I'll never forget that experience. It completely changed me, not overnight, but it started a process in me as I began searching for what was behind it all.

PLAYBOY: When and how did you begin that search?

FONDA: It was 1968. There were soldiers in Paris at the time, deserters from Vietnam, young men who had enlisted in the service and had gone to Vietnam and left because they couldn't deal with what was happening there anymore. I met some of them in Paris and I talked with them. Then I began to read. I read Bertrand Russell's *War Crimes in Vietnam* transcripts, a book by Jonathan Schell called *The Village of Ben Suc;* I got subscriptions to *Ramparts* and *The Village Voice.* Paris was in a state of siege. Most everyone I knew was in the streets, but my eyes were on my own country; the occupation of Columbia University, the '68 convention riots in Chicago.

Gradually I realized that my place was not as a married woman on a farm in France any longer, that I wanted to come back here. I had a purpose in coming back. I wanted to find some way that I could be part of what was going on. For the first time in my life, I realized that people were finding a way to create change. I didn't know what it was; all I knew was that people were beginning to feel powerful again, and I wanted to be part of it.

PLAYBOY: When you returned to the U.S. late in '69, you immediately embarked on a cross-country tour that created a lot of publicity because of the things you said. Why did you make that trip?

FONDA: I realized when I came back to the United States from France that I didn't know this country at all. I knew New York and California, and vaguely Omaha, because that's where my father comes from, but I didn't know the rest of the country and I decided that one way to start finding out about it was to drive through it. Because I'd spent time with soldiers in Paris, I became very interested as I traveled in what was called the GI movement. I didn't really understand what that was in the beginning. I remember telling someone I was going to be driving across the country and he said, "Oh, you should go to the coffeehouses." I didn't even know what the coffeehouses were, but I learned that there were soldiers organizing, putting out newspapers and opening coffeehouses where other guys from the base could go and talk about conditions in the military and about the war. I visited these places all across the country and talked with guys who had just come back from Vietnam. They knew more about the war than anybody else, in the sense that they felt the weight and horror of it in their guts.

I saw guys who will probably never be the same. You've read about the post-Vietnam syndrome. I've seen men suffering from it who can't even speak. They talk in whispers. They would whisper in my ear that they were incapable of doing anything except kill. I don't know whether everything they said was true or not, but I *do* know what a powerful effect it had on me to hear GIs talking about the atrocities they had committed against Vietnamese, the falsifying of reports and body counts. I participated with Vietnam Veterans Against the War in organizing the Winter Soldier Investigation in 1971. Over a hundred officers and enlisted men testified at the hearing about war crimes. Some testified to having participated in Nixon's secret invasion of Laos and in the 1969 raids against Cambodia. Yet the TV networks dismissed them as "alleged veterans."

I guess one of the most important experiences I can remember was arriving at a coffeehouse called the Oleo Strut in Killeen, Texas, where I found a group of men and women activists, GIs who were treating each other differently than I had ever seen people treat each other before. The men were fighting their male chauvinism. Women had assumed new positions of leadership. Responsibilities were shared. What I realized during the week I spent with these people was that all the words I had been hearing really meant something, that there really *was* an alternative way of living.

PLAYBOY: If you'd had doubts until then that all the words you'd been hearing really meant something, why had you already committed yourself to the movement?

FONDA: Well, prior to that experience, I had this feeling that I wanted things to *stop*. But I really didn't know what I wanted to replace them with. What I saw acted out in the lives of the people in the coffeehouses showed me the kinds of things I wanted to *start*. I began to see positive alternatives to work *for,* not just negative things to work against.

PLAYBOY: What do you say to the accusation that during this period when you underwent such a radical transformation, you were being used for promotional purposes, being manipulated by the movements that attracted you?

FONDA: It's true to a degree. But I kept coming upon people who were living life-and-death experiences: Their land was being taken away, or they were starving, or they were about to be shot or *had* been shot. These people weren't getting their stories out; they weren't being given access to the media; and groups of people would come and ask me to try to get some attention drawn to what was happening and I found it difficult to say no. On the other hand, I didn't trust the words I had to use. They were incoherent; they were unsophisticated; so I borrowed words from people who knew a lot of big political words, and they didn't sound good in my mouth. What I was seeing was real; I should have just relied on that realness and talked about it that way.

I was just trying to find a way to express what I was feeling—rage; the rage people feel when they've been lied to and suddenly realize it. The rage of someone who was, despite the cynicism and everything else, very idealistic about her country. I was very angry about the deception. My feelings came from inexperience, from being famous and, therefore, being asked to take an instant public position. They came from being a woman, unfamiliar with the need to be assertive. My outrage was also influenced by the fact that I was alone during this period. What you gain with experience and political maturity is the ability to be calm, the ability to understand that you have to

have a great deal of patience, that you have your limitations and that you can't do everything. You learn that without an organization, little can be accomplished.
PLAYBOY: It was also at this time that you began to speak out for women's rights. Tell us a little about the internal changes that turned you from a sex star into a feminist leader.
FONDA: I don't think of myself as a leader. I'm a woman who's changing. I think the problem women face is that we don't define our own lives, what it is we strive for, and consequently the means we use to get there are pretty well dictated by men. Recently, when I was having our new baby, all the workers in the hospital who did the shit work—who washed up and cleaned the floors and stuck a thermometer up your ass—were female and black, chicano or Asian. All the internists—anyone who had a dignified role—were white and male. It was just another reminder of the way women have been treated in terms of job opportunities.
PLAYBOY: But you've always been able to work and feel economically equal to men. What made *you* feel oppressed?
FONDA: For a long time, I *didn't* see how the women's movement related to me. I didn't even comprehend the concept of women's oppression. We get so used to certain things being the way they are that we consider them normal, inevitable. Three or four years ago, I would be asked periodically by groups of women to discuss my exploitation as a movie actress; I never knew what to say. It seemed to me that if you were an actress, you were a property that was packaged and sold and I saw that as normal. Looking back on it, I remember the first day I went to Warner Bros., when I was doing my first film there and a bunch of makeup artists were examining my face—checking it out to tell how they were going to make me up. I remember their looking me over, and I wasn't what they wanted.

When they got finished with me, I didn't really know *who* I was. My eyebrows were like eagle's wings and my mouth was all over my face. My hair wasn't the right color and had to be changed, too. Then Jack Warner, the head of the studio, sent a message down to the set that I had to wear falsies, because you couldn't become a movie star unless you were full-breasted. It seems silly today, given the consciousness that exists now, that I would accept that, but I just assumed these men were experts: They know, they've been doing it to women for years. So I allowed myself to be changed.
PLAYBOY: What made you begin to see things differently?
FONDA: I met women who had a new consciousness and they helped me understand the joy of not competing with each other, of being able to be open with and rely on other women. I also met a few men who had another attitude toward women, who weren't chauvinists. That made me think a lot and I was able to see the degree to which growth was literally stunted by concerns having to do with how we looked and what we had to do to be liked by men. The concern among women was always how they should relate to men.
PLAYBOY: Why?
FONDA: Because who wanted to relate to women? Women were losers. Looking back over my life and the women I had known, I realized the extent to which thwarted energy turns inward and eats you up like cancer. How many vital, vibrant, brilliant women have broken like dried wood because they were denied an outlet? And I became angry. The way I saw things a couple of years ago, men—most men, anyway—were the enemy. It became very difficult for me to deal with men at that time. I felt anger for me, for my mother and for all my sisters. I also felt a new compassion for women and a pride to be part of all these females who are holding their heads up,

saying, "We are strong and our strength has been denied, we are beautiful and our beauty has been painted over."

PLAYBOY: Tom, did you know Jane during the time she was feeling hostile toward men?

HAYDEN: No. That was before I knew her.

PLAYBOY: In view of your new compassion for women, and your period of hostility toward men, Jane, how do you feel about the upsurgence of lesbianism in the feminist movement?

FONDA: I don't want to get into that. I just think people shouldn't be persecuted for their sexual desires.

PLAYBOY: How do you feel about men now?

FONDA: I no longer think men are the enemy. They've been able to reap more benefits than women have, but most men are also victims of their own institutional role. They have the burden of being the provider, of being told that to be a man means being the stronger, the real go-getter. What a drag. Well, the only way we're going to make things fundamentally better is to do things *together*.

PLAYBOY: Tom, as a male leader of the left, did you have any trouble adjusting to the feminist awakening?

HAYDEN: I had tremendous problems. For anyone to discover a blind side isn't easy. My adjustment isn't over yet. I'm still working on it. It's a very tough problem involving almost a restructuring of your senses. You have to begin to truly listen to women and understand where they're coming from. You try to overcome all the subtle male things that make them feel trivialized, like talking to women in a certain way, giving them a kind of charming banter that you wouldn't carry on with a man. Maybe you should have conversations like that with men *and* women, but not *just* with women. It's a process that takes a long time, because the problem's so deep. Men have been treating women insensitively for generations. It was as difficult for me to begin changing those attitudes as it was for a lot of men who were first confronted with their chauvinism in the late Sixties.

PLAYBOY: When did you two meet?

FONDA: I had heard about Tom and some of his articles had affected me a lot. I like the way he writes; he's neither pedantic nor rhetorical. At a moment when there was a lot of confusion on the left about priorities, Tom's articles saying Vietnam was the strategic conflict were wonderful to read. They came at a crucial time: spring of 1972. The Vietnamese had launched their counteroffensive to destroy Vietnamization and Nixon was about to run as a peace candidate. Tom and I were both in Los Angeles, both speaking a lot and working with graphics and slides to help focus the issues, so we began to work together.

PLAYBOY: Tom, what first attracted you to Jane?

HAYDEN: It was a mutual recognition of the importance of Vietnam. I think, Jane, that immediately after your trip, you were in the same place I was, believing that we should dedicate ourselves to the war as *the* issue. I don't know entirely why, but going to Vietnam when you did, as the war reached a climactic point, made you come back feeling a lot more solidly about me, and I felt the same way about you, and it will probably take us years to understand that.

PLAYBOY: It sounds as if your relationship is based on the dedication you share about Vietnam.

HAYDEN: It isn't that our relationship is based entirely on Vietnam, but I think that just as Vietnam brings out genocidal characteristics in some people, it brings out the

better qualities in other people as well. And it magnifies feelings. That's what happened to us.
FONDA: We fell in love. It's a phenomenon that's not unique. Many people fall in love and don't describe the process in PLAYBOY. I could sit down and explain exactly why I'm in love with Tom, and why I'm very happy living with him, but I don't think it's appropriate here.
HAYDEN: Everybody should be concerned about what love is and how to make it work, but it isn't our specialty and we've been in love before and it hasn't worked, so we're not experts on the subject.
PLAYBOY: It seems surprisingly conventional and middle class for you to formalize your relationship by getting married.
FONDA: When I first met Tom, he said, "Who're you living with?" and I said, "God forbid, nobody." I was very cynical about relationships and I certainly never would have thought I'd be married again and have another child. But being in Vietnam had a very important effect on me. Here you are, an American in a country that's undergoing twenty-four-hour-a-day bombardment. Yet I have never been in a place where the life force was so strong, where people were looking forward so much to the future. As I met more and more people, I kept having this feeling that they were living *beyond* themselves. That manifested itself in many ways. Women were not only fighting with their hands, they were fighting with their bellies, having babies; it was a symbol of what this struggle in Vietnam represents. There was a poem that was written just before I got there, describing the 1972 spring offensive; it was a long poem written by a famous Vietnamese poet, and the last line was, "Nixon, we will fight you with all the joys of a woman in childbirth." That says so much about their struggle. They are giving birth to new hope for the people of the world.
PLAYBOY: What has all this got to do with deciding to marry Tom?
FONDA: Well, seeing it all made me want to have a baby. So I came back to the States and I just said to him, "Tom, I want to have a baby." Before I went to Vietnam, I had begun to spend a lot of time with Tom, and I fell in love with him. The stability and clarity that I had sensed in his writings come through also in his relationships with people, and he's as secure and gentle a person as I've ever met. It was this security that helped me past the cynicism I was feeling about all relationships. But after I came back from Vietnam, I felt much stronger, not only about Tom but about *life*.

It was due partly to the fact that Vietnam rekindled an enormous amount of hope in me. Hope in terms of people's individual capacity for change, recognition of the degree to which I had changed and an enormous sense of confidence in the possibility of people changing history. So why shouldn't two people who are involved in a struggle together and who are both confident of people's ability to change—why shouldn't they have a child together to participate in that atmosphere of new hope?
PLAYBOY: But why, as radical critics of the establishment, did you decide to make your relationship contractual?
HAYDEN: It was a step-by-step decision. I think when we both felt that we wanted to have a baby, many questions had to be answered—questions of responsibility to ourselves before a society. If we weren't married and this child were coming, what do you think the newspapers would print about Jane?
PLAYBOY: That Jane Fonda is going to have an illegitimate child. So what?
HAYDEN: Well, it's difficult enough to deal with the hostility directed toward radicals in general, but particularly toward her. And I think that while it's valid to have relationships without marriage, and children without marriage, you have to decide

what the priority problems are in your life and in what order you're going to solve them. We certainly aren't trying to promote marriage as an institution for people for whom it doesn't work. On the other hand, to frivolously reject marriage and all other institutions simultaneously means you're coming from a very isolated position. So when we decided to get married, we reached our conclusion in a kind of backward process. We said, "Well, we're going to have this kid. If we're not married, it'll cause all kinds of unreasonable criticism and divert attention from what we're trying to say. So maybe we better get married."

PLAYBOY: Would you still have gotten married if you hadn't been concerned about public opinion?

HAYDEN: I don't think I would have thought about it as carefully. I would have been able to duck it. But I'm glad it came up. I think it makes me feel more responsible, not for having gotten married, as such, but for having had to think it through more carefully. You know, a by-product of the alternative culture is that you don't have to think about relationships as permanent. If you start from the assumption that all relationships are temporary, then you can go ahead and have a series of them. And the end of each one will seem inevitable. It may or may not be so, but once you start from that assumption, you don't have to think too much and it becomes self-fulfilling.

PLAYBOY: Jane, how compatible do you find marriage with your feminist principles?

FONDA: Well in past relationships with men, it never occurred to me to ask the man to share certain responsibilities with me or to allow me space to grow. Women have always been made to feel that if you're married and you want to stay married, it's usually up to you to hold it together. So what you have to do is be "the best possible wife," and what that means is you have to be a great cook, be sexy, look good all the time and be a wonderful mother your husband can brag about.

PLAYBOY: Is that the way it was for you in the past?

FONDA: Yes, but I'm not saying that in my previous marriage my husband demanded these things from me. He didn't need to. Our culture demands it. Nor would he have refused to do certain things. It simply never occurred to me to ask him. With Tom's consciousness, because of his years working with and being criticized by women in the movement, we just automatically share responsibilities on every level—taking care of children, shopping, cleaning house, whatever.

PLAYBOY: Do you do all the work yourselves, with no hired help?

FONDA: The work gets done. We do it.

PLAYBOY: Since you were raised in a world of luxury, and left that life only a few years ago, it would be interesting to know what kinds of possessions you now have.

FONDA: Well, possessions used to be very important to me. They were like a fortress; it was a kind of security to have a lot of things. But I've given away or sold most everything I had, out of a need to be unburdened, and what we have now is stuff we need, that's all.

PLAYBOY: Do you own your house?

FONDA: Yes.

PLAYBOY: What kind of car do you drive?

FONDA: I have a Volvo and Tom drives a borrowed Volkswagen.

PLAYBOY: Tom, your background is much less familiar to the public than Jane's. Tell us something about it, about the experiences that led you to become a founder of SDS.

HAYDEN: I was born in a working-class family and raised in Detroit, although I lived in San Diego when I was four, while my dad was stationed there in the marines. I lived basically in a suburban neighborhood outside Detroit. I grew up and went to Catholic grade schools there. I was involved in sports and the high-school paper and wanted to be either an athlete or a foreign correspondent, so I could travel. There was no radical activity in my home town, to say the least. And I think in that environment, most people who rebelled didn't do so in political terms, because there *were* no political terms. McCarthyism had wiped out any semblance of a labor movement, or a left, in the late Fifties. We were attracted much more to figures like James Dean in *Rebel Without a Cause,* who were described by the establishment as being troubled malcontents with no apparent outlet or program. It was the same generation that was drawn to the work of J. D. Salinger, then went on to *Mad* magazine and, especially on the two coasts, into following the development of the Beats. Then, when the sit-ins began in the South, we found a way to rebel *with* a cause.

PLAYBOY: What made you decide to form SDS?

HAYDEN: It was formed in response, I think more than anything else, to the worldwide idea that students were making history. There were students demonstrating in Seoul, in Turkey, young intellectuals leading the Cuban revolution, black students sitting in a Woolworth's in the South. Students hadn't been taken seriously in American history or in past progressive movements; even in traditional Marxism, the student class has a very secondary role. We were attracted to the idea of students as agents of social change. SDS came out of ethnic social groups that hadn't been involved in American radicalism: WASPs, Catholics, the white middle class, Midwestern young people. America had reached such a limit of what it could offer to people that, suddenly, protest reached even those in the mainstream. Really, Nixon stole the idea of middle America from us, because the original SDS *was* middle America.

PLAYBOY: Jane, do you remember being aware of the forming of SDS back in 1962?

FONDA: No. I was in Europe and I was very apolitical during this time. As I remember, I became aware of SDS in 1968, and I first heard Tom's name while watching the Chicago convention riots on television.

PLAYBOY: What did SDS' first proclamation, the Port Huron Statement, say?

HAYDEN: It said, in general terms, that a society should be organized to ensure that every individual participates in decision-making, in choosing the form of government and representation he wants, and that he play a role in the vital issues that affect him—in the neighborhood, at work, and so on. It spoke the language of the whole political generation that followed.

PLAYBOY If you were writing a Port Huron Statement for *this* decade, what would you talk about?

HAYDEN: Well, for one thing, we need to make clear the deceptive and unworkable nature of our economy, since true democracy is incompatible with capitalism. You need only look at the headlines to see how true that is. Rule by the rich has created a country whose economy can't check inflation even though thousands of its citizens are suffering from malnutrition, a country that's unable even to provide sufficient energy to run itself.

PLAYBOY: Under what economic system would the nation flourish?

HAYDEN: You need creative jobs, a redistribution of income, workers' control and democratic public planning in combination. Our economic system is a global one, so the solutions to our economic problems have to be global. If we're using our technology and building factories in so many countries, then the peoples of the world are going to have something to say about decisions affecting our economy. I see the need for an economic system where private property is no longer legalized or tolerated, at least with respect to the massive and vital industries. But it's not a case for socialism, as it would have been fifty years ago, when the people of this country alone would have controlled our economy. It's a case for international change. This, I think, will come about through a revolutionary process that results in either a much-reformed United Nations or some other international system of planning and cooperation in which the *people* of the United States, not just the corporations, are represented.

PLAYBOY: Can you describe the kind of government you'd like to see in America?

FONDA: Well, participatory democracy would be revolutionary here. A society that didn't depend on racism would be, too. But I don't have any blueprint for what it's going to look like. One of the things we would hope for is that people had what they needed to live happily and healthily.

PLAYBOY: What do you mean by participatory democracy?

FONDA: A society and a government in which people have a true voice and can really determine the decisions that are made, thus forcing change that's really in their own interests. Rather than the situation that exists today, in which we go by the name of democracy but, in fact, the people aren't making the decisions and the decisions that are made *aren't* in the interests of the majority.

PLAYBOY: Would participatory democracy mean a decentralized federal government?

FONDA: No, not necessarily. As long as the federal government paid attention to the needs of all its people, rather than just to those of that minute percentage of the population that has most of the money.

HAYDEN: The question really is: Can a country as large as the United States be run any longer by a centralized elite? And the answer is, clearly, *no*. The system is falling apart. So we must ask what new institutions would reestablish order. The present system is literally suicidal. The oceans may dry up, the sources of oxygen may dry up, the remaining resources may disappear. I don't think there's a cubic foot of clean air over America at the present time. Private control of the economy is even leading to the ruination of the people who are making money from it.

PLAYBOY: Considering these urgent new priorities, aren't you tempted to turn your energies away from the diminishing issue of peace in Indochina?

HAYDEN: We think that the Indochina conflict has already been a decisive turning point in American history. Economically, it has precipitated the erosion of the dollar and proved that the United States cannot afford to fight long wars in other countries. Culturally, it has awakened millions of people. Politically, it has shown that as long as we support corrupt dictatorships in other countries, we will not be able to have an honest or democratic government here. We will have to have a government of secrecy. That's one of the lessons of Vietnam that must be learned. The long-term objective of our new organization, the Indochina Peace Campaign, is to make vivid these lessons of the war—through films, for instance. We're working on a full-length commercial film about veterans, their lives and families and that sort of thing—having people go to different base towns, military installations and hospitals around the country, researching the reality and involving lots of people in the film.

We've also put together an Indochina peace pledge that we hope will be adopted by political-office seekers and incumbents. This pledge has three basic points: one, to prohibit direct American reintervention in Indochina; two, to abide by the political provisions of the peace agreement; and, three, to stop all nonhumanitarian financial aid to Thieu and Lon Nol. By that, I'm talking about things such as their using U.S. dollars to build prisons and strengthen police departments. We want to encourage all kinds of citizens' groups and clubs to take this pledge and work to get politicians to endorse it. And Jane and I, among many others, are going to be spending a lot of time this year lobbying in Washington, at budget hearings and political caucuses, and in Congressional districts around the country, in the hope that the peace pledge will become a plank in the platforms of candidates running for office in 1974. You see, this is the first war that the United States isn't going to win, and the American people have a lot to learn from it. We can't afford to let them forget about it.

PLAYBOY: Still, don't you find a tremendous desire among people to do just that?

HAYDEN: Yes. But if you succumb to that feeling yourself, then you're only postponing a problem that's going to stare you in the face the next time you try to arouse anybody about anything. If we don't deal with painful questions, we can't make progress on any front. But I think a lot of people *don't* want to forget the war and are looking for therapeutic ways to make sense of it. Guys in VA hospitals, three million veterans and their families, intellectuals and artists. Have the German people forgotten the Forties? They can't forget those years. Neither should we forget *these* years.

PLAYBOY: Obviously you won't, and if you have your way, neither will the American public. But in the face of its mood of indifference toward the war, its continuing resistance to the basic reforms you demand and its personal hostility toward you as personalities, what keeps you going?

HAYDEN: I don't think it's a matter of choice; I didn't choose to be a radical. In fact, I don't even like the word *radical,* because when we select words to define ourselves, we must be up front and honestly explain the fundamental changes we want, but we shouldn't have to use words that isolate us. *Radical* is such a word. It connotes an extreme edge of society. It suggests an extreme alternative, one that causes the inevitable disruption of people's lives. I believe that if you want change, you have to be part of the mainstream, part of a kind of normalcy, if you will. Radical doesn't imply your goals; it identifies you with a means rather than an end. The word is entrenched, though, and you live with it. But it doesn't make me believe that what I want for myself and others is radical. I've felt from the beginning of my political activity that I was really just reacting to things in this society that were interfering with my life and the lives of millions of others. And as long as I have my life, I have to keep on fighting against that which interferes with it.

FONDA: I feel a very deep certainty about the possibility of people changing, and I have full faith in my feelings because of my own experience and because of what I see going on around me all the time. People can change, and as long as I believe that, *everything* is possible.

ROBERT REDFORD

December 1974

Interviewer: Larry Dubois

Had it been just ten years earlier, a conversation with the handsomest, most popular actor in America would have been a collection of studio stories and Hollywood clichés. But Robert Redford was part of a new breed who disdained the trappings of glamour and lived an outdoor, family life in Utah. He was outspoken about the environment, committed politically, "bankable" as few other superstars were—but he managed to convey the sense that he was, incredibly enough, sane and happy.

Of course, one reason he had preserved his sanity was that he'd avoided the hype of celebrity interviews and other perquisites of fame, so getting him to speak into a tape recorder took free-lance writer Larry DuBois almost two years of meetings, conversations, and outings before Redford would speak freely—and for a curious reason, as DuBois later recalled: "The first time I met him in his office in Los Angeles, *he* asked all the questions: Who was I, why did I want to interview him, how did I feel about this or that? He apparently liked to save his performances for the screen, and if I expected to find out about him, I was going to have to let him find out about me. The questioning was sharp and precise, his manner polite but firm and, well, suspicious. He didn't start to relax until he found out I was a Mormon from Salt Lake and finally he said, 'OK, what the hell.' "

Because the interview was done in bits and pieces, PLAYBOY editor Gretchen McNeese assisted both Fisher and DuBois in following through on some of the questions and in editing the piece. The sum of the parts, it might be argued with hindsight, adds up to a man who was evidently more than a movie star—and foreshadows his sensitive directing efforts of later years. As to the interview itself, it remains a paradox: virtually the only in-depth conversation granted by one of the most popular men in America.

He doesn't have the Mediterranean sensuality of a Rudolph Valentino, the rakehell charm of a Clark Gable, the suave sophistication of a Cary Grant or the ladykiller reputation of an Errol Flynn. But there's no doubt that thirty-seven-year-old Robert Redford is the most powerful male sex symbol on the screen today.

That's not a label Redford particularly relishes: He dislikes all labels, in fact. An accomplished dramatic performer (with several critically acclaimed stage appearances and one Academy Award nomination, for The Sting, *under his belt), Redford is a concerned environmentalist, a fiercely independent thinker and, in the words of one of his producers, "so smart he could be the first actor to be President." (Today that may not be a compliment.)*

Born in Santa Monica, California, in 1937, Redford went from Van Nuys High School to the University of Colorado, where he found himself majoring in mountain climbing, hunting and skiing, rather than in more conventional academic pursuits. He dropped out in his second year to spend thirteen months studying painting in Europe. Returning to the United States, he enrolled at the Pratt Institute in New York. Vaguely motivated by some idea of becoming an art director for the stage, he followed the suggestion of an instructor and enrolled in the American Academy of Dramatic Arts. The original notion was merely to obtain theatrical background, but once Redford tried acting, he was hooked.

While Redford was studying in New York, his heart was on the West Coast with young Lola Van Wagenen, a Utah girl he'd met in Los Angeles. Following a courtship conducted partly by long-distance telephone, they were married in 1958 and have since become the parents of three children: Shauna, fourteen; David James (Jamie), twelve; and Amy, four.

After impressing critics and directors in a series of supporting roles on stage and television, Redford landed the lead in the Broadway production of Sunday in New York *in 1961. His first big break came in 1963, when Mike Nichols cast him as the young husband in Neil Simon's comedy hit* Barefoot in the Park. *Six modestly successful motion pictures, including the screen version of* Barefoot, *preceded Redford's blockbuster breakthrough, when he was teamed with Paul Newman in 1969's* Butch Cassidy and the Sundance Kid. *That was the first time anybody stole a picture from Paul Newman, and it should have led to an unbroken stream of film roles. What it did provide was a chance for the unpredictable Redford to be very choosy. In the same year, he did a skiing movie,* Downhill Racer, *with his own production company, and a motorcycle film,* Little Fauss and Big Halsy, *and starred in* Tell Them Willie Boy Is Here. *Then he holed up in his secluded Utah home, refusing all movie commitments for a two-year period. Not until 1971, when he made* Jeremiah Johnson, *did he emerge from his self-imposed retirement—already the fourth such extended absence from filmwork in his career. Suddenly, there was Redford again, all over the marquees with* The Hot Rock *and* The Candidate *in 1972,* The Way We Were *and* The Sting *in 1973 and* The Great Gatsby *in 1974. In 1975, Redford will be seen in* The Great Waldo Pepper *and he'll shoot a Western about Tom Horn, the scout who tracked Geronimo in the Sierra Madres (the script to be done by William Goldman, who wrote* Butch Cassidy); *and he's bought the film rights to* All the President's Men, *the Carl Bernstein-Bob Woodward best-seller (first introduced in* PLAYBOY) *about the uncovering of Watergate. Despite this spurt of activity, Redford keeps talking about retreating back into his Utah mountain fastness. To find out if he really means it,* PLAYBOY *assigned free-lance writer Larry DuBois to track down the elusive Redford. DuBois' report:*

"Redford isn't really comfortable with any of the hoopla that goes along with his new superstar status, and so spending his time in front of a tape recorder, participating in the invasion of his own privacy, came very low on his list of preferred pastimes—somewhere down about where most of us would place going to the dentist. That may be why it took almost two years to acquire roughly eight hours of recorded conversation.

"The weekend I arrived in Utah was the last of the ski season, and what he mostly wanted to do was ski. So each morning, it was straight to the lifts, straight to the top and straight down again as fast as possible, hooting and hollering all the way. You don't have to be from Utah to understand why he loves living there. His home, which he and his wife built themselves, brick by brick, looks over those spectacular Wasatch Mountains where he filmed Jeremiah Johnson *and where he has developed a*

ski area called Sundance. The people in the area are pretty much unawed by celebrityhood, so it's easy for him to get away from its pressures. And those mountain roads, where there are few cars and even fewer highway patrolmen, are perfect for Redford's passion for driving his Porsche, his motorcycles, even the family station wagon, at truly immoderate speeds.

"We talked a lot that weekend—about Henry Miller and Hunter Thompson and skiing and Lola and art and self-discipline—you name it. He's a first-rate storyteller with the satirical eye of an editorial cartoonist: He loves to jump on himself, politicians, movie executives, anybody he catches indulging in any sort of phoniness or pomposity. But somehow we never got around to turning on the tape recorder, which was just fine with him.

"The next time we arranged a meeting was on the set of The Great Gatsby *in Newport, Rhode Island. He was in a very different mood, not loose and high-spirited at all. He was feeling suffocated by that high-society world he was immersing himself in on the set, and the locals in that status-conscious community tended to be impressed with Robert Redford. He was getting a lot of fancy invitations to a lot of fancy tennis clubs, and he gave off the feeling of a volcano that might blow at any time. His family was with him and, whenever he wasn't working, he wanted to be with them. So we shot a few baskets on the court at his rented farm and hung around the set for a while before I left early, as anxious as he was to be out of there. Later, he laughed at how constrained he felt living in Gatsby's world. 'It was like being in a straitjacket for eighteen weeks,' he said.*

"Finally, last winter, we got in some serious work, sitting on two canvas chairs in the middle of a big field outside San Antonio, Texas, where he was filming The Great Waldo Pepper, *which was much more to his taste in life-style, and he was enjoying himself enormously. Waldo Pepper is a slightly zany barnstorming stunt pilot of the Twenties, and Redford felt right at home in the part. He was getting especially high doing his own stunt work—things like walking on the wing of an old biplane at two thousand feet. God, how he loved that. Anyway, in between those wild scenes, we finally got his words on tape. They won't reveal everything you've always wanted to know about Robert Redford, but I think you will like, as I did, what they do reveal: He really is a good guy."*

PLAYBOY: Why were you so reluctant to do this interview?

REDFORD: I haven't had very good luck with interviews. I guess the press is fallible, human like all of us, but too often I've found myself in a situation where I felt the interviewer didn't have an open mind. He came in with a prejudice, or maybe just an angle on what I was all about, or should be all about. And when the interview comes out, the angle overwhelms it and I'll read about "Redford, the mountain man," or "Redford, the loner," or "Redford, the success." They make me look so perfect, so lucky, so one-dimensional. Nobody ever gives me credit for having a nightmare, for making people unhappy, for inconveniencing them. I can be terrifically irresponsible and selfish, but I don't see that coming through in an interview.

Besides, I think a lot of my privacy. I believe in separating my work from my private life, and I'd like people to judge me by my work, not by what they read about me. Especially if they get some kind of fix on me, such as that business about being a loner. That's not true. If I were a loner, I'd be living alone, and I'm not. But after people read a lot of stories about you, they think they know you; they've made up their minds about you before you even meet them. So whatever spontaneity their reactions to you might have had is lost. You've got this image, which is never more than partly accurate, standing like some great shield between you and other people, and that makes it harder to get to know them. So at one point I got so angered with these stereotypes that I just said, "All right. The hell with that. I just won't do interviews."

PLAYBOY: So why do this one? Do you think it will show you the way you really are?

REDFORD: I don't know if that's possible. Maybe the problem before has been that I haven't been completely honest with the interviewer, or maybe it's because I change from the moment I give the interview to the moment it's published. This PLAYBOY thing, I feel, is really the best of the interviews, because it's the straightest; it'll be accurate in terms of what I said. But it's true that I'm not the same person I was six months ago, or even twenty minutes ago. And if you can deal with that—like catching somebody who's riding through and grabbing a piece of that person—that's fine. As long as it's a whole piece of that person, and not a lot of fabricated phony imagery.

The real reason I originally agreed to do the interview, though, was that I had some things I wanted to say and I thought this might be a good way. An actor, after all, is a person who's capable of the same feelings that other people are. He can be just as up on issues, and just as passionate about world events, and about what's going on in the country, as anybody else.

PLAYBOY: Has it occurred to you that if you *weren't* famous as an actor, few people would be interested in reading about your opinions?

REDFORD: That's true. Fame is a two-edged sword. It gives you good leverage to do a lot of what you want to do, but at other times it feels like a plague. You can court fame like a lover, or fight it like a sparring partner. Either way, it's trouble. It's gotten so that when I meet people, I have this impression that they resent me—resent the way I look, maybe, resent my success. Sometimes it's not really justified, and that's even sadder. Let me give you an example. I went to a party the other night, which is something I seldom do. And I was feeling pretty good, looking forward to meeting some people I didn't know. So I went in and started introducing myself: "Hello. I'm Bob Redford. How are you?" and so forth. And this one guy gave me a real weird look, a sort of blank stare, like I was some scum he didn't want to be bothered dealing with. And I thought to myself, "Fuck you, then," and moved away. I found out later that he was so impressed by the fact that *Robert Redford* had actually come over and introduced himself that he was speechless. I misread his reaction and that's a shame. Maybe we could have talked together and come away with something.

Even with old friends, I sense a difference in attitude. One of the last outposts for me was Madison Square Garden. I used to love to go there and watch the Knicks. The Knicks are almost an art form to me, the way they operate, the moves they make. They play basketball as it's supposed to be played, as a team without any stars. Anyway, I used to be able to go to the Garden and sort of dissolve into the crowd; it was kind of like going home to me, to be able to go to the Garden and scream and yell with everybody else, and argue and piss and moan. But the last time I went, a crowd started gathering around me, and people were taking pictures, and the cops were trying to keep them back. I spotted somebody I knew sitting a few rows away, and during intermission I went over to say hello, because I hadn't seen him in several months. And the look on his face was incredible. Mixed with a certain pleasure in seeing me again was this absolute panic—pain at being brought into the spotlight and having the cameras snapping away—and that look told me: *Go away. Good to see you, but go away.* I understood that, certainly, but it was disturbing. That whole feeling of becoming an object rather than a person bothers me a lot. I don't mind being an object on the screen, because that's what a role is, something you've worked at creating. Off-screen, I'm not some kind of *thing*; I'm a human being.

PLAYBOY: You're also a sex symbol. How does it feel to know that so many women would like a piece of you for themselves?

REDFORD: Eh, I just wonder where they were when I needed them. Seriously, that sex-symbol business is a rather recent thing, and I just associate it with somebody who's up there on the screen, and not so much with me. So I can't admit to having a problem with it, really. But I hate being stared at, by anybody. Walking down the street, I feel like I'm in a head-on collision, that my life is getting narrower and narrower, and I wonder why I'm so uptight. Some of the reason, I think, is that I've lost the capacity to wander around anonymously—just hanging out, being loose, watching people and listening to them.

PLAYBOY: When did people start staring at you?

REDFORD: I think the first time I had that feeling was when that *Life* magazine cover story came out, back in 1970. I didn't know my picture was going to be on the cover, just that there was going to be an article inside. Well, I spent a lot of time indoors that week. I really couldn't wait for the week to be gone, because I couldn't bear walking the streets and seeing my face staring out at me from every newsstand. And sure enough, next thing, our house in Utah got robbed, and these tourists were wandering around all over the place. We put up a gate, then a fence, then a burglar alarm. Next come the machine guns and the turrets.

Mingled with that, sure, were some good feelings. You believed you'd gotten somewhere when you got on the cover of *Life* magazine. It meant you'd gained a certain amount of importance, a certain position in this world, so you had to be flattered. But mix that in with the problems it caused and it was a mixed bag. And the negative won out, I think. I don't know that covers on magazines aren't like Academy Awards, which I don't feel very good about, either. Never did, even before I was in the business.

PLAYBOY: Why not?

REDFORD: Well, you know I grew up in Los Angeles, and the Academy Awards seemed to me sort of like California politics. Weird. An awful lot of extravagance for nothing, and the awards were always getting won by people who had done better work before, or did better work later. The Oscars just reflect the opinion of Academy members. The guy who wins an award for a footrace gets it because he was the fastest guy on that track at that moment. That's the only kind of award I have any real respect for.

PLAYBOY: What do you do with all your money?

REDFORD: I don't have a whole lapful of it. That's a fantasy that's mostly been perpetrated by the press. This past year and a half, doing four films back to back, is the longest I've ever worked since I've been in the business. I've had a lot of problems in the past; I've gone in cycles, sometimes gone two years at a time without working because I just didn't want to act, or it took that long to develop something that I really wanted to do. I'd certainly *like* to be very rich. Just because I like nature and I like wearing Levi's and I have a disdain for certain material things doesn't mean for a second that I don't want to be the richest guy in the valley. By God, I think I could enjoy that without making myself soft. I think I could resist the temptations of success, like having an entourage of maids, butlers, things like that. But no matter how you slice it, this business of being a Jeremiah Johnson, like that character in the film—of going up to this place I have in the mountains, backpacking and living off a horse—can't be done without money. Money is the single most dominating element in our society; you can't live without it. We are, as a society, completely tied to economics. It's a damning thing, a frustrating thing, but I think it's worth the fight. I really do. I think you've got to have certain fights in your life, or you just vegetable out.

PLAYBOY: You still haven't said what you'd do with all that money you don't have, if you had it.

REDFORD: I'd travel, and I'd buy land and build things on it. I'd like to use the money to create a little freedom in my life, as Howard Hughes has done. I like Hughes. He's doing fine. I was glad they blew that what's-his-name, Irving, out of the saddle on his hoax, because it meant Hughes could buy some more time before he had to appear in public. There's a guy who's managed to keep his privacy.

PLAYBOY: If you're so hooked on privacy, why continue in movies, the single art form that's most guaranteed to rob you of your immunity from curious stares?

REDFORD: If you know the answer to that, you've solved the riddle of the Sphinx. I have only a kind of half-assed answer, which is that I suppose if the pressure gets bad enough, I'll just pack acting in and do something else. Right now, I like to think I act because it's the thing I do best; and there are things I really want to do in films that I haven't done yet. Things like my next film, *All the President's Men*, which I feel strongly about because of my beliefs about the whole Watergate mess.

PLAYBOY: Isn't there a danger that the Watergate scandal will be very old news by the time the movie comes out?

REDFORD: The Watergate scandal itself is like being in a hotel room with a Gideon Bible. It's just there for everybody to see and know about. You're absolutely right that there would be no point in making a movie about Nixon. That's all been documented very nicely. What interests me, though—and this is what *All the President's Men* is really about—is how the whole thing was uncovered through the persistence of investigative reporting, which seems to be a dying art in this country. I, for one, think there ought to be more of it. As a responsible, civil-rights-minded citizen, I want to see more investigative reporting that says, "Hey Agnew, cut the shit. We've got the facts here." "Hey, Dick, how come you said this yesterday and you're doing this today?" That kind of reporting is a terrifically important part of our democratic system and I want to know why so many papers lay back on the facts, what kind of taboos existed, what a newspaperman has to go through to get his story. Besides, I think that Bob Woodward and Carl Bernstein of *The Washington Post*, whose story *All the President's Men* is, have given us one of the top suspense yarns of our generation, which nobody would *believe* if it weren't documented with facts.

I think, really, the newspaperman is our one hero figure at the moment. Following these guys around in Washington, as I've done a bit lately, I learned how difficult it is to be a newspaperman, because you're always a moving target. You're in the business of grabbing history on the run, and sometimes you grab lightning on the run. You're gathering so much information so quickly, so constantly, that it's very difficult to be accurate every time, so you run the risk of getting shot down by each person you refer to in print. But with all their flaws—reporters tend to be lazy and sloppy sometimes—they also tend to be honest. You can't say that about the government.

PLAYBOY: What do you think would have happened in this country if Watergate hadn't been uncovered?

REDFORD: I think we were heading for some kind of Orwellian nightmare, and that it was blown apart just before it went over the line. They were getting everything so nicely stacked: Supreme Court appointments, trying to take over the FBI, the whole mentality that said dirty tricks could be equated with national security, the concessions to big business interests. One concrete thing we should get out of Watergate is campaign-spending reform. That was one of the reasons I made *The Candidate*: to show how our political process, as it now stands, shapes the kind of leaders we get.
PLAYBOY: At the time you made *The Candidate*, some politicians said you were being unrealistic, unduly hard on the political process.
REDFORD: That makes me laugh, because given recent developments, *The Candidate* pales in comparison with reality. I mean, there's something drastically wrong with a system that can produce, as the country's leader, a man who twice in his political career had to go on national television to tell the people he is not a crook. What *The Candidate* showed was that power does corrupt, and that once a guy gets power he's likely to insulate himself from the people in the street. Nixon, too, is the type of man who's been screened against humanity. I have a gut-level feeling about politicians that goes way back, that there's nothing to see in their eyes. They all talk as though they're addressing a room filled with forty thousand people; there's no sense of one-to-one relationship. With few exceptions—and there are some, because I do have acquaintances in politics whom I like—I find politicians extraordinarily shallow people. Maybe it's by necessity, because they're always going to a lot of luncheons, making a lot of speeches, shaking a lot of hands; but whatever the reason, they just lose the ability to deal with individual people. I can see why so many of the eighteen-year-olds didn't vote. If I were eighteen and I picked up a newspaper and saw that this person's been indicted, that person's been cheating, this guy's undergoing a tax audit, and everybody's living in a state of corruption, I'd turn my back and go to something else. We're still being served up the same tired old hash like Rockefeller and Jackson and Ford, and I say they're cast in the same mold. It's a mold that has to be gotten rid of. I'm not saying they're income tax cheaters, but that they're part of the old system, and unless the system changes, just give me a backpack and I'll go live in the mountains.
PLAYBOY: With all the films you have out now, do you worry about becoming overexposed?
REDFORD: Sure. But it's out of my hands. I can't help it if Columbia Pictures decides to release a film I've done for them in October and Warner Bros. decides to release a film I've done for them in November, even though they may have been two years apart in the making. If I produce the film, I try to control the timing of the release, because I'm afraid I might become a drug on the market. The four films I've just done, though, have afforded a lot of variety in the roles. That interested me. They weren't always the Sundance Kid in a different situation. I mean, you can really play the Sundance Kid in a detective story; you can play the Sundance Kid in a Western; you can play the Sundance Kid in a film about business; you can be the hired gun in any kind of tough situation. I was comfortable being the Sundance Kid, because there was something *simpâtico* there, but I wouldn't want to play that role again next time.
PLAYBOY: *Butch Cassidy and the Sundance Kid* is the kind of film that looks as if the actors had fun making it. Did you?
REDFORD: No film is a laugh a minute, because you always have problems. But for the most part, it was the most consistent fun of any film I've ever done. Paul Newman is a

very generous, giving actor who was at his happiest when the whole thing was working. Not just his part, but everything. George Roy Hill, the director, is scared to death of horses, and he's the tightest man on earth. That was wonderful, because it made us charge him on our horses whenever we got a chance, try to maneuver him into paying the tab in a restaurant.

PLAYBOY: You said you felt comfortable playing the Sundance Kid. Why?

REDFORD: I had a strange identification with him that I can't quite put my finger on. There was a time when I was very young that I didn't think it would be so bad to be an outlaw. It sounded pretty good to me. The frontier wouldn't have been a bad place to be in the 1880s, it seemed to me. You didn't turn your back on too many people, but the atmosphere was free and you carved out of it what you could make out of it. One reason I liked *Butch Cassidy* was that it pointed out the fact that a lot of those people were just kids, doing what they did—robbing banks, holding up trains—as much for the sheer fun of it as for anything else.

PLAYBOY: Didn't some of the critics take *Butch Cassidy* apart because of that sense of fun, saying it wasn't realistic?

REDFORD: They were wrong about that. There are a lot of old people around, especially here in Utah where I live, who remember having met the real Butch Cassidy and his Hole in the Wall gang. And what they say is that Butch and the boys loved life so much they couldn't be contained. They robbed banks, they were wild as hell, and they had a hootin' time, and they liked each other. I've met Butch's sister, Lula, who's a buff on Westerns, and when she saw *Butch Cassidy*, she said it captured an honest-to-God emotion that's missing from most films on the West, that feeling of fun. Those guys got into so much trouble because they were having too much goddamn fun. When a guy just got *too* drunk and shot another guy's head off, he didn't necessarily mean to. The critics may not have liked *Butch Cassidy*, but obviously the reviews didn't make any difference, because the film was very successful.

PLAYBOY: The critics generally, though, have been fairly kind to you, haven't they?

REDFORD: Yes, I would say so. But some people have me labeled as a kind of upper-class WASP all-American boy—winning, successful, intelligent, assured, born of wealth and position. Typecasting is always a curse in this profession; I once played a young Nazi and for a short period after that, to many people, I was this guy who just came over from Munich, and I'd be fine once I learned the English language. Then I played some psychotic killers on television, and I had to fight to land a comedy role. "Well, he's a great killer, but does he have a sense of humor?" So it's always a hassle. But this business of being overprivileged really makes me burn. "If you didn't look as if you had graduated from Harvard, we could believe you as a garbage collector." Well, I've got news for those people: I did collect garbage. I don't know what the inside of Harvard looks like; the closest I ever got to Harvard was getting the *Harvard Lampoon*'s Worst Actor of the Year award. I never got through college, never got good grades. I wasn't a bastard son born in Hell's Kitchen, but I did grow up in a less-than-privileged neighborhood, and I did run with a grim crowd for a while. I had my share of trouble, and I was exposed to a jail cell a time or two.

PLAYBOY: What for?

REDFORD: Oh, just your basic WASP juvenile delinquency. I wasn't your fair-haired boy. Never combed my hair; couldn't, because I had too many cowlicks. No one ever thought I was good-looking; I was always too messy. Someday I'd like to compare notes with these people who think they've been through more in life. I had all kinds of jobs, all kinds of stupid jobs, got tossed out of a lot of them. Now that I look back, I realize that a lot of my problem was simply that I was growing up in Los Angeles—a city that was beginning to look like the front and back end of a Hollywood set, with a great facade in front supported by stilts behind—in the Fifties, an era that somebody has described as an age in which the bland was leading the bland. You could tell a man by the shine of his shoes, we were advised, and I just couldn't buy that.

PLAYBOY: Tell us about some of the jobs you got fired from.

REDFORD: Oh, had my ego been a little smaller, I probably would have gone and jumped off a bridge, thinking there wasn't anything in life I could do successfully, because I got fired from everything. I got fired from Von's supermarket in Van Nuys because I couldn't stuff groceries into a bag. Couldn't stuff groceries into a *bag*! I worked at the Standard Oil refinery, started as a roustabout laying pipes, and I ended up sleeping in trenches. So they canned me from that job and put me in the barrel-reconditioning department, and I started playing games with the barrels instead of just taking them off the stack and walking over to the truck with them and loading them onto the truck. I found that by spinning the barrel a certain way, I could curve it, pretty much like a bowling ball, right into the slot by the truck. When I knocked down a whole truckload of barrels doing that, they decided to get me out of the barrel department and put me to work doing something with bottles. And I broke a whole load of bottles, pushing them off the end of the dock while I was looking up at the sky. The sky interested me; the bottles didn't. I was lucky they didn't put me on a boat and ship me out to sea! Then I was fired from a couple of jobs as a carpenter's apprentice because I was always crawling under the foundation to grab some sleep. I was a failure at everything I tried.

PLAYBOY: Why didn't you finish college?

REDFORD: Thought it was a waste of time. I dropped out of the University of Colorado during my sophomore year. But I never liked school, don't think I really began to learn much until I left. Most of my teachers were bureaucratic types tied to silly rules. "You must print on this side of the paper." "You must use this kind of line on your paper." "You must use this kind of pencil." "This is your textbook." "This is your seat in the second row." It was so regimented it was awful, and I didn't like it. Didn't like the other guys who followed the rules, either. I remember at my high-school graduation, the guy who was the student-body president was giving a speech. I was reading *Mad* magazine through the whole ceremony. I was a slow reader. And this guy got up and talked about ideals and started to cry, and I just had this weird kind of premonition: *This guy ain't going to make it.*

PLAYBOY: Were you really a slow reader?

REDFORD: Well, I never liked books used as a form of instruction. I liked 'em on my own terms, just for enjoyment.

PLAYBOY: What kind of books interested you?

REDFORD: Fantasies, fiction. I responded very strongly to Henry Miller's work; I think because he seemed to me to be breaking all the rules of conformity. I liked his irreverence. And he was carnal, and I was going through what I thought was a very carnal period. His love was as strong as his hate, and both were full-out there for everybody to see. And later, when I spent some time bumming around Europe, I identified with him, because he had had a pretty grim time in Europe, too. I used to drive up to Big Sur and go past his house a lot. One time I even walked up to the gate, but I couldn't bring myself to go in.

PLAYBOY: Why?

REDFORD: Because at the time I didn't have anything to give *him*, and I was very taken—and still am—with the concept of a fair exchange of ideas. I don't feel I have the right to go up to somebody who's famous and say, "I like your work, so here I am: Entertain me." If I meet a physicist, I hope I can tell him something about movies, because I'm interested in physics. If I sit with a Barry Commoner, I don't feel it's fair to say, "OK, lay it on me, Barry, where's technology taking us? How have we fucked ourselves up?" unless Barry has some interest in movies and how they work and I can tell *him* something. So I couldn't go talk to Henry Miller.

PLAYBOY: Did you ever meet him?

REDFORD: In a strange sort of way, years later. I was in Santa Monica, driving along, and I pulled up to a crosswalk just as the light changed to green. It was a bright summer day, and all these kids had just gotten out of school and they were a little crazy, like kids are when they've just gotten out of school, and they were honking their horns and yelling at this old gent who was walking his bicycle across the street, hadn't made it across by the time the light changed. I pulled up next to the guy and I saw that he was Henry Miller, wearing knickers and a tweed jacket and cap and dark glasses. And it all came together right there in the middle of Sunset Boulevard: Henry Miller and all these punks yelling at him, things like, "Hey, move it or milk it," "Haul ass, old man," "Get off the road," stuff like that. And I was filled with eighty million things to say to the guy, but what I did was I hung out over the door, looked at him and said, "Take your time, Henry," and drove off. That was my meeting with Henry Miller.

PLAYBOY: Driving cars is pretty much of a consuming passion with you, isn't it?

REDFORD: Yes. I love to drive around the country; my mind opens up a lot when I'm on the open road. When I'm driving alone, I get so high, I talk to myself.

PLAYBOY: Aloud?

REDFORD: You bet.

PLAYBOY: What do you talk about?

REDFORD: Whatever comes to mind. Driving, to me, is serious business. Not that cruising-around stuff like I used to do in high school—with your arm out the window and pretending to watch the road while you're looking out for girls. I mean really driving, and that takes a lot of concentration. There's such a release, not unlike coming off the top of a mountain on skis when you're really loose and you know you're ready, that this run has really got it. It's all going to come together, you're going to make all your best moves, and you really let it fly. You let all the stops out. It's the same thing in a car when you just take a breath and say, OK, I'm going, and you just pile through the night or the day. It's a great high.

Even in a city, figuring out the lights and how to play them, maneuvering through traffic, allowing for ways to handle the guy who might run a red light—that's exciting to me. I once made it through all the lights on Park Avenue in New York, from Seventy-second all the way down to that Grand Central Building overpass at Forty-sixth Street, without stopping once. I'd always had a fantasy about doing that, because those lights are always stopping you on Park Avenue. So one night I did it. Must have been around two o'clock in the morning, and what I had figured out was that you have to get going faster and faster in order to catch each light before it turns red. I was up to over a hundred miles an hour; it's awful to contemplate. That was ten years ago, and my hands get sweaty when I talk about it now. I went barreling into that overpass like some giant dragon, just belching exhaust fumes, with sparks and rubber flying all over hell. I didn't think I was ever going to get geared down. I did a big S inside and just had to pull over afterward and wait for my heart to come back down from my mouth.

PLAYBOY: You were alone in the car?

REDFORD: Oh, yeah. It's better to do something like that alone, because you don't want to make someone else nervous, or hurt anybody. I suppose some people would consider that Park Avenue thing as reckless driving, but it was an incredible experience, because it had always been one of my fantasies. I have a lot of fantasies about driving.

PLAYBOY: What are some others?

REDFORD: Well, a long time ago, when I was a student in New York and stuck there without any money, the only way I could get away was by car, and I did a lot of driving from coast to coast. I'd start feeling good about the time I'd leave Chicago, along around Elgin, Illinois. And that good feeling increased when I'd get into Iowa. And Nebraska was just terrific. Omaha was one of the best spots for me. For years, I've bought Porsches from a dealer in Omaha just so that I'd have a long drive to the Coast after I picked up the car. Anyway, I always felt good on these trips through Colorado and Utah and Nevada. I just loved that big space. It has a real power to it, like a Henry Moore sculpture. The air took on a form of its own. Then I'd start to get antsy about the time I got into Arizona, and as I got to San Bernardino, just before you dip down into all that smog and shit that is Los Angeles, I'd start to go way down, feel real bad, and not want to go any further. I'd slow the car, stop more frequently, anything to prolong the pleasure of being outside the gates, so to speak. And then when I got to L.A., I'd crash for three or four days. Nothing could bring me up. Finally, I started to develop this fantasy about driving from one end of the country to the other, which always felt good. And when I got to New York, just before the Lincoln Tunnel, I'd just pull a big U right there at the toll station and head right back to the West Coast. And just before San Bernardino, it'd be another U. But in my fantasy, L.A. kept getting bigger and New York kept getting bigger, until pretty soon New York went all the way to Chicago and L.A. came right after Utah, and eventually they cover the whole country. The only spot left was Nebraska, and I had visions of just spending the rest of my life driving endlessly in a circle around the state of Nebraska.

PLAYBOY: Do you really feel that uncomfortable in New York and Los Angeles?

REDFORD: With New York, I have a kind of love-hate relationship. There is something quite tasty and honest about New York, because it's dirty, really dirty. If things are going to get really foul and ugly, they're going to get foul and ugly in New York first, and I'd rather be where the action is. The bad things that are happening in London and Rome now happened in New York twenty years ago. Pretty soon, I think, the London bobbies will start having to wear guns, and all the development going on outside Rome will eventually engulf the beauty of the city, and it won't be such an Eternal City anymore. I couldn't stay in New York forever, but after a certain period away from the city, you begin to get restless for its grit, its edge, its unexpected surprises. In New York, you know you're alive.

Now, Los Angeles, well, as a young kid, I loved Los Angeles. I thought it was a fabulous place, and I really believe it was. It was beautiful; I remember being able to see the mountains from miles away, and smelling fragrances in the air that you can't smell anymore. But L.A. was being poisoned, really, from the time World War Two ended. Los Angeles was our first victim of technology, our first warning of the environmental crisis. After the war, L.A. was the end of the rainbow for so many people that everybody was coming there to spend their newly gained money, to sell their new inventions, to drive their new cars. L.A. as a receptacle just couldn't take all this; it cracked under the strain. All the new industry that came in—nobody bothered to think about what effects its chemicals were having on the air. When the freeways came, that really bothered me. I *never* liked the freeways. They were too smooth; didn't have enough wrinkles in them. By the time I was sixteen or seventeen, Los Angeles had changed. I began to feel that there was nobody at home in L.A. anymore, and that's one of the reasons I left. I started driving or hitching around the country whenever I could.

PLAYBOY: Where did you go?

REDFORD: Vegas, lots of times. I used to love the smorgasbords there. I'll never forget, though, one of the most embarrassing experiences of my life happened in Las Vegas when I was about seventeen. I was supposed to meet this girl there, and I wheeled into town and went into the hotel to find out where she was, and they said she was out by the pool. So I went out by the pool, and there I saw all these fat, middle-aged slugs lying around. All the money guys—promoters, advertisers, publicity people—they were lying around the pool getting tan, to make it look as if they did a lot of swimming, but what grabbed me was that they never went into the water. The first thing that hit me was, Hey, I don't have much money—I guess I had about twenty-five bucks on me—but I don't have to take a backseat to these guys. They're all just lying around, probably have a heart condition. But I needed some kind of entry, something to make people pay attention to me. So I figured, Well, the thing I got to do is get up on that high dive there and really dazzle their minds a little bit, go through a few good moves. So I climb up and walk out to the end of the high board—I figure I'll go in dry, you know, to make it all the more impressive—and get ready to do this one and a half. So when I feel that all the eyes are on me, I go into my move. What I didn't know was that those boards in Vegas had so much spring. I knew the instant I hit that thing that I was in trouble. The moment I sprung into the air, I thought, My God, I'm going to the moon! Anyway, I came over and around and over again and landed flat on my back. It hurt so much I was crying under the water. I never wanted to come up, and when I did, there was that horrible moment when people were just looking away, you know? And my back was beet-red. I felt as if there were a seam up my back. It was just very clear that whatever plans I had had to establish any kind of position with those people were just blown. I got out and walked around the pool, trying to keep my back turned away from everybody, and just slunk away. I never did get to meet the girl I was going to see. I was never one for hanging in after a great moment like that.

PLAYBOY: Does that sort of thing happen often?

REDFORD: Often enough. Another time started out, coincidentally enough, in Las Vegas, but it ended up in a Texas hamburger stand. That was in 1961, in the days when I used to play golf, and I'd been at the Tournament of Champions in Vegas and I had to go to Texas on some family business, so I just decided to put some miles on my Porsche. I went into the Silver Slipper, loaded up on grub at the smorgasbord, got behind the wheel and just drove fifteen hundred miles, from Vegas to Austin. Stopped for gas and that was it; had a few beers, didn't eat.

PLAYBOY: How long did that take?

REDFORD: Day and a night. I got into Austin about 10:30 at night and I was like a zombie, because I'd been pushing that car to full performance the whole time. I literally had to pry my hands off the wheel when I pulled up at an outdoor hamburger joint. I was starving, *had* to have something to eat, even though I knew I looked berserk. So I went up to one window and said, "I-want-a-hamburger," in a robot voice. I could see the girl at the counter looking at me, and I realized that *everybody* was looking at me, because I was sort of weaving from my legs' being cramped up behind the wheel so long. So I put my hands in my pockets, waiting for them to fix my hamburger, trying to appear cool. I decided to stretch a little bit, to let them know I'd been driving for a while, and I stretched and wahhh! banged my head against the glass so hard it stunned me. This time everyone looked up. Well, I didn't want anybody to think I had done anything crazy, so I just started pounding my head against the glass, again and again, as if to say, *Yes, this is what I do, just like you scratch your ear; it's just my thing.* That whole experience was weird.

PLAYBOY: Was it only the driving, or had the beers on the empty stomach gotten to you?

REDFORD: No. I only had a couple. There was a time when I drank pretty heavily. Before I went to Europe, in 1956, and after I came back.

PLAYBOY: You went to Europe to paint, didn't you?

REDFORD: Yes. I was in Italy, in Greece, in Germany. I traveled a lot. It was a great education in a lot of ways, but there was a big low in Italy. I guess what I was doing was testing my self-discipline, and finding out what I could do without the benefit of the crutch that alcohol had become. But I was living in a very, very small room in Florence. I had only one outfit and I wore it constantly. I spent a lot of times alone—I mean, *really* alone. I went long periods without eating, mostly because I didn't have any money, but I enjoyed the fasting. I was willfully putting myself into a bleak situation, and I got into some wild trips. I'd sit in a chair for hours on end, not moving, just letting my mind go. I'd pick a small part of the room and concentrate on it for hours to see what happened. And finally, I was getting into honest-to-God self-induced hallucinations. It was exciting, but then it got frightening because I thought I was losing control of it. I started to conjure up physical symptoms of madness and sickness. I was getting these odd visitations from strange creatures, and it certainly wasn't anything I could share with anybody. I was too young and I didn't feel like any of my friends could understand.

So it was a completely solitary experience. Everything was going into me, and nothing was coming out except in the painting; and when I felt that the professor I admired most was rejecting my painting, it was a terrific blow. So much was happening to me mentally that I couldn't deal with it, and I began thinking very heavily about death and darkness. I remember one particular time lying there in that little room, puffing away on cigarettes all day, and thinking that no one anywhere knew where I was. I was completely alone, and I started thinking about Las Vegas, and it made me crazy. I could hear the slot machines, and I could see the Cadillacs pulling up and the guys with the sharkskin suits stepping out with the chicks on their arms, and I was hallucinating like mad. It was then that I realized how much you can really do on your own, and the idea of drugs and liquor couldn't carry much weight with me after that. But I was just so messed up it was ridiculous, and when I left Italy to hitchhike pretty much wherever a ride would take me, nothing seemed to matter. I had no desire to go home. I just wanted to move. And it was very frustrating when I came home after that experience. In about a year, I felt like I'd aged and become an old man. No one could relate to what I'd been through at all, and so it went back inside me, and I started drinking worse than ever because I didn't have anyone to share that incredible experience with.

PLAYBOY: Was that when you met your wife?

REDFORD: Yes.

PLAYBOY: What were you doing when you met her?

REDFORD: Dying. Just dying a little bit every day. Heading right downhill, and almost enjoying it. The worse it got, the more I kind of liked it. I really didn't have the energy to come out of it.

PLAYBOY: What do you think would have happened if you hadn't met Lola then?

REDFORD: I have a hunch, which probably sounds melodramatic, that I might have gone under in some way. Walked in front of a truck, thinking about the moon, maybe. I just don't know. The fact is that I *did* meet her. I needed to talk to someone who could understand what I'd been through, and Lola's attitude was so fresh and responsive that I started talking, all night long for a long time. She was genuinely interested in what I had to say, at a time when I really needed to talk. There were nights when we would walk around Hollywood Hills and start talking, like after dinner; walk down Hollywood Boulevard to Sunset, then up Sunset to the top of the hills, then over to the Hollywood Bowl and back and watch the dawn come up, and we'd still be talking. I had always said I'd never get married before I was thirty-five, but my instincts told me that this was a person I'd like to go through life with. So we got married.

PLAYBOY: When was that?

REDFORD: September 1958. We've been married sixteen years now, and as time goes on, I begin to realize we're sort of a museum piece, just by virtue of the fact we're still married. It's hard to be married, to make a marriage work, but the rewards are awfully rich if you can. There's an exchange that gets deeper as you go on, and it's very fulfilling. A lot of people can have relationships that go on for four or five years and then come apart, or they can just go their own way and have other relationships. That's just as acceptable, but I just happen to like the way things are going for me as is.

PLAYBOY: Has having children changed your relationship in any way?

REDFORD: What the kids did was make me realize that I could broaden my capacity to love people. There was a time when I didn't think I wanted kids. I used to have trouble expressing affection. But having kids made me find out that I can love one child as much as the next, and then a third child as much as the the other two.

PLAYBOY: What do you expect to pass on to your children as advice on how to live their lives?

REDFORD: Don't expect anything, and learn to enjoy the surprises, because they're goddamn enjoyable. I will lay on them the things I think they should know, but it's up to them what they do with it. I wouldn't want them ever to feel they had to go along with peer pressure, which is very dangerous. If they can just develop their own thinking, their own way of doing things, I hope I'm big enough to go along with them. One thing I hope I can give them is a sense of roots, growing up here in Utah. I felt no roots at all, growing up in Los Angeles. Living in Los Angeles is like living someplace on a two-year lease. You feel no sense of permanence.

PLAYBOY: What was it that made you settle on Utah for your home?

REDFORD: I was exploring the West, tramping around a little bit, hitting the road, and I came to this place, and I remember saying to myself, I really want to build a house here, right here on this spot that I think is the most beautiful spot I've seen so far. I know there must be a lot of people who say the same thing when they're passing through some beautiful piece of territory, but they pass right on through the woods and only keep the place as a memory. That wasn't for me. I wanted to do it and I didn't care what it took, what sacrifices had to be made; and I was going to do it *then*. It was wildly inconvenient, actually; my career was going badly and I didn't have any dough. Besides, I had my doubts about my ability to build the place myself because I already had a record of being a klutz as a carpenter's apprentice back in high school. For another thing, I had signed to do a Broadway play—*Barefoot in the Park*—and I had only four and a half months before rehearsals began. Starting on the house was a monumental decision, but I made it. And it was a good move. It was the beginning of so many meaningful things that have happened to me; helped me learn so much about myself.

PLAYBOY: In what way?

REDFORD: I learned to care for things I never thought I cared about. For example, I used to hunt; hunting was very important to me at one time. But while I was working on the house, deer would come down and feed in the mornings, you know, and migratory birds would come around, and I started looking at birds and animals from a different viewpoint. That changed my whole attitude about killing animals. And I got very, very deep into the experience of living outdoors, being organically connected with the land. I guess I'd always had strong feelings about the land, but they'd been dormant; now they were becoming explicit. And I could express them in building the house, working with my own hands, putting up a stone wall.

Of course, not everything went according to plan. There were some great accidents in building the house. A stairway ended three steps before it was supposed to, so we had to improvise, do something with the space. I got so much into the experience of building the house that I never once gave the Broadway play a thought. I didn't want to go to New York. I wanted to stay and finish the house, and when the winter came I wanted to sit inside and see if the walls were going to fall off, or if the glass was going to crack, or whether the forty-foot fireplace I built was going to crumble into the thirty-five tons of rock that I had collected myself. I wanted to find out if it was going to stand, to get a reaction like Frank Lloyd Wright must have felt after that earthquake in Japan, when he got the telegram saying his Imperial Hotel was one of the few buildings in Tokyo still standing. So the night before I left for New York we were still working, with lights and lanterns, putting the last of the rocks in place. Then I got on the plane; and when I landed in New York, it was like a reentry from space, which I didn't handle well at all. Everything seemed speeded up. Everybody was talking too fast and too loud. I felt as if I were about fifteen feet tall and a total idiot, as if everything I was doing was in slow motion. And when we went into rehearsals, I just couldn't adjust to it; the play seemed stupid, silly, lightweight. I tried to get fired from the play, told Mike Nichols, who was the director, to get another actor. I did everything but lie down on the stage.

PLAYBOY: What did Nichols do about it?

REDFORD: He's a very smart man, an extremely smart man, and something of a psychologist as well. He didn't know *why* I didn't want to act, but he understood the *fact* that I didn't want to act—and furthermore, that I *should* act. He was determined that I was right for the part, and finally he said to me, "Look, I know what you're doing. And I can only say that you're not going to be fired from this part. If you want to go out on opening night with a script in your hand, then that's the way it's going to be. So it's kind of up to you, I don't think you can afford not to do your best." So from then on, I kind of straightened out. But what I really wanted to do was to get back to the house and our two acres of land.

PLAYBOY: How much land do you have now?

REDFORD: Eleven hundred acres at the original place, plus an interest in the Sundance resort, which is another three thousand acres. Then we just bought a fifty-six-acre farm in southern Utah at the mouth of a canyon. It's an old horse palace, with an indoor riding arena, a place for rodeos, forty-one stables and a racetrack, but the principal thing is that it provides fifty-six acres for crops—corn, sugar beets, tomatoes and alfalfa. I need to have land around me, to farm—because I'm really afraid we may be heading for a famine—and just to walk through, just to sit down on, get in touch with the elements. We're running out of elements; we're abusing them so badly that people can't relate to anything. I think being away from the land is screwing up most people's psyches.

PLAYBOY: How can you reconcile this concern for the environment with the building of a resort, which most ecologists would deplore?

REDFORD: Sundance isn't an ordinary resort. We're developing an area that is anti-development. We're trying to enhance the beauty of the place, not destroy it; emphasizing the ecological underpinnings of the area. There is one other owner at Sundance, incidentally; I'm just the one who gets most of the publicity, because I'm an actor. One time they asked me to speak to a bunch of bankers about Sundance, and I'm not much on public speaking, but I agreed to do it. Now, Utah is quite a conservative area; I think the bankers there have a tremendous distinction in that they think they can somehow take their money with them. They sure are sitting on a big wad. They don't put it into the state and they don't send it outside the state. God knows what they do with it. So I was a little uptight about talking to the bankers, because I thought the way they were doing business in this state was prehistoric. Besides, I didn't think they really wanted to hear me give a speech. Didn't they really want to see me stand up and pull a fast draw, maybe, or find out if I'm actually six feet tall or only five feet, six, or whether I'm really pudgy and wear a hairpiece? Well, one of the other owners, who's a very dear friend of mine, wrote out something nice for me to say. But the moment I got up and looked down at the paper, I knew that speech had to go.

I started out with about the first four lines—you know, "Well, it's a pleasure to be here tonight"—and that's when I put the paper down. What I said to them was, "What are you guys sitting on your money for?" I said, "I would like to talk to you about how tough it is to do business with the bankers in this state." My friend was wilting in his chair, but I went on. What I said was heartfelt and not a put-down or anything, more of a question. Like: "I don't understand. You explain it to me. We come from outside the state; we want to improve the state. We want to build a development here that we think is unique. And we get no help or encouragement from you. You manage to treat people like they're invaders from Mars, and you find it difficult to give up ten bucks. And meanwhile, all the development that you people scream and yell about wanting to bring into the state is being developed by outside money: Texas money, Seattle money, California money, New Orleans money. Where's the Utah money? I mean, are you planting it, or what?" It was kind of an old-fashioned harangue, went on for about a half-hour I guess, and I finally just sat down, kind of puffing.

PLAYBOY: What was the bankers' reaction?

REDFORD: Well, they clapped, and everyone started to pile out. They came up to me like you do at a wake, when you look at the body in the coffin, and shook my hand. And I thought, Well, this is going to be interesting, because they're really going to jump on my bones. They'll say to me, "Who in the hell do you think you are? Some two-bit actor coming into an arena you know nothing about, telling us how to bank?" But that's not what happened. What *did* happen was that they came up and said, "Sure was an interesting talk. Say, tell me, you know in *Butch Cassidy,* when you guys jumped off the cliff, did you really make that jump yourself?"
PLAYBOY: We won't ask if you did. But after making four movies in a little more than a year, what are your plans?
REDFORD: I'm going to spend as much time as I can in Utah with my family. I guess after all is said and done, I'm happiest in the mountains and the West. And we've started designing a new house up at our new place. I'm so excited about it I can hardly wait to get to work on it. It's going to make even more interesting use of space than our first one. We'll have water coming down from a spring above, and we're going to try to use solar-cell heating and maybe a windmill for electricity, so the main thrust of its energy will be from natural sources. I hope to do as much work on the house as I can myself.
PLAYBOY: And what do you plan to do with yourself after you've finished the house?
REDFORD: I'll think about that when the time comes.

ROONE ARLEDGE

October 1976

Interviewer: Sam Merrill

Perhaps the single most influential figure in sports for two decades was neither a coach nor an athlete but an executive with the ABC television network. Roone Arledge had, with little personal visibility, changed the way sports were played, the way fans watched them, when and where sports were played, and how much athletes earned on and off the field. It was Arledge who, for good or ill, gave the world the instant replay, football on Monday nights, and Howard Cosell forever. Arledge's innovations would eventually change the face not only of sports but of television itself.

Several years after this interview took place, Arledge, to the surprise of almost everyone, was named to the presidency of ABC News *and* Sports. And it was his promotion that brought the fledgling ABC news operation into direct rivalry with the other networks for the first time. This makes it all the more interesting that Sam

Merrill, PLAYBOY's interviewer, decided to pursue an unlikely line of inquiry and asked a then-preposterous question of a sports producer: "What would a Roone Arledge news program be like?"

This interview appeared the month before Jimmy Carter's was published, and in retrospect it may have been overlooked in the glare of publicity attending Carter's famous election-eve remarks. But it was Arledge, with his inhuman schedule of travel and work, whom the editors and journalist remember as being one of the hardest subjects ever to pin down—harder, even than the next month's subject, who was a presidential candidate during a campaign. But once found, Merrill remembers, Arledge was easy to talk with.

Between 1960 and 1976, Roone Pinckney Arledge has spun out a dizzying succession of top-rated sports shows, including Monday Night Football, ABC's Wide World of Sports, *six of the past eight Olympic games,* Monday Night Baseball, The American Sportsman *and* The Superstars. *He has also "line produced" every minute of every Olympic telecast on ABC. In the process, he advanced to network vice-president in 1964 and to president of ABC Sports, Inc., in 1968. ABC Sports is now the most profitable production company in television and Arledge, whose 1975 earnings approached the one-million-dollar mark, is reputed to be the industry's highest-paid executive. But names of shows and numbers of dollars do not accurately express the impact of the man who has either invented or pioneered the use of virtually every major technical advance in sports coverage. One of Arledge's most famous electronic toys, the instant replay, has profoundly altered the way sports events are viewed and may soon change the way they are officiated as well.*

Arledge's contribution to TV sports has been verbal as well as technical. His 1961 description—first written on the back of an airline ticket—of the sports experience as "the thrill of victory, the agony of defeat" has passed into the language and when, later that year, he refused to sign any contracts that included the traditional announcer-approval clause, ABC became the first network to allow critical commentary to accompany its play-by-play.

But of all the innovations Arledge has brought to the sporting scene, he will perhaps be best remembered for having hired an obscure New York attorney whose voice reminded Arledge of Eddie Bracken and who had, by 1965, done enough local broadcasting to get himself blackballed by the national network. That Arledge invented Howard Cosell is indisputable—but whether he is to be praised or damned for it is a question still open to debate.

Sam Merrill followed the nomadic producer from New York to L.A. and back, discussed sports, technology, and Cosell with the former third-string college wrestler who has been called "the creator of the electronic sports revolution."

PLAYBOY: This year, besides your regular schedule of programs—*Monday Night Football* and *Baseball, Wide World of Sports* and others—you're also the producer of both the Winter and Summer Olympics. Hasn't it all been rather frantic?

ARLEDGE: Producing the Olympics is a lot like competing in the Olympics, except that your event lasts twenty hours a day for two weeks. But I enjoy it. Performance under pressure is what sports is all about: You create an artificial situation that is fraught with incredible tension, then see how people perform. It's exciting, exhilarating.

And, of course, when it's the Olympics, everything is magnified by the largeness of the games themselves. If Howard Cosell berates some poor coach on *Wide World of Sports*, we'll get a few letters about it. If he does it at the Olympics, it's an international incident.

PLAYBOY: You mean like the international incident you created at the Winter Olympics in Innsbruck—something about Polish hockey jokes?

ARLEDGE: Right. I was in the studio when a hockey score came in—Russia, 16: Poland, 1—and I thought, "My God, can you imagine what that Polish goalie went through? It must have been a nightmare." So we set the highlights of the game to music as a joke, pucks flying past this poor guy from every angle. It never occurred to me that because he happened to be a *Polish* goalie, people would take it as some kind of ethnic slur. But the Polish embassy and every Polish civic group in America was suddenly clamoring for equal time. And all because everything you do in the Olympics is magnified so intensely. The pressure is enormous.

PLAYBOY: During this year's Summer Olympics, you had a hand in the making of a new star—Nadia Comaneci, the Romanian gymnast. What did you think of her perfect scores?

ARLEDGE: I think Nadia's—and Nelli Kim's—perfect tens will ruin the sport. They imply not only that they can never improve but also that no one will ever perform better than they did. The sport may become stultified. It certainly has been cheapened.

PLAYBOY: But Nadia herself said she hopes to improve anyway.

ARLEDGE: She's capable of improving, but because of those scores, I don't think she will. Why risk failing at more difficult maneuvers when she's already been judged perfect? She'll never be awarded a 10.1.

PLAYBOY: You once described the Olympic experience as "communal." What did you mean?

ARLEDGE: There's a desperate need for total reliance on other people during an Olympic production. We take over the entire prime time of the network for two solid weeks of *live television*. And the audiences are unprecedented. In Munich, forty-nine of the fifty top-rated half-hour segments each week were the Olympics. So I just have to *know* that if someone goes out to do something, he is going to get it done correctly, get it done the way I want it *and* add something of his own creativity as well.

PLAYBOY: You must get to know your people pretty well in a situation like that.

ARLEDGE: That's why the Olympics are so great for an organization. You get to watch people in action, see how they react under pressure. And, as a communal experience, the absolute worst thing that can happen to a producer is for him to walk into the videotape room and be treated like a VIP—the chairman of the board making his tour of the studio. There's got to be an equality of roles.

PLAYBOY: At Innsbruck, some ABC executives criticized you for demonstrating too *much* equality by barricading yourself in the video room when you should have been out pressing the flesh with the sponsors.

ARLEDGE: The network brought a lot of guests to Innsbruck. They stayed at one of the most beautiful hotels in the world up in Zeifel and spent their days skiing and their nights partying. Meanwhile, the production people were working day and night, many of them never even getting out of the video room to see what Innsbruck looked like. I decided to stay at the Holiday Inn with the basic troops and didn't go to a single cocktail party. The advertising people were a little angry.

PLAYBOY: Wasn't that as much for psychological reasons as for convenience?

ARLEDGE: I suppose so. I didn't want the people who actually make the shows good—which is why the sponsors buy them in the first place—to think I was living it up in the Alps while they were sweating it out in the tape room.

PLAYBOY: Doesn't that point up the biggest problem you've had in recent years, the schizophrenia of being an executive producer? What *is* an executive producer, anyway—an executive or a producer?

ARLEDGE: Both, usually both at the same time. The image that ultimately appears on the tube is what TV is all about, so for me, the most rewarding and exciting part of my job is making pictures and words that move people. Not selling time or buying rights or making schedules. But the bane of this industry—the problem we face that magazines and newspapers don't, the problem that leads to so much of television's gutlessness—is that we have to buy the rights to an event before we can produce anything. So I end up spending more and more time on rights and scheduling each year. Which is a shame, because during a major sporting event, the action isn't in the commissioner's box, where every other TV executive sits, but in the mobile unit. That's the place to be.

PLAYBOY: Speaking of the technical end of the business, let's discuss some of the electronic wizardry for which you originally became known. The instant replay, for example. How did that happen?

ARLEDGE: In 1960, I was doing a survey for a college football game in the Los Angeles Coliseum with an engineer named Bob Trachinger—

PLAYBOY: Bob Trachinger? Isn't he that bearded guy in the commercials?

ARLEDGE: That's him. "More chief engineers choose blah-blah-blah than any other color TV." Trach is one of the most brilliant guys in the business, our head man on the West Coast now; but at the time, he was just a working engineer. Anyway, after the survey, we went over to a place called Julie's for a few beers. I asked him if it would be possible to replay something in slow motion so you could tell if a guy was safe or out or stepped out of bounds and Trach immediately began sketching on the napkins. We talked and sketched and drank beer that whole afternoon and when we were finished, we had the plans for the first instant-replay device.

PLAYBOY: The top people at ABC must have been pretty excited when they saw those napkins.

ARLEDGE: On the contrary. Trach's superiors at ABC engineering thought he was crazy. They were opposed to the idea and wouldn't give him any development money. So he literally took funds that were supposed to be used for something else and developed the system. Incidentally, Trach is also the guy who developed the underwater camera for me. He's just an extremely creative guy.

PLAYBOY: Do you remember the first time you used the instant replay?

ARLEDGE: The first use was during a Texas–Texas A & M football game. It was a lousy game and the instant replays were justifiably unmemorable. But the first important use came the following weekend, during a Boston College–Syracuse game. That was a terrific game and, at one point, Jack Concannon, a sophomore quarterback, was trapped in the pocket but ended up running seventy yards for a touchdown. Six or eight people had a shot at him and we replayed the whole thing in slow motion with Paul Christman analyzing the entire play as it unfolded. Nobody had ever seen anything like that before and the impact was unbelievable. That moment changed TV sports forever.

PLAYBOY: Back in the early Sixties, when you were producing the old AFL football broadcasts, you used to pull all sorts of weird technical stunts.

ARLEDGE: I'd prefer to call them experiments, but, yes, I guess we did play around a lot. Since nobody was watching anyway—particularly when the NFL was on opposite us—we had the freedom to try new things. That's how we invented the isolated camera, just by fooling around during one of those early AFL broadcasts. Much of the space-age coverage we supposedly pioneered on *Monday Night Football* was actually developed on our AFL telecasts in the early Sixties. Nobody knew about them because nobody was watching.

PLAYBOY: You were also the first guy to put sound into TV sports.

ARLEDGE: It's hard to believe now, but back in the "golden age" of the NFL, you couldn't even hear the ball being kicked. Yet sounds are very much a part of the experience of a game: the clatter of the lines converging, the sound of the quarterback barking signals. So when I began producing football for TV, I knew I had to get those sounds on the air.

PLAYBOY: But not *all* the sounds of the game are acceptable to the FCC.

ARLEDGE: That's true: and, at first, we used a two-second tape delay: but I never liked that, because you'd see the huddle break and they were halfway up to the line by the time you heard them clap and say. "Let's go." So finally I just said the hell with it and went live.

PLAYBOY: Have you ever gotten into trouble for any of those live sounds?

ARLEDGE: A couple of times. You know how a stadium will sometimes quiet down all of a sudden until, for a brief moment, there isn't a sound? That happened to us once in the Cotton Bowl. Absolute dead silence. Then some guy in the stands started screaming, "Get going, you motherfuckers!" It came over the air with better quality than we were getting from our announcers. Another time, a Florida A & M running back named Bob Paremore was taken out of the North-South Shrine game and said, "Awwww, sheeee-it!" But when that sort of thing *does* happen, the complaints usually come from league and network officials, not from the fans. Fans know what a game is supposed to sound like.

PLAYBOY: No one would deny that by wiring sports for sound you brought the TV viewer a lot closer to the stadium experience. But haven't you also gone overboard occasionally? We've heard rumors that, in 1972, you put a miniature microphone in the Olympic torch to catch the sound of the flame being lit at the opening ceremony. Is that true?

ARLEDGE: It is true, and perhaps we did go a *little* overboard with that one.

PLAYBOY: Did you do it again at Montreal this year?

ARLEDGE: We tried, but this time it wasn't possible.

PLAYBOY: As TV's major sports producer, you've created a lot of media heroes—and one very notable media villain. Exactly how did Howard Cosell happen?

ARLEDGE: Howard was a lawyer who had represented a number of athletes, including Willie Mays. He'd done some local radio and TV sports and had tried many times to get on national television. But, to tell you the truth, he was blackballed.

PLAYBOY: Why?

ARLEDGE: Well . . . a lot of it was anti-Semitism. But many other people just hated his guts on general principles—personal reasons.

PLAYBOY: But you hired him despite the blackball.

ARLEDGE: I was tremendously impressed by the fact that he had developed a great rapport with the athletes and that he'd done it on his own. When a guy is with a major network or magazine, the athletes have to, you know—

PLAYBOY: Kiss his ass?

ARLEDGE: Sure, because he's important. He has the power of his medium behind him. But Howard had achieved that power on his own. So, for that reason, and because I thought he had a funny voice, I hired him to do the pregame show on our ill-starred baseball telecasts of the mid-Sixties.

PLAYBOY: Why do you say ill-starred?

ARLEDGE: Because the broadcasts were poor and the ratings were worse. But I shouldn't blame the stars. They were OK. We were lousy.

PLAYBOY: But Cosell was good?

ARLEDGE: I thought he did a hell of a job. He got players to do things they'd never do for anyone else. Once he even got a pitcher to demonstrate his spitball. So, despite the hate mail and the little remarks from network executives, when I began to produce boxing, I decided to give Howard a try. And Howard had never been a fight announcer, but he knew Floyd Patterson and a lot of other people. And he did very well.

PLAYBOY: What do you mean by "the little remarks from network executives"?

ARLEDGE: When a guy is blackballed, you hear all kinds of things. Some people just say, "I don't think you ought to use him anymore, you know what I mean?" Others are more specific, like, "The sponsor's wife hates him and everybody at my country club thinks he's a loudmouth Jew."

PLAYBOY: You mentioned anti-Semitism before. About how much of the antagonism toward Cosell would you attribute to that?

ARLEDGE: It's hard to say, because Howard embodies the entire anti–New York feeling people have around America, and a large part of that feeling is based on anti-Semitism. Howard did an innocuous little piece about New York on his show last fall that Bob Lipsyte of the *Times* wrote with him. It said to the rest of the country that we're no different from you. That we've made our mistakes but they're only a little ahead of your mistakes, so don't treat us like an enemy. The piece lasted less than a minute, but by the time Howard had finished reading it, the switchboard was lit up with over five hundred long-distance calls. Can you imagine how upset people have to be to spend the money to call in from Kansas and then wait on the line maybe ten minutes just to tell some poor operator how much they hate Howard Cosell?

PLAYBOY: But if people hate Cosell, why do you keep him on the air?

ARLEDGE: I keep him on the air because I think he's a good honest journalist. And to illustrate just *how* honest he is, even when I was the only guy in the business willing to hire him, he still persisted in bad-mouthing me. He once said publicly that "*Wide World of Sports* is important if your idea of journalism is Jim McKay yodeling on a mountaintop." Howard characterized us as a bunch of kids playing with cameras who tried so hard to get more blimp shots than anyone else that we missed the journalism.

PLAYBOY: We agree that Cosell is honest, but what about his effect on the ratings?

ARLEDGE: Apparently—assuming the ratings are accurate—Howard is the man middle America loves to hate. Some people watch because they love him, while others watch hoping to see him fall on his ass. But *everybody* watches. Many of Don Meredith's fans on *Monday Night Football* were people who enjoyed seeing the down-home Texas cowboy insult the brash New Yorker.

PLAYBOY: So, for various reasons, you hired Cosell as your boxing announcer. And from there he developed his famous relationship with Muhammad Ali. How did *that* happen?

ARLEDGE: It happened because Howard was really the first guy in the media to publicly defend Ali during his years as a draft resister and he was the *only* one to call him

Ali immediately after he changed his name. So, naturally, Ali would talk to Howard and not, for example, to Dick Young of the New York *Daily News*, who continued to call him Cassius Clay until quite recently.

PLAYBOY: What's it like to work with Muhammad Ali?

ARLEDGE: He's a strange man: very childlike but also very honorable. And he has the world's shortest attention span. In the middle of talking to him, he will suddenly begin playing with something or looking out the window and you'll be absolutely certain he didn't hear a word you said. But six months later, when even *you've* forgotten what you said, you'll discover that not only did he hear and remember it but he intends to hold you to it down to the last detail. Ali keeps his commitments and expects others to keep theirs. In that sense, he's an ideal athlete to work with—completely reliable. But before you tell him anything, make sure you can say it in less than six seconds. Otherwise, he'll start fiddling with your stapler in the middle of a sentence and make you feel like a total idiot.

PLAYBOY: Ali certainly helped Cosell achieve national prominence. But Cosell also received a great deal of notoriety during your coverage of the 1968 Olympics at Mexico City.

ARLEDGE: Right after the Tommie Smith–John Carlos "black-fist affair," Howard alone got both of them into our studio for an in-depth interview. Then he attacked the U.S. Olympic Committee and the International Olympic Committee for overreacting. That was the event that brought Howard into focus as a national personality. But *Monday Night Football* made him a star.

PLAYBOY: A *star*?

ARLEDGE: We deliberately set out to create a special role for Howard on *Monday Night Football*. The analogy I always use is Dorothy Kilgallen on the old *What's My Line?* show.

PLAYBOY: In other words, you wanted him to antagonize people.

ARLEDGE: But only in the course of speaking his mind and making things happen.

PLAYBOY: Did you ever feel he antagonized people a little *too* much?

ARLEDGE: Sure, but that's only natural. There are people in this country for whom football isn't a game but a religion. They want Ray Scott to tell them the down and yardage and maybe Pat Summerall to say. "That was a zig-out." But beyond that, they don't want their religion disturbed. They certainly don't want Howard criticizing everybody, or Don Meredith saying about football, as he did one night, "There must be more to life than this." To some people, football *is* life and Howard has had quite a few death threats because of things he's said about somebody's favorite player. On several occasions, we've broadcast the game from a control booth full of FBI agents.

PLAYBOY: That's pretty bad.

ARLEDGE: There's worse. I probably shouldn't tell you this. I've never even told Howard—

PLAYBOY: Oh, go ahead.

ARLEDGE: There's a bar down South where, during the football season, all the regulars put in a few bucks a week and on Monday night they buy an old TV set and a load of buckshot. Then they draw lots and, the first time Howard's picture comes on the screen, the winner gets to blast the TV set to smithereens. Then they all get drunk and watch the game on another set.

PLAYBOY: Do you, personally, *like* television?

ARLEDGE: Let's say I don't think its potential is being properly utilized. I mean, do

Mac Davis, Tony Orlando and *Laverne and Shirley* really represent the ultimate use of this medium?
PLAYBOY: But commercial TV as we know it is a mass medium. Look at your own career. You do the Olympics every four years. You do demolition derbies somewhat more often.
ARLEDGE: I believe we've proven in our best sports coverage, and I *know* it's been proven in certain areas of the news, that you can appeal to a mass audience without appealing to the lowest common denominator.
PLAYBOY: In general, what do you think of TV news?
ARLEDGE: I think news, like entertainment, is done better elsewhere. It is my understandably biased opinion that TV does sports better than sports is done anywhere else but that everything else is done better in other media.
PLAYBOY: What would a Roone Arledge news program be like?
ARLEDGE: The first think I'd do as a news producer would be to hire a staff of investigative reporters. Television did nothing with Watergate, perhaps the biggest news story in the history of our nation. That's because Watergate was essentially an investigative story. John Mitchell didn't hold a press conference to reveal he was one of the co-controllers of Nixon's secret fund, so naturally, television newsmen had to read that in the papers. Also, I'd try for a more interesting format. Newspapers are always wrestling with their formats in an attempt to enhance reader interest. But TV thinks news has to be dull to be credible. Another thing I'd do as a news producer is personalize world leaders the same way I personalize sports figures.
PLAYBOY: Presumably, the networks do that on their panel shows.
ARLEDGE: Right. Three discussion programs that are carbon copies of one another. I simply cannot believe the only format in which a world leader can be presented to the American people is around a desk with three people asking him questions at one o'clock on Sunday afternoon.
PLAYBOY: What would you suggest?
ARLEDGE: I'd do one-minute press-conference-type interviews on the six-o'clock news and hour-long documentaries on prime time. That way, on a daily basis, we could get to know who these people are. During our Olympic coverage, we routinely run documentary profiles of the athletes. The next morning, Americans know not only what people like Olga Korbut and Dorothy Hamill look like but where they come from and, to at least some extent, what kind of people they are. But until the Senate hearings, ninety percent of the American public didn't even know what Bob Haldeman looked like, let alone what he did and thought. He was the second most powerful man in the country and we had the most powerful medium in the country, yet somehow, a man like that was able to remain anonymous.
PLAYBOY: The most powerful man in the country was also America's number-one football fan. Did you ever meet Richard Nixon?
ARLEDGE: On several occasions. The first was at a Texas-Arkansas game for the national championship. I was supposed to meet my wife in Hawaii that weekend, but when Nixon decided to attend the game, I felt I *had* to produce it personally. I would never have forgiven myself if something had happened to the President and I wasn't there.
PLAYBOY: Because you felt you could have helped prevent an assassination?
ARLEDGE: No, because I wouldn't have wanted anyone else making the decision on how to cover one.

PLAYBOY: You are nothing if not professional.

ARLEDGE: Incidentally, stranding my wife in Hawaii like that proved to be the last straw in our marriage. Soon afterward, she divorced me. But getting back to Nixon, Texas won the game and after congratulating the team, the President went into the Arkansas dressing room to give the players a little talk. It started out with the usual locker-room clichés, just another politician giving another speech. But then Nixon began discussing defeat in the most intensely personal terms. It was extremely moving, since, as we all realized, he was actually talking about himself. But the next time I met Nixon, just four days later, it was plain weird.

PLAYBOY: What happened?

ARLEDGE: The afternoon before a football dinner Nixon was attending, I got a call saying the President would like to see me. I went up to his suite in the Waldorf Towers and everyone said, "Oh, yes, the President is expecting you." So I walked into this huge room, figuring there would be about a hundred other people in a reception line. But the room was empty; just an American flag, the Presidential flag and one man: the President of the United States. It was a rather awesome experience. We spent more than half an hour together, talking about sports. At first, I thought, This is awfully nice of him. He wants to put me at my ease by talking about something I'm familiar with. But after a while, I began trying to change the subject to other things that interest me a lot more than sports: music, theater, the problems of our cities. But Nixon kept coming back to sports. Finally, I realized that he wasn't trying to put me at ease, he was trying to impress me with his knowledge of sports trivia. While he was rattling off the times of quarter-milers in the 1936 Olympics, I remember saying to myself, I can't believe it. The President of the United States is trying to impress *me.*

PLAYBOY: Let's go back a moment to your development of innovations in televising games: Did you run into much opposition from the sports establishment?

ARLEDGE: Sure. Techniques that are now considered standard, such as the instant replay, slow motion, showing the faces of the players, even superimposing the names of the players on the screen after a good play, were called gimmicks when we introduced them.

PLAYBOY: Do any particular incidents come to mind?

ARLEDGE: The first time we put a camera in the dugout was at Yankee Stadium. Before that, no one was doing field-level shots. But I wanted the kind of dramatic close-up from a human perspective—not foreshortened because the camera is in the upper deck—that has become standard now. Well, Red Barber was doing the local telecast for the Yankees and he turned his cameras on us and did a whole editorial on the air. He announced to his viewers, "Ladies and gentlemen, you are witnessing something that has never happened before in the history of baseball. The sanctity of the dugout has been violated."

PLAYBOY: While revolutionizing the visual aspects of sports broadcasting, you were also making some important changes in the way events were announced. You have even been quoted as saying that sometimes sportscasters talk too much.

ARLEDGE: That's why Dick Button is so good. He's an expert who knows when not to talk. When something is truly beautiful to look at, a play-by-play becomes an irritating intrusion between you and the event. It would drive me crazy to watch Baryshnikov dance and have to listen to somebody babbling in my ear: "Now watch his left foot. He's going to jump and, as he turns, listen to the music change key."

PLAYBOY: But because of the size and variety of the TV audience, sometimes an announcer *has* to explain something that for millions of sophisticated viewers might seem academic.

ARLEDGE: Would you believe that when we first covered Wimbledon, very few Americans knew even the basic rules of tennis? It was embarrassing, but Jim McKay had to go on the air and explain that love means zero and the object of the game is to keep the ball inside the white lines. Can you imagine how that must have offended veteran tennis fans?

PLAYBOY: *Wide World of Sports,* which premiered in 1961, was really the show that made you and, as you've said, it's been your proving ground for the techniques you use in covering the Olympics. How did that show get started?

ARLEDGE: In 1960, the major-league baseball owners still clung to their old blackout rule. They restricted the telecasts of major-league games to minor-league markets. As a result of that great humanitarian gesture, which contributed to the destruction of the minor leagues, the three networks were fighting over only forty percent of the country, since sixty percent was in the big-league markets. ABC decided that was silly and assigned me to come up with a year-round sports show that could fill the void and not have to worry about the blackouts. That show was *Wide World of Sports.* The idea was to travel to the world's greatest events and try to capture whatever it is that makes those events fascinating. We combined the techniques of documentary filmmaking—so viewers could get to know the performers personally—with coverage designed to make you feel as though you are there.

PLAYBOY: *Wide World of Sports* has covered some pretty weird events over the years. How do you find them all?

ARLEDGE: It's easy now, because people come to us with them. But when we were starting out, that was one of our biggest problems. I knew NBC had a large microfilm library with a lot of the information I needed and I gambled on two things: first, that nobody there knew I was gone and, second, that nobody there knew what I looked like. So I sent Chuck Howard, who was then a production assistant and is now vice-president of ABC Sports, over to NBC to go through their files and list all the sports events we might be interested in. I told him whenever anyone asked who he was, to say he was me. It worked, and so I began traveling all around the world, signing up events for *Wide World of Sports.*

PLAYBOY: And that's how *Wide World* got started?

ARLEDGE: Not exactly. Because when I returned to New York with the rights to everything from the Japanese All-Star Baseball Game to the British Open, to the Twenty-four Hours of Le Mans, no sponsor wanted to buy the show. At ten minutes to five on the afternoon of the day the show was going to be canceled, Ed Sherick, who was then the head of sales for ABC, had the guts to use NCAA football as a sledgehammer to sell time on *Wide World of Sports.* He made R.J. Reynolds Tobacco Company buy the new show before he'd let it have a quarter of college football. So, *Wide World of Sports,* now the longest-running sports show in television history, came within ten minutes of never getting on the air.

PLAYBOY: You were the first American producer to do a show from the Soviet Union: the 1961 U.S.-Russia track meet. Acquiring the rights to shoot in Moscow must have been the bureaucratic experience of a lifetime.

ARLEDGE: Rights? What rights? We were just naïve and crazy enough to fly a hundred tons of equipment into Moscow without official clearance or permits or anything. We got all set up overnight and taped the meet the next day. I had never been to Russia before, couldn't speak the language—we weren't even sure what kind of electricity they had. But everything went well and we ended up with Russian soldiers in the control room—not arresting us but watching to see if Valery Brumel could break the world's high-jump record. That first trip was easy, but each successive time we've been back there the—if you'll excuse the expression—red tape has gotten a little thicker.

PLAYBOY: Weren't you also the first American to do a show from Prague after the revolution?

ARLEDGE: That was also without permits, and we were even shooting stuff at the palace. We thought we'd be arrested at any moment.

PLAYBOY: But you weren't?

ARLEDGE: Fortunately not. It would have been difficult to explain the girl we were smuggling across the border in our mobile unit. Especially when she turned out to be a double agent!

PLAYBOY: Last year, when the U.S.-Russia track meet at Kiev was canceled because of a contract you had signed with a Soviet agency, the AAU accused you of everything from selling out the American athletic team to ruining détente. What's your side of that story?

ARLEDGE: I paid the Soviet radio-television committee fifty thousand dollars for the broadcast rights, but the AAU people claimed that since we were giving the money to the Russians instead of to them, they could no longer afford to send our athletes to Kiev. So they postponed the meet.

PLAYBOY: There must have been more to it than that. According to news reports, you later offered to charter a plane and fly every American athlete to Russia at your own expense, yet the AAU still insisted on canceling the meet. Why?

ARLEDGE: It turned out that what the AAU was *really* concerned about was getting free junkets for its own officials. They wanted to send one official for every two athletes. And when I refused to underwrite all those junkets, they refused to let the athletes go.

PLAYBOY: Do you find it generally more difficult to deal with amateurs than with professionals?

ARLEDGE: Yes, with one notable exception. The former commissioner of the National Basketball Association was the most difficult man I have *ever* dealt with.

PLAYBOY: We assume you're referring to Walter Kennedy.

ARLEDGE: Yes; I feel he acted deceitfully in his negotiations with us. Actually, Pete Rozelle is the only sports commissioner who can sit down and tell you something and you know it's going to stick. Bowie Kuhn, though he is not deceitful, doesn't have Rozelle's authority.

PLAYBOY: Because Rozelle is a stronger man than Kuhn?

ARLEDGE: Perhaps, or perhaps the football owners are enlightened enough to realize that they all gain strength when their league has a strong commissioner. The baseball owners tend to be self-motivated most of the time—crotchety and either unaware of anyone else's problems or, if they are aware of them, they don't give a damn. With the exception of football, most pro sports groups cannot agree on anything among themselves, so we can hardly expect to agree on how to treat the outside world. The baseball-team owners are just a loose confederation of carny operators and robber barons, with a small sprinkling of enlightened statesmen thrown in.

PLAYBOY: Do you think the baseball owners actually want a weak commissioner?

ARLEDGE: I'm sure of it. Several years ago, when they made their much-publicized nationwide search for a new commissioner, the baseball owners *talked* about hiring such people of real or presumed stature as Hubert Humphrey and—before Watergate—Richard Nixon. But who did they end up with? General William Eckert, the unknown soldier. Don't get me wrong. Bowie Kuhn is a good man. But the owners never intended to give him any power when they hired him—and they didn't. So even if I were to sign a binding contract with Kuhn, I'd still have to wait and see if the owners would let him live up to it.

PLAYBOY: In 1973, when you announced that you had acquired the TV rights to this year's Summer Olympics for twenty-five million dollars, NBC protested that you had made the deal "through secret and noncompetitive procedures . . . contrary to the best interests of the people of Canada, the American TV audience, and the games themselves." Rumors were also circulated that your price tag included some heavy bribes.

ARLEDGE: There were all sorts of accusations of under-the-table payments, illegal contributions to Canadian political parties and everything else. Of course, nothing was ever proved. We'd have been pretty dumb to get involved in anything like that.

PLAYBOY: But bribery does happen occasionally doesn't it?

ARLEDGE: Not to me. Who do you think I am, one of Nixon's friends? The point is, even if I'd *wanted* to bribe somebody, I didn't have to. The Olympic people wanted to go with us all along. That's what infuriates the other networks. It happened when we signed Montreal and it happened again this year after we signed Lake Placid: CBS president Bob Wood fired off telegrams to the Olympic committee, every congressman and senator in New York, the governor, even the President, raising the phony issue that we did not acquire the TV rights through sealed competitive bidding.

PLAYBOY: Well, you didn't.

ARLEDGE: Because sealed bidding is almost never done in television. I don't see NBC putting Bob Hope up for sealed bids every year or CBS doing it with *All in the Family*. There are continuing relationships in this business.

PLAYBOY: But the Olympics are different. Since public funds were needed to build most of the facilities in Montreal and will be needed to build at least some of them at Lake Placid, don't you think there is a public responsibility to have competitive bidding so the municipality can raise as much money as possible?

ARLEDGE: No, because, in a sense, money itself is a phony issue. Let me give you an example. NCAA basketball was just renewed by NBC. We'd talked to the NCAA and had told them we were interested, but we never even got a chance. They just sat down in a room with NBC, said they were happy with the job that network had done last year, told NBC how much money they wanted, negotiated a bit and the deal was made. There was nothing unethical about that and, although I was sorry we didn't get our shot at it, I certainly didn't scream to Congress that, since many of the colleges are supported by public funds, the NCAA has a responsibility to raise as much money as it can through competitive bidding. The point is that the NCAA was happy with the way NBC had treated them. That was worth more to them than the possibility of a few extra dollars. Besides, with sealed bidding, there is also the possibility of *fewer* dollars, since the seller has abdicated his right to negotiate. And, of course, with sealed bidding, there's an opportunity for collusion among the networks to keep prices down. Collusion, like bribery, has been known to happen.

PLAYBOY: So, in the case of the Summer Olympics, the people of Montreal believed that you could provide certain benefits that the two other networks could not.

ARLEDGE: Well, we *were* able to offer them our track record at producing Olympic Games in the past.
PLAYBOY: NBC produced the 1964 and 1972 Olympics from Japan.
ARLEDGE: Very unsuccessfully, I might add. The Japanese government spent over one billion dollars on each of those Olympics—1964 was particularly important to them, because it was supposed to be their welcome back into the human race after World War Two—and it was pathetic how little impact the NBC broadcasts had. They were done in fifteen-minute increments late at night and practically nobody knew what was happening. We've done every other Olympics: Innsbruck in 1961, Mexico City and Grenoble in 1968, Munich in 1972, Innsbruck and Montreal this year. And, in each case, the impact has been tremendous.
PLAYBOY: Nice of you to say so.
ARLEDGE: The fact remains that we did thirteen and a half hours in prime time from Innsbruck—which even I believe was more time than necessary—and the reviews and ratings were tremendous. Our success with winter sports in prime time surprised most people in the TV industry and even some at ABC. So, putting yourself in the place of Mayor Jean Drapeau, who had to spend 1.3 billion dollars and whose goal was to publicize Montreal, which network would *you* have picked?
PLAYBOY: You're a persuasive salesman.
ARLEDGE: Unfortunately, selling one's network takes up a good deal of a producer's time.
PLAYBOY: Getting back to the alleged scandals in acquiring TV rights to the Olympic Games—
ARLEDGE: If you must.
PLAYBOY: If the Lake Placid deal was really on the level, why didn't CBS and NBC move to get the 1980 Winter games even *after* you proved at Innsbruck that winter sports could capture a big viewing audience in this country?
ARLEDGE: I don't know, but after Innsbruck, we kept waiting for the two other guys to contact the Lake Placid people. It was like waiting for the other shoe to drop. But they never did. Finally, the Lake Placid committee sent telegrams to NBC and CBS saying that, since they hadn't heard from them in over six months, they were proceeding with us. That's when those two networks began screaming to Congress, the President and God, not necessarily in that order.
PLAYBOY: What you've been describing is essentially behind-the-scenes work. Even though you've brought about some profound changes in television, practically no one knows what you look like and your name is hardly a household word. Does the relative anonymity of a producer's role ever bother you?
ARLEDGE: Sometimes. After I've worked twenty hours a day to produce the Olympic Games, even my own father has said, "Gee, that was a great show Jim McKay put on."
PLAYBOY: You mentioned the kind of news show you might present. What other kinds of programming would interest you?
ARLEDGE: Well, considering my addiction to ballet, I can think of ways to produce *that* that would make it exciting.
PLAYBOY: How?
ARLEDGE: Well, apparently Baryshnikov and Nureyev had never met before a year ago January, when they were in New York at the same time. I think that, if we'd been given the opportunity to explain the rudiments of dance—as we explained gymnastics and figure skating at the Olympics—people would have really gotten into a kind of

big-money shoot-out between two top stars. And the result would have been a piece of videotape that people would be watching a hundred years from now.
PLAYBOY: When you say shoot-out, surely you're not implying that you'd open with a blimp shot of Lincoln Center, then cut to an isolated camera on Nureyev's big toe.
ARLEDGE: Of course not. And neither am I implying that after every leap, three judges would hold up signs saying 5.6, 6.3 and 5.8. As in sports or news or anything else, producing ballet would simply mean getting the shot the viewer really wants to see, not the shot that proves you are an electronic wizard.
PLAYBOY: But some of the shots you've gotten over the years *have* required a lot of electronic wizardry. How do you determine when you are getting the shot the viewer wants and when you have gone beyond it to become, in Cosell's words, "a bunch of kids playing with cameras"?
ARLEDGE: The answer is simple: You must use the camera—and the microphone—to broadcast an image that approximates what the brain perceives, not merely what the eye sees. Only then can you create the illusion of reality.
PLAYBOY: In other words, you distort reality in order to make it seem real.
ARLEDGE: Exactly; but you must exercise the restraint to stop before it becomes *sur*-real.
PLAYBOY: This is beginning to sound a little circular. Let's cut to a concrete example.
ARLEDGE: Take auto racing. When you're at Le Mans, the entire atmosphere is charged with the vivid sensations of speed and danger. But put a camera in the middle of the Mulsanne Straight, where the cars are traveling well over two hundred miles per hour, and all you see is this dot that gets a little bigger as it approaches. The perception of speed is absent. So we put slave cameras much closer to the track than any spectator could ever get. They give the television viewer that zip and roar, the sensation of speed the live viewer would perceive simply by watching that little dot grow larger. That way, we are not creating something phony. It is an illusion but an illusion of reality.
PLAYBOY: *Wide World of Sports* routinely compresses three-hour events into eight-minute segments. And people seem to love it. But that doesn't seem to be even an illusion of reality—just a snippet.
ARLEDGE: There's certainly some truth to that, but it depends upon the setting. People eagerly watch the long, nonaction segments of the Olympics, heavyweight championship fights and the world series. But in sports they aren't that familiar with, or in events that aren't that important, people do enjoy the knowledge that something different will be coming on every ten minutes.
PLAYBOY: In addition to catering to an ever-shortening attention span, do you feel you are oversaturating the airwaves with sports?
ARLEDGE: Oversaturation is a danger faced by everyone in the media. PLAYBOY now has to compete with all its would-be emulators and TV is glutted with forty-three cop shows that have replaced forty-three Westerns. In every area of every medium, you can reach a point of surfeit, when numbness sets in.
PLAYBOY: Has sports numbness ever set in on you?
ARLEDGE: I must confess that it has. On the weekend after New Year's you generally have at least two NFL championship games and four or five—sometimes six or eight—bowl games. And by the end of that weekend, I have this composite image of forty-seven tumbling catches in the end zone, twenty-six explanations of why you've got to have both feet in bounds and, really, it's all just a blur.

PLAYBOY: Would you say, then, that sports have peaked on television?
ARLEDGE: No. In fact, I'd say the TV audience for sports will continue to grow for quite some time, but there's going to be a lot of weeding out. Some bowl games have already vanished. A football league and a basketball league both folded this year. Tennis went from being wildly underexposed to being wildly overexposed. There *may* never even be a TV audience for hockey.
PLAYBOY: But hockey is such a successful sport.
ARLEDGE: Not on television. NBC and CBS made big mistakes with hockey and I'm not knocking them. I could have made the same mistake. I enjoy watching hockey and every time I go to Madison Square Garden, there are seventeen thousand people there. But it's the same seventeen thousand people all the time. In the New York TV market, you need one million viewers, not seventeen thousand. So, you see, the weeding-out process is already under way.
PLAYBOY: But don't you think television has the power to create tastes, even create an entire sport, if it's left on the air long enough?
ARLEDGE: No.
PLAYBOY: Many media experts have credited you with creating the sudden American taste for gymnastics.
ARLEDGE: Gymnastics came along when Americans were just beginning to become aware of their bodies, and the personality of Olga Korbut came along when the women's movement was getting into athletics. TV *can* create a personality, but it *can't* create a taste the public isn't ready for. Americans were ready for golf when Arnold Palmer appeared on television. He was the swashbuckling hero who would be six strokes down, hitch up his pants and charge. People who didn't know a putt from a sand blast could root for him. But, like Bobby Fischer, Palmer would have soon faded into obscurity if an interest in the game didn't underlie an interest in the personality.
PLAYBOY: Your *Monday Night Football* announcing team certainly became personalities—in fact, they almost became folk heroes. Did you expect them to work together that well, or was it just a fortunate accident?
ARLEDGE: Of course I knew what each would do individually, but the magic of their group personality developed spontaneously over a period of time. And there were adjustments. Few people remember that our original play-by-play announcer was Keith Jackson, not Frank Gifford, or that Don Meredith wasn't very funny the first year. And the public's response to Howard that first year was unbelievable. I'd come to work on Tuesday morning and the office would be filled with sacks of letters demanding that we throw him off the air. And I'm not talking about letters that began, "In my opinion . . ." I'm talking about letters that began, "We the undersigned . . ." and ended with three hundred names. But toward the end of the first year, letters praising Howard began to equal the ones that asked, "By what right does that Jewish boxing loudmouth come off criticizing *my team*?" And, of course, Howard was the guy who eventually drew out Don Meredith.
PLAYBOY: When and how did that happen?
ARLEDGE: Toward the end of the first year, St. Louis beat the Cowboys 38–0 and Meredith was moaning, crying; he was a man in anguish and with Howard to egg him on, his human qualities really came across. Don won an Emmy largely because of that show and it made him a star.
PLAYBOY: Sometimes your announcing "stars" overshadow the game itself.
ARLEDGE: Yes, that's true. When *Monday Night Football* comes to town, some cities

build parades around our announcers and ignore their own teams. *Monday Night Football* is a traveling circus.

PLAYBOY: Meredith and Cosell were a perfect match: the pompous city slicker and the sly country fox. How would you characterize their very different senses of humor?

ARLEDGE: The difference was illustrated clearly the night we had Agnew on the show. Howard likes the loud, pretended-to-be-overheard remark. While strolling through the Baltimore Colts' dressing room with the Vice-President, Howard said, "In other words, Mr. Agnew, it is your position that black ballplayers should no longer be allowed in the NFL?" And, to his credit, Agnew came right back with, "I didn't say there should be none, I said we were considering a quota." But Meredith waited until he was on the air—he was a little high that night, which always made him even more irreverent than usual—and said, "Hi there, Mr. Vice-President. Nice to meetcha. You seem like a nice fella, but I'd never vote for ya. I notice you're wearing a Howard Cosell wristwatch."

PLAYBOY: Was Meredith a little high often during a show?

ARLEDGE: Well, occasionally.

PLAYBOY: Did Meredith's irreverence ever get you in trouble?

ARLEDGE: Only when he called the President of the United States Tricky Dickey.

PLAYBOY: Was Meredith difficult to replace?

ARLEDGE: Very. Now, Don is an entertaining guy, a hell of a guy, and over the course of a season, he'll come up with five or six truly memorable remarks. But, because *Monday Night Football* is larger than life, people remember Don as being hysterically funny all the time. So the guy who replaces him feels compelled to reel off twenty-eight knee-slappers in the first quarter. And if he doesn't, everybody says, "Hey, he's not as good as Don Meredith." But Alex Karras has been terrific and the ratings have been better.

PLAYBOY: On *Monday Night Baseball,* aren't you trying to do the same thing with Bob Uecker that you did with Meredith?

ARLEDGE: In a way, except that Uecker is a much funnier person than Meredith or Karras or Garagiola or, in my opinion, anyone who has ever injected humor into sports.

PLAYBOY: Yet Uecker hasn't been that funny on the air.

ARLEDGE: I know. The format may not be quite right for him or, as with *Monday Night Football,* it might just take time.

PLAYBOY: You mentioned Garagiola a moment ago. What do you think of his work?

ARLEDGE: Garagiola is funny, but he's a very strident humorist. You get the impression Joe comes in with a list of stories he's going to work into the game.

PLAYBOY: What's your view on the "jock rights" movement—specifically, the labor disputes that have afflicted baseball this season?

ARLEDGE: I can't tell you how repugnant the notion of owning and selling human beings is to me. Sports is the only area of modern life where people are traded or sold for money. The word *owner,* when applied to a man, conjures up images of slavery.

PLAYBOY: Yet fans boo ballplayers who favor modification of the reserve clause.

ARLEDGE: It has always astonished me that the sympathies of so many working people instinctively go to management. The fan, who is himself a wage earner, behaves as though he owns the franchise.

PLAYBOY: Assuming America's pro-team owners don't regulate themselves—which, based on past performance, seems a fairly reliable assumption—what do you foresee? Chaos?

ARLEDGE: Worse. I think the government will get involved. Nobody wants a Federal Sports Commission, but I think we're headed for one.

PLAYBOY: Why would a Federal Sports Commission be so awful?

ARLEDGE: Chaos would be replaced by political corruption: "We'll get this bill passed if you put a franchise in Birmingham, Alabama." A Federal Sports Commission would *run* sports. Of course, sports aren't apolitical now. Why do you think Congress lifted the NFL's blackout rule?

PLAYBOY: OK, we'll bite. Why?

ARLEDGE: Because political leaders were sick and tired of not being able to get tickets to the Redskins games. Complaints from the fans had little to do with it. If the same situation had existed in Cleveland, we'd still have a blackout rule today.

PLAYBOY: Nevertheless, the government doesn't operate the pro leagues and you seem satisfied with that arrangement. Yet you do not seem satisfied with the way private enterprise has handled the sports industry.

ARLEDGE: I'm troubled by what is really an ethical, not an economic, question: To what extent does the private ownership of a public facility conflict with our traditional American values? We condition our children to identify with their community, particularly with the sports heroes of their community. Politicians run for office while waving the home-team banner. Local sportscasters, who are paid by the team and whose job it is to sell tickets, imply that it's the fans' civic duty to support the home team. If we allow something that important to be created in people's minds, two questions arise: One, is private ownership compatible with a public enterprise? And two, should any standards of excellence—or at least competence—be required?

PLAYBOY: And how would you answer those questions?

ARLEDGE: I don't know; but assuming private ownership *is* compatible with operating a civic institution, should the owner of the Metropolitan Opera be permitted to move to Milwaukee because he can get a better deal there? I don't think so.

PLAYBOY: Your second question sounds rather idealistic. We've never heard anyone suggest that owners meet standards of excellence in order to retain control of their ball clubs.

ARLEDGE: A TV station is granted a regional monopoly, just like a sports franchise. And, like a sports franchise, that monopoly is usually a very profitable thing. But in order to keep its broadcast license, a station is reviewed every three years and has to prove that it operates in the public interest. It also has to demonstrate a certain degree of competence. And I approve of that practice. When a public facility is privately owned, there has to be a way to make sure the community standards are being met.

PLAYBOY: Would you like to own a ball club yourself?

ARLEDGE: That might be an interesting experience but one I will probably live without—certainly as long as owning a ball club means owning the employees, too.

PLAYBOY: You're almost as well known for business acumen as for technical expertise and your income is reputed to be awesome. Would you mind telling us where you invest your money?

ARLEDGE: Lately, I've been investing rather heavily in divorce.

PLAYBOY: On second thought, perhaps we should go elsewhere for financial advice. But we will ask you who your favorite athletes are—and why.

ARLEDGE: Bill Russell is probably number one. Not only did he exhibit total mastery of his sport but he was also an innovator. Due solely to his presence, the game of basketball Russell left when he retired was different from the game he found when he began playing. And Russell is also an important person in America. I've been after him for years to run for office. I think he'd make a great senator, or President, for that matter. Another favorite is Jack Nicklaus and for similar reasons: his dominance of the game he plays and his personal qualities.
PLAYBOY: Nicklaus is an unexpected choice. The two of you are hardly friends. He has generally sided with the USGA in your frequent disputes with that organization.
ARLEDGE: Nevertheless, I admire Jack's integrity. Golf is, in many respects, the purest sport, because it is the only one in which the player must penalize himself. If your caddy moves the ball in the rough, you must call it on yourself. That happened to Byron Nelson in the U.S. Open and he lost the tournament by one stroke. You just know that Nicklaus would do the same thing, even if no one on earth could possibly have seen his ball move. It's interesting to ask yourself what you'd do in a situation like that.
PLAYBOY: Any other favorite athletes?
ARLEDGE: One more: O.J. Simpson. Although he is the greatest running back in football history, his basic modesty hasn't changed since he was a junior at USC. Incidentally, O.J. could have broken the reserve system wide open when he graduated, but he chose not to.
PLAYBOY: How?
ARLEDGE: He was the most-sought-after college player of all time. He could have marketed his services for millions of dollars, and he *wanted* to play for Los Angeles, where he lived, where he was already a hero and where he could have made a fortune in endorsements. But, instead, he went to Buffalo and took whatever Ralph Wilson felt like giving him, which wasn't much. He played on a lousy team with a lousy line for a coach who wouldn't let him carry the ball. It was only luck that, after years of frustration, Buffalo finally changed coaches and drafted some good linemen. Otherwise, O.J.'s entire career would have been ruined—by the reserve clause. Unless both sides get together, there's never going to be any sanity in professional sports.
PLAYBOY: Are you sorry Simpson didn't smash the reserve clause when he had the chance?
ARLEDGE: I'm not sure.
PLAYBOY: Had you been his business manager, what would you have advised him to do?
ARLEDGE: Smash the reserve clause.
PLAYBOY: Of all the shows you've produced, what would you consider the greatest moment, the single most important image you have ever beamed out to the world?
ARLEDGE: The word *important* may seem to require some justification in this context, since individually, both sports and television are essentially trivial. But when the two are combined, they can become *very* important. And I think my most important moment came during the 1963 U.S.-Russia track meet in Moscow. In those days, the meet was a titanic international struggle, with the conflict between the two systems as the underlying motif. And in that particular year, the U.S. and Russia were trying to put together the first meaningful arms agreement of the Cold War. Khrushchev and Harriman were negotiating day and night, but at the very end of the meet, the two of them came out to Lenin Stadium to watch Valery Brumel, the great Russian high

jumper, try for the world's record. It was getting dark and a light rain had begun falling. Brumel was down to his last attempt. He sprinted toward the bar, leaped and made it. There was a momentary lull as ninety thousand people waited to see if the bar would topple. It didn't, and the crowd exploded. I turned our cameras on the chairman's box and Khrushchev and Harriman were jumping up and down, screaming, hugging each other. That was the single most important image I have ever broadcast. Two old men. Enemies who spoke different languages and couldn't even agree on a way to prevent the world from blowing itself up. Yet there they were, embracing like brothers on world television at the simple act of a man jumping over a bar.

ALEX HALEY

January 1977

Interviewer: Murray Fisher

This is, hands down, the magazine's sentimental favorite. As the first PLAYBOY interviewer, and the man who conducted interviews with the two most significant black leaders of the Sixties—Martin Luther King, Jr., and Malcolm X—it was not only fitting but ironic that Haley should be the first (and so far, the only) interviewer to become a *subject*. Even more appropriate is the fact that G. Barry Golson asked Murray Fisher to conduct the interview. The reader will recall that Fisher was the editor who originated the Playboy Interview, and was thus Haley's boss and Golson's predecessor.

One reason among several that *Roots* became the phenomenon that it did in 1977 was Haley's personality and his ability as a storyteller. Beyond his writing and research abilities, Haley could sit back and talk—in the same spirit of oral-history tradition as his ancestors possessed—about the people from Africa who were brought to America. It was this ability to paint word pictures aloud—in small pieces on television, in longer versions on the lecture circuit, and at a full and definite length in this PLAYBOY interview—that predisposed an entire nation to tune into the TV version of *Roots*.

As for Fisher, he had collaborated for so long and so intimately with his old friend that one day Golson approached him as he was transcribing his Haley tapes in a PLAYBOY office. At one point, Fisher turned off the tape and continued typing for a minute or two. Golson glanced over Fisher's shoulder and saw that it was a particularly moving moment in Haley's description of his journey to Africa. Golson decided to play fact checker: "Are those last couple of sentences of Alex's precisely accurate? I heard where the tape cut off and you went beyond it." Fisher cocked an eyebrow at Golson, switched on the tape recorder, and they listened as Haley's unmistakable voice pronounced the exact words Fisher had typed moments earlier.

If it weren't for the fact that it's a true story, Roots *might well be the Great American Novel. In the months since its publication, it has been compared to both* Moby Dick *and* War and Peace, *and at least one reviewer called it "among the most important books of the century." Doubleday, its publisher, ordered the largest print run ever for a hardcover book (two hundred thousand), which sold out in a matter of weeks, and there are indications it may become the first book in history to sell over one million copies in hardback—even before Dell brings out the paperback version.*

Its author, Alex Haley, will undoubtedly become a household name later this month, when ABC-TV broadcasts the first episode of a twelve-hour series based on Roots, *making it the longest and most expensive (six million dollars) dramatic television production ever aired. Now fifty-five and living modestly in Los Angeles, Haley is in the midst of a mammoth publicity tour of his book, but in the past several months he found time for a series of conversations with a man who also has a special place in both* PLAYBOY*'s and Haley's history. He is Murray Fisher, former assistant managing editor of this magazine, who assigned Haley the first Playboy Interview and shaped the format of the feature. It was both their professional relationship and their personal friendship that led Haley to ask Fisher to be his editor on* Roots, *a task that has occupied no small amount of Fisher's own time over the twelve-year period it took Haley to write the book. Now a contributing editor to* PLAYBOY, *Fisher conducted this interview with his old friend and colleague as "a labor of love." It is Haley's story, but one that Fisher knows almost as well as his own. His report:*

"In the 12 years since Alex had asked me to help him edit Roots, *we'd met to work on it in New York, Chicago, Los Angeles, Miami, San Francisco, New Orleans, the West Indies—just about everywhere but the place it all began: Henning, his home town in rural Tennessee, where he'd first heard the stories as a five-year-old on his grandmother's front porch. Now, at last, the book was published, and he had embarked on a promotion tour that included—among its forty-nine interviews and public appearances in twenty-nine cities in thirty days—a half-day stop in Henning to film a television documentary of the prodigal son's return to his 'roots.' He invited me to join him there. 'Where will I find you?' I asked. 'We'll be moving around town. Just ask the first person you see.'*

"He wasn't hard to find. On the lawn in front of a small white frame house were a crowd of people, cables, cameras and parked cars, and at the center stood Alex, surrounded by interviewers peppering him with questions while the camera crew prepared to shoot him walking up the path to the front door for the third time, each from a different angle. 'Some homecoming,' I said when we were out of earshot. 'I know,' he said. 'It's been just Grandma's house all my life, and now with all those lights and those reporters, suddenly it's a media event. But I guess I'll have to get used to that kind of thing. Now that the book is out, I'm beginning to realize that the stories I heard from Grandma—sitting in that very rocker right up there on the porch—don't really belong to me anymore. So I've decided to keep that chair; next time you come to my house, it'll be on my front porch.'

"In 1873, soon after Alex' ancestors had arrived in Henning by wagon train from the plantation in North Carolina where they had lived as slaves, most of them had become founders of the New Hope Colored Methodist Episcopal Church—where the documentary's final scene was shot that night at a special service held in honor of the town's most celebrated citizen.

"It was recently rebuilt in the gleaming white architectural style of a suburban

corporate headquarters, and waiting for him inside the new church, dressed in its Sunday best, bathed in the brilliance of quartz movie lights, sat the entire congregation, filling every pew.

"Glad to be there, but feeling a little out of place—though perhaps less so than the jeaned and bearded film crew from L.A.—I slipped in and found a seat in the back. A moment later, the doors opened and Alex started walking down the aisle toward the pulpit, followed by his younger brothers George and Julius, who had been invited by the TV people to make it a 'family reunion.'

"A black boy of about ten in the row ahead, staring at Alex with shining eyes, asked, 'Is that him*?' He didn't have to wait long for an answer; later, everyone in that church was giving him a standing ovation. The cameras, of course, were rolling. Looking a little sheepish, Alex sat down on a bench behind the pulpit beside his brothers, and Fred Montgomery, a deacon of the church, an alderman on the town council and a lifelong friend of Alex', led the purple-gowned choir and the congregation in a rousing spiritual. Then a white aide to Henning's mayor got up to say a few words about the pride everyone in the community took in its native son.*

"Then, standing nervously with one arm on the piano for support, a teenage girl, obviously her high school's valedictorian, recited tremulously a short speech she had not only memorized but undoubtedly written herself. By the time she got to the end, she was looking at the audience rather than the floor, and she said loudly and firmly, 'What Mr. Haley has done for us—and for the world—will remain eternal.'

"The congregation was on its feet again, and it was Alex' turn to speak. In that deep, down-home baritone he can pour on like honey over biscuits, he told them about his search for roots, 'a story that began right here in Henning just two blocks from where I stand.' It was a shorter, but more personal version of the dramatic and deeply moving speech that's made him one of the most popular speakers on the lecture circuit for the past ten years—a speech he's made so often that passages from it have become almost a narrative litany of oral history. Parts of it even turned up in his answers to my questions. But there in that Henning pulpit, he added something new: an obviously heartfelt tribute to his home town.

" 'It's not a pretty place,' he said. 'There's nothing very special about it. But to me it's a symbol of small-town America, the birthplace of those old-fashioned virtues that are our deepest strengths as a nation—like compassion for your fellow man: Even to this day, there isn't a door in Henning where somebody cold or hungry would get turned away. Values like respect for your elders—needing them, caring for them, listening to them; they've got a lot to teach us all.'

"There's no question that Alex had missed his calling as a fundamentalist preacher; or maybe he hasn't. Every few sentences were interrupted with outcries of 'Say it!' and 'Amen.' And when he was finished, people were weeping, cheering, applauding, rushing up to touch him, shake his hand, gush out their thanks.

"He couldn't afford to be late for a speech to five thousand teachers later that night in Memphis. But he's constitutionally incapable of brushing people off, and it was half an hour before he could make it to the door. Dazed with exhaustion after two weeks in a different city every night, he lapsed into silence and sat with his eyes closed almost all the way to the Mid-South Coliseum. Arriving just in time to be rushed onstage, somehow he managed to crank himself up into delivering another rafter ringer; and the crowd went wild again.

"He couldn't get back to his hotel until three A.M.; his plane was leaving at 7:30. As

he trudged with me down the hall to his room, he was nearly out on his feet. 'If only they wouldn't come at me so,' he said. We went on to talk about that for a few minutes more, while he sat on the edge of his bed and pulled off his shoes and socks, and then I said good night. Though this conversation was the last in the twenty hours of taping sessions we'd recorded, I decided to make it our first exchange in the interview—for it seemed to foreshadow a new life for Alex that promised not only wealth and fame but elevation, in some mysterious way, to the mythic stature of a spiritual leader.

"The following personal opinion may compromise my credibility as a journalist, but frankly, I value more highly my credibility as a friend of Alex Haley's for fifteen years. And the simple fact is that I consider him the finest and most decent man I've ever known. If we have to have a spiritual leader, we could do a whole lot worse."

PLAYBOY: The reaction you've evoked in public appearances since the publication of *Roots* has often been almost worshipful. How does that make you feel?

HALEY: It disturbs me. My most devout hope was to write a book that would move people, and apparently I've succeeded. But I truly feel that I was merely a conduit for a story that was *intended* to be told, and I know that it's the story I tell, not *me*, that they're responding to. If only that response weren't so intense. A few weeks ago, I was talking with friends at a small party in Los Angeles, when a young black woman I'd never seen before came rushing up to me, grabbed my hand and fell to her knees, bubbling her gratitude. All I could think of to do was tell her to *stop* it and pull her to her feet. Things like that aren't just embarrassing: they're unsettling. She just didn't understand that what *Roots* is saying to black people, especially—is that once you find out who you really are, you don't have to go down on your knees to *anyone* anymore. If people are starting to look at me like I'm some kind of Gandhi, all I can say is: I'm not qualified for the job; and even if I were, I wouldn't want it. All I did was write a book, and I'm the same guy now that I was before I wrote it.

PLAYBOY: But that book has become a runaway best-seller and on January 30, it will debut in an unprecedented twelve-hour television adaptation for which a nightly audience of at least fifty million is being predicted. You may be the same guy you were before, but don't you think all this is bound to change your *life?*

HALEY: It already *has*. Hell, I feel like I'm living somebody *else's* life. After fifteen years as a journalist, I'd gotten used to a certain life-style; hustling for a buck, waiting for the phone to ring with an assignment, wangling my way past secretaries to interview their bosses. Now, all of a sudden, I'm going to be paying someone as much to handle my finances as I used to *make* in a year. The phone is ringing off the wall with invitations, such as to join assorted dignitaries for lunch at the State Department and dinner at the White House, queries from writers for magazines that used to reject my stuff, wanting to do stories on *me;* and now PLAYBOY is making me its first interviewer ever to be interviewed by the magazine. And, just to wrap up the irony, I'm being interviewed by you, the guy who used to be my editor at the magazine.

PLAYBOY: Does that bother you?

HALEY: After all those years at the mercy of your blue pencil, I'm looking forward to it. The only trouble is, by this time we know each other so well that I know what you're going to ask before you open your mouth, and you know what I'm going to say before I open mine. So why don't we save ourselves the trouble of talking? I'll write your questions, you write my answers and we'll just *mail it* in.

PLAYBOY: Good idea. But just for the sake of appearances, why don't we go through the motions of taping an actual conversation?
HALEY: Just as long as you promise not to ask leading questions. I've *heard* about you PLAYBOY interviewers.
PLAYBOY: We'll give you the same consideration you always offered people when *you* were doing interviews.
HALEY: In that case, forget the whole thing.
PLAYBOY: Fine, just as soon as we finish the interview. You were talking about what success has done to your life.
HALEY: Well, I'm being inundated with requests to appear on television shows hosted by stars whose *publicists* never used to return my calls, with letters from universities asking me to accept honorary degrees and address their graduating classes. I find myself being eased into plush leather armchairs and offered cigars in executive sanctum sanctorums that I couldn't have broken into with TNT a few years ago. My daily calendar, where I used to scrawl my grocery lists, is blocked out from breakfast to bedtime for meetings with people who want my name, my permission, my support, my endorsement, my commitment, my involvement and especially *money*—to underwrite everything from stuff like *Roots* T-shirts and Afro-American tour groups to worthwhile social causes and promising television and movie projects, some of which I plan to pursue as head of my own production company later this year.
PLAYBOY: You're not complaining, are you?
HALEY: I'm having the time of my life. I've never felt happier, younger, stronger, more energetic and alive than I do today—because I set for myself a task that seemed impossible, and yet somehow I completed it. It took twelve years, but I feel it was worth every moment of it, because *Roots* tells a story that's needed to be told for two hundred years. That was reward enough for undertaking it, but I'm happy to say that *Roots* is going to earn me something far more tangible, as well as precious: financial independence.

After being harassed by debt for more years than I care to remember, I now feel beyond a reasonable doubt that I will never have to waste another moment worrying about rent, taxes, alimony, the lot of it. I mean, it's funny that at this very moment, while I'm here talking to you, I'm sitting and folding my own laundry. But by the time this interview appears, I'll finally be in a position to buy what I've always longed for—the *time* to spend on things I care about that I used to have to spend on things I *didn't* care about.
PLAYBOY: Do you think success may spoil—or stifle—Alex Haley?
HALEY: I pray not. Not as long as I remember who I am and where I came from. Every time I catch myself getting annoyed when I have to wait outside some studio for a while because the limousine is late, every time I pick up the phone in some fancy hotel to order a steak from room service rather than run down to the coffee shop for a hamburger, which I'd actually enjoy just as much, I think about Miss Scrap Green and Fred Montgomery and all the other good people I grew up with back in Henning, Tennessee, and I wonder what they'd say if they could see me now. And I'm glad they can't. Because their values are still my values, and they always will be. No matter where I go or what I do with my life, no matter how many books I write or movies I produce, I'll always be "Miz Haley's boy" to them, and that's the way it ought to be.

A while ago, just after I had been interviewed by a television host who introduced me as "the author of one of the great literary works of our time," I went home to visit the family and as I was walking down the street one morning, I met this old man—the ageless kind every small town has—going the other way. " 'Mornin', sir," I said. You just don't pass anyone in a small town without saying hello. "How do," he replied, stopping and squinting at me. "Ain't you Miz Haley's boy?" "Yes, sir," I said. "Ain't seen you aroun' for a while," he said. "What you doin' with yourself nowadays?" "I'm a writer." "What you write?" "Books." "How you do that?" "Well, it's kind of hard to explain." "Write somethin' for me, then." "I'm afraid it doesn't work quite that way." He considered that for a while, and then he said, "Well, if you was to tell me you was a lightnin' bug, I'd 'spect you to light up."

Ever since then, whenever I've been tempted to feel important—and there've been a few times—I just remember that old man. Henning is what keeps me honest. It's my roots, and those roots run deep—from my Grandma Cynthia's porch all the way back to Africa.

PLAYBOY: Wasn't that the porch where your grandmother told you the stories about your family that led to the writing of your book?

HALEY: Yes, it was. Whenever I go home to visit Henning, I always go over to the old house and sit on that porch for a while. The new owners don't seem to mind. Grandma's long gone, of course, but while I'm sitting there—in the same white wicker chair she used to rock on while she talked—I remember all the stories she told as if it were yesterday.

PLAYBOY: How long ago *was* it?

HALEY: About half a century now. The earliest I can remember hearing them was a year or so after my grandfather Will Palmer died, when I was around five. Grandma had lived for that man ever since the day they'd met thirty-eight years before, and when he died, something inside her went along with him. She'd always been a lively woman, but from then on, she took to sitting out on the front porch and just rocking for hours at a time. Since my mother was off teaching school and my father had taken over Grandpa's lumber mill, I spent most of my time alone at home with Grandma.

But after a few months, she began inviting various sisters, nieces and cousins around her age—Aunt Plus, Aunt Viney, Aunt Liz, Aunt Till, Cousin Georgia and a few others—to come and keep her company. They'd arrive from exotic places like Dyersburg, which was all of twenty-five miles away; Inkster, Michigan; St. Louis; even Kansas City; and they'd stay for a few weeks, sometimes the whole summer, often five or six of them at a time, cooking, knitting, talking and puttering their way through the day. Every night, after the supper dishes had been washed, just around dusk, as the lightning bugs were beginning to flick on and off above the honeysuckle vines, they'd all drift out to the porch and settle down in their favorite rockers—with me scrunched up on the floor behind Grandma's—and they'd pick up where they left off the night before, with her taking the lead, telling stories about the family.

PLAYBOY: Tell *us* a few.

HALEY: They were just bits and pieces, weaving back and forth through the years. Some were from Grandma's own life and Grandpa Will's—how the leading white businessmen of Henning, in a historic decision, had turned ownership of the town's only lumber company over to him when its drunken white owner had brought it to the brink of bankruptcy, and how he had gone on to become one of the town's most respected citizens. Only a generation before, they recalled, the same town's white business community had forbidden Grandma's father, Tom Murray, to open a blacksmith shop, so he'd built up a thriving trade with a rolling shop—an anvil and a forge on a wagon—which he drove from farm to farm.

After emancipation, it had been Tom who led the family—his half-Cherokee wife, Irene, and their eight children, his seven brothers and sisters and *their* children—across the Appalachians in a wagon train from "the Murray plantation" in Alamance County, North Carolina, all the way to Henning. They'd been lured to this backwoods settlement in western Tennessee, Tom had said, by his father, George, who'd returned from his travels as a freedman with tales of a "promised land" with soil so rich that "if you plant a pig's tail, a hog'll grow." Proud of his ancestry, George had kept alive the stories of the family he'd heard from his mother, Kizzy, by repeating them as a ritual at the birth of each new child by his wife, Matilda. But he was hardly a dutiful father and he earned a justified reputation as a ladies' man—and as a high-rolling gambler on the fighting cocks he had trained since boyhood for his massa, Tom Lea.

PLAYBOY: Hence his nickname, "Chicken George"?

HALEY: Which he carried with him proudly to his death, along with a derby hat and a rakish green scarf, which he wore like a trademark. Time and again there on the porch, I heard how Massa Lea had finally lost almost everything he owned in a wager to an English nobleman, who took Chicken George off to England as his gamecock trainer for three years. When he left, it seems that Massa Lea lost more than a cockfighter. When George was a boy, Kizzy had told him that he'd been sired by Massa Lea, who had raped her on the night of her arrival at the Lea plantation. At sixteen, she'd been sold away from her parents for helping a boy escape from the plantation of Dr. William Waller in Spotsylvania County, Virginia, where she had been born and raised. Her mother, Kizzy told young George, was the big-house cook, Bell. And her father—the furthest-back person anyone in the family ever spoke of—was a man they called the African.

PLAYBOY: Did they know any more than that about him?

HALEY: They said he had been brought across the ocean to a place they called Naplis, that he had tried four times to escape from the plantation of his first owner, Massa John Waller, and that after his fourth attempt, he was offered the choice of castration or having a foot cut off. Because he chose the foot, said Grandma, "I'm here to tell about it." The African told Kizzy that the massa's brother, Dr. William Waller, had bought him, nursed him back to health, put him to work in his garden and later had him serve as his buggy driver. Though John Waller had named him Toby, the woman said the African had always angrily insisted that the other slaves call him by his real name, which they pronounced "Kin-tay."

As Kizzy grew up, according to the old ladies on the porch, Kin-tay taught her words from his own language. He called a guitar a *ko*, for example, and as they rode in the buggy past the Mattaponi River near the plantation, he'd point and say something that sounded like *Kamby Bolongo*. The thing Kizzy remembered most vividly—and passed on to Chicken George, who later told *his* children, and so on down to me—was that when Kin-tay was a boy of about seventeen "rains"—his word for years—he had been out in the forest, not far from his village in Africa, chopping wood to make a drum, when four men had set upon him, beaten him senseless and marched him in chains to the ship in which he was taken to America and sold into slavery.

PLAYBOY: Did those stories make much of an impression on you at the time?

HALEY: I loved them, but I didn't *live* them, as Grandma did. With Grandpa gone, those stories were the most important thing in her life and she told and retold them—to the point where she and my mother actually had words about it. "I'm sick of all that old-timy stuff!" Momma would exclaim. "Why don't you quit talking about it all the time?" And Grandma would say, "Well, if you don't care where you come from, *I* do!" And they might not speak for two or three days.

PLAYBOY: Why didn't your mother want to hear the stories?

HALEY: She was the first person in our family who ever went to college. You see it in every poor immigrant group that's come to this country; the first thing its members want to do as they begin to make it is to forget their homeland—its traditions and its culture—and to fit in with the new one. Momma wanted nothin' to do with no Africans, and even less with slaves; she was embarrassed by all that. But to a little boy like me, it was just a bunch of stories, like the biblical parables I heard every week in Sunday school at the New Hope Methodist Church. They were more exciting, of course, because some of the people in them were sitting right there on the porch. But most of the family they talked about—Tom Murray, Chicken George, Kizzy, the African—were just characters to me, like Jonah, Pharaoh, David and Goliath, Adam and Eve.

PLAYBOY: When did the stories begin to mean something more to you?

HALEY: It took about thirty years. I had grown up and gone to college for two years and then joined the coast guard as a mess boy not long before World War Two broke out. During the long months at sea, I passed the time by writing letters to everyone I knew—maybe forty a week—and after a while, I caught the bug, and started writing for *publication*; or tried to. I spent eight years writing some part of every single day before making my first sale to a magazine. When I finally retired—chief journalist—after twenty years, at thirty-seven, I moved to Greenwhich Village, where I planned to make it as a free-lance journalist; I guess I thought I'd pick it up by osmosis, simply by *living* in that writers' colony. But it didn't come quite that easy. One day, I was down to exactly eighteen cents and two cans of sardines when a friend called me with the offer of a modest but steady job in the civil service. I took a deep breath and turned him down. The very next day, a small check arrived in the mail from some magazine, and I managed to hang on long enough to begin selling regularly. Those two sardine cans and that eighteen cents, by the way, are framed and hanging on my wall even to this day, as a reminder of how close I came to the end of the line. Anyway, it was around that time that you assigned me to conduct an interview for PLAYBOY.

PLAYBOY: That was the very first interview we published, in September of 1962.

HALEY: With Miles Davis. Which taught me a little bit about jazz as well as journalism. But my association with Malcolm X, the second interview you assigned to me, led to my collaboration with him on my first book, *The Autobiography of Malcolm X*. I remember his telling me very calmly, as he read the finished manuscript two years later, that he'd never live to see it published—and he was right.

In a way, I have PLAYBOY to thank for setting my second book, *Roots*, into motion, too. It was soon after the Malcolm book came out, and you asked me to interview Julie Christie, who was making a movie in London. While I was there, waiting for an appointment—which never came about, as you know—I kept myself busy taking guided tours of the city. One of them stopped at the British Museum, where I found something I'd heard about only vaguely but which now entranced me: the Rosetta Stone. I immediately read up on it and learned that it had been found in the Nile delta in 1799, inscribed with three texts: one in Greek, the second in a then-unknown set of characters, the third in ancient Egyptian hieroglyphics, which it had been assumed no one would ever be able to decipher. But in a superhuman feat of scholarship, a

Frenchman named Jean Champollion had matched the two unknown texts, character for character, with the Greek text and proved that all three were the same, thus cracking the code and opening up to the world much of mankind's earliest history, which had been recorded in—and hidden behind—the mystery of those hieroglyphics.

PLAYBOY: Why did all that fascinate you so?

HALEY: I wasn't sure. I felt that key which had unlocked a door to the past had some special significance for me, but I didn't realize what it was until I was on the plane returning to the U.S. In the stories Grandma and the others had told me, there were fragments of words from an unknown tongue spoken by the African who said his name was Kin-tay, called a guitar a *ko* and a river *Kamby Bolongo.* They were mostly sharp, angular sounds with K predominating. Undoubtedly, they had undergone some changes in pronunciation as they had been passed down across the generations, but it seemed to me that they had to be phonetic snatches of the actual language spoken by my ancestor and that if I could find out what that language was, I might be able to unlock the door to my *own* past.

When I got home, I knew there was somebody I had to see. Of all the old ladies from the porch in Henning, only one was still alive: Cousin Georgia, who had been twenty-odd years younger than the others. She was in her eighties now and living with her son, Floyd, and daughter, Bea, in Kansas City, Kansas. I hadn't seen her in several years and she was ailing and bedridden, but the moment I mentioned my interest in the family stories, she jerked upright and started prattling away: "Yeah, boy, dat African say a guitar a *ko* and he call a river de *Kamby Bolongo* an' he was out choppin' wood, intendin' to make hisself a drum when dey cotched 'im." It was like echoes of the stories I'd heard during my boyhood.

When I told her that I wanted to see if I could find out where Kin-tay came from, which might reveal the identity of our ancestral tribe, she became so excited that Floyd, Bea and I had trouble calming her down. And as I left, she told me something that galvanized me—something that has driven and sustained me ever since: "Boy, yo' sweet granma and all of 'em—dey up dere, watchin'. So you go do what you got to do."

PLAYBOY: What *did* you do?

HALEY: I soon discovered what I already feared: that because there was little tradition of family continuity among blacks, there were very sparse genealogical records of black families—certainly none of the kind that can enable some white families to trace their ancestors as far back as the *Mayflower* and across the Atlantic to wherever they came from. In the first place, newly arrived Africans were divested of their born names and given slave names—as Kin-tay had been renamed Toby. Thus were they robbed of their past, beginning a process of psychic dehumanization that was compounded with the frequent breeding of slaves like livestock and the sale of their offspring—often before birth. It was not uncommon for a slave to grow up without knowing his own father. Not many got to know their grandparents. For family stories to go back, as ours did, to great-great-great-great-grandparents was almost unheard of. But because there were no established avenues for corroborating those stories, I had to kind of start from scratch.

PLAYBOY: Which was where?

HALEY: Well, one day, while I was in Washington, D.C., on a magazine assignment, I went to the National Archives. Remembering that Grandma had said she was born on the Murray plantation in Alamance County, North Carolina, and figuring that the family had to have lived there around the time of the Civil War, I asked a black attendant for the census records of that county for the year 1870. They were on microfilm, and I threaded the first roll through the machine and began to turn the handle. There before me were columns of names in old-fashioned script, where the Ss look like Fs, and those people—head of household, wife, children, grandparents—began to parade past. The lists seemed endless, and by the end of the second roll, my curiosity was rapidly diminishing. The thought that I'd ever run across a familiar name among so many countless thousands seemed hopeless and I got up to leave. I gives me the quivers to think how, if I *had* left, none of this would ever have happened.

But as I was walking out, I passed through the genealogical-search room and I happened to notice that, unlike the reading rooms of most libraries, where people are sitting back relaxed and comfortable, everyone there was bent intently over old documents, some with magnifying glasses. And the thought came into my head: *These* people are all here trying to find out who they *are*. I turned around and went back to the microfilm room and picked up where I had left off. Some rolls later, as I was slowly turning the crank, I suddenly found myself looking down at the name "Murray, Tom, Blacksmith, Black," and beneath that the name "Murray, Irene, Housewife, Black," and beneath them the names of their children, Maria Jane, Ellen, Viney, Matilda and Elizabeth. Matilda was Aunt Till from Dyersburg, Elizabeth was Aunt Liz; I'd eaten her biscuits for years. They were Grandma's older sisters; she hadn't been born yet. I was staggered. To see those names right there in an official document in the same building that houses the U.S. Constitution somehow made it very real—and made it *matter* in a way it never had before. That thought gripped me—and still does. I had stumbled upon incontrovertible evidence that I, my family, we black people, indeed, did have a past, a heritage; it just wasn't very well documented.

PLAYBOY: So that challenged you to keep going?

HALEY: It surely did. Between magazine assignments, I spent the next few months commuting to Washington from New York, searching in the National Archives and the Library of Congress for further confirmation of the family story, and slowly I found it. In bits and pieces. In time, I discovered that those old ladies on the porch had been incredibly accurate; they hadn't known it, but they were oral historians of the highest order. Piece by piece, I began to fit it all together about everyone in the family—except for the African. There was simply nothing to be found anywhere about a slave named Kin-tay, and even if I could find some record of him under the name Toby, that wouldn't help me find out where he came from. Slave traders were interested in the value of their property, not in its origin. I knew that those shreds of African words passed down by the African would have to be the key. If I had known then what I know now—that maybe one thousand tribal tongues are spoken in Africa—I would have given up on the spot. But since I didn't know the odds against me, I forged blindly on.

PLAYBOY: In what direction?

HALEY: Well, it seemed logical to seek help from as wide a range of Africans as I could find, so I began to hang around the lobby of the UN Building in New York around quitting time. It wasn't hard to spot the Africans. In the course of two weeks, I managed to buttonhole maybe two dozen of them. Everyone listened to me for a moment—and then took off. I couldn't blame them much; what kind of impression could I make trying to blurt out some alleged African sounds in a Tennessee accent—sounds that very possibly might have been distorted beyond recognition across the two hundred years they had taken to reach me?

Finally, I told my problem to a lifelong friend from Henning, George Sims, who happens to be a master researcher. He promptly went into the Library of Congress and shortly brought to me a list of people recognized for their knowledge of African linguistics. The credentials of one of them, a Belgian Ph.D. named Jan Vansina, impressed me so much that I called him for an appointment at the University of Wisconsin, where he was teaching. He had written a book, *La Tradition Orale*, based on research conducted while he was living in African villages. I thought he might be just the man to help me, if anyone could. And he gave me an appointment to meet with him in Madison.

Dr. Vansina listened intently as I told him my story—every syllable of the sounds, everything else I could remember, buttressed by what Cousin Georgia had recently told me. He was particularly interested in how the sounds were passed along from one generation to the next. I told him there had always been one person in each generation who was keeper of the story: First it was Kin-tay, then Kizzy, then George, then Tom, then my grandma Cynthia and, finally, me. When I was through talking, he said he wanted to sleep on it and invited me to spend the night.

PLAYBOY: Did you get any sleep?

HALEY: Not much. I didn't think he would have asked me to stay unless he felt some good reason for it. The next morning at the breakfast table, he said to me, with a very serious expression on his face: "The ramifications of the phonetic sounds preserved down across your family's generations could be immense." My heart all but stopped. He said he had consulted by telephone with one of his colleagues, an eminent Africanist, Dr. Philip Curtin, who concurred with him that the sounds I'd conveyed were in the tongue spoken by the Mandinka. or Mandingo, people. The word *ko*, for example, he said, probably referred to the *kora*, one of the Mandinkas' oldest stringed instruments. But the phrase *Kamby Bolongo* was what clinched it. Without question, he said, in Mandinka, the word *bolongo* meant a large, moving stream, such as a river, and preceded by *Kamby*, it probably referred to the Gambia River. Almost certainly, my African ancestor had been from the Gambia. I'd never heard of it.

PLAYBOY: Did you say so?

HALEY: I was too excited to hide my ignorance; so I asked and he showed it to me on a map—a small, narrow country about midway on the west coast of Africa, bordered on three sides by Senegal and bisected by the Gambia River. I was determined to go there, preferably on the next plane; but I couldn't just pop up in Africa! I wouldn't know where to go, whom to talk to or how to ask. I knew I had to find someone who knew more than I did about the Gambia, which was almost literally nothing.

PLAYBOY: Another research job for Sims?

HALEY: I didn't have to ask him. As fate would have it, only a week or so later, I was asked to speak about my Malcolm X book at Utica College in upstate New York; it was my first paid lecture. I got one hundred dollars for it, which would be about one-tenth of my round-trip air fare to the Gambia. Afterward, talking with the professor who'd invited me to speak, I told him about my quest—and my plight—and he said he'd heard there was an outstanding student over at Hamilton College, about half an hour's drive away, who came from the Gambia. I drove up there and fairly snatched him from a class in economics. His name was Ebou Manga and he was the

blackest human being I had ever seen. He seemed reservedly amused as I poured out my story in a rush of words, but when I asked him to accompany me to the Gambia—at my expense—his fact lit up and he said yes on the spot.
PLAYBOY: How did you intend to finance that expedition?
HALEY: I had no idea where I'd get the money for my *own* ticket, let alone his. But it fell into my lap like manna from heaven two weeks later, when you paid me for an interview. I'd already obtained a visa and the very next day, Ebou and I were off to Dakar, where we changed to a lighter plane and flew on to a small airfield in the Gambia. From there, we drove in a van the rest of the way along a rutted two-lane highway to the capital city of Banjul, which was then called Bathurst.

Ebou's father, Alhaji Malik Manga—they are a Moslem family—soon arranged for me to meet with a group of men who were knowledgeable about their country's history. So once again, I told my story. When I had finished, they seemed most interested in the name Kin-tay. "Our country's oldest villages," they told me, "tend to be named for the families that settled them centuries ago." And on a map, they pointed out a village called Kinte-Kundah and, nearby, another called Kinte-Kundah Janneh-Ya. The Kinte clan—of which my ancestor was undoubtedly a member, they said—was an old and well-known family in the Gambia, and they promised to do what they could to find a *griot* to help me with my search.
PLAYBOY: A *griot*?
HALEY: I cocked my ear at that one, too. They said *griots* were oral historians, almost living archives, men trained from boyhood to memorize, preserve and recite—on ceremonial occasions—the centuries-old histories of villages, of clans, of families, of great kings, holy men and heroes. Some, they said, were the keepers of certain family stories so long that they could talk for three days without ever repeating themselves. When I expressed astonishment, they reminded me that every living person goes back ancestrally to some time when there was no writing, when the only way that human knowledge got passed from one generation to the next had been from the mouths of the elders to the ears of the young. We in the West, they said, had become so dependent on "the crutch of print" that we had forgotten what the memory of man was capable of.
PLAYBOY: Did they find a *griot* for you?
HALEY: Yes, but it took months. I returned home to await developments—and to devour everything I could find to read about Africa. It embarrasses me to think how ignorant I was about the people and the culture of the earth's second-largest continent. Like most of us, black and white, I formed my impressions of Africa and of Africans mostly from *Tarzan* movies, *Jungle Jim* comics and occasional leafings through old copies of *National Geographic*. So from morning till evening, I pored over book after book about African history and culture, and every night, before I turned out the light, I studied a map of Africa I'd put beside my bed, memorizing the location of each country, its rivers and major cities. Finally, a letter arrived from the Gambia, which I almost tore open. My contacts there had found a *griot* who might be able to help me, and they'd put me in touch with him if I would return at my earliest convenience. Man, I went nearly wild with excitement—and then frustration. Where would I find the money? I was ready to work my way across as a cook on a freighter—that had been my job for several years on U.S. coast guard cutters—when a last resort occurred to me. I wrote to Mrs. DeWitt Wallace, cofounder with her husband of *Reader's Digest*. I had met her at a party several years before and she had said very

kind things about an article I'd written for them. Told me to get in touch with her if I ever needed help. I figured she was just being polite, but I had nothing to lose, so I wrote her a letter. To my astonishment, Mrs. Wallace arranged for me to meet with a group of *Digest* editors to see what they felt about my project. I talked passionately and nonstop for about three hours, as if my life depended on it, and in some strange way, I felt it did. They came through—with a three-hundred-dollar monthly stipened and "reasonable necessary travel expenses."

PLAYBOY: Sounds like a dangerously ambiguous phrase. They didn't know you very well, did they?

HALEY: I guess not. But they do now—and I think they've forgiven me. Anyway, two days later, I was back in Banjul, tape recorder and notebook in hand, chafing to get to the *griot* they'd found for me. "His name," they said, "is Kebba Kanji Fofana, and he is a *griot* of the Kinte clan." I was ready to have a fit. "Where is he?" I asked, I suppose expecting to find him waiting somewhere nearby, flanked by a PR man and an interpreter. They looked at me quizzically. "He's in Juffure, his village in the back country upriver," they replied. If I intended to see him, it soon became clear, I'd have to do something I'd never dreamed I'd be doing: organize a kind of modified *safari!*

PLAYBOY: The great black hunter?

HALEY: You go straight to hell. This was totally serious business! It took me three days of bargaining and endless African palaver to assemble everything and everyone I was assured I couldn't do without for the journey. By the time I'd hired a launch for the trip upriver, a lorry and a Land Rover to make the journey overland with provisions and a total of fourteen companions, including three interpreters and four musicians—

PLAYBOY: Musicians?

HALEY: I was told the old *griots* didn't like to talk without musicians playing in the background. Anyway, by the time I got all that together, I felt like Stanley setting out in search of Livingstone. I tried to imagine the reaction back at the *Digest* accounting department in Pleasantville when they saw *this* item on my expense account.

PLAYBOY: What did you find when you reached your destination?

HALEY: You've heard of the expression *peak experience?* That's what I had in Juffure. We put ashore at a little village called Albreda and set out across hot, lush savanna country, and finally we were approaching Juffure's bamboo fence, beyond a grove of trees. Little children playing outside ran in to announce our arrival, and by the time we entered the gate, everyone in the village—about seventy people, plus maybe half as many goats—had converged on us from mud huts. Among them was a small, wizened man in an off-white robe and a pillbox hat; somehow he looked important and I knew he was the *griot* we had come to see and hear.

The interpreters left our group to talk with him and the other villagers swarmed around me, three and four deep all around, and began to stare. For the first time in my life, every face I saw was *jet-black*. And the eyes of every one were raking me from head to toe. As my own eyes dropped in embarrassment, my glance happened to fall on my hands. I felt ashamed.

PLAYBOY: Why?

HALEY: It was the color of my skin—because I wasn't black. I was brown, the product of forced interbreeding under slavery; I felt impure among the pure. Finally, one of the interpreters came over and whispered in my ear, "They stare at you because they have never here seen a black American." They had been looking at me not as me,

Alex Haley, an individual, but as a symbol for them of a people—twenty-five million of us black people—whom they had never seen, a people who lived in a land beyond the ocean, as unknown to them as they were to us.

Just then, the old *griot* turned from the other interpreters, strode through the crowd and stopped in front of me, his eyes piercing into mine. Seeming to feel that I would understand his Mandinka, he looked straight at me as he spoke, then fell silent while the translation came: "We have been told by the forefathers that there are many of us from this place who are in exile in that place called America. . . ." With that, he sat down on a stool across from me, the people gathered round, and he began to recite the ancestral history of the Kinte clan. This was a state occasion, an extremely formal and stylized ritual that dated back unchanged far into antiquity. As he spoke, he leaned forward, his body rigid, and the words would issue from deep within him, like a solid thing, as if carved in stone. After two or three sentences, he would stop, sit back—his eyes seeming opaque, his expression unreadable—and wait for the translation. Then, as if summoning all his strength, he'd lean forward and begin again.

PLAYBOY: Were you tape-recording all this?

HALEY: Indeed, I was, along with the background chatter of monkeys, parrots, goats, chickens, children, and the like. But you could hear him droning through it all. Even in translation, it sounded much like Biblical recitation: So-and-so took unto himself the wife So-and-so and by her he begat . . . and begat. . . . He was talking about people and events 150 or 200 years ago—who married whom, their children in their order of birth, then whom those children married and *their* children, and so on.

PLAYBOY: How long did that go on?

HALEY: For about two hours, there under a broiling sun, bathed in sweat, buzzing with flies. I'll just sum his story up as briefly as I can. The Kinte clan, the *griot* said, began back in the 1500s in a land called Old Mali. After many years, a branch of the clan moved to Mauretania and, from there, one son, Kairaba Kunte Kinte, a Marabout—or holy man of the Moslem faith—traveled south to the Gambia, where he eventually settled in the village of Juffure. There he took his first wife, a Mandinka maiden named Sireng, by whom he begat two sons, Janneh and Saloum. He then took a second wife, Yaisa, by whom he begat a third son, Omoro. When Omoro had thirty rains, he took a wife named Binta Kebba, by whom he begat four sons, named Kunta, Lamin, Suwadu and Madi. Here the *griot* added one of the many time-fixing references in the narrative that is how they identify the date of events: "It was about the time the king's soldiers came. . . ." Then, as he had done perhaps fifty times earlier in the course of his monologue, he added a salient biographical detail about one of the people he was discussing: "The eldest of these four sons, Kunta, went away from this village to chop wood—and he was never seen again."

Well, I sat there feeling as if I were carved of rock. What that old man in back-country Africa had just uttered dovetailed with the very words my grandmother had always spoken during my boyhood on a porch in Tennessee, telling a story she had heard from her father, George, who had heard it from his mother, Kizzy, who had been told by her father, the man who called himself Kin-tay: that he had been out, not far from his village, chopping wood, intending to make himself a drum, when he had been set upon by four men and kidnapped into slavery.

PLAYBOY: How did you respond?

HALEY: I must have looked as if lighnting had struck me, because the *griot* stopped midsentence and leaned toward me with concern and bewilderment. Somehow, from my duffel bag, I managed to pull out the notebook in which I had recorded that very passage of the family story, as Cousin Georgia had retold it to me at her bedside in Kansas City. When the interpreter read what was written there, it was all he could do to control himself sufficiently to translate it. The *griot's* eyes shot wide and he leaped up, exclaiming loudly to the others while jabbing at my notebook with his forefinger. A shock wave seemed to go through the crowd, and without an order being given, every one of those seventy people—man, woman and child—formed a giant human ring around me and began chanting rhythmically, moving counterclockwise, lifting their knees high, stamping up reddish puffs of dust. Then a woman holding a baby to her breast burst from the circle and came charging toward me, scowling fiercely, and thrust her child toward me almost roughly in a gesture that said, "Take it!" No sooner had I clasped it to my chest than she snatched it away and another woman was pushing *her* baby into my arms, followed by another and another—until, in a couple of minutes, I'd say I had embraced a dozen babies.

PLAYBOY: What did all that mean?

HALEY: I had no idea. I was too dazed to do anything but stand there. It wasn't until a year later that I was told by Dr. Jerome Bruner at Harvard, ironically enough, that I had been participating in one of the oldest ceremonies of humankind, the laying on of hands. They were telling me in their way, he said, "Through this flesh, which is us, we are you and you are us."

I don't remember much of what happened after that—except for a photo that was taken of me standing with several of my sixth cousins, direct lineal descendants of Kunta Kinte's younger brothers. And when we left a few hours later by Land Rover, my mind was still numb. As we careened down the pitted back-country road toward Banjul—dust pluming up behind us—I saw nothing, heard nothing, felt nothing around me. But in my mind's eye, from the journals I had been reading, I began to envision, almost as if it were a film, how my great-great-great-great-grandfather—and the ancestors of every single black alive—had been enslaved. I could hear their screams in the night, see the flames from torches licking at their thatch-roofed huts, hear their screams as they dashed outside into a rain of clubs and cutlasses wielded not only by white slave traders but also by traitorous fellow Africans who were in the hire of the whites. I could smell the blood and sweat as the survivors were linked neck to neck by thongs into processions—called coffles—which often were a mile in length before they reached the beach areas near where the slave ships waited.

I seemed to feel their horror as they were branded, greased, shaved, then lashed and dragged, screaming, clawing at the beach, biting up mouthfuls of sand, in their desperation for one last hold on the land that had been their home. I saw them thrown like firewood into longboats and rowed out to the waiting slave ships, shoved and beaten down into stinking holds and chained onto rough wooden shelves. I heard their moans as the ships weighed anchor and they began to move down the river toward the sea.

My mind was still reeling with this nightmare vision when we came in sight of a village up ahead. The driver slowed down as we drew closer, for there were hundreds of people waiting, and every one of them waving and shouting.

PLAYBOY: What was going on?

HALEY: Somehow, word had reached them of what had happened back in Juffure. As the Land Rover crept through the throng, their cacophony of shouting engulfed us. And the face of everyone—from robed elders to naked little boys to wrinkled old crones with toothless gums and breasts like belt straps—was wreathed in a smile. I found myself standing up and smiling and waving back: but it wasn't until we were about halfway through the village that I understood what it was they were all chanting: "Meester Kinte! Meester Kinte!"

Let me tell you something: I've never been considered overly emotional, but when I heard what those people were shouting, I threw my hands in front of my face and started to sob like I hadn't done since I was a baby.

I was weeping in grief—not only for the anguish of the ancestor I embodied for those cheering Africans but also for the suffering of his descendants down through the generations. But I was also weeping in joy, for I felt that through me, his great-great-great-great-grandson, Kunta Kinte had finally come home. And because of him—his courage, his pride, and the tenacity of his determination to keep alive the memory and the meaning of his roots as a free man in his own land—all of us who had come after him had finally rediscovered who we were.

PLAYBOY: Seems like a good subject for a book.

HALEY: That's right, wise guy. When I arrived in New York, I went to Doubleday and told them that every black American goes back ancestrally to someone who was taken, as Kunta was, from some village, chained in the hold of some stinking ship, sold onto some plantation to live out his years in slavery—and had children whose children's children's children are still struggling for freedom. So the story of any one of us is really the saga of us all. I told them I wanted to write that story in a book called *Roots*. They told me to go ahead.

PLAYBOY: Did you visit Cousin Georgia to tell her the news?

HALEY: Listen, let me tell you one of the major reasons why I feel that this book *Roots* was simply meant to be. Just before leaving on that second trip to Africa, I had visited old Cousin Georgia, who was in the hospital, recovering from a stroke, and in her dramatic, deeply religious way, she'd exclaimed to me as I prepared to leave: "Boy, I'm jes' a soldier on God's battlefield, an' I been *hit!* But you go on!" But now, when I came off the plane and telephoned my brother George, he interrupted my greeting to tell me that while I was gone, Cousin Georgia had died—at the age of eighty-three. Later, after making time-zone calculations, I realized that she had passed away literally within the very *hour* of my arrival in Juffure. I truly believe that as the last survivor of those ladies who had told the family story on that porch in Henning, it had been Cousin Georgia's job to oversee me into our ancestral village—and then she'd joined the others up there watchin'.

PLAYBOY: Did that inspire you to go on?

HALEY: That, combined with the mystical nature of my entire experience in the Gambia, filled me with a sense of mission and fired me with an obsessive passion I have felt ever since.

PLAYBOY: Where did that passion drive you next?

HALEY: Before I knew where to go next, I had to piece together what I'd learned so far, like clues in a detective story. From what the old ladies on the porch had told me, the ship that brought the African across the ocean had landed at Naplis, which had to be Annapolis, Maryland. And now I knew that the ship had to have sailed from the Gambia River. What I *didn't* know were the only things that really mattered. What ship? And what voyage?

PLAYBOY: How did you manage to track them down?

HALEY: The *griot* had told me that Kunta had disappeared "about the time the king's soldiers came." Projecting backward six generations to Kunta, that must have been somewhere in the mid-eighteenth century. And since slavery was first and foremost a maritime industry conducted predominantly by England and her American colony, I figured there might be a record somewhere in London of a military expedition to the Gambia around that time. I was right. After weeks of digging among British parliamentary records, I discovered that a group called Colonel O'Hare's forces had been dispatched to protect Fort James on the Gambia River from attack by the French in the spring of 1767.

So now I knew approximately when Kunta's ship left. Somewhere among the many thousands of voyages logged in shipping records during the two centuries that the slave trade flourished, there must be the record of a voyage by some ship from the Gambia River to Annapolis in the spring of 1767.

PLAYBOY: Where did you look?

HALEY: I soon discovered that various repositories here or there in London held a maze of old shipping records, some dating back to the sixteenth century; and included were countless records of slave ships. Hardly pausing to eat or sleep, I breathed dust and squinted over yellowing records for nine hours a day every day for the next seven weeks. Finally, in the British Public Records Office one afternoon, I was about halfway down a list of thirty-odd sailings in my 1,023rd set of records when my finger traced a line that read: "*Lord Ligonier,* registered in London, Captain Davies, sailed from the Gambia River July 5, 1767, destination Annapolis"—with a cargo that included 140 Africans.

PLAYBOY: What was your reaction?

HALEY: For some reason, it didn't seem to register right away. I jotted down the information, stuck it in my pocket and went next door for a cup of tea. I was just sort of sitting there, sipping away, when it hit me. I still owe the lady for the tea. Without even stopping off at my hotel to pick up my bag, I grabbed a taxi, told the driver, "Heathrow!" and got the last seat on that day's last flight to New York. All the way across the Atlantic, I could see it in my mind's eye—a book I'd come across several months before in the Library of Congress: *Shipping in the Port of Annapolis, 1748–1775.* Before I slept, I was going to have my hands on that book. And I did. Turning to ship arrivals starting in September 1767—allowing at least two months for the crossing—I found it in ten minutes: The *Lord Ligonier* had docked in the Port of Annapolis on September 29, 1767. In the Maryland Hall of Records, I looked up ship arrivals for that date, and there was the cargo manifest for the *Lord Ligonier.* On it were listed "3,265 elephant's teeth, 3,700 pounds of beeswax, 800 pounds of raw cotton, 32 ounces of gold and 98 Negro slaves." Forty-two had died en route.

PLAYBOY: Almost a third. Wasn't that an incredibly high fatality rate?

HALEY: It was about average. The slaves on the *Lord Ligonier* were stowed "loose pack," as they called it, on their backs, shoulder to shoulder, on shelves. When they were shipped "tight pack"—on their sides, up against one another like spoons in a drawer—the death rate was even higher.

PLAYBOY: Then why would they be shipped that way?

HALEY: The reasoning was that since more slaves could be fitted on board tight pack, the ship still might arrive with more salable merchandise alive.

PLAYBOY: What was the cause of most of the deaths?

HALEY: Disease and debilitation, from being forced to lie in their own excrement and vomit, chained together at the wrists and ankles on shelves four or five deep for an average of two and a half months. After a few weeks—bitten by rats, infested with lice, often bloated with tapeworms ingested in tainted slop, rolling back and forth on the rough planks beneath them—they were a mass of ulcerated and often gangrenous wounds so deep, in some cases, that muscle and bone showed through. Some died of beatings; others were killed in insurrections; and a few threw themselves overboard to the sharks rather than wait to get eaten in Toubabo-Koomi, the land of white cannibals to which many thought they were being taken. What's surprising is not that so many died but that so many *survived* the nightmare.

It's ironic that, percentagewise, more whites than blacks died on the slave ships. The *Lord Ligonier* left Gravesend, England, with a full crew of thirty-six and arrived in Annapolis with eighteen. Whites were less resistant than blacks to many diseases, but most fell victim to the same afflictions that killed their captives: every week or so, the crew members had to scrub off the slaves and muck out the holds.

PLAYBOY: Were they well paid for that kind of work?

HALEY: On the contrary, the crewmen earned around two or three shillings a day—if they lived to earn *anything*. The fewer of the crew to survive the journey, the fewer of them had to be paid. More crew members than slaves died from floggings by brutal captains and mates: they were recruited—in some cases, shanghaied—human dregs of the waterfront and were regarded as far less valuable than their black cargo.

Shipowners and the great insurance companies that bankrolled the trade found it enormously profitable, however. Nor did the slave-ship captains do badly, either. In fact, they earned far more doing that sort of dirty work than they ever could have done at the helm of a warship or a tea clipper. Most of them were castoffs from military service or trading lines, competent sailors who had been disgraced or dishonorably discharged for drunkenness, insubordination, and so on. They had to earn a living at the only thing they knew—the sea—and it was a lucrative one. But many of them seemed to be ashamed of it. I learned in my research that some of our favorite hymns were written by retired slave-ship officers. "*Amazing Grace,*" for example, was written by an ex-first mate named John Newton. The familiar line "I once was lost but now am found" takes on a poignant new significance in that light.

PLAYBOY: How did you find out about all this?

HALEY: By reading scores of slave journals, captain's memoirs and especially the records of the antislavery society. One of the most revealing tidbits I unearthed in this way was the fact that the surest mark of veteran slave-ship captains and mates was the number of human teethmark scars they carried on their lower legs—sustained while doing their job, which was to keep as many slaves as possible from dying, and to patch them up well enough to command a decent price on delivery.

PLAYBOY: What sort of price would an average slave command?

HALEY: That would depend on the state of the market at the time, but the principal determining factors were obviously age, strength and health. The tribe a slave came from also sometimes made a difference to knowledgeable buyers. The Wolofs, who were quick, intelligent, natural leaders but proud and defiant, tended to sell for less than members of other tribes that were regarded as more tractable and hardworking. In 1767, an average fieldhand in prime shape was worth anywhere from five hundred to eight hundred dollars. Though they weren't capable of the same kind of hard work, female slaves often commanded more than a thousand dollars, especially if they were young and attractive, because they could both provide pleasant diversion for their masters and increase their inventory of human livestock by breeding children.

PLAYBOY: Were you able to discover Kunta Kinte's sale price?

HALEY: About $850 is my best guess, based upon then prevailing prices in the Maryland and Virginia area. But I found a specific record of when and where he was sold. In the microfilm records of the *Maryland Gazette* for October 1, 1767—two days after the *Lord Ligonier* docked—I found an advertisement in the far-left-hand column on page two, announcing its arrival and inviting interested parties to an auction in Annapolis three days thence of its cargo: "98 choice, healthy slaves."

PLAYBOY: Was there any written record of those sold at the auction?

HALEY: Not that I could find. But I already knew who had bought Kunta, if the family story continued to prove as accurate as it had so far. Grandma had said Kunta had been sold to a "Massa John Waller," who named him Toby, and later, after his foot had been cut off, he had been sold to John's brother, Dr. William Waller, who put him to work in the garden at his plantation in Spotsylvania County, Virginia.

Since slaves were considered property, just like a horse or a plot of real estate, I reasoned that there might possibly be a record of Kunta's sale from one brother to the other somewhere among the state legal deeds on file in Richmond. So I began searching through those documents, starting a few months after his original purchase, to allow time for his four unsuccessful escape attempts. Finally I found a deed—dated September 5, 1768—transferring 217 acres of land from John to William Waller. On the second page, like an afterthought, were the words, "And also one Negro slave named Toby." I sat staring at the document, unable to believe my eyes. It was impossible, but I'd done it: traced a man who had been dead for almost two centuries all the way from his home village in western Africa to a plantation in Spotsylvania County, Virginia. I felt like leaping up and shouting back across the years to Grandma and the rest of the ladies on that porch: "It's true! It's all true! Every word of it. It really happened just the way you said! We've found him!" One less detail in the family story, one missing document in my search to confirm it, and the trail could have petered out anywhere along the way. Somehow, just enough fragments had survived from what the African had told Kizzy, and what she and the others had passed on down through the generations, to lead me finally, there in that Virginia library, all the way back to my great-great-great-great-grandfather.

PLAYBOY: Were you ready to begin writing the book?

HALEY: Hardly. I had traced my own ancestor all the way from freedom in the Gambia to slavery in Virginia, and I knew the outlines of the family story pretty well from that point on. But if *Roots* was going to stand a chance of transcending the story of one family and becoming the saga of an entire people, I knew I'd have to find out what it had been like not only for Kunta Kinte and his descendants but for millions like them on both continents from that time to this. I felt my job now was to immerse myself in research in two vast areas: tribal life in Africa and slave life in America. Since Africa's where the story began, I decided to study it first.

Most of what I'd read so far had been written by outsiders, predominantly white missionaries and anthropologists, and even among the most knowledgeable and well-intentioned of them, the tone was somewhat paternal and condescending. Their insights and observations were inevitably limited by the cultural chasm separating them from their subjects. So I began going back to Africa, maybe fifteen or twenty trips. Setting out with my interpreters into the back country, I'd arrive in a village with a gift of kola nuts or something and ask to speak with the most-honored elders. And I'd sit for hours with three or four of those old men, asking them about their boyhoods—and about whatever they could recall their fathers telling them about *their* boyhoods. I was digging not only for firsthand cultural history but also for personal anecdotes that would illuminate the life-style and the character of these people: sensory impressions of taste, touch, smell and sight that would help me bring the story to life in a way that the reader could not only appreciate but at least vicariously *experience*.

PLAYBOY: How much of what you learned conflicted with your preconceptions about Africa?
HALEY: Most of it. The worst misconception I had—in common with most Americans—was conditioned by the cartoon image of Africans as semisimians with bones through their noses, swinging from trees and dancing around fires over which missionaires were cooking in big pots. What I found out about my own ancestors, the Mandinkas—a fairly representative tribe among the thousands in Africa—was that they were a poor people, most of them simple farmers at the mercy of the harsh elements of western Africa, which range from flood to famine. They live in what we would consider primitive conditions, and during the hungry season they sometimes eat rodents and even insects to stay alive. But they are a highly civilized and sophisticated people who are brought up to be aware of, and proud of, a rich cultural heritage, and they have a deep respect for the value of all life. Most are devout Moslems, the men are literate in Arabic and not only conversant in their own language but schooled from childhood in Koranic recitation.

Conditioned as I was to think of Africans as savages, I was deeply moved when I learned about the age-old Mandinka ritual of child naming, which is still practiced in the back country. On the eighth day of his life, a newborn child is brought out before the people of his village in his mother's arms and held up before his father, who whispers three times into the infant's ear the name he has chosen: it's the first time that child's name has ever been spoken aloud, because the Mandinka people believe that *each human being should be the first to know who he is*. That night, the naming ritual is completed when the father takes his child out beyond the village gates and holds the infant above him with his little face turned toward the heavens. "Behold," says the father, "the only thing greater than yourself." As a black American, brought up to regard myself as second-class at best, my knowledge now of that simple ancestral declaration has profoundly changed the way I feel about my value as a human being.
PLAYBOY: How long did it take you to collect that kind of firsthand research?
HALEY: Perhaps four years; then another six months organizing it into dozens of notebooks, including one for each year of Kunta's life in Africa, distributing every shred of information I'd been able to find on everything from weapons to kitchen utensils, from morning prayers to evening campfires, from birth to death, into what I feel is as comprehensive and authentic a profile of African cultural life as has ever been assembled.
PLAYBOY: Were you as meticulous in researching the slave life in America?
HALEY: Maybe more so. It certainly *took* longer. There was hardly anybody to talk with who had direct experience of the period I was interested in, and the culture itself, unlike that of back-country Africa, had changed beyond recognition. So I had to rely almost entirely on reading. Digging long and deep in sources that had the ring of validity, finally I unearthed solid material—out of antebellum memoirs, diaries, personal correspondence, and the like, by slavemasters and -mistresses; out of the Library of Congress, the Library of the DAR, the Widener Library at Harvard, the New York City Library's Schomberg Collection in Harlem, the Moreland Collection at Howard University, the Fisk University and Morehouse College libraries, and a good twoscore other specialized source places—my quest, my mission, being to get at the *truth* of slavery. I read the works of prominent ex-slaves such as Frederick Douglass, Sojourner Truth, Harriet Tubman and Phillis Wheatley, an African girl who

grew up to become a celebrated poet. But the most invaluable—and heartbreaking—research I used in the book was gleaned from the transcripts of several unknown interviews with completely unknown ex-slaves that had been conducted by unemployed writers as a WPA project during the Thirties. Many of them are in a book titled *Lay My Burden Down,* which I recommend to anyone interested in the true and terrible story of slavery as told by its last survivors.

From all this reading, I finally amassed a staggering mound of research, which I then began to condense and classify into a second set of dawn-to-dusk, life-to-death, A-to-Z notebooks that constitutes, I think, a portrait of plantation America at least as exhaustive—and fully as authentic—as my research on tribal Africa.

PLAYBOY: Did what you found out about slave life in the South force you to revise any more preconceptions?

HALEY: Many—but most of them, I'm happy to say, weren't my own. The worst of them, of course, was the popular white stereotype of slaves as ignorant wooly-heads who grinned and shuffled around the plantation with nothing on their minds but sex and watermelon: a lot of whites still think that way about us. But the *fact* is that most slaves were innately as smart as their masters, and not a few who got the chance at freedom and an education went on to excel in those fields they were allowed to enter.

But there wasn't a single slave who wasn't smart enough to lull white folks into thinking he was ignorant. As long as they were thought to be dumb, they'd pretty much be left alone. What whites seldom realized was that through a highly effective grapevine, nearly every slave out in the cotton fields learned in minutes just about everything that went on in the "big house," even behind closed doors. House slaves eavesdropped on most words their masters and mistresses spoke; they suckled babies, changed the bed sheets, fed their owners and then emptied their slop jars. Yet their masters knew next to nothing about *them.*

PLAYBOY: What about the old stereotype that slaves were lazy and shiftless? Did your research shed any light on that?

HALEY: The facts are that they were worked *very* hard six days a week, usually from dawn till long after dark. House slaves, of course, didn't have the same kind of backbreaking responsibilities as those who worked in the fields; some of them, in fact, grew close to their white owners and enjoyed special privileges, rather like house pets. But field slaves were worked sometimes until they literally dropped dead. It's not surprising that they took every chance they could get to lighten up whenever they thought the overseer's back was turned: or that after emancipation, they tilled the same land with more dedication as sharecroppers than they had as slaves.

PLAYBOY: Didn't the special treatment accorded to house slaves alienate them from field slaves?

HALEY: It didn't exactly create a bond between them, but more important than the fact that one group sweated in the fields while the other wore starched uniforms, fanned the "missy" with ostrich feathers and ate leftovers from the master's dinner table was the fact that they all recognized they were enslaved together. If any of them showed the slightest disrespect toward any white—or was even *suspected* of it—they'd all suffer the same consequences.

PLAYBOY: What kind of consequences?

HALEY: Beatings were administered regularly by overseers, and often by white layabouts who happened onto slaves out alone on the road or in town. But all kinds of unimaginable cruelties were commonplace, for the most capricious pretexts. Ears were cut off for eavesdropping and hands for stealing, genitals for real or imagined evidence of any untoward interest in a white woman.

A particularly sadistic case among the hundreds I documented in my research was about an attractive young slave girl who had been raped by her master. When he died, his wife, who had been forced—like so many plantation wives—to endure in silence the humiliation of his infidelity, took a poker and beat the girl nearly to death: broke her jaw in several places, put out an eye, disfigured her for life.

But the atrocity I remember most vividly was the chopping off of Kunta Kinte's foot by those poor-white "pate-rollers" who caught him after his fourth attempt to escape. I found myself morbidly obsessed with it. Over and over in my mind's eye, I watched as Kunta, bound by his waist to a tree, struggled vainly to escape as his right foot was tied firmly across a stump. I saw the ax flash up, then down. I heard the thud, the horrible scream, saw his hands flail downward, as if to retrieve the front half of his foot as it fell forward, gouts of blood jetting from the stump. It was like a recurrent nightmare: I could see it, hear it. But I couldn't *feel* it. Finally, after studying the physiology of the foot, I began to internalize the agony he must have felt as the ax sliced through skin, tendons, muscles, blood vessels and bone and thudded finally onto the stump. Only then did I feel that I could write about it. And only when I did was I able to purge myself of the obsession.

PLAYBOY: In *Roots,* you describe another attempt to emphathize with the sufferings of your ancestor, when, boarding a freighter bound, as the *Lord Ligonier* had been, from western Africa to America, you spent every night of the crossing stripped to your shorts, lying on the rough planking of the dark hold. Did that help you lose yourself in the character—and his ordeal?

HALEY: I don't know. My discomfort, of course, was sheer luxury compared with what he went through. I felt I had to do *something* to make it more real for me, but lying there night after night seemed to drive me deep inside *myself,* instead of him. I couldn't seem to get inside his skin so that he could cry out, through me, the agony he had endured. And that agonized *me.* But even beyond that, I felt myself sinking into despair over my inadequacy to the task I had undertaken, at my effrontery in taking it upon myself to tell the saga of an entire people. I had been working on the book for years. I was beginning to think I'd never finish. Finally, one night, I found myself standing at the aft rail of the ship, looking back at the waves behind us, and very slowly, not with despair but with a sense of exhilaration, it began to dawn on me that the solution to all my problems lay just one step before me. All I had to do was slip between the rails and drop into the sea that had been my home for twenty years; it would only be fitting that the birthplace of my career as a writer would be my burying place as well. It would all be over and I could join the others up there—Jesus!—*watching* me at that rail about to bury forever the past they had sent me out to find. So help me, God, I began to hear their voices talking to me—Grandma, Tom, Chicken George, Kizzy and Kunta Kinte—and they were all saying quietly, "Don't do it, son. Go on. Have faith. You're gonna make it." With all my strength, I pushed myself back from that rail and crawled on my hands and knees back across the deck to the companionway. And that night, in my cabin, I sobbed my guts out. After that, when I sat down at my typewriter and began to write, it flowed, it poured out of me like lava, the whole story of the slave-ship cruise, and I hope it hurts to read it as much as it did to write it.

PLAYBOY: In your zeal to relive the story so totally, did it occur to you that you might be getting carried away by it?
HALEY: I *knew* I was getting carried away. I was lost in it, hopelessly in love with it. In the single-mindedness of my determination to track down every lead that might take me to something I thought I had to know or feel, I went days at a time without food, nights without sleep, months without touching a woman. Carrying every scrap of research I'd collected along with me in a pair of very heavy satchels that never left my side, I traveled maybe half a million miles, interviewed hundreds of people, read hundreds of books, pored over thousands of documents in more than seventy archives on three continents. I could have gone on that way forever, never satisfied that I'd learned quite enough, always hoping that tomorrow I'd stumble across one more piece of evidence that I couldn't do without.
PLAYBOY: What stopped you?
HALEY: I simply ran out of two basic commodities: time and money. I was exactly four years behind my deadline for delivery of the manuscript, and though no one knew it, except you, I'd actually *written* only the African section and the slave-ship crossing. The eternal optimist, I would always convince myself that I'd be able to sit down and grind out the rest in six months of eighteen-hour days at the typewriter. But then I'd run out of money—I'd lost all of my credit cards and friends to borrow from—and I'd have to stop work on the book entirely for weeks at a time to go on the lecture circuit, *talking* about the book, to earn enough money to get back to it for a few more months. I must have spoken before more than a million people about "My Search for Roots" over a period of several years, and people were beginning to say that the book was just a shuck to get me lecture bookings. Even friends like you, who knew better, began to lose patience with me.
PLAYBOY: But not faith.
HALEY: Well, yours lasted longer than mine. Finally, in exasperation, my attorney, Lou Blau, told me, in so many words, to just stop runnin' my mouth about it, take the research I had—which was enough for ten books by then—get off on some desert island somewhere and *write* the goddamn thing. I swore I would and promised—for the last time—to deliver it in six months; Doubleday gave me some money to live on until then. Squirreling myself away in a remote hilltop cottage in Jamaica, West Indies—beyond the reach of telephones—I sat down to do just that.

But as the months passed, I found that mail and telegrams were managing to find me—and nearly every one seemed to be an announcement from some collection agency that I'd better pay up or else; or a command from the IRS. It was hard to find a single creditor who was willing to accept my honest explanation that all those debts had accumulated—and couldn't be paid off yet—because of my desperate efforts to research and then write an important but seemingly interminable book. What with one thing or another, when I sat down and figured out what I owed various people and institutions, it was a total of around a hundred thousand dollars, including late charges, and just realizing that had what you might charitably call a deterrent effect on my creative output. If I didn't find a few bones to throw to the biggest and hungriest of those wolves howling at my door, I knew I wouldn't have a typewriter to finish the book on or a roof to do it under.
PLAYBOY: Since you *did* finish, you must have found a few bones. Where?
HALEY: I did something I'm not proud of, but if it hadn't worked, I'd be even less proud of it. With just a few days left before my six months were up—knowing that I'd need

at *least* another six months to finish—I wrote the first twenty pages of the next section of the book, polishing each and every word until it gleamed, and also the last few pages of the book, where I tell everybody what it all means. I didn't really have any *idea* what it all meant at that point, but I made up something that sounded good, and then I typed up about 750 pages of my research to the same margins, stuck them between the first twenty and the last few pages, numbered them all in sequence, put a big rubber band around the whole thing, stuck it in a satchel and took the next plane to New York, arriving in the office of my editor, Lisa Drew, exactly on deadline day.

Sitting at Lisa's desk, chitchatting for the first five or ten minutes, I could see her glance fastened hypnotically on that satchel at my side, so at the appropriate moment, I opened it up. I pulled out this massive manuscript and set it before her on the desk. Her eyes narrowed warily as I explained that it was still just a rough draft but that I'd brought it along to reassure her that I was making progress. Then she began to read the first page, then the second and the third, and she began to smile, wider and wider. But when she kept on turning pages, I started talking and kept talking, faster and faster, asking so many questions that she finally began just skimming and then riffling around page fifteen. Then, as I knew she would from long acquaintance, she turned to the last page and read it carefully. I'd really poured it on at the end, and when she looked up, it was with moist eyes and a tremulous smile.

While she was still in a tender mood, I apologized abjectly for letting her down once again, after crying wolf so many times. All the more so because I would have to ask her one *last* time for another six-month extension—and another modest advance on my royalties, just enough to buy groceries, pay the electric bill and keep me in typing paper until I'd put the final polish on the manuscript. Flinching, sighing, but obviously impressed by the apparent existence of a rough draft for a book she had just about decided she'd never see, she authorized a check—for considerably less than I'd asked for, of course—and sincerely wished me good luck and Godspeed. And a warning that this was the last penny I'd see until the final draft was in her hands exactly six months from that day.

PLAYBOY: Was it?

HALEY: Delivered on time or the last penny I saw?

PLAYBOY: Either.

HALEY: Neither. One way or another, I managed to eke out enough of both time and money to finally finish the book—about a year later—but not without pulling one last shameless ruse. The last hundred pages of the manuscript, which I turned in to Doubleday as finished copy only five days after the final, final deadline—when I was told bricks would begin to tumble from the roof of the Doubleday building—were actually a kind of novelized synopsis of the actual copy I intended to write while the manuscript was being typeset. When I received the galleys for correction about a month later, I simply substituted my two hundred new pages for the last hundred pages they had set in type. They fumed, of course, but it *was* incomparably better than the original version. I offered to pay for the cost of resetting—hoping they'd have the kindness to turn me down, which they did, since they knew I'd have to ask them for another advance to do it. But as things are turning out, it looks as if neither Doubleday nor I will have to hassle over the printing bills.

PLAYBOY: Or any other bills, it would appear, since *Roots* seems destined to become the best-seller of the season—and perhaps, when the twelve-hour television adaptation debuts at the end of this month, one of the best-sellers of all time. After all those years of dodging creditors, how do you feel about the prospect of becoming a millionaire?

HALEY: Well, I still owe enough money that it'll be a while before I see a dollar without somebody else's fingers attached to it. But when it starts rolling in, I'm pretty sure I'll prefer it to poverty. The main thing I look forward to is being able to go to the mailbox and find a few checks in it instead of a pile of window envelopes with notes inside that begin: "Final notice: If you fail to call this number within twenty-four hours. . . ." Apart from that, and the creative independence it'll buy for me, the only reason I'm really excited about making some money is so I can fix up my backyard and maybe get me a nice stereo system for the living room. That's about it.

PLAYBOY: Will you laugh all the way to the bank over some of the criticisms that have faulted *Roots* for having a "pulpy style that smacks of conventional romance"; for your reliance on the use of a slave dialect that becomes "wearing and ludicrous"; for devoting too much of the book to Kunta's "boring" life in Africa, which one reviewer found, "for all its troubles, a primal Eden"; and for glossing over the more recent generations of your family in "a hasty, sketchy, unsatisfactory way"?

HALEY: When almost all of the reviews received by a book are as admiring, and in some cases adulatory, as those written about *Roots*, you've got to expect your share of potshots from some quarters. They roll off. But if you want me to comment on the specific criticisms you mentioned, I'll be glad to. As for my pulpy style, I'd rather describe it as I intended it to be: simple, direct, descriptive, dramatic—a style well suited to the story it tells, I think; and many other reviewers seem to feel as I do. The use of slave dialect, too, is not only intentional but authentic; some critics may find it ludicrous, but the fact is that that's the way those people talked. Should I have made them speak the king's English like their white owners? Differences in language were both symbolic and symptomatic of the vast gulf between slave and master. The reason I devoted the first 126 pages of the book to Kunta's life in Africa, which some critics found both long and boring, was that so little has been known up to now in the West, by white or black, about the depth and richness of African culture, which I happen to think we can all learn something from. I also wanted to plant Kunta's roots so deep, as I told the story of his life from birth to capture, that the wrench of his being torn from the soil of his homeland would be as heartbreaking for the reader as it was for me. As for depicting Juffure as a primal Eden, maybe it was, and still is, compared with America's urban jungles; but I certainly made no attempt to romanticize the harsh realities of tribal life in western Africa.

PLAYBOY: How about the criticism that the book glosses over the more recent generations of your family?

HALEY: I'd be inclined to agree with that one. I wish I'd had another year or even two to flesh out the lives and characters of Tom Murray and his family and all the others who came after them, all the way down to me, as I had been able to do with the rest of the book—from Kunta and Kizzy through Chicken George. The latter part of the story is just as rich as all that went before, and maybe someday I'll have the chance to go back and do it the justice it deserves. But the reason I didn't do it is that time, as I said earlier, simply ran out. Multimillion-dollar book publication and TV production plans had been set irreversibly into motion, and there was finally no way to resist them any longer. But the whole story is still there; I don't think the impact or the importance of the book has been diminished in any significant way.

PLAYBOY: The final—and most frequent—charge is that, despite all your attempts to document the history of your family, *Roots* can't really be called nonfiction, because

so few specific details could be corroborated that much of the book is a work of imagination.
HALEY: That's the one thing it's *not*. All the names and dates are real. All the major incidents are true, and the details are as accurate a depiction of what happened to my family, or to thousands of families like us, as years of research can achieve. When it comes to dialogue, thoughts and emotions, of course, I had to make things up; but even those inventions are based as much as humanly possible on corroborated fact. Call it "faction," if you like, or heightened history, or fiction based on the lives of real people.
PLAYBOY: However they choose to classify it, most reviewers have been ecstatic, hailing *Roots* as everything from "the epic of the black man in America" to "a book of such colossal scope that it arouses not only admiration but awe." Are you embarrassed by all that approbation?
HALEY: If I were, you couldn't tell whether I was blushing anyway. But what can I say when I see words like *colossal* and *epic* applied to a book I spent twelve years of my life working on? That's the kind of thing any author would *dream* of having said about his book, and now that such a dream actually is coming true for me, it's a little hard to believe. But because *Roots* is more than just a book I happened to write, because it has come to represent far more than just the story of my family, I find myself able to step back and see it—above and beyond any personal considerations and whatever literary merit it may have—as something that really *is* an epic: the colossal epic of a people.
PLAYBOY: Some readers feel the book isn't the story of the black man but of *man*. Was that your intention—and is that your hope?
HALEY: It was and is. On its most literal level, it is the story of both my family and my people, for the ancestors of all of us were brought over here in the same way. But as I wrote it, another dimension began to emerge. Besides feeling that *Roots* might help restore to black people some sense of their identity and pride, I felt it might also help the descendants of their owners, and all peoples everywhere—Russian and Chinese, Catholic and Protestant, Arab and Jew—face the facts about the atrocities committed time and again, throughout history, in the name of everything from King Cotton to Almighty God. All of us, at one time or another, are both victim and oppressor, and fate seems to be rather capricious about who plays which role at any given time.

Black or white, for those of us here in America, this is our home. Except for the Indians, who already lived here when we arrived, the ancestors of all of us came across that same ocean on some ship. We must learn not only to live together but—by learning to see one another as *people* rather than as stereotypes—to love one another. That will happen when we face what we are and what we've done and then forgive one another—and ourselves—unconditionally, for everything.
PLAYBOY: That's a beautiful speech. But do you really think that will ever happen?
HALEY: The truth? In the fifty-five years I've been around, I haven't run across any great signs of a new awakening. On an individual basis, yes; now and then, a spontaneous act of kindness and understanding, here and there heartwarming cases of genuine brotherhood—like our own fifteen-year friendship, if you'll allow me to get personal. But I can't say that I feel too optimistic about the perfectibility of mankind. On the other hand, I'm encouraged by the tremendous upswelling of emotion that *Roots* seems to have set in motion, an emotion that—to judge from the outpourings of sometimes even tearful gratitude I'm encountering wherever I go these days—seems to be not only cathartic but, in some way, *healing*. If people hadn't wanted and needed that,

hadn't been ready for it, in some deep way, I don't think the book would be nearly as important as it seems to have become.

PLAYBOY: Aren't people also responding to some pretty old-fashioned virtues in *Roots?* Whatever else it may be, isn't the book a kind of tribute to the family unit as a force of continuity in human society and the repository of its values?

HALEY: Say that again slow and let me write it down; I didn't know how profound I was. But, yes, to me the family has always been the source and heart of every culture. I didn't set out with that thought in mind as one of the messages of the book, but I guess it is. In the forty or so years since I grew up in Henning, the family has been shrinking and drifting apart as America has moved from the country to the city, from huge, messy old homes echoing with the noise of three generations to closet-sized, four-hundred-dollars-a-month apartments for swinging singles eating TV dinners alone in six-hundred-unit high-rises; from sitting on front porches, listening to grandmothers tell family stories like the ones I heard, to sitting in suburban rec rooms with baby-sitters while Mom and Dad go out; from screen doors left unlocked to steel doors triple-locked; from walking home after school by way of the fishing hole, the sandlot and Miss Scrap Green's house, where she'd always have a plateful of hot cookies waiting on Thursday afternoons, to riding home through cursing mobs behind the barred windows of school buses with armed drivers.

I don't mean to run down urban America; I live in Los Angeles and I drive a Mercedes. And I don't want to romanticize our past; when I was a boy, we did without a lot of conveniences—like electricity—that have made life easier for everyone, and I grew up in a segregated town. But there's no question that somewhere along the way between then and now, we've lost something very precious: a sense of community, which is nothing more than a congregation of *families*. Everybody in town knew everybody else in town; there wasn't much privacy and there weren't many secrets, but there was no such thing as loneliness, anonymity, psychiatry. People didn't think about "role models" or worry about losing their identities. They weren't so anxious to leave home and go "looking for themselves" in the big city when I was growing up. They usually wound up doing more or less what their fathers and mothers had done and spent their whole lives within a mile of where they were born. And felt good about it.

It was small-town America, and it was pretty much the same in Henning, Tennessee, as it was in Plains, Georgia, or Emporia, Kansas. I say *was* because the binding hardships that created them and the simple pleasures that held them together *are* slipping away, dying off even in the back country, along with all those square values like trust, decency, neighborliness, patriotism. Even those of us who never grew up there, as I was fortunate enough to do, feel a sense of loss and longing, as the media and the supermarkets and the exurban industrial complexes slowly homogenize the land from coast to coast.

PLAYBOY: Do you think that process is inevitable—and irreversible?

HALEY: Probably, but I don't think it's inevitable that the moral and spiritual values that give meaning to our lives—that we most cherish in ourselves—have to disappear along with the rural America that nurtured them. This sense of self-worth can be revived and sustained—but only by restoring pride in who we are and what we mean to one another. We need, among other things, to start holding more family reunions; however sophisticated we become, that's where we all come from, and we can't afford to forget it. But my fondest hope is that *Roots* may start a ground swell of longing by black, white, brown, red, yellow people everywhere to go digging back for their own roots, to rediscover in their past a heritage to make them proud. Man, that would make me feel ninety feet tall—to think I was the impetus for that!

PLAYBOY: You don't expect people to go through the kind of ordeal you did, do you?

HALEY: No, just go rummaging through those old trunks up in the attic, in those old boxes under the bed; and don't throw anything old away if it has to do with the family. But the first thing they ought to do is simply open their ears. The richest source of family history you could find anywhere in the world is the memories of your parents and your grandparents—memories that will tell you things you never knew or have long since forgotten about yourself; but perhaps even more importantly, they will reveal to you, perhaps for the first time, the true identities of those who gave you life—and shared theirs with you for so many years. This will make them feel needed, relevant, *alive*—and that will bring out the same response in you. And almost certainly, this exchange of caring will deepen the blood bonds that can make a close-knit family the strongest social unit in the world. And in ways that will be understood best by those who belong to such families—the kind that eat together, stand up for one another, share births and deaths—it may leave you profoundly changed. The giving and getting, the sense of belonging and contributing to something larger than yourself, to something that began before you were born and will go on after you die, can make it possible for you to *accept* life in a way that makes you wish the whole world could realize how easy it is to feel as you do, and wonder why they don't. That's what having roots—and writing *Roots*—has done for me. I pray that *reading* it—and then reaching out for their families to join in a search for their own—will do the same for everyone.

PLAYBOY: One last question: What do you think your ancestors would think about all the acclaim over *Roots?*

HALEY: I hope they would approve. I often think of the Mandinka belief that Kunta's father expresses in the book: that there are three kinds of people living in every village: those you can see, walking around; those who are waiting to be born; and those who have gone on to join the ancestors. That idea was brought alive for me recently while I was on the set, watching them shoot the TV series based on *Roots*. I found myself wishing Grandma and the others could be there, too. I could almost *see* Grandma, wearing that hat she reserved for state occasions such as a revival meeting—the one with the feather like an apostrophe on it—and I could just *hear* her making her own private commentary on the film: Her father wasn't *that* fat, her grandfather wasn't *that* bald. And then I suddenly realized that she really *is* watching, along with Tom, Chicken George, Kizzy, Kunta and all the rest. *All* of them are up there watchin'—and not just over me now, but over all of *us*.

TED PATRICK

March 1979

Interviewers: Jim Siegelman & Flo Conway

The name may not be familiar to many people, but Ted Patrick turned out to be an important and timely interview. During the late 1970s, the magazine's editors had wanted to explore the growth of religious cults in America. The Hare Krishna, Scientologists, "Moonies," Synanon, and other groups had been receiving mounting press attention both for the abuses they were accused of—"brainwashing," and in some cases, violence—and for the tactics employed against them—chiefly the unlawful practice known as "deprogramming."

After considering, and rejecting, the idea of interviewing one of the cult leaders (editorial control was always demanded), PLAYBOY's editors decided to go in the other direction. The interview subject would be Ted Patrick, a zealous and driven tenth-grade dropout who had become the cults' chief enemy in his crusade to kidnap cult members and snap them back to independent thinking. It was a touchy issue, not only because Patrick had aroused the wrath of civil-rights groups and religious leaders, but at the time, some of the more militant cults had threatened and harassed publishers and network executives who had been responsible for negative reporting about the cults.

PLAYBOY editor Golson asked Jim Siegelman and Flo Conway, authors of a recent book on religious brainwashing and cults, to conduct this interview. The lengthy introduction to the subject and the interviewers' remarks are reprinted here in full to explain a complicated subject.

What was uncanny is that both the interviewers and the editors were skeptical of Patrick's often-sweeping claims about the harm caused by *all* the cults, and his contention that many were armed and had the potential for violence. On November 6, 1977, Patrick said to the interviewers: "You take some of these cults. . . . These people will do anything they are told to, including killing themselves, their parents, police, political leaders, *anybody* they feel is necessary." Less than two weeks later, with the interview still unfinished, Jim Jones and his followers killed an investigative party including a congressman and reporters, and then perpetrated the most gruesome mass-murder–suicide ritual in American history.

Despite the tragic vindication of Patrick's warnings, the editors felt Patrick had not been grilled sufficiently on the civil-liberties aspect of his actions, so Golson joined the interviewers in a hotel room (after the Guyana massacre) to ask some final questions of Patrick. The interview was finished as the television set in the room showed the images of the corpses being returned to the United States.

As this book goes to press, Ted Patrick has been in and out of prison on kidnapping charges and doubtless will continue to spend as much time in courtrooms defending his technique as he does practicing them.

Few social movements in American history have been quite so baffling as the rise of the religious cults of the Seventies. Who would have predicted a decade ago, when America's campuses were in upheaval, that within two or three years, those same young college students who had been organizing, marching, and even fighting in the streets for peace abroad and civil rights at home would now be selling flowers on street corners, hawking books in airport lobbies and selling life insurance and vacuum cleaners from door to door in the name of such unlikely "causes" as the Holy Spirit Association for the Unification of World Christianity, the International Society for Krishna Consciousness, the Children of God, the Divine Light Mission, and the Church of Scientology?

And who, in his wildest imagination, could have made up a more horrifying story than the murders of a U.S. congressman and three newsmen, to be followed by the mass suicide and murder of over nine hundred followers of Jim Jones's People's Temple in the jungle of Guyana three months ago? But even before that, it wasn't just the names of those new religious groups or even their divergent philosophies and beliefs that were beginning to perplex people. There was something about the members that was surprising and disconcerting. Many of the parents of those individuals, alarmed by the changes they said they had witnessed in their children, began to claim that they had been "brainwashed" by one cult or another. They told of their children's shaving their heads, changing their names, signing over their money and possessions to their group leader and denouncing their families and society as a whole as agents of "Satan's world." For their part, however, the young cult members denied all allegations of insincerity or skulduggery. They claimed that they had found peace, love, and happiness in their new religious groups, and that their freely chosen forms of worship, however unusual, were entitled to full protection under their First Amendment right to freedom of religion. In response, desperate parents began kidnapping their children from the cults in an effort to divert them from their new beliefs. Cult members started suing their parents and having them arrested for violating their constitutional rights. Law-enforcement officials, attorneys and judges were stumped by the legal predicament, and the news media reported the proceedings with a mixture of skepticism, confusion and mild amusement.

Ted Patrick seems to be one of the few persons who have steered an unwavering course through the various controversies. Right or wrong, the notorious figure who prides himself on the nickname Black Lightning has been waging a no-holds-barred, one-man crusade against the cults since 1971, helping parents abduct their children from them and practicing his controversial "deprogramming" technique on unwilling subjects. His goal was to free them from what he termed cult programing or mind control and return them to their families, their schools and the world they had abandoned. From the beginning, Patrick's deprogramming techniques have met with furious opposition from almost every camp. The various cults have opposed his every action as a flagrant violation of their members' personal freedom. The majority of clergymen and leaders of larger organized religions have also decried Patrick's activities as dangerous transgressions of religious freedom that may lay the groundwork for still broader inquisitions. And both the legal community and the media have condemned deprogramming.

For Patrick, however—and maybe for Patrick alone—the distinction is an easy one: freedom of religion versus what he calls freedom of thought. His claim is that cult rituals and techniques destroy the cult member's ability to think and make choices for himself. When that happens, he says, the individual is no longer entitled to his constitutional right to freedom of religion. It then becomes his parent or guardian's right, even duty, to remove him from the cult.

Patrick's argument is unprecedented in American legal history: Our society does not acknowledge as he so readily does that an individual can be stripped of his free will or that he can be induced to say or do anything in the absence of actual physical coercion. Since 1971, Patrick has been arrested and convicted on numerous charges, including kidnapping and unlawful detention; and he has served time in New York, Pennsylvania, California and Colorado.

In several important trials, however, Patrick has won. In one celebrated case in Seattle in 1974, the court ruled that the kidnapping of a cult member by Patrick acting as her parents' agent—was a justifiable act committed to prevent a greater harm. In a more recent case in Rhode Island in 1978, where a lawsuit for unlawful detention was dismissed, the court ruled that deprogramming itself was not an illegal act.

At forty-eight, Ted Patrick is a most unlikely person to be setting court precedents and attracting the attention of leading psychiatrists and psychologists. He has had no formal legal training nor background in medicine or mental health. On the contrary he is, by his own admission, "a tenth-grade dropout with a Ph.D. in common sense."

Following his first highly publicized abductions and his initial, almost incomprehensible deprogrammings, Patrick achieved instant notoriety and nearly universal condemnation. Nobody, it seemed, accepted his claim that the cults were dangerous and damaging to the minds of their members. And nobody believed that his deprogramming technique was different from the brainwashing methods he attributed to the cults.

Within the past year, however, many people have begun to reassess the things Patrick has been saying since the early Seventies. Last August, eleven members of the Church of Scientology were indicted for infiltration, bugging and burglarizing the offices of the Justice Department and the Internal Revenue Service in Washington. In October, after an eighteen-month probe, the House Subcommittee on International Organizations recommended that a federal task force be established to investigate Korean evangelist Sun Myung Moon's Unification Church for violations of U.S. currency, immigration, banking, tax, arms-export-control, and other laws. And since last fall, representatives of Synanon, the once-respected drug and alcohol rehabilitation center, have been suspected of committing a number of terrorist acts, including attempting to commit murder by placing a four-and-a-half-foot rattlesnake in the mailbox of a Los Angeles attorney who had won a three-hundred-thousand-dollar judgment against the group. Then, of course, there was Guyana, with its incomprehensible ritual of faith and carnage.

Patrick has deprogrammed members of almost all those groups and hundreds more from the estimated three thousand religious and pseudo-religious cults that have been active in the United States in this decade. Since 1971, he claims to have deprogrammed nearly sixteen hundred people from the "big five" international cults—Krishna, Moon, Scientology, the Children of God, and the Divine Light Mission—and from religious groups, fringe therapies and extremist political groups as varied as their names: the New Testament Missionary Fellowship, the Worldwide Church of God, Dianetics, Transcendental Meditation, the U.S. Labor Party, and the Move.

As psychologists, sociologists and the press have latched onto the convenient new buzzword cult *and have applied it to encompass everything from radical socialists to charismatic Christians, so, naturally, has public confusion ascended to dizzying heights. How does one distinguish between a cult and a legitimate religious movement? What constitutes freedom of thought and how does one determine if a person is under some form of mind control? What medical and psychiatric criteria should be established for the regulation of deprogramming? And what legal safeguards must be instituted to protect the individual from personal abuse and the society as a whole from anarchy, on the one hand, and inquisition on the other? To broach some of these questions, and with the hope of unraveling the enigmatic personality and activities of Patrick,* PLAYBOY *executive editor G. Barry Golson (who was himself in on some of the questioning) called on free-lance writer and veteran interviewer Jim Siegelman and on Flo Conway, a communication researcher with eight years of doctoral study in group dynamics and interpersonal relations. Together, Siegelman and Conway have been studying various cult movements for more than five years. Last year, they co-authored* Snapping: America's Epidemic of Sudden Personality Change, *an exploration of the impact of cult religious rituals and therapeutic techniques on the workings of the brain. Siegelman and Conway report:*

"This was not our first encounter with the infamous Ted Patrick. We had interviewed him twice before in connection with our research: once, in early 1977, while he was serving a one-year sentence in Orange County Jail in California, and again, briefly, several months later, in the Denver jail, where he had gone voluntarily to serve out his remaining time on an earlier kidnapping conviction. On both these occasions, however, and in those surroundings, we were unable to get a complete picture of the man and his technique.

"The hardest part of the Playboy interview turned out to be just tracking him down, but we managed to intercept him between deprogrammings. He was en route from Miami, where he'd just deprogrammed a seventy-three-year-old woman from a nameless Christian cult, to New Jersey, where he was scheduled to confront a young Hare Krishna member who had been lured home by his anxious parents. When we got to Patrick, we locked him in a hotel room in midtown Manhattan and over the next thirty-six intense hours proceeded to conduct our own deprogramming of sorts.

"We found Patrick to be a much less forbidding figure when not in prison garb and under harsh lights. In fact, his physical appearance didn't seem at all like the thing to strike terror into the heart of a Moonie. He takes his work seriously, but not life in general; and we found him to be a most pleasant person to spend two days with.

"We had no premonition, of course, that twelve days after our last session with him. events in Guyana would make Patrick's seemingly melodramatic prophecies come true in a terrible way. We were able to talk further with him after the Guyana murders and suicides, but we'll start with what he had told us earlier."

(The following portion of the interview was conducted on November 4, 5, and 6, twelve days before the massacre and mass suicide by People's Temple cultists in Guyana.)

PLAYBOY: You've been convicted and imprisoned for kidnapping and unlawful detention. Yet you continue to engage in your deprogramming activities, holding young people against their will and attempting to change their religious beliefs. How do you justify kidnapping and violating people's First Amendment right to freedom of religion?

PATRICK: What I do is not kidnapping. What I do is *rescuing*. When I deprogram a person, he has already been unlawfully imprisoned. His mind has been unlawfully imprisoned by the cult. But the cult members don't know a psychological prison from a physical prison. They don't know right from wrong, because their minds have been destroyed.

PLAYBOY: You may call it rescuing. Most people would call it kidnapping—and a felony.

PATRICK: What most people don't know is that I only go in with the approval of the person's parents; and the courts have recognized that a parent cannot kidnap his own child. The charge that is usually brought against me is unlawful detention, or holding a person against his will, which is not a felony but a misdemeanor; and I have been acquitted on that charge many more times than I have been convicted. And what most people aren't aware of is that most states have a law of justification that permits a person to do something that would ordinarily be considered illegal if he was committing that act to prevent a greater harm, the greater harm being what is happening to the mental and physical health of the person in the cult. In the common law, this doctrine is centuries old. It's called the lesser of two evils, and judges in New York and Washington have acknowledged this with regard to deprogramming. In Seattle, the only time I was ever tried on felony charges, I was acquitted hands down. In fact, the federal judge there said that if the parents had not tried to get their daughter out of the cult, they would have been "less than responsible, loving parents."

PLAYBOY: So then you're claiming that you haven't broken the law, is that right?

PATRICK: That's right. The courts have recognized that what I'm doing is legal under the law of justification.

PLAYBOY: But you don't deny that you have taken the law into your own hands?

PATRICK: I have taken the law into my own hands, but I haven't broken it.

PLAYBOY: That's a fine semantic line. What about the two times you have been convicted and imprisoned for your deprogramming activities? Why aren't those legal rulings as valid as the two you just cited?

PATRICK: Because I never should have been convicted. In the biggest case, against a Hare Krishna girl in California, I didn't even take part in that deprogramming. The girl had gone home of her own free will, and I was just asked to go in for a few minutes to see if I could help. When I arrived, I didn't say a thing to her—only asked her her name, and I never touched her. Then she threw a glass of water in my face and jumped up and ran out of the house. She wasn't even going to press charges until her leaders told her to. Then I was tried in Orange County, one of the most racially prejudiced areas in the country; and the jury didn't even try the case. The judge called all the shots and I wound up with the maximum sentence.

In the other case, in Denver, I had been placed on probation, but when I was convicted in California, the judge revoked my probation and sent me to jail.

PLAYBOY: What makes you so certain that the people you deprogram aren't there of their own free will? How can you claim that they haven't sincerely dedicated their lives to these new religious movements?

PATRICK: Because I have proof. The people themselves are my proof. I've deprogrammed hundreds of people from these groups, and when I deprogram them, they come out of it and tell the truth about what has happened to them. They say that they have been duped, brainwashed, hypnotized and mesmerized by the cult. That's the proof, the people themselves.

PLAYBOY: Don't the people in these groups say that they are there of their own choice?

PATRICK: Yes, but that's because they have been programmed to respond that way.

PLAYBOY: That's an easy out. How do you know that they have been programmed? Isn't it just your word against theirs?

PATRICK: No, and I can prove it with a simple discussion. I don't even need to deprogram a person to present proof that he has been programmed. All you have to do is put us in a room—a living room, a courtroom—and allow me to talk to that person, and I can show that he is under mind control. In almost every case, you'll see that he can't think for himself, that he can't make decisions. You'll see that he can't even answer a simple question that requires a yes or no answer, that it is psychologically impossible for that person to hold a normal conversation.

PLAYBOY: Aren't most of the people who get involved with these groups psychologically disturbed to begin with?

PATRICK: No; on the contrary, they are some of the brightest, most intelligent kids in the country. Of course, you find some kids in any group who are naïve and idealistic, and others who have been approached at particularly vulnerable times of their lives—they've just lost their girlfriend or they're down on their luck. But the vast majority of the people I have deprogrammed are intelligent, outgoing, popular kids. Many of them are sensitive, artistic; others are handsome and athletic. A large proportion of them come from Catholic and Jewish backgrounds where religion was a strong part of their family upbringing. But all of them are searching for something, searching for better ways to make the most out of life, searching for the same things most of us are searching for.

PLAYBOY: So, for a lot of people, cults must provide some sort of answer in terms of that search.

PATRICK: They'll tell you they've found God, or the truth. They'll tell you they find friendship and love in a group. Lots of "God bless you" and "We love you, brother," and putting their arms around you and hugging you. But that is after they've been psychologically kidnapped. It's not the so-called love and friendship that hooks them. They're already mesmerized at that stage. No one can claim he's found an answer to anything when he's a willing slave, when he's given up everything he owns to unseen masters he doesn't even know, when he's spending eighteen and twenty hours a day lying and cheating and raising money. When they come out, when they get deprogrammed, they all say that it *wasn't* an answer, that they were miserable and filled with guilt and hate—not love.

PLAYBOY: You're throwing out a lot at once. Let's take things one at a time. First, you talk about "cults" as if it were a brand name everyone were supposed to recognize. Just whom do you mean when you use the term *cults*?

PATRICK: I mean the Moonies, the Hare Krishna, Scientology, the Divine Light Mission, the Children of God, the Tony and Susan Alamo Christian Foundation, the New Testament Missionary Fellowship, the Way International, and hundreds of other groups in the United States that use techniques of mind control that destroy their members' free will. NBC estimated that there were ten million cult members. My figure is closer to twenty million.

PLAYBOY: You claim that cults damage a person's mind. What kind of evidence do you have to back up that charge?

PATRICK: Many of the kids who were in the Children of God when I started investigating it are being kicked out now, because they've reached a point where they are no longer able to serve the purpose of the cult. After years in the cult, the members' minds cease to be, and they develop a mental condition, become a vegetable or become suicidal. Only recently have the cults begun to kick people out. Then they go back to their families and sit around the house like vegetables. Recently, I had three who were gone to the point of no return. They had to send them to a mental hospital, because there was nothing I could do with them. Their minds had been completely destroyed.

PLAYBOY: What do you mean destroyed? Physically?

PATRICK: Mentally and physically. In one case, the parents knew before they called me that they were looking for some miracle. There was one boy who had a long beard and hadn't left his room for weeks. He had a jug in there and he urinated in it. He hadn't eaten in fifteen days when I got there. I made him eat, but I couldn't help him. They had to put him in a mental hospital.

PLAYBOY: Have you heard of any kids who have died as a result of being in cults?

PATRICK: Oh, yes. Plenty of them die and plenty of them commit suicide. There's just so much a human mind can take. A lot of Moonies have died. Two fell down an elevator shaft at the New Yorker Hotel. Another committed suicide. There have been others who have been so fatigued that they have gotten in car wrecks. Then there are some cases where cult members have gone insane and killed each other. They have the capability of destroying themselves or someone else.

PLAYBOY: Presbyterians fall down elevator shafts, get into car wrecks and commit suicide. What does that prove?

PATRICK: Presbyterians aren't programmed to use violence to further their aims the way cult members are. Two members of Synanon were recently accused of putting that snake in an attorney's mailbox—I deprogrammed the first people he got out of that group. Other cults have started training their members to use guns. *Every* one of these cults has the capability of turning into another Manson family, and, in fact, they're more dangerous than Manson, because Manson wasn't organized. You take some of the cults with tens of thousands of members. Those people will do anything they are told to do, including killing themselves, their parents, police, political leaders, *anybody* they feel is necessary.

PLAYBOY: That seems very exaggerated. Since you referred to the Manson murders, which occurred nine years ago, don't you really think the cult movement has died down somewhat?

PATRICK: No, it's getting bigger every day; it's getting stronger and stronger.

PLAYBOY: Why does one read so little about it?

PATRICK: Because people are afraid. Those in the anticult organizations are afraid of being sued. They're afraid of bad publicity. And the cults are going after them now, threatening them, arming themselves.

PLAYBOY: How bad do you think it is going to get?

PATRICK: I don't know. It's getting pretty bad now. I think it has already gotten way out of hand, but nobody is going to do anything until something bad happens to great numbers of people. I'm convinced of that.

(The next portion of the interview took place several days after the Guyana events.)

PLAYBOY: How did the murders and suicides in Guyana affect you?
PATRICK: I feel very sad. I've said it would take something like this to wake people up, but it makes me very, very, very sad to see what happened.

But I also feel strongly that those people shouldn't be blamed for what they did. Congress, the government officials who refused to investigate those cults years ago are responsible. Important members of the ACLU, the National Council of Churches, and everybody who has supported those cults are responsible. They're the ones who killed those people. The blood is on their hands.
PLAYBOY: Were you aware of the People's Temple before the tragedy in Guyana?
PATRICK: Yes. For years, I had tried to get people in Washington to do something about the People's Temple. Jim Jones had been on *my* list for a long time. I had had numerous reports and requests for help, but nobody could move on them, because nobody could locate the individuals. I came close to deprogramming one sixteen-year-old girl, but before I could get up there, she disappeared. She vanished. Then, when we found out that she was over in Guyana, it was too late to do anything.
PLAYBOY: Did you hear any reports of violence prior to last November?
PATRICK: Yes, as far back as '74. Many people knew about it, especially in San Francisco. It was known that they had beaten people up and killed people. They killed people long before they left for Guyana. It was a report of one such killing that started Congressman Ryan on his investigation.
PLAYBOY: Do you think the potential for Guyana-type violence exists in other cults?
PATRICK: Unquestionably. The potential exists in the Moonies, in Krishna, in Scientology—and they are much larger and much better organized than the People's Temple. Each talks about eliminating its enemies. The Reverend Moon has said that those who oppose him will die—that's a quote: "Many people will die." I deprogrammed a Krishna who told me that he had been taught to flee anyone who was "being blasphemous," to kill that person or, if all else failed, to kill himself. At one time, Scientology's so-called code of honor stated, "Never fear to harm another in a just cause." They also had a fair-game policy that stated, "Enemies of Scientology may be tricked, sued, lied to or destroyed." Interestingly enough, the People's Temple is reported to have had its own fair-game doctrines. When you confront them with those policies, all the cults deny that they are meant to be taken literally, but there is plenty of evidence to the contrary.
PLAYBOY: What about suicide pacts in the other cults?
PATRICK: I already told you what Krishna teaches its members to do if they should feel threatened. I've also heard about Moonies who were instructed to slash their wrists rather than face deprogramming. I know of one instance where that did, in fact, occur.
PLAYBOY: Do you think we could have a tragedy here in this country on the scale of what happened in Guyana?
PATRICK: I think they're going to start happening like wildfire.
PLAYBOY: Murders and mass suicides?
PATRICK: Yes. Those organizations are multimillion-dollar rackets, and if Congress is forced by the public to do something, the cults are not just going to give up their paradise without a fight.
PLAYBOY: You're not claiming that anyone who is in a cult is potentially a killer, are you?
PATRICK: Potentially. And I don't mean the way you and I could potentially kill. I

mean *real* potential. Cult members can only do as they're told. They can't question anything. So if their leaders tell them to kill someone else or kill themselves, they'll do it.

PLAYBOY: That's quite a dogmatic statement. You don't see any gray areas, any possibility that some cult members may be more heavily indoctrinated than others?

PATRICK: Of course, there are degrees of mind control. But I do believe those major cults have the potential of doing what Jim Jones did or what Charles Manson did. The Jonestown suicides and murders weren't anything compared with what's going to happen. There's going to come a time when *thousands* of people are going to get killed right here in the United States.

PLAYBOY: Sounds like a paranoid's fantasy.

PATRICK: Paranoid or not, I warned of things that sounded much more fantastic eight years ago. This means violence could take place without firing a shot. Water supplies could be poisoned. They could make blackouts happen. They could stage underground operations that would involve killing many people.

PLAYBOY: They *could;* anybody could. Saying so doesn't constitute proof. Let's stick to what you know about firsthand. For instance, you've deprogrammed about a hundred Krishnas, by your count. And you've told us they've used violence against you when you've had them locked up in a room with you. Well, so might most people. But what evidence do you have that a peaceful cult like the Krishnas actually programs its members to be capable of violence, especially when there have been reports that the Krishnas have dropped some of their Eastern trappings and have moved toward the mainstream of respected religious sects?

PATRICK: The temple leaders teach them that when argument fails, violence may be necessary. Hell, they feel they have a divine sanction to kill.

PLAYBOY: Facts, Mr. Patrick, facts. Do you have that in writing? Is there a Krishna manual that orders the members to do as you claim?

PATRICK: The facts are that every Krishna member I've deprogrammed, from temples across the country, has told me the same thing. The one question I always ask—it's part of my standard list—is, "Would you kill for your faith?" or "Would you kill for your leader?" They say yes.

PLAYBOY: How many of them have said yes unequivocally?

PATRICK: Almost every last one of them.

PLAYBOY: Every last one of them has said he'd *kill* for his leader?

PATRICK: Yes, and I can go further. I make it a point to ask them, "Would you kill your *parents*?" And they say yes.

PLAYBOY: That reminds us of the test of Abraham in the Bible. Any deeply religious person might tell you that at a hypothetical level.

PATRICK: Perhaps, but virtually all cult members say the same thing. I've videotaped most of the more recent deprogrammings, so anyone can see for himself. Just the other day—to change cults for a moment—I deprogrammed a girl from the Divine Light Mission. I asked her, "Would you kill your*self* if the Guru Maharaj Ji told you to?" She hoo-hahed around for a while, and I asked her again: "If the Guru walked into this very room right now and told you to kill yourself, would you do it?" She said yes. That's on tape, too.

PLAYBOY: That's only what they're telling you. It doesn't constitute proof that they're capable of violence.

PATRICK: But that's the point. If they were thinking for themselves, admitting something like that would be the last thing they'd tell Black Lightning. That's ammunition for me. The fact is that they respond to that question that way because they've been programmed to say that. They *can't* say anything else. As to whether or not they'd carry it out, there's only one way to prove *that*. . . . Here's another example: A wealthy psychologist I deprogrammed from a tiny Christian cult on the West Coast had two beautiful children, a daughter seven and a son nine. I asked him, "If someone came into this room and put a knife to your children's throats and told you that if you didn't stop going to these cult meetings, if you didn't give up your faith, he'd slice their throats, yes or no, would you let them die?" Without frowning or anything else, he told me, "Yes. Anything that would interfere with my serving the Lord . . . " He meant that. He *meant* that.

PLAYBOY: If what you're saying is true, if these cults really do put people under mind control, how is it possible that they have been able to attract so many willing participants in recent years?

PATRICK: They do it with deception and with love. These people have the ability to walk up to you on the street and talk to you about anything they feel you're interested in. Anything—sports, politics, religion. But they rarely tell you who they really are or what group they're with. Their technique is to get your attention and your trust, and the split second they get your trust, they can create a kind of on-the-spot hypnosis.

PLAYBOY: Come on. People can't be hypnotized that easily. Give us an example of what you mean.

PATRICK: OK, take Krishna, for example. Many times I have watched them at the airport. They come up to you, stand inches away and talk to you or they touch you on the shoulder. Then they stare you straight in the eye. If they can make eye contact and get the person's trust, then they can put him in a brief hypnotic trance and get twenty dollars from him, just like that.

PLAYBOY: That's going against what many experts on hypnosis say. How can you claim a person can really be hypnotized as easily as that?

PATRICK: We have a natural ability to slip into this unconscious state. We use it every day. I'm sure anybody who has ever driven a car has driven up to a traffic light in an unconscious state of mind. You stop on red and as soon as the light turns green, you pull off. Then, once you're through the light, you snap back to consciousness and look back to see whether or not you've run a light. When you went through it, you were acting in an unconscious state of mind. Everybody does the same thing when he gets up in the morning and goes through his daily routine. But cult recruiters take advantage of this to place suggestions in your mind. You may walk away from them and say they're stupid or crazy, totally unaware that they've already started working on you. Days later, you may feel a strong urge drawing you to look into the cult. Your mind has already been opened to suggestion.

PLAYBOY: Once a person is drawn to a cult, what techniques are used to keep him there?

PATRICK: They use a combination of fear, guilt, hatred, deception, poor diet and fatigue. First they isolate you from your family, then they isolate you from the world. They give you a very poor diet and very little sleep, and that's where the brainwashing begins. They sit up there twenty-four hours a day, saying over and over that everything outside the cult is evil, that it's Satan's world. They program you with repetition until you have no desires and no emotions left. You feel no pain, no joy, no nothing. They destroy everything about you. Then, in order to keep a person in that frame of mind, they make it impossible for him to ever think or act on his own, and they do that with self-hypnosis, autosuggestion. That kind of self-hypnosis comes in a million different forms, and every cult uses it. It can be induced by repeating a chant, a word, a group of words, by meditation, yoga, tapes, records, the Bible, the cult's books, any card in the deck.

PLAYBOY: Are you saying that the chanting and meditation cult members do are really done under hypnosis?

PATRICK: That's right. The reason most people don't believe that, though, is that when you talk about hypnosis, they relate it to its clinical form, in which somebody sits you down and tells you that he is going to hypnotize you. But in the cults, nobody tells you that you're being hypnotized, and every time you begin to think or have doubts or any emotions at all, the cult teaches you to hypnotize yourself. It tells you that your mind is evil, that thinking is the machinery of the devil and "If you think, you stink!" Then it tells you that you are supposed to use your mind only to serve God—and God is always the leader—or that you are supposed to use your mind only to read the Bible or to do whatever they want you to do.

PLAYBOY: But still, Moonies, Krishnas, Scientologists . . . you're certainly tarring every one of those groups with the same broad brush.

PATRICK: They *all* use the same set of techniques to turn their members into zombies.

PLAYBOY: But couldn't many of those same claims be made about the Catholic Church or any other strict religious order that makes demands on its members' time and energy? How do you distinguish between a cult, as you use the term, and a legitimate religion?

PATRICK: You look at the facts. Organized religions—Catholicism, Protestantism, Judaism—don't totally cut people off from the world. They don't teach people to hate their parents, their government, and everything and everyone but them. They don't teach people to lie, cheat, steal and beg in the streets. They teach you to honor your father and mother, to love your neighbor as yourself and to do unto others as you would have them do unto you. You can't compare having a child in a cult with having a child in the priesthood. When you enter the Catholic Church to become a priest, first you've got to qualify. Then they tell you exactly what you're getting into. You know what you can do and what you can't do. If you go to become a priest or a nun, you know you aren't going to be able to get married. You know you've got to study for so many years. You know exactly what you're going to do before you go in there. But these kids don't know what they are getting into. They find out after the mind control begins, after they have been hypnotized.

(The rest of the interview, with the exception of the final section, was conducted before the Guyana tragedy.)

PLAYBOY: You've been skipping around, using examples from various cults. Which cults are the ones you find dangerous?

PATRICK: Every one of them. *Every* cult uses the techniques in some form.

PLAYBOY: Then let's get down to specifics. Take the Moonies, for starters. What do they believe, what techniques do they use and what do you feel is wrong with them?

PATRICK: In my opinion, the Unification Church is public enemy number one as far as the cults are concerned. Moon calls himself a Christian, but his movement has been denounced by Christians the world over. In truth, he is a wealthy Korean industrialist who wants to rule the world. He's said that over and over again. In 1973, he said, "I will conquer and subjugate the world." In another speech, he said, "The present United Nations must be annihilated by our power." And in 1974, he said, "Every people and organization that goes against the Unification Church will gradually come down or drastically come down and die. Many people will die—those who go against our movement."

That man is a multimillionaire with factories in Korea that make munitions, air rifles, pharmaceuticals and titanium products. He owns vast amounts of real estate in the United States, hotels, mansions, a daily newspaper in New York, two big yachts; and he has bought up huge fishing operations in Massachusetts, Maryland and Alabama. He has between seven thousand and fifteen thousand full-time members in this country who work for nothing or next to nothing; and all of them believe he is the Messiah, the Lord of the Second Advent who will come from the East. That's how he controls them. He makes the whole world out to be Satan, then he proclaims himself to be God and the world of his cult to be the only path to salvation. The Moonies come up to you on the street and they start working on you with what they call love bombing. They smother you with love, warmth, friendship and total acceptance. But they're so deceptive. They don't tell you who they really are, they say they're with the New Age Fellowship or the Creative Community Project. They have a doctrine called heavenly deception that instructs them to say anything they have to to further Moon's mission. Then, once they get you into the group, they start indoctrinating you with the Divine Principle, Moon's version of the Holy Scriptures, which claims that both Adam and Jesus Christ failed in their missions on earth and that Moon has been sent to earth by God to breed a new ideal race of men who are free from sin.

PLAYBOY: What about the Hare Krishnas?

PATRICK: Krishna is one of the most dangerous cults in this country—as well as one of the richest. It preaches a life of strict asceticism and self-denial, forbidding sex. Krishna's form of mind control is through chanting, plain and simple. They get up at three or four in the morning and start chanting, over and over, *Hare Krishna, Hare Krishna, Hare Hare,* fingering their prayer beads to keep count. They chant two to five hours a day, then go out on the street to recruit members. They sell books, pamphlets, incense, orange juice. They hire advertising agencies and travel around the country training their members in high-pressure selling techniques.

PLAYBOY: So far, you haven't mentioned anything that either nuns in a convent or a typical businessman might not endorse. What about the Church of Scientology? The press has reported that eleven of its leaders were recently indicted on charges of infiltrating the Justice Department, stealing documents from government offices, and bugging IRS meetings. But there has been relatively little reported about their beliefs and practices. What do you know about them?

PATRICK: Scientology is probably the biggest cult in the country, perhaps the world. It's estimated that there are sixty thousand members in the U.S. and more than three and a half million worldwide. It was founded in the Fifties by a former science-fiction writer named L. Ron Hubbard, who created a new vocabulary to describe and cure people's mental and emotional problems. He talks about "clearing" people of traumatic experiences and "aberrational behavior," and of universal spirits called Thetans that are reincarnated in every person on earth. Top-ranking Scientologists I have deprogrammed told me that they believe they could leave their bodies at will and travel through space and that they had all been friends trillions of years ago on other planets.

They have filed multimillion-dollar lawsuits against people who have criticized the cult. And, like the rest of the cults, they bring in millions and millions of dollars each year. They have a huge estate in England, more than two dozen centers in the United States, including a big celebrity center in Hollywood, where they have recruited movie stars and rock stars, football players and jazz musicians; and they use their names and pictures to recruit more members. They *don't* tell you that Charles Manson studied their techniques when he was in prison in the early Sixties and that he probably used a lot of what he learned to get women to join his family.

When the FBI raided Scientology's offices a couple of years ago, it found blackjacks, pistols, eavesdropping and lock-picking equipment, knockout drops, and files on federal judges, government officials, lawyers, journalists and parents of kids in *other* cults. They had a file on me marked OPERATION BLACKOUT and a memo about stopping publication of my book. They had one on Paulette Cooper, who wrote a book called *The Scandal of Scientology*. It was marked OPERATION FREAK-OUT and its purpose was to "get PC [Cooper] committed to a mental hospital or a prison"—which they almost succeeded in doing. They had one on the American Medical Association marked A.M.A. DOOM PROGRAM.

PLAYBOY: We haven't discussed any of the Christian cults you named. Do those groups use mind control, too, and if so, how is what they do any different from the practices of other evangelical Christian sects?

PATRICK: The Children of God, the New Testament Missionary Fellowship, the Tony and Susan Alamo Christian Foundation, the Way International, and every other Christian cult use the Bible as a form of self-hypnosis. The Bible is the most misused book in the world. They take verses out of context, they twist them around and they make you keep your head in the Bible until you get so engrossed that you become mesmerized. Most of those groups use the charismatic practice of speaking in tongues as their primary technique of mind control. They teach you how to speak in tongues—there's nothing magical about it—and they tell you to do it all the time. Even when you're talking to someone, you're supposed to be thinking in tongues. Plenty of other Christians speak in tongues, but they do it only once a week or so and the effect lasts for only a little while.

PLAYBOY: What do you consider a tolerable degree of speaking in tongues?

PATRICK: These cults do it *all* the time, until people can't get it out of their minds. Then, as usual, they send the kids out on the street to raise money. In the Children of God, some of their prettiest women have been turned into "Happy Hookers for Jesus." Some of the other groups have farms and communes where the members work around the clock and sleep on wooden floors and turn over everything they have to their leader—their money, cars, personal possessions.

PLAYBOY: How are those Christian cult practices different from other evangelical rituals? Take Billy Graham, for instance. Would you call him a cult leader?

PATRICK: No, Billy Graham is not a cult leader. He doesn't teach hate, he doesn't isolate his followers from the world and he doesn't turn them away from education or their families. However, Billy Graham does use many of the same techniques as the cults to get a lot of money from people. Billy Graham's whole thing is making money, and he is a genius at it. But I've never seen Billy Graham do anything to help anybody. I never heard of Billy Graham going to the site of a flood or a city that had been wiped out by a tornado and holding out a helping hand. The only thing I have ever seen Billy Graham hold out is a begging hand.

PLAYBOY: Would you say that his followers are under the influence of mind control?

PATRICK: A lot of them are. They don't think he can do anything wrong. They don't worship God, they worship Billy Graham. Whatever he says is the Gospel. That is the same kind of adoration you find in the cults. I disagree with Billy Graham on a lot of things, especially when he says you've got to have the Word. Well, you don't have to have the Word—and that means the Bible. The Bible will drive you crazy if you take it literally.
PLAYBOY: Do you consider some of the political and therapeutic groups that don't call themselves religions to be as objectionable as the cults? Have you ever deprogrammed anyone from, say, est.
PATRICK: Oh, yes, I've done them all. I don't care which ones you're talking about, they *all* use the same techniques. Est uses a lot of Scientology. Synanon uses fear, guilt and physical intimidation. TM uses a very damaging form of meditation—
PLAYBOY: Wait a minute. You think TM is dangerous?
PATRICK: TM is one of the most damaging forms of meditation. It's also one of the biggest cults in the nation.
PLAYBOY: But don't millions of Americans—housewives, executives, artists—practice TM every day without any adverse side effects?
PATRICK: If they do it just twenty minutes twice a day, they usually don't have any problems. Three-quarters of the people I deprogram tell me that their first experience with cults was with TM and that it opened their minds to all types of suggestion. TM doesn't care what people do, it doesn't want to start a lot of communes, but it prepares people to be taken into other cults.
PLAYBOY: That sounds like the old argument that marijuana leads to heroin.
PATRICK: Well, I happen to think there may be a lot more to TM's chief guru, the Maharishi, than just opening people up. My personal belief is that he is one of the top people involved in a conspiracy to meddle seriously in world politics.
PLAYBOY: You better explain that.
PATRICK: All right. I've had a number of calls to deprogram TM instructors who have been in the organization for many years. I got a call last week from a woman who said her son, who is a TM instructor, was part of a team of fifty that the Maharishi is sending around the world to bring calm to areas of political turmoil. He wrote her a letter from Guatemala, where they had been sent at the request of a group of wealthy Central American businessmen; and they were convinced that their going down there and meditating was bringing peace! They claimed responsibility for stopping the strikes and riots and getting the newspapers publishing again. They had been to the Middle East and they claimed they were responsible for the peace talks there. When the woman called me, her son was on his way to another secret mission to Rhodesia. He told her they were instructed to keep those operations very quiet.
PLAYBOY: Let's go back to Synanon for a minute. What happened when you deprogrammed the first kids who were brought out of Synanon?
PATRICK: Synanon is one of the worst cults I have ever been involved with. They made everyone cut his hair so you couldn't tell the men from the women. They trained people to use guns. A fifteen-year-old boy told me that they talked about killing and about suicide. They said never give in or give up.

I deprogrammed three members of Synanon at one time. Their parents were in the cult, the mother had died there, and they were taken to their grandmother. When I got to the scene, I couldn't tell the girl from the two boys. Their heads were shaved and all three were wearing men's clothes. They had already done a lot of damage. They had torn up furniture. They made almost five hundred dollars' worth of telephone calls on their grandmother's bill. The grandmother had left the house, because she was afraid one of them was going to kill her.

PLAYBOY: How did you handle them?

PATRICK: Well, I don't care who they are, how large they are. They can be black belts in karate, weigh 250 pounds—I always let them know who's the boss. When I step in there, I get that straight from the very beginning, especially with the guys. I work on the theory that a human being is just as good as you make him and as bad as you let him be. So I went in there and I told them, "Look, now I want all of you to sit right down and don't move an inch. Keep your damn mouths closed, and I don't want no bullshit from you." I said, "Now I'm not your grandmother. If any of you jump up, I'm going to put you out of action real quick." Then they became just like three little babies with me. I don't care how big they are, once I show them I'm boss, they always become like babies.

PLAYBOY: What did you do then?

PATRICK: The next thing I did was to separate them. I realized that the strongest one was the girl, and I always try to take the toughest one first, so I put each of them in a separate room and started with the girl. She was a brilliant girl and she spoke very well, and she made fun of the way I talked. But if they want to get nasty, I can get nasty, too. I was prepared to use whatever method was necessary. I've got better techniques now, but sometimes I have to revert to my old techniques, where I get real nasty with them. It's the only way to gain their respect. So I just told her, "Girl, you're a bitch. You've got the gall to talk to me that way and you don't even know me. You're sitting there looking more like a man than your two brothers. You're in a cult that took a beautiful girl and made a lesbian out of her"—I really got *down* with her—"you hate your own grandmother. You would kill your own grandmother for this leader. You take orders from that no-good son of a bitch, you will eat his shit." When I started talking about her leader, she really got steaming mad. That's what brought her out of it, though.

PLAYBOY: Did you ever lay a finger on her?

PATRICK: No, but if it had been necessary, I would have put her out of action. I told the two boys, "If you so much as move, I'm going to put you on your ass so quick it will make your head swim."

PLAYBOY: From the description of the threats you use, some of your techniques don't seem very different from those you claim the cults use. How *is* cult deprogramming *different*?

PATRICK: Deprogramming is opening up a person's mind so that something other than the programming of the cult can go in for the first time in so many days, weeks, months or years. The cults' type of programming consists of putting suggestion into a person's mind, constantly, until they've destroyed his ability to think. They take a person's mind away from him and make it impossible for him to act on his own, and they teach him self-hypnosis to keep him in that trance. I restore the individual's free will and his ability to think. That's the difference. I bring him out of the trance. I force the mind to start working again.

PLAYBOY: How do you do it?

PATRICK: I force them to think. When I deprogram people, all I do is shoot them challenging questions. I hit them with things they haven't been programmed to respond to. I know what the cults have told them, so I shoot them the right questions and they get frustrated when they can't answer. They think they have the answers, they have been given answers to everything, but I throw them off balance and that forces them to begin questioning. I get them to start comparing and evaluating, and that is the key, because that makes them start thinking. Then once they start thinking, they deprogram themselves. They come out of it and their minds start working again.

PLAYBOY: How do you choose your subjects?

PATRICK: I don't solicit any work. I never go to anyone's parents. They always come to me.

PLAYBOY: How can you tell if a parent's claim is legitimate?

PATRICK: When they come to me, it's always with a legitimate claim, because when a parent comes to me, I know he's reached bottom. First they go to their religious leader, their spiritual leaders, the minister, and they don't get anything there. Then they go to their legal adviser, their attorney, and they don't get anything from him, because he doesn't know. Then their psychiatrist, the family doctor, the police, the FBI, their congressman, senator, the President, the U.S. Attorney-General. When they finally come to me, I'm the bottom of the barrel. They have struck out everywhere.

PLAYBOY: Yet many people claim that what you do is not deprogramming but *re*programming, forcing an individual to change his religious beliefs to those of his parents or to those that society deems more acceptable.

PATRICK: They don't know the facts. I don't tell anyone *what* to believe in. I don't tell him anything one way or another. As I said, I get the mind working again. They can live their own lives.

PLAYBOY: How can a person be sure someone isn't going to have him kidnapped and deprogrammed by you simply because he doesn't think the way someone wants him to?

PATRICK: I don't go out and take a person just because he doesn't think the way somebody wants him to. Before I agree to deprogram somebody, I conduct a thorough investigation. I look into his entire history and I ask a lot of questions that enable me to evaluate the situation.

PLAYBOY: How does deprogramming work? Give us a typical example.

PATRICK: OK. When I start a deprogramming, I don't need to know anything about the cult. If I didn't know the name of the cult, it wouldn't matter at all. You can bring someone to me and I can read his mind, to a point where I know not what he is thinking but *how* he is thinking, how his mind is working. I watch the mind.

PLAYBOY: What do you mean? The mind isn't visible.

PATRICK: No, but I can see the mind in a person's face. Whatever you are—a genius, a wino—is going to show up in your face. If you can read a person's face, you can practically tell his entire personality. Their eyes are not always glazed, either. They've gotten beyond that point to where their pupils are no longer dilated. Those are the ones who have been in the cult for a long time. Then you have to watch how they answer even the simplest questions.

For example, a person may say to me that he has been in a cult for six years and that everything he did was for God and that everything he gave, he gave to God. And I'll say, "You gave all your money to God? You gave fifty thousand dollars to God? How did you give it to Him? Did He come down to pick it up, did you send it special delivery? Or did you send Him a letter? How did you give all that money to God?" And if he tells the truth, he's got no answer, because he's done nothing for God. Everything he did was for the leader.

PLAYBOY: Can you get the person you're deprogramming to admit that?

PATRICK: No, because everyone in the cult looks upon the leader as God. Even if they admit he's not God Almighty or the Messiah, they say he alone is appointed by God or God speaks through him only. Then I say, "Well, how did God appoint him?" Or I refer them to the Bible and I say, "Well, if what you're telling me is true, then what about the fourteenth chapter of John, where it says, 'I am the way, the truth and the light: No man cometh unto the Father but by me'?" And I say, "Your leader claims he's the way, the truth and the light. Which one is telling the truth?" And every time, I don't care what cult they are from, they say neither one is telling a lie.
PLAYBOY: What do you do then?
PATRICK: I don't let it stop there. I go into detail on everything the cult has programmed them to say. I keep hitting them with challenging questions that show them they don't know right from wrong, that they don't know it's wrong for a person to destroy somebody's free will and program him to beg and lie and cheat, that they don't know it's wrong to hate your parents and wrong to isolate yourself from everything and everybody. When they see that they don't have any answers, they start searching for something to say. That forces the mind to start thinking again and they come out of it.
PLAYBOY: Is that it?
PATRICK: Yes, it's just talk. You push the mind with questions until you break through.
PLAYBOY: How do you know when you've broken through?
PATRICK: From the first time I lay eyes on a person, I'm watching his face. Then I start moving his mind, pushing it with questions, and I keep pushing and pushing. I don't let him get away with the lies he's been told. Then there'll be a minute, a second, when the mind *snaps back* and he comes out of it. The only way I can describe it is that it's like turning on the light in a dark room or bringing a person back from the dead. It's a beautiful thing, the whole personality changes, it's like seeing a person change from a werewolf into a man. Where they showed no emotion, you can see feeling again. One minute it's like talking to a stone wall; the next you are able to reason with them. They're able to relax and respond with intelligent answers.
PLAYBOY: You mentioned that you often threaten to put someone "out of action." The cults have accused you of actually using force and brutality in your deprogrammings. How do you reply to those charges?
PATRICK: A lot of cult members get very violent, especially at the beginning of a deprogramming session. Krishna members have spat in my face and called me a demon. One girl came at me with a kitchen knife, someone else came at me with a broken bottle. The Moonies, as I said, tell their people to slash their wrists rather than talk to me. But the only thing *we* do is restrain them, to keep them from hurting me or hurting themselves.

The cults tell their people that if I ever show up, I'm going to rape them, beat them, drug them, lock them in their closets, put ice down their backs, stuff chicken bones down their throats, deprive them of food and sleep. Those are the stories circulating about Black Lightning. They don't realize that they're making my job easier. They come in scared to death of me, find out that I don't do what I'm accused of, and suddenly they're wondering, Why? So their minds start to work again. They'll say, "Don't touch me! Don't touch me!" and I'll just sit back and deprogram them just like that.
PLAYBOY: It can't be as simple as that. Would you give us a more detailed example of a deprogramming?

PATRICK: All right. Let's take a Moonie deprogramming. I remember one in particular; the fellow had been on the dean's list at a good Eastern college before he dropped out to join the Moonies. His parents got him to go home by telling him that his cousin was getting married and his grandfather from Israel was going to be there, but he figured he would go home for a few days, play it cool, and take a thousand dollars out of his bank account to give to the cult. When we surprised him at the airport and got him into the car, he didn't struggle at all. He withdrew into himself, stared straight ahead and started praying to the Reverend Moon for protection. Another deprogrammer talked to him for six hours before I went in, but nothing would go in. He didn't say a word. He sat on the edge of the bed with a smile on his face, but he didn't speak, he didn't move a finger.

Finally, I went into the room and said, "Hello, I'm Ted Patrick." I sat down on a chair across from him and got close enough so that our knees were almost touching. Then I stared him in the eye and got right down to it. I said, "You think you are a Christian. You think you are doing the Lord's work. But you don't worship the Lord. You worship Moon. Did the Lord ever tell you to hate your father and mother? Where does it say in the Bible that you should hate your father and mother? Where does it say that? And where does it say in the Bible that you should spend all your life, twenty hours a day, out on the street cheating little old ladies, lying to them and robbing them of their money? Christ told the rich man to give away everything he owned. But he didn't say, 'Give it to me.' And he didn't say, 'Give it to Moon.' "

Then I reached down into my briefcase and took out a picture of Moon and a felt-tip pen. I drew a pair of horns on his head, then a mustache, pointed ears, and as I was doing that, I kept talking. I said, "Why would you give up your mind? God gave you that mind, a good mind, a brilliant mind. You are a brilliant boy and you have everything going for you. Why would you give up that mind to worship Moon? You're not doing the Lord's work. You worship this son of a bitch. See him? There's your god. Satan the snake!" Then I ripped the picture into pieces and tossed them into the boy's lap.

I kept going. I said, "You think God can't speak English. Why's that? Think about it, Why?" I said, "You're not going to talk. That's OK. You want to smile at me. Well, I'll smile right back at you. We'll smile together. I've got nothing else to do. I can stay here three, four months. Even longer. Nobody's going anywhere." That's very powerful when I say that. Even though it rarely takes more than three days, once I convince them that they're going to be there forever, they begin to weaken.

I kept throwing questions at him. I said, "How can Moon be the Messiah if he was born of woman? The Bible says Christ was born of a virgin. We know Moon wasn't born of a virgin." It wasn't until the next day that he even started to talk. Then he kept repeating, "You don't understand. You're distorting the truth. The answer to that is in Divine Principle." But I knew Moon's Divine Principle better than he did. I tore him apart on Divine Principle. Then I played tapes for him of other Moonies I had deprogrammed in which they talked about how they had been duped. And I showed him newspaper stories about the mansion Moon lives in while his followers sleep on the floor and eat peanut butter. I kept asking him, "Where does the money go? Where does the money go?" But he couldn't answer. Finally, his parents went into the room with the other deprogrammer who was there. His father said, "I don't know what they've done to you, but I'll stay here for six months to get you out. If it means my job, my career, my life, I'm prepared to do it." Then they asked him, "Who do you love more? That pimp—or your father?" And he said, "My father. I love my father," and he got up out of his chair and hugged his father, and both of them started to cry. The cap was unscrewed. He was out of it.

PLAYBOY: What about the charges that have been made on television that you have been known to drug or sexually abuse your deprogramming subjects?

PATRICK: There's no truth to them. You know, we're dealing with kids from some of the best families, and their parents are responsible people, not skid-row bums. We're dealing with some of the most brilliant minds in the world, and the parents are not going to bring in anyone who is going to harm their child. There's no way we would hurt them. We don't drug anybody—their minds are already messed up. We try to give them the best food and we encourage them to sleep as much as possible in order to rebuild the mind. The parents are present throughout the deprogramming, and if you want more proof, you can see for yourself. I've videotaped hundreds of deprogrammings I've done in the past few years.

PLAYBOY: What happens to someone after he is deprogrammed? Does he go back to the life he led before he joined the cult?

PATRICK: When we deprogram a person, we restore his ability to think and make decisions, but he is still going to have problems for a long time to come. There's a lot more to deprogramming than just talking to the individual. In most cases, you've got to deal with every problem the whole family has ever had. It could be a small problem they had in the past that has become magnified. Sometimes the parents need to be deprogrammed more than the kids.

PLAYBOY: Do you find that many young people go into those groups because their parents have been too narrow-minded or too strict?

PATRICK: Not as a rule, no. But I find a lot of cases where parents will try to raise a child to be what they want him to be, not what the child wants to be. They want the child to live for their happiness, not for his own happiness. Then, after the deprogramming, they tell him who to marry, what school to go to. They don't realize that his mind has been damaged. It has deteriorated, and the mind doesn't heal like a regular sore or a cut or an operation. I deprogrammed a very brilliant girl in Canada who called me after three and a half years to say that only then, for the first time since she had been out of the Divine Light Mission, did she feel completely normal again. That is why every person I deprogram goes through a period of rehabilitation.

PLAYBOY: What happens during rehabilitation?

PATRICK: Rehabilitation is like if you don't run your car for six months or a year and the battery runs down, you jump it to start it, but then you don't turn the key off right away or it will go dead. You let the motor run long enough to build up its own power and recharge itself. Well, the mind is the same way. If you have been incapable of thinking and making decisions for so many days, weeks, months or years, once you get the mind working again, you've got to keep it working until the person gets in the habit of thinking and making his own decisions. After deprogramming, a person tends to float. He'll slip into a trance state without even knowing it. I don't care how strong they come out of it, they'll still float. That's why I say we're dealing with a person with a damaged mind. During rehab, we keep a team with the person at all times. When they slip into that trance state, you can always tell by the hypnotic stare and you bring them out of it by getting them to do things, by talking to them and keeping them busy, and by getting them to go places and keep actively using the mind. When we go out to dinner, they have to decide what they want to eat; if we go to the movies, they have to choose what we are going to see. In the morning, we ask them, "What are you going to do today, go to the beach, go swimming, play records, go for a walk?" They have to make the decisions.

PLAYBOY: How long after the deprogramming will a person "float" like that?

PATRICK: It varies. Some float for two or three days; others float for two or three months. Some never recover completely.

PLAYBOY: You've made some pretty harsh charges. In view of your lack of formal education and the serious nature of the work you are engaged in, don't you think people have a right to ask what qualifies you to speak as an expert on the human mind?

PATRICK: I think my experience and the proof I have presented speaks for itself. I've deprogrammed almost sixteen hundred people. I have a success record. Each and every person I've dealt with qualifies me to do what I'm doing.

PLAYBOY: What about your highly publicized failures? Haven't there been numerous reports of cult members' going back to their cults after they were deprogrammed?

PATRICK: Well, I'd say of the sixteen hundred I've deprogrammed, fewer than thirty have returned to the cults, and most of them escaped before we had a chance to take them through the full process of deprogramming and rehabilitation. Only about five people that I know of went back after going through the full process, and even they wouldn't have gone back if their parents had done what we told them to do.

PLAYBOY: How do people escape?

PATRICK: Somebody lets his guard down and they break out. They jump out the window or slip out the door. When I deprogram someone, I work with a security team. We have somebody accompany the person to the bathroom. Then at night, one person sleeps across from him and another sleeps in front of the door.

PLAYBOY: You seem to have quite a system. When did you first get involved with the cults?

PATRICK: At the time I was working in San Diego as special representative for community relations for Governor Reagan. I didn't have any time for my family. We couldn't be together and do things like we used to, so starting in '68, I used to rent a hotel suite at the Bahia Hotel on Mission Beach. Every Fourth of July, we would entertain our family and friends for three days. We had a ball every year. But then, in 1971, they had a big fireworks display at the amusement park across from the hotel. My kids and their guests wanted to go to the amusement park, and I said, OK, but be back in the hotel after the fireworks. Afterward, everybody was present and accounted for except my oldest son, Michael, who was fourteen at the time.

After about an hour and a half we got worried. We organized teams and went all over the beach looking for him. Finally, after about four hours, we went back to the hotel and started calling the police and local hospitals, when Michael walked in the door. The first thing I noticed was his eyes. The pupils were dilated, and the first thing I thought about was drugs. I went to take hold of him and he told me, "Dad, we were on our way back to the hotel when some people stopped us on the street and asked if we believed in God and if we had Christ in our hearts and if we knew that Christ died on the cross for our sins and if we were happy at home. Then they said they had a family and they called it the Children of God and that the world was going to end within seven years and that they were the chosen family and if we weren't in their family, we were going to burn in hell. But if we joined the Children of God, we wouldn't ever have any more problems. We wouldn't ever be sick or have to go to school, because it was of the devil, and we wouldn't ever have to be bothered with our parents anymore, because they are of the devil. The only thing we would have to do is live in peace with God."

I told him he was stupid for standing up there talking to them for four hours. And he said, "Every time we'd go to walk away, they grabbed us by both arms and started repeating Bible verses and trying to get us to stare them back in the eye." He said, "You know, they had very strange eyes. I've never seen anyone's eyes like that before. And every time I went to look in their eyes, I got dizzy, like the sky was turning around and around." He said, "I thought they were something from outer space." At that point, I got very angry and said, "Look, Michael, don't you say another word. You come home four hours late telling this fantastic lie."

PLAYBOY: You didn't believe him?

PATRICK: No one believed him. We read some of the material they had given him, but it didn't make any sense to me. I was going to send it up to Sacramento the next day to be checked out, but by then I had forgotten about it. When we got home from the beach, Michael went to his room and stayed there. He stayed up there with his head in the Bible, and his eyes looked like he had had a dose of LSD. After about a week of that, my wife called me at the office and said I should go home and talk with Michael. I said OK. This was a boy who had never read the Bible before. If someone had told me that could happen in my family I would have called him a liar. And Michael was the last one it would happen to. He was an outdoor boy. He holds two titles in karate, a track scholarship, plays football, basketball. Nothing could keep him in the house.

So I went home and asked him, "Michael, are you sick?" He said, "No." "Do you feel bad?" "No." "Are you angry with somebody?" "No." "Well," I said, "Michael, this is not you." Then he started telling me about how the world was going to end and we were going to burn in hell and all material things were of the devil and my wife and I were of the devil. And I said, "Mike, I don't want to hear that. I know I've been working hard and haven't been home. Are you on drugs?" And he really blew his stack. He said, "I just want to be alone and read the Bible!" I said I didn't see anything wrong with that.

Then, about a week later, a woman came into my office in San Diego to turn in a complaint. Her son had disappeared. He was last seen on the Fourth of July on Ocean Beach. Then, five days later, she got a call from him saying, "Mom, I found God. I'm not coming home anymore. You are all of the devil." It was the same thing my son was saying, but it didn't hit me right away. She had found out where her son was and went up there to see him, and when they brought him down, five people were with him. Every time she would ask him a question, the leader would answer. And she said, "Mr. Patrick, you know, all those people are nothing but zombies. They have very strange eyes, and every time I looked in their eyes, I got dizzy, like the ceiling was turning around and around."

That's when it struck me. Everything hit home. It upset me so bad I called my wife, and it upset her so bad she told my daughter to bring all the children inside and lock the doors. When I got home, I said to Michael, "I want you to take your time and tell me everything you can remember about that night." We stayed up all night, talking about every detail. And he came out of it. He changed completely and went back to being a normal human being.

PLAYBOY: Was that your first deprogramming?

PATRICK: Yes, but I didn't know it at the time. The next day, I dug in and started calling everybody, trying to get information. In two weeks, I had talked to fifty-two people who had lost kids or relatives to the Children of God. Then I started reading everything I could find on brainwashing, mind control, black magic and psychic power. I talked to everyone from witches to professors, trying to find out what they were doing, how they were putting people under and whether or not what people were telling me was true. It was unbelievable. I wrote up a report to give to the governor's office, but I had to see for myself. So I called my boss and said, "I've got my report ready, but there's one thing missing: Before you make me an appointment with the governor, I want to go in and infiltrate this group." My boss said, "Are you crazy?" And he said, "Ted, I know you when your mind is made up, but remember, if something happens to you in there, I don't know anything about it." I said fine.

Well, I went in with the intention of staying a week. I stayed four nights and three days and I was hooked. I started thinking, these people can't be wrong. I must be the one who's wrong.

PLAYBOY: How did you infiltrate them?

PATRICK: I went out to Mission Beach, where they had their bus. They served coffee, tea, cookies, sandwiches and cake. But I didn't eat or drink anything, because I had reason to believe they had put something in the food. Several years later, authorities in Bellevue, Washington, did find amphetamines in the cookies the Children of God were serving at their public meetings. But when they started talking, I started saying, "Praise the Lord!" and "Thank you, Jesus!" So they thought I was really hooked. Then they drove the bus up to their place at Santee, where there must have been two or three hundred people. Everyone came running out of the house, hugging us and blessing us and saying, "We love you, brother." You'd think that was the greatest thing in the world. Then we went inside and sat on the floor and they started preaching, talking for hours, reading verses from the Bible out of context. They'd never give direct commands, always indirect suggestions. For example, they wouldn't come out and say you should hate your parents. They would quote a Bible verse out of context to make it read, "He that hates not his father, mother, brother and sister cannot be a disciple of Christ."

It was a pitiful scene. Everyone there was so spaced out. If someone fell asleep, another person would punch him in the ribs. When one guy would get through talking, somebody else would go up and talk for hours and hours. You couldn't go to the bathroom without having somebody next to you. You were never alone. And everything was Bible verses. You had to memorize six Bible verses before you could eat in the morning. Even while people were sleeping, they had tape recorders going, Bible verses over and over. They had records playing in the kitchen for the people who were washing dishes. After three days, I began to feel myself weakening. I didn't want to eat too much of their food, and with so little sleep, there's just so much a human mind can take. I began to think, There's no way these people can be wrong. The world *is* going to end in seven years. All material things *are* of the devil. I began hallucinating, seeing angels and Christ and all the things they were talking about.

PLAYBOY: How did you finally get away?

PATRICK: After three days, they thought we were all hooked to the point of no return and they gave us a little free time. I got to thinking, I better get the hell out of here. I told them that I had fifteen thousand dollars in the bank—which I didn't—and that I wanted to go home to get my bank book and my car and my things and bring them all back. So they sent two guys with me in a van and as we were going by the bus station, I said, "Look, let me go in here and call home to make sure nobody's there." When I got away from them, I called a taxi and went out another door. I made it out OK, but

I was so confused for six days. I would leave home at 7:30 in the morning and find myself sixty, seventy miles away. I had to stop and figure out where I was and how I had gotten there. It took me four months before I was back to normal. All the Bible verses were constantly ringing in my mind. That's the power of suggestion.

PLAYBOY: Did you submit your report to the governor?

PATRICK: I not only gave him my report, I took an entire delegation with me to Sacramento: mothers, fathers and people who had been in the group and gotten out.

PLAYBOY: What did Reagan say when he read your report?

PATRICK: The only thing he could do was refer me to the state attorney-general's office, the top law-enforcement agency in California. I went up there and spent many hours with the attorney-general's representatives. But they didn't believe anything I said. They kept asking, "Can you prove this?" They refused to investigate. On the plane back to San Diego, I remember thinking to myself that the only way we were going to get anything done was to do it ourselves.

PLAYBOY: Who? You and the parents?

PATRICK: Yes. I called a meeting the very next night. The place was packed with more than fifty people, and I told them, "OK, I'm not going to lie to you and tell you that my meeting with the attorney-general's office was fruitful. To be frank with you, they're not going to do a damned thing." I had sent a copy of the report to Nixon and Mitchell. We'd been to the police and the FBI. I said, "You're going to have to make up your minds tonight whether you want to fight this thing or just go home and pray about it and hope that everything works out all right. I'm doing all I can do legally. Now, if you want to fight it, I want to make it crystal clear, you've got to be willing to do what is necessary and the hell with what is legal. They're operating illegally in a legal world. We've got to do the same thing. And the first thing we've got to do is get somebody out of there and see what makes them tick. But you're not going to get them out by persuading them to go home. You're going to have to go in there and bodily *rescue* your child."

PLAYBOY: As a government employee at that time, did you have any misgivings about breaking the law?

PATRICK: Oh, yeah, but I knew we had to and I was prepared to. I didn't know what I was getting into, really. I kept thinking once we got somebody out, I would report to the governor and it would be all over. I kept waiting for it to end, but it just kept getting bigger and bigger.

The following Sunday, I got a call from a lady in Miami. Her daughter, a straight-A student at USC, had dropped out of school and joined the Children of God. The mother had spent over two thousand dollars hiring private detectives. I told her, "The only way you are going to get her out is to go in there and bring her out bodily." And she said, "Will you help?" And I said yes. We went up there one night and they happened to be having a meeting and the girl was sitting on the floor. When the door opened, she saw her mother and came to the door and we grabbed her, locked her arms down at her sides, got her in the car and took off. The whole thing happened so fast she didn't know what hit her. But when her mother went to kiss her, the girl slapped her almost unconscious. She said, "You bitch, you're not my mother!" She yakked and yakked all the way back to San Diego, saying, "You're all going to burn in hell," and repeating Bible verses. We checked into a hotel and just started talking to her, telling her everything we knew about the cult. After two days, she came out of it. Her eyes and everything changed. It was like seeing a person return from the dead. She started crying and she embraced her mother for about five minutes. Then she told her mother she was sorry. They just stood there crying and everyone was hugging and kissing. It was a very emotional thing. I said, "Now, you see, she is deprogrammed."

PLAYBOY: Was that the first time you used the word?

PATRICK: Yeah, and the word got around. We held a press conference and I started getting calls from all over the country. Reagan had to hire an extra secretary just to handle the inquiries.

PLAYBOY: Do you mean you were abducting kids and deprogramming them while you were still working for the governor?

PATRICK: Yeah. I started deprogramming in '71 and I didn't resign until November of '72.

PLAYBOY: Were you getting paid to do that at the time?

PATRICK: No. I wouldn't even accept donations, because I was afraid of a conflict of interests. I told people to put in a prepaid airplane ticket for me, but in each case, I would spend fifty or a hundred dollars out of my own pocket. I'd be in Texas one day and New York the next and maybe Ohio the day after that. That is where I got the name Black Lightning, because the cults never knew where I was going to strike next.

Eventually, the work load got so heavy it began to take up my time. I had to make a decision whether or not I would quit my job and spend my full time deprogramming or remain with the governor's office and give up deprogramming completely. Finally, it got so hot and heavy I knew that even if I stayed with the governor's office, I would probably be asked to resign. So I left my job. I lost my business, my house; I almost starved to death in 1973. I had a wife and six children and I knew that I could lose everything. I could be arrested. I could serve time in prison.

PLAYBOY: Why did you risk all that?

PATRICK: I was getting calls from all over and there was no way I could leave those parents with no place to go and nothing to do. There was no way I could turn my back on them, and already I had begun to get threats and letters written in blood and telephone calls from people claiming to be Satan. Then people began calling with kids in other cults. They were coming in like flies—Krishna, Scientology, the Moonies, the Tony and Susan Alamo Foundation. I didn't know at the time I was taking on the world alone. I figured if I resigned from the governor's office, I would get all kinds of support from the parents and the churches and the law-enforcement agencies. I was never so mistaken in my life. I found that I was left out in the cold with no support. Nobody would touch me with a ten-foot pole. I had received help with every kind of movement I had been in in the past. I'd had community support, police support, NAACP support. You can kill a judge or a policeman, rape forty women, do everything under the sun, and you are still going to get support from the ACLU, the churches, the left or the right or somebody. But in this nobody gave me any help. Nothing.

PLAYBOY: Why not?

PATRICK: Because of freedom of religion. Everybody is afraid of it. It's one of the biggest rackets the world has ever known, this religious bit. I had taken on a giant. It was not just a San Diego deal anymore; many of the cults had become worldwide operations.

PLAYBOY: Did you ever try to bring any of this to the attention of anyone in Washington?

PATRICK: In 1973, I took a petition to Congress. I explained the whole movement and what I was doing and I asked Congress to form a committee under the House Judiciary Committee, like it did during Watergate, and conduct a full-scale investigation. People who had been in and gotten out or anybody who could contribute anything to this investigation could come before the committee. Then we could prove everything. But they refused to investigate the cults, so I asked them to investigate *me*. But they still refused. Since I was in Washington, I figured I would visit the FBI and give them a copy of my petition. They were very nice. They suggested I go to the attorney-general's office, but when I went down there, I found a Scientologist working in the front office. That is just what they were indicted for last year—infiltration of the Justice Department. Then I went to serve my petition to Carl Albert, who was not only Speaker of the House at that time but Acting Vice-President of the United States. Agnew had just resigned. I went into his office to tell him about Scientology's infiltration of the Justice Department, and who did I find in his front office—three Moonies!

PLAYBOY: How do you know they were Moonies?

PATRICK: I recognized all three girls from previous encounters.

PLAYBOY: What were they doing there?

PATRICK: They were operating right out of his office. At the time, I couldn't believe it, but it was in the papers a couple of years later. Now nobody talks about it anymore.

PLAYBOY: Did you ever get a meeting with Carl Albert?

PATRICK: No. He was in there, but he wouldn't speak with me. He referred my petition to the Rules Committee, which was just like throwing it in the trash basket. I never heard from them. I never heard anything.

PLAYBOY: Did you find Moonies working in many congressmen's offices?

PATRICK: Yes. If they did the Korean investigation right, they'd probably find that the entire Korean operation was a lot more serious than Watergate will ever be. At least one hundred senators and congressmen were paid off.

PLAYBOY: Now, wait a minute; what's that got to do with the Moonies?

PATRICK: A Moonie I deprogrammed was a top person on the Unification Church's public-relations team. She told me she saw a cardboard box filled with envelopes containing anything from ten to a thousand dollars as contributions for congressmen. Another Moonie I deprogrammed corroborated that and said he saw at least one congressman being handed one of the envelopes at a Washington party. You see, the Moonies started off with a hotel suite in Washington, and it was their PR team's job to approach every congressman and senator and lure him there. That was all they did. They didn't care how they got them there. Once they did, they were served good food, and there was dancing and anything else that followed. It was a fabulous hotel suite, and in it were beautiful American, Korean and Japanese girls, and once those girls got them into the hotel suite, it was their job to get them into bed. Whenever they had sex with those girls, it was taped, and then, a few days later, they would call them up.

PLAYBOY: Do you know for a fact that those kinds of things went on?

PATRICK: Yes, I deprogrammed some of the top people from the Moonies' PR team. Moon himself had those girls line up and strip so he could inspect them. They had to perform and parade nude.

PLAYBOY: Who told you that?

PATRICK: Several girls I deprogrammed.

PLAYBOY: Have you deprogrammed any of the girls who claim to have had sex with congressmen while they were members of the Unification Church?

PATRICK: Yes.
PLAYBOY: How many?
PATRICK: One who admitted it. I deprogrammed others who could probably tell you more about it, but I don't know if they would want to. I think many of them feel ashamed to admit that they were involved. A lot of them were Korean and Japanese girls.
PLAYBOY: How many members of Congress do you think had sexual relations or other illicit dealings with Moonies?
PATRICK: If they investigated this thing right, at least a hundred senators and congressmen would go to jail.
PLAYBOY: What do you think Moon was trying to accomplish in Washington?
PATRICK: That I don't know. I do know that Moon is not a South Korean. He was born and raised in North Korea, and he spent time in prison in North Korea and possibly in China. It is my opinion that Moon is a wolf in sheep's clothing, with all his talk about anticommunism. I think he knows that if he came here as a Communist, he couldn't get anyone to join him. But if he came as an anti-Communist, he could get a lot of people. Now he's buying up all these fishing companies. Can you imagine what he could do to people just through food, canned food, if he chose to?
PLAYBOY: Let's stay away from some of your more farfetched conspiracy theories, if you don't mind. Now that the House International Organization Subcommittee has reported that it suspects Moon of a number of illegal activities, don't you think the government will agree to investigate the Unification Church?
PATRICK: No, I think it's going to be quashed just like the Korean payoff scandal was. I think the Moonies concentrated on paying off the Democrats because they were the majority party in Congress. They controlled the Korean investigation and they are going to be the same ones to control any cult investigation. I was the one who exposed Moon in the first place, back in '73, when he was holding those rallies in support of Nixon. Nobody believed me then; he had letters from politicians, policemen, judges endorsing his world crusade.
PLAYBOY: If the Moonies really have done the things that you claim and that the House subcommittee has charged, what should the government do about Moon and his organization?
PATRICK: The government should completely disband the Moon organization, and the money and property should be given back to the people Moon got it from. A lot of people went in there and gave millions of dollars, everything they owned in the world, and most of them worked without pay.
PLAYBOY: And what about all the Moonies who are now in this country? What would happen to them then?
PATRICK: They should be deprogrammed. But it won't happen. Congress is not going to touch Moon. It's not going to touch any of the cults.
PLAYBOY: What about the executive branch of the government? Have you tried to contact President Carter?
PATRICK: Carter? Yeah, I've tried every President. Not only President but every U.S. attorney-general. They're not going to do anything.
PLAYBOY: What did they say to you?
PATRICK: Nothing. They didn't even answer my letters. But they answer Sun Myung Moon. They answer Krishna. Jimmy Carter sent a signed letter to Krishna congratulating them on their book and the work they are doing. Krishna put it up on every wall. Go to their Detroit temple. You'll see it.

PLAYBOY: Why do you think the government refuses to challenge the cults?
PATRICK: Because they've got the money. These cults are very powerful. They can buy anything or anybody.
PLAYBOY: You've told us what you think the government should do with the Reverend Moon. What do you think the government should do about the cults in general?
PATRICK: The first thing it should do is have an independent investigation and it should be conducted in public hearings like Watergate was. It should let everybody who has been in a cult or who knows anything come before it and testify. Then it should pass laws to protect people from being psychologically kidnapped. We also need some laws governing fraudulent business practices in the name of religion. I'd like to see a law passed that removed the tax exemptions from all churches. Let's say a law that taxes all religious organizations, just one percent of their income. There isn't a legitimate church in the country that can't afford one percent, and it would allow us to see what's going on inside. Many of them flourish partly because they are not accountable for their money; they are immune to all governmental checks and balances. Then they should pass laws to protect the First Amendment from abuse, to prevent people from using the First Amendment as a license to kill, steal, lie, cheat, push drugs and rip off the public. The cults are using the First Amendment to overthrow the country. They're using it to destroy human beings.
PLAYBOY: But, again, aren't you the one who is abusing people's freedom? Aren't you the one who is depriving them of their First Amendment rights?
PATRICK: I will fight and die to protect the First Amendment. That is what I am fighting for. I believe a person should have the right to worship the way he pleases, but when someone destroys your free will and your ability to think and takes your mind, you don't have any more rights. They have destroyed your human rights and your constitutional rights. And I haven't broken the law. These people have been rescued, not kidnapped, and we have a law of justification that states that a person is justified in committing an apparently illegal act in an emergency to prevent a greater harm, if it is the lesser of two evils. We now have conservatorship laws to give parents custody of their children when they are in that state of mind. Those laws didn't exist before I started what I am doing.
PLAYBOY: There are a lot of people who won't grant you that premise. They say it is impossible to take away a person's mind.
PATRICK: Well, have they heard about Hitler and Mao Tse-tung? Do they know what happened to Korean prisoners of war, or what's going on today in Russia and China?
PLAYBOY: What do you tell people who say that it can't happen here?
PATRICK: Well, it *is* happening here, and the techniques they are using are more sophisticated than ever. But don't take my word for it. Find out yourself. Where facts are involved, there's no excuse for ignorance.
PLAYBOY: Let's talk about the cults' reaction to your campaign against them. What was their response when you started?
PATRICK: They came back fighting. They disagreed that they programmed anyone. Every cult agreed that all the rest of the cults were bad, but they denied that *they* did those things. Each one said *it* was the good one. Krishna said Moon and Scientology were bad. Scientology agreed that the Moonies and the Children of God were bad. Brother Love down in Florida said, "I agree with Ted Patrick that the Moonies and Krishna and all of those cults are bad. But we don't deal in brainwashing. We deal in washing the soul."

PLAYBOY: We've mentioned the criminal charges the cults have filed against you, what about lawsuits?
PATRICK: I've been sued so many times I've lost count. Right now, I'm fighting a fifteen-million-dollar suit from Sun Myung Moon, a few million dollars more from the New Testament Missionary Fellowship, two and a half million dollars from Krishna, and I don't know how many million Scientology is suing me for. I've got over sixty million dollars in lawsuits pending at the moment, and I've already spent over two hundred thousand dollars in legal fees. But more and more people are beginning to understand what is going on.
PLAYBOY: You mentioned money. There have been a lot of rumors about the exorbitant fees that deprogrammers charge. Just how much *do* you get for your services?
PATRICK: Well, no matter what you start, somebody's always going to come in and make a racket out of it. There are some people out there now making a racket out of deprogramming. I know of cases where people have paid thirty or forty thousand dollars to have their child deprogrammed, and in two of those cases, I was called in to do the deprogramming and they paid me less than two thousand dollars.
PLAYBOY: What are your expenses for a typical deprogramming?
PATRICK: It costs me a good three to four thousand dollars every time. That figure is made up of transportation and hotel costs, car rental, food, telephone calls, out-of-pocket expenses, and what I pay people on my security team.
PLAYBOY: How much profit do you make on deprogramming?
PATRICK: I've never charged more than ten thousand dollars for a deprogramming—and I may come out three thousand ahead or I may come out six thousand behind. All of this is very expensive, especially the transportation, and I pay my people very well. I get my money up front and I tell the parents that we can't guarantee anything, any more than a doctor can guarantee anything. But I never leave a person hanging. If he needs some kind of follow-up, I don't charge.
PLAYBOY: What about the mental-health community? What has its response been to your work?
PATRICK: Most of them are totally unaware of the situation. They're still hanging on to their old beliefs that no one can be hypnotized against his will and that there's no way you can get a person to do things other than what he wants to do in the first place. They don't know anything about mind control or the type of hypnosis we are talking about. If you ask most psychologists or psychiatrists, they would disagree with what I'm doing, but some of them know I am right. I've got them coming to me by the dozens to learn my technique.
PLAYBOY: Psychiatrists are studying your methods?
PATRICK: Yeah, now. Psychiatrists and psychologists, doctors, attorneys. Everyone is coming to me. They admire my work, but they won't take a stand. They're worried about their credibility. They're worried about ruining their reputations. They're afraid of being labeled, of being sued, of losing their licenses. They're afraid of a lot of things. Everybody is afraid of the word *deprogramming*. Again, it's fear of appearing to meddle with freedom of religion.
PLAYBOY: What about people who have studied brainwashing in China and Russia? Won't they lend you their support?
PATRICK: You know, I have met all the so-called experts on brainwashing. They make me glad I didn't go to school or to college. Those people don't realize that you don't have to use torture to brainwash people today. There's no torture anymore. It's all done with love and kindness—and deception.

PLAYBOY: What about the ACLU and other civil-liberties organizations? Have any of them come to your defense?

PATRICK: The ACLU stands behind every cult in the nation. It defends all of them, but it won't defend me.

PLAYBOY: Why should they? Isn't it reasonable to assume that the ACLU sincerely believes you are abridging cult member's First Amendment rights?

PATRICK: It would be reasonable to assume that, if it was being reasonable itself. But the ACLU is not interested in listening to reason. It has never really investigated the claims the cults make against me. I have invited it many times to travel with me and observe me in action, but it has refused. I feel that, at the national level, the ACLU has been heavily influenced by the cults. It has practically become part of the whole movement. The ACLU defends every cult as if it were a legitimate religion.

PLAYBOY: As perhaps it should, at least until a particular cult is proved *not* to be a religion. Look, doesn't every form of religion use some kind of conditioning, or even hypnosis, no matter how subtle?

PATRICK: Everybody uses those techniques. Every parent, every teacher is a hypnotist, but it's their obligation to program you to know right from wrong. Every preacher, every salesman, the news media are all hypnotists, because they, too, have a certain amount of control over people. But the same techniques can be used for good purposes or for evil, and there are too many irresponsible people today using them for evil purposes.

PLAYBOY: Yet it remains true that most of the people who oppose deprogramming are not in religious cults but in major organized religions. What do you say to someone who says, "My God, if they're deprogramming kids from cults, I may be next!"?

PATRICK: They can think what they want. If they think what I'm doing is bad, I would fight and die for their right to hate me. They can think I'm a no-good son of a bitch, as long as they've come to that opinion of their own free will.

PLAYBOY: That doesn't answer the question we asked. How do you know if someone's using his own free will? What criteria do you use to determine if someone needs to be deprogrammed?

PATRICK: Being programmed is the only criterion. If you haven't been programmed, you can't be deprogrammed, and you can tell if someone's been programmed, because that person has undergone a complete personality change. All of his old values have been changed.

Look, we can be engaged in a conversation on religion or politics, and you can have your opinion and I can have mine. We may sit up here all day and all night and discuss it, but you're going to leave with your opinion and I'm going to leave with mine. You may be able to persuade me one way or the other, and I may be able to sway you, but you won't have any fear whatsoever of discussing something with me. You would stand up and fight for what you believe in. If you've been programmed, there is no way you would be willing to discuss anything with me other than what you'd been programmed to discuss. It would be psychologically impossible.

You know, people talk about natural resources and the energy crisis and all that, but this cult movement is destroying one of our country's most important natural resources: our young people, our future leaders. If the cults continue for the next five or ten years, instead of producing some of the most brilliant minds and leaders the world has ever known, we are going to have nothing but a bunch of idiots.

PLAYBOY: Would you say that it is primarily young people who are vulnerable to these techniques?

PATRICK: Everybody's vulnerable to them. Hell, we live in a controlled society, to a certain extent. When we go into a store, someone else has already decided what we should buy or what style we should wear. But at least with a free will and a free mind, you are able to reject. A person in a cult can't reject anything. He doesn't have that power. He can only accept.
PLAYBOY: How can people protect themselves?
PATRICK: Knowledge is your only protection. People should become knowledgeable about brainwashing and on-the-spot hypnosis. They should participate in educating other people; they should stand up for what they believe is right. If their representatives don't do anything, they should vote them out of office; they should get out there and campaign against them. We've got to get these old rotten, gutless politicians out of office, because if you've got weak leaders, you're going to have a weak country.
PLAYBOY: Do you think history is going to regard you as a hero or as a villain?
PATRICK: Well, it's like Mark Twain said, anyone who comes up with a new idea is always called a crank. A lot of people have invented or contributed things and never received any credit, especially the blacks. If I had been white and developed a technique like this, I don't think I'd have had the same problems. I would have had more support. Being black has made it much harder.

(The final portion of this interview was conducted after the events in Guyana.)

PLAYBOY: Earlier, you predicted the outbreak of violence affecting large numbers of people. What happened in Guyana appears to have borne you out. In view of that, do you have any final thoughts on what steps the government should take with regard to some of the other cults you've talked about?
PATRICK: I think the goverment should disarm those cults before they take over the country. They should arrest every cult leader I can think of—because that says a lesser evil is forgiven if it was intended to erase a greater evil, or I get prosecuted. But, look: I don't just go and kidnap a person on a hunch or on the parent's word. There are a lot of things we research before we move. We grill the parent and go over the whole history of the child—what he was like before, why the parent thinks it *is* a cult, what kind of personality changes occurred, when he dropped out of school, whether the parent tried to visit him, whether the parent visited the leader and what the leader said, what the neighbors observed and so forth. We do our homework so we *don't* make mistakes.
PLAYBOY: But no matter how scrupulous you say you are, what's to prevent deprogrammers, or police, or anybody, for that matter, from moving against people who behave oddly? How can you have laws that will protect the rights of eccentrics?
PATRICK: Well, first, there should be a national justification law that spells out very clearly what steps can be taken for what purpose to prevent a greater evil. Next, if a parent or a spouse notices someone's personality undergo a sudden change, and sees all his property being handed over, and the other criteria I've mentioned, he should be able to obtain—cheaply—a conservatorship. That just means that the parent has the right to have the child under observation by a psychiatrist or proper authority for, say fifteen days, to determine whether the person is acting free of mind control. That would protect both sides of the First Amendment.
PLAYBOY: We're not so sure it protects the First Amendment, but let us put it to you another way: If you happen to be wrong, what's to protect people from someone like *you?*

PATRICK: Nothing. Under the justification law, as I said, a mistake is a mistake if it's well intentioned. And, considering the alternatives, having the opportunity to prod someone into thinking for himself can't be too bad a mistake. We have a lot more laws right now protecting the guilty than laws that allow us to protect the innocent.
PLAYBOY: On the subject of legal remedies, what about another appeal to President Carter?
PATRICK: He isn't going to do anything. I'm more pessimistic than ever on that score. Hell, Jimmy Carter's sister is one of the biggest cult leaders in the nation. Ruth Stapleton uses all the same techniques they do. She's nothing but a cult leader.
PLAYBOY: Why is she a cult leader if Billy Graham isn't?
PATRICK: Because she programs people. I've seen her do it in meetings, and she's got a mailing list like you wouldn't believe. I also have reason to think she's using the same technique on members of the goverment. I saw one Cabinet member on TV talking about he was born again through Ruth Carter Stapleton. He looked just like a Moonie, glazed eyes, the works.
PLAYBOY: Which Cabinet member?
PATRICK: I honestly don't recall. It was a news show, on CBS.
PLAYBOY: That seems like an irresponsible accusation, especially since you've repeatedly admitted that many people and institutions may use techniques of persuasion similar to those used by the cults. Almost no one would doubt that Ruth Stapleton is using her techniques for benevolent purposes.
PATRICK: All right, I'll grant you that she may be a good cult leader, but that's what she is, nonetheless. She uses hypnotic techniques in her faith healing and many of her followers endow her with godlike powers. More so than the followers of Oral Roberts or Billy Graham.
PLAYBOY: What have you proved, though? You haven't said anything that would suggest Ruth Carter Stapleton—or any of the other religious figures you mentioned—has used those techniques for anything but benevolent purposes.
PATRICK: But that's my point. All the cult leaders who have gone bad started with benevolent purposes. Jim Jones was a highly respected political and social activist, and who knows when he started using his techniques to enslave his followers? Certainly not his followers, who were in no state to be able to judge for themselves.

Jim Jones wasn't a behind-the-scenes cult leader like the Krishnas or Scientologists have. He was more the TV type of cult leader, visible and wise to the media. He started out as a public figure in San Francisco before he took his people to Guyana. He was like Oral Roberts in terms of his style, which is why he was able to get those endorsements from everyone from Rosalynn Carter on down. Although I don't believe Oral Roberts could ever become as warped as Jim Jones, I'm just saying we should know about those techniques and crack down on them when there is evidence that they are being misused.
PLAYBOY: Are you still pessimistic about the government's doing anything about the situation as you see it?
PATRICK: I think it will do a *little* something—and then let it ride. There are too many congressmen and elected officials involved in it all—directly or indirectly—for anything more than that to be done.
PLAYBOY: One impression we can't help having is that you're as much a zealot about your beliefs as those you say you're combating. Looking back at the past eight years, have you *ever* had any qualms about what you've been doing?
PATRICK: There was one real moment when I had to look at the price I'd pay. Here I

was, a tenth-grade dropout, making three times more money than I'd ever expected. When I had to decide whether or not to stay with this movement, I had to face the fact that I could get killed, my house could be bombed, my family could be harmed, I could lose everything I had, I could be arrested and thrown into jail, I could be hated and crucified in the press. That was the price, and I've paid most of it. And the fact that I accepted the challenge means I've accepted the price.

PLAYBOY: But what about the issue of the ends justifying the means? Haven't you ever felt any doubt as to whether or not it was right to break the law, no matter how good your intentions?

PATRICK: Maybe to some people I have broken the law, but I prefer to think that I am performing a service, a public service, which no one else is willing to perform. It's hard to find other areas of the law where there aren't perfectly feasible alternatives to taking the law into your own hands, and anyone who thinks I enjoy all those legal battles, the convictions, the jail sentences, must be crazy. But I know that the only way to develop blueprints for legislation to govern the cults is to produce evidence about what is happening inside them. No law-enforcement agencies will launch an investigation because of the First Amendment. A dog won't run from the smell of a skunk the way a politician will put his tail between his legs and take off at even a hint of controversy in the religious area. Believe me, before I started taking kids out bodily, I tried everything. I went to the governors, the Congress, the attorneys-general, the Speaker of the House, the President. All I ever got were sympathy cards.

But it's not just the cowardice of Congress and so-called experts that protects the cults. The churches of America have to shoulder the blame. A lot of clergymen of various faiths have sat in on my deprogrammings. They've seen firsthand what is going on, yet they refuse to take a stand. There is a moral vacuum in some churches of this country, and I think it's this vacuum that the cults are rushing to fill.

PLAYBOY: Does it matter to you that a lot of people who read this, and may sincerely be concerned about the dangers of some cults, will nevertheless dislike what you've been saying and quarrel with the generalizations you've made?

PATRICK: Most people aren't going to believe me, anyway. Until it happens to them, they aren't going to pay much attention. I don't really care if people refuse to believe a lot of what I've said in this interview. If they've read it, at least then someday when they're confronted with the cult phenomenon in their own lives, a lot of what I've said will flash through their minds. And it may help protect them.

WILLIAM SHOCKLEY

August 1980

Interviewer: Syl Jones

There have been a number of Nobel Prize winners interviewed by PLAYBOY, but none so adversarially as physicist William Shockley. One of the most controversial scientists of the twentieth century, Shockley was awarded the Nobel for his work in creating the transistor, but spent most of the 1960s and 1970s in a field in which he was *not* educated—genetics—advancing theories that in effect stipulate that blacks are inferior to whites. Even during the progressive Sixties, when radicals of every stripe were welcome to speak at American campuses, Shockley was one of the few whose very name could cause bannings and boycotts.

Shockley's notoriety would seem to have made him a perfect subject for a forum of last resort such as the Playboy Interview. But Shockley was in fact a problem to the magazine's editors. It wasn't just that the feature had a strong tradition in favor of civil rights (the first Playboy Interview was with a black man, Miles Davis, conducted by a black man, Alex Haley); it was that Shockley, unlike a cretin like Klan leader Shelton, made racist points that were not obviously refutable by laymen. Ordinary journalists were unprepared to interrogate Shockley with enough expertise to put the complexities of race and genetics into perspective.

When a writer, journalist, and young playwright from Minneapolis named Syl Jones contacted Golson at PLAYBOY with the news that he not only wrote about science but had made Shockley's theories a personal field of study, Golson felt a good opportunity had arrived. When it also turned out that Jones was black, it was clear that the opportunity was ideal. What followed was a dramatic and memorable encounter.

Fifteen years ago, William Bradford Shockley went public with his theory that "retrogressive evolution," or dysgenics, was occurring among American blacks—meaning that less intelligent blacks were having more children than those of significantly greater intelligence. His pronouncement, which amounted to a claim of black genetic inferiority, touched perhaps the most painful nerve that still exists in American society. After all, this was not a member of the Ku Klux Klan or the Nazi Party mouthing racial obscenities but an eminent scientist, a Nobel Prize winner at that, who was reviving an argument most Americans hoped had been forever discredited.

At first, in the wake of the nation's urban riots, and in the midst of legislative efforts to rectify past racial injustices, Shockley's theories were discussed seriously—if scathingly—mainly in the scientific community. The public at large took little heed. For one thing, it was pointed out in popular accounts, Shockley's 1956 Nobel Prize was for physics—he helped discover the principles that made possible the transistor—so why should his dabbling in the field of genetics be taken seriously?

In addition, when scientists responded, they did so in such uncharacteristically abrasive terms—as they continue to do today—that Shockley's reputation as some sort of "mad scientist" prevented any dispassionate public discussion of his ideas. Three professors at Stanford, where he sought to teach a course in dysgenics, wrote: "The essentially genocidal policies [Shockley] has seemed to propose are not only painful for black people to hear but are abhorrent to all decent people whatever their skin color." The National Academy of Sciences wrote, "Dr. Shockley's proposals are based on such simplistic notions of race, intelligence and 'human quality' as to be unworthy of serious consideration by a board of scientists. . . . It is basically vicious to evaluate individuals on the basis of the group to which they belong."

But in 1969, Dr. Arthur R. Jensen weighed in with scholarly and statistical support for Shockley's dysgenic thesis. By then, Dr. Martin Luther King, Jr., and Robert Kennedy had both been felled by assassins. Lyndon Johnson, the leader of what now seems a naïve Great Society program, had been replaced by Richard Nixon. If Shockley wasn't quite respectable, the climate of the nation was such that at least people would listen to him—in some cases.

The man whose mind could range from the intricacies of electrical conduction to the problems of genetic reproduction was born in London in 1910. He graduated from Cal Tech in 1932 and got his Ph.D. at MIT. He worked at Bell Laboratories from 1936 to 1954 and it was in that year that he and fellow scientists John Bardeen and Walter Brattain discovered the principles of the transistor. The importance of the transistor was not publicly recognized until two years later, with the designation of the Nobel Prize. Shockley acted as president of Shockley Transistor Corporation from 1958 to 1960 and slowly shifted his attention to a new—and inestimably more controversial—field.

Bolstered by Jensen's highly publicized article in the Harvard Educational Review *and subsequent studies, in which he asserted that black children were less capable than white children of "level II [abstract] reasoning," and that blacks as a group scored fifteen points below whites in IQ tests, Shockley toured the country, speaking at colleges on both coasts, spreading his dysgenic notions wherever he could find an ear—and in some cases even where he couldn't. He was often shouted down by militant black and white students at campuses such as Brooklyn Polytech, Sacramento State, and Stanford, his home campus. In 1972, he was denied a request to teach a course on dysgenics at Stanford on the grounds that he was not a qualified geneticist, a charge he has never sufficiently refuted.*

Shockley's lifework has been in electronics and electrical engineering. He is so highly thought of in those fields that the Institute of Electrical and Electronics Engineers awarded him its Medal of Honor and the ten-thousand-dollar prize that accompanies it. In so doing, the IEEE made it clear it was not endorsing Shockley's dysgenic views. Writing in the institute's newsletter, past president Jerome Suran said, "If there's one person who's had the most impact on electronics in this century, it is Dr. Shockley. However, we are in no way endorsing or even sympathizing with his efforts in other areas."

To take on the difficult assignment of interviewing this contentious, brilliant scientist, PLAYBOY *tapped Syl Jones, a Minneapolis-based science and medical writer who has long had an interest in the man and the subject. He also happens to be black.*

We made the assignment before Shockley delivered yet another public shock—this one involving sperm banks. Here is Jones's report:

"I first met Bill Shockley in 1974 as part of an assignment for Modern Medicine *magazine. I tracked him down by telephone and tried to arrange an interview, but he was extremely difficult. He'd had bad experiences with reporters in the past quoting him out of context or misquoting him altogether. Shockley tape-records his telephone conversations and once told me that he and his wife, Emmy, often analyze the recordings over dinner. He had turned down many reporters on the grounds that they were not competent to understand his theories. By the time I reached him with my request, I was fully prepared. I had read almost everything that had been written by and about Shockley and his theories.*

"He was pleased that I knew something about him but demanded that I study his theories and submit to a series of telephone quizzes before he would agree to an interview. These quizzes almost always involved fairly complicated mathematical analyses of statistics designed by Shockley in support of his theories. After a few weeks of this grilling, he agreed that I was competent to interview him.

"But there was still more. He wanted personal information on my background. Where had I been born? Where had I gone to school? How many brothers and sisters did I have? Long before this point in the process, most others reporters had written Shockley off as a kook and had given up. I was tempted to do the same. But something intrigued me: Never once did he ask my race or make any kind of racist remark, and he had no idea I was black. I didn't tell him, because I was hoping for a confrontation. In October 1974, I got my wish.

"When a white photographer and I showed up at Stanford for the interview, Shockley instinctively reached to shake the photographer's hand with the greeting, 'Hello, Mr. Jones.' It was a wrong guess that seemed almost to stagger him. Obviously stunned by my blackness, he insisted that I submit to one final test, concocted on the spur of the moment concerning the application of the Pythagorean theorem to some now-long-forgotten part of his dysgenic thesis. Somehow, I came up with a satisfactory explanation, and Shockley had no choice but to grant me the interview. Since that day, he has consistently viewed me as 'the exception that proves the rule' of black inferiority, a designation that he, in all innocence, believes is true.

"For the Playboy Interview, Shockley and I met three times, twice at his home and office on the Stanford campus in Palo Alto and once in Minneapolis. Shortly before the second session, Shockley called my home and left a message that he wanted to speak with me. I tried calling back, but no one answered. A day later, Shockley was off on another adventure: In 1977, he had responded positively to a request from Dr. Robert Graham, eyeglass entrepreneur and student of eugenics, to donate sperm to the newly formed Hermann Muller repository, named in honor of the Marxist geneticist. In February 1980, he made that donation public in a story first published in the Los Angeles Times. *Shockley had called me the night before his revelation to ask if I thought he should tell the world.* Manchester Union Leader *publisher William Loeb, a close personal associate of Shockley's, advised him to release the information; his lawyer advised against it, and even Graham thought it a bad idea to mention any of the Nobelists by name. But now Shockley himself seemed eager to be before the public eye.*

"The media's reactions to Shockley's revelation have been resoundingly negative. But he insists that hasn't bothered him one bit. His purpose in telling the world

about this incident was to get another forum for discussing 'human quality' problems.

"The main points to keep in mind while reading this interview are:

"1. Historically, blacks as a group have scored fifteen points lower than whites on IQ tests. But Shockley's evidence to the contrary, there is still no general agreement that IQ tests measure raw intelligence.

"2. Shockley believes that the fifteen-point difference is primarily reflective of a basic genetic inferiority on the part of all blacks, whether American or not.

"3. Critics of Shockley say he is perverting science for his own racist, political reasons and that he is only the most recent link in a long chain of scientific racists.

"4. Shockley claims that low-IQ individuals are responsible for lowering the average IQ of society, a phenomenon he has dubbed the 'dysgenic threat.' To combat that threat, he has proposed the provocative Voluntary Sterilization Bonus Plan as a 'thinking exercise,' the details of which are revealed here.

"And, finally, anthropologist Claude Levi-Strauss, writing in Society *magazine, expressed some thoughts that may help place this interview in its proper context. Speaking of the futility embodied in the search for truth in the social sciences, where the data are often soft, he said: 'But if we are able to make even some limited progress toward wisdom, then we may be . . . more ready to resign ourselves to the general truth that science will remain forever incomplete.' "*

PLAYBOY: In February of this year, Dr. Shockley, you revealed to the world your participation in Dr. Robert Graham's Nobel-laureate sperm bank. You have donated your sperm to Dr. Graham's repository and have admitted your participation publicly. The news media reacted to your admission with both shock and ridicule, so let's start by discussing that.

SHOCKLEY: Shall I give you the standard questions?

PLAYBOY: If you like.

SHOCKLEY: The standard questions are, "Where are these sperm banks going to go?" and "What's the objective in trying to produce a superrace?" and "Isn't this what Hitler tried?" and "Who are *you* to be donating your sperm?" and other questions of that sort.

PLAYBOY: Let's double back to those questions and start with our own. How did you get involved in this Super Baby experiment?

SHOCKLEY: I don't call it a Super Baby experiment and I object to your doing so.

PLAYBOY: That's not our term; every newspaper in the country has called it that.

SHOCKLEY: Well, that is clearly a misrepresentation of my purpose in participating in Graham's program.

PLAYBOY: Fine. What *was* your purpose in offering your sperm to Graham's repository?

SHOCKLEY: Let's get this straight. I didn't offer. I responded to Graham's request. In 1965, I was in the news after expressing worries that the genetic quality of our population might be declining. My first contacts with Graham occurred shortly afterward, in 1966. Graham had started even then to canvass some of the Nobel laureates about the prospects of contributing sperm to a proposed repository. The actual opportunity to contribute came my way some twelve years later. Also, in 1965, I had met a man who had already made the decision, with his wife, to seek a highly qualified sperm donor in order to improve the probable quality of his children. His wife shared his views on the matter. To my way of thinking, they are a very rare case in having come independently to this decision to seek out a sperm donor.

PLAYBOY: Wasn't that an unnatural step to take?

SHOCKLEY: I agree that the idea seemed unnatural, but this man's arguments stood up very well. He was an unassuming fellow and not particularly impressive, but the more you listened to him, the more sense he seemed to be making. He said, "I don't expect to do everything for my child. I propose to teach him social values and to love him and to care for him. And I want him, or her, to have the greatest possible opportunity in life. If somebody can furnish sperm that gives a greater likelihood of success to my child than I would be able to give, then I'd have no qualms about arranging for a donor." What he said all hung together.

PLAYBOY: Maybe so, but you'll have to admit it's a minority opinion.

SHOCKLEY: I don't see that a minority opinion should be regarded as an adverse thing. I'm sure that as a black writer, you carry a certain number of these yourself. And Einstein carried some for quite a while, too.

PLAYBOY: Let's get back to how this whole thing began. We're trying to understand how you bring up a subject like donating your sperm to a repository. Did you and Graham sit down and hash it out over drinks, or what?

SHOCKLEY: This wasn't exactly a new idea. Graham had been in contact with Hermann Muller, the Marxist geneticist, and this was actually Muller's idea, which he proposed long ago. I really don't know the history. Graham knows such things much better than I do.

PLAYBOY: What was the general reaction when Muller proposed it?

SHOCKLEY: Muller came in for a great deal of castigation. He made the tactical error of trying to draw up a list of people he considered optimum donors, which included some people who later ended up looking pretty unattractive.

PLAYBOY: Such as?

SHOCKLEY: I've forgotten who they were. Whether he had Karl Marx or Lenin or somebody else in there, I'm not sure.

PLAYBOY: Graham got involved because he knew Muller? What was *his* interest in something like this, which is outside his field?

SHOCKLEY: Graham's interest in the declining quality of people goes back at least to the Sixties, when he wrote a book called *The Future of Man*. He did studies of what went on during the French Revolution and the elimination of the elite class, which probably removed some of the brilliant people of France. I don't know that one can say France has significantly less intellectual potential now than it did before the Revolution, but this is what some of Graham's studies were concerned with. Anyway, Graham had for some time been urging more intelligent people to have more children. We had talked about these things and my concern about possible downbreeding, or dysgenics, struck a responsive chord in him. I knew about his plans for a sperm bank and when it was set up, I had no particular problem in making a decision. This all happened about 1977, I believe.

PLAYBOY: How many other Nobel laureates have donated their sperm to that repository?

SHOCKLEY: To the best of my knowledge, there have been two others. The repository contains sperm from five individuals, two of whom I don't know anything about—but they are there for some reason of Graham's, which I have not explored.

PLAYBOY: Three women have already been inseminated, according to press reports. How were those women chosen?

SHOCKLEY: Graham has been advertising for women in a publication sponsored by the Mensa Society. Mensa is a group of individuals who all have IQs in the top two percent. But neither Graham nor I regard the Mensa population as being an ideal group. We both have the notion that, by and large, Mensa members have nothing going for them to speak of aside from a high performance on IQ tests.
PLAYBOY: But isn't that what you're looking for? High IQ as an indication of intelligence?
SHOCKLEY: Graham is looking for creative people.
PLAYBOY: Creative people? Why Nobel-laureate donors, then? Why not artists, writers or actors?
SHOCKLEY: The Nobel laureates can be said to be more distinguished in terms of creativity than in terms of IQ. Certainly, they are distinguished in both categories but far more so in the creativity area.
PLAYBOY: Aren't there other positive traits society is in need of? Such as intuition, physical strength, honesty? And how are those related to high IQ?
SHOCKLEY: There is definite positive correlation between practically any high-quality human trait and IQ. A number of these things, including honesty, resistance to temptation to cheat on tests and physical capacity, in high-IQ children, compared in a positive way with their contemporaries. Now, this doesn't mean that IQ necessarily is the best trait to breed for, but I don't know of any other trait that has such a highly positive correlation. There are other sperm banks where you can specify things like hair color, eye color and height. I'm not sure if you get information about the donor's educational attainment or IQ. But I have nothing against these other traits you mentioned. It's just that in selecting for high IQ, you are likely to get these other things anyway.
PLAYBOY: Your bias is definitely toward the intelligentsia, isn't it?
SHOCKLEY: It takes many good traits to make a good society, and if we were able to isolate these traits and prove that they were heritable, then it would be good to select for these values. It might be very attractive to set up specialized sperm banks for that purpose, but obviously, you couldn't get too specialized. One could not set up a sperm bank that would be intended to select people with a high inclination to become celibate priests, for example. This characteristic would have eliminated itself from the gene pool, assuming it could be shown to be heritable.
PLAYBOY: How do you define creativity?
SHOCKLEY: The Nobel committee is essentially looking for discoveries and inventions "of greatest benefit to mankind," that occurred in the recent past. So if you examine that, you find that one definition of creativity might be the creation and delivery of something new and valuable. Nobel laureates in science certainly meet those standards.
PLAYBOY: As to the three women who already have been inseminated—
SHOCKLEY: When I last spoke with Graham, it was not known if any of these women had yet become pregnant.
PLAYBOY: Newspapers reported that the women were due to deliver this year.
SHOCKLEY: I've seen such news stories, too. I am not aware that they have any basis in fact.
PLAYBOY: Odds are that at least one will get pregnant. Let's assume you're the father. Are you going to know who the mother is?
SHOCKLEY: The arrangement is that Graham knows everything on both sides and neither side knows anything about the other side.

PLAYBOY: Might this situation create some psychological problems for the child?
SHOCKLEY: It might. But I wouldn't think any more than adoption would. I also think the child would be better able to have an objective view of the situation than an ordinary child would. Furthermore, there is the other side of this, which speaks to the fact that we are not trying to produce a superrace. I might point out here that before I even allowed my name to be linked with this experiment, I insisted on stating that we were not endeavoring to produce a superrace, but I was entirely in accord with Graham's objective of producing more intelligent, productive, creative people. I also went on to say that my emphasis is on reducing the human misery that may be developing at the bottom end of the IQ distribution. And I tried then to emphasize the difference in the distinction between these two positive influences on human quality; namely, the positive eugenics that Graham is talking about and the antidysgenics that I have been emphasizing.
PLAYBOY: If the genetic theory behind this idea really worked, wouldn't we be able to judge the success of it by looking at the children Nobel laureates have already produced, for example?
SHOCKLEY: Yes, and there was a famous study done on this back in the Twenties by Lewis M. Terman. He picked a thousand children from the California schools who were in the top one percent of the IQ distribution. Then this so-called gifted group was followed for about thirty-five years. At the end of that time, they had about twenty-six hundred children. Terman's project was able to measure IQs of fifteen hundred of these. The median IQ of those children was about 135. I made drawings showing how well these IQs fit the pattern of normal distribution for the general population. And not one of these fifteen hundred children fell into what is known as familial mental retardation—that's retardation that results from the tail of the normal distribution. Actually, there were thirteen retarded children in this group of fifteen hundred, but these included Mongoloids and other children with physiological problems.
PLAYBOY: What about your own children? How did they turn out?
SHOCKLEY: In terms of my own capacities, my children represent a very significant regression. My first wife—their mother—had not as high an academic-achievement standing as I had. Two of my three children have graduated from college—my daughter from Radcliffe and my younger son from Stanford. He graduated not with the highest order of academic distinction but in the second order as a physics major, and has obtained a Ph.D. in physics. In some ways, I think the choice of physics may be unfortunate for him, because he has a name that he will probably be unlikely to live up to. The elder son is a college dropout.
PLAYBOY: Do you see your children very often?
SHOCKLEY: Not very often. No.
PLAYBOY: Do they know about your activities?
SHOCKLEY: My daughter perhaps knows more than the others of my activities in these areas. But as far as my sons are concerned, it's mainly the things they see in the papers.
PLAYBOY: Incidentally, what's your IQ?
SHOCKLEY: I don't know.
PLAYBOY: You've never known your IQ?
SHOCKLEY: I had IQ tests made by Terman in connection with the gifted-children study when I was about ten. Then my IQ was about 130.
PLAYBOY: So you were actually part of the Terman gifted-children study.

SHOCKLEY: I was not accepted for the Terman study, because my IQ was not high enough. Terman missed two Nobel laureates; I was one, Luis Alvarez of Berkeley was another. We were both tested for this program.
PLAYBOY: What was Terman looking for in terms of IQ?
SHOCKLEY: I think 135 or over. I suspect my IQ is higher than that by now, but I have not done a test on it.
PLAYBOY: Do IQs improve with age?
SHOCKLEY: There have been cases in which there has been marked improvement of IQ over the years. I have heard that Einstein was not a very bright student in his early years. I'm not sure what his IQ was in his adult life, but I would be rather surprised if it weren't quite high.
PLAYBOY: What are your children's IQs? Do you have any idea?
SHOCKLEY: No, I don't.
PLAYBOY: What about your parents'?
SHOCKLEY: Terman measured my mother and, as I recall, it was above 150.
PLAYBOY: To come back to Graham's experiment in breeding, what's the value of it if not to add more knowledge about the effects of this kind of eugenics?
SHOCKLEY: I consider the real experiment to be sociological, and that experiment has been accelerated by the publicity surrounding the Nobelist sperm bank.
PLAYBOY: Now that the reactions have come in, are you sorry it was tried?
SHOCKLEY: Not at all. There has been a clear demonstration of an important truth about our nation's intellectual community. This truth is that a Dark Ages dogmatism blocks objectivity about human-quality problems.
PLAYBOY: Dark Ages dogmatism? That's strong language.
SHOCKLEY: The evidence for Dark Ages dogmatism is found in press reports of interviews with scientists about the sperm bank. These suggest emotional judgments rather than reason. Most eminent scientists, including Nobelists, have condemned Graham's program with the words weird, pretty silly biological nonsense, ridiculous, ethically and morally repulsive.
PLAYBOY: So much for the inherent intelligence of Nobelists, right?
SHOCKLEY: I think these reports suggest that sperm recipients may be hoodwinked into thinking that genius babies are guaranteed. Dogmatism won a KO decision over science in one report suggesting that a child's mental endowment would be *completely* uninfluenced by the father's own mental powers. The Dark Ages dogmatism suggested by these reports would, if transferred from man to horses, amount to saying that breeders of race horses have all been hoodwinked when paying the stud fees demanded for Kentucky Derby winners.
PLAYBOY: Yes, the general reaction of the press to the whole idea of "intelligent sperm" has been devastatingly negative. Columnist Ellen Goodman accused you of conceit and we're wondering: Is it possible you're on an ego trip, trying to play superstud, just to get the resulting publicity?
SHOCKLEY: That comment raises two issues. I'll dispose of the ego-trip aspect first. After Phil Donahue introduced me to his audience a few moths ago, I thanked him for not bringing up the superman issue. To put it in perspective, I rose to my full five-feet-six-inches height, removed my jacket, turned a full circle and explained that a superman description would need to be expressed as "superman plus twenty pounds."
PLAYBOY: That's a nice PR gimmick, but it doesn't answer the question. The fact is,

this revelation of your participation in the sperm bank has brought you a great deal of publicity. It seems to us you may have planned it that way.

STOCKLEY: No, I acted on the spur of the moment in making the donation. But I deliberated and consulted, as you know, before deciding to identify myself as a sperm-bank donor. Furthermore, I insisted that the original sperm-bank story in the *L.A. Times* quote me as saying that I didn't think of myself as the perfect human being or the ideal donor, and also that, although I supported Graham's positive eugenics aim of more people at the top of the population, my own focus is on reducing the misery at the bottom. By these statements, I laid a foundation for emphasizing the dysgenic threat when subsequently interviewed about the sperm bank. The results have been rewarding to me.

PLAYBOY: Why is it so important to you to talk about the so-called bottom of the population? And what people are at the bottom, in your opinion?

SHOCKLEY: It's important to me because of the tragedy at the bottom end of the population, which is particularly severe for the blacks, but also probably occurs for the *chicano* population—maybe to a comparable degree—though I am not as conversant with the *chicano* case. The same thing probably occurs for some Appalachian whites. What I'm talking about here is poverty, crime, unemployment and a host of other human miseries that impose heavy burdens on society and bear most heavily on the babies who are born into suffering as a result of this misery.

PLAYBOY: What about these so-called human-quality problems? You have repeatedly said that the quality of the human race is declining in this country because "society is not doing enough research into the genetic factors that make people what they are." What caused you to make that observation?

SHOCKLEY: One key incident in 1963 stands out. It involved a San Francisco delicatessen proprietor who was blinded, or nearly blinded, by an acid-throwing teenager with an IQ of 65. This teenager was one of seventeen children born to a woman whose IQ was 55. I asked myself what people I knew who had families that large. I could think of none. Apparently, these large families were those of people who were not making it in our society, so that those with the least intelligence were having the most children. The more I talked to people about this, the more alarmed I became. No one was willing to look at this subject objectively, dispassionately. This is what drew me into the whole question of dysgenics, or retrogressive evolution.

PLAYBOY: Why focus on some acid-throwing teenager who happens to be black? The majority of mass murderers in this country have been white and not all have been low-IQ morons. Hitler apparently had a high IQ. What does that suggest to you?

SHOCKLEY: It suggests that any trait, either extremely good or extremely bad, would be highly enhanced by a high IQ, because the individual having that high IQ would possess general abilities to get things done.

PLAYBOY: But it seems to us you emphasize that anecdote about the black teenager more than any other. Why?

SHOCKLEY: He was in California at the time when I was involved in considering the question of whether the abortion laws should have been liberalized. He came from a rather large family of relatively ineffective people. His crime made the news, of course, and my attention was drawn toward him as an example of problem makers' multiplying faster than problem solvers. It was simply an accidental circumstance that brought this into focus for me.

PLAYBOY: All right, let's define dysgenics.

SHOCKLEY: It's an important word to get into the vocabulary of the public. Dysgenics is evolution without progress, retrogressive evolution, which decreases the quality of the species. It is caused by the excessive reproduction of the genetically disadvantaged. In 1967, in *Sex Versus Civilization,* demographer Elmer Pendell proposed that civilizations decline because problem makers multiply in greater percentage than problem solvers. This is what I fear is happening to intelligence in our society.
PLAYBOY: Is that just your opinion or do you have facts to support it?
SHOCKLEY: The seventeen children of the low-IQ mother are one example. The fact that she was black warns that the dysgenic threat is most severe for blacks, and statistics from the 1970 census back up this conclusion. When socioeconomic classes are listed, college graduates come near the top and rural farm families near the bottom. Black rural farm women average 5.4 children, early three times as many as the 1.9 for black women college graduates. Now, on the average, the woman who graduates from college has a better brain, for hereditary and genetic reasons—one more suited to education—than does the rural farm woman. And 1.9 children per woman is not enough to maintain that part of the population. It looks as if the numbers of problem solvers of the black minority may be decreasing. As for the problem makers, I have heard at least two anecdotal stories from responsible observers about women who have said they would have babies to increase their relief income. But I have found no good published evaluation of this matter. One sociologist has written that the percent of Aid to Families with Dependent Children (AFDC) that goes to parents whose parents in their turn were AFDC recipients has doubled twice from five to ten to twenty percent in the past twenty years. If something doubles every ten years for a century, it will become a thousand times larger—an alarming prospect.
PLAYBOY: But the comparatively rapid social advancement of blacks during the twenty-five years since the Brown desegregation decision, when some of the artificial environmental barriers that impeded progress were removed, proves the falsity of your dysgenic analysis.
SHOCKLEY: Blacks have caught up with whites to a substantial degree during that time. But, as Dr. Arthur R. Jensen's new book documents, the incidence of mental retardation for black children in school has not decreased as it should if theories about better education due to integration were working out. The socioeconomic gains of blacks compared with whites eliminated about one-third of the deficit in family incomes.
PLAYBOY: That's not true. The gap in incomes between blacks and whites has actually grown because of inflation's effect on the dollar.
SHOCKLEY: My analysis used what I have called an offset method based on percentages of black and white families in matched income ranges. The dollar values are not used. What I find is that the gains all occurred between 1955 and 1969 and after that, progress stopped. Is dysgenics involved? It's something to worry about.
PLAYBOY: Isn't the answer to this to spend more for remedial education and job training, instead of conjuring up the "dysgenic threat"?
SHOCKLEY: If environmental efforts now being put forth are not at an optimum level, they should be increased. But that emphasis should not continue to prevent research on genetic factors. If genetic factors affecting the IQ or motivation are involved, then future taxpayers will suffer from this dysgenic trend. But those who will suffer most are the babies born to these families—babies who may be so genetically disadvantaged that they can't escape from these bad environments. In effect, they are genetically enslaved to a life of frustration. A question that might well be asked is, for

example, Are fertility rates, like the 5.4 children for rural black farm women, even higher in city slums? I have not found a penetrating study on what may be the root cause of urban decay. Nobly motivated humanitarianism that prevents objective studies' being done on these tragic matters, which affect whites as well as blacks, is humanitarianism that has gone berserk. One question that I've mentioned is whether welfare mothers have babies to increase their income. Berserk humanitarianism may put taboos on such research. I once asked an investigative reporter to do some research on this subject through the Welfare Department. He was unable to complete his report due to the Welfare Department's uncooperative efforts. They evidently felt this was a taboo subject.

PLAYBOY: But the bulk of evidence you and others bring to bear on this subject of black intellectual inferiority comes from IQ testing, does it not? And isn't it a known fact that the black minority in this country has suffered from years of social neglect, abuse and poverity? All of which is reason enough to expect low performances on IQ tests.

SHOCKLEY: But these environmental deficits don't explain the details of the tragedy. One of the standard erroneous representations about my position is: "Dr. Shockley says Negroes have lower scores on IQ tests and therefore are racially inferior." That is an entirely inaccurate statement, setting up a straw man that can easily be knocked down. My opinion is best represented in this statement: My research leads me inescapably to the opinion that the major cause for the American Negroes' intellectual and social deficits is hereditary and racially genetic in origin and thus not remediable to a major degree by practical improvements in environment. That statement is based upon research that puts together a whole pattern of things.

One example concerns *components* of the IQ test and not simply the total scores. A significant example is supplied by studies done under the direction of Gerald Lesser at Harvard. He went into the New York school system and tested students who were white, black, Chinese, Puerto Rican, and Jewish. His IQ test was divided into four components. The most striking findings, from the point of view of my interests, concern the component of the test on which almost all sociologists would say that blacks would perform worst because of cultural disadvantages; namely, the verbal part. Actually, the verbal component turns out to be the part on which black children score highest. On the other hand, the components that involve analytical reasoning—even things that involve day-to-day reasoning, like how many pennies are in a nickel—on those things the blacks are more retarded than whites of their age group. In other tests, this same pattern of retardation has been borne out. In other words, black children don't have much comparative trouble with questions like, Who discovered America? and Who wrote *Romeo and Juliet?* But they do have problems with things like, Which way is west? and How many days are in a week?

PLAYBOY: In other words, things that require noegenetic reasoning are more troublesome for blacks. Is that what you're saying?

SHOCKLEY: What does noegenetic mean?

PLAYBOY: It's a term developed by Charles Spearman that refers to the application of educative or inductive reasoning.

SHOCKLEY: You mean something that involves the use of cognitive skills?

PLAYBOY: Right.

SHOCKLEY: Yes, these tend to be more troublesome. Another kind of test stands out in my mind, and this one has been documented by Jensen in one of his books. It's a test of memorization ability done on white and black children in the California schools.

The child is shown a set of twenty familiar objects, such as a ball, a book, a brush, a toy car—one at a time. Then the child tries to recall as many as possible. This is called a free-recall test. At this stage of the test, there is no difference between the black and white children on performance. By the fifth time the children went through this test, it became obvious that the white children were remembering better. The reason for their better performance was this: The white children, as the test series progressed, were mentally classifying the items into a group of balls, a group of books, and so on, as an aid to memorization. Black children weren't nearly as apt to do this or to do as good a job at it as were whites.

PLAYBOY: You said these items were common to the children's environments. Were they two separate groups of items, one for black children and one for white children?

SHOCKLEY: In Jensen's California experiment, they were objects that are common both to Richmond, California, and to Berkeley.

PLAYBOY: But that assumes that the white children and the black children in that part of California live in the same environment.

SHOCKLEY: Still, the point is that on the first few rounds of the test, the two racial groups showed negligible differences in the performance. Hence, one concludes that the items were equally familiar to both groups. Otherwise, why should the performance have been so nearly equal?

PLAYBOY: You conclude, then, that—

SHOCKLEY: That the difference in performance is in the processing of the information, which requires cognitive skill, rather than in the familiarity of the items.

PLAYBOY: The subject of the relevancy of IQ testing has been debated endlessly and may never be resolved. But getting back to this dysgenic-threat thesis of yours, it's fair to point out that your theories have been aimed for the most part at black Americans, whom you have labeled genetically inferior as a group. In fact, you called this "The National Negro Tragedy." What is your motive in using such inflammatory terms?

SHOCKLEY: I don't know where you got that National Negro Tragedy phrase. It's not mine and doesn't convey my position. The phrase that I now use is the The Tragedy for American Negroes. My emphasis is on the tragedy for the Negroes themselves arising from their greater per-capita representation in statistics for poverty, welfare, educational failure and crimes. The relief burden related to these statistics could be called a National Negro Tragedy if the intent is to focus upon the concerns of taxpaying citizens. But that is an unfair focus. I believe society has a moral obligation to diagnose the tragedy for American Negroes of their statistical IQ deficit. Furthermore, this is a worldwide tragedy, and in my opinion, the evidence is unmistakable that there is a basic, across-the-board genetic disadvantage in terms of capacity to develop intelligence and build societies on the part of the Negro races throughout the world.

PLAYBOY: Wait a minute. Let's boil that down a bit. At the nub of what you're saying is the belief that blacks are inferior, right?

SHOCKLEY: If you, personally, were representative of the Negro population as a whole, rather than belonging to Lord knows how high a top-level fraction of it, then we wouldn't have these troubles. There are many individual exceptions, of course, as I have said many times. What disturbs me most about this situation is that black people are going to suffer most because of their disadvantages. The real losers are going to be the genetically disadvantaged babies. Their disadvantages result from what I've tried

to emphasize by calling it an unfair shake from a badly loaded parental genetic dice cup.
PLAYBOY: That's colorful, but what does it mean?
SHOCKLEY: Actually, it's more as if the baby got a genetic five-card poker hand that was drawn not from a full deck but from a ten-card deck made up of the two hands holding the genetic cards of the parents. If both parents had high hands, for example, the chance of the baby's getting two pairs or, even better, a full house, would be pretty good and the worst possible draw would be one pair. This oversimplified genetic explanation suggests how high-IQ parents will tend to produce not-quite-so-high-IQ children, while sometimes producing a dumb one. Sometimes parents blame themselves when one child falls far below his sibling in making grades. Actually, genetic models predict that in about ten percent of all two-child families, the IQs of the children will differ by 20 IQ points or more. Knowledge of this fact might keep some parents from trying to push the slower child beyond his capacity, which may do the child far more harm than good. At the other extreme, if the parental ten-card deck is composed of two worthless four-card flushes, both in the same suit, one child in twenty would have a good chance of being a high-value flush. This suggests how a single, highly gifted child may show up in a large family even though all the other children are below average.
PLAYBOY: If such a tragedy exists—and you yourself have pointed out that only fifty percent of the people you've talked with will admit that there is a tragedy for American blacks—doesn't it have as much to do with the white power structure in this country as anything else? The "tragedy" could not exist in a vacuum.
SHOCKLEY: Let me put my thoughts in perspective. A similar sort of tragedy certainly exists in Africa in terms of famine areas where planning has been inadequate. One aspect of the tragedy in America, which seems to me to be hard to blame on the white power structure, is the tragedy of the black spouse-killing-spouse homicide rate. If this is caused by frustration due to the belief that blacks have been treated unfairly—as the general prevailing sociological position would inculcate anyone who listens to it—then, certainly, widespread resentment could exist and more instability could lead to marital quarrels. My research on statistics shows that the spouse-killing-spouse mortality rate is about thirteen times higher per capita for the blacks than for whites. I don't believe the same thing occurred with the American Orientals at the time the power structure was saying that they couldn't buy houses in the same area as other people in California, back during World War Two.
PLAYBOY: Certainly, you're not comparing the history of Oriental Americans with that of black Americans. Blacks have been exploited in America for generations.
SHOCKLEY: I'm not convinced that it takes even one generation to adapt to changes from situations that have lasted for many generations. I know a man—an Aztec Indian—whose family had been out of touch with white civilization for, I think, a hundred or two hundred years. This fellow had never had any experience with things that dealt with modern technology and his father had been enslaved. He came from a culture of blowgun and Stone Age level, isolated from modern civilization. He didn't enter school until the age of ten, yet at twenty-one he had acquired an electrical-engineering B.S. and a physics M.S. His brother is a successful journalist in Mexico City. This example supports my conviction that fantastic cultural deficits can be overcome in a fraction of one generation by individuals with outstanding inherent determination and intelligence.
PLAYBOY: You're comparing an anecdotal story of an Aztec Indian with a whole race

of people and saying the Aztec case proves a genetic disability on the part of blacks. Would you agree that there are similar individuals in the black community who have overcome environmental handicaps? Many, in fact?

SHOCKLEY: Absolutely. And these people have certainly existed in our society for at least a century.

PLAYBOY: If you agree, how does that fit with your view of blacks as a genetically enslaved race?

SHOCKLEY: My point is, the environment and the discrimination have not stopped some blacks who have the ability from progressing, so I don't see why it is necessarily stopping all the rest.

PLAYBOY: Very interesting. But what does that have to do with the relationship between the badly loaded genetic dice cup and what you call the American Negro Tragedy?

SHOCKLEY: Tragedy for American Negroes, if you please. The relationship is that in some cases the cards are stacked or the dice are loaded, so to speak, so that the likelihood of drawing really good genes for intelligence and other behavioral traits is much smaller for some groups of people than for others. This is patently unfair. These people end up at the bottom rungs of the socioeconomic ladder through no fault of their own. This is the fate that is now befalling a disproportionately large fraction of the black minority. This fate will become worse if dysgenic effects result from the 5.4-to-1.9 ratio found in the 1970 census.

PLAYBOY: In what way is this a tragedy for all blacks, if these dysgenic conditions affect only the low-income end of the black population?

SHOCKLEY: The tragic disadvantages of those at the low end probably act as a disadvantage to those at the high end because the color-coding effect comes in. People may then react to all blacks unfavorably as a result of some experience with those at the low end of the scale.

PLAYBOY: But that has nothing to do with objective science.

SHOCKLEY: That's right. One might respond subjectively to all blacks in just the same way that some people believe that all redheaded people are emotionally volatile.

PLAYBOY: That's called prejudice, isn't it?

SHOCKLEY: Well, it may or may not be. Perhaps one has intuitively picked up something about redheaded people that is perfectly sound. In the case of the black situation, carrying the reactions one might have to black street-gang types over to black academic-faculty types would be a prejudice.

PLAYBOY: How do you feel about prejudice?

SHOCKLEY: Prejudice that is not supported by strong facts is both illogical and not in accordance with truth. The general principle that truth is a good thing applies here. Some things that are called prejudice, which are based on sound statistics, really shouldn't be called prejudice.

PLAYBOY: Give us an example of that in the context of our discussion.

SHOCKLEY: It might be easier to think in terms of breeds of dogs. There are some breeds that are temperamental, unreliable, and so on. One might then regard such a breed in a somewhat less favorable light than other dogs. Now, some of the business prejudices against blacks, the pragmatic man-in-the-street prejudices, are not incorrect. The man in the street has had experience and knows what to expect from blacks in business. If one were to randomly pick ten blacks and ten whites and try to employ them in the same kinds of things, the whites would consistently perform better than the blacks.

PLAYBOY: Of course. The majority of whites have better access to education, influence, money and other environmental elements that help ensure success in our society.
SHOCKLEY: Well, I've already said that I've been led inescapably to the conclusion that these problems are more related to genetics than to environment.
PLAYBOY: Earlier, you mentioned Africa and said this dysgenic threat was a worldwide problem. You believe it affects all Negroids, regardless of their environment?
SHOCKLEY: I put my chief emphasis on the tragedy for *American* Negroes. The book *Race and Modern Science* contains the best study I've seen on blacks outside this country. In his chapter, Stanley Porteus, a Hawaiian psychologist, describes how he and his colleagues used a maze test on tribes in Africa and Australia. They found the natives to be intrigued and challenged by the test. They tested various tribes and found very big differences among them in performance. Some Rhodesian tribes—Ndau and Wakaranga—were more advanced, while some of the Bushmen were at the low end. From the data, which are given in mental-age equivalents for these tribes, I conclude that the Bushmen were down around an IQ of 50 and the others are up to somewhere around 80. None came closer than ten IQ points of my estimate of about 90 IQ for California Negroes.
PLAYBOY: Few scientists working in the fields of genetics, anthropology or psychology agree with you. Many of them have said that your theories are blatantly racist.
SHOCKLEY: Let me point out that this attitude did not exist at the turn of the century. Many eminent and thoughtful scholars expressed the same ideas that I am attacked for. Alexander Graham Bell wrote a pamphlet on improving the human race. Stanford's revered president David Starr Jordan stressed the same theme in a book, *The Blood of the Nation*. The situation had changed by 1962, when eminent anthropologist Carleton Coon proposed in a book that Negroes were substantially behind whites on an evolutionary scale and said that he would discuss brain differences in his next book. In the next book, he retracted his offer because of pressure on him. Coon has told me that these attacks undermined his health and led to early retirement from Harvard. This suppression of inquiry on matters related to dysgenics shows up in book publishing. Under the subject "eugenics," the Stanford library card file has many acquisitions from 1900 to 1930 and practically none from1930 to now.
PLAYBOY: You'll have to admit that eugenics is widely held in disrepute and is barely a legitimate science. You won your Nobel Prize for your work that led to development of the transistor. Why should anyone listen to a person who's a Nobel Prize winner in physics on the subject of genetics?
SHOCKLEY: There is an old saying: Wisdom from the mouths of babes.
PLAYBOY: Babe? At seventy?
SHOCKLEY: Wisdom from the mouths of babes means that occasionally, truths can come from an unlikely source. This is like the *Encyclopaedia Britannica* or some other profound mathematics book being produced by monkeys typing in the British Museum. If there seems to be merit in the things that are expressed, one had better look at them.
PLAYBOY: The likelihood of a monkey typing the *Encyclopaedia Britannica*—especially when he knows more about bananas than about encyclopedias—is infinitesimally small.
SHOCKLEY: If you ask, Why should anybody listen to someone? well, why should anyone have listened to Einstein when there were no relativists at the time?

PLAYBOY: That's not the first time you've mentioned Einstein in comparison to yourself. Einstein is considered a genius. Are you a genius, in your opinion?

SHOCKLEY: Insofar as genius may be sweat and effort, perhaps. I would not like to try to define exactly what a genius is or to say that I necessarily belong to that class. Certainly, there have been very great technological developments that have followed from very simple observations that anyone might have made if he had been there at the time. My track record is definitely somewhat better than that. But in terms of people such as Einstein, Newton and Maxwell, I would say they belong to a higher level of genius. The contributions I have made are more technological.

PLAYBOY: And now your contributions to this new field of eugenics have brought you notoriety and censure from some of your academic colleagues. How have you had to deal with suppression of your ideas?

SHOCKLEY: I was put on notice very early that few would take kindly to my raising questions that are usually swept under the rug. My interview "Is Quality of U.S. Population Declining?" was published back in 1965. It was reprinted in the Stanford Medical School alumni journal. Stanford's "faculty, the department of genetics" objected with a letter to the editor brandishing the words *malice, mischief* and *myopic* against me. An eminent friend of mine in the National Academy of Sciences explained to me that the mere fact that I had memtioned both Negroes and IQ in one and the same paragraph led my critics to label me a racist. The geneticists' beautifully and forcefully written letter pained me greatly when I first read it. Since then, I have enjoyed reading it aloud to friends, with rhetorical flourishes, preferably over cocktails, so as to dramatize its Madison Avenue merits. My presentations have been suppressed many times by disruptions or cancellations, sometimes only a day or so before I would have left home to keep the engagement.

PLAYBOY: Didn't common sense tell you that linking an entire race—black, white or green, for that matter—to intellectual inferiority would be opposed as racist by many people? And that it would invite censorship?

SHOCKLEY: The genetics-faculty letter did more than any other thing to make me face up to dealing with the racial issue. A related incident occurred earlier, when I was preparing a paper that didn't deal with racial questions at all but simply with mental retardation. While preparing my lecture, I questioned one of my fellow Nobel laureates about the possibility of the worldwide dysgenic threat. I proposed to him that human genetic quality—almost certainly definable to some meaningful degree—was declining. His responses were vague, unclear. I finally said, "I think what you're saying is that this question is so bad you will not try to answer it." He agreed with that interpretation. I thought that was a deplorable attitude to take.

PLAYBOY: In your own mind, how do you explain the fact that so many people disagree with your theories about black genetic inferiority?

SHOCKLEY: I think that two basic premises underly the rejection of the concept of genetic inferiority of humans, no matter whether the concept is applied to individuals or to races. One is the American ideal that stems from the "created equal" phrase in the Declaration of Independence. That phrase was intended to apply to social rights but is popularly misinterpreted as equality in genetic endowment. This is biologically ridiculous. It asserts that man alone, of all species of mammals, is made up of individuals all genetically equal—equal at least in potential for socioeconomic success in our society. The second premise is what I have labeled the Apple-of-God's-Eye Obsession. AGEO for short. In Galileo's day, this obsession held that God must have put the Garden of Eden at the center of the universe. Galileo's conclusion that the earth moved around the sun was an intolerate heresy. Darwin's evolutionary theory that man was a descendant of primates was a comparable heresy. The version of AGEO that blocks objectivity about racial or dysgenic questions combines these two premises. AGEO adherents hold that God created all mankind with equal dignity and equal potential, and that God could not have done anything else. These views are so widely held and accepted that they have set up taboos that prevent research. This is an example of berserk humanitarianism. As a result, there are many scientists who agree with me but dare not speak out—dare not "come out of the closet," as one psychometrician has told me.

PLAYBOY: Let's assume that the dysgenics threat is real and the quality of the human race is declining. What would you propose as a solution?

SHOCKLEY: I proposed a thinking exercise about ten years ago called the Voluntary Sterilization Bonus Plan. What it does is to offer people who may be carrying genes that are defective, including those for intelligence, a bonus for voluntarily agreeing to be sterilized.

PLAYBOY: That sounds vaguely familiar to us. Does it remind you of any particular mass movement within the past forty years?

SHOCKLEY: Forty years takes us back to Hitler's concentration camps and gas chambers. Your question has often come to me from lecture audiences in the form, "You're talking about eugenics. That's what Hitler tried, isn't it?" Incidentally, during the war against the Nazis, I did operations research and was awarded the Medal for Merit with a citation signed by President Truman. The real lesson from Nazi history is that the First Amendment, which permitted uncovering Watergate, is the best guard against totalitarian abuses. The Hitler reference is one standard question often used to shut off discussion of eugenics or antidysgenics. A second, similar question is: "What's the definition of the perfect man?" And a third question is: "When the committee to define the perfect man is set up, how can I make sure to be appointed to it?" If one accepts that any conceivable remedy for dysgenics would be worse than the illness, then there would be little purpose in diagnosing the tragedy we've been discussing, except as an intellectual parlor game.

PLAYBOY: OK, that's fair. How would your Voluntary Sterilization Bonus Plan work?

SHOCKLEY: Every time I have discussed the Voluntary Sterilization Bonus Plan, I have described it carefully as a *thinking exercise* rather than as a legislative proposal. It shows that we don't have to define what the perfect man is and that no authority is deciding who can have children. It's a voluntary choice by the people themselves. It does not require Hitler's concentration camps. There is an inducement, but nevertheless, its acceptance is voluntary. The amount of the cash bonus would vary. In some cases, it would be zero. For example, income-tax payers, who tend to be somewhat successful already in society, would get no bonus. All others, regardless of sex, race or welfare status, would be offered a bonus that would depend upon best scientific estimates of any genetically carried disabilities that they might have. Those would include diabetes, epilepsy, hemophilia, Huntington's chorea and other genetically transmitted illnesses. A dysgenic increase of these afflictions is probably now occurring, owing to advances in medicine that overcome evolution's pruning actions. There would also be bonuses for lower-than-average IQs.

PLAYBOY: A lot of people are affected by those so-called undesirable genetic traits that might be passed on from one generation to another. Do you have any of those traits that you might pass on yourself?

SHOCKLEY: I am not aware of any. No hemophilia, no epilepsy, no Huntington's chorea, no diabetes.
PLAYBOY: So nothing that you are aware of that would be passed on to a child through the sperm-bank program?
SHOCKLEY: I was short one tooth on the lower jaw, and I think maybe one wisdom tooth. I'm not sure those are real disadvantages.
PLAYBOY: How much money would those people receive for agreeing to sacrifice their right to have children?
SHOCKLEY: My thinking exercise proposes a figure of a thousand dollars for every IQ point below 100. That may sound high, but thirty thousand dollars put into a trust for a 70-IQ moron, who might otherwise produce twenty children, might make the plan very profitable to the taxpayer. If three of these hypothetical children ended up in institutions for the mentally retarded for life, it might cost the taxpayers nearly three hundred thousand dollars to take care of them. Furthermore, if we offered ten percent of the bonus in spot cash, it might stimulate our native American genius for entrepreneurship.
PLAYBOY: Several states in the South have sterilization programs for those who are mentally retarded or otherwise judged unfit by society. Many of those programs call for forced sterilization. What do you think about them?
SHOCKLEY: I think that they have been very unjustly derogated. Objections to these programs are based on the same berserk humanitarian beliefs and Dark Ages dogma that refuse to accept the fact that people may obey breeding laws that are similar to those of animals. I remember one man asking me if I favored sterilization of the retarded and then proceeded to say that he had a loving, compassionate retarded daughter and he didn't see why she shouldn't have children. To my way of thinking, this is a clear case of humanitarianism gone berserk. Why should a child be brought into the world under those adverse genetic conditions just to fulfill the compassionate and warm feelings of the retarded mother, in this case?
PLAYBOY: What bothers many people is the fact that *your* thinking exercise seems aimed at blacks in particular. That's why the Nazi parallel has been raised by those who are normally dispassionate and detached in these matters. Your theories amount to scientific genocide of the black race.
SHOCKLEY: What I am intending to do is reduce human misery for the people involved. And this proposal cuts across all racial and ethnic-group lines. Certainly, in terms of numbers, more whites than blacks would be involved, though the *percentages* for black retardation are higher. As to the Nazi reference, I think everyone agrees that their methods were profoundly inhumane. I believe that true humanitarianism extends further than the Christian version of the golden rule of "Do unto others as you would have them do unto you." I feel that true humanitarianism is best expressed by Jainism: "In happiness and suffering, in joy and grief, we should regard all creatures as we regard our own self." In other words, true humanitarianism is concerned with even nonhuman forms of life.

Nobel laureate Albert Schweitzer carried this to the extreme in acting on his principle of reverence for life by trying to avoid stepping on insects and transplanting weeds and things of that nature. But I believe he drew the line at withholding antibiotics from a sick patient because of his reverence for the life of bacteria. Incidentally, Schweitzer spent the last part of his life running a hospital for blacks in Africa. He wrote, "With regard to the Negroes, then, I have coined the formula: 'I am your brother, it is true, but your elder brother.' " For this, Schweitzer has been called racist. I think that a logical, true humanitarianism replaces Schweitzer's reverence for life with concern for the memories of emotions stored in the neurological systems of one's fellow creatures. The Nazis had no regard for concerns like these.

PLAYBOY: And you, unlike the Nazis, are concerned with the feelings of your fellow creatures?

SHOCKLEY: Yes.

PLAYBOY: Are you familiar with Kipling's philosophy about the white man's burden?

SHOCKLEY: In a general way. Kipling applied this to India, did he not?

PLAYBOY: No, to the Philippines, but it has been more widely applied to white paternalism toward all Third World people.

SHOCKLEY: It would be interesting to know how the general welfare in India actually fared before and after the British occupation there.

PLAYBOY: We're asking because your Jainist attitudes seem like warmed-over paternalism toward blacks. That quote from Schweitzer, in particular, reflects a rather odious view. Do you share Schweitzer's view of blacks? How does this reflect your humanitarianism?

SHOCKLEY: You've asked that question before. We do take seemingly brutal measures that we regard as humanitarian with certain animals. If we eliminate all predators of deer, they might become too numerous and run out of food and starve to death. I think a situation not too different from that might exist in some of the most primitive tribes, possibly the Bushmen tribes. If one were to build up a civilization around those people and try to fit them in, it's quite possible that it might lead to a very miserable situation for children of that society, who might then lead very tragic lives. I think society has a moral obligation to diagnose these conditions and take corrective measures.

PLAYBOY: Your use of animal imagery is clearly inappropriate. The fact is, it's incredibly conceited for one group of human beings to make life-and-death judgements like that over another group of human beings.

SHOCKLEY: But there's nothing novel about that. That's what we do on all sorts of food-and-drug laws. To protect people from their poor judgement in buying drugs. The extreme case is the law on cancer drugs. Even though the cancer cases may be relieved of some symptoms, the laws say certain drugs cannot be used to treat cancer. In California, the law even prescribes what kinds of treatments are legal for cancer. So there is no great novelty about government's taking this view. Only when it comes to something like human quality and the possibility of doing research into it are there taboos and thought blocks erected.

PLAYBOY: Let's be clear on this: You are trying to balance your concern for human feelings on the one hand with your strongly held belief that something must be done to stop this genetic backsliding. Correct?

SHOCKLEY: Thanks. That's a good summary. But one aspect deserves special emphasis. Human intelligence is one of the finest, most admirable products of evolution. Intelligence is necessary to ensure that humanitarian and compassionate endeavors do not go astray. We should respect intelligence and do all we can to prevent a dysgenic deterioration of it.

PLAYBOY: Let's discuss Arthur Jensen, the Berkeley psychologist you mentioned earlier. You've been referred to in the press occasionally as a disciple of Jensen, who advanced the theory that black children are less capable of level-two or abstract reasoning. He's been in the news recently as a result of a new book defending IQ testing. What's your relationship with him?

SHOCKLEY: We first met in 1966, when I spoke at the Center for Advanced Study in the Behavioral Sciences at Stanford. Jensen was a member of the audience. I regarded him as a resource person, because he had been reading and writing in the field for decades and had a very scholarly approach. In his *Harvard Educational Review* article in 1969, he used words from parts of a paragraph I had written a year or so earlier having to do with the "dysgenic threat" and "genetic enslavement." But as far as I know, that's the only time that he has emphasized that particular point. Whereas I have put my emphasis on the area of social obligations and psychometric research, Jensen's focus has been much more on the tools for analysis and the scientific validity of the results.

PLAYBOY: But you basically share the same beliefs about blacks, don't you?

SHOCKLEY: I'm not aware of whether Jensen would agree with my main conclusions or not.

PLAYBOY: His book takes a rather hard line in favor of IQ tests. Jensen says IQ tests are not biased against any group of Americans for whom English is the first language. Is that an opinion you share?

SHOCKLEY: I would not want to give blanket endorsement to that point of view without studying it more. I believe it might be possible to make an intelligent estimate of the degree to which environmental deprivation might actually be producing a bias in the intelligence scale for children. There may be a few general-information questions that show a specific cultural bias toward whites, such as, "What color is a ruby?" But I would postulate, without having looked into this in much detail, that questions like this one would make a difference of only two or three IQ points, at most.

PLAYBOY: Some IQ test questions are obvious cultural setups. One, in particular, that strikes us as invalid is, "If you see smoke coming from a neighbor's house, what should you do?" The answer to that question depends on how you were socialized, what your parents have told you to do, not on your general intelligence.

SHOCKLEY: There was one example of this kind of question brought up in CBS's program *The I.Q. Myth.* The question was, "If a child smaller than you hits you, what should you do about it?" This was supposed to be an example of a culturally biased question. As it turned out, this was one of the easier questions for blacks and certainly did not give evidence of being culturally biased.

PLAYBOY: The so-called correct answer to the question is, "Don't hit the child back, because he's smaller than you."

SHOCKLEY: I'm pretty sure that was not the only correct answer. There may have been several.

PLAYBOY: In any case, isn't the point that these answers reflect a value system based on white society and have nothing to do with intelligence?

SHOCKLEY: That doesn't stand up. The fact is that the blacks have acquired these values from their environments just as well as the white children have. Furthermore, they gave more correct answers on that question than they had on the average for all of the other questions.

PLAYBOY: What we're really talking about is the assimilation of values as reflected by an IQ test. Not necessarily the use of any cognitive skills. A child isn't stupid just because he answers that question another way.

SHOCKLEY: The question is whether the elements involved in developing cognitive skills are entirely cultural or whether there is a basic genetic predisposition. Many cases have been cited of gifted children who start learning how to read with very little stimulation whatever. This is obviously due to genetics. I don't see why the same sort of thing shouldn't apply to cognitive skills. It's the consistent pattern of observations like these that lead me to what I call my "inescapable opinion" about the black IQ deficit.

PLAYBOY: In the past, you have indicted the scientific community for not researching ideas about black genetic inferiority. We're not saying there is a problem as you've described it; but if there were, who would be responsible for investigating a genetically disadvantaged race?

SHOCKLEY: I would say the responsibility to do this kind of thinking rests primarily with those who are most intellectually capable of it. In terms of race, a disproportionate fraction of the white population can do this compared with the black population. So the white population is most responsible. But one particularly distressing circumstance is implied by news stories about intelligent blacks' moving into the suburbs to avoid ghetto or slum areas. Some reports indicate that they seem withdrawn rather completely from a concern for their less fortunate brethren. I have often said that the people who would be most important for me to try to reach are the black intellectuals of this country.

PLAYBOY: How can you expect to reach black intellectuals when your rhetoric smacks of racism?

SHOCKLEY: The smack of racism attributed to "my rhetoric" lies in the ears of the listeners. It is not present in my written or spoken words. The word *racism* carries with it a connotation of belief in the superiority of one's own race, plus fear and hatred of other races, and lacks any hint of humanitarian concern. What I am intending to do is to promote raceology, the study of racial problems and trends from a scientific point of view, and this approach is quite different from racism. One black student told me after we talked that he no longer thought of me as a Klansman or Hitler and that I had guts for facing up to a problem no one else would face.

PLAYBOY: That's nice, but you are still making qualitative judgments about an entire race, are you not? You believe quite simply that whites as a race are superior in intellect to blacks.

SHOCKLEY: Statistically, yes. But not in individual cases. Let me repeat that I always try to qualify statements about black racial IQ inferiority by saying that there are many blacks who are intellectually superior to many whites, and that the Caucasians are not necessarily the world's most superior race. In terms of the percentage of the population who can achieve eminence and make great contributions in science, American Jewish scientists are an outstanding fraction of the scientific community and on a per-capita basis are represented, I think, at least ten times higher than is the population as a whole. American Orientals also are overrepresented.

PLAYBOY: Of course, Jews aren't a race. But doesn't the tightly knit social structure of Oriental and Jewish families have more to do with their success than genetics?

SHOCKLEY: What makes their social structure tightly knit?

PLAYBOY: Tradition, customs, learned experiences—their environment, in other words. But we're asking you.

SHOCKLEY: Why shouldn't it be genetics? It certainly is in the animal kingdom. Take, for example, the cuckoo bird, which has this very unusual habit of never hatching its own eggs. That's certainly not an environmental factor. The weaverbird, which hangs its nest on a limb with a piece of horsehair that is tied in a knot. They have raised weaverbirds with robin foster parents and never let them see a horsehair for several generations. Then, if you give them a horsehair, they know exactly what to do with it. That's undoubtedly a built-in genetic trait. I see no reason to think that family patterns don't stem from genetics.

PLAYBOY: What about Orientals: Is it possible they are the "superior race," assuming there is such a thing?

SHOCKLEY: They are certainly not inferior. Furthermore, even when discriminated against in the Twenties, Japanese schoolchildren in California on two verbally weighted tests showed very small IQ deficits and actually outperformed whites on a less verbal one. The massive 1966 Coleman report on 645,000 students showed Orientals about five verbal IQ points below whites and on nonverbal IQ, a share above in grades nine and twelve.

PLAYBOY: All right, here we are back to square one again. Dr. Shockely, aren't you essentially a white supremacist?

SHOCKLEY: No, I am not a white supremacist.

PLAYBOY: If that's the case, why have you allowed yourself to be used by right-wing-extremist groups who promote white supremacy? For example—

SHOCKLEY: I have appeared a few times prominently in such right-wing publications as *Thunderbolt,* a newspaper supported by the States Rights Party, or closely tied into it. It's not a Ku Klux Klan publication, but it is definitely anti-Negro and anti-Semitic and very much white supremacist. I find these views in conflict with my version of the golden rule. But on two points I put *Thunderbolt* ahead of much of the American press. First, I believe it is not hypocritical, though it does express erroneous views. Second, it sometimes publishes valid news that I don't find elsewhere. I also believe that the net result of getting the truth out will be good and that misinterpretations will be corrected.

PLAYBOY: But if these people are misusing your theories, why haven't you put a stop to it?

SHOCKLEY: If someone has stolen your car and is driving it recklessly, why haven't you put a stop to it? I have not given priority to a study of extremist groups, but I have this view about them: Those groups view black problems from the perspective of racism, not from that of scientific raceology. Their focus on black crime would be on its brutality rather than its contribution to the Tragedy for American Negroes.

PLAYBOY: You've mentioned black crime before, as if its existence supports your claim of black genetic inferiority. Does it?

SHOCKLEY: The important issue is the role of crime in the Tragedy for American Negroes. The people who suffer most from black crime are blacks themselves. I mentioned earlier the high spouse-killing-spouse ratio. A young black male in Harlem is more than a hundred times more likely to be a homicide statistic than a male in Denmark. These are aspects of the tragedy that raceology reveals.

PLAYBOY: As to crime and race: Aren't there tribes in Africa in which crime is almost unheard of? Anthropologists who have studied those tribes point out that their environment tends to discourage crime. On the other hand, there are studies in this country showing that our cities tend to breed crime. Obviously, there's a strong environmental relationship here. How does that fit in with your racial thesis?

SHOCKLEY: I don't know of any studies showing such a lack of crime. I do know of some showing that certain tribes tend toward intertribal warfare. Some researchers postulated that this bellicosity was caused by a lack of protein, but that didn't seem to be true once they actually looked into it. With respect to urban slums' breeding crime, the question of a cause-and-effect relationship needs to be researched much more carefully. Do people remain in the slums because they have a low IQ, which is highly correlated with a high crime rate? I tried looking into this myself once. I asked a law-enforcement agency if it would search its files and give me a reference to anything that had been written on the correlation between IQ and crime. They claimed there was nothing available. I went to the Stanford Library in one afternoon and produced two studies in which hundreds of prisoners had their IQs tested in two separate studies. As I recall, the median prisoner IQ was about 85, or one standard deviation below normal. Of course, someone could argue that high-IQ people who commit crimes don't get caught. That might be one explanation, but I doubt it.

PLAYBOY: To return to the central point: There is no question that the KKK and even the Nazis have used your data for goals that are political, destructive and have nothing to do with humanitarian idealism. Given your goal of reaching the so-called black intellectual community with your theories, how can you allow yourself to be misrepresented by those white-supremacist groups?

SHOCKLEY: Your emphasis that we must "return to the central point" is a new experience for me. I do not recall anyone making the point before, and certainly not as persistently as you have just now, that I will be irresponsible if, in your words, I allow myself to be misrepresented by white-supremacist groups. Let me assure you that I make no efforts to allow myself to be misrepresented. My efforts instead have been to communicate the concerns and findings that we are discussing as accurately as I can. That, as far as I am concerned, is the central point of this interview. I would then hope that this accuracy would suffice to reach the intellectuals, black or white, who should think responsibly about the dysgenic threat in general and its relationship to the Tragedy for American Negroes in particular.

PLAYBOY: What attempts have you made to reach black intellectuals, and with what results?

SHOCKLEY: If I think that one over, I will end up with a pretty long list. Near the beginning are Dr. Alvin Poussaint and Donald Warden, a San Francisco attorney and radio host. James Farmer, Roy Innis and Frances Cress Welsing have appeared with me on TV programs and I have tried to be as precise as I have been here. My correspondence with Roy Wilkins in 1973 was, perhaps, my most diligent effort to open a line of communication. Mr. Wilkins regarded me as a threat to Negro progress greater than the KKK, according to press reports of a speech. In that case, I responded with both a press release and a letter to Mr. Wilkins. I asked him to choose one hundred to two hundred black intellectuals for blood tests and I pointed out if this showed they were no more Caucasian than the national average, then, and I quote from a news story: "This new scientific fact could correct unfair discrimination that now prevails on the opinion that Negroes obtain their intelligence from white ancestors."

PLAYBOY: Some anthropologists say that race is such a fuzzy concept that it would be pointless to try to find out how much Caucasian blood American blacks have. What about that?

SHOCKLEY: One proof that I don't have to be a geneticist to work on these problems is my 1973 paper in the *Proceedings of the National Academy of Sciences* on the determination of the percentage of genes in Oakland blacks that come from white ancestors. I refined the best prior estimate of twenty-two percent obtained using a particular blood type called Duffy's gene. I reconciled that with an estimate of twenty-seven percent for another blood type and obtained a new best value of twenty-three percent. As far as I have heard, my 1973 paper is still the most advanced on this subject.

PLAYBOY: What was Wilkins' reaction?
SHOCKLEY: Mr. Wilkins rejected my proposal but made no reference to your central point about white-supremacist groups. Biology professor Richard Goldsby and I are on first-name terms after a number of public debates but no closer to agreement on the main issues. Carl Rowan and others were also approached. This interview with you is the latest of my serious attempts.
PLAYBOY: Reaching the black intellectual community is nearly an impossibility for you. Harvard psychiatrist Poussaint, one of the best-known, most-respected black professionals in the nation, says that your theories have hurt the black self-image and that blacks tend to take them to heart and feel that they are personally inferior, not as a group but as individuals. Would you comment on that?
SHOCKLEY: Yes. I think that there may be some truth to what Poussaint says, and this is a very sad state of affairs. If a very substantial fraction of the black race is made up of people who have limitations in objectivity of character so that it is impossible for them to accept reality, then disclosure of this dysgenic threat could be a very devastating thing for them, and that would be tragic. But one alternative can be even more tragic. That would be to set up an artificial milieu in which blacks are protected, as some people might be in mental institutions. If such a lack of objectivity exists and if the blacks most susceptible to it are increasing most rapidly because our society is afraid to do the needed research to diagnose the problem, then it's a pretty deplorable state of affairs. It indicates fear and a lack of faith in the power of reason and the existence of humanitarianism—attitudes that I do not share. Where there is a serious illness that needs to be diagnosed before treatment can be wisely made, I see no excuse for withholding the contributions that reason may provide.
PLAYBOY: Your faith in humanitarianism seems unrealistic to us. For example, what logical reason would blacks have for showing faith in humanitarianism when, as a group, they have suffered from severely inhumane acts for generations? And why would most whites who know the history of blacks, and whom you blame for "not doing the needed research to diagnose the problem"—why would they put faith in humanitarianism's winning out over racial hatred and injustice? It never has before, so why would it now?
SHOCKLEY: Well, I have faith that if one brings facts out and presents them properly, sound answers will be found. I may be wrong about this, but not only is this a faith that I have, but it is probably an element of faith that any religious person should have. If he believes that God is involved in this situation, then he is compelled to have the same faith I have.
PLAYBOY: Really? Why?
SHOCKLEY: Because the Apple-of-God's-Eye Obsession says that God has set up the world to be fair to man and to be good to him.
PLAYBOY: But *you* don't believe that, do you? You apparently don't believe in God.
SHOCKLEY: I think that some of these philosophical views are broader than the belief or nonbelief in God. I think these things came about through evolution. In terms of my humanitarianism, you wouldn't say that the blacks in the United States are worse off than they are in almost any African country, would you?
PLAYBOY: Worse off in what way?
SHOCKLEY: Healthwise.
PLAYBOY: No, not for the most part. But blacks in America have been exploited and deprived of their basic human rights.

SHOCKLEY: How about Idi Amin?
PLAYBOY: An isolated instance.
SHOCKLEY: Or how about the civil war in Nigeria?
PLAYBOY: Civil war is one thing, slavery is another. So is genocide.
SHOCKLEY: Is there no black slavery of blacks in Africa now?
PLAYBOY: Perhaps, but how do these digressions help us understand your faith in humanitarianism? Your faith seems somehow unconnected to historical and present-day reality.
SHOCKLEY: You could have some faith in terms of the elimination of slavery, the enactment of affirmative-action programs, the wiping out of Jim Crow laws and things of this sort. But blacks can also conclude that these things will turn around and get worse if dysgenics are at the root of the problem. And, on that basis, it may be very difficult for blacks to share my faith in humanitarianism. Nonetheless, I'm reminded of the dictum of Herbert Spencer: "The profoundest of all infidelities is the fear that the truth will be bad."
PLAYBOY: Do you believe that?
SHOCKLEY: I think I concur with that, yes. It expresses rejection of a lack of faith in reality. To have such a profound lack of faith in the world is being unfaithful to the very nature of one's existence. That is what it means to fear that the truth will be bad. The truth about Watergate, for example, was a very bad thing. But getting the truth may have been a very good thing.

If one can perceive some kind of a tragedy potentially developing—then one should seek some way of dealing with it that minimizes human misery. For the worries that I express about dysgenics, this aim may very well be best achieved by limiting the number of babies that come into the world under adverse circumstances. The same solution has often been recognized, but not implemented, in underdeveloped, and perhaps undevelopable nations.
PLAYBOY: That kind of humanitarian social Darwinism may be well and good, but it doesn't deal with real-life situations. Take, for example, the white woman who was thinking of marrying a black man. This is a documented case. Somewhere on the East Coast, she heard you speak about black genetic inferiority and she became afraid that her children by this black man might be born inferior. She threatened to break off an otherwise good relationship. She went to a therapist and asked for advice. This kind of reaction seems to be the real potential tragedy, Dr. Shockley—that white people could actually come to believe that black people as individuals are inferior to themselves and will inevitably produce inferior offspring.
SHOCKLEY: Do you know what answer the therapist gave her?
PLAYBOY: The answer was that she shouldn't be concerned about your theories, that they were irrelevant. And that the question itself was inherently racist.
SHOCKLEY: Well, if she had been asking about races farther apart than blacks and whites, and if more facts were known, the therapist might very well have said that the chance of having a mentally retarded child as a result of this vast divergence between the races might be very substantial. I doubt if it is for black-white matings, because if it were, the result would be known. The probabilities might be much larger for very different groups.
PLAYBOY: But we're describing an emotional crisis in a woman who reacted to your theories. Obviously, asking a question about mental retardation in black offspring in the context of your theories is tantamount to questioning the very humanity of a people. Certainly the humanity of the black individual she wanted to marry.

SHOCKLEY: Well, it is quite true that these are very painful thoughts. They are things that strike centrally on one's whole viewpoint toward life and the universe. Objective thinking on this subject is blocked by the Apple-of-God's-Eye Obsession, as I mentioned earlier.

PLAYBOY: But you still haven't answered our question about this white woman. Wouldn't it be a tragedy for whites to believe that black people as individuals were inferior to themselves and would inevitably produce inferior offspring? And isn't this an example of that kind of racist thinking?

SHOCKLEY: I'm not saying that this is not a tragic situation, you understand. But what are the facts? If you pick two black people at random in the black population and mate them and produce children, and you take two white people at random in the population and mate them and produce children, the existing statistics fit into this pattern that I call an inescapable opinion that the black children will be, as far as the IQ tests are concerned, inferior to the white children. Now, then, you say, suppose people come actually to believe this. It seems to me you are saying, "Suppose white people actually came to believe what you, Shockley, believe."

PLAYBOY: But you keep saying your purpose is to limit human misery. The example of the woman is one in which you may have caused human misery.

SHOCKLEY: I would say even greater misery will result, and is now taking place, because of society's refusal to investigate the dysgenic threat.

PLAYBOY: Are you for or against interracial marriage? Not as a scientific experiment but as a social reality?

SHOCKLEY: I'm going to say I certainly would not oppose an interracial marriage in any particular case that might come up. But I wouldn't advocate it as a policy. One would have to know more about these facts.

PLAYBOY: Do you think there ought to be efforts made to increase marriages between black men and women of high IQs?

SHOCKLEY: I don't see why not. It would be applying positive eugenics to encourage more births in that part of the population.

PLAYBOY: Do you believe in equal opportunity for all people, black or otherwise?

SHOCKLEY: Yes. I believe in the created-equal assertion of the Declaration of Independence, when it is interpreted in terms of equal political rights, but I would qualify it some: I don't think the right should be given equally to everyone to have children, if those people having children are clearly destined to produce retarded or defective children. This puts an unfair burden upon society. But when I talk about that burden, my standard language emphasizes the fact that the ones who suffer most are the children themselves.

PLAYBOY: But we're asking about equal opportunity, not the right to have children.

SHOCKLEY: Can you have equal opportunity if you don't have the same capacity as someone else to utilize it?

PLAYBOY: The fact that you can't go through a door doesn't mean that it shouldn't be open. Don't you agree with that?

SHOCKLEY: That's right. But you may also be led to demand that there should be a wider door. If the door is too narrow for you to go through, you can certainly assert then that, although the door is open for you, you are not given equal opportunity. Is the trouble really with the door or with the width of the man?

PLAYBOY: Suppose we are talking about a handicapped individual. Handicapped by society or by himself. And the doorway to success is not designed to accommodate his wheelchair. Should the door be redesigned to accommodate the man?

SHOCKLEY: This does not lend itself to an absolute and general answer, because if one follows the open-door approach, then one would say that a man should have equal opportunity to visit anyone he wants, and every house should be built with a ramp for his wheelchair.

PLAYBOY: No, we're talking about equal opportunity in institutions such as colleges, corporations, etc., that have a responsibility for administering equal rights.

SHOCKLEY: An individual may be limited in his capacity to exploit his opportunity for equal rights. Black students who get into college certainly have equal rights to learn. They are exposed to equal lectures. They may be brought in by quota systems and are underqualified both by training and in their basic ability to grasp the material. Then, although they are given the equal opportunities and, indeed, the extra advantages of remedial courses, they won't be able to make the most of them. They can reasonably conclude that something phony in the system is frustrating them. When society endeavors to enforce equality of achievement by methods like these, then the result may be a sort of induced paranoia on the part of blacks. I see this as possibly related to the high spouse-killing-spouse rate we have discussed.

PLAYBOY: Wouldn't it be better for society if you shifted your focus and your energies from the dysgenics question to the goal of equal opportunity for all? Then we might have an equal basis for making qualitative judgments.

SHOCKLEY: To my way of thinking, that is basically not a very astute observation at all. I could at most add only a minuscule contribution to the efforts already under way. I'm perfectly certain I am unique among the Nobel laureates in saying that I feel an obligation to face this problem, the dysgenic aspect or threat. Nothing that has occurred in the past several years has made me feel that my approach is unsound. This situation places me in a position like the one I occupied when my team was probably almost alone in trying to create the transistor. And the dysgenic problem is of greater importance than that was. It has been around since the days of the Greeks. It has been discussed many times and no satisfactory solutions have been found. The transistor will, in due course, probably be replaced by something else, just as the vacuum tube has been replaced by the transistor. But the human-quality problems I'm talking about are going to be with us until some new stage arrives. Possibly, it may be genetic engineering on the DNA code or cloning or things like that. But I think these are so distantly foreseeable that they amount to distractions in discussions like this one. Anyway, if we can prevent dysgenic deterioration of intellectual capacity, future generations will be that much better able to think about genetic engineering.

PLAYBOY: It might be helpful for us to know something about the tenor of your personal relationships with blacks. It could give us some insight into your motives.

SHOCKLEY: I basically haven't had much personal contact with blacks, but I can remember some.

PLAYBOY: What were your impressions?

SHOCKLEY: The earliest recollection I have of any close association with blacks was in my teens. We had a black maid—I think her name was Genoa, as I recall—and my mother and I were both very fond of her. Also, when I attended Hollywood High, there were black students there.

PLAYBOY: How did you get along with them?

SHOCKLEY: I didn't have much contact with them. All I remember about them is that they were active in sports. Later on, when I moved to New York—actually, Madison, New Jersey—we had a maid or housekeeper who was black. She wasn't very efficient, that's what I remember most about her. I also recall that while my children were going to school, I happened to find out that the president of the high-school student body was black. I thought that was a constructive social development.

PLAYBOY: That's interesting. Anything else?

SHOCKLEY: Well, there's something I hadn't thought about until you asked me just now. One night while I was living in Madison, we found a black boy, about eight years old, sleeping in our garage. I tried to drive him home, but he couldn't or wouldn't find the way. The police finally took him off our hands. They seemed to feel he'd been a victim of some kind of child abuse.

PLAYBOY: What about more recent contacts, outside of your well-publicized encounters with Roy Innis and other professional blacks in a business setting?

SHOCKLEY: Well, in 1961, my wife and I were in a hospital for months in casts after a head-on collision. Most of the nurses who took care of us were black, and the quality of their care stood in marked contrast to that of the white nurses. My wife and I were most impressed.

PLAYBOY: What was it that impressed you so highly?

SHOCKLEY: They gave us the best care and were the most natural and comforting that I had. In fact, while my cast prevented me from doing so, they were the ones who cleaned my rear end properly.

PLAYBOY: One of the more troubling parts of your theory has to do with the degree of white blood you claim effects the genetic intelligence of blacks. Do you really believe there are intelligence differences between light-skinned blacks and dark-skinned blacks?

SHOCKLEY: Industrialists who have operated in Africa have told of the greater value of mulattoes over pure blacks as employees. But where race mixing has gone on for generations, only a statistical correlation would be expected between skin color and performance. Judgments about individuals would be dubious. Actually, skin color alone does not provide the best measure of white ancestry. J. R. Baker in *Race* considers morphological features, in addition to skin color, and concludes that many eminent American Negroes have substantial fractions of Caucasian ancestry. The conclusion seems to me to be borne out by blacks seen on TV—for example, by many black newscasters.

PLAYBOY: That's interesting, but how is it pragmatic for the man in the street, who doesn't understand statistics?

SHOCKLEY: The pragmatism comes in when a businessman says, "I know I have had bad luck hiring three blacks, and so I am going to avoid hiring blacks if I can." Here again, science may offset unfairness by developing valid aptitude tests that see deeper than skin color.

PLAYBOY: Is your opinion based on personal experience you have had with blacks?

SHOCKLEY: It is based mostly on conversations with successful businessmen. Two of these described specific aspects of their problems. I have also obtained a similar impression from general reading. A third item is my own research, which proposes a mathematical model to explain why an increase in IQ raises earnings less for blacks than it does for whites. Its name, the cooperative-correlation model, is much shorter than its explanation.

PLAYBOY: Do you feel that certain scientific groups that should be dealing with this issue are simply ignoring it?

SHOCKLEY: Yes. My primary target for this criticism is the National Academy of

Sciences. Another group I would single out specifically consists of the tenured members of faculties and departments of anthropology in the country. Most of these anthropologists tend to maintain that race is a myth and there can't possibly be any differences in intelligence or anything else deeper than skin color. They will go further, of course, and say that even if there were differences, there wouldn't be anything one could do about it. Both of these statements are irresponsible.

PLAYBOY: Most of your critics assume that there is some ulterior motive for your highly inflammatory views, such as racism or some political intent. Is there? And how do we know that you don't have any secret political ax to grind? That you aren't a racist wolf in humanitarian sheep's clothing?

SHOCKLEY: I guess I really don't know how you can convince people of that. Eminent political figures have tried with great eloquence and expressiveness to convey such impressions, sometimes quite successfully, sometimes even when untrue. I wouldn't pretend to have the expertise that politicians have. One characteristic that would make me an unlikely candidate for a covert racist ideology is my not entirely unrecognized lack of tactfulness in some areas. The outspokenness that I have is, I think, by and large, not in keeping with a man who has any skills in being deceptive in political matters. That would be about the best argument I could give.

PLAYBOY: Even so, you are undoubtedly aware that some people would sooner see you in prison than allow you to express these opinions, though the First Amendment protects your right to say what you have said. Do you have any thoughts on freedom of speech?

SHOCKLEY: The words that define the First Amendment seem to me to be some of the most important words put on paper by man. I compare their significance in the political arena with statements in science like Newton's third law of motion: "For every action there is equal and opposite reaction." I have stressed the point that the First Amendment was a lesson that the German people didn't learn during Hitler's time. I don't believe he would have lasted if the First Amendment had been in place in Germany.

PLAYBOY: Do you worry about reprisals?

SHOCKLEY: Not really. As my wife has often said, to do what I do, you must have three things: honesty, a secure professional reputation and financial security. I have those three things and thus have no excuse not to try to communicate what I believe will benefit mankind.

PLAYBOY: How are you hoping readers will respond to the concerns you have raised in this interview?

SHOCKLEY: I am hoping that it will trigger someone who is sitting on the edge of making a decision, saying, "I should take a stand on this." He might then take action. Get a proposition on a ballot or organize a demonstration. I don't know who it would be. My main theme in this interview has been that the diagnosis of racial problems can be done and that good things might happen as a result of open-minded research.

PLAYBOY: What if, in the final analysis, you are proved wrong about all of this?

SHOCKLEY: I've got my answer for that one: My chagrin over a scientific setback would be more than offset by the fact that these new scientific results would go far toward eliminating what would have to regarded, then, as an unwarranted prejudice against blacks.

PLAYBOY: That's very interesting. Perhaps more than any public figure in the history of this nation, you have been booed off speaking platforms at college campuses, hung in effigy and generally greeted as bad news. How did you feel when that began to happen to you?

SHOCKLEY: I think the first time was at Sacramento State in 1969 or so. There were people dressed in Ku Klux Klan uniforms and I remember a man coming up to the platform and offering me a Nazi salute. Then there was the situation at Brooklyn Polytechnic Institute, where there was a twentieth-anniversary meeting of the scientific honorary research society Sigma Xi. They had asked me to speak and I accepted and told them the title of my talk, which had the words *race* and *dysgenics* in it. A week before I was to give the talk, they called and asked me to speak on physics. I refused. The net result of this was that they canceled the whole meeting and sent out about five hundred telegrams one day before the scheduled meeting.

PLAYBOY: You were involved in a rather famous dispute at Leeds University in England, weren't you?

SHOCKLEY: Yes. Someone thought the transistor deserved to be recognized, and so I was invited to accept an honorary doctor of science degree from Leeds in May of 1973. I was in London in February of that year to lecture to electrical engineers to commemorate the twenty-fifth anniversary of the transistor. I can remember well that it was February, because the most dramatic incident occurred on my sixty-third birthday, the thirteenth of the month. Lord Boyle, the vice-chancellor of the university, invited me to have cocktails at the Carlton Club, the noted conservative club in England. He and I had a pleasant conversation for a few moments, and then he said: "Dr. Shockley, when we decided to award this degree, we were not aware of your other interests." I at once began to wonder about this and said, "Lord Boyle, are you leading up to saying that when I come to Leeds University you would like me to behave in some way other than I would normally behave, or are you saying you'd like me to forget the whole thing?" He replied, "A frank question deserves a frank answer. We'd like you to forget the whole thing." After I broke that story to the press, the news coverage in England was comparable to that of Graham's sperm bank here. David Frost interviewed me as the first of a new series.

PLAYBOY: Did it ever occur to you that you might actually get hurt at some of those disruptions?

SHOCKLEY: Yes. There was one occasion when I saw a man in the audience with something that looked very like a sword cane. I've been a little concerned in other situations but not very much. Incidentally, I've acquired great confidence in the competence of the police and security forces.

PLAYBOY: After fifteen years of this and at the age of seventy, Dr. Shockley, one would think you'd be rather tired of this crusade. Any rewards you have received must be intensely personal in nature, since the world has not exactly welcomed your theories with open arms. What we're wondering, finally, is how you feel about the work you have done and how you would characterize the risks involved in being a "raceologist," as you have described yourself elsewhere.

SHOCKLEY: As I have said before, I don't feel myself that the risks are very large. Young scientists would jeopardize their careers by doing research or expressing views like mine. Such risks have been much smaller for me. I have felt that this fact places an obligation on me to continue. One fellow scientist, whom I meet every year or so, usually greets me with, "Well, here you are again. I didn't know whether you would be here another year." Actually, I have had very few threats. Although sometimes in the press I may not come across accurately, I find that most people, or at least most who talk with me, accept the fact that my intentions are good. I believe this goes a long way toward eliminating the type of hostility that might otherwise exist. As for my personal motivations to continue pressing this subject despite my advanced age, I once used a letter-to-the-editor opportunity, while responding to a column in *Presbyterian Life* identifying me as a disciple of Hitler, to discuss it in these words: "During the last five minutes of my life, should I have my intellectual powers intact, I hope to consider that since engaging in this campaign, I have used my capacities close to their maximum potential in keeping with the objective of Nobel's will of conferring greatest benefit on mankind."

G. GORDON LIDDY

October 1980

Interviewer: Eric Norden

At the time PLAYBOY published this interview, Gordon Liddy was still known as the "sphinx" of Watergate. He had just broken his silence with the publication of *Will,* his autobiography and Watergate memoir, and although it enjoyed a short stay on the best-seller list (and would later be turned into a television movie), Liddy had not yet found out what was marketable about himself. What does a disbarred lawyer and former White House plumber do when most of the country thinks he's a lunatic?

One answer may be suggested by the aftermath of this interview. Eric Norden, veteran of the exhaustive and definitive PLAYBOY interview with Nazi Albert Speer in 1970 (see Volume I), spent two weeks with Liddy, taping while Liddy made appearances to promote his book. Most interviewers he met, both on television and for print, asked Liddy the standard Watergate questions, and Liddy became an expert at the short, clipped, provocative answer. With Norden, however, he was given a chance to develop his thoughts and was asked to probe a little deeper into himself. What emerged was a rounder, fuller self-portrait of the man. He also found out, from the enormous PLAYBOY reader reaction to him (especially among college-age readers), what a colorful pose he had struck.

Every generation has its Tallulah Bankhead—a self-consciously outrageous character people love to be shocked and dismayed by. Liddy may have learned this around the time Norden was interviewing him, for shortly after the piece appeared, Liddy became a huge draw on the college speaking circuit. Standing before audiences who were ten years old at the time of Watergate, he would recycle much of the material he tried out with PLAYBOY—to the gasps and hisses and applause of his college listeners—and he found he had a new career.

As this book goes to press, Liddy, who is also a security consultant, had taken the process a step further by teaming up with another bright and unemployed gentleman:

Timothy Leary. In a series of lucrative and highly publicized debates, the two old ideological foes (Liddy had arrested the drug guru back in his FBI days) relive their differences in an endless rerun. What often makes Liddy the victor in these encounters is a gritty kind of integrity that is evident in this interview.

The press had been gathering since three A.M., and by eight A.M., there were over a hundred reporters, photographers and television cameramen camped on the steps of Connecticut's Danbury Federal Prison. When the door finally opened and a slim, wiry man with thinning black hair and a bristling mustache slipped out, he was almost swallowed up in the swirling, shouting crowd. As newsmen jostled one another for position, the newly released inmate embraced his attractive auburn-haired wife and stowed his prison gear in the trunk of their son's 1971 Ford Pinto. "How does it feel to be out of jail?" one TV newsman called over the din. The object of their attention snapped, "Was mich nicht umbringt, macht mich starker." *There were blank stares from the crowd until a reporter who knew German translated: " 'What doesn't destroy me, makes me stronger.' It's from Nietzsche." The Pinto pulled out of the prison driveway, hotly pursued by five Ford Granada press cars, and a screeching seventy-mile-an-hour chase ensued until the driver of the lead car finally shook off his pursuers after a series of nerve-shattering maneuvers that left his wife collapsed in tears in the front seat. "God," she snuffled finally. "After all these years, you haven't changed at all." She sighed, "I don't suppose you ever will."*

Her husband smiled fondly at her. "Bet your ass, kid!"

It was September 7, 1977, and G. Gordon Liddy had just been released on parole after serving fifty-two months of a twenty-year prison sentence for having masterminded the break-in at the headquarters of the Democratic National Committee in Washington's Watergate complex on June 17, 1972.

George Gordon Battle Liddy was born on November 30, 1930, in Hoboken, New Jersey. It was the Depression, but the Liddy family was well-off, and there was always a maid in attendance. His father was an internationally respected lawyer. Gordon attended parochial and prep schools (where his IQ was measured at 137 to 142, in the genius range) and graduated from Fordham University, subsequently taking an ROTC commission during the Korean War. Much to his regret, he was not sent overseas with his fellow artillery officers, due to a ruptured appendix, and instead served out his time at an antiaircraft installation in Brooklyn. After the army, Liddy graduated from Fordham Law School, winning election to the prestigious Law Review, and in November 1957, he married Frances Purcell. (They have five children, three boys and two girls.) Liddy joined the FBI in 1957, serving as a field agent and bureau supervisor until September 1962, when he resigned for financial reasons. He then worked at his father's prosperous Wall Street law firm until 1966, when he accepted a post as assistant district attorney in Poughkeepsie, New York (in Dutchess County, which Liddy describes as "somewhere to the right of Barry Goldwater").

Liddy quickly won considerable local attention for his unorthodox trial techniques, including discharging a gun into the ceiling of the courtroom during a dramatic plea to the jury. He became a local celebrity when he led a raid on the Millbrook, New York, headquarters of Dr. Timothy Leary, the psychedelic guru and LSD proselytizer.

In 1968, Liddy contested the Republican Congressional nomination in the 28th

District, running on the campaign slogan, "Gordon Liddy doesn't bail them out; he puts them in." He lost narrowly (fifty-one to forty-nine percent) to a moderate, Hamilton Fish, but won the admiration of local GOP leaders. With the support of his sponsors, close friends of the new Attorney-General, John Mitchell, Liddy was rewarded after the elections with a job as special assistant to the Secretary of the Treasury with special responsibility for narcotic and firearms control. He was forced out of the Treasury Department in 1971 after a speech against gun control before the National Rifle Association. But he was subsequently attached to the White House, where he organized a special counterintelligence squad that ultimately gained notoriety as the White House Plumbers' Unit. In December 1971, he moved from the White House to the Committee to Re-Elect the President, which he served as counsel until the aftermath of the Watergate break-in, where five of his operatives were arrested, including CREEP's security director, James McCord. Liddy was subsequently charged with one count of conspiracy, two counts of burglary, two of intercepting wire communications and one of intercepting oral communications. He refused to testify against his associates and Judge John Sirica imposed the stiffest sentence on him of any of the Watergate coconspirators: twenty years in prison and a forty-thousand-dollar fine. President Carter commuted the sentence in mid-1977 and Liddy was freed on parole shortly afterward.

In 1979, Liddy published a novel, Out of Control, *a spy thriller that received decidedly mixed reviews. But when his autobiography,* Will, *was published under conditions of strict secrecy and quickly climbed best-seller lists across the country, the reviews seemed to polarize even more sharply. Clarus Backes, book editor of* The Sunday Denver Post, *wrote with evident surprise, "Fully prepared to hate it, I carried the book home with me one evening and found myself completely enthralled. . . . It is one of the most engrossing and thoroughly honest self-revelations that I have ever read." Bob Woodward wrote in* The Washington Post, *"There is almost an embarrassment of riches in the book. . . . A hundred little facts and inferences convince me that he has been as honest as he could be." But literary hatchets were also being sharpened for Liddy. In the* New Republic, *Alan M. Dershowitz, while conceding that "Liddy is an excellent writer and a fascinating character," nevertheless condemned the book as "the* Mein Kampf *of a failed* Führer," *while Christopher Osborne, writing in New Hampshire's* Leisure, *waxed practically apoplectic: "Liddy is a very sick man. His autobiography . . . makes no attempt to vindicate his sordid and despicable life. On the contrary, it seems to revel in calm disclosure of his insanity. . . . His time was in Germany during the Thirties and Forties."*

To determine what had ignited this latest storm of national controversy over G. Gordon Liddy, PLAYBOY *sent novelist Eric Norden to interview him. Norden, who had spent considerable time with other Watergate figures such as James McCord (and whose previous interview credits include director Stanley Kubrick in September 1968 and former Nazi Albert Speer in June 1971), reports:*

"The first thing that struck me about Liddy was his sense of humor. It was a discordant note in the image I had built of him as a steely-eyed fanatic, and it was to permeate a great deal of the interview. It's hard to believe that someone who jokes with you over the pomponettes de truffe surprise *at New York's fashionable La Côte Basque, where we met for an initial exploratory lunch, could calmly blow you away over the soufflé and cognac. Liddy also was smaller than I'd expected, though obviously in excellent physical shape, as befits someone who does one hundred*

pushups every morning. We had a pleasant lunch, and as we parted, I had difficulty remembering I was in the presence of someone who had been described by Theodore White as 'a thoroughly dangerous man'—and dubbed by the press as 'the Darth Vader of the Nixon administration' and, appropriately enough, 'The Sphinx.' But Liddy was talking now, and volubly.

PLAYBOY: Throughout your trial and nearly five years' imprisonment, you maintained a stoical, name-rank-and-serial-number silence, and on your rare interviews after release, expressed contempt for your Watergate coconspirators who published books on the subject, vowing never to follow in their footsteps. Why did you change your mind?

LIDDY: There were a number of reasons, both personal and legal. As early as July 1973, the late columnist Stewart Alsop wrote me a letter arguing very persuasively that I should tell my story because, in his words, "I had a debt to history." Alsop was a fine writer whom I regarded highly both for his war record—he was an outstanding veteran of the OSS—and because he had terminal cancer and was confronting his pain and imminent death with great bravery. I took the position then that he was probably right about my debt to history, but it wasn't a demand note due today. You've got to remember that at that time, our containment strategy, what the press dubbed "stonewalling," was unraveling pretty rapidly but still hadn't totally collapsed, and I continued to nourish the hope that the President could be insulated from the scandal. If that had happened, of course, I *never* would have written the book.

PLAYBOY: But Nixon was forced out of office in 1974. Why did you wait until 1980 to publish your book?

LIDDY: Well, that pertains to the legal aspects. I had to wait until the statutes of limitations had expired before I could tell the full story without endangering the liberty of any of my former colleagues.

PLAYBOY: And your own?

LIDDY: Yes, and my own as well.

PLAYBOY: Some of your critics have speculated that, despite *Will*'s disarming candor, you have not revealed some matters of grave import because the statutes of limitation on those particular illegal acts have not yet expired—or, as in the case of murder, never will.

LIDDY: Well, obviously, if I were concealing a homicide, I'd hardly reveal it to PLAYBOY or anybody else. Of course, I am not.

PLAYBOY: According to Magruder, your former White House superior, you *are*. Magruder wrote in his autobiography that you had confided to him that you once murdered a man while in the employ of the FBI.

LIDDY: That's absolute nonsense. And let me point out that Jeb Magruder, apart from being a thoroughly spineless wretch who always seemed on the verge of crying for his mommy, is a liar, a perjurer. No, I'm sorry to disappoint the romantic expectations of your readers, but I do not come to you red of tooth and claw, with a double row of notches on my six-gun. I would be prepared to kill—not murder—either in the armed forces of my country or in defense of her national security, but I have never been called upon to do so.

PLAYBOY: And yet your book abounds with plots to murder opponents of and defectors from the Nixon administration, ranging from Jack Anderson to E. Howard Hunt—

LIDDY: None of which came to fruition.

PLAYBOY: Do we detect an unspoken "alas" at the end of that statement?
LIDDY: If you're a mind reader, you tell me.
PLAYBOY: Why in God's name did you want to murder Jack Anderson in the first place?
LIDDY: I'd prefer to term it justifiable homicide, since murder is a legal term for a specific type of homicide that by its very definition is unjustifiable. But, in any case, let me stress that it had nothing to do with his political opinions or his policy differences with the Nixon administration. I recognize that reasonable men can differ on such matters, and I have no trouble with the concept of a loyal opposition, in press or parliament. I will say, though, that I have very little respect for the type of advocacy journalism we've seen in the United States since the late Sixties which in my view is an ideologically motivated corruption of traditional objective journalism, one that pretends to be reporting the news while it is subtly manipulating and slanting it.

Anderson is one of those mutant strains of columnist who are half legitimate, because he occasionally labels his own opinions as such, and half deceptive, because he also passes off biased interpretations and selective information as straight reportage. At one point, Anderson's systematic leaking of top-secret information rendered the effective conduct of American foreign policy virtually impossible: He blew one of our finest technical sources of information abroad by disclosing that we had found a way to intercept car-to-car conversations between Brezhnev and Kosygin and other top Soviet officials as they drove through Moscow in their Zil limousines. But no move was taken against him until E. Howard Hunt informed me that one of his columns had fatally—quite literally—compromised a vital U.S. human intelligence asset in the Middle East, a man who as a result of his disclosures was being tortured, or was possibly already dead, even as we spoke. Anderson had finally gone too far and he had to be stopped. Not for what he wrote but for what he did, and could be expected to continue to do.
PLAYBOY: Casting Anderson as a villain who caused the death of a U.S. agent is an effective rationale for silencing him, but the fact remains that his removal would have spared Nixon considerable political embarrassment. Wasn't that the real motive?
LIDDY: No, it certainly was not, even though I recall George Bernard Shaw's observing that assassination is the extreme form of censorship. But, Jesus, man, if we'd tried to whack out every Washington reporter and columnist who had it in for Nixon, then the National Press Club would've held nothing but wall-to-wall memorial plaques. No, we moved against Anderson for no other reason than that he had exposed and destroyed a man who had put his life on the line for the United States, and there was no other way to stop him from continuing that kind of conduct.
PLAYBOY: Anderson strenuously denies having done any such thing.
LIDDY: No, he doesn't. What he *does* do is say over and over—and I've been on two or three television and radio shows with him recently where he repeated the same line—that he never "revealed or identified a CIA officer." Now, the man in question was not a CIA *officer,* he was a CIA *agent,* an agent in place, as it's called, a foreign national in the agency's employ overseas. Anderson desperately sticks to that tortured formulation, because it's not a technical lie. Just like that other secular saint of the American liberal establishment, old Maximum John Sirica, he's scared of getting his halo tarnished.
PLAYBOY: How did you two get along when you met on a television show?
LIDDY: Anderson appeared a bit nervous, but I shook his hand and told him, *"La*

guerre est finie." It was something like those postwar reunions when *Luftwaffe* and RAF pilots get together over a stein of beer and swap stories of dogfights during the Battle of Britain. At least, in *my* mind it was.

PLAYBOY: Nice of you not to carry a grudge, since you only tried to murder the man.

LIDDY: No, never actually tried. It never got to that.

PLAYBOY: Why not?

LIDDY: We worked out a plan, but it was ultimately never approved by our principals. Hunt and I started the ball rolling by meeting a physician from the CIA, who was introduced euphemistically as a specialist in "the unorthodox application of chemical and medical knowledge."

PLAYBOY: Meaning an expert in killing people.

LIDDY: Crude, but not inexact. Anyway, we had lunch over at the Hay-Adams across from the White House and discussed various methods of killing Anderson, including coating the steering wheel of his car with an LSD solution sufficiently potent to cause a crash, which we rejected as too chancy, and "aspirin roulette," which we also turned down.

PLAYBOY: Dare we ask?

LIDDY: Aspirin roulette is intelligence jargon for a rather common assassination technique, which entails the substitution of an ordinary aspirin or other headache-remedy tablet in the target's medicine cabinet with a look-alike that is actually a deadly poison.

PLAYBOY: Sounds lovely. Why was it rejected?

LIDDY: Too iffy again. It would be only one out of fifty or maybe even a hundred tablets, and months could go by before the target swallowed it. But most important was the danger that an innocent member of his family might take the pill.

PLAYBOY: Very scrupulous of you. What did you finally decide on?

LIDDY: A simple if un–James Bondish method, which I'd learned in the FBI. Let's say an FBI agent was penetrating a foreign embassy to crack a safe and steal a onetime cipher or some such for the National Security Agency, and suddenly an employee returned earlier than he was supposed to and was about to endanger the mission. Well, other agents would have been following everyone assigned to that embassy and they would have intercepted him before he reached the building and staged a common street mugging to divert him. In Anderson's case, we merely decided to make it a lethal mugging.

PLAYBOY: Who would have done the job?

LIDDY: It was initially decided to assign it to some of our Cuban-exile assets, but then Hunt began to worry that our principals would deem it too sensitive a matter to be entrusted to them. So I volunteered to do it myself.

PLAYBOY: Just like that?

LIDDY: No, not just like that. But I thought about the matter, considered the damage that Anderson was doing, for whatever motives, to the security of this country, and decided that, if the Cubans were ruled out, I was the best man for the job, considering my own FBI and martial-arts training. We didn't want to make it look like anything more than another Washington street-crime statistic, remember, so no sophisticated weaponry could be employed.

PLAYBOY: How would you have killed him?

LIDDY: Oh, I would have knifed him or broken his neck, probably. One of us would have died, no doubt about it. But, as I say, we never received the final green light.

PLAYBOY: Were you relieved or disappointed?

LIDDY: I was neither. I was acting on the instructions of my principals, and I was prepared to follow those instructions either way they went.

PLAYBOY: You really see nothing anomalous, much less frightening, about two aides to the President of the United States cold-bloodedly plotting to assassinate one of the country's leading reporters?

LIDDY: I know it violates the sensibilities of the innocent and tender-minded, but in the real world, you sometimes have to employ extreme and extralegal methods to preserve the very system whose laws you're violating.

PLAYBOY: Including murder?

LIDDY: Drastic problems sometimes demand drastic solutions. Look, let me give you an example. Philip Agee, the CIA defector, has effectively exposed and compromised dozens of our intelligence agents around the world, and one of his revelations led directly to the assassination of the CIA station chief in Athens, Richard Welch. This one man has done untold damage to the worldwide security interests of the United States. And what have we done about it? Nothing. Fifty years ago, Henry Stimson scuttled an effective American intelligence effort on the grounds that gentlemen don't read other gentlemen's mail. The pendulum seems to have swung all the way back to that position, and the Russians couldn't be happier. They've tried to destroy the American intelligence capability for thirty-five years, and in five years we've done the job for them, with the help of a few posturing demagogues like Frank Church. I just wish someone would point out to the good senator that the world is not run by the League of Women Voters.

PLAYBOY: Returning to Philip Agee for a moment, how would *you* deal with him? Would you, in CIA parlance, "terminate him with extreme prejudice"?

LIDDY: You're damn right I would. If I were back serving in some capacity in the American intelligence community and I found Agee living comfortably abroad, outside the reach of our law and continuing his revelations, I would strongly recommend that he be assassinated. And were I given the task, I would undertake it, and feel completely justified in so doing. But let me stress that his killing would not be retributive but preventive, to forestall further disclosures that would damage the security of this country and endanger the lives of its intelligence agents. The same rationale I employed in the case of Mr. Anderson.

PLAYBOY: You'd be willing to kill a man you've never met solely because he was on the opposite side of the political and ideological fence?

LIDDY: No, my friend, because he's on the opposite side of the *trench,* in a political-military war between the United States and the Soviet Union that is crucial to our survival as a free nation, and no less vicious because it's undeclared. I hope we don't have to wait until the skies over New York are black with missiles to understand that fact and act on it. And if we continue our current posture of head-in-the-sand appeasement, I'm afraid that may very well be the case.

PLAYBOY: And you'd feel no qualms, much less remorse, about liquidating someone like Agee?

LIDDY: No more than swatting a fly. Of course, our government has been so weakened we no longer have the will for such action, even though we retain the human and technological capability. And the Russians, who are thoroughly ruthless and realistic about the pursuit of their own national interests, know it. But there would be nothing intrinsically evil or immoral about such an act. Just the opposite. The French have a saying, *"Cet animal est três mêchant; quand on l'attaque, il se dêfend."* Roughly translated, it means, "This animal is very wicked; when attacked, it defends itself." When the CIA and other intelligence agencies tried to defend us effectively against our external enemies, they were mercilessly pilloried by the press and Congressional committees, and their most seasoned agents prematurely forced into retirement. Now, after Ethiopia, Angola and Afghanistan, a few alarm bells are dimly ringing in Washington and there's even a halfhearted effort to refurbish the kennel. But it's too late. The animal is no longer wicked. It's just toothless.

PLAYBOY: You also planned to murder one of your old buddies and fellow Waterbugger, E. Howard Hunt. Surely, Hunt was no enemy of this country.

LIDDY: At the risk of belaboring this point once again, I would personally never characterize it as murder, because murder by its very definition is *unjustifiable* homicide, and I never would have considered the act in the first place if I had not deemed it eminently justifiable. Hunt had become an informer, a betrayer of his friends and associates, and to me there is nothing lower on this earth. As Nietzsche put it, there is but one sin—cowardice. Hunt deserved to die.

PLAYBOY: Here was a man who had once been your good friend, who was now broken in mind and body, grief-stricken over his wife's death and ground down by the rigors of prison life. And so he violated your code and turned state's witness. Couldn't you have forgiven him that and summoned up sufficient compassion to forget, if not forgive?

LIDDY: Forgiveness, as Mark Twain once said, is the fragrance a rose leaves on the boot that has crushed it. But I'm afraid you're being naïve as well as sentimental. It wasn't a question of my personal feelings about Hunt, though God knows if he'd stayed a man, I'd have done everything in my power to help him. It wasn't even a question of my detestation of informers, even though I'd point out that we all went into Watergate with our eyes open, were willing to benefit from success and should have been equally willing to face failure with fortitude. No, the stakes were much higher than that, my friend. Hunt knew too much, not only about Watergate but about other matters of state, including CIA secrets. It seemed perfectly plausible to me that my superiors might wish his elimination, and I was prepared to execute those orders without a moment's doubt or soul-searching.

PLAYBOY: Perhaps it is sentimental, at least in your book, but the question of friendship does seem an important consideration here, since none of your other "targets" were close to you personally, as Hunt had once been. E. M. Forster wrote, "If I had a choice between betraying my country or my friend, I hope I would have the courage to betray my country." Is such a concept totally alien to you?

LIDDY: Yes, but only because I *do* value friendship, like personal honor, so highly. I would find betraying a friend as unthinkable as betraying my country, and the conundrum would never arise, because the only time I would turn against a friend would be when he had forfeited that friendship by betraying *our* country. And that, of course, is precisely at the root of my feelings about Hunt.

PLAYBOY: Nixon and the political fortunes of his administration are not exactly synonymous with the national interests of the United States, are they?

LIDDY: Well, under the circumstances, and in the light of what's happened to this nation since—and because—Nixon was forced from office, I think you could make a very good case that the two were so inextricably linked that Hunt's betrayal constituted an act at least of regicide, if not of outright treason.

PLAYBOY: Do you feel the same way about Dean?

LIDDY: Yes, but even more strongly. For all of Hunt's weaknesses and failings, it would still be manifestly unfair to place him in the same category as Dean or Magruder. Next to them, Hunt is a giant. I wouldn't even talk of him in the same breath, much as I condemn his betrayal. The difference between Hunt and Dean is the difference between a POW who breaks under torture and aids the enemy and Judas Iscariot.

PLAYBOY: You've been alone with Dean only once since he testified against the White House, and you've said that you contemplated killing him then. How close did you actually come?

LIDDY: Oh, it was just a fleeting thought, now one of those sweet memories that one loves to treasure. God knows, he would have been no loss. What happened, actually, was that in October of 1974, federal marshals escorted me to the offices of Watergate special prosecutor James Neal for an interview and told me to wait in Neal's office, as he was expected shortly. I went in and shut the door behind me and, lo and behold, there was Dean sitting behind the desk. He looked up and I could have sworn he was about to wet himself. His eyes darted all around the room, but I was between him and the door and I could see that he was absolutely terror-stricken. My first thought was that here was the ideal opportunity to kill the bastard. I saw a pencil on the desk and all it would take was a quick thrust through the underside of his jaw, up through the soft palate and deep inside the brain. And simultaneously, I wondered if this were a setup, if someone had arranged for me to be alone with Dean, anticipating exactly such a denouement. But then, on more somber reflection, I ruled that out. Nixon had been out of office for two months, I had received no instructions from my old superiors and, in any case, his killing could only damage the chances of Mitchell, Mardian and others in their forthcoming trials. No, revenge might be a dish best supped cold, but this was positively stale. The whole thing had just been a weird, stupid error. So I exchanged a few inconsequential remarks with Dean, he stammered a reply and I stepped aside so he could gather his papers and scurry out the door. I think he aged considerably in those three or four minutes.

PLAYBOY: Let's put Dean aside for a moment and consider the method you considered using to kill him—

LIDDY: Good idea. A pencil's always a more interesting topic of conversation than John Dean.

PLAYBOY: If there weren't several pencils on the table between us right now, we might ask you not to interrupt. But seriously, you're a student of unarmed combat, and in your novel, *Out of Control,* you describe an attack by an Oriental master of the martial arts as follows: "Such was the power ot T'ang Li's thrust that his fingers kept right on going through the wet pulp of the man's eyeballs and the shell-thin bone at the rear of the sockets to penetrate into the warm, moist, unresistant softness of the brain itself." Was that just poetic license, or could you kill a man with such a single blow? And we stress that it's a purely theoretical question; there's no need to demonstrate.

LIDDY: You cringe very nicely. No, it's true that I've trained in the martial arts for many years, initially at the FBI, where I first learned to kill a man with a pencil, incidentally, and was taught to blind and maim and in general employ my body's "personal weapons," as my instructors called it, against an opponent's "vulnerable areas." Later on, I studied under a red-belt master of the high T'ai Chi who could rip out your throat or disembowel you with a backhand slash. A fascinating character. So that scene was based on fact, though I've never duplicated it in real life.

PLAYBOY: What are the most effective ways to kill a man without employing a conventional weapon?

LIDDY: Well, they are innumerable, depending, of course, on the skill of the practitioner. For someone with no special training, our old-faithful pencil is *very* efficient, just your common garden-variety standard wooden pencil with a good sharp point and a strong, substantial eraser. The eraser's quite important, actually. With those prerequisites, and if you can reach your opponent, any novice could kill his enemy in one second or less. But I don't want to go any further into the details, lest we have a sudden rash of pencil killings in junior high schools across the country. Assuming, of course, that adolescent males concentrate on PLAYBOY's interviews.
PLAYBOY: In *Will,* you describe an encounter in a California prison with a Mongolian master of the martial arts who instructed you only reluctantly, after warning that "You are a very violent man, I can see it in your eyes." Was he right?
LIDDY: Oh, yes. But I've learned to suppress my violence, and control it. And remember, as any true master of the martial arts will tell you, the most powerful weapon I have is this. [*Taps temple with index finger*] The physical body is the vessel of the intellect, and the strongest muscles are useless without the guidance, the supercharger effect, of a trained and disciplined mind.
PLAYBOY: As long as we're on such a murderous topic, is there any such thing as an untraceable poison?
LIDDY: Yes, there are a few, in the colloidal family, and they're known—and used by—the intelligence services of the superpowers. But they may not be untraceable for long, since there's recently been a considerable forensic breakthrough in that area. But generally, you know, even traceable poisons are *not* traced, unless there's reason to suspect foul play. Most autopsies are *pro forma,* unless the forensic pathologist is on his toes and already suspicious; so if you use a poison that simulates the symptoms of heart failure, say, you're generally home safe and dry.

There's a wide range of poisons that can be manufactured simply at home, without complex laboratory technology. Give me several cigars, for example, and in a short while I'll have extracted enough pure nicotine to kill a man with a few drops in his food or coffee. That was how I was going to handle Hunt, in fact, if the signal had come down from on high. But, once again, I don't want to spell out the process in any detail, lest I put ideas into the heads of any impressionable adolescents in your audience.
PLAYBOY: You have one hell of an opinion of the young people across this country.
LIDDY: Realism, my friend, realism. If people know how to do something, no matter how nasty, sooner or later somebody's going to do it. It's the nature of the beast.
PLAYBOY: Moving from the martial arts and exotic poisons to more prosaic means of mayhem, you are not only proficient in the use of firearms but also an avid gun collector and outspoken opponent of all gun-control legislation. In fact, Peter Prescott of *Newsweek* went so far as to call you a "gun fanatic." Is that a fair description?
LIDDY: About as fair, I'd say, as my describing a writer like Peter Prescott as a "typewriter fanatic." As far as I'm concerned, to enjoy hunting or target-firing weapons, or to collect them, is no more unusual or unhealthy than admiring and enjoying the use of any beautiful piece of machinery, like a Daimler-Benz engine or a fine Leica camera. If that makes me a fanatic, then all I can tell you is that the gentleman's definition of fanaticism differs from the standard dictionary definition and is a reflection of his bias rather than his intellect. And there certainly is a bias against gun users and their rights on the part of the urban liberal intelligentsia, which is always lobbying to deny guns to law-abiding citizens, even though they would always remain

available to the criminal on the flourishing black market or through theft. The proponents of such nostrums should contemplate the failure of Prohibition in the Twenties.

PLAYBOY: You say you're not a gun nut, but didn't you wear a pistol to your own wedding?

LIDDY: Yes, a small, concealed .38 snub-nosed revolver. But I was an FBI agent at the time, and wearing a gun was second nature to me. In fact, shortly after our wedding, my wife gave *me* a beautifully gift-wrapped magnum revolver as a present.

PLAYBOY: Are you carrying a gun right now?

LIDDY: Another admirable cringe. No, obviously I am not, as that would constitute a violation of my parole and jeopardize my freedm needlessly. I do have an air gun that I still practice with, a Walther LP 2 Olympic grade air pistol, which is highly accurate and practically recoilless. Using target sights, and employing a pointed projectile preferably coated with pure nicotine, I could shoot you dead at a range of ten meters, or approximately thirty-three feet. It's as silent and lethal as a fine throwing knife.

PLAYBOY: Sorry we asked. But speaking of knives, you wrote in *Will* that you carried a switchblade with you on the night your men broke into the offices of Daniel Ellsberg's psychiatrist in Beverly Hills. If the burglary had been interrupted by police or passersby, would you have used that knife?

LIDDY: First of all, it was not a switchblade, melodramatic as that sounds, but a Browning clasp knife. But I would have used it only as a last resort. I was in radio communication with our men inside the building, and if I'd seen a third party approaching, I would have instantly alerted them and then attempted to divert the intruder's attention.

PLAYBOY: How?

LIDDY: Nonviolently, if at all possible. Say we had some bad luck and a cop appeared on the scene. There was no outward evidence of the break-in to tip him off, but if for some reason he'd heard the breaking of glass and decided to check the building, I'd have made my presence known and diverted his attention from the men inside once I'd tipped them off. I'm a good runner, and I could have led him a merry chase.

PLAYBOY: But let's say you had the bad luck to encounter the only cop on the Beverly Hills police force ever to qualify for the Olympic decathlon and he outran you. Would you have surrendered?

LIDDY: No, that would have placed the mission and my principals in jeopardy, not just me. I would have attempted to incapacitate him nonlethally, if at all possible. Remember, there's an awful lot of ways of taking somebody out without using deadly force. The knife was an absolute last resort, to be employed only after I'd exhausted all other options.

PLAYBOY: And if you had?

LIDDY: I've already told you that I was prepared to take all necessary measures to protect my men and our mission. I did not arm my self gratuitously, but neither would I have used my weapon unless absolutely necessary to protect myself.

PLAYBOY: But you were prepared to kill if absolutely necessary?

LIDDY: Yes, I've told you I was.

PLAYBOY: It's precisely this kind of ruthlessness, which casually encompasses homicide as just another option, that has so alarmed your critics. For example, Herb Klein, who served as White House director of communications during the Nixon administration and who hardly fits the stereotype of a bleeding-heart liberal, reviewed your book recently in the *Los Angeles Times* and charged that you had adopted "a Mafia-like attitude placing Liddy above the law. . . . The book reads like gang-war fiction." How would you answer him?

LIDDY: Well, we *were* fighting a war, a civic war, in those days, a far more serious one than the typical gangland squabble over who controls numbers and drugs in this or that section of town, or who had intruded on somebody else's turf. The stakes, as we saw it, were the security and very survival of this nation, and we were ready to take strong measures in its defense. If that's Mafialike, so be it.

PLAYBOY: You reveal in your autobiography that while in prison, you got on well with a number of actual Mafia leaders, including the unnamed one to whom you entrusted the contract on Hunt. Did they consider you a kindred spirit?

LIDDY: First of all, I'm not going to characterize anyone as Mafia. That's a label pinned by federal and local prosecutors on people who may or may not be involved in organized crime, and I know from my own experiences that it's not always accurate. But it is true that I arrived in prison after defying all three branches of the United States government, executive, judicial and legislative, and my refusal to become a rat had preceded me. Nothing is despised more in prison than an informer, remember, and, conversely, nothing is admired more than the so-called stand-up guy, in jailhouse parlance, who refuses to turn in his associates. So I did find that a number of people who had been accused of involvement in organized crime approached me and expressed a certain degree of respect for my behavior. And, as it turned out, we did get on very well, because we had some values in common.

PLAYBOY: Considering the Mafia's obsession with *omertà,* the traditional Sicilian code of silence, their penchant for liquidating enemies, their ruthless pursuit of *vendetta* and their fanatic code of personal honor, wouldn't you have made a good *mafioso,* perhaps even a godfather? And is it still too late?

LIDDY: It's nice of you to search out avenues of employment for me, since they tend to be somewhat limited to someone who has been in prison on a felony conviction. I'll be sure to refer your suggestion to my parole officer. Actually, there was one amusing incident in that vein that took place in prison in California, where I'd come to know Bill Bonanno, who'd been the protagonist of Gay Talese's best-selling book *Honor Thy Father.* One Christmas Eve, two of Bill's hulking friends showed up to escort me to midnight Mass in the prison chapel, even though I was no longer a practicing Catholic and had not planned to attend. I sang the hymns lustily, and at a small party Bill threw afterward, he gave me a hearty *abbraccio* and said, "I *knew* anyone whose mother's name was Abbaticchio hadda be OK: right, boys?" Everybody laughed and he went on: "What I like about this guy, it's the only kinda singing he knows!" So, yes, we certainly did have a bond on that level.

PLAYBOY: Your critics would contend that you had far more in common with the Mafia than a mutual scorn for stool pigeons—i.e., a dedication to the principle that the ends justify the means.

LIDDY: Well, I've never denied that. When the issues are significant enough, the ends *do* justify the means. And, in fact, most people in this society operate on just that assumption, though a lot of them gloss it over with a shimmering veil of hypocrisy, like John Sirica. Didn't *The New York Times* believe that the end justified the means in the Pentagon Papers case, when it published purloined top-secret government documents? And didn't the civil-rights and antiwar demonstrators believe that the ends justified the means when they broke the law by sit-ins at lunch counters or burning their draft cards? Sure they did, and at least in the civil-rights movement, they were prepared to go to jail for their convictions. It was only when we countered the illegal actions of the antiwar movement with some of our own that they tore their hair and rent their raiments and screamed, "Police state!" and the whole thing turned into a morality play. All a question of whose political ox is getting gored, of course. When I'm in a war, I can respect my opponent, no matter how strongly I detest his convictions. What I cannot stand is hypocrisy.

PLAYBOY: That's the second analogy you've made between your conduct and that of a soldier in wartime, and throughout your trial and imprisonment, you certainly conducted yourself as a POW trapped in enemy territory. If you were a soldier, weren't your only enemies fellow Americans of differing political views?

LIDDY: That's easy enough to believe if you conveniently distort the facts of recent history. Everybody today knows that in the late Sixties and early Seventies, we were involved in an exterior war in Vietnam, but they tend to forget that we were also embroiled in an undeclared civil war at home. And unless you can understand the nature of that struggle and the issues it posed for the administration in Washington, you'll never be able to understand my motives or the motives of my associates in undertaking the actions and running the risks we did. We were up against a formidable constellation of forces in those days, an alliance of influential elements of the media with a so-called counterculture that represented a Weltanschauung and life-style that were utterly repugnant to me. It was as unthinkable to me to let the country succumb to those values as it would have been for a Japanese officer reared on the code of Bushido to contemplate surrender in 1945.

PLAYBOY: And so you became a kamikaze, and ultimately self-destructed over Watergate?

LIDDY: No, I joined people who believed as I did in a well-justified counteroffensive against the forces of civil disorder that were sweeping the country in those days. And I have absolutely no regrets about my decision to do so. Ultimately, our side won out and crushed the revolutionaries, which is one salient reason why what's left of the left has never forgotten or forgiven Richard Nixon. But our very victory has to some extent obscured the gravity of the situation as it was seen in Washington in those days.

PLAYBOY: Aren't you drastically exaggerating the true dimensions of civil unrest in order to justify your own violations of the law? Sure, there were antiwar demonstrations and civil disobedience and some incidents of terrorism by crazies like the Weathermen; but can you seriously argue that the country was teetering on the brink of a revolutionary upheaval?

LIDDY: In my opinion, you're seriously *under*estimating the threat. We didn't have a crystal ball at our disposal in those days that would inform us that mass student opposition to the war would peter out after the end of the draft, or that the racial cauldron in the big cities would eventually simmer down. We had to act on our best intelligence assessment of the forces arrayed against us, and that assessment was far from encouraging, particularly when you consider the revolutionaries. Remember, we knew that those same forces had caused Lyndon Johnson to abdicate his office, and we were not prepared to see a similar scenario in the case of Richard Nixon. We drew the line and chose to fight back.

PLAYBOY: You never had any doubts that the antiwar movement posed a serious threat to this country and its institutions?

LIDDY: Never for a moment. They were the shock troops of a movement and value system I despised, and as far as I was concerned, if they were going to succeed, they would have had to march over my dead body. And I always felt justified in taking any action necessary to thwart them. I remembered Cicero's dictum that laws are inoperative in war. And I knew we were at war.

PLAYBOY: In the course of your crusade to save the Republic, was there any ethical line you would have drawn? And, as a "good soldier" in Nixon's army, what do you think of the so-called Nuremberg precept that the execution of an illegal and immoral order constitutes a crime under international law?

LIDDY: I do not believe in "blind obedience" to authority. On the contrary, I believe that the individual has a responsibility to pursue the dictates of his own conscience and own reason, even when they counter the interests of the state. Man, after all, has free will. A concentration-camp guard at Auschwitz or in the Gulag cannot absolve himself of responsibility for his acts simply on the grounds that he was "obeying orders." I've explained why I'd be willing to break the law under extraordinary circumstances, but there is a point beyond which I would not go.

PLAYBOY: What *is* that point?

LIDDY: Well, anything that is *malum in se,* evil in itself, as opposed to something that is *malum prohibitum,* or wrong only because there is a law against it on the statute books.

PLAYBOY: That appears to be a rather Jesuitical distinction.

LIDDY: Well, the Jesuits have had hundreds of years to ponder such questions, so I wouldn't dismiss them too lightly, but the distinction between *malum in se* and *malum prohibitum* is a very real and vital one when considering the role of man's conscience in relationship to the law.

PLAYBOY: Would you give us an example?

LIDDY: OK. A classic example of *malum in se,* something that's evil in and of itself, would be the sexual abuse of a child. I don't need to refer to the statute books to know that is wrong, nor would the public at large. Now, to take another extreme for purposes of illustration, let's say I was driving through the Nevada desert one day, where I could see a hundred miles in either direction, and suddenly I approach a red octagonal STOP sign. If I drove through it, as I would, I would clearly be committing an illegal act, I would be violating the law. But absent an Eleventh Commandment enjoining, "Thou shalt not go through an octagonal red sign with the word STOP on it," my action would be morally irrelevant. Of course, there's a wide range of gradations involved between such a harmless infraction and an ultimately heinous crime such as raping a child, but there are vital distinctions between the two kinds of violation that should and must be made.

PLAYBOY: But wouldn't murder—which you've admitted plotting, if not executing—clearly fall under the category of *malum in se?*

LIDDY: Only if you refuse to accept the distinction I made earlier in our conversation between justifiable and unjustifiable homicide. And even if you resort to Judaeo-Christianity for ethical guidance, a similar distinction would have to be made. We're taught that the commandment reads, "Thou shalt not kill," but, in fact, the literal translation from the Hebrew reads, "Thou shalt not do *murder.*" To illustrate the point, let's carry this concept of *malum in se* over to the political area we've been discussing. I've said I would have been willing to kill Jack Anderson or Philip Agee. Now, let's say in 1972, before the New Hampshire primary, somebody had approached me and said, "Liddy, we want you to whack out Ed Muskie, he's gaining in the polls and he's a real threat to this administration in November." Well, I wouldn't have touched that one with a ten-foot pole—no pun intended. I disagreed totally with Senator Muskie's domestic and foreign-policy positions at the time, and if he'd been nominated, I would have fought him politically every inch of the way. But he was and is a decent, patriotic American who was not out in any way to damage the interests of this country, and it would have been a pure case of *malum in se* for me to move against him. On the other hand, if he had won the nomination and somebody said, "Liddy, infiltrate an agent in Muskie's headquarters and find out what he's up to," I certainly would have considered it. That would have been traditional in American politics. It would, in fact, have been another case of *malum prohibitum.* So the difference between the two is very important to me, and I would always draw the line at *malum in se.*

PLAYBOY: The problem is that you, G. Gordon Liddy, are arrogating to yourself the right to decide what laws should or should not be broken. Isn't that in a very profound sense subversive of the constitutional principle that this is a government of laws and not of men, and no one, from the chief executive on down to the humblest citizen, is above the law?

LIDDY: No. Ultimately, each of us must be accountable to his own conscience. One must consider the facts and make a prudent judgment. Remember that the Constitution is just what the Supreme Court—a group of men—says it is. And that court gave us, among other decisions, Dred Scott [a landmark pro-slavery decision]. I'll take my own conscience, thank you.

PLAYBOY: You're a student of history, with particular interest in ancient Rome and Greece. Do you recall Juvenal's maxim, "Who is to guard the guards against themselves?" And doesn't that apply to G. Gordon Liddy?

LIDDY: Well, I'm no longer a guardian. But, in the final analysis, the people have to do that themselves, by participating in the political process and keeping a sharp eye on the men they elect to govern them. If the majority of the people feel their leaders are abusing that power, they have the option of turning that particular bunch of guardians out of office. They had the chance with us in 1972, and you remember the results.

PLAYBOY: You mentioned Muskie as the kind of man you would never have considered harming, for which dispensation he's doubtless grateful. But another picture of your relationship with Muskie is painted by former high-ranking CIA official Miles Copeland, who claims your agents spiked Muskie's punch with a particularly virulent dose of LSD shortly before he broke down and wept outside the offices of William Loeb's *Manchester Union Leader* during the critical 1972 New Hampshire primary, an event that effectively ended his candidacy.

LIDDY: I'm afraid you're exploring the farther shores of political paranoia on that one. There's no truth to it whatsoever.

PLAYBOY: And yet you've been quoted as having said shortly before campaigning began in New Hampshire that your agents were prepared to pull some "rough stuff" in that contest.

LIDDY: I wasn't referring to *that* kind of rough stuff. I ended up with responsibility for Donald Segretti, you know, though I never recruited him, and he was up in New Hampshire with his bag of so-called dirty tricks, operating against the various candidates. But his stock-in-trade was nothing more serious than glorified fraternity-house pranks—disrupting campaign scheduling, canceling motel reservations, that kind of thing. Nobody connected with us would even have thought for a second of slipping LSD to the senator. Of course, with all the post-Watergate paranoia that's still floating about, I'm surprised we haven't yet been blamed for the sinking of the *Lusitania.*

PLAYBOY: Maybe it's "post-Watergate paranoia" and maybe it's not, but in the course of a CBS radio commentary at the height of the Watergate scandal titled *Thinking the Unthinkable,* newscaster Dan Rather commented that it was time to ask "some of the tough questions about such characters as Hunt and Liddy and their Cuban contacts and whether they had at any time any connection with Lee Harvey Oswald. . . ." How do you feel about being accused of a possible role in the assassination of President Kennedy?

LIDDY: I initially would have assumed it was just one more example of the hysteria surrounding Watergate, but I subsequently learned why Rather asked that question. When I first appeared on *60 Minutes* in 1975, Mike Wallace told me off camera that CBS News possessed a photograph of the crowd in Dealey Plaza taken contemporaneously with President Kennedy's assassination, and that one individual bore a striking resemblance to me when his features were magnified. Prior to my appearance on *60 Minutes,* CBS had the photo and negative checked by the top experts in the country in an attempt to verify my presence at the time, presumably by comparing photographs of me with the shot from Dallas, and they couldn't do so. But apparently the story had been floating around the higher echelons of CBS News for some time, and that's where Rather picked it up. Why he threw in Hunt's name as well, I can't tell you.

PLAYBOY: Where were you on November 22, 1963?

LIDDY: In my law offices in Manhattan, though I'd been in Dallas a number of times prior to that. I know you're disappointed, but I'm afraid I can't place myself in the sixth-floor window of the Texas School Book Depository, zeroing in on the motorcade through the sights of a Mannlicher-Carcano.

PLAYBOY: In 1977, your sentence was commuted by Carter. What do you think of him, both as a man and as President?

LIDDY: As a man, I think the popular conception of him as good and decent and sincere is probably correct, and personally, I'm grateful that he commuted my sentence. He'd certainly get my vote—for parson. But as a President he's been an absolute, unmitigated disaster. You see, a moralizer like Jimmy Carter is fine at delivering orotund sermons, but he doesn't understand the way the world works and, just as bad, he doesn't understand the way the United States works. If you view the U.S. government as one vast complex diesel engine, which I think is a pretty fair analogy, then Ted Kennedy at least knows how to operate the machinery, even though he might drive it in the wrong directions. But ol' Jimmy doesn't even know the ignition key from the exhaust pipe. Hell, he wasn't even that effective governing a state like Georgia, and he's totally lost trying to run Washington. Oh, he's great at spouting pious platitudes, but to be a President, you've first and foremost got to be a good *mechanic*. You've got to operate that goddamn machine or the whole thing's going to come apart. Now, to take a leaf from Jimmy's book, you could call in the Pope from Rome, the chief rabbi from Jerusalem, the archbishop of the Anglican Church from Canterbury, the president of the Baptist World Alliance and the Ayatollah Ruhollah Khomeini from Qum or wherever he's presently holed up, and they could all keep circling that huge diesel engine day after day, chanting their prayers over it, and the mother's still not going to turn over. Faith is fine, but it's no substitute for expertise and leadership. And Carter's got neither.

PLAYBOY: That seems a rather harsh caricature. And why emphasize the President's private religious beliefs?

LIDDY: Because they aren't *private* anymore, damn it; they're at the root of his whole

Easter Bunny approach to running this country. Jimmy Carter just doesn't understand the world as it is; he still believes you can look the other way and the problem will disappear. He's not prepared to face the harsh problems, whether inflation or recession at home or Soviet aggression and American military weakness abroad. I mean, if he were on a yacht for a summit conference with Maggie Thatcher of England, Giscard d'Estaing of France and Helmut Schmidt of Germany and that yacht capsized and they were all in the drink together, I can just picture what would happen when a dark fin started cutting through the water toward them. Thatcher, D'Estaing and Schmidt would all shout, "Jaws!" and do everything in their power to scramble up for safety on the inverted hull of the ship, while Jimmy would just continue paddling around, saying, "Gee guys, it's Charlie the Tuna!" No, I'm sorry, but the requisites for leadership of a great power are brains, brawn and balls, and I'm afraid Carter is singularly lacking in all three departments.

PLAYBOY: Some of your critics would contend that Carter's brand of morality is infinitely preferable to the kind of ruthless *Realpolitik* you preach and practice.

LIDDY: I'm sure they would, and I'd say they were deluding themselves. Look, let's face reality. Politics, and in this context I'd include the conduct of a superpower's foreign policy, has by its very nature to be amoral. Not immoral, amoral. It cannot be conducted by a man who wears his sainthood on his sleeve and who is superbly equipped to deal with the hereafter but emotionally totally unprepared to deal with the harsh realities of the present-day world. And I'm particularly alarmed when a man like Carter bases his foreign policy on the way he *wishes* other nations to be, rather than on the basis of how they actually behave in the world as it is. I don't mind Carter talking to God. It's when God answers back, and tells him something different each day, that I get really worried.

PLAYBOY: You don't believe in the brotherhood of man, we take it.

LIDDY: Sure, I do. Cain and Abel! Abel and Cain! No, come on, you know precisely what I mean. All of Jimmy's lovely idealistic pipe dreams are fine emanating from a pulpit, but they don't cut any ice in the serious international arena. The Russians would just contemptuously echo Stalin's derisive question in World War Two: "How many divisions has the Pope?" The Carter policy from the inception of his Presidency has been one of weakness—economic weakness, political weakness, military weakness. And he has been as much a disaster for this country as Neville Chamberlain and his appeasers were for England in the Thirties. The only difference with Carter is that he doesn't even *know* how much he's surrendered. He's a classic case of noble intentions gone berserk and reminds me of Emerson's description of the pious humanitarian liberal of his own day: "We mean well and do ill, and then justify our ill-doing by our well-meaning." And, you know, it's interesting to reflect, in a historic context, that Great Britain began to decline as a world power and ultimately lost her empire when her own people fell victim to a very similar blend of romantic humanitarianism and evangelical religion. But at least Britain held on to her empire for almost two hundred years on the momentum of her former dynamism, like a red-giant star before it collapses into a white dwarf, and it was only the debilitating and bankrupting aftermath of World War Two that finally forced her to relinquish the last of her greatness. It's taken us less than twenty years of mismanagement and self-delusion to reach a comparable nadir of power.

Whether we like it or not, we are already in a state of strategic and conventional inferiority, and there's little likelihood the situation will improve appreciably in the near future. It's not just Carter's fault, either, though he has a lot to answer for. The fact is that a great many Americans, including significant opinion-molding elements of the media, have been living in Cloud-Cuckoo-Land as far as national defense goes. It's the Charlie the Tuna syndrome all over again—if we just ignore the bad news, it'll go away. As in Afghanistan, reality has an unpleasant habit of waking us up with a rifle butt hammering at the door in the middle of the night. The only question is if we'll learn our lesson in time, and if our national will is sufficient to face the challenges ahead. In the long run, you know, a nation's psychology is far more crucial than its military hardware. My Oriental instructor in the martial arts taught me that the outcome of a battle is decided in the minds of the opponents well before the first blow is struck. We certainly saw that in the France of 1940. The French had more troops, more tanks, more guns than the Germans, more of almost everything except the fanatic and disciplined *esprit de corps* of the German fighting man. Hitler's secret weapon wasn't the brilliant and imaginative coupling of Panzer and Stuka in concerted ground-air attack; it was the courage of the individual Wehrmacht soldier, each of whom carried blitzkrieg in his breast. Can you imagine what Rommel's Afrika Korps would do with today's volunteer army, the army that "wants to join you," as the recruiting posters said? Jesus, they'd chew us up and spit us out in no time flat. We couldn't fight our way out of a wet paper bag today.

PLAYBOY: The admiration for the German fighting spirit you've just expressed, and your general fascination with all things German, is an underlying leitmotiv of *Will*, and has assumed sinister overtones in the eyes of some critics, who accuse you of being a closet Nazi sympathizer. Could they be right?

LIDDY: They couldn't be more wrong. It's true that I do admire the mentality of the northern Teutonic races, not only their fighting spirit but also, and equally important, their work ethic and sense of discipline. I find all those values admirable, and have always identified with them. But I have absolutely no sympathy for Adolf Hitler and Nazism. Remember, German history spans thousands of years, and the twelve years of the Third Reich was no more than a historical aberration. One of the many tragic aspects of the holocaust is that the very German virtues I have enumerated—discipline, efficiency, the ability to subordinate emotion to duty—were perverted into the organized annihilation of millions of innocent civilians, not only Jews but gypsies and Slavs as well. To me, that is the antithesis of all the things I admire about the German martial spirit, and it is a stain on German honor from which the country will take many years to recover. But in fairness, I can also admire the sheer courage and military genius of German soldiers like Rommel who took no part in such atrocities, and maintained their and their country's honor intact. But for Adolf Hitler and the psychopathic scum in the concentration camps who butchered babies on an assembly line because they were born into the wrong race, I have nothing but contempt.

PLAYBOY: Many of your critics have speculated, nonetheless, that if you had been born in Germany, you would have made one hell of a Nazi.

LIDDY: What can you really say to something like that? I mean, shit, I'm just as interested in the extraordinarily deep and rich culture of Japan, and equally fascinated by the traditional Bushido code of the samurai warrior. What're they going to say about that? "Oh, Liddy would have flown a Zero at Pearl Harbor"? Come on.

PLAYBOY: If you had been born in Germany and been of fighting age in World War Two, would you have served in Hitler's armies?

LIDDY: Well, that's all extremely hypothetical, of course. Here you are slapping me down in another culture and another time and asking how I'd behave. Would I have been conditioned by my society into accepting Hitler as a savior, as our German maid did in the Thirties? I certainly hope not, and, in fact, I suspect just the opposite. I can accept and serve authority I respect, but against authority that I despise, I quickly turn to rebellion, as I did in the slammer when I fought the prison administration tooth and nail. In the case of Germany, you must remember that I'm a political conservative, and I respect tradition and the values of Western culture, and so I think it far more likely I would have joined those conservatives and Catholics who tried to overthrow Hitler. Like Carl Goerdeler, or Count von Stauffenberg, the heroic German officer who had lost an arm, hand and eye on the Eastern front but returned to almost blow Hitler to smithereens at Rastenburg during the July twentieth plot in 1944. And who, needless to say, was executed by the Gestapo shortly afterward. But yes, like Stauffenberg as well, I'm sure I would have fought for my country, probably in the Luftwaffe or a Panzer division. But it's all sheer speculation, of course. Next you'll be asking where I keep my Iron Cross!

PLAYBOY: If Hitler had abjured anti-Semitism and genocide, could you have supported him?

LIDDY: No. It would have made his regime less loathsome, of course, but he'd still have been a dictator, and Nazi Germany would still have been a totalitarian state. Again, as a conservative, I support the concept of a society that, whenever possible, is voluntary and noncoercive. As I explained when discussing the upheavals of the Sixties, there are times when the state, to preserve that very humane society, must intrude into the privacy and freedom of the individual, but it should be done as sparingly as possible, and only in response to a clear and present danger to the very stability and security of the society. A totalitarian state, by its very nature, *permanently* imposes itself as the master of the individual, and thus is inherently abhorrent to me. Some, like Nazi Germany and Stalin's Russia, are bloodier than others, but all are ultimately destructive of the human spirit.

PLAYBOY: Your abhorrence of Hitler's genocide certainly sounds sincere, but it only makes your own fascination with the Nazi era more perplexing. For example, if you really loathed everything Hitler stood for, why did you go out of your way to arrange a special screening of Leni Riefenstahl's classic Nazi propaganda film, *Triumph of the Will,* for a group of top White House aides?

LIDDY: Well, you've got to understand the background to that. John Ehrlichman and others who had run Nixon's 1968 campaign were always regaling people about what great advance men they'd been, and what giant rallies they'd organized, with balloons going up in the air by the hundreds, and on and on *ad nauseam*. I got so bored hearing about those "mammoth rallies" of theirs that finally I said, "Hey, you guys, you want to see a *real* rally?" They took the bait and I set up a private screening of *Triumph of the Will* at the National Archives for the entire White House staff. It really is an impressive film you know, there's no doubt that Riefenstahl's a cinematic genius. Well, about fifteen people attended, and they sat there watching hundreds of thousands of storm troopers marching in mass formations under Albert Speer's spectacular stage management, a vast field of people standing to sing the Horst Wessel *Lied* at night as giant antiaircraft spotlights beam pillars of light through the clouds overhead, creating a luminous, cathedral-of-stars effect. In short, a really overwhelming display. And finally, when the lights came on, there was a moment of awed silence, and then from the back of the room a voice breathed reverently, "Jesus! What an advance job!" My point, it seems, was taken.

PLAYBOY: Forgetting for a moment the obvious negative connotations of the word *fascism*, and keeping in mind your professed detestation of Hitler's genocide, don't you, in fact, embody most of the traditional values of Italian and Spanish fascism, if not of Nazism—i.e., duty, honor, love of fatherland, military *élan* and semimystical exaltation of personal and national will and destiny, strong anticommunism, genetic determinism, contempt for the herd, etc.? And, thus, couldn't you fairly and objectively be termed a fascist in that sense?

LIDDY: No, because if you're going to be at all precise and objective in your evaluation of comparative political systems, then fascism refers to a specific political movement that evolved in Italy in the Twenties and was subsequently emulated in various countries in Europe and Latin America. It embodies the concept of blind obedience, the corporate state, dictatorial, centralized one-man rule, and a host of other totalitarian mechanisms and concepts that are all anathema to me. And I certainly don't think that some of the qualities you enumerate, such as duty, honor, love of country and military strength, are exclusive attributes of fascism. Indeed, when I was growing up, they were much praised and universally aspired-to virtues in this country. I hope they will be again. But that certainly does not make me a fascist of any stripe.

PLAYBOY: Why did you sing the Horst Wessel song at the top of your lungs to a black audience in prison?

LIDDY: Because I had become the subject of racial prejudice myself while in the Washington jail, shortly after my initial conviction. I ran a daily gauntlet of racial slurs from the predominantly black prisoners, and even though I told myself it shouldn't get under my skin, it finally did. I was in deadlock, so I couldn't even challenge to a fight the prisoners who hurled their taunts through the bars. I had my opportunity to strike back one morning when a guard escorted me to the showers. As I walked down the catwalk, a chorus of jeers greeted me: "OK, baby, if you want racist, here's racist!" I knew the words to the Horst Wessel song by heart from childhood, when I'd first heard it from Germany on our family shortwave radio, and I have a fairly strong voice. So when I reached the showers, I burst into full and rousing song, my voice booming through the cell block: "*Die Fahne hoch!*" I sang. "Raise the flag!" As I went on, screaming out my frustration through the echoing tiers of the prison, the jeers and catcalls began to fall off. "*Die Reihen dicht geschlossen!* . . . " The din gradually silenced, and by the time I reached the second verse of the Horst Wessel song, my voice was the only one that could be heard in the cell block. It was almost eerie, because I'm sure there was not one other man in that prison who understood one word of what I was singing. But they all got the message.

PLAYBOY: That initial hostility you encountered from blacks changed pretty rapidly as you began doing free legal work for black and white prisoners alike, and challenging prison administrators in the courts on questions of prisoners' rights. In fact, you ended up becoming something of a hero to inmates of both races. Did your experience in prison change any of your own racial attitudes?

LIDDY: Not really, because I had always abhorred racial prejudice and bigotry, even though I'm perfectly willing to answer back in kind when I'm on the receiving end, as the incident I just related indicates. But I think racism is one of the most stupid and ultimately *wasteful* of all human vices, because it denies a man's potential and worth for something as superficial and frivolous as the color of his skin. Throughout my life, I've had good and productive relationships with blacks. I also tend to particularly admire the virtues of the northern races, perhaps out of frustration with my own genetic composition. I have more Irish and Italian genes than German, and my hot Southern blood has always caused me serious problems with my temper, which it took me a long, hard struggle to govern. And I also happen to prefer the Nordic type of woman, as an aesthetic preference. I hardly think that *Gentlemen Prefer Blondes* can be condemned as a racist pronunciamento! But I also think blacks should take pride in their African ancestry. My God, if I could demonstrate I had some Zulu blood, I sure as hell would be proud of it, because the Zulu warriors were some of the finest fighting men on the face of this earth.

PLAYBOY: Leaving black-white issues aside, throughout your book you express a fascination with genetics and eugenics, even to the point of cold-bloodedly selecting your prospective bride according to the contribution she would make to your "family gene pool." How did she feel about that?

LIDDY: Well, it was not exactly an element I played up in our courtship. But even though it wasn't the most romantic of all considerations, I think it's a valid one, nonetheless. There's a good deal of truth to eugenics as long as you don't carry it to extremes, as we've done in the past with involuntary-sterilization plans and that kind of dangerous scheme, with all its potential for abuse. It had taken me a long time to build myself up from a puny, sickly child, so I wanted my own children to have a running start. That's why I determined that my smartest course was to marry a tall girl of Celtic-Teutonic ancestry who also had a terrific mind. And, as a result, I have five strong, athletic and bright children. Of course, all those considerations have to be coupled with a mutual emotional compatibility, but they were definite factors in selecting my mate.

PLAYBOY: Didn't you also run a security check on your wife's background through the FBI's central computer before you married?

LIDDY: Purely a routine precationary measure.

PLAYBOY: Did your wife know of your security check on her, as well as your evaluation of her as potentially good breeding stock?

LIDDY: Oh, yes, we discussed it. But it never upset her. After all, it's probably the least of the problems she's had in our marriage. Next to being sent away for twenty years, what the hell is a little security check, right?

PLAYBOY: Did your four and a half years in prison have any negative effects on your marriage?

LIDDY: Well, it certainly wasn't an easy period, but you'll remember I had selected my wife very carefully, and she came through the whole ordeal with flying colors. She was really tremendous, the way she brought up the kids and kept the family together. She went back to teaching, in the Washington, D.C., school system, and her salary managed to keep our leaky financial boat afloat. The kids all worked and chipped in their share, too.

PLAYBOY: How badly were you hit by the legal fees for your several trials?

LIDDY: Oh, I was wiped out. When I got out of prison, I owed three hundred thousand dollars in legal costs, plus the forty-thousand-dollar fine our old pal John Sirica had imposed, which President Carter didn't waive when he commuted my sentence and made me eligible for parole. I had to swear out a pauper's oath and I lost my license to practice law, of course.

Fortunately, due to the two books I've written, I've managed to cut the debt down to two hundred thousand dollars and royalties from the sale of *Will* should reduce it further. I'll be happy just to wake up one morning and say to Frances, "Eureka, honey, we're plain flat broke at last!"

PLAYBOY: How did you handle prolonged sexual abstinences during your imprisonment?

LIDDY: With some variations, I took the old tried-and-tested ice-cold-shower route, I exercised a great deal, and I also severely restricted my caloric intake, which I discovered also reduced my sexual appetite. Again, it's a question of willpower.

PLAYBOY: What was the impact of your imprisonment on your relationship with your children?

LIDDY: Well, the single most important thing was that I was out of their lives during their formative period of adolescence, which, naturally, I regret. But there again, my wife did a marvelous job of bringing up the kids, even while she had to hold down her schoolteaching job. And without sounding like an indulgent father, all the kids have turned out great; they're all uniformly high achievers.

PLAYBOY: Your children seem remarkably well adjusted, considering the pain and anxiety they must have experienced during your trial and imprisonment. Were they also spared the misery and insecurity you experienced as a child, and describe at length in *Will?*

LIDDY: Oh, yes, they had normal, healthy and happy childhoods. Nothing like the hell I went through. But then, they're all strong kids, mentally and physically.

PLAYBOY: In the book, you dramatically recount that unhappy and terror-ridden childhood, and take apparent pride in your grueling campaign to conquer your "weaknesses" and overcome your morbid fears by turning yourself into a fearless machine trained to kill without emotions. But couldn't your critics equally well depict that entire process as profoundly neurotic, as well as an extirpation of those very values and emotions that produce a well-integrated and mature adult?

LIDDY: My critics are quite obviously free to do as they choose and to make what interpretations they wish. But I pay so much attention to this area in *Will* precisely because it's at the root of who I am, and how I became what I am. I am, in a very literal and noneconomic sense, a self-made man. And therefore, if you wish to understand me, you must first try to understand the struggle I waged with myself as a child. It was a kind of psychic guerrilla war between the person I was, and despised, and the person I wanted to become. And it was a terrifically difficult period in my life, which I remember with no more nostalgia than I would a car crash. Fortunately, it was a battle that I ultimately won.

PLAYBOY: What was at the root of that inner struggle?

LIDDY: Well, let me fill you in on the background. I was a sickly, puny and miserable little child. I suffered from a serious bronchial condition, which necessitated spending long hours under a tent breathing medicated steam, and I consistently flunked my tuberculosis patch test. I didn't have asthma, but there was something badly wrong with my lungs, and to this day X rays show scar tissue. For a while, I was so ill that my father, who was a very successful international lawyer, was afraid he might have to transplant the entire family to Arizona, which would have been disastrous for his practice. Now on top of all this, I was born into a family of very high achievers, as my mother used to make clear to me when discussing our relatives and our family history. But she never made invidious comparisons between them and the pathetic little invalid to whom she was spooning broth. She didn't have to. I made them myself. And to add further to my self-loathing, I was absolutely riddled with fear, obsessed and consumed with it. I literally lived in terror.

PLAYBOY: What kind of fears?

LIDDY: You name it, I was afraid of it. I was paralyzed by thunder and lightning; I feared fire and electricity; the dirigibles that passed over our house on the way to Lakehurst made me shake and gibber; I was afraid of moths, ever since one cast a terrifying giant shadow on the wall of my room as I lay wheezing in my steam tent; I was deathly afraid of rats; I feared the leather harness my grandmother used to beat me with; I feared my own left hand, as my mother tried to force me uncomprehendingly into right-handedness; and most of all, I feared God, the God of my good nuns at parochial school, Whom I was taught was omnipotent and terrible in His punishment of sinners, and Whom I knew was sitting up there with a thunderbolt just waiting for the right minute to whack out this contemptible little crying coward of a kid named Gordon Liddy. I was, in short, afraid of my own shadow, and I knew that I couldn't go on living like that. So at the age of six or seven, I decided to do something about it.

PLAYBOY: What?

LIDDY: The thing I most dreaded: stand and confront my fears, and vanquish them. The problem was, I had so *many* goddamned fears that I knew there was no hope of taking them on all at once. So I realized that I'd have to face them one at a time. And to do this, I realized I'd need something called willpower. I'd learned the importance of that from the priests at Sunday Mass, and also from listening to Adolf Hitler with our pro-Nazi German maid Teresa over the Emerson shortwave radio.

PLAYBOY: Some critics contend that childhood flirtation with Hitler was the beginning of a lifelong infatuation.

LIDDY: No, not at all, it had nothing to do with Hitler's political message, which I was hardly competent to comprehend at the age of six or seven, though I'd picked up enough *Deutsch* from classmates in our predominantly German New Jersey neighborhood to get the gist. It was the combination of the stirring German martial music and the incredible self-confidence and *power* Hitler's voice radiated that had such an overwhelming effect on me. I mean, he is generally regarded as being the most effective orator of the twentieth century, and just as his words mesmerized the masses in Germany, so they influenced me. Here was the very antithesis of fear and cowardice, a towering figure of sheer primitive force and determination, quite literally an exemplar of the "triumph of the will." And after the broadcasts, Teresa explained to me that Adolf Hitler had resurrected his nation on earth and delivered it from fear! Those last words truly galvanized me and gave me hope for the first time. If Adolf Hitler could free Germany from fear, then I could free myself. What a great nation had accomplished, one seven-year-old boy could emulate. It would require pain, and suffering, but I now accepted the breathtaking idea that *I could become anything I wanted to be*.

PLAYBOY: So you became the nicest storm trooper on the block.

LIDDY: Oh, come on, I didn't give a hoot for Hitler's politics. I didn't know what politics *was*. And I derived a similar psychic shot in the arm from the fireside chats of FDR, particularly his message that "the only thing we have to fear is fear itself." That really struck home. But those broadcasts were certainly catalysts in my decision to conquer my own terror, to metamorphose myself.

PLAYBOY: How did you go about it?

LIDDY: Like a war, one campaign at a time. For example, to conquer my fear of thunder, I waited for a big storm and then sneaked out of the house and climbed up a seventy-five-foot oak tree and lashed myself to the trunk with my belt. As the storm hit and chaos roared around me and the sky was rent with thunder and lightning, I shook my fist at the rolling black clouds and screamed, "Kill me! Go ahead and try! I don't care! I don't care!" As the storm subsided, I heard my father ordering me to come down. As I lowered myself to the ground, he shook his head and said, "I just don't understand you." "I know," I said.

I repeated this kind of confrontation over a period of years, mastering one fear after another. I was afraid of electricity, so I scraped off an electrical wire and let ten volts course through me; I feared heights, so I scaled high buildings with one of my friends; I overcame my fear of the dirigibles by visiting the palisades, where the great *Hindenburg* would have to pass just a few hundred feet above me, so close that the ground shook under my feet from the roar of its four huge eleven-hundred-horsepower Mercedes-Benz diesel engines. And I went on down the line of my fears, testing myself against them over and over again until finally they were vanquished. And all this time I was also building myself up physically, exercising, bicycling, running, and finally, by my teens, I ended up being on the state championship cross-country team. By the time I graduated from prep school at the age of seventeen, I was physically in excellent shape and psychologically self-assured to the point of cockiness. It hadn't been easy, but I had won. Like a plastic surgeon operating on himself. I had grafted on successive layers of strength and courage until I was at last able to face the world.

PLAYBOY: Probably the most dramatic, and certainly the most celebrated, example of the lengths to which you were willing to go to overcome your fears was the incident in which you ate a rat. Would you describe that for us?

LIDDY: Well, I didn't eat the entire rat, just the hindquarters. Of course, the genesis of that repast was my inordinate terror of rats, which abounded on the Jersey wharves along the Hudson River near my home in West Caldwell, some of them as big as cats. Then one day when I was eleven years old, our pet cat caught and killed a rat and deposited it proudly on our back doorstep as a trophy. Well, I'd been reading about how some American Indian tribes ate the hearts of the bravest of their enemies in order to ingest their valor, and suddenly the idea came to me, why not do something similar with my old rodent nemesis? I assembled a makeshift barbecue out of some bricks, cooked the dead rat for about an hour, then skinned and ate the roasted haunches. After I buried the remains, I saw our cat and smiled to myself, thinking that henceforth rats would have to fear me as much as cats.

PLAYBOY: Now to the most profound and far-reaching question of this interview, What does rat meat taste like?

LIDDY: Stringy and rather tasteless, as I recall. I certainly never acquired the taste, though the *Washington Star* polled the top French chefs in Washington after my book came out and the consensus of culinary opinion was that while I might be competent in other areas, I was a distinct flop at preparing rat. I really felt very chagrined. One chef, as I recall, was quite indignant that I had broiled the beast, contending that the only proper way to serve rat is roasted. Everyone had his own recipe, but they were all down on mine. Ah well, I've never pretended to be Julia Child. *Chacun à son goût.*

PLAYBOY: Over the years, you've not only broiled rat to test your willpower, you've broiled yourself, toasting your hand and forearm over an open flame to prove your powers of endurance and immunity to pain. Isn't that carrying the whole business pretty far?

LIDDY: Well, that began as an effort to overcome my fear of fire as well as pain, so I started burning myself with cigarettes and candles to see if I could stand it, initially just searing myself and then enduring more serious burns. Actually, this is a form of self-testing well known and understood in the East but largely unknown to Western civilization. As I built my will, I subjected my body to doses of pain much as a weight lifter builds his muscles by lifting progressively heavier weights. After severely burning the tendon in my left hand, however, almost to the point of incapacitating myself,

I realized I would have to be more careful. And, of course, I would never burn my gun hand.

PLAYBOY: Of course. But incidents such as your mortification of the flesh by fire have led to some of your more psychiatrically oriented critics to suggest that you feel a compulsion to demonstrate a "supermacho" image in order to overcome deep-rooted sources of personal insecurity, perhaps even lingering subconscious doubts about your own masculinity. How would you respond to them?

LIDDY: Well, those anonymous critics of yours might do well to ponder Adlai Stevenson's observation that he who throws mud generally loses ground. No, this was a means of testing and perfecting my will, and in my case, it proved eminently successful. And I stress, in *my* case. I'm not advocating anyone else emulate me, and I certainly wouldn't suggest that everybody go out and toast his hand over open flame like a marshmallow. I'm only saying that for me it was a useful tool. As for this whole business of being macho or supermacho, of which I've been accused frequently, it's just not true. Of course, macho was originally a perfectly respectable Spanish term for a manly man, a designation I'd feel perfectly comfortable with, but in recent years it's been expropriated as a code word by the women's liberation movement and twisted into a pejorative Archie Bunkerish caricature of the loutish, leering male who believes that the only natural position for women in this world is horizontal. A kind of *Kinder, Kirche, Küche* attitude, which I certainly have never subscribed to. In fact, the type of woman I appreciate and respect is not only physically attractive but strong-willed and intelligent, certainly not the submissive dumb-blonde type, or "airheads," as my kids would call them. I believe that such women are every bit as capable of intelligence, strength, discipline and perception as a man.

PLAYBOY: For better or worse, your public image is still that of a nut case, and it's doubtful that the success of your autobiography will alter it appreciably. Does it bother you that millions of people think you're rowing with one oar?

LIDDY: Not in the least. As I said earlier, I've never been concerned with image or reputation, only character. I've tried to be ruthlessly honest about my life and my values and my motivations in *Will*, and that's all I can do. From there on, it's up to the reader to make his own judgments, and if he concludes that I'm loosely wrapped, so be it. I would not be displeased, of course, if after reading the book and this interview, people will understand me a bit better, even if they disagree totally with my politics and my actions.

PLAYBOY: Nonetheless, a number of critics have made a Freudian analysis of your book and concluded that not only your hand burning but also your willingness to be a human sacrifice on the alter of the disintegrating Nixon administration is evidence of a strong streak of masochism in your character. How would you respond?

LIDDY: I'd respond with the words Joseph Stalin addressed to Leon Trotsky at a Communist Party Congress in Moscow at the height of their struggle for power in the Twenties: Everybody has a right to be stupid, but some people abuse the privilege. And just let me add a serious note here. For any of your readers who think that my childhood struggles with myself or my later attempts to build my will and endurance were just eccentricities, harmless or otherwise, I'd suggest that they put themselves in my place in a filthy and sweltering prison cell, stripped naked under solitary confinement and at the mercy of dumb and often brutal captors. I did not succumb to that pressure-cooker atmosphere, because I had spent my youth, however unwittingly, preparing for just such an eventuality, as if I had been in training for a battle I never knew would be fought. Prison held no terrors for me, because I had already conquered my own weaknesses. Watergate and its aftermath only tempered steel that had been forged in the furnace of my inner struggle forty years before.

PLAYBOY: We've deliberately avoided recapitulating the minutiae of Watergate, because you've covered it in such depth in your book and in radio and television interviews around the country. But there are a few areas of interest that you have not touched on, including H. R. Haldeman's contention that "the overwhelming evidence leads to the conclusion that the break-in was deliberately sabotaged." Could Watergate have been a setup?

LIDDY: No, I don't believe so. I don't think there was anything more sinister involved than bad luck and bad timing. Of course, the conspiracy buffs will maintain that the break-in was deliberately bungled as part of some massive conspiracy of agents and double agents and quadruple agents to topple Nixon, but I just don't believe it.

PLAYBOY: Not only conspiracy buffs maintain there was more involved at Watergate than meets the eye. Again, H. R. Haldeman suspects that "the CIA was an agency hostile to Nixon, who returned the hostility with fervor," and adds that throughout the Watergate investigation, "the multiple levels of deception by the CIA are astounding." Haldeman tends to support the thesis that Watergate was, in fact, a highly sophisticated CIA plot to destroy Nixon—in effect, the CIA's first domestic *coup d'ètat*. Could he be right?

LIDDY: It's very, very unlikely. First of all, there *was* friction between Helms and Nixon, but it wasn't the deadly, bitter type of feud that this CIA-conspiracy scenario presupposes. It was more of a question of bad chemistry between Helms and Nixon, and, in fact, general bad chemistry between the CIA and the administration. Traditionally, you know, the CIA has been a very WASPish, Ivy League, old-school-tie-type organization, and Richard Nixon's entire background was very different. He didn't feel comfortable with them, and vice versa. But to extrapolate from that to a full-fledged conspiracy theory verges on paranoia.

PLAYBOY: Proponents of the theory that the CIA manipulated the Watergate break-in and cover-up for its own ends suggest that Jim McCord, a former CIA security chief who was intensely loyal to the agency, deliberately sabotaged the Watergate break-in in order to cripple the Nixon White House and frustrate its attempts to centralize control of the intelligence community.

LIDDY: Yes, and I think they're dead wrong. McCord may have bungled the taping of the internal doors, all right, but remember Hanlon's Razor, which is a maxim that states: "Never blame on malice that which can be fully explained by stupidity." It's true McCord was very loyal to the CIA, but I just can't accept the concept that he deliberately set out to be caught, and I don't believe he was a double agent who cold-bloodedly betrayed his colleagues. I do condemn his decision to break ranks with the containment strategy. But I think he was at the point of cracking from the strain of imprisonment, and his actions were those of a desperate and obsessed man. He even felt that the CIA had abandoned him, and as a deeply religious man, he wanted to get back on the side of the angels. But I don't believe for one moment that he deliberately sold us out.

PLAYBOY: Haldeman implies that Hunt was a serving CIA agent throughout the period he was involved in Watergate. Is he correct?

LIDDY: Hunt might have been, yes.

PLAYBOY: And Charles Colson was equally convinced that Hunt was spying on the White House for the CIA.

LIDDY: Spying is a somewhat loaded word. He might have relayed information back to

Langley if he was still on the CIA payroll, which I do not know to be a fact, but I doubt there was anything sinister or conspiratorial about it.

PLAYBOY: Isn't that exactly what you would be saying if you were, in fact, a secret CIA agent?

LIDDY: Yes, I suppose it is. It just happens to be the truth.

PLAYBOY: Haldeman wrote in his book *The Ends of Power* that you and Hunt were "getting directions . . . on behalf of the CIA and the CIA's silent partner, Howard Hughes." He adds that "we didn't know that a CIA employee was, in effect, running a White House team." Were you and Hunt, as Haldeman implies, serving as stalking-horses for the CIA? Or, even more seriously, and as some Watergate investigators suspected, were you really a secret CIA agent yourself, a kind of agency Trojan Horse within the White House, rather than the Nixon loyalist you professed to be? And isn't it conceivable that you "stonewalled" your way through court and into prison not to protect Nixon but your actual superiors in the covert-operations arm of the CIA?

LIDDY: That's absolute nonsense. I've never been a CIA officer of any sort, and I resent the accusation that I was operating against the interests of my President. I believed then and I believe now that he was a splendid leader of this country, and I think the extraordinarily disastrous last three and a half years under Jimmy Carter has only served to demonstrate by contrast how superb was the Presidency of Richard Nixon. I think I'm more of a Nixon loyalist than Haldeman not only is but ever was.

PLAYBOY: Throughout the course of this interview, you've been relaxed and cooperative, even under occasionally harsh questioning, and you seem genuinely pleased by the success of your best-selling autobiography. In fact, all the time we've been together, you haven't issued a single assassination threat or gouged out one eyeball. Is it possible that the Gordon Liddy so many liberals love to hate is finally mellowing?

LIDDY: [*Chuckling*] If you really think that, then why did you hide all the pencils? Anyway, the Liddy family crest is, or at least should be, *Nil illegitimis carborundum*—"Don't let the bastards get you down." But no, seriously, this has been a most pleasant and enjoyable discussion, and you have offered me no offense and I, of course, have responded in kind. I am no danger whatsoever to anyone who does not wish me ill. Had you behaved differently, of course, I might have responded in kind, and more in keeping with the somewhat sensational image you suggest I have. But I don't think I'm mellowing. I've lived on the razor's edge all my life and don't intend to jettison my beliefs or values now. I've paid too heavy a price for them. In any case, I find life a tremendously exciting, perpetually renewing adventure. I'm never bored, thank God, and I'm always searching for one big dragon to slay. Of course, the lesson you learn is that dragons are Hydra-headed, and as soon as you kill one, another springs up. Which, of course, is what makes the game worth the playing. God, wouldn't it be a drag if all that came along was a pussycat?

PLAYBOY: Nietzsche, whom you admire, wrote that "he who fights the dragon becomes the dragon."

LIDDY: Tell that to Saint George. All I can do is pledge to make it a fair and honorable fight. That's all anyone can do in life.

PLAYBOY: Gordon Liddy, were you born in the wrong century? Are you an anachronism?

LIDDY: No, I don't think so. I'm not saying I wouldn't have enjoyed living in ancient Sparta, and I would certainly be right at home as a *condottiere* in Renaissance Italy, hopefully in the day of Machiavelli, whom I consider the greatest political philosopher

of all time. But I'm quite content in this century, not that I have much choice in the matter. I know a great many people do consider me a throwback and an anachronism, but if the virtues and values that I respect and to which I adhere are outdated, then I suspect that there are millions of anachronisms in America who share the same value system and, if put to the test, will demonstrate it. I really have a tremendous amount of faith in the people of this country, and I think that once they shed the scales of illusion that currently afflict them and see the world as it really is, we will once again be capable of a remarkable national cohesion and dynamism, such as we saw in the course of the Second World War. And I'm glad we have that potential, because I believe another war is imminent.
PLAYBOY: Will you be in the front ranks?
LIDDY: Well, let's put it this way. Shortly after the disaster at Pearl Harbor, a new chief of naval operations was appointed, Admiral King, who up to that time had enjoyed a reputation as the meanest son of a bitch in the service, and for that reason had been sent out recruiting in Iowa, as the saying goes. Now, all of a sudden, *he* was the new chief of naval operations, and the Washington press corps rushed to his office and asked, "Admiral, how do you explain this phenomenon of your sudden ascendancy, passing over so many senior officers?" And King said, "When the bullets start to fly, they come looking for the sons of bitches." And perhaps, when the bullets start to fly again, they'll come looking for me. When and if they do, I'll be there.
PLAYBOY: When the French Foreign Legion, which you admire, was marched out of their headquarters at Sidi bel Abbès in Algeria under guard for their role in an abortive military coup against De Gaulle, the men defiantly sang one of Edith Piaf's famous songs, "Non, Je Ne Regrette Rien"—"I Regret Nothing." Would you agree with their sentiments?
LIDDY: Agree? It's my goddamn theme song!

ROBERT GARWOOD

July 1981

Interviewer: Winston Groom

His name may be among the less familiar in this anthology, but Robert Garwood lived through an experience that puts into relief an entire era. Garwood was the U.S. marine once called the White Vietcong, accused of being a traitor by his fellow soldiers and of having fought against them. He was released under mysterious circumstances by the North Vietnamese only in 1979, and through the myriad legal proceedings and court-martial that awaited him, was generally unavailable to the press.

Writer Winston Groom was put into contact with PLAYBOY after he had secured an informal agreement with Garwood to write a book or movie script about his collaboration and fourteen years of captivity. Groom agreed that a full-length Playboy Interview would be a useful way of eliciting Garwood's story, but neither he nor editor Golson expected that the result would be as moving and dramatic as it was.

Garwood is a shy and tentative man, but under Groom's sympathetic but firm questioning, he emerges as oddly articulate. His is the story of a young, raw, uneducated boy from Indiana who enlisted without knowing what he was doing, ended up driving a jeep in a country he'd never heard of, was captured a few days before his Vietnam tour of duty was up, and spent fourteen years in the hands of the Vietcong trying to justify a war he never understood. It is the strength of this interview that the reader comes away not necessarily knowing whether Garwood was a weak and pathetic turncoat, or, given the circumstances so reluctantly and painfully described, he was the entire American experience in Vietnam writ small.

In early 1979, six years after the North Vietnamese officially released the remaining American prisoners of war, the State Department received word from a Scandinavian economist who had recently visited Hanoi that he had seen and spoken with a man who had told him, "I am an American. Are you interested?" The economist, a Finnish banker, also produced a note nervously scribbled by a tall, dark-haired man who had given his name, rank and a marine-corps serial number.

The man was Private First Class Robert Garwood, missing from his unit since 1965 and, by most accounts, presumed dead. The note sparked an international diplomatic furor that resulted in the return to American hands of a man the marine corps felt was perhaps its most notorious turncoat of the Vietnam War.

The accusations against Robert Garwood included leading Vietcong troops in combat against American soldiers, propagandizing them with a bullhorn, verbally and physically abusing U.S. prisoners held by the enemy, desertion, writing antiwar leaflets and various other charges that, had he been convicted of the most serious of them, might have put him before the firing squad.

The man who two months later stepped off the plane and into the waiting hands of the marine corps was hardly everyone's idea of a typical traitor—if such a character exists. Gaunt and confused, Garwood, then turning thirty-three and slightly balding, faced microphones, television lights and flashing cameras and said with a noticeable Vietnamese accent, "I'm glad to be home."

Garwood was something of an enigma then, as he remains today—not only to those who have followed his internationally reported trial but to himself as well.

One of the oldest in a family of nine children, Garwood grew up on what might be described as the wrong side of the tracks in a small Indiana town. As a youngster, he lived a fairly ordinary life, playing the usual pranks but occasionally getting into trouble for them. He did not do well in school, except to show an aptitude for foreign languages; but by the time he was seventeen, he was considered a problem child by his father, a printer, and was turned over to authorities. While he was living in a juvenile detention center, he encountered a marine-corps recruiter who persuaded him to enlist. That was in 1963, before the war in Vietnam had assumed major proportions for the United States.

Garwood's tour in the marine corps wasn't exactly exemplary, but it wasn't that bad, either. He was busted once for being absent without leave and wound up as a jeep driver with an outfit stationed on Okinawa. Shortly before his tour of duty was up, he was shipped out to Da Nang, Vietnam, to join his division headquarters' motor-pool section. It was there that Garwood disappeared one day, only a few days before he was due to be shipped back to the States and released from active duty. He says he was captured by Vietcong troops while on assignment to pick up an officer in the field. The marine corps alleged that he had been absent without leave and suggested he had been visiting a whorehouse when he was taken prisoner. In any case, a few weeks after he was reported missing, Vietcong propaganda leaflets signed by Garwood began turning up. The marine corps still carried him on its books as missing, and although several times over the years, as more information came in about him, it tried to have his status changed to that of deserter, he was not officially charged with that crime until he was released by the North Vietnamese in 1979.

The marine-corps case against Garwood was a touchy and disagreeable matter from the beginning. Years after a war everyone would have preferred to forget, the corps was faced with the prospect of court-martialing a man for events that had occurred a decade earlier. Furthermore, the general feeling among civilians who responded to news stories of Garwood's release seemed to be that he had "suffered enough" and should be left alone.

On the other hand, there had been a lot of publicity about the case; and some of the allegations against Garwood—especially that he had carried arms for the enemy in a time of war—were so serious that the corps was afraid of the precedent that might be set if he were simply let go. A board of inquiry was appointed by the commandant of the huge marine base at Camp Lejeune, North Carolina, where Garwood had been assigned after his return. The witnesses who could be found were interviewed, and gradually a case was built against him. Many of the original accusations, however, were never substantiated—particularly the ones pertaining to Garwood's having led Vietcong troops against American forces; and the charge of desertion was subsequently dismissed by the military judge at the trial. However, the marine corps felt it had enough evidence to warrant a court-martial, based on testimony by former American POWs that Garwood had, over an eighteen-month period ending in late 1969, collaborated with the enemy while he was in a POW camp deep in the jungles of Vietnam.

The specific allegations were that Garwood had lived outside the compound where the other POWs were held, fraternized with the North Vietnamese guards, propagandized the POWs, interpreted for the North Vietnamese, worn a North Vietnamese uniform, carried a weapon and guarded American POWs. At one point, he is supposed to have struck an American POW with his hand and told another, "I spit on you!"

Garwood was eventually represented by John Lowe, an established trial attorney in Charlottesville, Virginia, and Vaughan Taylor, a former military lawyer. They decided not to attack the government's prima-facie case against Garwood but to rely solely on the psychiatric defense of insanity brought on by the "coercive persuasion" (once called brainwashing) of his North Vietnamese captors.

To prove their case at the court-martial, Lowe and Taylor put several well-known psychiatrists on the stand, each of whom testified that Garwood, because of his traumatizing experience, lacked the capacity to realize that his collaboration with the Communists was wrong. But the marine-corps prosecutors put on psychiatrists of their own to counter that testimony and Garwood was convicted on February 5, 1981, by a court of five officers of collaborating with the enemy and of assaulting a POW by hitting him with his hand. The other charges were dismissed. The sentence Garwood received was relatively light: a dishonorable discharge from the marine *corps and forfeiture of his pay and allowances from the time of conviction. In dispute presently is the matter of more than $120,000 in back pay covering the fourteen years Garwood spent in Vietnam, and a special military board has been set up to adjudicate that matter.*

Because he never took the witness stand at his trial, Garwood's version of his experience has never been told. To get this exclusive story of Garwood's fourteen-year odyssey, PLAYBOY *asked novelist Winston Groom* (Better Times Than These, As Summers Die*), who served as an army officer in Vietnam, to conduct the interview. Groom files these impressions:*

"I first met Bobby Garwood in the summer of 1979, a few months after he had been returned to America. It was an odd place for a meeting arranged by his lawyer at the Larchmont Yacht Club, a fancy establishment in a small community half an hour from New York City. The incongruity of the setting still strikes me: Here was a man who had spent almost all of his adult life under primal conditions in Southeast Asia, and he was walking around with me past the tennis courts and ritzy suburban trappings in one of New York's fashionable playgrounds. We had lunch on a terrace under the trees and ordered from a menu that included elaborate salads and veal piccata. Bobby ordered a cheeseburger.

"He spoke then with a heavy Oriental accent, with a glottal diction in which the tongue is pressed against the roof of the mouth to form the variations of Vietnamese syllables. In our subsequent meetings, I have noticed that his speech patterns have become much more Americanized—except when he is under stress, and then he returns to the Asian style.

"We talked for several hours and then we walked under some trees because it was a hot day. He squatted down, Oriental style, and explained, 'This position is very restful if you can get used to it.'

"I next met with him at Camp Lejeune, a sprawling marine-corps training center and, I might add, one of the most unattractive military bases I have ever seen. It was in the spring of 1980 and we had some long sessions with the tape recorder. Bobby was still waiting for the court-martial to begin, and it was obvious the strain was taking its toll. In the intervening time since we had last met, he had been befriended by a local family—the Longs—and was heavily involved with them. A few months before, Dale Long had been killed by a drunken driver; and Bobby was spending a lot of time with Donna and her children. He had also purchased an automobile—a red 1957 Chevrolet—in which he had installed a tape deck, with music straight out of the Fifties and early Sixties.

"I interviewed Bobby again not long ago: The court-martial was over and he seemed more relaxed and relieved. He is currently undergoing psychiatric care at a Virginia institution and trying to figure out what to do with the rest of his life."

PLAYBOY: What was your reaction to the verdict in your court-martial?
GARWOOD: Well, basically, I guess I was relieved that it was over. Sixteen years of fighting for your life, you know?
PLAYBOY: At the trial, you had to listen to the testimony of the witnesses against you. Didn't you have an urge to get on the stand yourself to tell your side of the story?
GARWOOD: Yes, I did. I had the urge, but at the same time, I just wasn't sure I could come across right.
PLAYBOY: Were you following the advice of your lawyers in not testifying?
GARWOOD: No, not entirely. It was mostly my decision; those were times that are not

easy to talk about. I just wasn't sure I could hold up. I didn't want to make a spectacle of myself, you know, or break down emotionally, or physically, or whatever, on the stand. Trying to recall those years, the questions that could be fired at me—it was just too many bad memories for me.

PLAYBOY: You hadn't seen the witnesses—your fellow prisoners—in thirteen or fourteen years, since you had been in Vietnam together. What was your reaction to seeing them again?

GARWOOD: Actually, a lot of compassion. I was very happy to see them, because one of the things that ran through my mind all those years was, How many of us made it out? I was very saddened that a lot of my good friends didn't make it out. I felt a lot of compassion toward those who did survive like me, they were just forced to relive the whole thing all over again. And that's very hard, very hard to do.

PLAYBOY: Do you think they understood your situation when you were over there?

GARWOOD: No, not entirely. I don't think they even understood their own situation.

PLAYBOY: What about the court? Do you think the officers were fair in their judgment?

GARWOOD: I asked myself that many times. I try to put myself in their place, though it's difficult, because of, well, their intelligence, their background, their schooling—but just as a layman or, you know, a marine, I think they had to weigh their sympathy and compassion against their professional responsibility. I think it was a very tough decision for them to make. But because they were career officers and marines, even though they had sympathy and compassion for me, there was just no way that they could neglect the professional responsibilities. And knowing that, it was much easier for me to accept.

PLAYBOY: Now that the court-martial is over, you're undergoing psychiatric care for a while. Do you feel that you need it?

GARWOOD: Definitely so. Yes.

PLAYBOY: Why?

GARWOOD: I find it very hard to adapt and communicate with the world now. That's been true in the last couple of years. I tend to lock myself out from the world. There are times when I've been places or I've said things or done things that I don't remember. It just makes me realize more and more that I'm just not as well as I thought I was. I don't have a life now, really. That's one of the biggest bridges I have to cross—getting psychiatric help to find out who I am and just what I can do with my life.

PLAYBOY: As an accused collaborator, did you encounter a lot of hostility during these past two years?

GARWOOD: You say "a lot"—no.

PLAYBOY: Some?

GARWOOD: The mail, for example—I'd say close to ninety percent of the mail I received was not only favorable but very, very sympathetic and supportive. It came from doctors, lawyers, preachers, Vietnam vets, ex-POWs—I mean, every walk of life in the United States. The only ones I got that you'd call *bad mail* were from people who didn't really condemn me, but they said they felt I could have been stronger than I was.

PLAYBOY: When you returned, it must have been something like Rip Van Winkle. What was your reaction? How had America changed in fourteen years?

GARWOOD: It shocked me. It shocked the shit out of me.

PLAYBOY: What in particular?

GARWOOD: Everything, almost. Everything seemed so alien to me: the dress, the speech—the frankness of speech, really. Back fifteen, twenty years ago, a person speaking to another guarded his speech so no four-letter words came out. It was more like an etiquette kind of thing, you were more careful about that then. And the attitude about what you'd show, it was limited, so to speak. And now it's—I don't know how to say it, but I noticed that there is a lack of caution. In things like dressing—dressing and speech, and in attitude. Especially the little things, I don't think you'd notice them as much as I have.

PLAYBOY: Such as?

GARWOOD: Well, one of the first things that freaked me out, the first thing I focused on, was the girls. Their hair, you know, it wasn't taken care of like it was way back then. I mean, it looks like somebody stuck their finger in a light socket. And all the girls are in pants. There aren't dresses.

At first, it was a real hassle. You really had to look very close to distinguish between a man and a woman. And usually the only way you could tell that was by the . . . bust. Or the way they walked. And sometimes even by the way they walked you couldn't tell. Yeah. That was really weird to me.

PLAYBOY: Who was the first female, aside from family, whom you talked with when you came back? Even a casual encounter.

GARWOOD: Casual encounter? When I went to the hospital. Yeah, that was the hospital at Great Lakes Naval Station.

PLAYBOY: Nurses?

GARWOOD: Yeah, nurses. Actually, later I dated one of the nurses that took care of me. She came to my home town and dated me. She was the first American girl I dated.

PLAYBOY: How long had it been since you'd seen a Caucasian woman?

GARWOOD: Since North Vietnam.

PLAYBOY: We're asking about this because about a year ago, while you were waiting for your court-martial to begin, you were charged by the state of North Carolina with molesting a seven-year-old girl. The incident took place, according to reports, when you were driving the girl home from church. We realize that the case has not yet been resolved, but what can you tell us about it?

GARWOOD: I can't say much, because my lawyers don't want me to comment before it's settled. But I can say this: There was *never* any misconduct by me toward the girl. I had known her family for four or five months before the charges were made. And right up until they made those charges against me, her father was scheduled to be a character witness for me in my court-martial trial. I'm one of the oldest in a family of nine myself, and I've always been very protective of young children. I don't have any idea why she would make those untrue allegations against me.

PLAYBOY: And that's all you can say?

GARWOOD: At this time.

PLAYBOY: Your life has obviously been chaotic since you returned; did you *know* you were going to be accused of collaboration when you came back to the U.S.?

GARWOOD: You talking about before I left Vietnam Before I left Vietnam, no, I had no awareness at all.

PLAYBOY: When did you realize you were in trouble with the U.S. military?

GARWOOD: When they read me Article Thirty-one. In Bangkok. Instead of receiving a handshake or a "Welcome home," immediately it was Article Thirty-one, and I "had the right to remain silent" and all that. And I said, "Wait a minute, what the hell's going on?" I had arrived in Bangkok on the Air France plane. It was funny, you see, because when the Air France plane picked me up in Saigon, the French people, they really welcomed me—God, I mean, it was something. They really welcomed me, with champagne and the whole bit.

PLAYBOY: This was the crew of the Air France plane?

GARWOOD: Yeah, the French crew. And I really felt free. I'd fought for so long and the day had actually come, and still I couldn't believe it. Believe me, it was a great *sharing*. Then we landed in Bangkok and the U.S. ambassador came on the plane, and introduced himself, and told me that I had to come with him, and there was the guys with military security and the reporters and everything. I more or less expected the reporters to make a big thing out of it—that I spent fourteen years in Vietnam and got back, that I was probably unique and all that.

PLAYBOY: What was your reaction when they read you your rights the first time?

GARWOOD: At that time, I had no lawyer, or at least I didn't know I had one. Actually, there was a marine lawyer there, but I didn't understand that. But the charges—it shocked hell out of me. Goddamn. It was kind of a deep emotional thing. I was shocked and then I figured, Oh, well, maybe it's just like a security precaution. Hell, they don't *know*. . . . Maybe they think I was brainwashed or some shit and they're just being careful. And then I was just so goddamned happy to be out of that country. I guess the overwhelming happiness of my own situation just overruled the disappointment. I thought, What the hell, I've been in a foreign land, there's been a war, fourteen damn years, and I'm still alive.

PLAYBOY: Let's talk about those fourteen years and go back to the beginning, to the day you were captured. What happened that day?

GARWOOD: It was September 28, 1965. Tuesday. I'll never forget it for the rest of my life. That's when my heartaches began. It was like the world exploded in front of me.

PLAYBOY: How old were you then?

GARWOOD: Nineteen.

PLAYBOY: Where were you? What time of day was it?

GARWOOD: It was in late afternoon. That morning, I went on my usual jeep run for G-Two (the battalion intelligence section). I was at Third Marine Division Headquarters on the direct perimeter of the Da Nang area. It was near a village they called Dogpatch. That's what we called it, anyway. My company went there as an advance unit.

PLAYBOY: How many marines were there at that point?

GARWOOD: In the Da Nang area, not that many, maybe twenty thousand, I'm not sure. They'd only been there a few months.

PLAYBOY: Where did you drive the jeep that day? And what did you do?

GARWOOD: Well, the dispatcher called on the squawk box and said G-Two wanted a driver. So I reported to G-Two, and I didn't even get a chance to get out of my vehicle. An officer came right down to me. He said, "Report to recon at Marble Mountain and pick up an officer. He's gotta go home on emergency leave; plan to take off very shortly. He'll be waiting for you at Marble Mountain."

PLAYBOY: What was Marble Mountain?

GARWOOD: There was fighting over there. Sort of like we ruled it by day, they ruled it by night. It was about five miles away.

PLAYBOY: How were you to identify the officer?

GARWOOD: He'd be waiting for me. This recon unit had just arrived there.

PLAYBOY: So you set off for Marble Mountain about what time?
GARWOOD: If I remember, it was probably about four o'clock.
PLAYBOY: Go on.
GARWOOD: All right. Marble Mountain had a kind of reputation, especially with recon units, which usually went where the action was. I was kind of worried. I thought, Damn, I'm a short-timer, you know? Getting ready to go home—that's all I was thinking on my way there. All I needed was to get wiped out now, get blown up by a mine or some shit, and it's going to be my damned luck. I only had a few days to go. I was kind of scared . . . probably a whole *lot* scared, a lot more than I would admit, really. When you're getting short, you don't want to do nothing, go nowhere. When you first get there, you're gung ho, but when you get down to them last days, man, I mean, you count every day and every hour. You hear a firecracker go off, man, you hit the first foxhole you see. You just get so close to the ground, man, you're smaller than the grass is. It's paranoid. So I started going out, and I asked for directions on the way.
PLAYBOY: Whom did you ask?
GARWOOD: Marines along the route. I'd stop and yell, "Hey, where's the recon at?" And they'd say, "*What* recon? We've got all kinds of recon units out here. Which one do you want?" And I said, "Oh, shit. That's all I need."

I stopped another guy and asked, "Where're they at?" He just pointed toward Marble Mountain. "Just go that direction, you'll find them. And if you don't find them, they'll find you." So I kept going and going, and got to a bridge right there on Route One. And there was a marine and an ARVN (a South Vietnamese soldier) posted as sentries on the bridge. They told me there were a couple of recon units in the area, including one across the bridge.

Well, I still had a couple of hours of daylight, so I figured I'd go ahead and check the one across the bridge. There was no way I was going over there, on the other side, when it started nightfall, you know? Windshields make mighty big targets.

Time was very precious. About the time I hit the bridge, it was 4:30. And I said, "Well, what the hell." So I shot across the bridge, and I remember the guard told me, he said, "Hey, man, don't be caught over there. In about another hour or two, it's going to be dark."

So after I crossed the bridge, I didn't see nothing. I didn't see no goddamned recon units or *nothing*.
PLAYBOY: What was the terrain like?
GARWOOD: Palm trees and a village. Fishing village was what it was. I went down the road and then the road started breaking up and it became like—sand. I was going pretty slow, pretty cautious, and I see no friendly military, but there was villages and everything. Then I came to a stretch where, hell, there was *nothing,* no people. I mean, there were signs of life—you could see the smoke coming out of the little hootches and everything—but you couldn't see a damn thing. So I took the road that veered off toward the beach, because under the palm trees, banana trees and the coconut trees and all that, it was getting kind of dark, and it was kind of scaring me, so I wanted to go out toward the beach, where it was light. I figured I'd be safe there. But then the road just played out entirely, just stopped in a little clearing.

It got kind of scary. You know, the sun was going down, there was no people. I was getting scared shitless, so I turned the jeep around and was going to head back toward our lines. I'd seen there was a lot of gunnery placements on the beach. And, uh, just as I turned the jeep around, this old man came out.

PLAYBOY: A Vietnamese?

GARWOOD: Yeah, a Vietnamese. He was an old man, with a beard, and he was waving to me, saying something in French and Vietnamese. I just stopped and looked at him. He just smiled. Then he came over to the jeep and he pointed to my weapon, like he was asking for my damn .45, you know. I said to myself, This guy must be nuts. He's crazy. I told him to go away.

PLAYBOY: Who did you think he was? Vietcong?

GARWOOD: At that point, I wasn't even sure what a VC *was*. I'd had no contact with the VC before. I wasn't in combat status. I was a driver. Then the ARVN and the VC look sort of alike, you know. And all of a sudden, they, like, came out of *nowhere*. They had camouflage, and they wore shorts, black shorts, and, uh, well, at first, you know, when I first saw them, man, it was like a sigh of relief, I thought it was an ARVN patrol.

Most of them had their weapons pointed down at a forty-five-degree angle, but this one kid had his weapon pointed directly at me. Then I started looking at the weapons. Man, those weapons were *not* American weapons. And the ARVNs, usually they were outfitted with M1 carbines or Thompsons or M14s, but these weapons, man, these were real weird weapons. Some were long, some were short. I never seen them before.

I just kept looking and they didn't say nothing. I looked around and I was completely encircled.

Something just clicked in my mind, just instant fear. I thought to myself, Oh, shit. Something's wrong. It ain't what's supposed to be. They weren't smiling. They were very, very serious.

PLAYBOY: What'd you do then?

GARWOOD: I dropped my hand down and released the holster. I wasn't really that familiar with .45s, other than that I knew how to fire it, how to load it. When I put my hand down, that one kid saw me—I swear to God, the rifle he had was longer than he was. He looked as if he was going to fire it, so I dove.

PLAYBOY: You dived out of the jeep?

GARWOOD: Well, it was like a dive and a crawl, because I had to go across the seat. And when I did that, man, all hell broke loose. I mean, shit, automatic weapons and everything. I hit that sand and I tried to bury my head, and then it kind of ceased. I remember one guy came charging up with a bayonet or something, with a blood-curdling scream.

I think I closed my eyes and I just shot the damned .45 at him with both hands. I figured if I missed him, hell, it was over anyway. But I didn't, I hit him, and there were two loud screams. I fired again, and then immediately after I fired the second shot, there was a burst of automatic fire. At first, I didn't feel any pain, I felt just like going to the dentist and you know how they shoot you with this stuff and your whole mouth is numbed up. That's how my arm felt. Then I saw the blood and I rolled under the jeep—

PLAYBOY: Where were you hit?

GARWOOD: It was right here. Twice, right here. [Indicates right arm above the wrist] And I just commenced saying the Lord's Prayer. But they grabbed me by the boots, pulled me out. I think they wanted to kill me right there, but one of them—he looked like he was a little older—said something, and so they laid off. They told me to take my clothes off.

When I started taking my uniform off, way off in the distance, in the ocean, there

were one or two helicopters, they were coming in toward land. The Vietnamese saw this, and they started talking jibber-jabber and motioned me to stop taking off the clothes, and they took me—half dragged me and I half ran. I was scared shitless. I couldn't see in front of me. I stumbled and fell—there was all kinds of commotion.
PLAYBOY: Where did they take you?
GARWOOD: Into the village. I vaguely remember hearing the engine of the jeep. Somebody was driving it away or something. And I remained there when the helicopters went over. They made me lie facedown, pointed a gun to my head. About five, ten minutes later, they took off my uniform and my boots and tied my hands in the back. The old people came up and were shaking their fists and pointing at the guns, and they pointed at the planes—I mean, they were really angry. Damn—I thought I would get a public execution or something. I was in my white skivvy shorts and shirt.

They took me away maybe about an hour from there. Everywhere we went, the people were waving at me and spitting on me and throwing rocks.
PLAYBOY: Where were they taking you?
GARWOOD: West, toward the mountains. I remember when we crossed Route One, at night, because there was a cross fire. We were caught right in the middle of it.
PLAYBOY: Cross fire? Between whom?
GARWOOD: Evidently, the ARVNs or Americans had some VC, because we got right in the middle of this rice paddy and just all hell broke loose. Tracers and all. Well, I plopped down, and the VC just laughed their asses off, because I was scared. It was worse than the obstacle training back in the States. Scarier than hell.
PLAYBOY: Did you keep going all night?
GARWOOD: Yeah, we went all night. It rained; I was very cold. I was hungry, I was tired, and everywhere I went, especially that night, everytime we come to a village or somewhere, there was a group of people, they'd bring lanterns and they pinched me, they'd feel my hair and feel my body—it was real weird.
PLAYBOY: Did you have anything to eat?
GARWOOD: At that point, no, they didn't give me nothing. They didn't give me nothing to eat till the next morning. The next morning, they brought me a small bag of cookies and a soda. They was like Vietnamese cookies and they tasted like shit. They kept me in a little boarded hootch-type thing. And that's when the guards brought me the soda and cookies.
PLAYBOY: You were staying put during the day and moving at night?
GARWOOD: That's pretty much the way it worked. They tried to interrogate me and everything, but no one spoke English—they speak French and some phonetic English. But I couldn't make heads or tails of it.
PLAYBOY: Did you speak any Vietnamese at that point?
GARWOOD: A little. Very little. I didn't let them know that I did.
PLAYBOY: Go on.
GARWOOD: They took me in boats, down rivers, across rice paddies, sometimes where there was fire or artillery, and I was going right in front of it. I mean, I was scared out of my wits.
PLAYBOY: How many days were you on the move before you reached the first prison camp?
GARWOOD: About a week or ten days.
PLAYBOY: How far do you suppose that was from where you were captured?
GARWOOD: Maybe ten, fifteen miles.

PLAYBOY: Were you in the mountains at that point?
GARWOOD: We just kept going up and up. Finally got to a compound, sort of. There was a little bamboo cage with metal bolted into it, a large chicken coop, I'd say. Or something like you'd keep a wild animal in. So they put me in this. There wasn't no roof on it, so they got some leaves and they put them over it like a cover.
PLAYBOY: What did they do then? Did they try to interrogate you or did they just leave you alone?
GARWOOD: No, not at this time. I was very worn out and I had leech bites all over me. I was very tired, and I was weak, because I didn't eat much. I lost a lot of blood. They took care of my wounds. I mean, they bandaged them, wrapped them up the second day. They didn't really take care of them until the third day, when they cleaned them out with alcohol. Raw alcohol. When they did that, the wounds started bleeding again, but a guy who spoke half English said if it starts bleeding again, that's good, because the infection will come out. They wrapped it in a dirty bandage. Later, it got infected. That's why it's such a big scar [Holds up arm].
PLAYBOY: What did they give you to eat?
GARWOOD: Cookies and soda pop. They thought all Americans ate was junk food. Finally, I got across what I really wanted, I guess. They tried to feed me rice, but when they give me that other damn stuff—
PLAYBOY: *Nuoc mam* [a potent sauce made from fermented fish]?
GARWOOD: Yeah, *nuoc mam;* I'm going to throw up. Well, I thought it was some kind of poison; I'll be damned if I was going to eat this shit.
PLAYBOY: How long were you in that cage?
GARWOOD: Until we left the camp. They never really built a hootch for me. I slept on strips of bamboo. Nobody ever spoke to me. I was there maybe five, six weeks.
PLAYBOY: Did you still think that they were going to execute you?
GARWOOD: Yeah, I really did, because they always made a point to show me their weapons. It was constantly like they was just going to blow me away, but they just weren't ready to do it *yet.* I felt strongly I was going to die. I mean, I was completely convinced of that.
PLAYBOY: You say nobody made any attempt to communicate with you, but wasn't it at that first camp that they tried to get you to sign some leaflets for propaganda?
GARWOOD: About the second or third week I was there, there was a dude—just appeared out of nowhere—whose name was Mr. Ho. He showed up with a couple of bodyguards and proclaimed himself to be a professor of English, which I believe, because he spoke English better than I could.
PLAYBOY: Was Ho a political officer?
GARWOOD: Well, all he told me was that he was a radical socialist. He said he wasn't a Communist and he wasn't a capitalist but that he was against what the U.S. was doing to Vietnam. He was very sophisticated. Very clean.
PLAYBOY: Was he a North Vietnamese?
GARWOOD: No. He had South Vietnamese *looks.* Wore black pajamas.
PLAYBOY: What did he say to you?
GARWOOD: He introduced himself and said that we'd be talking later, and he went out. The next day, he asked me how I had been treated since I had been captured. Actually, I was afraid to tell him that I was treated badly, so I said that, uh, under the circumstances, all right. And he didn't press the situation, torture me or anything like that.
PLAYBOY: What did he want to know?

GARWOOD: I think he was just trying to get to know me.
PLAYBOY: He wasn't interested in anything military?
GARWOOD: Nope, just to get to know me. He was feeling me out. Yeah. And, uh, he asked me how long I had been in Vietnam. I can't remember it at all. I mean, I was trying to answer him, but I wasn't. And he sensed it right away. And he told me, "All the questions I'm asking you, I know the answers already, so it won't do you any good to avoid it." He said, "You either talk to me or you can talk to someone else. And the someone else who comes to talk to you may not be so nice as I am." So he got his point across. I was trying to make him understand that I'm a marine, and I'm an American military man, that I was sworn to do certain things and that I can't say anything that I'm not supposed to.

He said, "Yes, I know all about your code of honor, but it doesn't do you any good here in Vietnam. You invaded our country, so, therefore, we consider you a criminal. If you do your best to be a friend to the Vietnamese people, then we'll treat you as a friend; but if you do your best to be an enemy, then we'll treat you as such."
PLAYBOY: Was he interrogating you in your cage?
GARWOOD: Yeah.
PLAYBOY: What else did he want?
GARWOOD: Well, actually, not much. He said, "I'm not going to press you too much today, give you time to think about it, to remember you're in the jungle, we have captured you, you're our prisoner and we can do with you what we want." He was there for about a week and I talked to him every day. He kept persisting, persisting, so I figured, in the end, I'm going to have to tell him some kind of story, or he's going to start turning the screws. So I made up a bullshit story that I was a general's aide, told him my family was very rich back in the States. I tried to build up that I was very important, so they'd maybe try to get some ransom or they wouldn't kill me.
PLAYBOY: How did he react to that?
GARWOOD: He was very crude about the whole thing. He said, "Because of people like you, your capitalist family, thousands upon thousands of Vietnamese are being killed every day." I mean, man, he cut me down bad.
PLAYBOY: When did he urge you to sign leaflets?
GARWOOD: Just before I left. He told me that he'd just got a report back from the guerrilla unit that captured me. First he asked, "What religion are you?" I said, "I'm Baptist." He said, "All right, if you're Baptist, then you know your Bible says, 'an eye for an eye,' right?" I said yeah. He said, "Well, I'm told you have killed two Vietnamese. What do you think about that?"

I said, "They were shooting me, and I shot back in self-defense." He said, "You cannot claim self-defense, you invaded our country. You killed our people. Now, if you had killed someone in the United States, what would have been your punishment?" I said, "Well, you go to jail and, possibly, execution." He said, "What makes you think that we shouldn't do the same?"
PLAYBOY: He was trying to scare you.
GARWOOD: He didn't *try;* shit, he *succeeded.*
PLAYBOY: To what purpose? Why do you think he was trying to scare you?
GARWOOD: At that point, I don't know. I was very, very confused. I was scared 'cause I thought they was trying to prepare me for what eventually was going to happen. Later on, I felt that I really screwed up. I thought, Oh, shit, I throwed up to them that my parents and my family was really important. Man, they're going to make it out, and make a damned public execution and broadcast it all over the world. Got rid of

one more big capitalist and all that shit. By that time, I was thinking, Why didn't I just come out and tell them that my father was a worker?

PLAYBOY: What did your father do?

GARWOOD: He was a printer. My whole family was workers. I'm poor as hell.

PLAYBOY: But you did, finally, sign some propaganda leaflets, didn't you?

GARWOOD: Yes.

PLAYBOY: Why?

GARWOOD: Well, first, Ho didn't tell me anything about any leaflets; he wanted me to write what they called my autobiography. I told him that I couldn't do that, that I was sworn by a code of conduct not to give him anything more than my name, rank and serial number. He said, "I'm going to flat out tell you now: We do not recognize the Geneva agreements. The United States has not declared war on Vietnam, so the Geneva Accords—and your code of conduct—do not apply." He got very angry when he said that. And he told me, "If you don't write it now, then you'll write it later."

PLAYBOY: So you wrote the autobiography?

GARWOOD: I stuck to a bullshit story and wrote the autobiography. Actually, I told him I was a chaplain's aide.

PLAYBOY: Chaplain's aide?

GARWOOD: Oh, he got me for that, too. Because he came back and said, "Do you know what a chaplain's aide is? A chaplain is actually the biggest CIA agent that your government has. His job is to counsel troops when their morale is very low, to get them to fight."

PLAYBOY: What about the leaflets?

GARWOOD: He had made out this document that said "Fellow Soldiers Appeal." He wrote it and then asked me what I thought about it. I said, "I'm sorry, I can't sign it." He said, "Well, do you think the military's going to come in here and save you? Do you think the marine corps's going to remember you, after you're dead and buried?" He kept playing on it like that. "Nobody gives a shit about you. As far as the marine corps goes, you're just cannon fodder, and you're going to be buried in the sand with thousands of other cannon fodder, and nobody's going to know your name, or remember you." He kept playing this spiel, his spiel. I said, "I'm sorry, whether it's true or not, I've got my own conscience I've got to live with." So he didn't force his hand then. He said, "I'll give you time to think about it and I'll be back here very shortly."

But then I developed dysentery real bad. And they wouldn't give me any medicine. They said they didn't have any. It was hard for me to converse with them, anyway, and I got real sick. I was going to the latrine up to maybe fifteen, twenty times a day. Blood was coming out and I couldn't eat. I was very weak. Ho came back about a week later and he pulled this sympathy act, you know. But I got even worse, until I really thought I was going crazy. I started going to the state where—I don't know—I accepted the fact I was going to die.

PLAYBOY: Go on.

GARWOOD: Well, Ho came down and gave this big spiel, and showed me a leaflet where he said two army dudes had been captured, and been released, and they had signed, and they had written these leaflets. He said, "See, these people now are back in the States with their families, and nothing has happened to them." He said, "You have nothing but your own survival." He said, "You're not going to be hurting anybody."

PLAYBOY: Then you signed your leaflet?

GARWOOD: Eventually, I signed it. It was just so much propaganda. I knew, as an

American, nobody would pick it up, except as a damn souvenir or something, nothing serious, anyway.

PLAYBOY: You mean they'd think it was a joke or wouldn't be persuaded by it?

GARWOOD: Well, yeah, because nobody knows an American like the Americans do. It was a bunch of bullshit. You don't think somebody's going to cross over for their damned leaflet.

PLAYBOY: So you thought it would be obvious that you had signed it under duress.

GARWOOD: Right, because right on the leaflet it said, POW, prisoner of war, and my name. So, automatically, when Americans saw that "prisoner of war," they assumed you had to sign it, you know, you were forced to. Meantime, I figured, There's still some chance; if I get some of my health back, I'll be able to escape.

PLAYBOY: Did you really think that by signing that leaflet they might release you and send you back to the States?

GARWOOD: No. It was just like a stay of prosecution.

PLAYBOY: You mean a stay of execution.

GARWOOD: Execution, prosecution. . . .

PLAYBOY: So you signed one leaflet?

GARWOOD: Yeah. That's right.

PLAYBOY: How long was that after you were captured?

GARWOOD: Pretty close to two months, I guess.

PLAYBOY: And you were still living in the cage?

GARWOOD: Immediately upon signing this, they got the medicine and give it to me, because my health was just about to the point where I could barely walk around. Then I was moved to the second camp.

PLAYBOY: During those first couple of months, did you try to escape?

GARWOOD: Yeah, about a week after I was captured. We were traveling along the riverbank, toward the mountains. And the guards that were on me—

PLAYBOY: How many were there?

GARWOOD: At times there was as many as ten, and at other times there was only two or three, including one small guy.

PLAYBOY: Were you tied up?

GARWOOD: My hands were tied behind my back and there was a rope around my neck, which one of the guards had in his hands. We traveled all day and half the night. Well, one day, we got to this pagoda with steps that led down to the river.

We were resting on these steps and it was about midnight. It was cold and they told me to lie down on the steps to get some rest, but I didn't sleep. The small guard, who was maybe fourteen or fifteen years old, was six or seven steps above me. The other guard went away and I didn't have the rope around my neck, all I had was my hands tied. The little guy eventually dozed off to sleep. So I rolled down one step and waited for his reaction, because, usually, if I even moved, he said something. He didn't say nothing, so I rolled down another step. I was right near the water's edge and he was still in the same position. I just rolled from step to step and rolled into the water, and went downstream, along the bank.

I kept listening, but I never heard anything from the guards. I don't know when they found out I was gone. I moved pretty fast. My hand hurt bad, my arm was swollen. I was gone quite a distance. It was hard for me to keep track of the time, but I speculate it was maybe four or five in the morning, because I remember the roosters were crowing, but it wasn't light yet. And I was feeling my way along the bank and trying to find somewhere to hide during the day. I thought the river would go back in the direction we came from, to Da Nang, or, if nothing else, out to the ocean. You know, there was American river patrols, all kinds of stuff like that. I figured I'd run into somebody.

Well, I was feeling my way around the bank and I bumped into something, a goddamned sampan, or a boat, and it's got all these Vietnamese in there, and it woke them up, and they shined a flashlight and saw me and started yelling and screaming. I was recaptured instantly.

PLAYBOY: Were they VC or just villagers?

GARWOOD: I think they were guerrillas, because they had weapons. The guys in the sampan, I don't think they knew where I came from. A lot of jibber-jabbering going on—like they thought they'd been the ones who captured me, that maybe I'd parachuted or something. I don't think they knew that I was actually captured and had escaped.

Anyway, I was a prize possession, just sitting around, and, God, then there was people coming out of nowhere. And then I saw this little guard, he showed up again. And he was jumping up and down, wanting to kill me. He said he was going to blow my brains away or something. The other guerrillas, they were laughing about it. And then four or five other guys clothed in black—strong, muscular, looked like weight builders, you know—they escorted me. They pushed and shoved and pointed rifles, like I should be shot for what I tried to do, and shit like that.

PLAYBOY: All right, let's move forward again to Ho and the autobiography.

GARWOOD: Wait, there's something else. Before I got dysentery, and before Ho left, they took me back down the mountain to the plains. There was a village surrounded by rice paddies. There must have been a hundred people, if not more. Regular villagers, people working in rice paddies. They were carrying rice up the mountain. And they'd point at me, and they'd laugh at me and say, "Ooo Ess"—Ooo Ess was U.S.—and stuff like that. I found out they had brought me to make a movie.

PLAYBOY: A movie?

GARWOOD: Yeah. A reenactment of the capture. At the camp with Ho, this girl came in who could speak English fairly well. She told me that she was going to make a movie. She said they wanted a reenactment of the capture. First, I kind of laughed at her, and she got really pissed and she screamed, "You laugh at the people?" I said no. So they took me out in the middle of the damned rice paddy, put me in the middle of it, surrounded by VC guerrillas, and they shot up in the air and all kinds of bullshit, and then the VC came in the middle of the rice paddy, got me by the arms and dragged me out of the rice paddy. And that was the end of the movie.

PLAYBOY: Then what happened?

GARWOOD: They gave me something to eat and took me back to the mountain again. The next day or the day after that was when I started to develop the dysentery.

PLAYBOY: And then Ho came back?

GARWOOD: That's when he got me to sign the leaflet. As soon as I signed it, he left. And then they gave me medicine.

PLAYBOY: Did the medicine clear up the dysentery?

GARWOOD: It did after about a week. It didn't stop altogether. It was down to where I was going about twice a day, maybe three times a day, but I could eat. I was able to eat rice, you know, and they gave me some brown sugar and I was getting a little of my strength back. It was up to the point where I was able to walk, but I didn't let them know. That's when I decided to try to escape again. See, dysentery is a very, very fatal disease. They're scared shitless of it. I noticed that every time I had to go to the latrine, they'd always stay a distance from me. They'd never get close to me. And there were certain guards that wouldn't even follow me, except just to the edge of the path, that was maybe forty feet to the latrine well.

When I started getting better, I didn't let the Vietnamese know I was getting better. Every time I went to the latrine, I tried to stay as long as I could, to see how long it took before they called me. Sometimes, with certain guards, they would call me periodically about every five or ten minutes. Then there was this one guard who didn't call me at all. And I was getting my strength back.

PLAYBOY: What were they calling you, by the way?

GARWOOD: Bo. Bo.

PLAYBOY: For Bob?

GARWOOD: Yeah, and a lot of them called me Me—"Hey, Me, Me, Me." For American.

PLAYBOY: So, at some point, you decided you were going to use that as a way to escape.

GARWOOD: Right. The longest I stayed there was about a half-hour, and the guard never even called me. And so I was hoping a half-hour would give me enough time to get down the damn mountain. I was getting scared that they were going to use me, and when they weren't going to use me no more, they was just going to get rid of me. So I figured, Man, my time's getting shorter and shorter, and what the hell if I'm shot now or later? And there was still a chance. Some kind of a slim chance.

There was a creek behind the latrine and I thought the creek must've led down to the plains where they took me and filmed this movie thing. So maybe, just maybe I could work my way, because at night there was artillery from Da Nang. And if I just followed that direction, just maybe I could come upon one of the patrols or something. Maybe I'd just luck out, you know. My damn luck had been so rotten so long and, goddamn, it couldn't be that way all the way. It was a big chance, but I was really desperate.

Well, it was in the evening, it had started to get dark and I went to the latrine, and I lucked out with that guard. Actually, I hadn't planned it just then, not until I saw who the guard was, and it was like a split-second decision right there. I'll try it now or might never get the chance again. So I went to the latrine like I usually do. The stream was right behind me, so I just started following it. I tried to run, and I stumbled, and it was daylight but getting dark, so you could just barely see your way. And I stumbled and fell on the rocks and I was gone maybe for better than a half-hour.

PLAYBOY: Down the mountain?

GARWOOD: I mean, it seemed like forever to me. And I heard shots ring out—bang!—bang! I heard voices and shouts—it looks like they found out I'm gone. So I tried to go faster. Anyway, this damn stream went around down the mountain—it was nothing but rocks and slippery—I fell several times and busted my ass. I had no shoes, I was barefoot. Cut my feet. I went all night like this, and it was getting on to the morning, and I knew I was going down, because I could look up and I couldn't see the top of the mountain. I found a big rock, a big overhang, and got under it. I wasn't even at the base of the damned mountain yet and I was going all fucking night!

It was just light enough so you could see where you were going, and then they found me. They started raising hell and everything else. I didn't say nothing, I just curled up under that rock like a porcupine or something and figured I'd get beat to death. They was yelling and screaming. They'd been waiting for me at the base of the damned mountain. Because they went down the path and I went down the stream. Down the path was probably a very short distance, and down the stream, you zigzag. I was weak, anyway, and then they hit me and all that shit. I had bumps and bruises and there was some blood, and I felt real sure that I was going to be executed. But they put me back in the cage and didn't give me nothing to eat the next day.

Then it wasn't long after, about five, six days, they moved me.

PLAYBOY: What direction did they move you in? Did you have any idea?

GARWOOD: North. It was at night. I could see the lights were flashing against the skyline. I guess it was Da Nang Air Base. A couple of weeks, moving north.

PLAYBOY: That would have been when—in December 1965?

GARWOOD: Or late November.

PLAYBOY: When was it that you saw your first fellow American?

GARWOOD: I'd arrived at the second camp about two, maybe three weeks before I saw my first American. That's when they brought Ike [Eisenbraun] in.

PLAYBOY: How had he been captured?

GARWOOD: He was a special-forces captain in the Pleiku region. His outpost was overrun by the VC. The guy was in bad shape. He'd been captured about five, six months. Yeah, Ike came in and he was pitiful. I was so damn happy—he was a godsend. I mean, I wanted to talk to somebody, just to *have* somebody to confide in, somebody I could turn to, because I never had been in a situation like this before. And I was really lost.

PLAYBOY: You said he was in bad shape; how bad?

GARWOOD: He was sick; his feet were swollen. He had—what do you call it?—nutrition edema; and he had diarrhea.

PLAYBOY: Did they put you in the same hootch?

GARWOOD: Yeah. And he was always sick. I had to care for him, wash him, like that.

PLAYBOY: Did the two of you get along?

GARWOOD: He was the best. But he was just on the verge of death then. We remained together until he died about a year and a half later.

PLAYBOY: What went on in that second camp?

GARWOOD: Not much. The guards made us go and get wood for their kitchen, but Ike couldn't go, so I carried the wood for both of us. There were also some ARVN prisoners there, and they released about twenty of them.

PLAYBOY: Why did they release them?

GARWOOD: Because they had become "liberated." They would say the progressive stuff or whatever, that they were going back to fight for the "people's cause" and shit. I remember giving one of the ARVN prisoners my dog tag before he left.

PLAYBOY: Hoping the dog tag would make its way back to American lines?

GARWOOD: Yeah.

PLAYBOY: Did it?

GARWOOD: Yeah. I read it in one of the newspaper articles when I got back to the U.S.

PLAYBOY: So then they moved you to a third camp, right? Were you still going north?

GARWOOD: I don't know. It was triple-canopy jungle and deep in the mountains. You couldn't tell which direction.

PLAYBOY: How did they move Ike? By litter?

GARWOOD: No, he was able to walk, because I cared for him. I washed for him and bathed him and—I give him almost half my ration and his strength was able to build him up.

PLAYBOY: What was your ration at that point?

GARWOOD: Twice a day, one big bowl of rice, with some kind of jungle vegetables. Something *they* called vegetables; we called it weeds.

PLAYBOY: What was the next camp like?

GARWOOD: It wasn't very big. It looked like it had just been built. There were some ARVN prisoners. This camp was high in the mountains and under the canopy of the trees. They put us in a hootch.

PLAYBOY: For the record, would you describe what you mean by a hootch?

GARWOOD: It's a kind of a shed. There are bamboo walls and a bamboo roof. About fifteen feet wide and maybe forty feet long.

PLAYBOY: And how many guards were there?

GARWOOD: About fifteen, twenty, maybe.

PLAYBOY: How long did you stay there?

GARWOOD: Pretty close to a year, I guess.

PLAYBOY: Was Ike with you?

GARWOOD: Yes. And then, in July or August, Russ come. Russ Grissett. He was a corporal in the marines. He was in recon, too.

PLAYBOY: During that time, did they do anything to you? Did they try to get you to sign leaflets or propagandize you?

GARWOOD: They propagandized—yeah. They had an English interpreter there, too. He came from North Vietnam.

PLAYBOY: What was his name?

GARWOOD: His name was Hum. He spoke English, so you could understand him if you listened real careful.

PLAYBOY: What did he do?

GARWOOD: He brought a radio down and we listened to the Hanoi broadcasts. And he brought different leaflets and books and pamphlets that were printed by the VC and the North Vietnamese. Propaganda books.

PLAYBOY: Did they make you read them or did they just leave them with you?

GARWOOD: They were the only thing to read, really.

PLAYBOY: Did you consider escaping again?

GARWOOD: Yes, we both did. But we talked to the ARVN. Ike talked Vietnamese. We tried to size our chances and we felt that we had about maybe a twenty-five-percent chance of escaping. I'd tried it twice—Ike had already tried it twice, too. And we both failed. But Ike kept persisting that he wanted to do it again. But it got down to his health—we just couldn't make no time. I mean, first he was almost blind. He had lost his glasses. But what really bothered me was his health. He could hardly breathe at all and I could walk faster than he could run. I told him, "Ike, it's suicide. We don't know where the hell we are, and as far as surviving, that's not good odds." And I'll tell you, in my own mind at that time, I was just so afraid of being alone . . . I was afraid that he was going to escape and that he would die on the way or he'd be killed. Because Ike, goddamn it, he fought, he went down fighting. He never gave up. That's what I would say about him. I had a lot of respect for him.

PLAYBOY: It sounds as if you were discouraging him from escaping.

GARWOOD: At that point, I was young, I was real young, and when I was first captured, I was alone all the time. I was so afraid of losing Ike, so afraid of being alone again. Plus they told us that if we tried to escape one more time, that it would be automatic execution when they captured us. So I discouraged Ike almost every way I could about the possibility of trying to escape.

PLAYBOY: So you languished in that camp for almost a year, reading the enemy propaganda. Then what happened?

GARWOOD: They moved us again, because we were bombed. It was a B-52 strike. They had just showed us a propaganda film from North Vietnam. Right after the film, the damn camp was bombed.

PLAYBOY: It was just you, Ike and Russ?

GARWOOD: And the ARVN. The ARVN prisoners left before us. The next camp was a long way away.

PLAYBOY: And it was at that camp, the fourth one, that you left the American compound and began living with the Vietcong.

GARWOOD: Well, not . . . I guess you could put it that way, but I'd like to say what happened.

PLAYBOY: Go ahead.

GARWOOD: After we'd been in this camp a little while, Ho arrived.

PLAYBOY: The same Ho you had dealt with before?

GARWOOD: Right. And he proposed a deal. He came over with this big propaganda bullshit about the solidarity of progressive peoples, that there were such people in the United States and that they were considering releasing some of our POWs and, uh, thanks to the solidarity, they were considering me.

PLAYBOY: By the "solidarity," do you mean the antiwar movement back in the United States?

GARWOOD: Right. And, actually, I was kind of thrilled, but I was kind of disturbed, too. Just the thought of returning to America—returning to American control, American armies, was something beyond my grasp. It was something that everybody hungered for. Just the thought of it, being able to be free—under *any* circumstances. So Ho proposed the deal that, uh, he called a liberation. He said they would release me. All that would be required of me in return for my liberation was that they would announce that I had now become a "friend of the Vietnamese," and I would be taken to some villages where they would hold meetings, and I would tell these villagers that the American working class were actually in solidarity with the Vietnamese working class, that we weren't enemies and that it was only the capitalists that were waging war, and all that propaganda bullshit.

Well, I didn't agree right away. I told him that I would think about it, and I went back to Ike and I told him what happened. Russ, he didn't like it at all. Russ said more or less that it was against the code of conduct. So we discussed it and Ike said, "Hell, we've already signed statements and everything and, hell, nobody knows we're alive. And if just one of us can get out, then, if nothing else, they'll know we're still alive, that we're here, and they'll come looking for us." He said if it had been him, he would do it. And if it had been Russ, he would have ordered him to go. He said, "Since it's you, go. Do whatever you have to do to get out of here. Just get word out somehow that we're still alive."

I don't know, it kind of disturbed me. I had a small argument with Ike at that point. I said I'd rather that we all got out of there together, and maybe we could make some deal with them, where they'd release us all—you know, we'd cooperate with them in some way. Ike said no, they were not going to accept that. He said, "They've focused their attention on *you*. Just use it to the best advantage." I thought about it, and I thought about it, so I finally agreed.

It was like a mark, liberation, but it wasn't really liberation. I got up and gave a speech on friendship and said we're all together. Ho wrote it for me.

PLAYBOY: Was that in the camp itself?

GARWOOD: Yes.

PLAYBOY: Who was the audience?

GARWOOD: Ike and Russ and the ARVN POWs. Ho was there. They made a tape recording of it. It was like a preliminary. Actually, then I was not really liberated. But there was an announcement that I was now being considered a friend, and not the enemy anymore, as long as I cooperated. And so I was taken out of the compound, away from Ike and Russ. They built a small hootch for me. And I lived there.

PLAYBOY: Doing what?

GARWOOD: They used me. They used me like a pawn or a propaganda tool. Every time a new POW would come in, they'd point to me and say, you know, that I'd been progressive, and we'll let him go, he'll be released soon. They'd say, "Bob is a progressive American, and if you want to be like him, you have to abide by the camp rules, be a hard worker and probe your solidarity with the working class of America."

PLAYBOY: Did you continue your contacts with Ike?

GARWOOD: Yes, I did, several times.

PLAYBOY: Only several times?

GARWOOD: That was right after I was separated from Ike and Russ. But then Ike was separated from Russ. They put Ike in a hammock, right outside the compound.

PLAYBOY: Did they think he was too weak to escape?

GARWOOD: Possibly, but also, they told me that they were considering releasing Ike, too, because Ike by then was being much more cooperative. And I talked to Ike about it. He told me, "I don't think they're going to release me. But a little help, a little help, and they'd eventually maybe release one of us." So I told him, "They're using me as a damn tool, a propaganda tool." I asked him how far he thought they was going to go. He said, "Well, I don't know, but since we've stepped out a little, we'll have to step out all the way." Either they were going to release me or they were going to put me back in the damned POW compound. But Ike felt they wouldn't put me back in the POW compound, because this would only show the other POWs they were lying, that it was a bunch of bullshit. He said, "If anything, they will take you out of the camp and tell us that you've been liberated. But right now, whatever they tell you to do, do it. Because if you don't, then it's going to be worse on the other POWs."

PLAYBOY: Did you see Ike whenever you wanted to?

GARWOOD: No, I had to ask permission.

PLAYBOY: All right, so you were living in the hootch by yourself. How far was that from the compound where the other Americans were kept?

GARWOOD: About fifty or seventy-five feet. I was wedged between the guard hootch and the camp commander's hootch.

PLAYBOY: But you weren't in a cage or restrained in any way?

GARWOOD: Ah, no. Directly in a cage, no. To leave this hootch and go anywhere, I had to ask permission.

PLAYBOY: How did you eat?

GARWOOD: They brought my meals to me. My only duties at that point were to go get firewood for the guard kitchen.

PLAYBOY: Were you guarded when you gathered wood?
GARWOOD: I was guarded, yes.
PLAYBOY: When did Ike die?
GARWOOD: He didn't die until September [1967]. Actually, right after Ike died, that's when they took me away. They told me that he'd fallen out of his hammock and broke a couple of his rib-cage bones and punctured his lung.
PLAYBOY: Do you think that was true?
GARWOOD: No.
PLAYBOY: What do you think happened?
GARWOOD: See, I was going down to see Ike a lot. And they watched every move I made, because the only time I could see him was during the daylight. But toward August, I was getting frustrated and I was more persistent.
PLAYBOY: Persistent to see Ike?
GARWOOD: No, not to see Ike, persistent as to why I wasn't being released. I was more or less on hold right there. Wasn't allowed to go anywhere or do anything, except to gather firewood and manioc [a yamlike vegetable]. And I was really frustrated. They'd first told me I'd be released in about a month. And it had been four months already. I'd ask the interpreter, and he'd tell me, "Well, I don't really know, but I think that the front is waiting for an opportune time so that you may be turned over to an American peace committee. They'll probably come over to Vietnam and they'll turn you back over then, rather than turn you over to the CIA or the military."

Anyway, the day I heard about Ike dying, I asked to go down to the POW compound, and they let me. I talked to Russ. He just said that Ike fell out of his hammock and ruptured his lung.
PLAYBOY: What did they do with his body?
GARWOOD: The ARVN POWs went out and cut some bamboo and wrapped it around his body like a makeshift coffin and carried it to the clearing. There was myself and Russ and two other American prisoners, Luis Ortiz-Rivera and a marine named Bob Sherman. We insisted on digging the grave. But the guards got kind of angry when I started digging the grave; they told me I wasn't—you know—
PLAYBOY: You weren't supposed to dig a grave?
GARWOOD: No. They got kind of pissed about it. So Russ and Ortiz more or less dug it. Ortiz was the strongest, he was built like an ox. And Ortiz dug most of the grave. It was shallow, it wasn't real deep.
PLAYBOY: What was your relationship with Russ at that point?
GARWOOD: Russ Grissett. I wasn't overwhelmed with what a great guy he was.
PLAYBOY: You mean he didn't like the idea of your going off to be liberated?
GARWOOD: No. He thought if there was going to be a release, we all should be released together.
PLAYBOY: When you went down to the compound, did you talk to him?
GARWOOD: Yeah, I talked to him.
PLAYBOY: How did he react?
GARWOOD: I don't think he liked it too much.
PLAYBOY: So after Ike died, they moved you to a fifth camp?
GARWOOD: Right. It was just another prisoner camp. I thought they was going to release me then, but they didn't. They put me in a hootch right next to the kitchen—not in the POW compound. And very shortly afterward, they brought Weatherman in.

PLAYBOY: Who was Weatherman? An American?
GARWOOD: Yes; the VC told me he was a crossover, supposedly. I don't know. They introduced me to him as a member of the Solidarity Committee of the American People. Said he was drafted and immediately upon arriving in Vietnam, he came over to the people. So they said.
PLAYBOY: What was his rank?
GARWOOD: Private—Pfc., maybe.
PLAYBOY: What happened to Weatherman?
GARWOOD: They took him away. Right after Christmas. They treated Weatherman much better than they treated me; I mean, they give him new clothes and food, cigarettes—he was free to move about the camp.
PLAYBOY: Is he still alive?
GARWOOD: He's dead.
PLAYBOY: How long was it before the next American POWs arrived?
GARWOOD: Well, after about a month, there was Burns and then Corporal Zaltachy and Lance Corporal Hammond.
PLAYBOY: Where were they imprisoned?
GARWOOD: In the compound.
PLAYBOY: And you were living outside the compound, right?
GARWOOD: Right. But the week after Zaltachy and Hammond arrived, we all started out for the new camp.
PLAYBOY: How long did it take you to get there?
GARWOOD: A little better than a week. On the way to the camp, we met with two black American POWs.
PLAYBOY: Who were they?
GARWOOD: Willie Watkins, I believe was one, and Tom Davis. I'm not really sure. That was when I had my first contact with a weapon. We were going alone, and I was carrying all the gear, rice and cooking utensils. There were four or five guards and one of them had one of these little machine-gun-type things—I think it was Chinese—and he stripped it down, took the ammo and the firing pin out and told me to carry it.

It about freaked me out. At first, I wasn't going to carry it, because I thought that if we met some VC along the way, they'd think I was an American on patrol and blow me away. But the guards just laughed and said no, no way. I was scared shitless. But they thought it was hilarious.
PLAYBOY: So you met Watkins and Davis. Did they see you carrying a weapon?
GARWOOD: Yeah. They saw the weapon. The guards took the weapon from me, but I think it freaked the Americans out when they saw it. They asked me about it. I told them the guard told me to carry it, and I carried it. But they didn't like the idea, they thought I shouldn't have carried it. So I said, "What the fuck am I going to do, you know? I mean, hell, they're going to tell me what to do and I'm going to do it. I have no choice."
PLAYBOY: When did you arrive at the next camp?
GARWOOD: About the middle of February '68.
PLAYBOY: Who was in the camp when you got there?
GARWOOD: There was a lot of POWs—
PLAYBOY: All American POWs?
GARWOOD: Right.
PLAYBOY: Was that the camp in which most of the court-martial charges against you arose?

GARWOOD: Yes.
PLAYBOY: What was the physical condition of the other Americans? Were they in good shape?
GARWOOD: This was right after the Tet offensive. A couple of them had been shot up, but overall, their condition was pretty good.
PLAYBOY: What were you doing then?
GARWOOD: Nothing, really. When I arrived there, they showed me which hootch to live in, told me to stay there, let the camp commander come down and talk to me. After the evening meal—which they brought to me—the camp commander came down and told me that the situation was much different than it was before and that any time I wanted to talk to any of the Americans, I would have to let him know personally.
PLAYBOY: What kind of fellow was he?
GARWOOD: The camp commander? He was hard-line, but he never got what you'd call ferocious. Just strict. Reasonable. I mean, he'd listen to you, but you'd better not get smart with him.
PLAYBOY: When were you able to talk freely with the other Americans in the compound?
GARWOOD: After about a month, I was actually allowed to go down there by myself. All the time I was there with the prisoners, there was always a guard, he'd come popping in and out, or he was standing right there.
PLAYBOY: Were you helping to conduct interogations?
GARWOOD: Well, there was a first interrogation of a prisoner by the interpreter. Then there was a second interrogation, which included the interpreter and the camp commander, and sometimes I was ordered to be there.
PLAYBOY: What were they trying to find out?
GARWOOD: Mainly, besides name, rank, serial number, they would ask if the prisoner had a family, what state he lived in, when he joined the service, when he came to Vietnam, what unit he was with.
PLAYBOY: What was the purpose of that interrogation? What did they really want to know?
GARWOOD: Actually, nothing the POWs could have told them would have been of any value, as far as battlefield situations, because most of them had been prisoners for two months or more. And anything that had to do with the battlefield situation would have changed drastically in a month—I mean, it changed from day to day. So, really, the only purpose of the interrogation itself was to find out who the hard-core people were, who were the easy ones, so they could segregate them and break them down.
PLAYBOY: What was the attitude of the other American prisoners toward you? At least one soldier, named Port, had called you a traitor by then, isn't that right?
GARWOOD: He did. He called me that. But Port was delirious.
PLAYBOY: *Did* you consider yourself a traitor?
GARWOOD: At that point, no. It disturbed me, yeah. And even when he said it, I looked toward the other Americans and nobody said anything. But then we all just continued talking.
PLAYBOY: During that period, did you still have the feeling that they might release you?
GARWOOD: There was a slight hope—it was the only hope that I had. At that point, there was nobody I could turn to anymore. Ike wasn't there anymore—I used to be able to turn to Ike, but I couldn't turn to him no more.

PLAYBOY: How about Grissett?

GARWOOD: Grissett—Russ, he was getting really uptight. His mental stability was bad. He came to me several times to see if I had any influence at all, to try to get him out of the compound; he was going crazy.

PLAYBOY: One of the charges you were convicted of is that you physically abused a fellow prisoner. When did that occur?

GARWOOD: Well, it wasn't really physical abuse. David Harker himself acknowledged that.

PLAYBOY: Harker was the prisoner?

GARWOOD: Yes. He testified at my court-martial that he didn't consider it anything other than an insult or something.

PLAYBOY: What were the events leading up to the incident?

GARWOOD: Well, Russ was taking the brunt of a beating by the Communists for killing a cat, the camp cat.

PLAYBOY: Did they kill it to eat it?

GARWOOD: Yes. And Russ had been singled out to take the brunt of the punishment in which—well, two weeks later, he died from it. But, anyway, when I saw this—and I'm trying to picture in my mind what happened; I can't really remember exactly, you know—but I just went crazy when I saw Russ getting beaten, and I rushed into the compound and there was nothing I could do. Harker was standing in the doorway of one of the hootches. I brushed him aside with the back of my hand, which he said amounted to a slap, to his rib cage or his stomach. I went inside and said, "How the hell can you guys call yourselves Americans? Russ is out there getting beat. If you guys had stuck together, nothing would have happened." And we just stared at each other, and there was silence, and I left. And two weeks later, Russ died.

PLAYBOY: What about the charge that you verbally abused a Sergeant Buck Williams during one of the propaganda sessions?

GARWOOD: Williams was a career man. He'd served in the Korean War. He was tough. I guess the propaganda session you're talking about was when he referred to the South Vietnamese soldiers as ARVN. You weren't supposed to call them ARVN. You were supposed to call them puppets.

So Ho decided to make an example out of Williams. Ho told me that for the good of the class, everybody was going to have to criticize Williams. Otherwise, they would discontinue the class and everybody would be in the doghouse. So they reconvened the class and everybody started criticizing Williams. Then Ho said something like that Williams had been completely brainwashed by the capitalistic system and that he was hoping someday to retire on the blood of the Vietnamese people and stuff like that. Then Ho asked me, "Bobby, do you agree with that?" I said, "Yeah." Then he made me repeat it to Williams, too. But I apologized to him for it later. When Ho asked if you agreed with him, you'd better the hell agree.

PLAYBOY: Despite your explanations, you've been convicted of collaborating. Why do you think the other prisoners didn't collaborate—or do you think they did? Was your case special somehow?

GARWOOD: Yes, I think my case was kind of special, because the Communists didn't release me in 1973. If they'd released me with all the other POWs, there would never have been a court-martial, I'm sure of that.

PLAYBOY: Why? Do you think other prisoners collaborated but weren't singled out as you were for political—or other—reasons?

GARWOOD: I don't know the real reason behind that, other than what I've heard and

I've read. But I do know for a fact that there was a lieutenant colonel in the marine corps who came back in 1973—I'm not going to give his name; it's on record—but he had charges brought against him for mutiny, and several other very serious charges, more serious than mine. But his charges were dropped, and since, then, he retired from the marine corps and he's living a very respectable life, somewhere out in the West. There were numerous incidents like that.

PLAYBOY: One of the witnesses against you at your court-martial described you as the "white Vietnamese," referring to your personal habits while you were in the prison camp—the way you walked, laughed, squatted down in Oriental style. Is that true?

GARWOOD: It's probably pretty accurate. The psychiatrists who testified for me said it was part of my mental illness; that I unconsciously identified with the enemy, although I didn't realize it at the time.

PLAYBOY: When stories began appearing a couple of years ago that you were still alive, but before you were released from Vietnam, several men claimed you had led Vietcong troops in combat against American forces. What about that?

GARWOOD: It's totally untrue. And none of those accusations was ever made against me formally—at the court-martial—or even brought up in charges. One guy, for instance, stated he had seen me leading a band of Vietcong or something—but the man he described had blond hair and blue eyes. As you can see, I'm certainly not blond and my eyes are brown. Besides, in all of those alleged "sightings," I couldn't have been where they said I was, because I was in the prison camp.

PLAYBOY: To what do you attribute those allegations?

GARWOOD: The frustrations of war, I guess. I suppose they wanted to see *somebody* and I was a likely culprit. I don't think there was ever any American who led Vietcong. If there had been, I probably would have heard about it through the jungle grapevine.

PLAYBOY: There was another charge made against you at the court-martial that you had gone out with the Vietcong and used a bullhorn to urge American troops to lay down their arms.

GARWOOD: That was totally untrue, too. Those charges were made, but only because somebody allegedly said they overheard me saying it to somebody else, or something like that. The only time I came into contact with a bullhorn was when they [the Vietcong] had one of them and it didn't work and they told me to repair it. I looked at it and it was corroded and I told them to clean it up and it would probably work. All those charges were thrown out, but, damn, to hear some people tell it, I might have been running a bullhorn factory over there.

PLAYBOY: Going back to the charge that you carried a weapon, you said earlier you'd carried a dismantled, unarmed weapon once; but how many times, exactly, did you carry a weapon?

GARWOOD: I don't remember exactly—maybe five times.

PLAYBOY: Why?

GARWOOD: They told me to. At that point, I did pretty much whatever they told me to. If I'd refused, they'd have starved me to death or worse. That was the way it was.

PLAYBOY: What about the charge that you used a weapon to guard American prisoners?

GARWOOD: That was the times they gave me the weapon and told me to carry it. It was a different weapon each time and it was never loaded. I didn't realize what they were doing then, but they would give me the weapon and take me out on a trail and all of a sudden, we'd meet up with some new prisoners and the VC would say something like, "This is Bobby Garwood—see, if you'll be like him, you can get privileges," stuff like that. They always took the weapon away afterward. They were using me, but I didn't realize how much at the time. They were just using me.

PLAYBOY: Didn't you ever consider that it was wrong, or treasonous, to carry a weapon belonging to the enemy?

GARWOOD: No. I was trying to live. Besides, it wasn't hurting anybody. It wasn't even loaded.

PLAYBOY: What about the charge that you served as an interrogator for the Vietcong against your fellow Americans?

GARWOOD: That wasn't true, either. I did some interpreting, which means that I was a translator. I never interrogated anybody. Whenever the regular interpreter wasn't there, they'd get me to translate for them. Most of the time, it was just simple stuff—somebody would go to the prison compound and want to ask a question and I'd translate it. I think I actually *helped* the guys in the compound, because I would translate the questions and answers fairly—Vietnamese isn't an easy language, you know, and if somebody does it wrong, somebody could get in a lot of trouble. I always tried to make it sound the best it could—translating American to Vietnamese.

PLAYBOY: Were the other POWs aware of that?

GARWOOD: Not all the time. I don't know. Some people blame me because I learned the language. Hell, Ike taught it to me, and a couple of times I tried to teach it to the other POWs. You had to know the damned language to survive, I figured. Why is that such a crime?

PLAYBOY: Another of the allegations against you was that you wore a Vietcong uniform. What about that?

GARWOOD: I didn't wear any Vietcong uniform. I wore what they gave me to wear, because when I was captured, they stripped me to my skivvies. I had to wear something. So did everybody else. There was one accusation that I wore a badge, a "Ho Chi Minh pin," which they gave out to commemorate something—Liberation Day or something like that—but they gave them to everyone. Sure, I kept it, and wore it on my clothes, because I used the pin part, the sharp part, to take stickers out of my fingers and stuff like that. It was like a tool, a needle—there was a lot of bamboo around there and I kept getting slivers in my fingers.

PLAYBOY: You say you kept cooperating with the Vietcong because they were going to release you. When they didn't, why didn't you rejoin the other American prisoners in the compound? Did you even consider that?

GARWOOD: Yes, I did. I got very frustrated and very lonely. Especially the way they used me—kept making promises and kept evading my questions—the Communists did. Every time I'd bring up the prospect of being released, they gave me excuses: "We'll report to our superiors," "I'm sure it won't be long," "It may be in progress," even—stuff like that. And I was getting very depressed and very lonely, especially by what I saw down the camp—the life and the environmental conditions of the other Americans. It was getting really bad. The POWs were at each other's throats and—

PLAYBOY: There were approximately fifteen prisoners, correct? Of the fifteen prisoners in that camp, how many died?

GARWOOD: Approximately two-thirds of them.

PLAYBOY: How?

GARWOOD: The Vietnamese *let* them die. Of malnutrition and disease.

PLAYBOY: Do you think the Vietnamese could have prevented that if they had given them better food and better medicine?
GARWOOD: I feel that they could've, yes.
PLAYBOY: Do you think the Vietnamese saw that those people were ill and that they were dying?
GARWOOD: Definitely. You just didn't die overnight from that kind of thing. A week, two weeks or more—months. The Vietnamese always had excuses, you know. Saying it's so easy to die if a man wants to die, so let him die.
PLAYBOY: It's the weak who die?
GARWOOD: Yes, they said it's just so easy to die, here in the jungle.
PLAYBOY: So they didn't seem concerned about the health of the prisoners?
GARWOOD: Not to any extent. And this got to me. Because I visualized myself back in that compound and, damn, I could have gotten some illness and, like the other POWs, the same damn thing would happen to me. A lot of POWs were being put in the ground. It could have been me.
PLAYBOY: Were you getting better food, living where you were?
GARWOOD: No, I was getting about the same ration as the other Americans. But at certain times, I did—not from the guards or from the camp but because of my ability with the language; I was able to ask the *montagnards* when they came by. I could plead with them, beg them, trade them for anything like sugarcane or a banana or something like that, and sometimes they'd give it to me.
PLAYBOY: And were you able to steal from the guards?
GARWOOD: Many times.
PLAYBOY: Such as?
GARWOOD: Eggs, a chicken, anything. I would have stolen anything.
PLAYBOY: Were you allowed to leave the camp?
GARWOOD: Well, there was on instance when they took me into a village. They gathered the village people and gave a big speech—it was on a Vietnamese holiday. And they had me read a slogan saying the American people are in solidarity with proletariat Vietnamese people. Something like that. Then they ho'd three times and that was it.
PLAYBOY: They did what three times?
GARWOOD: They ho'd three times. Ho, ho, ho. For Ho Chi Minh, you know; it sounds like when we go hooray, hooray, hooray.
PLAYBOY: What other times did you leave the camp?
GARWOOD: I was on rice runs.
PLAYBOY: When did you leave that camp for the final time?
GARWOOD: I was gone for about two weeks on a rice run and then was ordered back to the camp, and the camp commander called me up and told me I would be relocated. I asked him why and he said that he didn't know but that I had made a lot of mistakes and I should think a lot and have some answers.
PLAYBOY: What were the mistakes, did he say?
GARWOOD: No.
PLAYBOY: Did you know?
GARWOOD: Well, I'd been stealing from the Vietnamese medics and guards. I'd steal from one guard's pack, put it in another guard's pack to create a disturbance among themselves. So when I'd steal something from the kitchen, the guards would suspect themselves.
PLAYBOY: So they considered you a troublemaker.

GARWOOD: Yeah, but they said it in harsher terms than just a troublemaker. Then this guy from the MCR-5—what they call the propaganda office—come down. His name, I believe, was Mic, and he started throwing a bunch of questions at me, asking if I didn't think I'd really pulled the wool over their eyes, shit like that. Then he said, "We know everything you've tried to do, but it didn't work." He said, "I don't know if you know it or not, but the other Americans distrust you very much, they really hate your guts—you don't think you've really accomplished anything, do you?" I tried to act innocent. But he told me to think about making a self-criticism. Then they moved me again. Uphill, very close to the propaganda headquarters.

PLAYBOY: Were there any other Americans there?

GARWOOD: Not that I could see. That day was the last time I saw Americans. It was late in 1969, September or October.

PLAYBOY: How long did you stay in that camp?

GARWOOD: Until 1970.

PLAYBOY: What was your function?

GARWOOD: Nothing, really. I didn't do a damn thing. Different people would come in and ask me questions—about the American POWs, who was their leader, who put me up to it—

PLAYBOY: Put you up to what?

GARWOOD: To stealing. And, also, what kind of information had I relayed to the other Americans? They wanted to know what kind of structure the American POWs had. They thought that there would have been a structure built and that I was aiding in the structure—by stealing and giving information.

PLAYBOY: What did you tell them?

GARWOOD: I told them that if there was any structure at all, I didn't know about it. Then Ho came and told me in straight out English that since the day I was captured, they suspected I was working for the CIA. So he says, "You think we're very stupid, don't you? You were captured driving a brand-new jeep, brand-new clothes, with a .45 and you're trying to say you're a Pfc. in the marine corps! We have your trip ticket. We know what a trip ticket is and we know what G-Two is."

And I just laughed and said, "I'm sorry, I think you're mistaken." And he says, "You slipped up the first time you talked to me—you said you were a chaplain's aide, and a chaplain is nothing more than a cover-up, a front, for the CIA."

PLAYBOY: What did they do with you then?

GARWOOD: Nothin', really. I was there until the middle of 1970, when the whole damn area was bombed by B-52s. I was wounded. I think practically all the damned camp was killed or wounded. I was unconscious—when I woke up, I was in, like, the dispensary. I had no clothes on at all and I was lying on the table, and they were bandaging my head and my back. The bomb fragments were in my back and in my head. I didn't even know the bomb hit, just like a big *blam!* I didn't see nothing else. I was deaf and I was almost blind. My sight was real blurry, but if you got close to me, I could make out, like, a face.

After three weeks to a month, my vision started coming back. They gave me injections to strengthen my eyes. But my hearing was bad and there was pus coming out of my ears. My wounds were starting to heal a little, but my body still hurt a lot. There were North Vietnamese troops in the dispensary, and when they saw me there, they started getting disgruntled and making complaints, saying they felt that it was wrong that they should have to receive the same medical aid and other things as an American—that's who they were fighting against.

So they moved me about five hundred feet from the dispensary to a really small hootch. I couldn't move. That was about the smallest thing they ever put me in. Then one day, they came to get me. It had been decided that I would be moved to North Vietnam, where there would be better medical care. I didn't say nothing, really. Whatever they said, I did.

PLAYBOY: What was your feeling at that point about the possibility of your release?

GARWOOD: Zilch.

PLAYBOY: So you went to North Vietnam in 1970. Did you travel on the Ho Chi Minh Trail?

GARWOOD: I don't know what the damn trail was. We called it the Ho Chi Minh Trail, they didn't. They called it the Strategic Trail or some shit.

PLAYBOY: How long did it take you to get there?

GARWOOD: Three months. Three months walking.

PLAYBOY: What happened on the way?

GARWOOD: My back was still banged up pretty bad, it had started getting infected and stuff, and they gave me some vitamin B-twelve injections along the way. One thing I noticed was they never let me rest at any of what they called the way stations. They always made me rest at either a *montagnard* village or a CP compound. Three months, walking all the way. My eyesight got a little bit better, but my ears, my hearing—you almost had to shout to me—I had a ringing sound like an ocean rushing and my ears were clogged up.

PLAYBOY: When you got to North Vietnam, what happened?

GARWOOD: They put me in a bus and moved me to a camp where I rested one day, and they put me in a military truck and took me to an army hospital. I remember the hospital was number five. They cleared out what looked like a damn storeroom—I'm sure that's what it was. They wouldn't put me on a ward, they put me in a storeroom. And put a bed in there. And they started treating my wounds. Eyes, ears, dysentery, back—I had a gut infection, all kinds of shit wrong with me.

PLAYBOY: How long were you there?

GARWOOD: About three or four months. Then they transferred me to the army hospital in Hanoi. Army hospital 108. Again, I was put in a small room—it looked like a damn prison section, but it's the ward where they keep all the people who have dangerous diseases—liver problems and chronic malaria, cholera, hepatitis—real diseases, I mean, killer diseases. They told me not to leave the room and not to talk to any of the patients. Every now and then, you'd wake up during the night, somebody was screaming—*"Aaagh!"*—they were going to die. It scared the hell out of me.

I was there till March 1971. When I got out, they came and picked me up in a Chinese type jeep and took me to a house—like one of those old houses way back that the Vietnamese landlords used to own. It had a brick wall built all the way around it. They put me on the upstairs floor and I remained there for about five or six months.

PLAYBOY: Doing what?

GARWOOD: Nothing. They just fed me.

PLAYBOY: Did you go out and walk around?

GARWOOD: Only in the backyard—it was really small.

PLAYBOY: Was anyone else there?

GARWOOD: There was an interpreter and a nurse and two security guards and one officer.

PLAYBOY: What did they interpret? Did anybody try to interrogate you?
GARWOOD: No, there were some officers who came down periodically and just checked on my health. I told them I was getting along fine. They brought a doctor about twice a month. He checked my ears and my eyes and my nose. I was in solitary there for about five or six months, and then a truck came up and they moved me to another location.
PLAYBOY: Who was there?
GARWOOD: Myself and the same people that was in the first house, the guards and the nurse. It was a house converted into a prison and all I did, I just sat around and listened to Hanoi radio. Just sat around on my ass.

Then my health came back pretty good. This was after almost a year in North Vietnam, and one day a jeep with two officers came up and I was moved to a camp at Sontay.
PLAYBOY: Sontay was where the U.S. military launched a raid to free POWs, wasn't it? The Sontay raid?
GARWOOD: Yeah. It was close by where I was. It was pointed out to me by the Vietnamese. They told me it was a very stupid American act.
PLAYBOY: Did they put you in prison in Sontay?
GARWOOD: No, they didn't—not actually in the prison. They put me about a mile away in the back of a mountain. They took me right through the city and, you know, as far as I was concerned, I didn't care if it was North Vietnam or not. It was the first civilization I'd seen in about six years and it flipped me out. I stayed in Sontay for a little more than three years.
PLAYBOY: Doing what?
GARWOOD: We had to grow our own vegetables.
PLAYBOY: You say we—who are we?
GARWOOD: Myself and the guards. We planted our own garden. That's what we did every day, just worked in the garden.
PLAYBOY: That brings you up to about 1974, right?
GARWOOD: Right.
PLAYBOY: By that time, there had already been the prisoner exchange. Did you know anything about that?
GARWOOD: Yes, a little bit.
PLAYBOY: How did you find out?
GARWOOD: Radio—Radio Hanoi.
PLAYBOY: What was your reaction? Didn't you think you were supposed to be released, too?
GARWOOD: I discussed it with the officer in charge when it first came up. This was before it actually happened. And they kept saying to me, "Nothing's been signed—wait until after the signing," always until after the signing. It was made known that there would be three groups—all prisoners would be released in three different time periods—A, B and C. And I finally came out and asked, "What group am I in?" and the officer, he just smiled and said, "You're not in any of them."
PLAYBOY: Did you ask why?
GARWOOD: He said, "I don't know. You ought to ask somebody else." He said, "You ought to ask my superiors."
PLAYBOY: Did you ever have a chance to ask his superiors?
GARWOOD: Yes, I did. It was just before the last release of POWs. They came to see me and the camp commander came over from the big camp. He asked what my

opinion was about the release and then told me, "This is a big cover-up by the U.S. government. You don't think we're going to fall for any of the U.S. government's tricks? We're not that stupid." He kind of had me baffled there for a minute. I couldn't figure it out. I'd heard it on the radio, there was going to be the exchange of prisoners. But now this guy is saying there wasn't. They would give names over the radio of the people, the POWs, so I asked him again, "When am I going to be released?" Well, he says, "You're in a different category." I asked what kind of category. He said, "We do not consider you a POW that has been captured." So I was a prisoner, a prisoner who was really not a prisoner—but I was.

PLAYBOY: Did you say what they considered you?

GARWOOD: He said they were still considering me some kind of spy, and they had not determined my status.

PLAYBOY: That was in 1973? And you stayed there in that little camp for—what?—another two years? After all the other American POWs had been released?

GARWOOD: Yes. And then, when they began closing in on Saigon, about midnight one night, a jeep came again and took me away, and I—wound up in Yenbay Province.

PLAYBOY: Where is that?

GARWOOD: That is way up north, near the Chinese border. It was very different. I was put into a very, very big POW camp.

PLAYBOY: Who were the other POWs?

GARWOOD: ARVN, Thais and Laotians.

PLAYBOY: Did they set you to work doing anything?

GARWOOD: Not at that point. After the fall of Saigon, the prisoners really started pouring in, thousands a day—every day. And then, right across the street, they started building this new camp and it was unique. They brought in bricks. They were building a damned house—like a house where the king would live. They built a wall around it and everything else and they built a watchtower like a miniature Alcatraz. And then they brought in dogs and I asked them, "Goddamn, what's going on over there?" They said, "Some very special prisoners are coming." A couple of weeks later, I was sitting there, just sunning myself, when three trucks pulled up and people started getting out and they all wore civilian clothes.

PLAYBOY: Vietnamese people?

GARWOOD: Yes. And they had suitcases and duffel bags and all kinds of shit. Some even had radios. I thought it was as weird as hell. I kept looking and then a couple of guards got friendly and we were talking and they pointed out that one over there is General Thi and that one is General Lam, and so on. I asked them "General of what?" They said, "The puppet army. We captured them in Saigon when we overtook the palace and we're bringing them here for reeducation." Then they took everything away from them. They confiscated everything, the radios, suitcases and all, and they issued their clothing like the clothing that they issued me.

PLAYBOY: Did you stay there in that camp?

GARWOOD: Yeah. It was getting close to 1976 now. I was beginning to think, you know, What the fuck am I going to do with the rest of my life? I might end up in Vietnam forever. What the hell am I going to do with myself, stay in this damned prison camp the rest of my life here in Vietnam or what? I had been there at the camp going on two years and it got to the point where they got a little relaxed. Once, I started talking to some of the villagers and I found out that this was the French prison camp from Dien Bien Phu and that the last French prisoners were not released until

1970—two hundred of them from that very camp. They were Moroccans, from the French Foreign Legion. Some of them even had families in the prison. They had married prostitutes. They were finally released in 1970.
PLAYBOY: So because of that, you didn't think your prospects at that point were so good.
GARWOOD: Exactly. I started thinking, you know, Jesus Christ, *they'd* been there since 1954 and not released until 1970—shit, that's almost twenty years. I figured if I've got to live this way, I might as well try to make my life easier. I'm just making my life harder this way. There was no way out.
PLAYBOY: You'd been captured for eleven years at that point?
GARWOOD: Right. Eleven years. I told myself, Jesus Christ, there is a possibility I'd be there twenty years or more, maybe the rest of my life. So I just thought to myself, Fuck it. The Americans have pulled out of here. I haven't seen no damned negotiations going on to find out if anybody is here or not, me included, and nobody has come to ask me, and I just felt completely deserted. I mean, wholehearted, totally, completely deserted. And my morale was low. So that is when I decided I would do *anything* I could to try to make my life easier in the camp, try to make it more comfortable.
PLAYBOY: What was your life like? Were you still guarded?
GARWOOD: Well, there were only two gates going in and out, but inside the camp itself, I was allowed to move freely as long as I didn't go within any of the small camps. I could move from my hootch to anywhere in the camp as long as I didn't go into any building without permission.
PLAYBOY: How did you eat at that point?
GARWOOD: I ate exactly what the guards ate.
PLAYBOY: Was there a mess hall?
GARWOOD: They issued me a mess kit and what I did was go down to the kitchen and I would give them my mess kit and they would fill it full of food and I went back to my hootch and I ate it.
PLAYBOY: How did you spend the evenings?
GARWOOD: The evenings? I'd sing to myself or play cards with the guards. They played, like, a Vietnamese poker—and solitaire.
PLAYBOY: Did they give you anything to read?
GARWOOD: They gave me some Cuban, Russian newspapers.
PLAYBOY: How about women?
GARWOOD: Taboo.
PLAYBOY: Did you ever manage to get around the taboo?
GARWOOD: I tried to and I got in a lot of trouble. It was back in '74, at the Sontay prison camp. The officer in charge of me had a wife. She was coming to visit her husband. She was in the army. Hell, all I did back then was masturbate. She came there quite often and she seemed to have a lot of sympathy for me. I could tell the way she talked to me and everything. She used to bring me candy. Her husband got on her case for it a couple of times. He was a lieutenant.

She was young, about twenty-four. Well, I immediately focused my attention on her. You see, at night, there was a couple of times I was left in that camp by myself with her, because her husband would go to meetings almost every night. I don't know what the hell the meetings were about. And the guards, a lot of times at night, they would take flashlights and they would go along the creek bank and catch fish and frogs and what have you, to cook in the soup, like a goulash.

The first night that we were left alone, I was scared. I wanted to, but I was scared. I knew all she had to do was just go up and tell somebody and they would blow my ass away or something. Then she made the first advance, she started talking, asked me about American women, you know, how American women kiss and how they make love, a bunch of stuff like that.

So I kind of got the idea what she was getting on to, but that first time I did not even attempt anything. But the second time, she was lying in the hammock and she took off her blouse, and then one thing led to another. I mean, hell, even if they blew me away, there was no way I could control myself. It was the first time in nine years I'd had a woman.

PLAYBOY: It must have been a strange feeling.

GARWOOD: Yeah. I went instantly. It was almost like a blink of an eye, really.

PLAYBOY: Did you see her again?

GARWOOD: Yes. When her husband came back, I was scared, because if he found out, he would blow me away in a second. Through all them years up until 1979, I was always scared, somehow he was going to find out and he was going to come back for me. But in 1975, I was transferred to the Yenbay camp and I never saw him again.

PLAYBOY: How else did you spend your time? Any sports?

GARWOOD: No, no sports at all. Basically, I just amused myself by trying to learn the Vietnamese language and culture so I could understand them better, so I could understand just what was coming down on me. It was one of those things that kept me from going really crazy.

PLAYBOY: Just how Vietnamized do you think you finally became?

GARWOOD: I always slept on a mat on the floor, I ate off the floor, squatted down like they did, drank out of old tin cups or bamboo shoots. When I started sitting in chairs again in the last couple of years, I'd get a backache.

PLAYBOY: At this point in the narrative, you were up north in that camp. How did you get back down to Hanoi?

GARWOOD: OK, it started in 1977. It had been two years since I'd seen any kind of civilization, so I just kept demanding, demanding, saying I would really like to go to Hanoi for just any holiday, so I could see some people, see some kind of civilization, you know. And they kept telling me that the security wasn't good enough, that it was very dangerous, that if anybody found out I was American—because the Vietnamese hate the Americans very much—my life would be in great danger.

This was always the excuse they gave me. Then, in '77, I got a real bad stomach ailment. They took me to the hospital in Hanoi, but I couldn't get in, they wouldn't check me in the hospital, and I had to stay in a house. It was about twenty kilometers from the hospital. I don't know how they found the house. I never inquired about it.

PLAYBOY: Who got the house? Whom were you with?

GARWOOD: Guards and an officer. Then they finally admitted me to the hospital in a special room that was away from the other people and I was treated. But I became very acquainted with these guards. They had never been in any kind of battle or anything and they came from pretty well-to-do families in North Vietnam. Just out of curiosity, they asked me, they said, "It would probably be pretty easy for you to walk into a hotel and nobody would ask you anything. You look like a Russian or a Cuban." Anyway, close to Christmas, they brought me to Hanoi and the officers, one lieutenant colonel, his name was Han, took me to a tourist hotel in downtown Hanoi for

Christmas dinner—which about flipped me out. And I found out, because I looked at the slip they had on the table, that it was a hotel just for foreign guests. I mean, they didn't have my nationality, nothing down there. Just foreign guest and the waitress joked with me like I was a damned Russian or Cuban or something. They explained that, you know, it was appreciation of the work I did and that I kept the machine running and all of that. They said, "Due to your progress, we have decided to treat you to a Christmas dinner." That was the first Christmas, anything close to Christmas, I had known in thirteen years.

Anyway, I excused myself and I went out. I went out among the other foreigners and nobody noticed me or anything and I just kind of wandered around and I stayed out maybe five minutes and then came back in. That's how easy it was. And I started getting a little brave. And so I got back with my guards and told them I was walking around all over the damned place and nobody said anything.

So we started talking and that's when the deal come up. One of the guards was a jeep driver. He was not actually a guard, he was a jeep driver and he says, "When you have the chance, do you like to drink beer?"

God, I hadn't had a beer in thirteen fucking years. "Do you like to drink beer?" I flipped out! I said yeah. He says, "Well, it's very dangerous, but we can do it if you cooperate." And, immediately, they were getting real friendly, buddy-buddy, so I just played along. The goddamned black-market racket was all it was.

The deal was they would take me to Hanoi, give me the money, I would go in the hotel and buy liquor, cigarettes and candy. On the black market, those were the most called for, and very, very high-priced. In return they would give me enough money to buy a pack of cigarettes and drink one or two beers.

So I played sick a lot and they'd take me to Hanoi and there were always the same guards when I played sick. They wouldn't admit me to the hospital, they would just give me medicine and I stayed in the same place about twenty-four hours and then I'd hop in the vehicle with the guards and go to the hotel and start buying shit. This went on until the time I got out of Vietnam. That is how I was able to pass the note.

PLAYBOY: The note that got you released. What happened that particular day?

GARWOOD: It had got to the point they were pretty relaxed. I think they thought that I wasn't so stupid as to try anything. Well, we went to the Victoria Hotel to buy the same commodities. As I walked in, there were four people sitting there eating their evening meal and I heard one man saying, "I'll be returning to Washington. . . ." It distinctly caught my attention, so I sat down at the first table. I listened to him talk. They had given me the money in an envelope and I took it out and on the back of it I wrote down, "I am an American. Are you interested?" And I wadded it up and I asked the guy for a cigarette and I dropped it in his lap.

PLAYBOY: You didn't say that you were a prisoner?

GARWOOD: At that point, I only said, "I'm an American. Are you interested?" And he got up and started to come over to my table and I got up the same time and motioned him over to the corner and he asked me some questions: "Are you afraid to return to the United States?" And I looked at him like he's some kind of a dumb shit or something. I said, "Are you crazy? Why should I be afraid to return to my own country?" So he didn't pursue that any further. He said, "What exactly do you want me to do?" I said, "I would like you to contact any American embassy or our U.S. military establishment and give them this note." At that point, he gave me back the note and I wrote down my name, rank and serial number and USMC. I said, "Just give them this and they'll know what to do." He says, "Where are you staying now?

Are you staying here in Hanoi?" I said, "No, I'm not. I'm in a forced-labor camp a hundred miles from here."

PLAYBOY: Who was he? Do you know?

GARWOOD: I know now. His name is Ossi Rahkonen. He is a Finnish banker or something, working for the World Bank.

PLAYBOY: How long was it after that episode that you heard you might be released?

GARWOOD: Approximately six weeks to two months. But almost as soon as I went back to camp, things started to change. Security got real tight, they wouldn't let me leave or anything. I figured, Oh, I screwed up. They found out. I'm in real trouble. My rations had been cut and conditions started really to become like they was in the mountains.

PLAYBOY: What was going through your mind about what might happen if they found out about the note you had passed? What were the worst possibilities?

GARWOOD: Well, I figured it would probably be a long, dragged-out interrogation—I don't know. It wouldn't be good, I was sure of that.

PLAYBOY: But, ultimately, the risk paid off. They let you go. How did that come about?

GARWOOD: They just come in one night and said to me, "You're going to Hanoi." They took me to Hanoi and put me in this little apartment, with four beds and a tiny table, and said, "You'll be meeting our commander soon." And the next day, they outfitted me with some new clothes—a damned tailor-made suit. I couldn't believe it. There seemed to be a lot of chickenshit stuff going on for the next few days, but the next thing I know, I'm getting on the Air France plane.

PLAYBOY: Stepping back from it all, how do you remember those fourteen years in Vietnam?

GARWOOD: They ripped my guts out. Actually, if you talk about human existence, there's not much of that left in me right now. They did that to me. They took fourteen years of my life away from me, and I've got no compensation for that. Even that I'm back in the United States, it seems like everyone's trying to put the brunt of the whole Vietnam War on *my* shoulders—not on Ho Chi Minh and all the Communists, or whoever the hell was responsible for it. All I know is I spent fourteen years in Communist prisons, and I would have gladly exchanged triple that time for any American prison, I'll tell you. And what did I do wrong besides putting on that uniform and going to 'Nam and trying to uphold what this government told me to do? My life has been destroyed, my family's life has been torn apart. It's just going to be nightmares until the day I die.

PLAYBOY: How do you feel about the Vietnamese people themselves now? What is your gut reaction?

GARWOOD: I'll tell you something. My heart, my soul burns, it aches. I'm more mature now, but still I cannot look at an Oriental without picturing myself trying to strangle or kill him or torture him in some way.

PLAYBOY: How do you feel about the marine corps at this point?

GARWOOD: I have no animosity toward them.

PLAYBOY: And you really feel you did nothing wrong?

GARWOOD: The only thing I really regret is that I might have thought about the other person more. I was young and there was a lot of confusion, but I wasn't ready to lay myself on the line—not to the extent where I thought I would be killed. To this day, it bothers me. Maybe I could have helped more, even if it had meant putting my ass on the line. I was in a better position than the other POWs, so I might have helped.

PLAYBOY: Aside from legalities, just looking at it morally, do you feel you've done anything that you should be ashamed of?

GARWOOD: No, I don't. But that's something that I'll probably be asking myself the rest of my life: Could I have done more? I saw eleven Americans die over there and it disturbed me, because I always felt that I could have been one of them. When I think back on it, this business about me deserting, or crossing over—it was a mixture of fear, revenge, survival, complete frustration. I had no one to turn to, no one to seek advice from. It was a situation that I never thought I could be in, and suddenly I was in very deeply and I didn't know to get out. I was just trying to survive.

PLAYBOY: How *will* you survive for the rest of your life, now that the court-martial is over and you've been dishonorably discharged?

GARWOOD: I went through so much shit in the past sixteen years that sometimes I want to give up and say the hell with it, you know. Just out of total frustration, isolation. When I was there, there was nobody to turn to, nobody I could talk to, nobody to give me advice, tell me what to do. I was completely cut off from the outside world and the years were just going by, and it seemed like there was no end. I was like some damned vegetable or a tree. They didn't give a shit. Every now and then, they'd water me and that was about it.

So, right now, I actually feel very fortunate, because I am still alive to this day, when I could very well have been dead. I'm thirty-five years old. You know, how many more years have I got in my life? I have no foundation. I have no wife or children. No job experience, career to look forward to. I guess there's still a few years left in my life before I reach forty. Maybe I can get some schooling, try to get some kind of a profession. You know, the first thing I did when I returned to the States was to get a haircut and put on a marine uniform. I didn't carry no placards, no antiwar demonstrations. I was very proud that I was accepted by the marine corps. And I have no animosity whatsoever toward the corps. Whatever happened during the past sixteen years was just a sequence of circumstances that were unavoidable. I thank God that I'm still alive to tell about it.

ORIANA FALLACI

November 1981

Interviewer: Robert Scheer

Oriana Fallaci's reputation had preceded her. Yes, she was perhaps the most famous—and feared—interviewer in the world, in addition to being a novelist and a political activist of great acclaim in Europe. But she was also supposed to be hell as an interview subject: vain, fiery, and domineering. It was therefore something of a surprise to Golson that the Italian-accented voice on the telephone was so friendly and personable.

Fallaci was quick to agree to a PLAYBOY interview, saying that she was an admirer of the form and that Golson's choice of Robert Scheer as interviewer was acceptable to her. Hadn't he been the one who had interviewed Jimmy Carter and Jerry Brown for PLAYBOY? That would make for an interesting combination. *Ciao.*

This was Fallaci's only understatement. Golson was looking for sparks when he introduced the two journalists, but later Scheer described the encounter as more like "throwing two Bronx alley cats into a gunnysack and letting them have it." Within an hour of Scheer's first meeting with Fallaci in a New York hotel room, Scheer was in Golson's office, exhausted, and Fallaci was on the phone to him, complaining that it would never work out.

The stalker of Kissinger, Khomeni, and Qaddafi was herself being stalked by a journalist who refused to be bullied. Scheer collected the requisite war stories, but then began to press hard on Fallaci's romantic defense of terrorism and anarchy, and then asked her to justify some of her more extreme examples of journalistic license. Conversations turned into screaming matches, and Fallaci threatened to halt the proceedings repeatedly. One time Fallaci said she was through, *basta,* but agreed to get together for a farewell luncheon with Scheer that Golson would host. After a bottle of wine, Fallaci was somehow convinced that she should attempt to finish the interview, and the two drove off together, muttering.

So much for process. The result, in the opinion of many journalists who volunteered opinions, is a classic encounter. It is an examination of what happens when the tables are turned on a skilled interrogator, and what was published has a great deal to say about news and literature and life. At the convention of managing editors sponsored by the Associated Press late in 1981, one speaker called this the best interview *ever* published. That is probably too much praise, but it is certainly one of the most memorable in PLAYBOY's history.

The Playboy Interview this month is with a woman who has done much to advance the interview form as a powerful journalistic tool—and, some might add, weapon. Oriana Fallaci is unquestionably one of the world's most provocative journalists, known for having exposed some of its most powerful and intransigent political leaders. She has a considerable following as a writer of both nonfiction and fiction, with her latest work being the international best-seller A Man, *a moving and deeply felt novel based on her lover, who was a hero of the Greek Resistance during the Sixties. But it is her interviews with the world's leaders, including the Ayatollah Khomeini, Henry Kissinger, Teng Hsiao p'ing, Yasir Arafat, the shah of Iran, and Muammar el-Qaddafi, that have made her famous.*

Fallaci often has been described as outrageous, brave and committed, and in almost every instance, her interviews become memorable bits of theater. She refers to her interview subjects as "those bastards who decide our lives." Elizabeth Peer of Newsweek *described her technique as follows: "She bullies, baits, charms and harvests disclosures of stupefying indiscretions from statesmen who ought to know better." One of those statesmen was our own Kissinger, who confessed to Fallaci that he pictured himself as a "lone cowboy entering a village . . . alone on his horse." This was widely interpreted as the definitive indication of Kissinger's massive ego, and he later described his hour with Fallaci as "the most disastrous conversation I ever had with any member of the press."*

Fallaci's political commitment—which she describes variously as "individualistic" and "anarchistic"—dates back to her childhood in the Italian Resistance during World War Two. Born in 1930, as fascism began to sweep across Europe, Fallaci developed an intense political consciousness that now is always with her. Here is not the objective or neutral reporting typical of American journalism but, rather, a series of encounters between an intensely opinionated interrogator and powerful men and women.

Her formative years were spent in a circle of anarchists-socialists-idealists in her native Tuscany, in which her father was a leader. After the war, she pursued a classical education, which included some years in medical school, but she dropped out to make her family some money as a journalist. To Fallaci, journalism always is a battle, if not a war—and she feels that way about life itself. This formidable woman has, in the course of her battles, produced three novels, five works of nonfiction and numerous articles and interviews, which she sells herself to Life, The Washington Post, The New York Times, *and newspapers all over the world. In the process, she has made news almost as often as she has reported it, rendering her an important participant as well as a pioneering journalist, which is precisely why* PLAYBOY *wanted to know more about her.*

Getting to know Fallaci and exploring her political and personal views turned out to represent a task as formidable as the woman herself. In the past, she has been known to lecture and intimidate reporters who attempted to ask her the sort of questions that she presumes to ask others. On one occasion, she had asked a New York Times *reporter to place off the record a personal detail of her life, but when it was published on the basis that it had already appeared elsewhere, Fallaci was outraged. When the* Yale Daily News *ran an unflattering picture of her, she refused an interview the next day with that paper, which prompted the college reporter to observe, "It's sad to see a person who writes about the use of power abuse it so blatantly."*

Obviously, a certain fortitude would be required in a reporter sent to put Fallaci through the long hours of give and take that go into a Playboy Interview. Our choice of Robert Scheer, a writer for the Los Angeles Times *was natural. Scheer is known to our readers as the man who conducted the famous Playboy Interview with Jimmy Carter, as well as those with Jerry Brown and John Anderson. Conservative journalist William F. Buckley, Jr., wrote a column last year likening Scheer to Fallaci, saying, "He can catapult an exchange into the shouting stage quicker than anybody since Huey Long." Just the sort to take on one of the irresistible forces in modern journalism. Scheer's report:*

"Our interview sessions were always on edge. Of course, in Fallaci's eyes, it was I who interrupted, while she just tried to inject a note of reasonable enlightenment, as befits a cosmopolitan Northern Italian. But if you ask me, it was the other side of her Italian temperament that emerged more frequently. There were frequent temper tantrums and just plain scenes. They began at the door to my room at the Drake Hotel in New York, when I first greeted Miss Fallaci with what she felt was insufficient good cheer and soon included the bellhop who took too long to bring her cigarettes. In fairness, her outbursts also embraced political topics about which she

feels passionate. Because her feelings were so often aimed at me in particular, rather than at the PLAYBOY *interviewer in general, I've retained the first-person flavor of those exchanges.*

"The interview sessions weren't all antagonistic. Fallaci is intelligent, well traveled and informed, and there was much in the way of profound and even occasionally brilliant commentary. But the mood was often hostile, and for the first time in my life, I found myself feeling sorry for the likes of Khomeini, Qaddafi, the shah of Iran and Kissinger—all of whom had been the objects of her wrath—the people she described as interviewing 'with a thousand feelings of rage.' I found myself feeling sorry not only for the subjects of her interviews but for mine as well, because the brute fact of the matter is that we do dish it out better than we take it.

"An interviewer must do many things to force a valid question that requires an answer. And Fallaci has her own well-practiced methods. She once said she stalks interviews as 'pieces of theater with a story inside.' Time *quoted her as saying, 'I make scenes, I yell and scream.' That's fine as a technique for breaking through the obtuse answers of a hack politician. An interviewer can defend bad manners as an effort to get at a larger truth, but when the tables are turned and one becomes the subject of the exercise—and I have been there myself and made a mess of it—then screaming can be nothing more than an effort to avoid the point of a question rather than answer it. As Peer observed of Fallaci, 'She can also bristle at any suspicion of criticism—a touchiness that is downright hilarious in someone so quick to attack.'*

"All of the above is by way of an explanation for the combativeness one will find in this interview. But enough of such carping. While it is true, as Fallaci admits, that she lives life at a shout, and while that may make for brittle dinner companionship, she is rarely boring and always on. This last quality, along with huge globs of conviction about almost any topic—from the correct path to revolution to the correct path to the perfect pesto sauce—has made her one of the world's most important journalists and a fascinating interview subject. But I'm not going to say I loved it. This was the first assignment I've done for PLAYBOY *over a ten-year period for which I feel I was underpaid."*

PLAYBOY: You're best known for the tough interviews you've published with some of the world's most powerful men and women. Let's start with possibly your most famous interview, the one with Henry Kissinger, in which he compared himself to a lone cowboy riding into a village by himself.

FALLACI: Don't let me speak about Kissinger again. It was in 1972, and they still persecute both of us because of it. I mean, even if we got married, we would be persecuted today over this point!

But as to the interview, it's a pity. He lost an opportunity to become my friend. He should have had the courage to stand by what he said. Instead, he said he regretted doing it.

It was only fifty minutes, and I thought it was a very bad interview. *My worst interview!* I almost did not publish it. In fact, everybody was surprised at the indulgence and tolerance I demonstrated toward him during the interview. But I do these interviews to understand the person, to study how power takes place. And I had not the time with Kissinger. I think, though, if he had not been so concerned with immediate success during his four years with Nixon, he would have gone down in history as one of the greatest American secretaries of state. I mean, the opening to China was real, historic, and it was him, not Nixon, who did it.

PLAYBOY: And his morality in the conduct of the Vietnam War?

FALLACI: Kissinger is beyond morality. The word would make him laugh. Men like him are amoral.

PLAYBOY: Who are other people like that?

FALLACI: Stalin. Nixon was *im*moral, a different thing.

PLAYBOY: What about your impressions of the Ayatollah Khomeini?

FALLACI: It may be a banal word, but the simple truth about Khomeini is that he is a fanatic. If you read my interview, you see that Khomeini is intelligent, unlike Arafat or Qaddafi. To me, a fanatic is *necessarily* an unintelligent person, but I must admit he is the one example that breaks the rule. I had thought to find an idiot, but I found a smart man. I began a question about fascism, comparing the people of Iran to the Italians under Mussolini, and the more I said, the more I thought, Oh, damn, he's not even going to know what I'm talking about, this complicated concept of fascism. But he knew. He answered me very well, he quoted Aristotle, he interpreted fascism in the Western sense. But then, of course, when I interrogated him about executing women for prostitution, he got very, very angry.

PLAYBOY: Your most famous moment with him came when you threw off the Moslem veil, the *chador*, and offended him. Why did you do it?

FALLACI: Because *I* was angry! You know what he said to me? God! I was wearing the thing, all seven meters of it, pins everywhere, perspiring, and I began to ask him about the *chador* as a symbol of women's roles in Iran. By the way, Bani-Sadr was translating from Farsi to French for us. So Khomeini says, "If you don't like the *chador* don't wear it, because the *chador* is for young, proper women." Bani-Sadr, the bastard, was laughing as he translated. I said, "Eeeeh! Will you repeat that?" I was reacting very strongly and Bani-Sadr was caught by surprise. "Ask him again!" I said. So Bani-Sadr whispers something to Khomeini, and he turns back to me and repeats the same thing. So I rip the veil off and I say, "This is what I do with your stupid medieval rag!" Khomeini had seemed so old and dignified, but when I did that, he jumped up like—have you seen those kung-fu movies, how quick they move?—like a cat, and disappeared. I remained sitting and called after him, "Where do you go? Do you go to make pee-pee?" Bani-Sadr was very frightened and said, "No, no, no, you must go. He has left."

I remained sitting there and said, "I don't go. I only have half an interview, I will not go." So I sat there for two or three hours—that was my strategy. I knew they couldn't touch me. When Bani-Sadr came to plead with me to go, I said, "You cannot touch me. You are Iranian, your religion says you cannot touch me. I'm going to stay until he comes back." Later, Ahmad, Khomeini's son, came in and said, "Please madam, you must go." He came back four times, four times, and finally he was desperate. He said, "If he sees you again tomorrow, will you go now?" By then, I needed to go pee-pee myself. "Ahmad," I said, "if you get him to swear on the Koran, I'll get up." So Ahmad went away for the fifth time, then came back and said, "Return tomorrow." I said, "He swore on the Koran?" "Yes, yes! Tomorrow at five."

Well, the next day, Khomeini did come in. I look straight at him and say, "Now, Imam, let's start where we left off yesterday. We were talking about my being an indecent woman. . . ." And Khomeini did something very interesting. You know, he never looks you in the face; he always looks at the floor, eh? Well, he looked straight back in my face with an amused smile! It was cute, because he couldn't laugh. So I continued, "Would you say that a woman like me, who had to sleep next to soldiers in combat in Vietnam, is an indecent woman?" And he says, "I don't know. *You* know what you did with the soldiers." It was so funny! Of course, I got angry again with him.

PLAYBOY: Of course. You also interviewed the shah before he was overthrown. How would you compare the two men?

FALLACI: The shah was not stupid, but he was less intelligent than Khomeini. Less politically shrewd. But in the matter of religious fanaticism, they were alike. I don't know why none of his other interviewers extracted this side of the shah's character—except for me. His religious obsession.

PLAYBOY: Religious obsession?

FALLACI: Yes; the shah entertained me for at least a half-hour out of the five or six hours we spoke in telling me about his visions. He said he actually *saw* the saints and prophets, that he spoke with them. When I wanted to make fun of him and said, "You mean you could shake hands with them?" he said, "Of course." I said, "If I am there with you, can *I* see them?" He said, "Of course you cannot. I can, because I am the elected one"—and blah-blah-blah. Well, this kind of stuff was also in Khomeini. I remember thinking the two or three times that Khomeini raised his eyes to me—they were also the eyes of the shah! They were opposite faces of the same coin.

PLAYBOY: After Khomeini, you were going to interview Bani-Sadr during the hostage crisis while he was still president of Iran, right?

FALLACI: Yes, he had interpreted for me and Khomeini and knew me well. I got a visa again, in spite of the fact that I was warned not to go. After the Khomeini interview, an Iranian newspaper had written something violent against me and published a photo of me that was torn in half. So, in a country where fifty percent are illiterate, all you have to know is that your photo has been published torn in half to be an enemy of the people. They know what it means. The people at *The New York Times*, who were sending me, were very nervous.

Well, I flew there and immediately was detained on the airstrip in Tehran. "You have no visa," they said. "What is that?" I said, point to my name. "That is *my* fucking name!" "So what?" they said, and started pushing me into a police room. So I started shouting, "You bastards!"—the kind of play I always do when I find myself in that situation. Usually, I count on the fact that my shouting will get them so tired they finally say, "Go away, go away."

Anyway, a man from the Italian embassy finally got me to my hotel. I keep myself hidden, because I don't want other journalists to know I'm in Tehran; otherwise, it happens, the same old story—Fallaci is here, etc. I finally get an official at the foreign ministry who ignores the fact that Bani-Sadr has promised me, in writing, an interview and calls me and the Italian government a nest of liars.

Then, a day later, I get a call warning that my life is in danger. It turns out that Bani-Sadr has given in to the militant students and is a total coward about seeing me. So I try to call Italy, to call the president of Italy, in fact, and they cut off all the lines. "Until when?" I ask. "Indefinitely," they say. So I went to another telephone and called London—which wasn't cut off. I dialed the first number in my telephone book, Ingrid Bergman's. I woke her up with the call and I said, "Ingrid. I call you from Tehran. Call Pertini [president of Italy at the time] and tell him I'm in trouble. *Ciao.*"

Ingrid was very smart. She got to the right people and they finally got me out and into London. Two days after I'm back, Bani-Sadr is in London for an economic meeting and he sends a message to me through my ambassador. "Psst. Tell Miss Fallaci that I ask to be forgiven, I really couldn't do it. There will be a next time." I just said, "Fuck Bani-Sadr. There will not be a next time. I will never grant him an interview!"

PLAYBOY: Before that, there was your interview with Qaddafi, which you've already mentioned.

FALLACI: That one was truly scary. Qaddafi is clinically sick, mentally ill, a certifiable idiot. You cannot deal with him. He made me wait three and a half hours outside his offices in Libya. He sits in the center office of his palace, surrounded by four or five circles of protective barricades, like German checkpoints. It's like entering a spiral. There are dozens of people standing around with machine guns. After the first hour, I wanted to go make the pee-pee, and I was stranded alone with my photographer in this huge library, but they didn't come to escort me to the bathroom. So I got infuriated—

PLAYBOY: Of course.

FALLACI: And I picked up this 1964 copy of *Who's Who*—the library was filled with books Qaddafi never read—and threw it against the wall to express my rage. Finally, Qaddafi came.

PLAYBOY: When did you become convinced he was insane?

FALLACI: You should listen to my tape. For ten minutes, ten full minutes, he is yelling, like a broken record, "I am the *gospel,* I am the *gospel,* I am the *gospel."* It's terrible, because he never stops, never stops. His face—his face is so out of this world while this is going on that I nudge my photographer to take the picture then. But the photographer was so scared he couldn't move his hands, and the interpreter was trembling, too. Finally, I interrupt him, which I almost never do and I said, "Stop! Stop! Do you believe in God?" That was the most surprising question I could put to him and he looked at me and said, "Of course; why do you ask that question?" I said, "Because I thought that *you* were God!"

He raised himself up and I thought, *Mamma mia,* good-bye, it's over. Whoever finds us again? Because he could do it. You know what happened to the manager of Alitalia in Libya? He just disappeared. Well, Qaddafi looked lost and confused for a moment, and then the interview went on and I knew I would not be arrested. But he *is* insane. He is obsessed with the color green, you know.

PLAYBOY: Green?

FALLACI: Everything around him is green. His handkerchief, everything is green. As we were sitting there, I picked up something—I forget what it was—that happened to be green, and something must have happened in his consciousness. He looked like he was going to strangle me. So I said, "Would you like it? Do you want this?" I gave it to him, and he took it. Immediately. He wanted it *so* much. He should be under the care of a psychiatric doctor. Dangerous, dangerous, dangerous.

PLAYBOY: Qaddafi is a good-looking man, isn't he?

FALLACI: No. They had told me that he was a good-looking man. I don't know, in the photos he looks better. But when you see him, he has this very stupid face. No matter what are the features, when the person is stupid, stupidity shows. He has very little, little eyes. In the photos, they are bigger. Then he has this enormous chin, enormous! His head is very narrow, because he has very little cerebral inside, very little. He is repellent. I have a physical hate for Qaddafi.

PLAYBOY: The reason I asked about his looks is that when you interviewed Arafat, you made a lot of his being short and ugly and having an obese stomach. And I wonder whether that is fair.

FALLACI: I don't care if it was fair or not. I didn't like Arafat. I think that Arafat is a phony!

PLAYBOY: Because he has an obese stomach?

FALLACI: No, no, no. That contributed to make his physical portrait.

PLAYBOY: You wrote about Golda Meir as if she were beautiful, yet by some standards she was ugly.

FALLACI: She *was* ugly, but I didn't *see* her ugly. Intelligence makes people beautiful.

PLAYBOY: But what is interesting is that when you talk about "ugly" Arafat, you say you are sympathetic to his cause. But Golda Meir, whom you describe sympathetically, is someone whose politics you reject.

FALLACI: Her Zionism, yes.

PLAYBOY: Why do you reject Zionism?

FALLACI: For the same reason that I reject the Catholic ideology and other ideologies. That is our fight in Italy against the Christian Democrats and the intervention of the Church. The theocratic state.

PLAYBOY: Why, when you interviewed Meir in your lengthy, friendly interview, did you not ask her one challenging question about Zionism?

FALLACI: You protest because I made *my* interview and not yours. I did not ask her the question *you* wanted, all right.

PLAYBOY: You wrote about the "fundamental justice" of Arafat's cause in the introduction to your interview with him. *Are* you sympathetic to his cause?

FALLACI: I understand his cause. Is it an answer? I understand his cause. And let's put it like this: I understand the cause of the Irish and I sympathize with the Irish. I understand the cause of the Palestinians. And I stop here because of several reasons that involve me, that mitigate the firmness of that judgment, for personal reasons and for political reasons. As everybody of my generation who is European, and particularly Italian, I cannot accept the blind hate and the contempt toward Jews. In the Resistance, we hid many of them. But it does not make me a crazy anti-Jewish person to say I am angry at the Jewish people for many things.

PLAYBOY: What are you angry at the Jews for?

FALLACI: For many things. If you want to take the example of America, how they hold the power, the economical power in so many ways, and the press and the other kind of stuff. . . .

PLAYBOY: You say that Jews control the media in America?

FALLACI: Well, you see Jewish names as directors of TV and newspapers. The owners, the directors, I never realized how it happened and how they came to control the media to that point. Why?

PLAYBOY: That's not true. Jews by no means own the media.

FALLACI: But listen, at *The New York Times,* they are all Jewish.

PLAYBOY: *The New York Times* is owned by an old German Jewish family that was even anti-Zionist at one point. Sure there are some Jews who are prominent in some papers. But you can go to most newspapers or the networks and find that that doesn't hold up. That's a European perception and it's just not true.

FALLACI: It is not true?

PLAYBOY: No.

FALLACI: OK.

PLAYBOY: Getting back to the subject of Arafat, what else didn't you like about him?
FALLACI: Arafat meets me with his automatic rifle, as if to say, "You know, with this rifle, I fight the enemy! I have just come from the combat." He didn't come from the combat! *Others* had been in the combat! And they were dead! . . . You know, I was told that he got married. I don't believe it.
PLAYBOY: In the preface to your interview with Arafat, you implied that he is a homosexual.
FALLACI: Yeah. Everybody knew it. Everybody would tell you. I don't imply it. He had at that time the most gorgeous young man I have seen in my life. He was a German. So handsome and so gorgeous and even behaved in a funny way with my photographer. He was a very handsome man and he never looked at me. He looked at my photographer. He was provoking him. He was doing things like that [licking her lips] and he was looking at him.
PLAYBOY: This smacks a little bit of character assassination. You admit that you couldn't come up with anything in the interview. You really couldn't get Arafat. So, in your introduction you get into personal attacks. You wrote: "His teeth are the teeth of a wolf."
FALLACI: What do you want to do? What do you want to do with me because I don't like Arafat? I don't like Arafat!
PLAYBOY: What if the introduction to this interview said Oriana has crooked teeth?
FALLACI: Let me see what I have written. [Reads from her collection] It is funny. It is amusing. It is amusing.
PLAYBOY: You wrote, "His fat legs and his massive trunk with his huge lips and swollen stomach." That's pretty tough stuff.
FALLACI: What do you care? Is he your friend?
PLAYBOY: I'm suggesting you didn't nail him in the interview, so you went a cheaper route. You wrote that it was an "unsatisfactory" interview because you couldn't get anything out of him.
FALLACI: Yeah, because he had nothing to say.
PLAYBOY: Not necessarily. For instance, he made contradictory statements. He said at one point, "We have to liquidate Israel!" Then, in another part of the interview, he said he has nothing against the Jews and he is *for* a democratic state.
FALLACI: Yeah.
PLAYBOY: Why didn't you ask him how he could be for both?
FALLACI: Because I had little time. You know how much it lasted? One hour. It was very short. When you have little time, you let them talk and you think you catch them later. But I never caught him later. I couldn't—he went away. He left with his beautiful, handsome German blond.
PLAYBOY: You sound as if you have a contempt for Arafat *because* he is a homosexual. Is there something about homosexuals you don't like?
FALLACI: They don't like *me*.
PLAYBOY: Why?
FALLACI: Maybe because I'm more manly than they are. I irritate them—I don't know.
PLAYBOY: You're more manly?
FALLACI: I'm—if we get lost into that subject, I am going to say something which makes me very unpopular. I don't know if I should look for other enemies; I have so

many already. But I'm not crazy about them, the homosexuals. You see them here in New York, for instance, moving like this [makes a mincing gesture], exhibiting their homosexuality. It disturbs me. It's . . . I don't know. Do you know the ones who have the high heels and put powder on and go to Bloomingdale's hand in hand, and they *squeak*?

PLAYBOY: It makes you nervous?

FALLACI: No, it doesn't make me nervous; I just can't stand them.

PLAYBOY: Heterosexuals can also be exhibitionists. They don't offend you in the same way?

FALLACI: Heterosexual means men that go with women?

PLAYBOY: Yes, or women with men.

FALLACI: Listen, here we get into the word *sex*. It's so boring. Anybody who makes an exhibition of sex, who makes exploitation of it, disturbs me. With PLAYBOY, I cut out the interview and sometimes other articles and I put them in the guest rooms of my country house because people are very happy to find them when they come in summer. It disturbs me to see all the nudity. It's like going to buy three pounds of steak. It is not puritanism, it's just a matter of aesthetics. Honestly, I mean, you at PLAYBOY are so liberal on certain things and you are so illiberal in the use of the naked women. Sometimes, to clear your conscience, you include also some naked men, but that disturbs me just as much.

PLAYBOY: To find sex boring says something about you; most people find it exciting—and most men seem to like the pictures in PLAYBOY.

FALLACI: It's boring for me. Listen, have you a PLAYBOY magazine here? Please, give it to me. I show you how boring it is. [Begins thumbing through a recent issue] It's always the same thing. I find *Vogue* much more interesting, because I like dresses. But this [points to a picture of a Bunny] is even aesthetically ugly. I shall never understand this uniform. I detest uniforms. Whether it is the military uniform, the uniform of the priest or the uniform of the Playboy Rabbit-Bunny, OK? And it makes this woman ridiculous.

PLAYBOY: The way you find homosexuals at Bloomingdale's ridiculous?

FALLACI: Listen, I don't want to be unfair to my homosexual friends, because I have a couple who are friends, whom I like very much, as they are very pleasant people, they're intelligent persons. But there is a form of fanaticism in them, of dogmatism, of exhibitionism, of Mafia sense, all what I despise. I mean, why should I reject it in political parties and accept it in the homosexual party? They *are* a party.

PLAYBOY: How are homosexuals a party? Or a Mafia, as you put it?

FALLACI: Listen, I should say this in Italian. When I'm tired, my English becomes lousy. This sense of comradeship which exists among, for instance, certain sporting people, or certain followers of an ideology, like the Communists. The Communists among themselves, whatever language they speak, they feel brothers. It's the sense of the parties, the strength, the real sense of the party. The homosexuals are the same. But theirs goes beyond the comradeship. It's kind of Mafia, and when they get together, for instance, in the artistic field, they are terrible, much worse than the members of a political party. Terrible, they use it, they're very strong. And I do not want to be obliged to love them. It's enough to let them live. I live my way, they live their way, to hell with it. But don't oblige me to love them.

PLAYBOY: The obligation is not to love homosexuals. But since you advance a conspiracy theory of homosexual life, and you liken them to the Mafia or to the Communist Party, you should be obliged to defend that.

FALLACI: It's a form of Mafia.
PLAYBOY: So defend that.
FALLACI: Tomorrow.
PLAYBOY: It's not to make you love them; it's making you be fair, making you be accurate.
FALLACI: Tomorrow I'll tell you.
PLAYBOY: You don't like being worn down in an interview?
FALLACI: I'm tired, I'm tired. Tomorrow I promise I'll do it. I'll elaborate tomorrow.
PLAYBOY: Have any of the people you've interviewed said to you, "Oriana, I'm tired of talking to you, I don't want to talk anymore"? Would *you* accept that?
FALLACI: I have never talked so long with the people. I never make an interview so long. Never!
PLAYBOY: Why is your journalism so consumed with politics?
FALLACI: I was always very political. You must understand that I made my first political rally when I was fourteen. I remember in Florence in the square outside the Palazzo Vecchio where the Medici lived, it was full of people and there was some rally, I don't know why, and they wanted to exploit me because I had been the key to the Resistance, etc. I remember very well how I was dressed. I had a dress in squares, red and white, and I remember this microphone and I remember the first words, because after, I was caught by terrible panic and I said, "People of Florence, it's a young girl who speaks to you! Listen to us young people!" And then I don't remember anything, nothing, nothing. I don't remember anything because I must have been talking or reading in the state of shock. I don't remember anything but "People of Florence"—and I loved it!
PLAYBOY: Who was exploiting you?
FALLACI: I was participating in the assembly of the Action Party, a kind of socialist party—an anarchist party that my father and brother belonged to. It was a very tiny party, where they were all generals, no soldiers. I guess I was the only soldier, I was so cute, and I wanted to stay with these people because they were all men and women of great culture, intelligent people, clean people, selected people who had been able to stand against fascism in prison. So I was drinking their words.
PLAYBOY: How politically active was your father?
FALLACI: My father was a craftsman, and during the Resistance he had been the military chief of the Action Party for Tuscany. And he belonged to the Central Committee, he was one of the leaders. Then my father disappeared. He had been arrested and was under torture for many days.
PLAYBOY: Where was your mother?
FALLACI: My mother had the guts to face the head of the Italian SS, who was a very famous torturer. He received her and said, "*Signora,* you can dress yourself in black. He will be executed tomorrow morning at the parterre." And my mother raised her arm and said, "All right, I shall dress myself in black, but if you are born out of the womb of a woman, you'll tell your mother to dress *her*self in black." And he said, "*Signora,* get out of here, I will arrest you, too." And she got out, very dignified. She was pregnant and she took her bicycle and she started on the bicycle and she lost the child in the street. That was a very fantastic story of my mother; she was a very tough woman, very sweet, though. If you saw her, you would say, "Oriana, you call this woman a tough woman?" My God, she was the symbol of what you call femininity, yet she was so tough.

PLAYBOY: How old were you then?
FALLACI: Twelve or thirteen. I was already working in the Resistance; everybody gave me orders, you know, all these big people. I was like a messenger, you know, those boys who bring the coffee, and they yell, "You do this, go buy a Coca-Cola." The problem is they didn't ask me for a Coca-Cola or for a coffee. They gave me, for instance, a hand grenade. "Take this hand grenade, go and take it to the group so and so." And I had to decide how to do it. For instance, for the hand grenade I had smart ideas; I was an intelligent kid. I hid the grenades in heads of lettuce.
PLAYBOY: How long was your father in jail before they let him out?
FALLACI: It was a few months.
PLAYBOY: They didn't kill him?
FALLACI: No, the Allies were coming up. It was clear the Fascists had lost, and they wanted to show some magnanimity; a certain lieutenant said to him, "I let you go, I know who you are; when the moment will come, remember that I let you go." I have seen so many things at that time. You know, when I speak in this country and they ask me, "What is the mark of your life?" and I say, "Resistance," I say it and I feel that they don't understand what I mean. But I really was a child of the Resistance.
PLAYBOY: The Resistance was a male environment; how did that affect your relationships with your mother and other women?
FALLACI: My mother was the *only* woman in my life. The influence that my father exercised on me was political in the full sense of the word, but also my mother, because she was a very good anti-Fascist, too. But in life itself, she influenced me much more. The talks with my father were political talks—democracy, socialism, fascism, Nazism, liberalism, Christian Democrats, the Republicans—all that. The facts of life I discussed more with my mother, even indirectly. For instance, it was my mother who put it in my mind that I should go to work. All mothers said, "When will you get married?" My mother never cared about that. She said, "When will you go to work?" I remember my mother, and I'm standing up in this bed, and she's crying and she says, "Don't do like me. Don't ever, ever, ever be a wife. Don't ever, ever, ever be a slave to a husband and children. Don't do it. I want you to go to work and I want you to travel the world and I want you to be independent. Go far away. Fly! Fly! Fly!" And she cried. That day was fatal to me, fatal, because I must have paid very much attention, maybe because she cried and her face was over mine; I have never forgotten those words. See? And she always pushed me in that sense. About marriage. When people ask me, "Why did you never get married?" I don't know how to answer, because it never occurred to me to marry anybody.
PLAYBOY: So you are a loner.
FALLACI: Oh, yeah, no doubt about that.
PLAYBOY: And you're also not happy if you're not on the edge.
FALLACI: You're right, you're right.
PLAYBOY: You seem to impose this context of a world undergoing perpetual resistance on everything you do. Is your vision the only way to look at life? Must it *always* be within a resistance?
FALLACI: You are telling me—or are you accusing me—that I make a war out of peace in any circumstances of my life, including work? Well, there might be much truth in it. The fact is that I regard life as a war. If you read [my book] *Letter to a Child Never Born,* the very first page, it portrays me very well. I say to this embryo within me, "Life is war, dead child." I describe life to this embryo to make him decide if he wants to be born or not, and I do it in such a way that the poor kids says, "To hell

with you, Mother, I'm not going to be born." Later in the book, there is this fantasy trial in her imagination, and she's condemned, and the one who condemns her is the child, who says to his mother, "How did you introduce life to me? Did you ever tell me that life can be sweetness and serenity and peace and the beauty of a kiss and an ice cream? You never did, you always told me terrible stories, fantastic stories, war stories, and why the hell should I be born to come into that?"

If I wanted to make me more sympathetic, I would try with all the politics I'm capable of to mitigate this, but then I would contradict myself. The truth would come out all the same, and so I am this. Besides, I'm always tired, I'm tired because I always live in tension. All I know is the war; I never knew the peace. I was born in the war, I grew up in the war, it was my school and here I am; it's a great limitation. I know at this point of my life to change is too late. I should have tried at least twenty years ago.

PLAYBOY: This insistence that life be lived on the edge runs through your latest book, *A Man*. Let's discuss the book's hero, Alekos. As an opponent of the Greek colonels' dictatorship in the Sixties, he resisted torture bravely but died some years later. He was clearly a man of courage, but he seemed to care for nothing but his revolution. By your admiration for him, you seem to imply that anything other than the great drama of life is inconsequential—

FALLACI: Number one, the man in this book and who really lived is contrary to what you say. If you had that impression, you are one of a tiny minority. I don't take you seriously for one moment when you say that. Number two, since I respect even the opinions I don't agree with, then if I gave you—or two or three other people—that impression, then I'm ashamed. Because Alekos was the contrary. What he was—he could not be blackmailed. He could not be blackmailed! Now, *I* can be.

PLAYBOY: Because you care about someone.

FALLACI: He did, too, for Christ's sake. You are unfair to this man!

PLAYBOY: In the book, there's not a single moment in which he feels responsible for another human being—not even you. He seemed to say he had a nobler goal than most people and any means could be sacrificed to it.

FALLACI: Can I answer now?

PLAYBOY: All the answers you want. The magazine can't publish every word we say, of course.

FALLACI: One second. If you don't publish my answers, then it's not an interview.

PLAYBOY: No publication can print every word of every interview. They're edited, of course. Don't you edit your interviews?

FALLACI: I published everything they tell me. Of course.

PLAYBOY: Every word?

FALLACI: That's why they're so long.

PLAYBOY: Then we'll have to direct this interview very tightly; we'll have to cut you off to stay on track.

FALLACI: You don't let *me* talk!

PLAYBOY: Go ahead.

FALLACI: I started to talk about repetitions in an interview. Obviously, sometimes you make people repeat something to be sure they meant it. For instance, when I interviewed [Polish Solidarity leader] Lech Walesa, he said if the government of Poland fell, Solidarity would go *into* the government. I was so shocked I asked him to repeat it. I said, Lech, I don't want to harm you, because what you said was dangerous, the Soviets will be reading this. By the way, he said more than that: He said not only would Solidarity go into government but he should become president. Since he is such a simple man, it was his way of expressing it. I said, Excuse me, Lech, I'm not going to write that you said you should become president, because you would be killed in a week. I'm not going to do that. And he said, OK, don't write it. So I asked him twice again if he meant that Solidarity should govern, and he said yes. Now, of course, I didn't include my three interventions in the published interview.

PLAYBOY: Why not?

FALLACI: [*Angrily*] I'm not capable of doing it! Listen, you are—you are too tyrannical. I'm tyrannical, too. We cannot go on. We can't go on like this!

PLAYBOY: As you said in your interview with Walesa, "I ask the questions." You're not conducting this interview.

FALLACI: This is not an interview, this is a fight.

PLAYBOY: Let's establish that if we go off on a tangent, if it adds nothing, if it's boring, we'll edit it out. I certainly don't have the authority to say that anything that comes out of your mouth will automatically will be published.

FALLACI: No, not all of it is good—not what I say and even less what I write.

PLAYBOY: Now, to get back to the theme of your book—

FALLACI: Yes, but you're hurting this man and it makes me very angry! You make me feel as if I give the wrong portrait of him. If I did, then I be damned.

PLAYBOY: What you say throughout this book is that his life defines the way a man should live. He resisted the dictatorship, he revealed nothing under torture. But, at the same time, he considered bombing the Acropolis to dramatize his point, he talked about taking American tourists as hostages. And you seem to endorse that.

FALLACI: It is obvious that I admire that man, or, if you prefer, that kind of man. If I didn't, I wouldn't have spent three years of my life with him or the three additional years it took to write the book about him. I admired that kind of man before knowing Alekos—for me, it came during the resistance to the Fascists in Italy. I like him, I like all men who resist. My father did it. Two others who were arrested with my father—one did, one didn't. When the one who didn't resist told me, ten years later, oh, I wanted to spit in his face. Oh, I do admire that kind of man. I do, I do, I do, I do! It is because of people like that that the world moves. I'm not a Marxist, you see. Marxism says it is movements, not individuals, who make the world move.

PLAYBOY: But to try to stay on the subject, what about the problem of means and ends? To consider kidnapping innocent American tourists in order to resist, that's a form of terrorism, and it's an important subject in the world today. . . .

FALLACI: OK. See, when talking like this with Americans, I feel a tremendous gap, something that divides us. I say this in sincerity and friendship, because I stay in the United States, nobody obliges me to; if I stay, it means I like it. But there is this void between us. We have different cultural perspectives. My concept of politics and everything is the experience I had as a human being, and the main experience I had in my life was the Resistance. I always go back to that. But you Americans don't *know* what that was, the Resistance. You see it in movies and in books, bad books, usually. So you will not understand when I say, "Yes, yes, under a dictatorship, you can take hostages, yes, you *can!*" For you it is monstrous. For me it is not. The French would agree with me; a German, a Russian, a Belgian, a Dane; not a Swede, maybe. But *you* will not! So the dialogue becomes impossible. You could also ask me, Why kill an eighteen-year-old German in 1945? Why? Was he responsible? I say to you, No, he wasn't responsible. So you kill him? I answer to you: Yes, I kill him—crying, but I kill him. And this is monstrous to you.

PLAYBOY: First of all, you have a condescending view of Americans, and that comes out in the book as well. You write, "America is made up of the rejects of Europe." That isn't true. Many of the people who emigrated to America were the most adventurous, and it was an adventure to come to this country. It was the most energetic of the Chinese who somehow ended up in San Francisco and to this day, it's the most energetic of the Guatemalans who crawl through barbed wire and somehow get to Los Angeles. But as far as the question of terrorism and hostages goes, I suspect the average Irish or French citizen would share my reaction to your view: It's not just that a hostage is different from a soldier, but there's a frivolousness with which revolutionaries consider taking hostages—and lives. It's as if the people to be used by revolutionaries weren't really living, human beings.

FALLACI: When I speak to you about this, I feel like when I speak to my little sister Elisabetta. And it makes me recall what Willy Brandt told me during our interview. He had the same problem with his children. They didn't care because they had not experienced what he had. So, in the same way, you are like the children of Willy Brandt and like my sister. You did not experience it, you do not have it in your consciousness. It is not an accusation. It is a fact.

You use the adjective *frivolous,* and it is gratuitously offensive. There were *not* frivolous episodes, I tell you. For Alekos *was* concerned about those people. I am talking about one part of him, you about another. When I asked him, "What does it mean to be a man?" he gives me an answer and asks me, "And for you, what does it mean to be a man?" I say, "Well, something like you, Alekos." His answer, what he means, is he's just a man; a man is a man when he is human, with all his frailties and limits and guilt and mistakes—and also beauties.

PLAYBOY: But you don't present him as just a man; this was your lover, the man you admire, you hold up to the world—

FALLACI: My *brother!* I prefer the word *brother* more than lover. Lover makes you think something like PLAYBOY, making jumps in the bed. No, he was my brother—

PLAYBOY: But he *wasn't* your brother.

FALLACI: Oh, yes, he was.

PLAYBOY: With all due respect, he was a man you gave in to, you were used by—

FALLACI: No, I was his accomplice.

PLAYBOY: Because of him, you took risks you didn't believe in. You went along with things you thought were crazy; you wrote that you thought maybe he was mad. You went along like some teeny-bopper, some sorority girl. You did what lovesick groupies have always done: You went along with *his* plans, no matter what you thought for yourself.

FALLACI: Look, if tomorrow you have a plan to kill Qaddafi, I come with *you* and follow you in the same way. Following Alekos' plans to resist the dictatorship is the same thing I did when I was a little girl with pigtails. I entered the Resistance as a kid and was discharged as a soldier. Let me tell you this episode; it will explain to you why I was not the slave of Alekos.

My work during the war, as you will find in any book about the Italian Resistance mentioning my name—and my *nom de guerre* was Amelia—was to accompany American and English prisoners who had escaped from concentration camps in Italy. I guided them to the Allied lines because it was a bargain we made with the Americans. The Americans would supply us with ammunition and other things we needed, but they wanted their prisoners back. You know . . . it seems that has been the problem of the Americans for the past fifty years of history—they wanted the Americans back from Italy, they wanted the Americans back from Vietnam, they wanted the Americans back from Iran.

So . . . what I did countless times, all alone as a kid, was to accompany Americans on my bicycle for sixty miles, and we saved many Americans and English and South Africans in that way. There is no need to tell you how dangerous it was, because anyone found in contact with an escaped prisoner would be executed immediately. And my mother was always frightened by this. My father, who did not live with us, because he was hiding, didn't tell her after the first couple of times I went. It was crazy at the time—to go past German roadblocks with men who spoke only English. I'm used to participating in something that might be crazy or not! I didn't feel used by Alekos!

PLAYBOY: But the point you make in your book—

FALLACI: I was like a sergeant following the lieutenant.

PLAYBOY: The point you make in your book is that Alekos was an example of other men around the world who resist authoritarian power. It's like a prism for everything you believe about courage and politics and life itself. It seems as if you're saying that the real test of a man is the courage to resist torture, to resist institutional power. The test of a man is never being a reformer, making the world marginally better. It's never being a parent, diapering a baby. You seem contemptuous of anyone who takes *small* steps. That comes out in your interviews: The people you are interested in are big political figures, they make history. Anything else in human experience doesn't seem to interest you.

FALLACI: OK, one thing at a time. About whether the test is diapering a baby—no, it is not the test, because that would be another book. I wrote *this* book, not another one. If you want that test, read my *Letter to a Child Never Born,* where the heroine is a woman and the test she has to face is of another kind.

PLAYBOY: Is that a test a man could face?

FALLACI: I let you talk when you put your very long question-accusation. Now you let *me* talk! I cannot do like this, because if you interrupt me, you do not want my answer! Why did you become a journalist and not a prosecutor-general?

Of *course* this book doesn't deal with the problem of diapers! I don't give a damn about the diapers of a child, because it was not the work of the character of the book. He had no children to wash anything for! The accusation, which was the real point you wanted to get to, is that I only deal—let's see if I understand it right—with exceptional people, I only care about people who do not belong to the crowd. Well, it is true and it is not true. It is objectively true, since all I offer to you is interviews with these people, and in this particular case, a book about such a man. It is not true if I recall to you that I do not make these interviews, or write this book, for those men—but for people who wash the diapers. To wake them up. To tell them, in the case of the interviews, who are the people who decide our life and death. Not necessarily bad people. Some are OK. Some are not. To tell them, in the case of this book, how much they are manipulated and how they are crushed in the preciousness of their individuality. How they must refind that individuality, because, as I say over and over, everybody is somebody. I don't know if it is good English.

In any case, I offer the extreme example of this man—extreme because I am not like him. I only write for the others as a moral commitment. I suffer when I write. It doesn't amuse me. I expose myself. I already told you I admire that kind of man; so what? Am I to be condemned? Yes, yes, I might be a little obsessed with courage. Something happened to me in my life—a trauma—when I was a little girl. The trauma of fascism and the trauma of resistance. This has marked my life, morally and culturally, and I cannot change it. I must be taken for what I am.

PLAYBOY: Then because of that, we should accept everything you say?

FALLACI: No, you should not. If you accept everything I say, you do the contrary of what I preach.

PLAYBOY: So those of us who didn't participate in the Italian Resistance cannot challege that view? What I am challenging is your view of courage. Individual acts of terrorism may be courageous, but don't they just alienate people and end up being self-defeating?

FALLACI: I feel helpless in talking to you, because even if you were a more tolerant interviewer, I feel as if I'm speaking Chinese. Take the Palestinians, for example. I feel they have no right to put a bomb in a bus with twenty-five schoolchildren—and I tell you that Alekos would never, no, never put such a bomb under a school bus. I would like you to recall that he never killed anybody, and the only violent act he did in his life was to put a couple of bombs that did not explode. What he did in Greece was to kill the tyrant, so to speak, which he did very well. And if I were courageous, I would do also. If I were courageous as he was, I would have killed Qaddafi when I interviewed him. I would have had the guts to die killing Qaddafi—but I didn't.

PLAYBOY: Who else among your interview subjects would you have killed?

FALLACI: Many others.

PLAYBOY: Which others?

FALLACI: I shall not mention anyone I have not yet been able to interview. I am not that stupid.

PLAYBOY: But which of the ones you *have* interviewed would you kill?

FALLACI: Let me think. Qaddafi for sure. I think it's a shame Qaddafi dies in his bed. Oh, God, if I had had the guts to do it! I should die with him, of course. Let me see. . . . You asked me for names; I'm a serious person, I'm not going to shout names like that. You probably expect me to say Khomeini, but I shall not. . . . Idi Amin, for sure, but I have not interviewed him.

PLAYBOY: That attitude may make good copy, but it also puts all journalists into question. Any time we interview someone, does that person have to fear he's going to be killed? Do you think we have the right to intrude this way?

FALLACI: To intrude in what sense?

PLAYBOY: To make history. You'll make history by killing Qaddafi.

FALLACI: No. I'll be protecting my life. He is a murderer. He is the man who helps the Red Brigades in Italy, who helps terrorists around the world, who wants a nuclear bomb for Libya. There are not many cases of absolute, personal dictatorships in our times like Qaddafi. I would say that was the case with Hitler. And I would think it was a tragedy for humanity that the attempt to assassinate Hilter failed.

PLAYBOY: But that doesn't really answer the question.

FALLACI: I didn't get a chance to *finish* answering! I never have the time to answer. Listen, *you* would make a very good dictator.

PLAYBOY: Calling me a dictator, what is that supposed to do? Make me say, "Sorry, I'll stop"? Is that to intimidate an interviewer so you won't get pinned down?

FALLACI: No, it's because I don't get a chance to answer. It's impossible! Let's just go have lunch instead of doing this interview.

PLAYBOY: Look, from the very start, you've taken offense that anyone should challenge this vision in your book of what courageous political action is all about. When I've raised questions about that, you've said it was because I'm an American, or I

didn't live in the Resistance, or I'm an egomaniacal interviewer. The fact is, many people have profound questions about this topic, would agree with my challenges, and you're just refusing to meet the questions head-on.
FALLACI: You're not attacking me. You're attacking him, Alekos. And I'm thinking, Oh, God, Alekos is dead, he cannot answer—
PLAYBOY: But it's not he, it's the idea we are talking about—
FALLACI: Please! Please! Please! [Screaming] You see? He doesn't let me talk! *Dio mio,* he doesn't let me talk!

[The interview was broken off at this point and resumed the next day in a more subdued atmosphere.]

PLAYBOY: It seems as if some people need perpetual revolution. . . . They need crisis, they need to think the world is falling apart; they're not happy if they don't think that fascism is coming or we're on the barricades.
FALLACI: I don't belong to them. I am more moderate than you think. I do not think that everything must be destroyed. On the contrary, I think there is much to preserve, to renew, to remake, to try to make better, to change, but not to destroy, in any field. I'm not Attila. When I see that in New York, you destroy those old buildings—for instance, an old hotel—I suffer. If you translate it into politics, it tells you something.
PLAYBOY: Still, you seem always to live your life as a shout, as if you were still at a rally, crying, "People of Florence!" whether you're getting a taxi or demanding to change a table or complaining about the wine. . . .
FALLACI: You're right—so what? You're right, I have nothing to answer. It's true. I've never been serene in my life. If you put me on a shore, of Acapulco or the Caribbean, beautiful shores, with this blue sea and the sky and the palm tree, and you say, "OK, Oriana, now you rest, take a rest for a week, come on, stay there in the sun," I might stay half an hour and then I begin to think, What a bore, nothing happens here. You say, "What do you mean, nothing happens? You have the beautiful sea, the beautiful sky, and what else do you want, pineapple juice with the rum inside?" And you give me the pineapple juice and when it is finished, I say, "What do we do now?" And you say, "Be quiet." I need things to happen.
PLAYBOY: Yes, you do. And it's obvious you love theatrics. You always make a scene at an airport or in a restaurant. You made a scene with Khomeini. But you know what you're doing and why, don't you?
FALLACI: I have a professional example which will please you a lot and which goes against me. When I was interviewing [Chinese leader] Teng Hsiao p'ing in Peking and he said something about Stalin, I let him talk a lot of time. But when it was over, I didn't take it. I felt the need to counterattack him. I said, "But Stalin"—and we got involved in a discussion so long about Stalin and it was such a waste of time, and Teng said at a certain moment, "Listen, let's do one thing." He was so cute; he said, "You remain of your opinion about Stalin and I remain about mine and we'll go on with this interview." And I said, "Yes, but that huge portrait of Stalin that you have in Tien An Men Square—why do you still have it up there?" That was around the end of our first encounter, which took place on a certain Thursday. I saw him again on Saturday and that morning, on our way to the Great Hall of the People, we passed through the square and I look up and there's no more Stalin! I couldn't believe my eyes.

When I entered again the Great Hall of the People, in this large room full of members of the government, I pulled another scene: My interview with Teng, it was not a private thing as we do now, or as I always do with the people I interview, but there were also TV people, newspaper people, photographers. I was *very* angry at Teng! I said, "I don't want them to stay here, the interview is mine, they are listening, they are going to steal it!" So he kept the government men and the photographers, but he sent away the newsmen. He was very nice, he was very cute.

PLAYBOY: By the way, do you think that a man could have gotten away with that?

FALLACI: Honestly, it might have helped, not only the fact that I'm a woman but that I'm a *small* woman. The point is that Teng, too, is very small; he's even shorter than I am.

PLAYBOY: You say it probably helped with Teng that you were a woman. What if a woman were interviewing *you?*

FALLACI: [Refers to an unflattering article written about her by an American journalist] When that fat woman reporter—do you want to know what is my problem when women interview me? If they are fat, be sure they will be nasty.

PLAYBOY: Why?

FALLACI: I don't know—maybe because I'm *not* fat. When they tell me how slim I am, I think, Oh, *mamma mia,* oh *Dio, Dio,* now I know she's going to write something against me. It's the story of my life in every country.

PLAYBOY: You really have a problem with women, don't you?

FALLACI: You see, it's the fact that I grew up among men. The only women I was familiar with were my mother and sisters. But outside the family, in the intellectual world, it was all men. So in school, in the Resistance, as a reporter, there were no women at all, just men. I never learned the art of dealing with women.

PLAYBOY: How do you get along with feminists?

FALLACI: I'm sick and tired of them. I used to say in the past that the biggest revolution of our time was the feminist revolution. I said it for a couple of years. Until they started breaking my balls and became really unbearable. It is their victimization that disturbs me. I think it's like a dictatorship: If you accept it, you deserve it. A dictator never becomes one if the people are not scared, silent cowards.

PLAYBOY: How did they start breaking your balls?

FALLACI: They don't treat with me anymore, they ignore me, they punish me. When *Ms.* magazine received the manuscript of *A Man,* they said, "We are not interested." So now I'm exiled, which is good, because I don't want anything to do with that fanaticism. It's fanaticism once again. What feminists really wanted me to do was stand up and say, "Look what I have accomplished in spite of all the men who were so nasty to me. . . ." I mean, I am living proof of the contrary. When you choose a few examples of women who did it in our time, you have to choose me, too. I'm not Joan of Arc and I'm not Catherine of Russia and I'm not Golda Meir. But I am one of those who succeeded. And they wanted me to say I had done it through my own heroism, in *spite* of men. But I said, "No, it is not so. It *helped* me to be a woman. It helped a *lot!"*

Two things have helped me—to be born a woman and to be born poor. They were the things that pushed me, pushed me. I have said that if my name were Orian*o,* if I were a man and had been born the son of the Duke of Marlborough, I would probably be a fucking idiot, because I'd have nothing to fight for. Plus having the temperament I do, it has made more news that I was a woman. If I had been Oriano writing the same things, maybe I would have been more slowly or less known. So the fact is that being a woman has helped and the feminists got angry. I said that I was sick of their victimization, always crying, "This happened because I'm a woman." I say, "No, it happened because you are no good, not because you are a woman."

PLAYBOY: So you've never been held back by "male-chauvinist pigs"?

FALLACI: I have always been uncomfortable about that—there is much truth to the issue of male-chauvinist pigs, but *I* have not been experiencing it. I must say that I have received in my life, from any point of view—including those who write about me—much more nastiness by the women than the men. If you find a nasty article about me, be ninety-eight percent sure it was written by a woman. Well . . . or by a homosexual.

PLAYBOY: That certainly brings up a familiar topic. What is it about you and homosexuals?

FALLACI: I remember once when I took my mother to London for the first time in her life. We were in front of Westminster Abbey and we saw these two workers, laborers, kiss each other on the lips. She almost fainted. She said, "Ccchhh. Is that what you always speak about, Oriana?" I said yes, so what? But no, I couldn't imagine two laborers kissing each other on the lips, making love. Those Bloomingdale's types that I cannot stand, or the homosexuals in Arab countries—it makes me sick. I can't imagine a homosexual in *any* position. When they swagger and strut and wag their tails, I can't bear them.

PLAYBOY: You, who claim to detest power and to root for the underdog, obviously associate homosexuality with weakness. You mentioned earlier that they don't like you because you're more manly than they are, so the implication is that they're weak and frivolous people.

FALLACI: No, I told you there are a few exceptions. I have very few friends among them, but, as the Latins say, it is the exceptions that prove the rule. When they love me, they love me madly, but most don't at all. And I never understood why, but lesbians hate me much more. The only lesbian who is nice to me is Kate Millet. She always sends me unbelievable artworks—from pornographic or lesbian exhibits, all that kind of stuff. I said, "Kate, why do you send me those things?" She said, "It's good." "It's *ugly,*" I said. Anyway, she's the only one who likes me. Yeah, they don't like me, thanks God.

I'm very happy that lesbians don't like me. I'm not so happy that [male] homosexuals don't like me, because, after all, they are men, and I like men better than women. See? Eh. I live well with men, that's the problem. Of course, in the field of love, you can be hurt by men, but you hurt them *also,* for Christ's sake!

PLAYBOY: But why do homosexuals make you cringe? You were physically recoiling a moment ago.

FALLACI: No, don't exaggerate. I don't care. They can do what they want. It's their exhibitionism that disturbs me. There is a very nice homosexual here in New York and I see him rather often and he is cute. Polite, intelligent and delightful. I would like to travel with him. Ooooo, I could go on holidays with him. How beautiful! You want to know why? So I have a man next to me and he doesn't bother me at night. He doesn't ask me anything. How cute. Cute.

PLAYBOY: Why don't you want to be bothered at night?

FALLACI: Because if you travel with a normal man, there is always a moment in which he may be attracted a little, make a gesture, and I say, "Oh, leave me alone." That will never happen with a homosexual.

PLAYBOY: You still haven't answered the question: *Why* are you so repelled by homosexuals, or by their exhibitionism, if you will?

FALLACI: I don't know. It's like seeing the beauty of the male body—and you will admit that the male body is much more beautiful than the female body—
PLAYBOY: No, I won't.
FALLACI: Oh, come on. There is no comparison! The Greeks understood that very well, for Christ's sake! And when homosexuals swagger—
PLAYBOY: You've never seen a female, a heterosexual female, swivel her hips?
FALLACI: I was trying to tell you, but you didn't let me say it! The male body has a different dignity than the female body. When the male swaggers it breaks the harmony, it hurts the dignity. It disturbs me. . . . You want me to think like you! You are doing to me what I did to Teng Hsiao p'ing, when he upset me and said I should remain of my opinion and he of his—and get on with the interview.
PLAYBOY: As long as you admit I'm not doing anything to you that you haven't done yourself as an interviewer.
FALLACI: But I was speaking of *serious* things when I fought with Teng. He liked Stalin! But you, you cannot bear that I am not in love with homosexuals.
PLAYBOY: Just rounding out the portrait, Oriana. You have a certain idea of maleness, and that connects to courage, to strength, to power—your field of study. Besides, you have a fascinating view of sex. What was it you said about it? That you found it boring?
FALLACI: Yes, it's boring. I have a friend, a very handsome and intelligent man who has many women. And he says, "Sex is an activity for porters."
PLAYBOY: For porters?
FALLACI: Yes, because all the blood goes down toward the legs, and the intellectuals, we need it in the head. It is not for us.
PLAYBOY: So assuming that even intellectuals occasionally have sex, what sort of man attracts you?
FALLACI: To love a man, it must be a courageous man. Once I was on NBC, doing the *Today* show to promote my book, and we got into a discussion of love, because Americans saw in the book a love story. So after a lot of talking, I became impatient and said, "Damn it! Don't you understand what I say? I'm saying I cannot love a fascist!" It had a great success, this thing. They loved it very much.
PLAYBOY: What about sex with a man who is not a fascist but whom you don't love, either?
FALLACI: That is my business. You will not come into my bedroom, I tell you.
PLAYBOY: You used the word *fascist* in this regard. It strikes me, in thinking about the Moral Majority, that it was the Fascists—and today the Communists—who were the most puritanical, who suppressed "sinful" behavior and homosexuals—
FALLACI: Yeah, the Nazi leaders, the hypocrites—how often they were homosexual! My God, damn it, what hypocrisy!
PLAYBOY: But one of the reasons PLAYBOY and others oppose the Moral Majority in this country is that those people equate their version of moral behavior with the good of the state—and that has elements of, if not fascism, authoritarianism.
FALLACI: Ah, you are putting up PLAYBOY as an opposition paper, eh?
PLAYBOY: Well, what do you think of the trend toward mixing puritanical religion and politics?
FALLACI: Maybe in America, not in Europe, thanks God. Churches are empty. Don't pay attention to those who go to St. Peter's Square—they are tourists.
PLAYBOY: But if America is where social movements start, Europe will catch up sooner or later and you'll find a similar revival of religion in state affairs.

FALLACI: That's not possible. History never goes back. No, no, no, no!
PLAYBOY: History is going back in America today.
FALLACI: Well, we make fun of you. I mean, in a country where the President of the United States, whoever he is, every time he opens his mouth, he has to mention God—well, my God! I mean, not even the Pope does that. It will never happen in Europe.

You know, Italy, in particular, is a pagan country. They are not religious. Maybe about half believe in God, but our Popes never believed in God. They forgot about it. You want to know how this new Pope, Wojtyla, was elected? When the other one died, all the Italian cardinals, they got together and said, "Hey! Any of us around here believe in God? Eh, Guido, you believe in God? No! Luigi, *you* believe in God? No! You over there? No! Well, we still got two countries where they believe in God—Ireland and Poland. Try Ireland first. Telephone lines all busy? Ho-kay, try Poland. Hallo, Wojtyla—you believe in God? You do? *Benissimo,* you come down to Rome, be our new Pope." This is a true story, Fallaci tells it to you.
PLAYBOY: Good story. When did *you* stop believing in God?
FALLACI: When I was twelve. I had very mixed feelings. What I said was, "I *don't* believe in God. Oh, my God! What will God do to me if He finds out I don't believe in Him?" That was my approach. But over the years, I find out it was sincere. I have the test that I don't believe in God. When I was covering the student riots in Mexico in 1968, I was badly wounded and had those three bullets in me—one here, one here and one here—
PLAYBOY: In your back, your side and your shoulder.
FALLACI: Yes, and I was losing blood, and I was fainting, not knowing if the fainting was death coming. I remember two things very clearly. I remember seeing my country house in Tuscany, which is very beautiful, like a Leonardo da Vinci panorama, and from my house you see these hills and mountains and the cypress . . . I saw all that. And I remember that I never thought of God. The concept didn't come to me, I didn't ask for help from God.
PLAYBOY: Did you come to these thoughts on your own?
FALLACI: I told you that half of Italy is pagan. In our house, our anticlericalism was so profound that our dog, each time the town church bells did dingdong, he got angry and was barking. Once, the priest came to our house to reproach us. He says, "No one is coming to church." My mother was ironing. She put the iron down hard on the board and she said, "*Priore,* don't come here to teach me life. Teach it to others. My family will always sow the good seed, because it is what it is. Good morning, *Priore.*"
PLAYBOY: When you mentioned nearly dying, you seemed almost resigned, fatalistic.
FALLACI: I love life. I mean, life is all, the only point of reference. So I am in love with life . . . but I'm very tired. I am tired inside. And when you see me do these things, you say, "That woman, how full of life she is!" But it is a kind of show I do with myself to fight the fatigue I have inside.

It started in 1976 and 1977, when they both died—Alekos and my mother. It was traumatizing. Something happened in my soul. You know, when you break a leg, the doctor comes, he puts the plaster on the leg, people come to visit and put the signature on the cast and say, "Poor Oriana, does it hurt?" Or you have a toothache: "Poor Oriana, did you go to the dentist?" But if you say, "God, I'm sad, I'm *so* depressed," people go, "Ahh!" They do. They do not take you seriously. So I always try to hide this broken leg of my soul, this broken teeth of my soul. Because people wouldn't understand.

But the more I have it, the more I live with it. And if you ask me, "What is the word you think most about during your days and nights?" I will say, "Death." Always. I calculate how many years, how many days remain to live for me. Twenty? Twenty-five? I say, "Eech, my God, they are few!" And the more I think, the more I adapt to it. If people do something nasty to me, I get very, very depressed. I'm very vulnerable. My vulnerability is equal to my strength, my so-called toughness, and when I'm down, I sometimes say, "Let death happen." But not suicide. It would be necessary for me to die in a decent way, with dignity—*for* something.

PLAYBOY: It's interesting that you admit to vulnerability, because the thing most people would associate with you is arrogance—as you've said, you sometimes use that professionally.

FALLACI: Yes, people think that I'm arrogant in a certain way. It is not arrogance. It's being uneasy—and not shy. It's a matter of uneasiness and a kind of . . . fear. Professionally speaking, it is, yes, yes, yes: fear, fear, fear. And this comes from being alone. My mother used to describe me as a very severe child—severe and isolated. I never played with the others.

PLAYBOY: It's hard to imagine you as a carefree child.

FALLACI: I wonder if I ever was. There is a story about my doll which will tell you. The Fascists in Italy would sometimes give out dolls to the kids, etc. I brought my doll home and my mother said, "Ahhh! What's that? A Fascist doll?" And she threw it out the window. Years later, when I was sixteen, I became a reporter. With my first paycheck, I gave most of the money to my mother, because there was need, but I reserved a small amount for myself. And with this money, I went to buy a very large doll. When I got it home, I gave it to my mother, because it was too late for me. She remembered my first doll and cried, and kept it for a long time. Today it is in my country house, dressed in red velvet.

PLAYBOY: Every time you mention your background as a sixteen-year-old girl, competing equally with men both in your profession and in the Resistance, you seem to be emphasizing how hard you had to fight to prove yourself. Is it too trite to suggest that is a battle you're still waging?

FALLACI: Well, with the Resistance, in particular, yes, it was my first great adventure. It was accompanied by fear, but it was a noble adventure. So I have been brainwashed, conditioned to love adventure, which explains so many things—including my encounter with Alekos, because he was the symbol itself of adventure. Today I make an adventure out of everything. And my interviews, which were once great adventures, are no longer a professional challenge. Let's admit it once and forever: I am more dedicated to my writing than to the interviews, because they are so easy for me. I *know* already what makes the interview—I don't know if I should say, because someone will try, stupidly. I cannot really explain it, except to say that they go beyond the tape recorder—its the *way* I conduct them. They are pieces of theater. I prepare the questions, but I follow the ideas that come. I build the suspense, and then I have *coups de scène,* do you understand? But they are very fatiguing. Do you believe that in some two-hour interviews I have lost weight? And, as I say today, they are no longer the adventure, the challenge.

PLAYBOY: You say your book writing is more important than your journalism. Do you still consider yourself a journalist?

FALLACI: This book [*A Man*] took me away from journalism. It's been a psychological withdrawal from journalism. When Alekos died, I had to decide whether to be a candidate for the Italian senate or get this book out of me. I chose to write this book. But for all that I've said, I don't consider myself out of journalism. I very proudly still consider myself a journalist. I love it; it's the greatest work in the world.

But what began to disturb me was that the journalism I fell in love with at sixteen was no more around me. I used to practice journalism as I had been told it should be done, as my uncle did. Like the doctors, you know, in the movies, old country doctors with the horse and buggy who deliver the children and the calves and the young horses and fix broken arms—do you remember? They still existed, those doctors, and they worked all day and night. And that was journalism, as I recalled it. Dedication! But around me, I saw instead the journalist becoming more and more pompous, with hours of work like people in the bank, you know—not on weekends, please. They don't give a damn, because they must go to ski. The more they become lazy, the more pompous they become, the more arrogant they become toward the world. They grew up with TV. I'll get into that later.

PLAYBOY: What do you mean by arrogance?

FALLACI: It is their lack of political commitment, and here I mean especially in America. I'm going to be hated, but it's what I really believe. The lack of political commitment is compensated by a kind of arrogance, which is the arrogance of the policeman. Journalists, especially the TV ones, address people as executioners: "Here I come, and I'm going to show you what I do to you, who you are," because they have the power, they have this tremendous pull in their hands, and they cannot be controlled. The press should control the politician, yes, but who controls the press? The old question, see?

There is this form of arrogance, which was particularly born in this country, which I remember because I experienced it the first time as a little girl working with a reporter at the daily paper in Florence. One day Anita Ekberg stops at the Grand Hotel with her new husband. She had got married that very morning. She still had the white dress of the marriage with one sleeve and the other arm bared, very beautiful, all this blond hair, very sexy, this tremendous bosom, etc. Immediately, they were surrounded by journalists, and there is one, a half-American, working for *Time* magazine in Florence—so imagine what a little correspondent *he* was—and he says, "When do you plan to get divorced?" She was married that morning! I froze. I felt like crying for her. I said to the correspondent, "Why did you dare? Why did you do it?" He said, "Because I am a journalist. I can put *any* question I want!"

That kind of arrogance extends to politics. I mean, it is extraordinary how, lacking ideas, journalists serve ideologies without questioning them or being aware of them. Ideally, a journalist, more than an astronaut, more than a judge, should be the perfect man or the perfect woman. We are more or less in the position of the judges and the policemen. So what detached me more and more was this disappointment with what the journalist has become today—a form of power; therefore, an abuse of power. We write so much about the abuse of power, and we are among those who commit most abuse of power. You understand what I mean?

PLAYBOY: I think you're exaggerating the power of the journalist, at least in this country. Because in certain situations—not necessarily the most important—if there's a sex scandal or some document comes out, yes, journalists can make life miserable for someone. But as far as power to raise serious questions that citizens have a right to examine, I don't see any great power of the press. Politicians can play off members of the press against each other—I'll give you the interview, I won't give it to you—and cut off press conferences at will. In this last election, you could go through a whole campaign with Ronald Reagan, and the press never really challenged this guy's view of the world.

FALLACI: Listen, I do not know if you suffered as much as I did, on the night of the debate between Carter and Reagan. I would have given a finger of my hand to be one of the persons who put the questions. I would have done so much! I was in Los Angeles for the promotion of the books. I prepared myself to watch TV as you prepare for the theater: I ordered the drinks, and I put them next to me, and I had my cigarettes, my lighter, everyting was—like a child, very excited. I couldn't believe! I shouted, "Ask him *that*—no, no, look what he answered! Why don't you ask? Why don't you do it?" The only one who said something, believe it or not, was Barbara Walters, because she tried, she said something. But the others—nothing, nothing. That day, if I were a citizen, I would have grabbed them and screamed, "You traitors! You were there for me, to represent me, and you betrayed me, as a citizen, you bastards! You parasite of powers, you are worse than them! At least *they* risk—you risk *nothing!"* Journalists don't risk. At least the leaders risk! Not only their life, because once in a while they get shot, but their reputation, all the shit that is thrown on them, the accusations, nothing is forgiven to them. For Christ's sake! And the journalists—who do what? Nothing!

But I have something to say more about the journalists and politics in your country, if you permit me. I followed very closely this last election. It was the first time that I spent all the time in this country. Before, either I was in Vietnam or somewhere, I could never follow. And I looked very well what happened this time. It seemed to me that the campaign was not really done by the politicians; it was done by the American TV. The most important guy in America in those days was not Reagan or Carter—it was Cronkite. My God! The night of the results, I saw something that was so repellent to my democratic sense I couldn't believe it: They started calling the elections when people were still voting! I shall never understand it. I told it to everybody in Italy. I told it to my father, he said, "Come on, it's not true. It's one of your American paradoxes." He still does not believe me. But besides that, do you remember the deference that Ford, Reagan, all of them, had toward Cronkite? "Yes, Walter, thank you, Walter, Walter, Walter." I *like* Cronkite as a person. I like Cronkite, I know him. I've interviewed him, he's cute, very nice, he's a very decent person. But I'd die to tell him today, "Listen, Walter, it was *unbearable* to see you that night, because you were the real President of the United States!" He stayed solemnly there on the throne of TV—because it's true, you have a monarchy in America. You have TV. An absolute, tyrant monarch. And I remember, poor Regean, he was so modest. He had not understood very well what had happened to him, that he had been really elected, until Walter Cronkite called him. So it seems to me that you have a system where journalists, who should be the bridge between the citizens and the power, become more powerful than the powers.

PLAYBOY: As someone who has interviewed some of the world's most powerful men, who do you think has more power—the President of the United States or the head of the Soviet Union?

FALLACI: The President of the U.S. In foreign affairs, he can make the decision all alone. In the Soviet Union, decisions are made by a group, a collective. I know that Brezhnev did not decide on the invasion of Afghanistan all alone. The president of France probably has more power than the President of the United States, among nonautocratic regimes. He has more power on paper; he can take *any* decision. He is king of France for seven years. But he is questioned more in France on foreign things than the American President is.

PLAYBOY: And how do you see Reagan wielding that power?

FALLACI: It is too early to tell about Reagan. He is determined, he has a few simple ideas. In Europe, we do not know how much knowledge he really has. But I think maybe he will be a parenthesis in our life, a stasis. He is determined, whereas Carter was intelligent, but I agree with Kissinger that determination is a better quality of leadership than intelligence that is undetermined.

PLAYBOY: And you're not worried in Europe about someone with a cowboy mentality having his finger on the nuclear trigger?

FALLACI: Well, I don't believe the Third World War will happen in the next three or four years. I think it *is* inevitable—Teng Hsiao p'ing said that to me and he is right. The Third World War will take place. But we can skip it now and go in peace for a few years more.

PLAYBOY: You say it matter-of-factly, almost cheerfully.

FALLACI: I'm infuriated! We are all infuriated in Europe, beause we will be the first ones to die! Because when you do your fucking Third World War, I doubt very much you will do it at home. You or the Soviets. You probably will not have to throw the nuclear bomb. Do you know why? Because you don't need it. You are going to make the war on our heads with conventional arms. The war will take place in Europe. You are preparing the genocide of Europe! Nixon's book, *The Third World War,* that's what's going to happen. You are *already* making the war—by proxy! China and the Soviets are already fighting by proxy in Southeast Asia, and aren't your puppets fighting your war elsewhere—in the Middle East, in El Salvador? It's already there, the proxy wars, and the big war will burst in Europe. Darn right. Of course I'm angry. You ask if I'm cheerful. For Christ's sake!

PLAYBOY: Let's return to your critique of the American press. What do you know about the American media, anyway?

FALLACI: American journalism was one of my first loves, because it was an aspect of my falling in love with America. America was to me what Paris was to my parents. But I mistook the quality of the paper for the substance of American journalism—really. We came out of the war and didn't have this heavy, shiny paper and those marvelous photos—*Life* magazine, etc. But as for substance, *mamma mia!*

Today, domestically, perhaps, journalism in America is good. But on the international scene, it's more complicated, and American journalists don't have a very deep political culture. My impression is that American corrrespondents reporting from foreign countries know very little and understand even less. Usually, they don't know the language. Why? Because of the imperialism, the arrogance, of the English language: You go everywhere and everybody speaks English; why learn other languages? Well, I can at least say the U.S. journalist is not lazy. The Italian journalist abroad *is* very lazy. He usually copies the major daily papers, makes a summary and that's it. Yes, he speaks the language because he has to read the newspapers and steal from them. The same goes for other European journalists.

PLAYBOY: What about journalism in Europe?

FALLACI: In France, with the exception of *Le Monde*—in spite of its pompousness and hypocrisy; it's easy to play the progressive abroad—the newspapers are the worst. As to English journalism, it would be stupid to ignore what the London *Times* has meant in the history of journalism. But the majority of English papers are shit. The most provincial of the whole world. You open the *Daily Express,* the *Daily Mail* and you see what there is. Nothing but stupidities about the royal family and that ridiculous wedding of Charles.

PLAYBOY: You're not much on royal weddings, is that it?

FALLACI: The horse who marries the blond girl? Who gives a damn if he gets married or not? Let me say I am not very sympathetic toward that family. I have nothing to say about the mother of the young horse, poor woman, but I have something to say of the father. When I was wounded in Mexico and I was in the hospital with three bullets in my body, Prince Philip was there, too, visiting. He was asked by a reporter what he thought about Fallaci being wounded in the riots. His answer was, "What was she doing there?" So a reporter came to me in the hospital for an answer to Prince Philip's question, What was I doing in Mexico? I said to the reporter, "Tell Prince Philip that I was doing what he has never done in his life—working!"

PLAYBOY: Getting back to European journalism as compared with American journalism—

FALLACI: Yes, I was getting there. You must admit that in spite of this, the London *Times, Der Spiegel, Le Monde* and several Italian papers are very well done. And in general, I would say the European press is better prepared to tell you the things of the world; the American press will give you abundance of information, of particulars, but never the full interpretation. At least in Europe, where newspapers have acknowledged political views, you know what you're reading.

PLAYBOY: Why should grinding an ideological ax be superior to trying to present the news factually?

FALLACI: If you insist on facts, then I insist that the choosing of facts is an opinion. I cannot imagine anything more arrogant than *The New York Times's* motto, "All the news that's fit to print." Who decides what's fit to print? Who? There is much hypocrisy in this motto of the *Times,* and I don't buy it. I also say, if *The New York Times* is so proud of its objective stories and interviews, then why do they publish me and want me so much? For instance, they publish my interviews, which are the most opinionated on earth. Someday they will have to explain it to me.

PLAYBOY: You touched briefly on television journalism, which is, after all, where most people in this country get their news. Many people compare you to CBS correspondent Mike Wallace, since you're both known as tough interviewers. What's your response?

FALLACI: Ridiculous. I'm a *writer* who does journalism. In no case can you compare me to a person who *performs* journalism for TV. Oh, he might write the *Divine Comedy* tomorrow, but—

PLAYBOY: You're talking about Mike Wallace, right?

FALLACI: I'm not going to pronounce his name, not if you torture me, not even if you kill me!

PLAYBOY: Yes, well, why not?

FALLACI: He did an ugly thing and I'll tell you what it was. After Kissinger devoted two pages of his memoirs to my interview, admitting he had done it out of vanity but saying that he was quoted out of context, since I had never played the tape for anybody, I got infuriated. *Time* magazine published the Kissinger excerpts, so I wrote them a letter saying that someone *had* heard the tape—meaning Mike Wallace. *Time* then got an answer from Mike Wallace, in which he admitted he'd heard the tape but the tape was "fuzzy." What fuzzy? If he wanted to get Kissinger on *60 Minutes* and be the servant of Kissinger, he's going to say a lie like this? The tape was far from fuzzy. He heard it when he was interviewing *me* for *60 Minutes.* They showed a photo of me—it looked like a 123-year-old woman; I don't know where they got that ugly photo! For that show, Mike Wallace asked to hear the Kissinger tape, then tried to fool me by putting a microphone on after promising not to use it. I interrupted everything and said, "Out! Out!"—it was terrible. But, in any case, when he did hear it, Mike Wallace was very excited and danced around the room, saying, "Oh, oh! If I didn't hear that, I would never believe it!" Fuzzy tape!

PLAYBOY: Getting back to television journalism in general . . .

FALLACI: A TV journalist, first of all, he has to be a showman. Because TV is made of images—you watch more than you listen, and even when you listen, you are distracted by the image, which isn't even static, it is in movement, and the more movement the better. So TV can give the headlines. If I want to know if the Pope has been shot, I open the TV. But if I want to know *how* it happened, who did it and why, I've got to read the written page, damn it!

I would also say, though, if I wanted to work for television as a journalist, which I love for its images and its immediacy, I would be a cameraman. On TV, the real journalist is the cameraman, who writes through images, who chooses who and what to point the camera at.

PLAYBOY: A familiar complaint from TV journalists is that they can't cover a story after a while because they're too well known. What about your own fame?

FALLACI: Yes, it is a problem. In my interview with Walesa, I arrived in Poland a week before the meeting and a girl at the airport recognized me—then the TV got the news and there were photographers at my next stop. I was desperate because a photo would appear so far ahead of my first meeting with Walesa—the secrecy was gone.

PLAYBOY: But you say that with a lot of pride in your voice, even vanity.

FALLACI: Pride, yes, vanity no. Very proud I am. I complain because to do this work you should be a transparent fly, and I am not that fly. I make news when I arrive. You have to admit it, sometimes it's the encounter of two celebrities, these interviews. But much as it disturbs me, I would be a hypocrite to say that I cry from despair. It is the result of a life of work.

PLAYBOY: But is it hurting your journalism?

FALLACI: It *is* hurting my journalism. Sooner or later, people recognize me, and not just in Italy or France or England or America, but in other countries, from Poland to Iran, from South America to Asia.

PLAYBOY: And it's not as if you haven't courted the fame. You speak at colleges, give interviews, you go on TV talk shows. . . .

FALLACI: Yes, but don't forget the TV and the university offers come because I was *already* a celebrity. . . . All right, I buy what you say for TV, but not for universities; that's not right. When I went to Yale—and now you can claim that I say it with satisfaction; OK, sure, damn it, yes! Ask anybody in Yale—I had crowds five or ten times as big as other people. The students didn't see me on TV; they had read my books, yes sir! I'm very proud of it, yes, yes, yes! The only degree that I have, I got here in America, and I never even finished the university.

PLAYBOY: Pride aside, how has fame—and success—settled on you?

FALLACI: I am totally incapable of dealing with success. It has been agonizing for me. I have never identified with stories of poor people from small villages who made it to New York or Paris—because I never said I wanted it. I was not even aware of the fame or success for a long time. I was traveling around the world, working. And then people began to stop me and say, "Are you a relative of *the* Fallaci?" And lately, *mamma mia!* In any city, I never make less than seven hundred, eight hundred people for a speech; it's unbelievable. In Yugoslavia, they had to close the doors to the theater—and the screaming outside! The same in Helsinki. I remember a doctor from Fort Lauderdale coming to me to say, "Do you know why we love you?" And these were his words: "You are possibly the most famous Italian we have now in America"—which is doubtful, because Sophia Loren is that—"because we don't believe in anybody anymore. You have such credibility!" Now, you must admit that is the most beautiful compliment you can receive. Another time, an old concierge in France said, "Oriana, do you know why we love you? Because you have been teaching us courage." Oh, *mamma mia!* If I think of all the times in my life when I was scared to death—and he tells me I have been teaching courage. I felt guilty and confused.

PLAYBOY: Let's get back to your most recent book, *A Man*. You say it's your most important work, that it contains what you believe about power and courage and what an individual must do with his life. Why does discussing it get you so emotional?

FALLACI: The book haunts me. I have resurrected a dead man, and now he doesn't want to die anymore. My life is B.C. and A.D.—like before Christ and after—only it has to do with before and after this book which obsesses me. When I became known as a reporter and was traveling around the world and began to earn a little money, I began to feel like the queen of England. It detached me from my political roots. I had been in Vietnam, in Cambodia, in Pakistan, reporting on wars and riots—and I had enough. *Basta!* I was fed up. Men are shit, they are garbage, they are bastards. What's the use? Then I met Alekos and it woke me up. He brought me back to political consciousness. And his death crystallized the message I tried to describe in the book: individual responsibility. It's the only answer. Ignore what the crowds say; if everybody is saying yes, you must say no. You are alone, OK. Tomorrow you will be two, then four and five and six. The one political message I have is the fight against indifference.

PLAYBOY: That message may be clear enough when there's a dictatorship, as there was in Greece, or a totalitarian state, as there is in Russia—

FALLACI: What I say about Russia is that for all we hear about solitary dissidents, they are such a tiny minority. There has been a dictatorship there for so long, with so little real resistance, you must ask yourself how much sympathy you can have for the Russian masses. Maybe they deserve what they have.

You know, I am reminded of the one interview I thought I won—but I was knocked out at the very last moment. I had interrogated [former CIA director] William Colby, putting to him some very hard questions. Just before we left the ring, I went down, because he said one very simple thing to me; Go speak with the head of the KGB and treat him as you have treated me. And he was right. No one resists because there is no one there to confront.

PLAYBOY: This message of yours, about individual responsibility and the struggle against indifference, is obvious enough in dictatorships, but how does it apply to a democracy?

FALLACI: As Alekos said, we are four billion people on this planet. If all those billions but one are oppressing one person, then we are all fascists. In America, you are obsessive about individualism—thanks God. All your epics—the epic of the cowboy, of the pioneers—all have to do with individuals, and it is charming. But when it comes to politics, to the participation of the citizen in politics, the individual is crushed. He can talk, he can write, he can even vote—but he does not participate in basic decisions.

PLAYBOY: So you dismiss town meetings, ringing doorbells for candidates, organizing to defeat or elect people? That's a pretty broad brush you're using to dismiss—

FALLACI: I was not dismissing. I was only speaking of the dramatic imperfections of democracy and I agree with Churchill, who said democracy was lousy but we having nothing better. Remember in my book that it is Alekos who cries in front of the Acropolis, "Give me a bad democracy, a sick democracy, but democracy!" The only thing I would like is a democracy which is not bad or sick.

PLAYBOY: That takes us back to the problem we had earlier. When you admit that your hero, Alekos, in resisting dictatorship as an individual, considered taking hostages and blowing up the Acropolis, I have to ask you again: Is that moral? Is it correct?

FALLACI: OK, you go back to that. OK, I accept it, I let you go back. You are obsessed by it.

PLAYBOY: Because it goes to the heart of your beliefs, because it touches on courage and responsibility and terrorism—

FALLACI: OK, OK, *I* am not the one who wanted to take hostages. I tried to dissuade Alekos until I gave up and said, OK, let's try. But I *knew* he wouldn't do it! I have to admit that since this interview began, I have found other American readers who have asked about the same point. And if you have not understood, it is my fault. It is the fault of the author—the author of a *novel,* I remind you. I exaggerated a minor thing, perhaps, and it was much more in his imagination than I tell in the book. It was crazy, it could not happen.

PLAYBOY: He was trying a bluff, in other words?

FALLACI: Yes, a bluff. I mean, he did have this quality, which is a very dangerous quality, of being a leader who can lead by the force of charisma, who can make other people follow him—

PLAYBOY: All right, so for three weeks since we started this interview, *that* was the statement you didn't want to make.

FALLACI: Because you didn't let me talk.

PLAYBOY: Come on, Oriana, it's a hard thing to admit. You tried to give moral and political reasons why men like Alekos should be admired and followed, and it all comes down to the fact that certain people can have a dangerous seduction over the rest of us—yourself included—and sweep us up in actions that may, in fact, be crazy or immoral.

FALLACI: But I don't buy your word immoral. Whether history recognizes them or not, yes, there are certain people who deserve to be followed. In Alekos' case, it never led to crazy things—that was just a fantasy—but there *are* occasions when violence is justified. Tyrants must be killed. But why must you persecute me for this? I remember when I did a story about the astronauts, I took a battery of intelligence tests and they were exhausting, they give me headaches. This is what you are doing to me. This is what you do with your fucking interview.

PLAYBOY: Poor Oriana, you never did this to anyone, right? What are your interviews if not a test of intelligence?

FALLACI: They're a test of force.

PLAYBOY: Now we're back on the topic of force, of power. It's interesting how much that term obsesses *you.* You dedicated your collection of interviews to your mother and to "all those who do not like power." In that collection, published in 1974, you wrote, "I see power as an inhuman and hateful phenomenon." Do you still?

FALLACI: That was written in 1973 and we are in 1981. Thanks God, an intelligent person does not remain attached to something without thinking about it. A person moves, changes, that's life. Only the dogmatic—the Communists, the Catholics—would repeat the same thing eight years later. While I was waiting for this last interview session to begin, I was looking at *your* collection of interviews [*The Playboy Interview*] and I read what Bertrand Russell had to say: "Contrary to the customary pattern, I have gradually become more and more of a rebel as I have grown older." Well, for once in my life, I belong to the majority, to the "customary pattern." In aging, I became wiser rather than more radical. By wiser, I mean seeing things more rationally, more coldly.

So eight years from now, I don't know what I'd say—I might be a dictator in eight years—but in 1981, I would have to define power as an inevitable curse. Why inevitable? Because when you put together a community, as small or as large as it may be, it needs to be organized to survive. And to organize, the community needs to delegate power to someone. Sometimes people take the power, which is the essence of dictatorship. Sometimes they are given the power, which is the essence of democracy. Now, we don't even discuss dictatorship—we disqualify it. But to discuss the best situation, if there are twenty of us in the community, surviving together in a cave, we have to organize against the dinosaurs, provide ourselves with warmth and food. So we organize and say, "You go get water, you tend the fire, you make the shoes, and you, over there, you make children. . . ." I don't like very much that one has to make children, but one has to, right? Because once she makes the children, she has to give milk. And when she gives milk, she cannot do other things. So I will be the one who makes the *shoes*.

Anyway, so the cave must have a coordinator. That means the coordinator is the power, and once you admit that, you admit that power is a necessary curse. When the use of power is not only legitimate but reasonable, then you have to accept that power. But you also realize that the moment he rules the other nineteen people, without wanting to oppress them, he oppresses them all the same. Why? Because if he says that the rule is no one leaves the cave after five P.M., because otherwise the dinosaur eats you, he's right, because he protects my life.

But wait! I am Oriana. I am hysterical, I am an anarchist, I want to go out and see the stars! So when they stop me on my way out of the cave, I suffer and feel oppressed. I curse the coordinator. I say, "If the dinosaur eats me, that's my problem!" Then he says the terrible thing: "Oriana, you are not master of your life. You belong to this community, you make our shoes, we *need* your fucking shoes and can't afford the luxury of having you eaten by the dinosaur!" So I am admitting that freedom doesn't exist to begin with and that, to a certain extent, oppression is a necessity for the community. *Someone* has to be oppressed.

PLAYBOY: That's quite a change from the angry, shouting, anarchistic Oriana Fallaci of ten years ago. It makes one think you would be more tolerant of Kissinger today—

FALLACI: Yes, I am much more tolerate in 1981 of all the Kissingers—plural—than I was ten years ago.

PLAYBOY: Having admitted that, would it tend to make you less of an adversarial journalist if you had to inteview those same people again?

FALLACI: No, it would make a more relaxed journalist.

PLAYBOY: And would it rob you of some of the passion and drama with which you confront people?

FALLACI: Yes, and for the better. Less dramatic and less theatrical but, in my opinion, better.

PLAYBOY: Nobody would guess it from this interview, but it almost sounds as if you're saying you've lost some of your fire—at least as far as journalism goes. That new tolerance of yours for power—

FALLACI: Eh, wait! All I said was, "I *understand* you, Mr. Power. But I'm going out of the cave anyway, to look at the stars. To hell with you!"

PLAYBOY: That seems a good place to finish. Anything you want to add?

FALLACI: Yes, I would like to cancel what I said earlier about homosexuals. I'm sorry I touched that subject. When you talk hours and hours like this, you always make mistakes. Wipe it out, please.

PLAYBOY: Hold it. Here we have Oriana Fallaci, who has published comments from the high and the powerful they wish *they* could retract, asking us to erase something *she* said.

FALLACI: Because it makes me sound illiberal, and God knows I'm not.

PLAYBOY: We can't tailor the questions or the answers to what makes you sound liberal. The fact is, it's an issue in your life—you mentioned it prominently in your Arafat interview—

FALLACI: Because I just mentioned it! I touched on it! If you insist on publishing it, you are making a tyrannical, fascist act!

PLAYBOY: It wouldn't be tyrannical; it would just be poor journalism not to publish it, something you'd never allow yourself. Besides, you didn't just touch on it—you expressed a series of opinions about male and female homosexuals.

FALLACI: Do you want this interview to educate people to intolerance, to lack of liberalism? In your magazine, you teach people to be more free, toward themselves and toward others. Why do you want to make propaganda for the other side?

PLAYBOY: Propaganda? Why? Because it turns out that Oriana Fallaci may be less than a perfect, one hundred percent liberal?

FALLACI: I think of my homosexual friends. I'm ashamed of having said it. I think you shouldn't publish what I said, because if you publish one of my mistakes, you encourage the oppressors. Oriana is not perfect, no! She is the less perfect being on this earth. But I am a political animal. Oriana is a character, a personage, and she should not encourage intolerance. It is not I who will suffer, it is they, the homosexuals. And they are innocent.

PLAYBOY: Don't overreact. Confessing to a personal distaste, a chink in your armor, won't necessarily unleash the oppression you fear. You, of all people, shouldn't be involved in retracting statements.

FALLACI: So you will not erase it?

PLAYBOY: No.

FALLACI: *Mamma mia,* I tried. [Shrugs] Maybe it will be my Kissinger-cowboy statement. You got it from me, you got it! [Laughter] Well, it took you twenty hours to do it with me. It took me only an hour with Kissinger. So I still win, OK?

Now let's go out and have a good Italian meal.

HENRY FONDA

December 1981

Interviewer: Larry Grobel

This interview, a rare one despite Fonda's apparently having been around forever, appeared at a time when the actor's family and friends feared the worst. He had been in and out of hospitals for the past several years, and had finished shooting *On Golden Pond* with every indication that it was his last film. At the same time, not only was the eagerly anticipated movie with his daughter Jane and Katharine Hepburn due out, but his biography by Howard Teichman was being published. So his granting of this, the only in-depth interview of his life, came at a time when he was taking a few symbolic curtain calls in front of a nationwide audience.

It is also an interview that could only have been conducted by Larry Grobel, a soft-spoken and sympathetic man who sat patiently by Fonda's bed day after day. Fonda's dedicated wife, Shirlee, had first met with Grobel and decided he would have the delicacy and tact to get her husband to open up—and to serve as a kind of therapist to the ailing actor.

In the months that followed the publicatin of the interview, Grobel stayed in touch with the Fonda family, visiting him the day after he received his long-overdue Oscar and, in general, becoming closer to the man he had helped to bring out in his twilight days. Fonda died on August 12, 1982.

The symbols in his Bel-Air home signify illness, recuperation, activity and creativity. There is a full-time male nurse with him as he slowly moves with the aid of a walker from one room to another. A hospital bed has been installed in a small room off the kitchen. Large cylindrical tanks of oxygen are delivered and stored in a corner of a bedroom. In another room, a new painting of a rumpled denim jacket hanging over a chair awaits his finishing touches. A half-read biography of Thomas Jefferson lies on a night table. On the dining-room table, 350 prints of several of his drawings are waiting to be picked up and sent to a dealer in New York and a gallery in Los Angeles for his first exhibition. And in the Galleria Room, his paintings, drawings and watercolors line the walls—still lifes of fruit, a scene from the set of one of his Westerns, a London rooftop, an oil of a potted geranium on a chair and folksy drawings that reveal the Midwesterner: a pitchfork and bridle, three hats, work shoes, a Levi jacket on a pole.

And then there is this: a drawing of a book opened to page 312. Resting on the top half of this page is a magnifying glass that highlights the last paragraph of Chapter 21. The final words, carefully printed in a hand that knows something of calligraphy, are these:

"On the highways the people moved like ants and searched for work, for food. And the anger began to ferment."

Below the magnifying glass, the words, much smaller, more difficult to draw, all still remarkably readable, continue: "It was late when Tom Joad drove along a country road looking for the Weedpatch camp. . . ." It is a page from John Steinbeck's The Grapes of Wrath, *and the artist is the man who brought Tom Joad to life in the 1940 film.*

It was the twenty-first motion picture of Henry Fonda's career, a career that has spanned six decades, including more than eighty films, dozens of plays, two TV series—and two children who have followed his path to acting, fame and fortune. Of all the plays and films he has made, it is Grapes of Wrath *for which he is most remembered. Tom Joad is a good, kind, decent young man who believes in a better life and who drives his family out West to find it. In his portrayal of Joad, Fonda left his stamp upon a character and a time.*

PLAYBOY *sent contributing editor Lawrence Grobel (whose interview with James A. Michener appeared in September) to talk with the legendary actor. Grobel's report:*

"Katharine Hepburn told Fonda upon their first meeting, 'It's about time.' I felt the same way about this interview. Henry Fonda's been with us so long it's almost as if we know the man—when in fact, we do not. As he is the first to let you know, he is not Abe Lincoln or Clarence Darrow or Tom Joad. He's had more than his share of personal tragedies, he's suffered through certain roles that he's ashamed of, and there are plenty of people who have angered him along the way of whom he remains unforgiving.

"But the man is a true professional, even in very ill health. Acknowledging that he hadn't wanted to do this interview and that his wife, Shirlee, had practically forced him into it—almost as therapy, it seemed to me—he was gracious and considerate and patient throughout, giving up six consecutive days to answer questions that were at times uncomfortable for him.

"Before I arrived, he spent fifteen or twenty minutes walking slowly around the house, so that the few hours we spent talking each day wouldn't be too much of a strain. His voice was hoarse from little use, but his memory was strong. While basically still a quiet and shy man who keeps things to himself, it was obvious that he had enough of being sick. Life, for Fonda, is when the lights are on him, when the camera is rolling, when there's a script to memorize; and he is eager to get out of his pajamas and robe and back into action. For him, it's worth while only when the show must go on."

FONDA: I'm deaf, so talk loud enough for me to hear your questions.
PLAYBOY: How loud?
FONDA: Well, I've lost forty percent of my hearing in both ears.
PLAYBOY: Do you wear hearing aids?
FONDA: What? [Laughter] I got them, but they're not working right. I've got to get to the doctor, but, shit, his office is in Hollywood and I can't get there now.
PLAYBOY: You're not very fond of doing interviews, are you?
FONDA: I don't look forward to it. I'm doing it because it's important and I've been persuaded. I said no for a long time.
PLAYBOY: Do you find it exhausting?
FONDA: No. Boring. I don't like to talk about myself, but that's the subject. Of course, I can also talk about the movie—*On Golden Pond*. It's something special. It's

unusual, moving, touching, funny. It was a brilliant script, a wonderful story. Katie Hepburn was magic. Jane playing my daughter was special.

PLAYBOY: Is it true that it was the first time you and Katharine Hepburn met?

FONDA: Yeah. I'd never met her. I knew Spence—not well, but I knew him—but I'd never met Katie. I met her at a meeting a month before we went into production. She came around to me and said, "Well, it's about time." From the first, it was as though we'd been working all our lives together.

PLAYBOY: How often does that happen with someone you haven't met before?

FONDA: Rarely.

PLAYBOY: Didn't Hepburn injure her shoulder and almost back off from the picture?

FONDA: She wouldn't have missed this chance, no way. We gave her three days off while we did other scenes, but beyond that, you'd never guess she had a problem.

PLAYBOY: Was Jane afraid of Hepburn when they met?

FONDA: I think maybe. She did well and conducted herself all right. They're very close today.

PLAYBOY: There's a scene in the film in which Jane meets you on the pond and attempts a reconciliation. Considering some of the differences you've had in the past, which we'll be getting into, was it a very emotional scene for both of you?

FONDA: Oh, yeah. It was working almost on two levels: with your own daughter and with an actress playing your daughter. Because of the context and the emotion of the scene, it could become very personal.

PLAYBOY: Since turning seventy, you've had an abundance of good parts, haven't you?

FONDA: There's nothing to say that when you get this age, you're not going to have some of the best things in your whole career. Normally, you're beginning to slow down and take either smaller parts or pictures that you wouldn't do otherwise; but for me it's just been four, five or six of the best things that I've had in my whole fifty-six years in the theater. There aren't that many parts for an old man, but when there are, I've got 'em and I couldn't be happier. And *On Golden Pond* is going to knock them right through the roof.

PLAYBOY: Didn't you make that film during the actors' strike last year?

FONDA: We didn't work for about three days, and then the producer got waivers for us. I'm not quite sure how, but we went back to work.

PLAYBOY: Did any of you consider not working because of the strike?

FONDA: If we didn't do *On Golden Pond* then, it was never going to get done.

PLAYBOY: Because of your schedules?

FONDA: It could only be done in the summer. If it weren't done then, we would have had to wait until the next summer, and who's to know whether Katharine Hepburn and I are still alive by then? You just couldn't afford to wait.

PLAYBOY: There hasn't been too much written about your illness, but what there has been has been somewhat sensational. Have you been irritated by what some of the media have written about you lately?

FONDA: Only the *National Enquirer* kind of shit, where you've got to talk to lawyers to decide whether you're gonna sue the shit out of 'em or forget it. The most recent one about me claimed I not only had a heart problem, I was riddled with cancer, and that's a crock, but it's bad publicity.

PLAYBOY: Why?

FONDA: Because the word gets out and the producers think you're not well and you can lose work on account of it.
PLAYBOY: You mean getting work is still a worry for you?
FONDA: It's the operative problem with actors. I'm not the only one. If you know what you're going to do next, even if it's a year away, you're OK. If you have no idea what your next job is, you think, Well, that's it! I won't work again!
PLAYBOY: Gossip and scandal sheets aside, what is the exact nature of your illness?
FONDA: Last year I began to have problems again with shortness of breath and unsteady on my feet. They put me in the hospital again, for three weeks. Nothing but tests. Every kind of test you could think of, trying to determine why my heart was reacting the way it was. They finally put me on a bunch of pills—I needed a pharmacy beside my bed almost with the number of pills I was taking.
PLAYBOY: Were you resisting?
FONDA: No. During all those examinations, there was a general feeling that my whole problem was that the outer coating that my heart is encased in had calcium on it, and they had to find out for sure if it was so. Eventually, they operated, found I didn't have a calcium problem, and while they had me open, they put a new pacemaker in. I came home and that's what I'm recovering from today.
PLAYBOY: Didn't you also have an operation to remove a tumor on your diaphragm a few years ago?
FONDA: Yeah. That was five or six years ago. It was growing out of my diaphragm and the doctor cut me between the ribs and took it out. Said it was as big as a grapefruit, benign but big.
PLAYBOY: Having gone through such an experience, do you fear death?
FONDA: Fear death? No.
PLAYBOY: Do you think much about it?
FONDA: No.
PLAYBOY: Do you feel you're making good progress toward full recovery now?
FONDA: Yeah. Everybody else does, too. The doctors all do.
PLAYBOY: Do you hate your diet?
FONDA: I sure do. I miss chewing on a kosher pickle. I dream about it.
PLAYBOY: What else do you dream about?
FONDA: I dream I can dance like Fred Astaire or Gene Kelly.
PLAYBOY: When you started acting, weren't you once offered a year's contract at a hundred dollars a week to be a dancing comic actor in an attempt to create another Astaire?
FONDA: In a way. Or Ray Bolger. Leland Hayward, who was the top agent and who could sell anything, was not excited about me as an actor and never indicated he wanted to handle me until the 1934 Broadway revue *New Faces*. That's when he made a deal with Dwight Wiman, who was a producer of musicals, who had an idea that he'd send me to Chorus Equity to dance and make a dance comedy. It was fifty-two weeks to a year, salaried, at a hundred dollars a week. That was unheard of, but I turned it down. My dream was not to be a dancer or a comic.
PLAYBOY: It was, obviously, to be an actor. In pursuit of that dream, didn't Joshua Logan call you the best-known unknown actor in New York?
FONDA: He did. In those days, I was religious in going from office to office. I never missed a day that I didn't go into a producer's or an agent's office. I never slowed down. All the casting gals and the secretaries got to know me so well, they'd just look

up and say, "Nothing, Hank." It was during that time that Josh said I was the best-known unknown actor in New York.

PLAYBOY: How discouraging was that?

FONDA: I never really was discouraged. There were others with me who were in the same position.

PLAYBOY: That was during the Depression. How did it affect you?

FONDA: I was barely aware of it. We were in a depression as actors all the time. It wasn't any different. We had no money. We existed on rice. No sugar, no salt. Nothing. You just boiled rice.

PLAYBOY: Yet you had a lot of confidence. After working in summer stock on Cape Cod, you've been quoted as saying you went to New York "damn sure" you were a good actor. What made you so certain?

FONDA: It doesn't sound like me to say that. I'll assume that I did, because I'd been playing the best parts written at that time for young actors and had been accepted by the local community and the reviews were always raves. I suppose that's what made me think of saying it.

PLAYBOY: When did you first get a feeling for words, which, after all, are what actors fall in love with?

FONDA: I don't think it happened until I was pushed on the stage of a little theater by Do Brando [a family friend and mother of actor Marlon Brando]. Up to that time, I was a painfully self-conscious, shy young man and had very little to say. I didn't think about words at all. Part of the whole attraction of acting was that it was therapy. I was wearing a mask. It was like hiding behind a character. I wasn't self-conscious at all in the theater playing a part.

PLAYBOY: When did it become something more?

FONDA: It was very gradual that the acting thing became a pull. What I was doing was acting with all of these fun people. I began to realize that acting was a game of make-believe: let's pretend. Like a young kid playing cops and robbers, cowboys and Indians. That's when I began not to think about becoming an actor but understanding what it was that is so exciting about acting. And it's still the fun that it was fifty-six years ago. It's still make-believe.

PLAYBOY: You never actually studied acting, did you?

FONDA: We were all learning by experience, by doing it. It never occurred to me or to anybody I knew to study. I wish I had. I wish I'd studied voice, particularly. I've never had a good voice. It doesn't always work. Right now, I lose my voice easily and with this recuperating and being an invalid, it gets weak and I have to force it. I don't think you learn to act in a school, but you get the opportunity to work.

PLAYBOY: Your acting often seems so natural and effortless, almost as if you're not acting at all. When did you become aware of the effect the theater can have on an audience?

FONDA: My first visit to New York was the most unusual week I'd ever had in my life. I saw nine plays in six days. They were the plays of the season and, as it turns out, the plays of any season. They were all special. It was one of those seasons in which everything was good: *Front Page, Coquette, Saturday's Children, The Constant Wife, Tommy*. One play I'll never forget was *Gods of the Lightning*, about Sacco and Vanzetti. Charlie Bickford was in it. It was so real that I walked out of the theater and scowled at cops. I'll never forget it as an experience. I totally forgot that they were actors. I very quickly realized there was a difference between watching an actor you knew was acting and watching somebody who made you forget he was an actor. I began thinking, That's the way I want to be. Please, God, don't let them see the wheels go around, don't let the machinery show. Whatever I do in preparation is to make it as natural and real as possible.

PLAYBOY: Were your parents opposed to or supportive of your acting ambitions?

FONDA: Only supportive. I was very lucky in my parents. You couldn't ask for a better father and mother. I remember being shocked to go East in 1928 and beginning to hear of contemporaries who hated their parents. I couldn't believe it.

PLAYBOY: Was your father the biggest influence in your life?

FONDA: I expect so.

PLAYBOY: Wasn't there a time, when you were fourteen, when he took you to witness a lynching?

FONDA: It was an experience I will never forget. This young black had been arrested on suspicion of rape and a mob started to collect. My dad's office looked down on the courthouse square and we went up and watched from the window. The mayor, the sheriff and his two assistants rode into the middle of this mob on horseback, trying to calm them. They damn near lynched the mayor. You couldn't believe that they would overpower the law, force their way in, get this guy out of a cell, drag him through the streets, hang him from a lamppost, riddle him with bullets and then drag him from the back of an automobile. It was so horrifying. When it was all over, we went home. My dad never talked about it, never lectured. He just knew the impression it would have on me.

PLAYBOY: Do you ever see your father in yourself?

FONDA: I've sometimes come on a shop window at a certain angle where you see a reflection and I've sort of instantaneously said, "My God, it's my father."

PLAYBOY: Did either of your parents live to see you in the movies?

FONDA: My mother never did. My dad was an invalid when I came out here. Fox Studio screened *The Farmer Takes a Wife* for him, so he did see one.

PLAYBOY: What did he think?

FONDA: By the time I got back to visit, it was not on the tips of our tongues to talk about. He'd talk about when he got well, he wanted to buy some property north of Omaha and raise chickens. I said, "Dad, that's what'll happen. I'll set it up for you." He died three or four weeks after my visit. [*Pause.*] When I think today that my mother died at the age of fifty-four and my dad at fifty-five, that's babies. To think that I've outlived my parents by more than twenty years. It's amazing.

PLAYBOY: How did they die?

FONDA: Mother had a blood clot and it killed her. I never was sure what the cause of Dad's death was. I just sort of have a vague idea that it had to do with his kidneys. I adored my father and mother.

PLAYBOY: Were you brought up in a religious household?

FONDA: I was brought up as a Christian Scientist. My grandmother was the first reader and a practitioner. If we got a cold, we'd call Grammy for help. We wouldn't go to a doctor. That's all I knew until I was out of college. Since then, I haven't been inside a church.

PLAYBOY: Do you believe in God?

FONDA: I'm an agnostic, which turns out to be a very hard thing to understand. I said it on a *Donahue* show once when somebody asked the question. Everybody thought it meant atheist. An agnostic means I don't know the answers. That's all.

PLAYBOY: When a seventeen-year-old Bette Davis wrote you a note proposing marriage, you didn't have an answer then, either, did you?

FONDA: When I was first in New York, I drove my friend Hunter Scott home from Princeton. He didn't want to stay at Princeton, so I met him in New York and we drove down to Princeton before starting our trip back. He had two girls and their mother with him, a Mrs. Davis and her daughters, Bobbi and Bette. Neither of them was particularly attractive, but Hunter was pinned to Bobbi. It turns out that Hunter was pinned to a girl in every city in the United States, almost. It was a thick, foggy night, but we got to Princeton and put them up at the Nassau Inn. The next day, we took the girls to look at the new Princeton stadium by moonlight. Now, I forgot to preface this by saying that Hunter had this great idea that we'd have this contest during our trip. Every time you would kiss a girl, you would get a score; the one who had the higher score won something. This was typical Hunter Scott. He was very juvenile and I'd just go along with it. Now, we've got the girls at the stadium and I'm in the back seat with Bette. I just met this girl and she doesn't really attract me. She wasn't a very pretty girl. But when Hunter got out of the car and walked into the stadium with Bobbi, I knew that he was going to be scoring. I have always been this very shy guy with girls. I went with the same girl for two years when I went to the University of Minnesota and I never kissed her. I'd get her to the door and was always too scared to kiss her. Anyway, now I'm in the back seat with this Bette Davis and some way or other, I just leaned over and gave her a peck, so that I was at least even with Hunter. That's all it was. The next day, we took them to the train, and before we left Princeton to start our trip, I got a letter that was written on the train, from Bette. In essence, it said, "I've told Mother and she will announce our engagement when we get home." I thought, Is that the way it happens? It scared the shit out of me. Never answered it. Never paid any more attention. Never heard anything more.
PLAYBOY: Soon after that, you got involved with a character named George Billings, who had made a silent film as Abe Lincoln and then hired you at a hundred a week to tour with him, doing sketches from Lincoln's life. Was that a lot of money for you then?
FONDA: The most I'd ever made. The most I'd ever dreamed of, and I didn't make that kind of money in the theater again for years.
PLAYBOY: Did you ever think that one day you'd wind up playing Lincoln yourself?
FONDA: No. When they sent me the script of *Young Mr. Lincoln,* I turned it down. I even let them test me as Lincoln. I went to the rushes with the producer and the writer the next day and this thing came on the screen and, shit, it was Lincoln! He started to talk and my voice came out of this character and I said, "No way, fellows." And they dropped it.
PLAYBOY: Until John Ford entered the scene and intimidated you into doing it.
FONDA: Months later, Ford was assigned the film and he sent for me. I didn't know Ford. I knew his work and I used to hang around the set, watching him shoot *Stagecoach.* I stood there at his desk like a guard with his white hat in his hand and he was the admiral. His first words were something like, "What's all this shit that you don't want to play Lincoln? You think he's the fuckin' President? He's a young, jackleg lawyer from Springfield, for Christ's sake." And that's how he intimidated and persuaded me.
PLAYBOY: Was Ford as great a director as people say he was?
FONDA: There will never be another Ford. He had instinctively a beautiful eye for the camera. He was so egomaniacal. He never would rehearse, didn't want to talk about a part. If an actor started to ask questions, he'd either take those pages and tear them

out of the script or insult him in an awful way. He loved getting his shot on the first take, which for him meant it was fresh. He would print the first take even if it wasn't any good.

PLAYBOY: That's how he shot that famous last scene in *The Grapes of Wrath*, in which you say good-bye to your mother and leave the work camp, isn't it? He didn't let you and Jane Darwell rehearse until he was ready to shoot.

FONDA: He would stop the rehearsal the moment Ma and I got into a position where the dialogue started. We never did rehearse the dialogue until we shot. Jane Darwell and I both knew that it was a hell of a scene. When he finally said, "OK, roll 'em, this is a take," we both sort of let the emotion take hold, and then we realized that that was all wrong. Don't let that emotion spill all over and become embarrassing. Hold it back. We played the scene like holding a horse that was trying to get away. The emotion was there in the back and it colored our faces, our looks, the tone of our voices, and that's all there was to it. We just finished the scene, cut it and walked away.

PLAYBOY: And Ford never said a word?

FONDA: He didn't have to. You knew how he felt.

PLAYBOY: Is that the film you're most identified with?

FONDA: I guess so. Yeah.

PLAYBOY: Do you feel there's a part of Tom Joad in you?

FONDA: No.

PLAYBOY: Steinbeck's wife has said that you became the personification of what her husband stood for. How would you interpret that?

FONDA: I don't know what John meant.

PLAYBOY: He apparently thought of you when he was writing certain of his characters.

FONDA: I can't believe that.

PLAYBOY: When did you get to know Steinbeck?

FONDA: After I'd done the film. I was in a restaurant and we just said hello, shook hands. We didn't fall all over each other. There were four or five others and we went on a tour of bars and got drunk and wound up at his apartment over on the East River and we were drunk at dawn. That's how I met him. He turned out to be a neighbor, only two blocks from my house in New York. We were never intimate or close. I think we had admiration for each other.

PLAYBOY: What did you think of him as a writer?

FONDA: I loved his work. I've read everything he's written. When he died, his widow asked me if I'd come back and read two of John's favorite poems. At the end of the services, I went into the little chapel and was with the widow. She handed me a tin cigar box that Steinbeck had lined with felt and it was his jewel case he had made for himself. In it were the gold studs and cuff links that he wore when he accepted the Nobel Prize. I have that upstairs; it's one of my prized possessions.

PLAYBOY: Wasn't it *The Grapes of Wrath* that forced you to sign a seven-year contract with Darryl Zanuck at 20th Century-Fox?

FONDA: Yep. I'd worked with Zanuck before, several times. I did *Young Mr. Lincoln, Drums Along the Mohawk* and *Jesse James* and he was always after a contract, but I wasn't interested. Until *Grapes of Wrath*. That was the bait.

PLAYBOY: He knew he had you?

FONDA: He said, "I'm not going to let you play Tom Joad if I can't control you." Well, bullshit. I did *Grapes of Wrath* and I followed it with some of the worst shit that I've had to do in films, so I'll never forgive Zanuck.

PLAYBOY: What kind of man was he to work for?

FONDA: The only times I saw Zanuck was when they'd cast me in some crock and I'd ask if I could see him. I'd go in there and object to it and say, "Why do I have to do this?" A couple of times, I was lucky enough to get off the lot and be lent over to Paramount or RKO or Warner Bros. to do *The Lady Eve, The Big Street* with Lucille Ball and *The Male Animal*. Except for those films, I didn't do anything else at Fox that I could be proud of until *The Ox-Bow Incident*, and that was made in spite of Zanuck. He hated it. Didn't want to do it. But by the time I got back from the war, he was taking bows for *Ox-Bow*. It had become a prestige picture.

PLAYBOY: Didn't Zanuck force Fritz Lang on you after you protested that you didn't want to work with him again?

FONDA: Because *Jesse James* was so successful, Zanuck said he'd do *The Return of Frank James*. He came to me and said he'd get Fritz Lang to direct it and I almost flipped out. He didn't seem the right man to direct an American Western at all. Not only that, I'd had such a bad experience with Lang on *You Only Live Once* I wasn't looking forward to it. I told Zanuck all those things and he said, "Well, he's learned his lesson." He wound up directing the film. He killed three or four horses because he didn't know when to stop running them. Ran them up hills at nine-thousand-feet altitude till their hearts would burst.

PLAYBOY: Despite not liking Lang, how did you feel about *You Only Live Once?*

FONDA: It was one of my best films. I recognized that he was one of the giants of our business and his films were incredibly good, but his attitude with actors was so wrong. He treated them like puppets. He wanted to pull the strings. He was very frustrated by sound, because he couldn't talk to them during the scene. He was off to the side of the camera, gesticulating.

PLAYBOY: You did *The Wrong Man* for Hitchcock; wasn't he like that as well? Didn't he feel that actors were cattle?

FONDA: Not Hitch, no. He was funny all the time. Hitch would come in and tell a funny story just before he'd say "Roll 'em" into a serious scene. I loved working with Hitch. He blueprinted every scene he did carefully with the production man and the assistant director and the script supervisor, so that any one of the four of them could have lined up the shot and shot it.

PLAYBOY: Which was totally unlike Ford. Which director did you prefer working for?

FONDA: I'd take Ford. He'd be at the top of the list. With Ford, you were never really sure. He kept things secret from his own script supervisor. He'd dream up little pieces of business in the car driving to location and never say a word to anybody. As soon as he got to the scene, he'd say, "Why don't you do this and do that? Put your feet up on the post. Change position." And they would always turn out to be the things that people would remember.

PLAYBOY: Did that rub off on your acting as well? Did you learn to improvise through Ford?

FONDA: No, I can't. I've got to have every word that's coming out of my mouth written and laid out.

PLAYBOY: Marlon Brando says if you can't improvise, you don't belong on a set. Would you say most actors can or cannot improvise?

FONDA: I don't really know. Jane's one who loves to improvise. I'm told that most of Al Pacino's pictures are improvisations. I don't know whether that's true or not.
PLAYBOY: Did you see Brando in *A Streetcar Named Desire* on Broadway?
FONDA: Oh, yeah. Memorable, memorable. I remember going backstage to see Bud and I was so moved I couldn't talk to him. I couldn't open my mouth. I was so emotional.
PLAYBOY: Since you knew his family and it was his mother who gave you your start, did you know he had it in him?
FONDA: I'd heard about this young kid who came from Illinois who was stirring Broadway. And I saw *Truckline Café*, in which he had a small part in one scene, but he had pure magic in that. But *Streetcar* knocked me flat.
PLAYBOY: Did you know him when he was a boy?
FONDA: He was just a baby when I worked with his mother. When he was six, they moved to Libertyville, Illinois. We kept in touch rarely. I'd only hear about Bud. He was only about fourteen, but it didn't seem like another day before I began to hear about this crazy son of a bitch in New York who was setting the town on its ear.
PLAYBOY: How good an actor is Brando?
FONDA: I don't think there's anybody better when he wants to be good. If he cares, I think he's absolutely the best.
PLAYBOY: Some critics say that about you.
FONDA: I don't think so. I actually feel quite limited. My Middle West accent is too pronounced. I can't lose it enough to play Restoration comedy or Shakespeare at all. I don't have a great ear. I can get away with east Tennessee or west Texas. I've even played a New Englander and got away with it and was proud.
PLAYBOY: Were you happy with your first film?
FONDA: I wasn't happy with the first three films I did. The first time I was pleased was with *The Trail of the Lonesome Pine*. [Director] Henry Hathaway and I did a lot of shit from then on for [producer] Walter Wanger.
PLAYBOY: How did you initially get involved with Wanger?
FONDA: I was under contract to Leland Hayward after I did the play *The Farmer Takes a Wife*, and he dragged me off to Hollywood for a few days and he sold me to Walter Wanger, who had no idea who I was, to make movies for a thousand dollars a week. Two movies a year in the winter and I could go back to New York in the summer. It was like everything on my terms and I was just dumbfounded. I found myself shaking hands with this stranger, agreeing on a deal. I remember walking away from the hotel with Leland and saying, "Now, am I bound by that? Can I get out of it?" Leland never let me forget that.
PLAYBOY: Did the movies interest you then?
FONDA: No. I had no ambition to be a movie actor. I thought, They're crazy. I'll take their money and go back to New York.
PLAYBOY: Is the stage still your first love?
FONDA: Oh, yeah. The theater.
PLAYBOY: Anyway, your move to New York was a few years after your marriage to Margaret Sullavan ended. How long had that marriage lasted?
FONDA: We were married the end of December [1931] and took an apartment in Greenwich Village. We must have been there three or four months before I moved out at her request. It was several months after that when she stopped off in Chicago on the way to California and got a divorce.

PLAYBOY: What was it—temperaments?
FONDA: I never was temperamental. She was very.
PLAYBOY: Were you close with her when she died in 1960?
FONDA: No.
PLAYBOY: Your second marriage was to Frances Seymour Brokaw, mother of Jane and Peter. How did you meet her?
FONDA: She was visiting Europe. I was doing a film with Annabella [*Wings of the Morning*] and Frances knew the producer, who brought her out to the set. I remember being photographed with her sitting in camp chairs. We had a chance to talk a lot. She was on her way to the Olympics in Berlin and the film was within a week or two of finishing. She said, "Why don't you join me in Berlin and we'll go to the Olympics?" I thought, Why not? We had a beautiful time. She was not only pretty but a fun person to be with. She enjoyed life. We enjoyed being together. She had had her Buick touring car shipped over on the boat and she said, "Let's drive around Europe." I said OK. From Berlin, we drove down to Munich, then to Vienna, Budapest, back to Munich, eventually to Paris, when I proposed. When we got back to New York, I met her family. We were married that first week in New York.
PLAYBOY: So you married within three months of meeting. Do you consider that a risky thing to do?
FONDA: Today I do. I obviously didn't then. We were very happy for twelve, thirteen, fourteen years, with a very successful marriage.
PLAYBOY: Soon after you were married, Jane was born. Did you feel close to her as a baby?
FONDA: I didn't get as close to Jane and Peter when they were babies as I did with [my adopted child] Amy years later. I used to go home from work and it would be Amy on my lap, get up in the morning and change her diaper. But there wasn't really that closeness with Jane and Peter.
PLAYBOY: Because you were working a lot?
FONDA: I *never* was not working, and a lot of it was far away. Many times I would be twelve weeks away from home and I'm sure Jane and Peter were getting to be an age when they wondered where Dad was and why he wasn't home like other dads. I've always regretted it a little bit. There were so many years when they were very young that I couldn't be with them—either because I was in the navy for three years or because I was on location. But I tried to make up for it. I took Peter fishing for a week the first vacation I had from *Mister Roberts*. That's when Peter became a fisherman, and he's a damn good one today.
PLAYBOY: When did they first get to see you in the movies?
FONDA: I don't remember with Jane. With Peter, their mother gave a birthday party and screened *Drums Along the Mohawk*. I wasn't there, but their mother told me afterward when the Indians were chasing Dad, it scared Peter so that he left the room and played out in the hall the rest of the afternoon and didn't go to the movies again for years. It was traumatic for him.
PLAYBOY: Does he remember it today?
FONDA: He remembers it and talks about it. During the war, I was in the Pacific and their mother had a party like that and showed *Chad Hannah*. It involved a circus and how I became a ringmaster. Peter sneaked up the side of the projector until he got to the screen and he put his hand up to touch my character. A couple of years later, when the war was over, I got home in the afternoon and the kids were still in school.

So I drove the station wagon to the school and parked it at the foot of the driveway. When Peter came down, he saw the car, then he saw me and he became very shy and walked slowly until he got up to the car and said, "Hello, Chad."
PLAYBOY: How old was he?
FONDA: Six.
PLAYBOY: Before you enlisted in the navy, you made a lot of, well, lousy pictures, didn't you?
FONDA: Just before the war, when it got closer and closer to the time that I knew I was going to be leaving and the studio knew it, they just crowded me into films and made as many as they could before I got away. Some of them were very forgettable. But you're under contract; you do what they tell you to do.
PLAYBOY: Didn't you also have to date actresses they told you to, to help keep the star system in the public eye?
FONDA: I only once dated somebody I was told to. Marlene Dietrich. It was very strange. I didn't know her and it was just like an assignment. She needed an escort to an opening, and I drove down to her house in my little Ford and waited for her to come down. When she did, it was the star's entrance down the staircase. We didn't go in my Ford, we went in her chauffeured limousine. I just sat there like a bump on a log. It was a typical opening night, lined with photographers. I remember this long walk beside Marlene Dietrich, being photographed a lot. We didn't have a great deal of conversation. She was a glamorous star. I don't remember her movies too much.
PLAYBOY: Getting back to your time in the navy, were you gung ho about the war?
FONDA: Yes. I was a typical eager beaver who wanted to shoot at Japanese. I wanted to go where the action was.
FONDA: How significant were those years?
FONDA: I didn't like one minute of them. A lot of it was going to school, learning navigation, signaling. I was on a destroyer for a year as a quartermaster; that's assistant to the navigator. That I enjoyed. I sailed through this boot camp for officers and came out at the head of the class. That impressed the shit out of people.
PLAYBOY: And you received a Bronze Star for helping sink a Japanese submarine.
FONDA: One of the things that I learned in my various schooling was antisub warfare: how to find submarines, where to look for them and what to do when you know there is going to be one in the area. Through our secret code, we were given the news that a submarine was taking off from Tokyo. I organized a marine squadron that searched a certain pattern. It was prearranged. Search planes flew another pattern and they found the submarine and sank it.
PLAYBOY: Do you still have the medal?
FONDA: Peter lost it. I'd given it to him.
PLAYBOY: Were you upset with him?
FONDA: No; it meant nothing to me.
PLAYBOY: How did you come to know about the dropping of the atomic bomb before it was dropped?
FONDA: We briefed the pilot about where he was going and what to look for. The next thing I remember was hearing about Hiroshima, which sort of took me back, I must say. I had no idea what kind of devastation it would create.
PLAYBOY: In retrospect, do you think it was the right thing to do?
FONDA: I can only wish that they had never thought of making it in the first place and that there was no problem today about nuclear fission or power stations or anything

else. I'm against all of it. I'm sorry that anybody who learned that it was possible said, "Let's go ahead." I wish they'd just said, "That's dangerous, let's don't touch it."
PLAYBOY: Do you think it will eventually destroy us?
FONDA: I wouldn't be surprised. Not necessarily as a weapon of war; but what are they going to do with the waste? They keep looking and trying to figure out what to do with it. In the meantime, we're getting more and more of it. That's where the danger is. Take the Love Canal, for instance. Jane and Tom were there and gave me details. That's so terrifying, and yet it's going on today. There are still companies that are illegally dumping poisonous waste in yards and don't say anything about it.
PLAYBOY: Do you think there's any way to stop it?
FONDA: I don't think it's possible. Too many people think it's progress.
PLAYBOY: Soon after you returned from the navy, you began a very successful run playing *Mister Roberts* on Broadway. Frances, however, was not well by then, was she?
FONDA: She was sick off and on for three or four years.
PLAYBOY: Did you find yourself losing your temper often with your children?
FONDA: I lost my temper a lot. I think they would say that.
PLAYBOY: Jane recalls your rages as being "terrifying—not Mediterranean rages but rages of frustration, tension and repression." She said they were as much against yourself as anyone else.
FONDA: I would guess. Uh, yeah.
PLAYBOY: Were you aware of how strong your rage was? Did it have to do with your personal or your professional life?
FONDA: I'm not sure I understand what Jane means, but I surely had nothing to be upset about in my professional life. My personal life was disintegrating, but very slowly. I wasn't even aware of it for a long time.
PLAYBOY: When *did* you become aware of it?
FONDA: After we moved East and I was doing *Mister Roberts.* That's when Frances first had to go to a home for disturbed people. It was not a place where you're committed, but she was in and out of there two or three times over a period of a year.
PLAYBOY: Did you ever know what caused her disturbance?
FONDA: No.
PLAYBOY: Was it difficult to live with her then?
FONDA: Well, it wasn't easy. A lot of that I've put out of my mind, so there's almost a blank. I never dreamed that it would be anything permanent. It was just a bore to have a wife who wasn't always well.
PLAYBOY: Is this difficult to talk about?
FONDA: It ain't easy. Frances' suicide is just never easy to talk about. I don't like to be reminded of what happened. It was a tragedy.
PLAYBOY: Were you at all prepared for that kind of tragedy?
FONDA: I don't know *anybody* in the family who was prepared for that.
PLAYBOY: How did Jane and Peter find out?
FONDA: They were ten and twelve—too young to be told the truth, so we just simply said that Mother had died in the hospital. They've both got their own stories about how they found out, hearing other children talk about it or reading it. I've been criticized for not telling them the truth and letting them find out that way. I still think I was right. Anyway, it was a tragedy and that's the way things happened.
PLAYBOY: When they found out, did they blame you? Were they angry with you?

FONDA: No. Oh, no. There was never dialogue about it at all. I never learned from them when they found out.
PLAYBOY: How much of Frances do you see in Jane and Peter?
FONDA: Very little.
PLAYBOY: You see more of yourself in them?
FONDA: Yeah. Frances' oldest daughter, Pam, lives in Rome, married to an Italian ambassador. She's very much like her mother.
PLAYBOY: In what ways?
FONDA: Looks. Nervousness, which Frances didn't show right away. But Pam is so jumpy that it makes you nervous to be with her.
PLAYBOY: On the day Frances took her life, you went to the theater that night to do *Mister Roberts*. Was that the most difficult performance of your career?
FONDA: Probably. Leland and Josh persuaded me that I should go on, that it would be the best thing for me. I was just too numb to argue or even think about it. I just went out and played the show. I would eventually have had to go back and pick it up. If I'd waited two days or a week, the first performance after that would have been tougher than the one I played.
PLAYBOY: *Mister Roberts* ran for almost four years. Isn't it unusual for an actor, especially a movie star, to stay in a play for that long?
FONDA: I am unusual. I don't know anybody else who likes long runs. Most actors say, "Shit, how could you do it night after night after night?" I enjoyed it. I wouldn't have missed a performance and didn't—seventeen hundred performances. And the last, at the Biltmore here in Los Angeles, was a better performance than the one on opening night—and opening night was as exciting as you could ask a theater to be. The audience went absolutely out of their minds, standing on their seats, hollering, whistling. It was the only time I ever had to make a curtain speech. They wouldn't stop applauding.
PLAYBOY: What did you say?
FONDA: Something like, "That's all they wrote. If you want us to start again at the beginning, we'd love to." And they went into convulsions all over again.
PLAYBOY: How could the last night be better than *that?*
FONDA: You've grown. If you don't grow in a part, you should get in another business. It should never become mechanical. I can tell right away when I'm in the audience if the actors are bored and they're listening and their eyes are on you if you are talking, but they're thinking, Where will I have supper tonight? You can't do that. It's a great concentration. It's a great discipline. It's a challenge in the theater that I enjoy.
PLAYBOY: Are you ever nervous before going on?
FONDA: Never. On the contrary. I'm called a neurotic son of a bitch by my peers because I don't go and throw up in a corner on opening nights. I can't wait! I'm gonna get out there and I'm not going to be myself and people aren't going to be looking at *me!* I'm going to be smart, like Clarence Darrow. A character, like Mister Roberts.
PLAYBOY: Logan, who co-wrote and directed *Mister Roberts,* has written that you were difficult to work with and that you dominated him. Did you feel that?
FONDA: No, I never felt that. I know Josh does. Josh was and is an awfully sensitive man. You can't criticize him at all. I did several times and it used to drive him right up the wall.
PLAYBOY: How different was the movie from the play?
FONDA: I was not happy with the film. Mainly with Ford, who I felt was the one man

in the world to direct it. Turned out *not* to be the one man. He was such an egomaniac. He didn't like to duplicate anything that Josh had done in the theater. He kept changing scenes. You can't play it for almost four years like I did and not become a purist. You don't fuck around with something that works as well as it did. We're lucky that he had his kidney attack and operation and he had to be replaced when the picture was half finished.

PLAYBOY: Didn't Ford actually hit you when you began to criticize his direction?

FONDA: Yeah. Leland said, "Pappy wants to see you." I went in and Ford knew that I was unhappy with the way he'd handled the scene that afternoon, and so he said, "All right, what's the matter? Let's have it." So I told him in the nicest way I could that when Leland asked me who should direct this film, I said, "There's only one—John Ford. He's queer for the navy, he's an outdoor man, an outdoor-location director, a man's director, everything you could think of. But Pappy," I said, "you're playing around with things that worked beautifuly in the theater and you're changing them." I don't know how far I got before he stood up and pushed me back over a table. It was more like a shove than a hit. Shit, I wasn't gonna fight the old man, so I just got up and left the room. A few minutes later, he came to my room to apologize, and from then on, it was almost embarrassing. He'd ask me before every scene, almost sarcastically, "Do you approve? Is this all right with you?" He stuck closer to the script from then on.

PLAYBOY: Logan wrote that James Cagney was like a Disney character in the film. Do you agree?

FONDA: No. But all the subtleties in the play were lost in the film and I blame Ford for that. It's hard to say these things about a film that everybody universally loved and saw twenty times. You can't tell them that you don't know what you've missed when you didn't see the play.

PLAYBOY: You've made a lot of pictures you weren't proud of, right?

FONDA: I did some awful, awful things and I'm ashamed of them.

PLAYBOY: What film was the most awful of them all?

FONDA: *Sex and the Single Girl.* I turned it down when it was offered to me. My agents talked me into it, because they said, "You son of a bitch, you're not going to make a living out of *Ox-Bow Incident*s and *12 Angry Men*s. They can win awards, but they don't make any money. In order to indulge yourself to do films like that, every so often you've got to be in box-office pictures." They were right. It was a terrible picture, but it was box office.

PLAYBOY: What was your role?

FONDA: I was married to Betty Bacall. I don't remember, really. I hated the director [Richard Quine], who never did anything else that I've heard of.

PLAYBOY: Earlier you said that *You Only Live Once* was one of your best films. What are some of the others you've liked?

FONDA: *The Grapes of Wrath* has got to be right up on the list. And *12 Angry Men* is one of the best; it's become a minor classic, known around the world. *My Darling Clementine* was a very special Western. *The Ox-Bow Incident* was a special film. *The Lady Eve.* A picture called *Slim,* a B picture but a very good film that was overlooked.

PLAYBOY: You've left out *On Golden Pond.*

FONDA: Oh, yeah. I think it may turn out to be the best thing I've done.

PLAYBOY: There's a lot of talk in Hollywood about this being your Oscar-winning performance.

FONDA: I never think about an Oscar.
PLAYBOY: Have you felt cheated that you've never won one for a particular film?
FONDA: Shit, no, it would embarrass me. The only time I was ever nominated, I got out of the country just to avoid having to be there. Getting the special Oscar was difficult, because everybody knows how I feel about the Oscar. Yet getting it the way I did was all right, because it was for a *body* of work, and that was an honor.
PLAYBOY: Was it also a moving experience for you?
FONDA: Yeah, because the audience was so sensational. They wouldn't stop applauding; it was a standing ovation. I kept standing there with Bob Redford for what seemed like five minutes before I could say a few words.
PLAYBOY: So if you're nominated this year you won't attend?
FONDA: No.
PLAYBOY: Not even if your wife insists?
FONDA: She can't. She says she's going to, but there's no way.
PLAYBOY: What if Shirlee and Jane and Peter all insist you go?
FONDA: I will *not* be there and put up with that shit! I watch it on TV and five contenders for Best Actor are all out there and at various times the camera will go to them for close-ups. . . . The idea of the camera coming to me while they're naming the other actors, then whoever wins kisses their wife or girl or husband and runs up there and takes it and makes a speech. . . . No way!
PLAYBOY: But if you did win it this year, you wouldn't turn it down, would you?
FONDA: No. I'll let Jane accept it or the producer . . . and I won't be as proud of it as I am of the special Oscar, but I won't do a George Scott, no.
PLAYBOY: You attended the ceremonies for the life-achievement awards presented to you by the American Film Institute and the Kennedy Center. Were they meaningful for you?
FONDA: The Kennedy Center was, particularly at the end, when they had a navy choral group onstage and they started singing "Anchors Aweigh" and then sang "The Red River Valley," which is *Grapes of Wrath.* I cried like a baby [Fonda's voice chokes], tears just streaming out of my eyes. I just couldn't stop crying. The navy group came up both aisles in line and they saluted, "Good night, Mr. Fonda." It just broke me up.

[At this emotional point, friend and fellow actor George Peppard enters the room. It is one of his regular visits. He puts a large tomato on the coffee table in front of Fonda. "That's my biggest," he says. "It's a beauty," Fonda says. "You always come at a time when I can't talk to you, George." George leaves, promising to call.]

PLAYBOY: Do you see many of your friends while you're recuperating?
FONDA: Jim [Stewart] comes out here about every three days to sit with me here. He's my closest friend. And Barbara Stanwyck always comes to visit when I'm not well. Sends the goddamnedest things to eat. She came the other day with five different boxes from a Beverly Hills dessert store. God, there were pecan pies and chocolate pies and lemon cake. I was madly in love with Barbara Stanwyck.
PLAYBOY: Was it a Platonic love?
FONDA: Well, we were both married, so it was Platonic. She was my favorite person. A damn good actress, too. I loved her then and I still do and Shirlee's learned to live with it.

PLAYBOY: While you're recovering, what occupies your thoughts?
FONDA: I think about my garden a lot, frustrated that I can't get out there. I was a naughty boy yesterday, because I took my walker out to the front of the greenhouse. I'd planted tomatoes and bell peppers and melons before I went in the hospital and they're all of them dried up. There's so much that has to be done and I'm just not ready. Shirlee caught me out there and just blew her stack. I asked her to put the walker in the back of the car and take me to the Westwood Garden Center, 'cause there're so many things that I can still get to plant. It isn't too late: lettuce, peppers, several other things. She wouldn't listen to it. Said, "You're not ready."
PLAYBOY: Shirlee's taking very good care of you. Would you say she's changed you any?
FONDA: In many, many ways. She is so outgoing, so extroverted. And I'm so introverted that she's been a great help to me.
PLAYBOY: Does she give you more confidence?
FONDA: I think so. She's a perfect companion for me.
PLAYBOY: How did you meet her?
FONDA: A mutual friend was working for Rogers and Cowan. They handled me at the time. He had to have a meeting with me and he didn't want to do it alone. He asked Shirlee if she'd come along. We went to La Scala. At the end of the dinner, I went off with Shirlee. She was a stewardess for American Airlines at the time and wasn't always in town. I used to drive out to the airport and pick her up when I knew she was coming in on a certain flight. We saw each other all the time and eventually she went with me when I had a location in Spain. We were together about three years. I didn't think I'd ever get married again. Then I thought, Well, shit, this is a very successful relationship, let's make it permanent and legal. I asked her and she went into shock.
PLAYBOY: Your reputation is that you never married your wives; they all married *you.*
FONDA: I'd say so. Except Shirlee.
PLAYBOY: So with women, you were more often the pursued than the pursuer.
FONDA: That's true.
PLAYBOY: Do you remember the first time you ever slept with a girl?
FONDA: The first couple of times was a prostitute and it was very unsuccessful. Turned me off.
PLAYBOY: In retrospect, are you surprised that you've been married five times?
FONDA: It not only surprises me, I'm ashamed. I'm really ashamed to have to admit to anybody that I've been married that many times. It just doesn't go with anybody else in the Fonda family.
PLAYBOY: After you married Shirlee, Jane thought you should go into psychoanalysis, because any man who married five times must be unhappy. Did you know she said that?
FONDA: No, but it doesn't surprise me. She'd be the first to say she was sorry she said it if she was reminded today.
PLAYBOY: How did your different marriages affect your children? Especially the third, to Oscar Hammerstein's stepdaughter, Susan, whom you were seeing while Frances was still alive?
FONDA: They liked her very much, got along well with her. She was wonderful with them and when we married, they moved in with us in our apartment in New York.

Susan was a very good mother for them. They were ten and twelve years old and she was a great help. They still adore Susan today. Didn't like Afdera at all. Who am I forgetting?
PLAYBOY: Just Shirlee.
FONDA: They adore Shirlee.
PLAYBOY: You once described your fourth wife, Afdera, as being one of the craziest persons you've ever known. In what ways?
FONDA: I don't like to criticize anybody in print and I'm just going to bow out and not answer. She's a character. I was going to say social butterfly, but it's more than that, because she had a compulsion for entertaining, which I never did a lot of, still don't; but we had dinner parties almost every night at the house in New York and when we lived in the south of France. There was a lunch every day for twenty to thirty people.
PLAYBOY: Did you know them all?
FONDA: No. If I did, I knew them casually as friends of hers, Italians, mostly.
PLAYBOY: How long were you married to her?
FONDA: About three years.
PLAYBOY: Didn't she introduce you to Hemingway?
FONDA: That was in Pamplona or Madrid. Afdera knew him and she took me. He was pathetic and it was sad to meet him. Ava Gardner was there. He was sort of half drunk, his beard was scaly, you could see scale on his skin. He just looked unclean.
PLAYBOY: Was he writing anything then?
FONDA: I don't believe so.
PLAYBOY: How long was that before he took his life?
FONDA: Several years.
PLAYBOY: Getting back to Susan for a moment, what was she like?
FONDA: She was a beautiful girl, like Alice in Wonderland. Long blond hair and she was gay, she was fun. I'm no good at this. You asked what she was like and I don't know how to answer.
PLAYBOY: Just what comes to mind when you think of her?
FONDA: We had a lot of good times until we went to Rome and she got bored. I was working and she was left alone a lot and by the end of the summer, she decided she was going home and she did and took Amy. By that time, we'd adopted Amy. And Jane and Peter had to go back to school, so she flew back with all of them and got them started in school and wrote me that it was all over.
PLAYBOY: How did you respond?
FONDA: I was heartbroken. I couldn't believe it. I begged her on the telephone not to give up, but it never worked again. I must say for years after that, we were very unfriendly. At least I was. I couldn't be friendly with her.
PLAYBOY: Can you see now that she might have had cause to leave?
FONDA: I don't blame *any* wife for having got fed up with me, because I was impossible. Shirlee's lasted nineteen years because I've mellowed and I'm easier to live with, obviously.
PLAYBOY: After you married Susan and went to the Virgin Islands on your honeymoon, didn't you have to rush back when you heard that Peter had shot himself with a Civil War pistol?
FONDA: We were getting ready to go to bed when one of the local natives who worked for the hotel came running in, saying he'd heard on the radio that my son had been in a shooting incident and that I should come home. Well, that's hard to understand:

shooting incident. What does that mean? He shot somebody? Somebody shot him? Not knowing anything more than that, Susan and I packed up, took a sailboat to where a main boat came from San Juan. In the morning, we flew to Puerto Rico on a flight that I chartered, where we caught a Pan American flight, still not having heard anything more. In Bermuda, I had a chance to call New York. I got Grandma Seymour on the phone and she gave me the details. Peter had shot himself accidentally. He was in grave condition but was not going to die. It was well after midnight when I got to the hospital and went into Peter's room. He was lying there with tubes in him. I stayed with him a couple of days until it was obvious that he was going to be all right.

PLAYBOY: Coming soon after his mother's tragedy and your remarriage, did you ever think he was depressed and that it might not have been an accident?

FONDA: No, because the story of what happened goes against all that. Peter had wanted a gun for a long time and I wouldn't get him one. I eventually bought him a .22 that he was to use only when we were together. We would go off into the woods and shoot at tin cans. Otherwise, it was kept locked in the closet. Now, Grandma Seymour was living with the children and one day Peter was going to the home of a friend's uncle and he wanted to take his gun. He said he didn't want to take any bullets, so his grandmother couldn't think of any reason why that wouldn't be all right, so she let him take the gun. They get there and the chauffeur drives them to a certain spot and waits in the car, with these three kids fifty feet away. One kid had an old relic pistol, the other kid had a shotgun. The three of them played with these guns, throwing things in the air and shooting at 'em. It's a wonder they didn't kill each other. The old relic was the only one that wouldn't shoot and Peter said, "Let me try." He took a .22 bullet from the other character and was trying to force it into the relic and it wouldn't go in. He had the barrel right in his gut and it went off. The chauffeur put him in the car and drove him to the hospital, which saved his life. So I just don't believe that it was anything but an accident.

PLAYBOY: Peter has been quoted as saying that a few years later, he was attacked by three hoods, who hung him on a fence in New York and drove nails through his hands. What do you remember about it?

FONDA: [*Angry*] Fucking' lie!

PLAYBOY: Peter tells that story.

FONDA: He's got the goddamnedest imagination and he's a compulsive liar. Now, I shouldn't say that about my son, but it's not a true story! It's not possible. He was living at home and that I would see this boy every day and not know he'd been crucified with nails through his hands? There's no way!

PLAYBOY: Why would he tell that story publicly? Was it to get at you?

FONDA: I don't know. He likes to fantasize, I guess. I remember his telling me that story and I believed it as he was telling it, late at night. It was a long, nightmarish story and I didn't begin to doubt it until later. Never talked to him again about it, but his wife told me that he had told her the story and then admitted it was not true.

PLAYBOY: Do you think he felt he had to come up with something like that to grab your attention?

FONDA: Who knows? *I* don't know.

PLAYBOY: Would you say that Peter's early use of drugs and Jane's early sexual activities were acts of rebellion against you?

FONDA: I think so, yeah.

PLAYBOY: Did you ever discuss it with them?

FONDA: No.
PLAYBOY: How long did their rebellion last?
FONDA: Not long. A year. They were both successful right away and it wasn't necessary to rebel after that.
PLAYBOY: Still, Peter was quoted as saying that while you depicted great American honesty, you had no way of telling them about your life; they weren't part of it.
FONDA: I don't know what he meant. I don't talk about myself a lot. That's all.
PLAYBOY: How did it affect you, though, to hear what your children said about you in public?
FONDA: It was all happening at a time when they made the decision to go into acting. It was a classic rebellion. I like to think I was smart enough to recognize it as such and not let it touch me. A lot of it did. I was hurt. But it didn't take long and they came to me and apologized for the things they said that were hurtful.
PLAYBOY: Have either of them ever come to you for professional advice?
FONDA: No, they don't come to me. We talk, but not in the sense of advice.
PLAYBOY: Do you feel closer to either of them?
FONDA: Not really. Jane is away so much. She calls all the time from China or London or Africa or South Africa. She'll come home and call to say, "I was coming this afternoon, but I can't, I've got to go to San Francisco to make a speech." So I don't see Jane as much as you would think I would. I don't see Peter that much, either, but he's more often in and out. But I always enjoy seeing them and being with them.
PLAYBOY: Have you seen all of your children's films?
FONDA: Yeah.
PLAYBOY: But you haven't seen all of yours, have you?
FONDA: No. That doesn't seem to me unusual.
PLAYBOY: Can you be objective when you watch them or are you a proud father?
FONDA: A little of both. Jane's films, particularly, I get totally taken in. They're so good. I think she gets better every time she goes to bat. There's nobody like her; she's unique. Peter's mostly are B pictures that not even he is proud of. Most of the time he says, "Don't bother, Dad, I did it for the bucks so that I can do this on my own," and then he'll do *The Hired Hand,* which is a little classic; a beautiful, beautiful film.
PLAYBOY: Jane's early films weren't very good. When did you start thinking she was good?
FONDA: Maybe *Klute.* The scene in *Klute* that I feel won her the Oscar was where she is talking to her analyst and the camera is on Jane. I remember thinking, Shit, what a writer to find those words, they are so real, so right. I asked her about it and she said it was an improvisation.
PLAYBOY: Not being a believer in the Oscars, what do you think of Jane's two?
FONDA: Proud, of course. I know it meant a lot to her, not only as an award but because it could mean money. Success for the films that she'd produced herself. They could make another million or so. That was important.
PLAYBOY: How important is money?
FONDA: It's very important. More important for Jane than for me, because she uses it in so many ways. Almost all the good money she makes goes to the Campaign for Economic Democracy. I just need money to be able to live this way and I've got to continue to make it. I can't start living on savings.
PLAYBOY: Has your salary risen dramatically over the years?

FONDA: I've pretty much gotten the same salary. Well, no, it increased. It's not the same as it was when I made my first films, when I got a thousand dollars a week. Then I got five thousand a film. Eventually, I got a hundred and then two hundred thousand. I can't think of one that made me more than another one.
PLAYBOY: Was it your need for money that led you to do those GAF commercials?
FONDA: I resisted it for many years. Like a TV series, it's a problem to find something that doesn't make you sick to your stomach. I sweated through seven years with GAF and was not unhappy when we quit. The one I did for Life-Saver was fun because we did it in Omaha on the block where I lived when I was eight, talking about those days. Two girls are looking at me and say, "Aren't you Jane Fonda's father?"
PLAYBOY: How would you describe Jane and Peter to the seven people in America who may not have heard of them?
FONDA: You ask questions that take such a long time for me to find answers. Jane is so smart that I'm in total awe of her—brilliant, talented . . . scary. She's got so many things going that I don't see how she keeps them all juggled in the air.

Peter is also scarily smart. He seems to know something about any question you ask him. He is also a writer-producer-director-actor. Spends most of his time on his ranch in Montana.
PLAYBOY: When the USO invited you to tour in Vietnam, how did your children react?
FONDA: Peter had very little to say about it. Jane didn't understand it at all. I had a lot of explaining to do to Jane, but I think she eventually understood. When the USO asked me if I would go on a handshake tour, I said I was opposed to the war. They persuaded me it didn't make any difference, we had thousands of troops over there and it would mean a lot to see somebody from home. We rarely were in an area in which there was gunfire. I don't know that I saw anything that shocked me or reminded me what a crock the whole thing was.
PLAYBOY: How did you react when Jane went to Hanoi and was called a traitor?
FONDA: I was very sorry. I thought she made a lot of mistakes. Told her so when she got back. She knew it and was learning every day. She was making mistakes and was trying hard to learn.
PLAYBOY: Were you upset that she went or about what happened once she was there and spoke on Hanoi radio?
FONDA: It was what she did when she was there that was upsetting.
PLAYBOY: Antagonized a lot of people.
FONDA: Oh, my God, I'll say.
PLAYBOY: How did you deal with that?
FONDA: I didn't have to deal with it.
PLAYBOY: Didn't you once say that she won't be satisfied until they burn her like Joan of Arc?
FONDA: I never said it. I think Vadim said it.
PLAYBOY: What was your opinion of Roger Vadim when Jane married him?
FONDA: I always liked Roger. He was a very civilized man, very smart. He's got a bad reputation with the ladies, and that may be so, but I visited them when they lived together in the country outside Paris and they were a very happy couple.
PLAYBOY: When Jane married Tom, did you like him?
FONDA: It took time.
PLAYBOY: Were you supportive of his politics?

FONDA: Oh, yeah.
PLAYBOY: Did you think he had a chance to win the Democratic senatorial nomination when he ran against John Tunney?
FONDA: He damn near made it. It scared the shit out of Tunney.
PLAYBOY: Could you see Tom as a future Presidential candidate?
FONDA: Tom Hayden? Tom could do anything he wanted to. He's so smart he scares you. I don't think he'll ever try it and I don't think he could make it, but if he did, he'd be good.
PLAYBOY: How about Jane for President?
FONDA: For President? Why not? Why not? She'd be good at anything she tried.
PLAYBOY: Would you be surprised if she entered politics?
FONDA: I would be. I don't think she has any ambition to and has said as much.
PLAYBOY: You didn't think she had any ambition to be more than a model, either. How do you think the media have treated Jane?
FONDA: She very gradually became the character the media have helped to build, and I don't know if I ever felt surprised about it.
PLAYBOY: Did you always support her?
FONDA: Oh, yeah.
PLAYBOY: We haven't really touched on your adopted daughter, Amy. What does she do?
FONDA: She's getting her doctorate in clinical psychology.
PLAYBOY: In a magazine article about her, she was quoted as saying, "In our family's careers, it's usually 'me, me, me'—and that drives me up the wall."
FONDA: I never thought of Amy reacting or realizing or thinking about that. I don't think it's true, except that probably to Amy, when she's with us, there's more talk about what Peter and Jane are up to than about what Amy's up to and that's why it seems like "me, me, me."
PLAYBOY: Are you close to her?
FONDA: Very, very close. I talk to her two or three times a week.
PLAYBOY: Are you also close to your grandchildren?
FONDA: Very. They come over all the time when they're in town.
PLAYBOY: Will there be a third generation of Fondas in the theater?
FONDA: Justin and Bridget [Peter's children] can't wait to be actors. They're fourteen and seventeen.
PLAYBOY: Brando said he doesn't believe movie stars can be artists. What do you think?
FONDA: I think De Niro is an artist; Duvall is an artist. It's such a special talent that they've got, what else can you call it?
PLAYBOY: How about yourself?
FONDA: I don't think about myself like that.
PLAYBOY: John Houseman, who directed you in *Darrow,* said that you always reach a point in a production when you become insecure and lose faith in the project. True?
FONDA: It's often true. Certainly with *Darrow*. I thought it wasn't going to work at all. It was awkward, being alone onstage and pretending you're talking to somebody else. I was very insecure about the play. I couldn't have been more wrong.
PLAYBOY: So once something's in rehearsal, you're no longer the best judge of what's right for you?
FONDA: Yeah.

PLAYBOY: Didn't Edward Albee write *Who's Afraid of Virginia Woolf?* with you in mind, only to have your agents reject it without showing it to you?
FONDA: I was told afterward that it was submitted to my agents for me and they never gave it to me. When I saw the play, I flipped out. It was the only fan letter I've ever written, to Arthur Hill, who played the part. Later, when they were getting ready to do the movie, there was talk for months about the casting: Bette Davis and I were often mentioned. Then Mike Nichols was assigned to direct it and he chose Elizabeth [Taylor] and Richard [Burton].
PLAYBOY: Did you like the film?
FONDA: Yes, I did. I frankly didn't think Richard was right for the part. I'm an admirer of Richard's, but it's very difficult for him to be vulnerable. That character is a very vulnerable man.
PLAYBOY: Vulnerable is one of the adjectives often used to describe you. What would you say your image was?
FONDA: I know people think of me as the typical American: trustworthy, loyal, friendly, full of integrity, and so on. And I know several directors who cast me against type for that reason. Joe Mankiewicz, who put me in *There Was a Crooked Man.* Quite an interesting part. I played a prison warden in the desert in 1880. There's a jail break and Kirk Douglas and this bunch shoot their way out and Kirk goes to where he hid the gold he'd stolen. It was in a hole and when he goes to reach for it, it's full of rattlesnakes and he gets bit and dies. I find him, throw his dead body over the back of the horse and the bags of gold over the saddle and start back. You assume I'm heading to the prison, but I ride across the Rio Grande into Mexico, which was an O. Henry kind of twist at the end. Joe cast me because I'd be the last person in the world you'd expect to do that.
PLAYBOY: Sergio Leone also cast you against type in *Once Upon a Time . . . in the West,* in which a rancher, his daughter and two sons are killed at the beginning and the camera slowly comes to the killer—and it's you.
FONDA: That's when I understood why Sergio would cast me in this son-of-a-bitch part—the worst son of a bitch that's ever been. Sergio could hear the audience say, "Jesus Christ, that's Henry Fonda," in shock, and that turned out to be absolutely true. It didn't do well in this country, but it played in Europe and South America for five years.
PLAYBOY: With all the cowboys you've played, how do you relate to horses?
FONDA: I'm scared to death on a horse. You can't be sure that it isn't going to step into a gopher hole or something and throw you on your ass and break your neck. Never happened to me, but I always felt it was going to.
PLAYBOY: Although you've been laid up for some months, are you still planning ahead? Looking at scripts?
FONDA: Oh, yeah. I don't *look* for anything; I read what's submitted to me. So few things are any good at all. I read a lot of shit. Script after script after script, it's just nothing. You don't even want to waste the time reading them.
PLAYBOY: At least you can always paint. Didn't one of your paintings go for twenty-three thousand dollars at an auction not too long ago?
FONDA: That just staggered me. Shirlee was on the committee for the Neighbors of Watts and she said she'd get me to do a painting. I took these two tomatoes from my garden that weren't quite ripe and put them on the windowsill and painted them. Called it *Ripening.* At the auction, everybody in the world was there. Frank Sinatra donated a gold cigarette box, an antique shop donated a Louis XV settee; somebody

else gave a thoroughbred colt worth maybe six thousand dollars. My painting was third from the last. There were about fifty objects. When the auction started, shit, the people weren't bidding at all, things were going for nothing. The Louis XV that ought to bring several thousand got a few hundred; the colt got a few hundred. I got madder and madder. When it got to my painting, I was ready to bid and get it back. I thought it might go for five hundred dollars. The first bid was eleven thousand! That's when I started to slide under my chair. Shirlee was jumping up and saying, "We're going to get a new schoolhouse!" The bids jumped to about fourteen thousand very fast. It narrowed down to two people bidding against each other and was knocked down to Norton Simon for twenty-three thousand dollars. The next day, he called and talked to Shirlee, just to say how happy they were to own it—and to tell me that you don't ripen tomatoes in the sun. He's the guy who should know—he made his first buck at tomatoes.

PLAYBOY: You also recently sold a series of four prints that you did. How did you feel about that?

FONDA: I'm still ambivalent. I thought the dealer was out of his mind, he wanted two thousand dollars for the set of four. Insanity! They're not worth it. I can't believe anybody would want one enough to pay that kind of money.

PLAYBOY: What painters do you most admire?

FONDA: Andrew Wyeth, his dad, his son. I own several Thomas Hart Bentons—an oil in the front hall, a lot of his lithographs and an original sketch from the *Grapes of Wrath* era.

PLAYBOY: What about music? Do you listen to much?

FONDA: I used to, but I hate the music that's being written today. I don't listen to rock 'n' roll. I was a jazz nut in the Thirties and Forties. To me, Benny Goodman and those groups—that was music.

PLAYBOY: Would you say you're guided more by passion or by intellect?

FONDA: By intellect. I don't . . . I don't really know. I wanted to say passion, but I think so much about decisions that it's got to be intellect, too.

PLAYBOY: We haven't touched much on politics. Since you and Jimmy Stewart are best friends, how do you maintain friendship, being on opposite ends of the political tracks?

FONDA: We learned a long time ago that if we were going to remain friends, we didn't talk politics. I first became aware of Jim's reactionary Republicanism when we were at the Stork Club and he started talking about what Roosevelt had done to the railroads—destroyed them. I said Roosevelt wasn't destroying anything, times were changing, we weren't still in an age when railroads were the whole answer; there were airplanes now. It began to be an argument. I realized then that we're not going to understand each other at all and I just stopped and haven't talked politics with him since.

PLAYBOY: How outspoken were you during the McCarthy era?

FONDA: The McCarthy era was just unbelievable to me. That's when I started to become less friendly with Duke Wayne and Ward Bond, who, I felt, hadn't known how to *spell* politics until then. They'd never indicated any political leanings, and suddenly these two characters are naming names of Communists in the business, putting them on black lists. I called them both on it, but it made no difference, of course.

PLAYBOY: Were you ever friendly with them after that?

FONDA: Never with Ward; I never spoke to him again. With Duke, a little warmer. He

was a very nice guy and had a sense of humor. He'd always kid me about Jane.
PLAYBOY: As a man who has played the role of President a few times, how many real ones did you know?
FONDA: I've met Roosevelt, Truman, and I knew John Kennedy intimately. He used to live at the Hotel Carlyle when he was in New York, about two blocks from my house. Afdera met him before I did and had a dinner party and he came. After that, he was at the house quite a lot at parties or just to come over and sit with a drink.
PLAYBOY: Was that when he was senator?
FONDA: No, President. We didn't talk politics. We were very social. He was an awful nice guy, easy to know. Funny. I enjoyed being with him.
PLAYBOY: Did you support Ted when he ran for President?
FONDA: Oh, yeah. But I don't think he'll ever make it. I don't think he should try.
PLAYBOY: Chappaquiddick?
FONDA: No question. A damn shame, because he's a good man.
PLAYBOY: What about some of the Republican Presidents?
FONDA: Couldn't stand Eisenhower. Nixon, of course, was just poison to me. I've hated Nixon for forty years. Started hating him when he whipped Helen Gahagan Douglas, saying she was a Red and a pinko. Such fuckin' lies. I knew her and I've just had nothing but hatred for Nixon ever since and will never understand how the son of a bitch was ever elected.
PLAYBOY: You think he belongs in jail?
FONDA: Sure.
PLAYBOY: Were you surprised he was pardoned?
FONDA: Not only surprised, I was shocked. I've never forgiven Ford for that. To think that Nixon was our President! He was such a crook.
PLAYBOY: Were you even more outraged when you found out the FBI under Nixon was tapping Jane's phone and opening her mail?
FONDA: I couldn't be more outraged. The name Nixon is enough to outrage me.
PLAYBOY: Briefly, we'd like to ask your opinions on some current issues, such as abortion and ERA.
FONDA: It's ridiculous that it's even a problem. ERA should be taken for granted. Abortion, that's up to the individual.
PLAYBOY: Gun control?
FONDA: I never will understand why people are against it. It's insanity to me that we don't have gun control.
PLAYBOY: Pornography?
FONDA: I'm not curious about pornography. I've never gone to a pornographic film. If people want it, give it to them. But I'm ashamed that there is a problem of pornography.
PLAYBOY: Gay rights?
FONDA: I don't think they ought to be put back in the closet, but there's a certain limit. You can't be a boy scout if you're known to be homosexual, and I agree with that. I'm not sure how I feel about the army and the navy. Homosexuals can make damn good teachers.
PLAYBOY: How concerned are you about Reagan?
FONDA: Reagan is a major concern. I think we're headed for disaster. I'm surprised there isn't more opposition. He upsets me so it's hard to talk about. He's got us on a path now that we're gonna be on for a long time.
PLAYBOY: Do you know him?

FONDA: Yeah.
PLAYBOY: Friend?
FONDA: Acquaintance.
PLAYBOY: Did you think much of him as an actor?
FONDA: No.
PLAYBOY: Is he much of an actor now?
FONDA: No.
PLAYBOY: How did he get elected?
FONDA: He's a hell of a speechmaker. He says the things people want to hear. He says them very convincingly and with what sounds like sincerity and he's talking a language that people haven't heard for a long time and it impresses them. *I* listen to a Reagan speech and want to throw up!
PLAYBOY: Let's, then, go from bad actors to good. Are there any actors you would have liked to work with?
FONDA: A lot. Brando, Pacino, De Niro.
PLAYBOY: What is it about them you like?
FONDA: That's asking me to analyze acting, in a way, and I can't do that. They're just exciting to watch.
PLAYBOY: You can't or you won't?
FONDA: I'm not good at it.
PLAYBOY: What about actresses? Are there any you regret not having worked with?
FONDA: No, I was very lucky, I worked with most of the exciting actresses around. Bette Davis, Joan Crawford, Barbara Stanwyck, Olivia de Havilland, Lucille Ball. All of 'em.
PLAYBOY: Among male actors, you never worked with Laurence Olivier. What do you think of his work?
FONDA: I'm a good friend of Olivier's and I think he's brilliant in his Shakespeare. But he's a mechanical actor. He admits he is. That's the way he works. He says he doesn't work from his heart, he works from his head. But he's awful damn good. He can be just as bad, and so can Brando. I mean, some of the things he's done recently are embarrassing. He wants to make enough money to put his kids through college.
PLAYBOY: Any other constructive criticism for members of your profession?
FONDA: I've become disappointed in Jack Nicholson recently. He started out to be one of the most exciting young actors we could have. Now, I don't like to hear myself say these things, because they're going to be printed. But I'm not close enough to him to tell him to straighten up.
PLAYBOY: Do you think he's destroying his career?
FONDA: If he continues like this, he will.
PLAYBOY: One of the most unpleasant Hollywood stories is about Joan Crawford, whom you knew. Her daughter's book, *Mommie Dearest,* has been made into a movie. How do you feel about that?
FONDA: I resent the book. I resent the daughter and the publisher and everything about it. I knew Joan during those days. Worked with her and was often at parties at her home, pool parties in the afternoon, when the children were there, and I never saw or heard anything that would give me a clue that the stories were true that the daughter wrote. I think whatever is truth about them has been exaggerated so that it makes her more of a monster than she was.
PLAYBOY: Do you dislike Hollywood books in general?

FONDA: I hate them. I didn't read it, but I hate Shelley Winters' book from what I've heard. Susan Strasberg's book; I didn't read it, but I'm told about it. I resent the shit out of Garson Kanin and his wife [Ruth Gordon]. They're making capital today and a good living on writing about people they knew and worked with, including Katharine and Spencer. Now, that was a well-known relationship; there wasn't anybody who didn't know about it. But the Kanins wrote about it in detail and they're supposed to have been good friends of Katie's. She'll never forgive them.
PLAYBOY: What about your own book, which Howard Teichmann wrote under your authorization?
FONDA: They've been asking me for years to write my story and I just was not interested. I couldn't believe anybody cared or would want to read it. I can't believe there's enough in my life that is interesting enough to make a biography. The only reason it was done is that Teichmann said, "It's gonna be written anyway, so you might as well cooperate," and that's why I agreed. I'm going to be curious to read it to find out why the publishers are excited. I'm curious about what I said and what friends said. He'd interview somebody and then call me to corroborate something and there wouldn't be a word of truth in it. It was their memory. It's the old *Rashomon.*
PLAYBOY: Didn't the book sell for $1,800,000, the highest price yet paid for an actor's book?
FONDA: And more than that by the time they add London's order and Canada's order, magazine serialization, paperback and everything else.
PLAYBOY: Well, for a man who's opposed in principle to that sort of thing, you're not doing bad. Do you think you like yourself?
FONDA: If I've made any sense at all in the days I've talked to you, you should understand that I don't like myself. I wish I were somebody better, smarter.
PLAYBOY: Yet you've played such likable characters.
FONDA: Look at the chances I've had to play and pretend that I'm Clarence Darrow, Mister Roberts, Tom Joad, all those wonderful people. For somebody who doesn't like himself, that's great therapy.
PLAYBOY: Do you like yourself more now than in the past?
FONDA: No.
PLAYBOY: What don't you like?
FONDA: I'm not able to be articulate with you and make a lot of good answers to your questions; that's one thing. I'm a lousy interviewee.
PLAYBOY: Not as bad as you think.
FONDA: Well, I feel I am. I don't feel I have good answers to anything.
PLAYBOY: Maybe you'll be surprised when you read this.
FONDA: Well, it will be you.
PLAYBOY: Let's say "us," with the emphasis on you. Brando also didn't think he was as articulate as his interview proved him to be.
FONDA: Well, I'll sure appreciate it if you can do that for me.
PLAYBOY: George C. Scott has said that the curse of an actor is that he continues to question how important he really is outside his narrow scope—
FONDA: See, that kind of answer is what I mean. I haven't got those good words.
PLAYBOY: Then let's ask you what worries you most as an actor other than not getting a part—what curse can you think of?
FONDA: I can't think of anything. I'm very proud. I guess because I've done well. I know I have respect and a good reputation. I'm proud of that.
PLAYBOY: And you'd like to be remembered as . . .

FONDA: [*Pause*] As a good actor.
PLAYBOY: Would you consider yours a happy life, in spite of what you say you feel about yourself?
FONDA: Not counting the tragedies that have happened, most of my life has been happy, yeah. I've been very lucky.

LECH WALESA

February 1982

Interviewers: Ania & Kristina Bittenek

The two women who walked into Golson's New York office in the summer of 1981 were unlikely candidates to pull off what would become a major journalistic coup. As it happened, the editor had been casting about for someone who would attempt to conduct an interview with Lech Walesa, the charismatic and elusive leader of Poland's Solidarity movement. Ania and Kristina Bittenek, sisters and fledgling journalists, proposed that they do just that—fly to Poland and return with an in-depth interview. Golson was skeptical, but decided to hear them out.

The two women described their background: They were experts on the history of Poland's labor movement, which began in the shipyards of Gdansk a year earlier; they were themselves of Polish extraction and spoke the language fluently; they had already met and interviewed Walesa's wife; they knew the people around Walesa, his aides and fellow Solidarity leaders. Golson was impressed, but said the only way he would risk sending them to Poland was if they could show him written proof that Walesa would sit for a Playboy Interview when they arrived.

To his surprise, the women turned up in his office several weeks later with a telex sent by Solidarity's press spokesman. It said that he would do his utmost to see that Walesa spent some time speaking with them for publication in PLAYBOY—and by the way, would they bring him one of those new Japanese tape recorders so he could make a record of his own meetings with the Polish authorities?

It wasn't ironclad, but Golson decided to send them over. For a week the two sisters pored over topics and questions in the PLAYBOY offices, then took off one afternoon in July for Warsaw via Kennedy Airport. And were not heard from for three months.

When Golson finally received a long telex from Kristina Bittenek, it was to explain that Walesa had been constantly on the move, had met with the Pope, then with the new head of the Warsaw government, and had been giving eight speeches a day all over the country. All that they had managed to get was a couple of hours on tape with him, and they knew that wasn't enough for an in-depth interview in PLAYBOY. . . .

Golson quickly telexed a reply to the sisters: After telling them of the magazine's concern for their whereabouts, he instructed them to translate and transmit the conversations they had recorded thus far with Walesa. As the telex clattered over the next several days, Golson was puzzled to see the machine go dead for several minutes in the middle of transmitting a Walesa answer on police actions in Poland. Since at that time there was relatively little censorship in Poland, it seemed odd that anything should interrupt the flow of copy; Golson made a note of it but did not dwell on it once the telex came to life again.

As it turned out, the dialogue was far more interesting, far more revealing than the Bitteneks themselves realized. Though the material was not as probing or far-reaching as the usual Playboy Interview, Golson decided it had an immediacy and a spontaneity that made it unique. The media in general had been presenting Walesa as a legend, a symbol issuing pronouncements about Poland and Russia. In the conversation with the Bitteneks, he was seen more clearly as the rough, untutored electrician that he was—with a wonderful gift for parable and humor and canniness.

Golson advised the sisters he intended to publish the material as the next available interview—in the February 1982 issue—and asked them to return home.

The February issue would be off the presses in late December. In one of those astonishing coincidences of timing that often seem to be a part of the Playboy Interview tradition, martial law was declared by the Polish authorities, censorship was reinstated in mid-December, and Lech Walesa was the object of the most intense speculation everywhere in the world. PLAYBOY had, in effect, Walesa's last interview as a free man, and it was chilling for readers to see him declaring, as almost his final words, "Poland was always a rather free country. . . . All of a sudden, we were ordered to love something else. We have freedom . . . in our blood and no one can hold us captive!"

By now his story has taken on the trappings of a legend. An unemployed Polish electrician named Lech Walesa scaled a fence at the Lenin Shipyard in Gdańsk, Poland, to join striking workers who were occupying the plant. Within days, he had become the leader of the strike and was demanding that the Polish government give workers the right to form free trade unions, unprecedented in an Eastern European Communist country. Six months later, Walesa had become one of the most powerful men in Poland, leader of the ten-million-member Solidarity union. By December, he was on the cover of Time *and spotlighted in its Man of the Year coverage for 1980.* Time *called him "one of the Communist world's most charismatic figures," and noted that "from his first appearance in the striking shipyard last August, Walesa showed an instinctive ability to inspire crowds and win their trust . . . [mesmerizing] audiences with a mixture of folksy quips and deadly serious admonitions."*

In the months since Walesa's rise to international fame and unprecedented power in Poland, the world has watched him lead his Solidarity union into a series of tough confrontations with Polish leaders. It has also watched the Soviet Union mass thousands of troops and artillery along the Polish border in a not-so-subtle reminder of what happens to Russian satellites when they stray too far from the socialist orbit.

*Throughout it all, Walesa (his name is pronounced Lek Vah-*when*-sah) has maintained a careful balance in his public image of international media celebrity interviewed by Walter Cronkite and humble, deeply religious Polish workingman. When he appears in public in Poland, he is the object of adulation, signing autographs and* *traveling with a squad of bodyguards. Yet his favorite response to admirers is often "I am not your master, I am your servant." To factory workers he has been known to say that "anyone who turns his head as I walk by isn't doing his job."*

Walesa has also managed to become adept at both public speaking and political infighting. In front of mass audiences who sometimes chant "Long live Walesa," he is calm, understated and given to parables and simple anecdotes that enhance his image as an average Polish worker with little formal education. Yet he has been able to motivate an entire country to stand up to Soviet domination and has become a symbol of Poland reborn. Within a few weeks after his rise to power in Gdańsk, he engineered a major strike that brought Poland to a standstill for exactly one hour. In public, he seems to draw out of all Poles latent feelings of both patriotism and Catholicism. He rarely misses daily Mass. He wears a medallion of the Virgin Mary in his lapel. When he appears in public to speak, a large crucifix is installed on the wall near him.

Recently, however, Walesa has become considerably more moderate and conciliatory and has taken a softer line on strikes. "Let us stick to what we have already achieved for the time being. Otherwise, we might lose everything," he told a group of workers who threatened another strike. "There is a danger that they might reply with tanks and rockets," he added, with no need to state who "they" were.

In negotiations with Polish officials, Walesa is known as a bargainer who speaks softly but carries enormous clout. In addition to fighting for free trade unions, he has managed to get government concessions for incrased wages, less media censorship and even radio broadcasts of Sunday Mass. He is always careful to deny that he is "antisocialist," insisting that he is a union man out to better the lot of the worker. Bringing down the government is not his aim, he maintains.

At the age of thirty-nine, Walesa seems an unlikely figure to be articulating a country's unhappiness with its rulers. Although he has been active in union activity in Poland since 1970, he seems to have come out of nowhere. The son of a carpenter, Walesa is an electrician by trade, who happened to be working at the Gdańsk shipyard in 1970 when bloody riots over the high price of food erupted and at least forty-five people were killed. Six years later, he was fired from his job at the shipyard for protesting too vigorously that the government hadn't made good on concessions granted to workers after the rioting. It was not the last job he was to lose for his labor activities.

However, by 1978, a Polish Pope had been installed in the Vatican and the climate seemed better for Walesa's ideas. He was instrumental in the formation of a small free trade union on the Baltic coast, and by 1980, another government decision that raised food prices led to another protest at the same Gdańsk shipyard and Walesa's climb to fame.

In private, Walesa strikes yet another balance between simple living and the accoutrements of power that have fallen to him. Critics say he has become a demagogue, interrupting others to voice his opinions and expecting them to be followed. The trapping of celebrity have piled up. He often travels by government-supplied helicopter, and a pipe or a cigarette, symbol of hard-to-get tobacco in Poland, is ever present in his hand. He and his wife of twelve years, Miroslawa, and their six children have moved to a six-room apartment from their former two-room flat, and Walesa's wardrobe now includes four suits in addition to the wrinkled one he invariably wore only a year ago. His salary is now $333 per month, about average for a *shipyard worker in Poland, and it is drawn from the Solidarity union he has been instrumental in founding.*

If his own personal life seems relatively sound, he is deliberately vague about where he intends to lead his country. He once told an interviewer that he had a vision for what he wanted Poland to become; but when asked to describe it, he replied, "Not in an interview." Even though he is a man of very little formal education, he has surrounded himself with some of the ablest advisers in Poland. With food shortages seeming to bring Poland to the very brink of catastrophe in recent weeks, Walesa is being put to perhaps his severest test yet. So far, he has managed to strike a balance between the hard-line radicals who want more reforms faster and the Russians who may be becoming increasingly restless.

To obtain an interview with one of the most significant figures in postwar Europe, PLAYBOY *sent Ania and Kristina Bittenek to Warsaw in October. The sisters are American journalists of Polish extraction (both speak fluent Polish) who have had extensive contact with Solidarity officials in the past tumultuous year.*

PLAYBOY: We've been waiting nearly three weeks to speak with you. Obviously, you've had many important things to do, but other journalists have been in and out. Do you have a problem with PLAYBOY?
WALESA: I'm not prejudiced against the magazine. I just don't have time. For now, I'm giving you ten minutes because you have been persistent. I am so tired, both physically and psychologically, that I want you to finally give me some peace. I'm giving you your ten minutes, so take advantage of them. You've already spent two minutes. Such is life. I can't satisfy everyone.
PLAYBOY: Then it wasn't a bias against—
WALESA: Who told you that?
PLAYBOY: One of the men in your press office.
WALESA: *Jezus,* the man is crazy. You can tell him I said so. I have never had a bias against anyone. You've now spent almost three minutes.
PLAYBOY: Seven more minutes is certainly not what we came to Poland for, nor what your people promised us, but we'll do what we can.
WALESA: Look, please understand, today I have a more important goal. I respect you. After all, the press made a star out of me. That makes me happy. I owe you a lot. Without you, I would be nothing, it's true. But I have my main priority. Now you've used up *four* minutes.
PLAYBOY: Here's our first question. Do you—
WALESA: All right, I take it all back! You can start over with ten full minutes. Let's see what will happen.
PLAYBOY: Fine. You're an interesting breed of political leader. You are at the head of a democratic process, which is new for Poland, but some of your tactics are those of a dictator. Do you consider yourself something of a benign dictator?
WALESA: No, I'm a *democratic* dictator.
PLAYBOY: What does that mean?
WALESA: Well, I know that I ascertain our goals in a democratic way: We agree on a framework together. But the *realization* of this framework, of these goals, is my business. I handle them in a dictatorial way. Do we understand each other?
PLAYBOY: Do you establish any restraints for yourself? Do you just bludgeon those in your way?

WALESA: No, I do not wage war, I do not conduct some great battle. For the time being, I do not shoot to get things done. I select my advisers, I rely on them. I use tricks, devices in order to accomplish the tasks I am given.
PLAYBOY: Given the fact that you established this framework of Solidarity a year ago, why has it taken so long to realize your goals?
WALESA: Come on. This is a movement that is ten million strong. You must realize what our geographical and political position is. You realize where we are.
PLAYBOY: All right, but that's true only as far as tactics go. We'll keep it general and ask you simply: What is your goal?
WALESA: My goal: for Poland to be Poland.
PLAYBOY: Meaning what?
WALESA: Meaning that Poland will be Poland when we shall speak what we think. We shall be richer than the Yanks, for instance. Because we *can* be. We are no stupider than you. Certainly not. We just live in a country that brought us up with different social models to follow. So we had to assume different attitudes. We learned *despite* our models, so that is why we are actually stronger, better off than you are. Still, one has to make the most out of what one is given. Whether we will or will not is a question. But I think we will.
PLAYBOY: How can you hope for that kind of prosperity, and especially that kind of freedom, as long as Poland is part of the Soviet bloc?
WALESA: We have attained one tremendous accomplishment: In the past year, we have survived. This is the greatest accomplishment of all. We survived for a year. This year we also showed them our hand, our aims, our goals. We signaled to them what we wanted. Next year, after this [Solidarity workers'] congress, we should begin to realize those aims. Then we shall be able to pursue the dream of this Poland that we have imagined.

I see two Polands: I see the one we dream of and, at the same time, I see the present Poland, beset with difficulties. I see the games each side plays, I see the variants of those games. But I am—*we* are—capable of winning every single variant of every game! I know, it sounds like phenomenal conceit [*laughs*] but there you are.
PLAYBOY: Given the pressures on you, how, specifically, do you intend to accomplish even a few of those goals?
WALESA: If I were to tell you that—

[An aide interrupts.]

AIDE: Don't reveal your tactics.
WALESA: I would help those who don't wish us well. So I won't do it.
PLAYBOY: All right, we'll go back to more general themes. You say you have a dream of what your ideal Poland would be. Can you describe it? What would your Poland be like?
WALESA: Independent, self-governing.

[An aide again interrupts.]

AIDE: Self-*financing!*
WALESA: A Poland in which one can speak, one can write, which one can leave, to which one can come.
PLAYBOY: In which military or trade agreements are made by free choice?

WALESA: No, no! The military does not concern us at all! We want to fight with the same weapons we are using now. With those weapons we can smash tanks, cannons, neutron bombs. And smash them we will!

PLAYBOY: For all your rhetoric, Poland is a shambles as we speak. What are your specific ideas for rebuilding the country economically?

WALESA: You must realize one thing: I lead this movement and my main task is to keep the movement together. We may quarrel and fight, but we must stand together. It is my job to keep it tight and strong. But I am not the alpha and the omega, the be-all and end-all. Specific problems will be solved by those I lean on, people who are wise, advisers, experts, people who have something to say. I must choose the best ideas after discussing them in a democratic manner. Specific problems will be solved by people in specific fields; for example, education, commerce, foreign trade. I would be some sort of peasant philosopher if I were to take all that on myself. I know nothing of such things. All I know is that Poland must be different from what it is today, based on sound laws and principles of profit. It is this I will squeeze out of the groups whose task it is to think about these things.

PLAYBOY: Are you afraid that despite your popular support, people will get tired of this struggle? After all, it's been more than a year and from a practical standpoint, things have gotten worse in Poland.

WALESA: One can get tired of many things. Even making love can tire you. So you should make an effort to concentrate on things that are both pleasure-giving *and* useful. Work can also be love, you know.

PLAYBOY: As it should be—

WALESA: And vice versa. Love can be nothing *but* work. [Laughs heartily]

PLAYBOY: We were in Poland last year and one of the things that have struck us most during this visit is that people on the street have stopped being afraid. Do you agree with that?

WALESA: Let me reflect on that. . . . I once heard about some kind of sea animal that commits suicide by swimming right up on the beach. I have this dread that it might be that *we* are doing a similar thing. You cannot just disregard realities and become happy and euphoric without wondering if it all might be wrong, this euphoria. And it would be tragic if it turned out that way.

But, at the same time, yes, we are *not* afraid. Because we have a soul. It is not a soul so much in the religious sense as in the spiritual sense. We have a goal. We know that man does not live by bread alone, that he's not automatically content when he's well fed and he has a lot of dollars. We know, somehow, that inner satisfaction is worth more, that there is nothing to be afraid of. We shall *all* go one day, anyway. You know, we have something that you people have less of. You have some of it, but not much.

PLAYBOY: And so you are afraid of no one?

WALESA: No, of no one, of nothing. Of God alone. I believe that.

PLAYBOY: Then, is it fair to say that since the formation of Solidarity, the threat is larger but the intimidation smaller?

WALESA: Let me put it differently. Someone could say that because Christ was crucified, it means he lost. He lost because he was crucified. But he's been winning for two thousand years. The fact that I lose today because someone breaks my jaw, or hangs me, does not mean I lost. It only means I lost physically, as a man. But the idea, whatever happens later, may prove to be a greater victory.

I can say that our victory is certain. Certain! I do not know how long it will take or how high the price will be, but we shall smash a few things over in *your* country. Because this is nearly the twenty-first century, and we can no longer think in the same old terms. Even you still think in such terms—threats, tanks, one worker killing another worker. If small things go my way, in fifty years I am convinced that someone could order us: Fight with this woman soldier. But we will kiss.

PLAYBOY: How would you like to be remembered? What would you like schoolchildren to read about in history books?

WALESA: It would be best if they left me alone, if they did not bring flowers to my grave. For it would all be artificial. Someone would have ordered the schoolchildren to be there, someone would have proclaimed it Walesa Day or something. The person brings flowers because he was told to, because someone praised me, when, in reality, the person never really knows whether I deserved the praise. No one ever got to know a man to his very depths and no one ever will.

PLAYBOY: You seem to have an ambivalent opinion of yourself. How do you see yourself as a leader? Are you a prophet? An accident?

WALESA: I see myself as a very unhappy man. A very unhappy man whom fate—with some help from me—has thrown into this position of leadership. I fell into it and only then looked around. Leadership *seemed* interesting, stimulating—until I saw what goes on behind the scenes. Once I learned all of that, I didn't like it at all. But, at the same time, I cannot get out of it. It would look bad and be wrong. If someone were to throw me out, I would thank him personally. When I am absolved of responsibility, I shall be a happy man. I would live differently.

PLAYBOY: What would you do?

WALESA: Fish, write books. I'd write books and earn money. Earn a lot of money. See other countries, travel all over the world in a big bus with a bathroom and everything. I'd like to have a lot of money, because now I can't —no, I'm *not* interested in money! I'd write, fish, travel, sight-see, make love, and so forth.

PLAYBOY: You say you'd write books, but you don't read much, do you?

WALESA: I'd like to, but I don't have the the time.

PLAYBOY: It's been rumored that you've never read a book; is that true?

WALESA: No, it's not true. For instance, I did read my primer in kindergarten. [His aides laugh.]

PLAYBOY: We'd better get back to our political questions.

WALESA: We are way over your ten minutes, but you are so nice I shall talk to you some more.

PLAYBOY: You're pretty charming yourself.

WALESA: Of course I am. [Laughs]

PLAYBOY: Putting aside the daily headlines, do you think you could put your revolt into a historical context?

WALESA: Well, some say that the history of the world turns in circles. I find that to be a bit so, a bit not so. People and conditions are different. If someone wanted to speak generally, he would insist that history turns in circles, but we are different because our grandmothers were different.

PLAYBOY: In what way?

WALESA: Oh, come on. They were different from us because we have travel and communications that let us get anywhere, hear anything, in a flash. But we still don't communicate or get there on time. Our grandmother could climb into a horse and buggy, make her trip and still find time for fun. We take a plane and are late.

PLAYBOY: We meant what differences were there with regard to your being Polish? Is there something about the Polish experience specifically that affects *this* period of history?
WALESA: As Poles? I answered that indirectly already. From bad examples we learned good things. Therefore, we are wiser than you, because you learned good things from good examples. We had a bad school in which to learn, but from ideology alien to us, we learned a new and splendid ideology.

Poles are best at everything! Although I don't know history, for I didn't study—as you may have noticed. I don't know my dates, and so on—I do know one thing: The system that was put into place here is as if you took someone to a place where it was very hot and dressed him in a heavy sheepskin. Poland was always a rather free country. To a large extent, we are democratic. We hobnobbed with France, England, America and others. All of a sudden, we were ordered to love something else. We have freedom, justice, and so forth, in our blood and no one can hold us captive! Many a time we paid an awful lot. After all those payments that have been made, now we have figured out something so as not to pay this time.
PLAYBOY: We read somewhere that you had the worst marks in school in history; now, here you are, creating history yourself. Doesn't it frighten you to be playing at these high stakes with your limited background?
WALESA: No. You have to look at me from a different standpoint. I was very gifted until the seventh grade—damn gifted! I just glanced at the material and learned it. But as more and more material piled up, I felt less and less like opening the books. I was always interested in something else: *not* in what was assigned to me, but whatever *I* wanted to learn. I always reached the same goals in a different way. But later I felt too proud to return—I had driven myself into a corner. So it isn't good to be *too* gifted, because you lose certain normal opportunities to get ahead. But I would still say it is better to be a bee that knows it has the ability to collect honey but does not rush immediately for the big beehive, where it can fall in and get stuck.
PLAYBOY: That's interesting, but it doesn't answer our question: How much do you trust yourself and your abilities as you make these historical decisions?
WALESA: I don't trust myself at all, that is the truth. I'm never convinced completely that what I'm doing is right. Everything can be turned around. What we imagine today to be exactly right, in fifty years people might say: What fools they were! Why did they do such and such? They could have done it differently! They didn't realize that the situation was favorable toward them. We punch someone in the jaw today and later on someone will say: Damn it, they were irresponsible! They could have gotten their way quietly. They could have made gains more slowly, less violently. You cannot say that this *is* the way or this *isn't* the way. You cannot! What seems right today, tomorrow may prove wrong. It's like with some writers: Some book is dismissed today, and later they dig it up. *Jezus* and *Maria,* how wise it is now! Why was that book ever banned or burned?
PLAYBOY: Do you think one of *your* books might meet that fate?
WALESA: Me? I don't know how to write.
PLAYBOY: What about all those books you're going to write when you retire?
WALESA: Who? Me? I'll talk the way I'm talking now. I'll say to someone, "Listen, write this down." And out of it should come a book. But not a boring one. It has to be interesting. It has to overturn the old theories. And, at the same time, describe them, restore them in order to overturn them. Ha! Such exactly is life—strange and paradoxical.

[An aide again interrupts.]

AIDE: You people asking about education and such cannot go beyond a certain viewpoint—
WALESA: No, no. They cannot leave their circle.
PLAYBOY: Our editor wanted us to ask about your personal background—
AIDE: People from the West, in general, think this way.
WALESA: Exactly—and, again, even this editor, who has more learning, more letters in his head than I do, who *should* know more, even he knows nothing. Practically nothing. Let your people finally understand that we Poles really have a damned good education—historical and otherwise. We are all doctors! At least, I'm already a doctor many times over [honorary university degrees].
AIDE: He has six doctorates!
WALESA: Exactly. And *I* make mistakes. [Laughs]
ANOTHER AIDE: Seven! Already seven!
PLAYBOY: For a man with a lot of weight on his shoulders, you obviously stay relaxed. How do you do it?
WALESA: I collapsed an hour ago, slept for an hour and now I am relaxed. But in another hour, I'll collapse again. I'll talk with you a while longer, but then I'll be finished. I put *everything* into these efforts.
PLAYBOY: Have you studied the labor movement in the U.S. and in the West generally? And, if so, what are the major structural differences with Solidarity?
WALESA: I am a spy of life. I spy on everything. I study all. Whenever I have time for it, of course. Now, I don't deliberate on American trade unions, because I can more or less deduce what they are like. Since America is a capitalist state, its interests are different; therefore, the unions are different. Some adhere to one party, others to another, still others say everyone else is doing things the wrong way. So I can imagine how and what things are over there. And I shall probably be right, provided I think logically: Take the conditions that they have, see the limits they have, who is in charge, what's at his disposal, etc. So I can imagine it all, provided that I concede it is a country with a different system of government.
PLAYBOY: Of course, but does that knowledge about unions in the West help you in any way work out the Polish model?
WALESA: It helps me avoid the mistakes that Western unions—in my opinion—make.
PLAYBOY: What are some of those mistakes?
WALESA: The American model cannot be directly compared with ours. Here we have one party, a monopoly in government, in administration, in money, in *everything*. In the United States, it is somewhat different, as it is in all other capitalist countries, so their models do not apply to us.
PLAYBOY: You don't see any possibility of securing a multiparty system in Poland, do you?
WALESA: Perhaps differently, if we do not limit ourselves to names. A number of political parties? No. But it could be accomplished differently. There can be a strong and vigorous organization of canary breeders, for example, who would be so strong, so beautifully efficient that it could rally people, close down stores. But it would not be political by name.
PLAYBOY: It would be a political force, in other words—
WALESA: Yes. That canary breeders' union would publicize its views that its elections

are wrong—because the canaries aren't participating in the elections, for example [the aides laugh]—and they will say, "Now, hold it, what sort of elections are these? Is this supposed to be democracy?" Yes, indeed. So the point is not in the words *political party*. For as soon as it is a political party, it immediately wants to take over the government—or so they claim here. But our canary breeders, by forcing new elections through publicity, do the same job.

PLAYBOY: And you wouldn't want to have the job done in a more formal, more obviously political way?

WALESA: No, no. Why bang your head against the wall when you can take a hammer and smash it against the wall?

PLAYBOY: We know this question may be loaded, but who or what is your bigger enemy in Poland—the party or the Russians?

WALESA: Neither. The enemy, our most vicious enemies, are ourselves. That's the answer. We must understand one another better. We must stop being so suspicious of one another. To trust one another and, at the same time, trust nobody—this is a complex problem. So we are our own greatest threat. We threaten ourselves when we fight among one another for executive position, tripping over one another as we run for the most important chairs.

PLAYBOY: To rebuild economically, what do you see as your greatest roadblock: the internal Polish system or—

WALESA: I find *no* roadblocks. There is no obstacle that cannot be removed. Everything can be surmounted, everything can be conquered—everything! It only depends on your choice of weapons, your choice of means, on the degree to which you are blinded by rage. I used to make such damn blunders! That is, I used to act this way [looks pugnacious and stubborn]: "What? No? Oh no!" And I would get it straight on the jaw. Finally, I came to the conclusion that that wasn't the way. Since I lost, it means I wasn't right. So now I turn it around and I think: Aha! I cannot defeat you today. OK, bye. Let's try it from another angle. And another. Then another still. And if I do not succeed, it means that I am not clever enough or am incapable of choosing the correct weapons.

To recapitulate: There are *no* obstacles that we cannot surmount. Of course, I don't mean such theoretical obstacles as reaching Jupiter in one jump or bringing the sun down with a rake, no. Only the realistic obstacles, the ones that you meet in everyday life, under normal conditions.

PLAYBOY: These are certainly not normal conditions. Why do you think the Russians still allow you to carry on? After all, for thirty-six years, things were done their way, and this is a very different situation for them.

WALESA: Because we outsmarted everyone. We learned from their models, we are their students, and no teacher can outsmart a good student.

PLAYBOY: You mean their tactics ricocheted? [Walesa and his aides laugh.]

WALESA: That's right.

PLAYBOY: As in the case of the farmers, perhaps? In Geneva, the Russians voted in favor of a farmers' trade union but later, in Poland, claimed that there was no legal basis for forming a union of individual farmers. Is that one example?

WALESA: I'm very tired now.

[There is an interruption and the question is not answered. The interview resumes later.]

PLAYBOY: There are other reasons, to be sure, but isn't the labor unrest at least partially responsible for all the shortages and for inflation?

WALESA: Of course it is. How could it be different? If I don't bake any bread and later say, "Give me bread!"—that is illogical. A baker cannot logically go on strike and then make a fuss because there is no bread. So, certainly; yes. But, at the same time, it is necessary to get to the root of why this bread disappeared, or why it was badly managed or badly distributed. This problem needs to be examined from several angles. We always hold that our work is wasted, destroyed, badly sold, etc. And in this, we see the main cause for the losses or shortages. We do not think it is because of how we work. We do not because, indeed, our work has been destroyed for many years—by building plants in the wrong places, by doing what was not needed, etc. This went on for such a long time that today we want to take care of these matters first. That way, we can get different results. Am I saying it right? Yes, I think so.

PLAYBOY: This question could only come from a country with food surpluses, such as America, but if consumers in cities go on strike or won't pay higher meat prices, doesn't that hurt the farmers who raise the livestock?

WALESA: No. You have to move in a real world, the one that we live in. But let's put it differently—in ten or twenty years, when we establish international contacts, when factories establish contacts with other factories, and so forth, I don't rule out the possibility that we would eat American meat instead of Polish. Because this or that manufacturer or processor will decide, No, they won't buy from Polish farmers, for they don't do it as cleanly or as well as the Americans. So the theoretical problem you raise is possible, but for the time being, there's no such danger.

PLAYBOY: This is a commonly heard criticism in the West: Walesa can get people to go on strike, but he can't get them to work. Why not?

WALESA: No, no, no! As I've told you, everything *can* be done, I can do *almost* everything! However, in order to play the game, one needs cards. Take the "free Saturdays" issue, for example. [The government required Poles to work on Saturdays. Solidarity successfully fought for revocation of the edict.] If during talks with the government I had been given the cards I wanted—and I did ask for them—the game could have been much more interesting and strong. But I wasn't given them. I did say officially: "Give me a card; I want to play."

PLAYBOY: We don't understand—you mean if the union—

WALESA: No, not the union, the government in this case. I cannot be more explicit. I needed cards, some cards that in the end we got anyway. But once again, the government party's pride wouldn't let them give us the cards just like that: "Here you are. You've got the better of the government—once again." The idea was not to give it to us.

PLAYBOY: "It" meaning more freedom for the union?

WALESA: No . . . we'll enslave ourselves on our own. [Laughs] No, at that moment, we needed the following: to supervise the storehouses that the government claimed were empty. We wanted to check them and say, "Yes, indeed. The storehouses *are* empty." What other card did I want? I wanted something else, I can't remember right now. . . . Anyway, had I got them, oh, that would have been beautiful, but they didn't give me any. Or, rather, they did, but not by dealing over the table, on the table, but *under* the table. Do you understand now?

PLAYBOY: Somewhat. Let's suppose the party discredits itself further at some point—

WALESA: I don't want that. I'll help the party once it starts to discredit itself or collapse. There are no other realities here. We cannot overthrow the party. We cannot take the power away from it. We have to preserve it. At the same time, tame it, and let it eat with us, so that it will relish what we create.

PLAYBOY: What then, if the party is still just as weak?

WALESA: I'll join the party.

PLAYBOY: You'll join the party? [Nervous laughter among Walesa's aides]

WALESA: We cannot let the party become very weak. We know that with control, with constant prompting of our wishes and with help, this party will do a good job and people will be happy about it. But we have to create the proper conditions for this party. The conditions it had up until now were *no* conditions. And that's why we have to educate the party. Under no circumstances can we overthrow it, for that would be a disaster for all of us. Therefore, we want it to subsist and, at the same time, we want to control its activities. We want to live. We want the party to serve us—and it will serve us. We'll teach it to.

PLAYBOY: By disaster, do you mean the Russians would not stand by any longer?

WALESA: No, no, no. Not the Russians. We would shoot *each other* down!

PLAYBOY: Without any party, you think Poles would shoot each other down?

WALESA: Yes! do you think that without the party I would not push myself for president? Or that my friend Jacek Kuron wouldn't also? Or [Leszek] Moczulski? Oh, come on! [Laughter around the room] We would all shoot each other down! We have no programs, we have no programs!

PLAYBOY: You can see no alternative to the party? The parliament? The courts?

WALESA: The parliament would fall apart too. Everything would fall apart. No, ma'am. Right now, the arrangement is such that the party watches everything. But later, if there were no party, everything would just scatter. It's as if you brought us a basket of ants. In the basket, the ants stay together; but try to empty the basket, and, *Jezus,* we'd never hold them!

PLAYBOY: What about Prime Minister Wojciech Jaruzelski? Would he be an obvious candidate to become president?

WALESA: I don't think so. Although it's hard to say. Hardly anyone who has tasted some power as I have tasted it, who understands it and who wants to be honest about it, when faced with the possibility of giving it up, will give up power that easily. He will not want to. *I* don't want power anymore. Although I'm not saying that I would not accept something . . . but I really don't like it. If you *knew* how much I dislike it . . . but, poor me, what can I do? What other choice do I have? None.

PLAYBOY: Do you agree that a workers' revolt is the one thing that genuinely challenges the Soviet system of control, since the Soviet system is supposedly based on the consent of the working class?

WALESA: I don't agree with that at all. The workers' movement does not challenge anyone. We ourselves challenge one another with this revolt. Who is responsible that things in Poland got to where they are? We are! Like a flock of sheep, we went to the polls, we applauded and shouted our support for each new policy. I shouted, too. When someone announced a meeting with a deputy or a councilor, we were the ones who didn't go. We went out for a beer instead. We elected decent people. At some point, I was even elected somewhere, and spat upon two days later. So this revolt is not a challenge to the Soviets but to ourselves. *We* are responsible for this mess. When some director did something wrong, all these people who looked on—where were they? So let's examine this revolt and we will find that we were the guilty ones. I was, too.

PLAYBOY: How serious is the split between the moderates and the radicals in the union? Have you become too much of a moderate for your hardliners?

WALESA: No, no. This is a great misunderstanding that I will try to straighten out. I am damned radical, but not suicidal. I am a man who has to win, for he does not know how to lose. At the same time, if I know that I cannot win today because I don't have a good enough hand, I ask for a reshuffling and then check whether I have gotten a better hand. I never give up. I'm damned radical, I repeat. But I don't walk into a stone wall with my eyes shut—I'd be a fool. There are some such fools, but not me. If I see that I cannot win today, I ask myself: Damn it, why is he stronger than me? Is there any other way I can get at him? And I try the other way.

In Bydgoszcz, some of our supporters were beaten up, and that made a lot of people think. Some party members, who are also people, thought, This is a bad affair—someday *I* could be beaten up as well. And so they end up supporting us. There was also a police— [Here the transmission of this interview from Warsaw to New York by telex was halted, from the Warsaw end. After a pause of several minutes, transmission resumed.] precinct that hadn't known about the beatings, and they supported us, too. So there is much evidence that in the end, we'll win, and here is my radicalism, a sensible one. I don't want to pay. I don't like to pay. I like to satisfy my appetite, but I don't like to pay.

PLAYBOY: How does your religion and the reality of a Polish Pope influence your decisions and actions?

WALESA: I believe in God. As a matter of fact, if not for my faith, I would not be here. I would have walked away a long time ago. What do I need this for? As things were, I lived like a human being. Now what do I live like? It is all so hard, so thankless, that it's beyond my strength. But I am religious, and thus I endure. And there's beauty in everything. Even in pain. One can enjoy everything. One only has to know how to enjoy.

PLAYBOY: Even if you cannot always be home for supper?

WALESA: Of course. So I am *enjoying* the fact that I didn't eat today.

PLAYBOY: We talked to your wife and she worries—

WALESA: She understands me less and less. My wife does not understand me; I don't know whether anyone at all understands me. . . . It's late now. I've given you so much time. I must go.

PLAYBOY: Just one thing more. Would you ever like to live in the United States?

WALESA: [Mockingly imitates a Polish-American accent] No, no. I like Poland and I am here. I will go, of course, because there are interesting things in America, pretty things, many snobs. [Laughs and returns to his normal pronunciations] I want to get to know all people, I want to go to the States, for we owe them a lot in general. . . . I'll check it out a bit, see how things are there, though I almost know. I know quite a lot.

ED KOCH

April 1982

Interviewer: Peter Manso

If anyone wanted to know what it was like to govern the capital of the world in 1982, one only had to talk to Ed Koch, the irrepressible mayor of New York City. Since his election in 1977, when New York's financial and psychological state was widely seen as moribund, the voluble, outspoken mayor had presided over a restoration that had balanced the municipal budget, made the city seem livable again, and in the process, transformed him into a national symbol of upbeat, feisty cheeriness in the face of urban blight.

Pinning Ed Koch down for a conversation wasn't considered a difficult journalistic feat. He was easily available, whether shaking hands on Manhattan streets, asking "How'm I doing?" or sitting back with reporters and charming them with blunt opinions and funny one-liners. But the Playboy Interview promised to be something different: Here was a chance to talk definitively about the state of the city and its mayor for a national audience, at great length, free of the caution and constraints that afflict politicians during a political campaign. Koch had, after all, just been reelected (in November 1981) by a seventy-six percent majority. And, as he never tired of saying, being the mayor of the most exciting city in the world was the only job he ever wanted.

Peter Manso, a former New Yorker who now lived on Cape Cod, was tapped to conduct the interviews and he and editor Golson agreed that Koch's relentless boosterism of the Big Apple was a topic worth probing in depth. There were many other subjects Koch would end up discussing with PLAYBOY—being Jewish in America, race relations, Reaganomics—but it was in his role as defender of New York City that the journalists felt Koch needed to be pushed. Surely, they speculated, Koch cannot be as much of a Pollyanna about the city's problems as he seemed; surely, the dirt and crime got to him, too, if only occasionally. . . . The fact that both Manso and Golson (who joined briefly in the questioning) had recently moved their families out of New York City gave the conversations a personal flavor.

At one point during an early interview session Koch rebutted a point Manso was making about suburban life with the retort, "Have you ever lived in the suburbs? . . . It's sterile . . . it's wasting your life." Manso returned to the theme later in the interview, suggesting that for many people who had tried living in the city, there existed an option of living more tranquilly in rural America. "Rural America?" Koch snorted. It was a joke, he said, to argue that people could escape urban problems by fleeing. Not only did the nostalgic vision of pastoral, rural America not exist, but the city's problems had moved to the suburbs as well. There was some further bantering back and forth over time wasted in subways versus time wasted in pickup trucks, and neither the journalists nor the mayor appeared to think anything unusual had been said. It came as no surprise that the mayor, who loved nothing better than a good argument, would defend his beloved city against the suburban hordes. Would La Guardia have done less?

The problem, of course, was that La Guardia never decided to run for governor of a highly rural and suburban state. About a month before the Playboy Interview with Koch was due on the newsstands, Governor Hugh Carey of New York State unexpectedly announced he would not run for reelection. Despite his wide popularity, Koch had repeatedly said he would never run for any office higher than mayor. (In fact, in the forthcoming PLAYBOY he had said he disdained the governorship because it required living in Albany, which was "small-town life at its worst.")

But during those several weeks Koch obviously saw something in Albany he liked. Seeing that there were no other candidates statewide who were remotely as popular as he, and spurred on by a friendly newspaper campaign, Koch decided to run. He announced three days before the first issues of the magazine became available.

There followed a firestorm of press coverage and political reaction unlike anything since the Carter interview in PLAYBOY six years earlier. In some respects, even though the interest was more regional, it was a more intensively covered issue than Carter's adultery-in-my-heart remarks. Rather than being seen as an uncharacteristic gaffe, as Carter's was, Koch's remarks seemed not only in character but enormously relevant to the central issue of the campaign: What does a fast-talking, smart-aleck, city slicker *really* feel about the state's nonurban voters?

Unfortunately for Koch, at least a partial answer was delivered at the polls later that year. Edged out by Lieutenant Governor Mario Cuomo, Koch's race for the governorship was over. Although the fact that he also lost New York City, which he loudly defended in the interview, is proof that his PLAYBOY remarks did not cause his defeat generally, it was nevertheless accepted that Koch's most telling interview, conducted in the world's media capital, was brought off by an out-of-town journalist working for an out-of-town publication.

Some time before New York City's mayoral election last fall, New Yorkers were treated to a widely publicized press photo. Hizzoner Ed Koch was seen loping across the Egyptian desert astride a camel, his famous smile framed by a burnoose fluttering in the wind—indeed, looking for all the world like Koch of Arabia. Shortly thereafter, while campaigning for reelection, Koch made an appearance at the Central Park Zoo and reporters wanted to know about his by-now famous ride. A TV reporter asked if hizzoner would now consider repeating the stunt, only this time with a nearby caged Bengal tiger. Koch paused, looked for an instant at the animal and then turned back, his smile still in place. "The mayor is not a coward," he intoned. "But neither is the mayor a schmuck!"

Another time, Koch was dedicating a new shopping center. Adept at working an audience, he seemed to have the crowd with him. Suddenly, a black member of the racially mixed group shouted, "We want John Lindsay!" Again Koch paused, to reflect on the reference to the former mayor, whose "liberal" administration Koch blames for many of the city's present troubles. Then he peered at the audience: "Everybody who wants Lindsay back, raise your hands," he commanded. A few hands went up. Koch leaned forward and bellowed: "Dummies!" The audience cheered.

Such stories characterize New York City's Edward Irving Koch. Recently reelected by an overwhelming majority, Koch has been credited with saving the nation's most celebrated city from bankruptcy when only four of America's larger cities have managed to remain solvent. A major accomplishment, certainly; but his flamboyant and uniquely outspoken style attracts as much attention nationally as his fiscal policies. For Roger Rosenblatt of Time, *he is New York's "nut uncle," his entire being "fused with the life of his lunatic city. . . . Koch can be brave, hilarious, generous, protective, occasionally gracious and more rarely, touching." He is the consummate showman, the master of well-timed one-liners, who, for* The New York Times, *has "defied enough conventional wisdom to fill a textbook." With his readiness to excoriate the "wackos," "richies" and "schmucks," Koch does not suffer fools gladly. But at the same time, he prides himself on being a man of the people, ready to listen to his constituents in movie lines, on street corners and at subway stops. He refuses to mince his words, even referring to himself as Mayor Mouth. He has provoked unions and management, blacks and whites, Jews and gentiles, while still retaining enough support to have run for reelection last fall with the endorsement of both the Democratic and the Republican parties. That he won with the largest margin in the city's history is the stuff of political legend.*

But not everyone loves Ed Koch. Among New York's traditionally liberal movers and shakers, there are those who claim that the improvements Koch boasts of having accomplished were at the expense of the poor, specifically at the expense of minorities. Koch, with characteristic bluntness, has indeed opposed racial quotas and busing; he has denounced "poverticians" and "poverty pimps" in the course of revamping the city's poverty agencies; and he has also opposed, in favor of slum rehabilitation, low-cost public housing in middle-class neighborhoods. Openly, unabashedly, he boasts of being the champion for the middle class, which has led more than a few observers to charge that he has forsaken his "liberal" roots.

When PLAYBOY *decided to plumb the Koch personality, we asked free-lance writer Peter Manso to conduct the interview. Manso was one of the principal brain trusters of the highly unorthodox Norman Mailer–Jimmy Breslin mayoral campaign in 1968, which he subsequently chronicled in his book,* Running Against the Machine.

PLAYBOY: As mayor of New York City, you've made national headlines and are probably best known for your blunt candor and outspokenness. Why, then, as we begin our first interview session, do you have two advisers at your side and your own tape recorder running?

KOCH: Simple. I don't want there to be any question as to what was said. We always have a member of our press staff at interviews, although we don't always use a tape recorder. On several occasions, reporters have made major errors on matters affecting the city, which they then had to correct when we produced the tape. It's never secret, however, and just as you're using one, I prefer it that way.

PLAYBOY: You represent New York and you don't want the city misquoted, is that it?

KOCH: Yeah, I think so. I don't want it to sound smug, but I've become identified with New York, and I think people like me and I think they like New York. A mayor can be a downer or an upper. I think I'm an upper. But I won't dissemble or deceive. I may remain mute on a subject. I don't have to offer myself to the caldron. But if I say something, I believe it.

When I first became mayor, it used to upset people; it drove my advisers crazy. They would have preferred more ambiguity, so I wouldn't ruffle so many feathers, but now they see it as a strength, not a liability. The important factor—what voters see in me—is intellectual honesty, meaning that I say exactly what I believe, even when it's not popular. I say it privately *and* publicly.

PLAYBOY: Which you claim accounts for your popularity among the voters, your recent landslide reelection. All that would suggest a decidedly high opinion of the electorate.

KOCH: What do you think I'm saying? I got more than seventy-five percent of the vote. A major part was my honesty, of course. In the past, I've admitted that maybe I ought to take tact lessons, which is a flip way of saying I don't have a bedside manner. I talk to all people exactly the same. Most politicians don't believe in this. They assume voters want pie-in-the-sky promises, but I've always worked on the premise that there's this extraordinary common sense out there. That was the slogan of my campaign: "Common sense." My opponents said to the voters, "Ask yourself the question that Reagan asked when he ran against Carter: 'Are you better off today than you were four years ago?' " But the voters in New York knew that wasn't the proper question. It was me who found the proper questions: "Did Koch get the biggest bang for the buck? Did he do the best possible with the reduced dollars available or was there someone who could have done it better?"

PLAYBOY: How much of the attention is paid to you and how much to the city itself?

KOCH: People are interested in New York and they're interested in me for whatever it is I add to it. But if it weren't me, there'd be attention paid because it's New York City. The place has a mystique. It's the largest city in the country, the city the newspapers report on. Things happen here that get attention; elsewhere, they're ignored. There's a sense of mystery, danger, all the things that go into this special city, with its seven and a half million people. It's so varied, so different. In 1964, Barry Goldwater made a remark that I think he now regrets, namely, that if it were possible, he would saw off the Eastern Seaboard—meaning, basically, New York City—and ship it back to Europe. Obviously, he was referring to the foreign influences here, the fact that we're made up of so many different groups. And it's that very diversity, those differences, that so intrigue people.

PLAYBOY: But you're aware that many people regard New York as a cesspool, even though they may be fascinated by it?

KOCH: It's a love-hate relationship, and depending upon the moment in time, it shifts. From 1975 to 1978, there was a lot more hate than love. Nowadays, I think it's turned around, starting with the Democratic Convention of 1976, when the Texas delegation held up its WE LOVE NEW YORK sign. The Bicentennial, with its tall ships, helped as well. I think I've contributed to the positive energy, too, and it's a sense that the city isn't standing still. This is what people tell me and I accept it.

PLAYBOY: Even though according to the census, almost one million people left the city between 1970 and 1980?

KOCH: Uh-huh, and they're coming back. How do I know? My sister came back two years ago. The middle class left because they had the wherewithal to leave and the services were deteriorating. Now that the services are improving, they're coming back. They found that they had traded deterioration for a sterile environment in the suburbs.

PLAYBOY: And they're prepared to put up with the dirt, the crime and the inconvience?

KOCH: Sure. Have you ever lived in the suburbs? I haven't, but I've talked to people who have, and it's sterile. It's nothing, it's wasting your life. And people do not wish to waste their lives once they've seen New York! I think we've gone through enormous changes, especially a change in outlook. Remember, under Lindsay particularly, the city's *raison d'être* was to be Fun City, Welfare City, anything but a business city. By creating a climate for jobs and profits in the private sector, we've brought about a big change. When I first suggested "Common sense" as my campaign slogan, my media adviser, David Garth, didn't like it; but now, he has no hesitation at all. It says everything, because in addition to describing me, it characterizes the city—what I take to be this new sense that we're not standing still.

PLAYBOY: By that, we take it that you mean things are getting better. But despite the city's solvency, there are many who feel things are getting worse, that city services are deteriorating.

KOCH: People compare New York City with the perfect city, with nirvana, with El Dorado. What you have to compare it with is other cities. We have estimated that we'll be spending thirty billion dollars over the next ten years to repair our infrastructure—far more, proportionately, than cities like Chicago, Boston, Detroit and a host of others. Does Detroit get the same kind of publicity?

PLAYBOY: What are you saying? That people have been misled, brainwashed by a negative press?

KOCH: No, I haven't said that about the press. In fact, I think it's terrific that people are so interested in us, that they want to come here, either to visit or live. But if you're gonna talk about New York City, you have to talk about it in the context of other cities, which raises a small difficulty. Namely, that there is no other city like New York City and its seven and a half million people. You can take several of our larger cities in the country—say, Boston and Chicago and San Francisco, plus the others—and fit all their population into New York. So while our problems are proportionately comparable to and in some cases even less than others', the dimensions here are so large that they become *sui generis*. From 1969 to 1977, we lost six hundred thousand jobs. That's one and a half times the size of Buffalo, the second largest city in the state of New York. In Detroit, they have twenty-four-percent unemployment! Do we ever hear about that?

PLAYBOY: But you're dodging our question: despite the statistics, doesn't the fact that many people see New York City life as a series of assaults—

KOCH: That's ridiculous.

PLAYBOY: Well, do women feel comfortable walking in the streets at night? Can anyone safely stroll through Central Park at night?

KOCH: How many women feel comfortable walking at night in Boston, or in Birmingham or San Francisco? When I lived in Washington, D.C., in 1969, it was scary, and if you walked the streets alone at night, you worried about it. But I have never—*never*—worried about walking the streets of the city of New York. Obviously, there are places you don't walk; I'm talking about my own residential area.

PLAYBOY: Your own residential area? Only recently, the daughter of [former] New Jersey governor Brendan Byrne was attacked down the street from Gracie Mansion.

KOCH: What are you saying? We're twentieth down on the FBI list of rapes. That means nineteen other cities are more dangerous.

PLAYBOY: Again, let's not keep talking statistics. Let's focus on impressions and perceptions, the years of negative publicity—

KOCH: We brought *that* on ourselves by our arrogance prior to 1975. We got our comeuppance when we suddenly found ourselves on the edge of bankruptcy. But New York is very appreciative that the rest of the country helped us when we were on our ass. We were chastened, and since the country helped us, there's a civility today that wasn't here before, an appreciation that we're living in a terrific city. It's obvious. Don't you agree with that?

PLAYBOY: A lot of people wouldn't, no. And probably, some New Yorkers would be a lot less polite about it.

KOCH: They'd think that I'm talking cant, is that what you're saying?

PLAYBOY: Cant, yes. But beyond that, they'd claim that the place often feels unlivable. Hostile, cynical and brutal.

KOCH: People who live in the city? Go talk to cabdrivers and cops. They have the best—

PLAYBOY: We did just that, coming over here to Gracie Mansion this morning. Talked to the cabbie—

KOCH: Yeah, what'd he say?

PLAYBOY: He said, "I'm carrying a gun." And it brought to mind Howard Beale in *Network,* the lunatic news commentator shouting, "I'm mad as hell and I'm not gonna take it anymore."

KOCH: Yeah, and not too long ago, some guy committed a robbery on Fifth Avenue and passersby beat him to within an inch of his life. The cops had to rescue him. [Laughs]

PLAYBOY: You're laughing now as you recall this. Why? Just how is it funny?

KOCH: I see humor in a lot of things. But my answer is akin to what I said to the cops after I was assaulted—

PLAYBOY: The incident at the doctors' convention, at the time you proposed closing Sydenham Hospital?

KOCH: Yes. I was addressing three thousand paramedics and doctors in the Hilton Hotel, and just as I began, some people got up to demonstrate. Suddenly, I felt a hand around my throat. It came from the rear. Then a fist socked me in the eye. There was something in the fist, and it was coming down my cheek. It turned out later that it was an egg, but at that moment, I believed I was the subject of an assassination. My adrenaline's working, obviously; I don't know what's happening and for all I know, I'm fighting for my life. So I grabbed the guy's hand and wrestled him to the ground. Turns out he was a doctor from San Diego, part of the demonstration, throwing eggs at me. I have this guy down on the floor and I want to kill him, I'm so angry. Then my security man comes to help me and he's holding the guy down and he sees that I'm set to kick him in the balls or in the head. Some vital place! I want to kill him! And my guard looked up pleadingly. Without uttering a word, he was saying, "Don't." And I didn't. But later, I described this feeling to a class of rookie cops, that I'd wanted to kill him because I thought he had tried to kill me. Instead, I eventually filed a criminal complaint and testified, and eighteen months later, the guy was given thirty days in jail and a thousand-dollar penalty. The judge told me that very few people in public life ever pursue such cases. But I had to do it. Otherwise, they'll do it again to somebody else.

PLAYBOY: Do you worry about assassination?

KOCH: When George Moscone, the mayor of San Francisco, was killed, I was asked for my reaction. It shook me because Moscone wasn't killed by a stranger; he was killed by somebody he knew, who had access to his office. The point is that you can have all the security in the world but you still can't protect yourself. I also happen to believe in the doctrine of *beshert,* which means "God ordains"—your life is laid out, predestined. Obviously, you're not supposed to make it easy for those who want to dispose of you—you don't throw yourself in front of a train—but nevertheless, when it's all said and done, I'm a child of God, as we all are, and whatever He wants to do with me, He will do with me.

PLAYBOY: Why be so fatalistic, even passive? Why not fight back?

KOCH: I understand the feeling—that's what I told those cops. Just like I understand the feelings of those people who beat up the robber on Fifth Avenue. That's why I laughed. I have the same feeling—me, the mayor.

PLAYBOY: Aren't there a lot of middle-class people who more and more approve of that kind of behavior?

KOCH: Yes, but we will not tolerate it. If someone engages in vigilantism, we're gonna put his ass in jail.

PLAYBOY: How did you feel about the film *Death Wish?*

KOCH: [Laughs] Oh, I thought it was terrific, but at the same time, I deplore what the guy did; it was vigilantism and, as such, unacceptable, intolerable.

PLAYBOY: But you also understood?

KOCH: Sure. You could identify with the guy's need for revenge, even though it's not permissible in a society of law. Still, I thought it was a terrific action movie.

PLAYBOY: Isn't it also deplorable—symbolic of everything we're talking about?

KOCH: Oh, please. Look, I like movies. *The Warriors*—very stylized, almost a ballet about gangs in the subways. It was wonderful. The fact that I would like *Death Wish*, though, doesn't mean I have to approve of its message.

PLAYBOY: What about the argument that self-defense *should* be permissible if the police or our laws can't protect people in the first place?

KOCH: It's unacceptable, just as unacceptable as a totalitarian society, where you have very little crime but also very few civil rights to begin with. I'm sure you'd be safer walking the streets in Moscow than in any major city in the United States. I also know that the Soviets have their *gulags*.

PLAYBOY: Your answers are consistent with the theme, so common in newspapers and magazines, that to be a New Yorker, you have to have a heartier, walk-through-the-troubles, grin-and-bear it attitude.

KOCH: Well, there *is* a feistiness and an ability to roll with the punches. But you can talk about the city of New York in a vacuum and come to any conclusions you want. Now, I think we're getting a hold on crime here and throughout the country. Everybody's concerned about it. You know my anecdote about senior citizens? When I was a congressman in 1973, I spoke to a group of senior citizens who wanted to know what I was going to do about crime. I said, "You're right, crime's the number-one issue. But, ladies and gentlemen, I know a judge who was just mugged, and guess what he did? He called a press conference and told reporters, 'This mugging will in no way affect my decisions in matters of this kind.' " An elderly lady stood up in the back of the room and called out, "Then mug him again!" [Laughs] It's a marvelous story; it always gets a response from people.

PLAYBOY: It *is* a good story. But your critics claim that your constant references to the middle class, to a reliance on what you call common sense, is just a buzzword, an appeal to white-middle-class fears and resentments.

KOCH: Bullshit! In prior administrations, it was taboo to talk about the middle class. It was part of the Sixties and Seventies syndrome that somehow, the middle class wasn't the group that you ought to court. "Who wants their lifestyle?" the rhetoric went. "Why should the middle class be elevated?" asked many of the radicals. So it startled a lot of people to have a mayor come in and say, "I think the middle-class life-style is *terrific*. I believe we oughta kiss the feet of the middle class for saving this town, since they're the ones who pay the taxes and create the jobs for the poor." And since I'm not able to do very much for them in terms of increasing services, at least they should know they have a friend in City Hall who wants them to prosper, who wants them to stay here and who doesn't take them for granted. Prior to my coming to office, it was always "What can we do for the poor, how do we expand welfare?" Recently, I testified before a legislative committee on homeles men and women, the sick people out there who sleep in the streets. One of the legislators complained about welfare centers that supposedly weren't giving out the necessary information, and then he demanded to know, "Well, are you going out there, Koch, to get people to apply for welfare and for Medicaid and telling them about all these programs?" I said, "No." Under Lindsay, they brought us to bankruptcy by going out and telling people to come in—"C'mon, get on the welfare rolls, you don't even have to file an affidavit." "No, I don't do that," said I to this legislator, who then accused me of violating my constitutional oath. I replied, "No, I don't think so, and seventy-six percent of the people recently indicated that they don't think so, either."

PLAYBOY: But popular or not, by emphasizing the middle class, aren't you practicing a kind of benign neglect of the poor?

KOCH: Look, it's the middle class, which pays the taxes, that allows me to spend fifty-six percent of our budget on twenty-six percent of the people, the poor. I know that jobs are the key, since lots of jobs have left this town, but we have 120,000 new jobs over and above those we had on December 31, 1977, and I know it's the middle class that has created those jobs. I mean, who do you think owns the factories, the stores and the places where jobs are created? It ain't the rich and it certainly ain't the poor! So I wish I could do *more* for the middle class. Why do you think they went down to Florida during the Lindsay Presidential campaign and put up this blimp with the slogan LINDSAY SPELLS *TSOORIS* [trouble]? Who do you think did that? The middle class, and not just the Jewish middle class. So now I'm saying to them, I'm not doing that to you, I understand your problems, plus the fact that when I upgrade the cops and the firemen and the educational system, I'm affecting the city as a whole.

PLAYBOY: By the same token, however, there is no blimp over Harlem saying, KOCH IS COOL.

KOCH: No, but there *is* a blimp over Harlem that says, WE'RE FOR KOCH; 60 PERCENT OF US ARE, because that's the way the black community voted in the last election.

PLAYBOY: We'll come back to that. But the so-called Sixties syndrome you refer to—you sound as if it offended you, as if the counterculture was a repudiation of everything you personally cherished.

KOCH: Yes, I think it was a license to do anything. What happened in the Sixties was that the values of integrity and hard work and industriousness no longer counted, were no longer perceived as worthy of reward. This even extended to government, where the attitude was, to hell with the middle class. It was a loss of balance. I don't know of any period when there wasn't something good and something bad, when we didn't move away from the center and then come back agan. In the Sixties, however, it went too far.

PLAYBOY: Does your appreciation of middle-class values, of hard work and responsibility, reflect your own upbringing?

KOCH: Sure. We were poor, and we all worked very hard. We lived in the Bronx, an all-Jewish neighborhood, low income, very safe. The rich one in the family was my uncle Max, who I think was a bottlegger in addition to being involved in the clothing business in Manhattan. Then the family moved to Newark, New Jersey, where another uncle ran the largest catering hall and dance palace in the city. Since my father's fur business had gone bankrupt during the Depression, he was given the hat-check concession, which became our major source of livelihood. I didn't get paid; I got an allowance. My mother and brother worked there, too.
PLAYBOY: Was money always a problem for you?
KOCH: Yes. I think our income was sixty dollars a week for five people. We never went hungry, though. Sometimes my father had to go out and borrow five dollars from somebody to make sure that Friday night was a good Shabbath dinner. We weren't religious, but Friday night was always terrific. There were times when he didn't have enough money, but even so, everything was stable and nice. My father was a much more accepting person. My mother was the stronger of the two.
PLAYBOY: Aside from the Bronx and Newark, were you exposed to other parts of the New York area when when you were growing up?
KOCH: When I was growing up, Manhattan was another planet! I didn't formulate it in my head at the age of seven, but what were you going to do in Manhattan? What was my mother going to do, go to the theater? Ridiculous! If she went to the theater, it was the Yiddish theater, on the Lower East Side. That's not the Manhattan most people talk about. Forty-second Street was Manhattan, and nobody lived there. I never heard of Park Avenue or Greenwich Village until I was in college.
PLAYBOY: You first left home when you went into the army?
KOCH: That's when I grew up, yeah. I became more self-aware because it was my first real exposure to different kinds of people and ideas, to non–New Yorkers, say. I enjoyed the cosmopolitan aspect of it.
PLAYBOY: Coming from this relatively insulated background, didn't you find the army a bit threatening? The great World War II novels *From Here to Eternity* and *The Naked and the Dead* both dwell on the anti-Semitism of the period.
KOCH: I never felt threatened as a Jew. I had only one anti-Semitic incident in the army, in basic training at Camp Croft, South Carolina. My platoon was about fifteen or twenty percent Jewish, a lot of them from New York, refugees from Europe, and what triggered it was that the Jews were not terribly athletic and found the obstacle courses difficult. The situation was made worse by this one smartass Jewish kid who would always have the answer when the sergeant asked a question. It irritated a lot of people. One guy in particular was constantly making anti-Semitic remarks, and I began thinking, I'm not strong enough to beat him up but I'm going to build my strength.

So I practice, getting stronger, until about the fifteenth or sixteenth week of basic training, when he makes another of these brutalizing comments. I walk over, grab him by the neck and say, "OK, when we get back to the barracks, you and I are gonna have it out." He says, "What are you talking about?"—'cause he didn't consider me Jewish, I could *do* the obstacle course, right? When we got back to the barracks, the Jewish kid who has created the problem now offers to help, and I say, "Get the fuck away, you prick! It's because of you I have this problem!" So we go out, me and the other guy, and we fight. There was a big crowd, fifty people or more. He knocks me down, I get up. I don't want this to sound like a movie, but he knocks me down again and again I get up. And I hit him. Finally we finish. He's won, of course, but for the next several weeks, there's not one anti-Semitic comment in the whole company. Not one. I felt terrific.

PLAYBOY: It really *was* a scene out of *From Here to Eternity.* Later on during the war, you supposedly became a de-Nazification specialist in Bavaria.

KOCH: That's an overstatement. After the war, I was in Bavaria, in a small military detachment near Würzburg. My job consisted of replacing public officials who were Nazis with non-Nazis. And believe me, if there was anything I could do to engage in retribution, I was going to do it. Replacing people in public office, confiscating property for the military government, taking over houses. There were always Germans coming in to tell you who the Nazis were, but they all claimed they had Jewish grandmothers.

PLAYBOY: Did you ever visit one of the concentration camps?

KOCH: Not during the war. I went to Munich in 1961 specifically to see Dachau. I don't know that I can even describe the experience. At Dachau, they have a little museum. . . . I was crying. I remember the camp itself was very hard to find—they sort of conceal it from you—but once I'd seen the furnaces, the crematoria, I didn't stay very long. Afterward, I was outraged, outraged that the world should have let this happen. And it did, no question about it. Every country participated. France, England, the U.S., all of them. It's an enormous blot on the record of every Western country that they didn't do something.

PLAYBOY: The abiding feeling of Jewish life is the specter of the Holocaust—

KOCH: It certainly is. Never again.

PLAYBOY: And you believe it *could* happen again?

KOCH: Absolutely. That's why I speak out when there's an atrocity in Paris or Austria or Vienna, or in Northern Ireland or Uganda, for that matter. *Every* country is capable of the vilest of excesses and almost every country has been. The Turks destroyed the Armenians in what is really known as the first Holocaust. The Spanish Inquisition expelled the Jews. In Ethiopia, they have destroyed blacks. Every country is capable of genocide.

PLAYBOY: As one of the country's most prominent Jewish politicians, you seem to feel the need or responsibility to speak out for Israel. How much of this is personal and how much is a factor of your being mayor of a city—

KOCH: That has more Jews than Tel Aviv?

PLAYBOY: Well, isn't it true that New York City is perceived nationally, perhaps with a taint of anti-Semitism to it, as a Jewish town?

KOCH: Do you really think so? Look at all our black Jews, all our Puerto Rican Jews, all our [laughs] . . . Irish Jews!

PLAYBOY: But seriously, you have come out very strongly in support of Menachem Begin's policies in Israel. You could be considered a hard-liner when it comes to Israel.

KOCH: Begin's an extraordinary man, even though he's occasionally perceived as a little too inflexible. I don't agree with everything he's done and I've said so. But when a nation like Israel has been under constant attack and you see its so-called allies running away out of fear of losing the petrodollar—I'm talking about the English, the Austrians and the French in particular—then what you're talking about are governments that have engaged in anti-Semitic actions. The best illustration is Lord Carrington, the British foreign minister, who's a schmuck. He claims that the PLO isn't engaged in terrorism. I say, thank *God* there's a Menachem Begin who has the strength to stand up for his people. Nobody's perfect, mind you, but if Israel had a more malleable prime minister, there'd be no hope; they'd just give way on everything.

PLAYBOY: How important to you is Israel's security?

KOCH: As a Jew who happens to be an American, I place American security first. I want to say it only once: These are my loyalties—the country, the city, *then* Israel. In that order.

PLAYBOY: As we said before, you're the best-known Jewish politician in America today—

KOCH: Isn't that nice! [Laughs]

PLAYBOY: You don't think the description fits?

KOCH: If I'm not, I'm one of them. OK.

PLAYBOY: Do you see anti-Semitism growing in this country?

KOCH: Yes. I certainly saw it in the attempt to smear the opponents of the AWACS sale to Saudi Arabia. But more broadly, there's a kind of ground-swell feeling that Israel no longer has the right to express itself. But what do you think Saudi Arabia was doing in the case of the AWACS? Prince Fahd or the royal family was supposedly given a room in the Senate Building while the AWACS vote was going on. So it's become a double standard. If the Jewish nation of Israel stands up and talks about its security, then it's attacked as being *too* Jewish, engaging in something that nobody else is doing, when in fact everybody else is doing it with impunity. Even more egregious is the line that the American Jewish community is part of some Israeli lobby. Well, so what? Why shouldn't we defend Israel? What should we do, go to the gas chambers silently?

PLAYBOY: What about the kind of remark that seems to be chic among some Europeans—Oriana Fallaci, for instance, said in her Playboy Interview that she believed the American media are controlled by the Jews.

KOCH: That's self-evidently false. Obviously, there are some Jews in the media, but here in New York, the most media-oriented city in the world, only one of the three newspapers has Jewish ownership. Anyone who says that the media are controlled by Jews is *meshuga* [crazy]. But I've heard that before. It's a left-wing point of view, part of the current anti-Semitism that comes from radicals. For example, I believe that Jesse Jackson has engaged in anti-Semitic remarks, and besides, he went to Lebanon and kissed Arafat on the cheek, gave his blessing to terrorism. I've never been supportive of Jesse Jackson; I *always* thought he was bad news on this issue. Obviously, he's done a lot of good things motivating black kids. But now we're talking about anti-Semitism. The key phrase today is anti-Zionism, which is used to conceal anti-Semitism. In fact, though, in this case, the two are one and the same.

PLAYBOY: Do you see anti-Semitism growing in Europe?

KOCH: Obviously, the bombings of synagogues in France were terrorist acts directed at Israel. True, they may very well have been terrorist acts directed at Jews, too. I'm not going to argue that. But no, I don't see it escalating in Europe in the sense that we've been talking about.

PLAYBOY: But you just said that anti-Zionism is the same as anti-Semitism.

KOCH: But in Europe, it isn't specifically related to the Jews. We're past that. They don't give a fuck about Jews! For most European countries, it's cravenness. What they care about is Arab money!

PLAYBOY: How do *you* feel about Arabs' buying up property in New York City?

KOCH: I don't have any problem with that so long as they're not able to buy up the

media. I'm not someone who says Arabs can't come in. In fact, I'd welcome them to come and buy the World Trade Center. They have the money; let them put it back on the tax rolls. I do very well with the Arabs who live in New York. Why? Because I've spoken out for the poor Lebanese, and even when I was in Congress, I condemned the slaughter of Lebanese Christians. I mean, it's criminal what's happened there.
PLAYBOY: Since you've publicly criticized Reagan's stance on Israel, what do you think, in general, of recent Presidents' attitudes toward Jews?
KOCH: Actually, I happen to believe that Ronald Reagan is very sympathetic to Jews. When he came to see me in 1977, he said, "I'm so pleased that you've spoken out against what Carter is doing on Israel." At the time, Carter people were participating in the UN resolutions denouncing Israel, and I think Reagan's statement to me was genuine, more than campaign politics. Fundamentally, he's a decent guy, though the people around him are terrible—Weinberger and Haig—though Haig himself is a mixed bag. Under Carter, there was Brzezinski, who was a very bad guy, as we subsequently found out when he revealed himself after leaving Washington.
PLAYBOY: What about Nixon? You are on record as saying he's an out-and-out anti-Semite.
KOCH: Oh, I believe that, just based on conversations in the Watergate tapes where he referred to Jews in a pejorative way. His comments were filled with anti-Semitic slurs.
PLAYBOY: And Ford?
KOCH: Ford was always very good on Israel, so I was shocked at what he did on AWACS. Carter, though, was never any good on Israel, but I cannot say he's anti-Semitic.
PLAYBOY: That seems tough on the man who engineered the Camp David accords.
KOCH: The Jewish community felt the same way I did. I'll give you an example. Hamilton Jordan and Pat Caddell and a number of others wanted me to speak on behalf of Carter to the Jewish community because they knew he was in trouble with the Jews. I said, "No, I won't do it." One of them said, "If you think *we're* bad on Israel, anti-Semitic, wait'll you see the Reagan people." And I said, "No, I don't believe it. I don't believe Reagan's anti-Semitic." They mentioned Senator Jesse Helms, and I said, "No, you're all wrong. Jesse Helms may hate Jews, but he *loves* Israel."
PLAYBOY: What about Jimmy's brother, Billy Carter?
KOCH: Oh, his brother was clearly anti-Semitic, sure. What do you want from a wacko?
PLAYBOY: You're quoted as having said, "If Carter had listened to my advice, he might still be President." How did you mean that?
KOCH: Remember, I was one of the first people to be for him early on in his first campaign. But even though I said I was going to vote for him, I was not going out to support him actively unless he spoke out for two issues in 1980. One was to take more of a pro-Israel stand; the other was to support the Moynihan Medicaid Bill, which would have provided greater federal sharing for New York City's Medicaid costs, which are breaking our back.
PLAYBOY: And you got no response?
KOCH: That's correct. I asked them to do it, and they wouldn't. They started to come around in the last ten days in terms of Israel, but by then, they'd already lost the Jewish vote.
PLAYBOY: Still, during the course of the Presidential campaign, you appeared suffi-

ciently sympathetic to Reagan to prompt a number of editorial writers to speculate on your real commitments. Would it be fair to say that while you supported Carter, in your heart of hearts, you were secretly pulling for the Republicans?

KOCH: No, that's not true. It's also unfair. What people don't understand is *why* I was hospitable to Reagan. Granted, there was a lot of criticism by my fellow Democrats, but I don't understand why people found it so unusual. I'd have been a horse's ass to refuse a Presidential candidate's request to be filled in on the problems of New York. I think it was helpful to the city; it was another instance of plain common sense. Courtesy never really hurt anybody, so far as I know.

PLAYBOY: Yet, in your Baltimore speech in late 1981, you called for the toppling of Reagan. Would you clarify your position?

KOCH: What's unclear? [Grins] I'm a Democrat, remember? I believe that we ought to have a Democratic government, a Democratic President. What's wrong with that? It's not inconsistent.

PLAYBOY: There have been national press stories that describe you and Reagan as the odd couple. Obviously, many people now feel that your policies are more in tune with the Republicans than with the Democrats.

KOCH: Look, Reagan is going to be the President for another three years. I have to work with him and I will, getting the most I can out of Washington for the city on an equitable, just basis. You cannot expect that someone whom you've been uncivil to is going to be helpful. I doubt that Governor Hugh Carey, for example, can get very much from Reagan, since it was thought that the governor was uncivil to him. But I wasn't rude, so now I have access to the White House; they respond to my telephone calls.

PLAYBOY: They may not, now that you've called for Reagan's defeat in 1984. Take Republican congressman Jack Kemp, for example. He supported you for mayor and reportedly arranged your initial meeting with Reagan. Now he's accused you of betrayal, hasn't he?

KOCH: Well, they can't figure me out. [Laughs]

PLAYBOY: You're laughing. Why?

KOCH: I always laugh at these things because people have *such* a hard time figuring me out. If they just exercised some common sense they wouldn't have any trouble at all. It's simple. I'm a Democrat. My loyalties are to the Democratic Party; everybody knows that. I've never concealed it.

PLAYBOY: But beyond being polite to Reagan, your friendliness to the Republicans certainly helped win their endorsement in the last election. Wasn't this a way of sticking it to liberal Democrats, those in your own party who are critical of you?

KOCH: I told you: It was common sense, it was political—

PLAYBOY: No, no, what we're getting at is what we've heard as your motto: "Forgive your enemies but never forget their names."

KOCH: That's not my quote. Mine is, "I'll never forget and I rarely forgive."

PLAYBOY: How much of this is real? How much of it is politics?

KOCH: It's both.

PLAYBOY: The part that's real would make you a very vindictive person.

KOCH: You call it vindictiveness, I call it justice. I believe in reward and punishment. I believe if someone kicks you, it should not be with impunity. I also have a high regard for loyalty and can't recall ever having been betrayed by someone I considered a friend.

PLAYBOY: What about former mayor John Lindsay? When he first ran, didn't he

promise to back you for City Council if you backed his mayoral race? And once he was in office, didn't he refuse to endorse you?
KOCH: He wasn't a friend. And don't you think he's paid for that? [Laughs] My sister said I should lay off him, that she began to feel sorry for him, so I quit and made peace with him.
PLAYBOY: There's a kind of glee in your voice. You like the debates, the arguments, even the heckling, don't you?
KOCH: I've always enjoyed debates—in high school and after law school, when I supported Adlai Stevenson and his campaign committee needed street speakers. You could go to any corner in the city and speak if you had an American flag, so I strarted doing that during my lunch hours. And I *loved* those street-corner debates. I found that I'm very good at it. Any time you get a heckler, it enhances your ability to move a crowd, and I delighted in those exchanges, just loved 'em.
PLAYBOY: What, the improvisational aspect of it? The theater?
KOCH: Yes, being able to turn things around and change the expected outcome. Even then, I rarely spoke from a script. I'm not a good reader. I'm much better now, but when I first read speeches, it was without emotion, without the electricity that comes from eye contact. If you're a good speaker, you're watching the crowd; you know what they're reacting to and you build on it.
PLAYBOY: Do you agree with those who have called you an actor?
KOCH: Let's define what you mean by actor. For me, the term means that the performance—performance here meaning the delivery—is polished. It has a beginning, a middle and an end. In that sense, yes, I'm onstage. Some people denigrate me by saying, "Gee, he engages in too much humor." I think that's ridiculous. Humor is terrific in public life—
PLAYBOY: Why are you defensive about it?
KOCH: Because of the silly deprecations of what I do, the cracks about Koch's "practicing government by one-liners." It isn't government by one-liners at all. I *can* demolish an opponent in one line, but that isn't the same thing as winning over the state legislature on Medicaid or pulling New York City out of bankruptcy. If I'm an actor, so be it; but don't think it hasn't been good and useful for the city.
PLAYBOY: Let's expand this a bit; maybe it will bring us closer to what's unquestionably your special style. Wasn't Richard Nixon a consummate actor?
KOCH: Nixon? He's a phony, I'm not. I'm me. My performance is not dishonest. His *always* was. Let me tell you, when I first met Nixon in 1969, he'd just been elected and had come around to address the House of Representatives. We suspended business and everybody stood in line to shake his hand. Fishbait Miller, who was then the doorkeeper of the House, says to Nixon as I'm stepping up, "Mr. President, this is one of *our* boys who took one of *your* seats away. Ed Koch, from the 17th in New York." I'll never forget it. Nixon put out his hand and said, "Lotta money in that district, Ed. . . . Lotta money." It was incredible. Here I am, the freshman congressman meeting the new President, who's grinning ear to ear, and this is all he has to say!
PLAYBOY: And his partner, Spiro Agnew?
KOCH: Look, Nixon was a bad man who violated the law; he was bad for the country. Agnew, though, I can describe only as *spittle.* I mean, Agnew is so far beneath contempt, he isn't a fit subject for discussion.
PLAYBOY: Well, if the electorate is as smart as you always claim, how could the country have put a couple of bad guys in the White House?
KOCH: We didn't know it then.

PLAYBOY: But you believe that the electorate has common sense, that folks have an instinct for making the right decision—
KOCH: Well, they're not always right. I said they're *mostly* right.
PLAYBOY: Do you see yourself as a kind of populist figure, the Everyman of Gracie Mansion?
KOCH: I don't like "populist" because it has an anti-Semitic aspect to it. But yes, I do see myself as a kind of Everyman. I don't want to get involved in critiquing my predecessors, but I don't believe any of them perceived himself as an ordinary human being.
PLAYBOY: What do you mean?
KOCH: Take John Lindsay, whose slogan was something like, "He's fresh when the rest of us are tired." Or, when he ran for Congress, "Pride of the district, hope of the nation." I say to myself, "This is *meshuga*!" Before that, there was Robert Wagner, who was the son of one of our greatest senators, the scion of a political family, quite well off, social and all the rest of it. He saw himself as the average joe? Come on!

I'll give you an even better example: When I first ran for Congress, in a Republican district, nobody believed I could win against the poshest, most social, wealthiest guy they could run—Whitney North Seymour, Jr. A guy with four names! *Oy*, and me, I only had two! But I won with fifty-one percent of the vote, I got seventy-five percent of the vote by the time I ran for a fifth term. After I left Congress, the area reverted to Republican. The same thing is true as mayor. I ran the first time, I'm six in a field of seven; I don't have a chance. The second time, they said, "Who's running against you?" Even though there *were* some vile attacks form some of my opponents during that campaign.
PLAYBOY: The most vile smear on you personally came during your first mayoral campaign, in 1977. Namely, the opposition slogan VOTE FOR CUOMO, NOT THE HOMO.
KOCH: Oh, sure. They were hand-lettered, nonprofessional posters. I never saw anybody carrying one, but I saw some on walls in Grand Central Station and on lampposts.
PLAYBOY: How did you respond?
KOCH: First, shock. Then anger that someone should stoop so low.
PLAYBOY: Had the question of your "homosexuality" ever come up before?
KOCH: In every campaign I've ever been involved in. There are always rumors when candidates happen to be single, male or female, and sometimes even when they're married. So that part of it wasn't a shock to me, it's typical of New York. What was a shock was having a poster put up so openly. VOTE FOR CUOMO, NOT THE HOMO! That had never happened before.
PLAYBOY: Were you asked to make a statement to the press?
KOCH: Only once, for TV. I responded by saying, "No, I'm not homosexual, but if I were, I hope I'd have the courage to say so, because I happen to believe that there's nothing wrong with people who are homosexual." Ten percent of the population is made up of homosexuals. What's cruel is that you're forced to say, "No, I'm not a homosexual," which in effect means you're putting homosexuals down, which I don't want to do.
PLAYBOY: Is the term *confirmed bachelor* a characterization that can be applied to you?
PLAYBOY: Well, I am a bachelor at fifty-seven. I've never thought of the term *confirmed,* but the probability is that—
PLAYBOY: No, no. The analogy would be to the priest, who remains celibate to devote

his life to his calling. Could being a confirmed bachelor be a way of putting all your energy into running the city?

KOCH: No, that's not the way I look at it at all. Whether or not I get married, I have not in any way taken a political vow that in order to do my duties, I foreclose marriage. That's ridiculous. What I have said on the subject is that marriage would be a plus, not for political purposes but because it would be nice to have the support that comes from a happy marriage. On the other hand, many marriages in the political sector are altogether unhappy. What the public gets as a result of my being single is obvious—it gets more hours of work out of me because I don't have to run home to the family.

PLAYBOY: How do you deal with speculation that exercising this kind of power can be a sublimation for sex and marriage?

KOCH: I assume that's a Freudian analysis and it may very well be correct, but it's of no concern to me. I remain convinced, without knowing the actual figures, that a substantial number of people voted for me thinking I was homosexual. Equally, a substantial number voted for me thinking I'm *not* homosexual.

PLAYBOY: *Are* you homosexual?

KOCH: No, I'm not.

PLAYBOY: Have you ever had a homosexual experience?

KOCH: I'm not going to discuss my private life with you. But you asked me that point-blank question and I've given you my response. A substantial number of people—again, I don't know the percentages—don't give a shit. It's not a factor one way or the other. They don't weigh it, they don't ask it, they don't think about it. So it's not something that distresses me anymore.

PLAYBOY: But at any point, has any of your advisers said, "You know, Ed, it would look better if you had a lady at your side to be your hostess"? Have you had any of that pressure in the past four or five years?

KOCH: No. Most people in my administration are friends and think I'm pretty good at running my own life as well as running the city's. Very few of them, if any—no, *none* of them—believe that in these areas, they're smarter than me.

[Koch's press aide comes in and interrupts.]

AIDE: Can I interrupt for one second? Carol Bellamy [New York City Council President] was on *Newsmakers*—

KOCH: Did she attack me?

AIDE: No, she didn't attack you, but she thinks maybe it would be a good idea for the city to take over the bus and subway system from the MTA. She's not sure, but she's leaning in that direction. You want to give the press a statement?

KOCH: All right: "I'm always interested in her advice because she's done *such* a good job on the MTA to date." [Laughs] No, no, let's put this in: "If this is one of her solutions, I'll certainly look at it."

PLAYBOY: OK, let's return to the public response to you—

[Further interruption]

AIDE: Can I just. . . . Let me read a version back to you, Ed: "I'm always interested in her advice. She's done a good job on the MTA." OK?

KOCH: No, no! 'Cause I know she *hasn't* done a good job. "I'm always interested in

her advice. She's been on the MTA board for four years, and I'd be interested in knowing how it's improved in that time."
AIDE: Oh, Jesus.
KOCH: You like that? What do you want to do? [Loudly, looking at the interviewer] She's a pain in the ass!
AIDE: How about, "She's been on the board of the MTA for four years. If she wants to suggest that as a solution, I'll certainly be happy to study it."
KOCH: Good. "She's been on the board for four years, she must have *some* insights. And I'm always interested." Work it out. Look, she gets a free ride on a whole host of things. That's what's upsetting to me, that she hasn't been subject to the criticism she should be. She's on that goddamn board; what's she done in the four years?*
PLAYBOY: Can we continue? Here we have the mayor of the most important city in the world, one of the best-known politicians in America—
KOCH: Isn't that nice to hear? [Laughs]
PLAYBOY: This august individual who—
KOCH: I'm *not* august—
PLAYBOY: Who uses a style and words that could well be considered undignified or unsuited to his office. The question is—
KOCH: By whom? Four percent? Those who don't like me? On that issue, the numbers are real small—
PLAYBOY: You've taken a poll on the public's response to your style?
KOCH: No, it's my own personal gut poll. Without any false humility, I've got a good intellect, not a superintellect. I'm no genius, just a good intellect—
PLAYBOY: What *is* your IQ?
KOCH: The last time I was tested, 123.
PLAYBOY: Not in the 160s?
KOCH: No. But I *use* people who are in the 160s. I have very good administrative skills. I'm able to use the talents of other people who are smarter than me in particular fields. If they were the mayor, though, they would destroy the city. Now, the talent that I have is reinforced by the fact that my reactions are those of ordinary people, common-sense reactions, as I've already told you. If I call Billy Carter a wacko, it's because everybody knows he's a wacko and it's probably what they've been calling him in private all along. The only person I upset with that remark was Jimmy Carter. I'm not going to get into the whole conversation between us, but he said, "Here I am, I'm under attack, and you call my brother a wacko!" The public, though, appreciated it.
PLAYBOY: Your lack of decorum lets people identify with you, is that what you're saying?
KOCH: Maybe. I see it as their realizing that I'm no different from them. They think, Koch is saying exactly what I'd say if it were me in City Hall. I don't want it to appear that I'm smart and clever because I'm not so smart and clever, but the people do feel a vicarious participation in government with me. They say to themselves, "Finally, there's someone who says what has to be said, exactly the way I'd say it if I were there."
PLAYBOY: Presumably, you're talking about New Yorkers now, a group hardly known

*This exchange took place a week before Koch told some New York City daily reporters in early December 1981 that he considered Bellamy a "horror show." In the ensuing local furor, he apologized and the two political rivals apparently made their peace.

for their decorum. What about the others? You're a national figure; and someone in the Midwest, say, might well be put off by the mayor of New York's using words like *wacko* and *schmuck*. You're confident that it's not you—or the city—who is going to be seen as wacko?

KOCH: Stop it! Midwesterners are just like anybody from the Lower East Side on the issue of my colorful language. What's wrong with the word *schmuck* anyway?

PLAYBOY: Well, what does schmuck mean?

KOCH: Schmuck means penis, but it's been accepted in American parlance today as another word for jerk. Nobody sees it as an obscenity or vulgarism.

PLAYBOY: But there are people who, nonetheless, accuse you of an intemperate style. Didn't you earlier say that the electorate wants its politicians to be better than itself?

KOCH: That accusation is made by people who don't like what I'm doing politically. If you've got guys like Arthur Schlesinger, who's worked for the Kennedys, or here in New York, Dick Wade, who's been aligned with Lieutenant Governor Mario Cuomo, then it's obvious, isn't it? Neither can get to City Hall, since I don't let them participate in anything I do. I wasn't for Kennedy and I defeated Cuomo in 1977, so of course they don't like my style. On the other hand, if I were pushing things they supported, I have no doubt they'd say I have a grand style.

PLAYBOY: What kinds of things? It's no secret that you've provoked a good deal of criticism on the issues. You've been called a "secret Republican" by *The Village Voice*—

KOCH: *The Village Voice* is a porno rag!

PLAYBOY: You say that because the *Voice* was one of your bitterest editorial opponents this past election. But even in a friendly cover story, *Time* magazine also used the phrase "crypto-Republican." If you don't like that term, do you agree that you fit the definition of neoconservative?

KOCH: I regard both those terms as a writer's conceit to sum up the idea that I'm outside the traditional Democratic mold. I'm neither neoconservative nor crypto-Republican. Reporters use clip files, and labels have a way of being repeated.

PLAYBOY: But you won't deny that you're a fiscal conservative?

KOCH: No, of course not. But I don't happen to consider that to be Conservative with a capital C or Republican with a capital R. If seventy-five percent of the country is for the death penalty, does that make it conservative? The most vocal spokesmen for the liberal point of view may oppose capital punishment, but they don't speak for the majority of liberals. Besides, what's liberalism? It's no longer what McGovern and Kennedy stood for. I doubt it ever was. The two of them just dominated the Democratic Party.

My priorities remain the same. The difference is that I won't borrow money for education, say, from our capital budget because that's fiscally stupid. In the Sixties, people spent money they didn't have. The result was that New York City nearly went bankrupt. Now we recognize that we have to prioritize. If there's more money, you spend more on cops and education and sanitation and so forth. If you don't have the money, you don't spend it, but that doesn't mean you look at cops, education or sanitation any differently than before. Anybody who's a mayor today *must* be a fiscal conservative. The problems facing our cities don't exist in a vacuum. If it were possible, I'd sentence every member of the Congress to one year as mayor, if only to make them understand the damage that we did. I include myself here; at the time, I had a one-hundred-percent ADA [Americans for Democratic Action] rating. You name it, and if it cost money, I was for it, so long as it was "good" for us. That is why I refer to myself as Mayor Culpa. We did a lot of damage, not intentionally—nobody intends detriment, right?—but there was damn little understanding.

PLAYBOY: This common fiscal dilemma—did it hit individual cities at the same time? How much of the problem was due to local mismanagement?

KOCH: Take New York. We began overspending in the last two years of the Wagner third term—namely, 1963 and 1964—then Lindsay came in. By overspending, I mean we spent more than we had in terms of providing services. You cannot provide services to an extent greater than taxes or other incoming revenues, and Wagner had already begun to use the capital budget for operating expenses, which then mushroomed. Under Lindsay, they took monies meant for street repair, for the bridges, sewers and school buildings and used it to hire cops and teachers and sanitation men. Then, big surprise! In 1975, suddenly, the banks that had been buying the city's paper closed the window. We were on the edge of bankruptcy. We'd become overextended. Part of it was the national economy, inflation, the cost of energy, OPEC and so forth. But the cities themselves became overextended. Like New York, they provided services they couldn't afford. It was almost epidemic, with everybody expecting more and more every year.

PLAYBOY: A case can be made that your fiscal conservatism really works in favor of big business, that it's a way of getting the banks and real-estate interests behind you. It's even been charged that you've sold out to them.

KOCH: *Any* mayor will be supported for re-election by the people with money in this town. If they think the race is going to be close, they'll even give money to both candidates! I'm talking about campaign contributions, not personal money. Now, it's no secret that the city's real-estate and financial institutions think I've done a good job and would like to see me remain mayor for another term. They didn't, however, support me four years ago.

PLAYBOY: Why do they like you now?

KOCH: Why? Because when I came into office in 1978, there were only two major construction jobs in the entire city. Today, there are 329. That comes as a result of businesses' saying, "We want to build in New York City; they're competitive, and they match incentives available anywhere." The best illustration is the American Telephone & Telegraph Company, which was considering moving its major offices to New Jersey. It asked for an abatement for a new two-hundred-million-dollar building, since with an abatement, its taxes over a ten-year period would be reduced from seventy-six million to fifty-six million dollars. The board that handles such matters therefore had to make a decision, weighing the fact that if American Telephone built in the city, there would be an additional fifteen hundred new jobs. The answer? Grant it the twenty-million-dollar reduction over a ten-year period, during which we will receive fifty-six million dollars in new taxes as well as benefit from the new job opportunities.

PLAYBOY: That's one side of it. But what about the charge that it is the real-estate interests that are making New York unlivable? Rents go up, the middle class is forced to leave.

KOCH: As I said before, the middle class is coming back. That's not to deny, though, that rents are unconscionable. The fact is that they would be even worse if we didn't have rent control and rent stabilization.

PLAYBOY: Where does it end, though? By reputation, New York now accommodates only the rich and the poor.
KOCH: Where does it end in the rest of the country? It's not just a local problem. There isn't new housing around today because of the high interest rates, and there's very little local government can do. We fight to keep rent stabilization and rent control. With one million fewer people than we had in 1970, according to the census, we have twenty-two thousand more apartments but not in all parts of the city. When you talk about the unconscionable rents, you're basically talking about the poshest areas—the Upper East Side, Upper West Side, the Village, Brooklyn Heights and Riverdale. If you want to live in other boroughs—in Queens, say—there are lovely apartments. They're not cheap, but they're nothing like how you're ripped off elsewhere.
PLAYBOY: So the middle class is returning but only to live in Queens?
KOCH: Partially, yes. Because it's no longer possible for middle-class people to live outside of rent-stabilized apartments. In suburbia, you used to pay forty thousand dollars for a home; now the average price is seventy thousand. What's the difference? They can live in New York City, only it means setting up new enclaves.
PLAYBOY: But won't some people be forced to move every time their area becomes "posh"—"gentrified," if you will?
KOCH: You have to understand, a city is constantly in flux. What we're talking about is the regeneration of certain areas. You don't use the term gentrification, because that implies you're driving people out. But if there are reasonable laws to protect the poorest of the poor and the elderly, then there's nothing wrong with this. The mayor's not a miracle man; he can only work with what he has. At this moment, my priority is to keep the city financially stable.
PLAYBOY: Of course, but you're on record as opposing low-cost housing projects for the poor as well.
KOCH: It's not that simple, and I've also been vindicated. You're obviously referring to the episode of the low-income project in Forest Hills, Queens. Fine. In 1971, when I was on the Congressional Banking and Currency Committee, which had jurisdiction over housing dollars, I went out there and said to myself, "This is crazy. You're gonna build three twenty-four-story buildings for some forty-five hundred tenants on welfare in a residential area!" Not to mention that it's in a two-fare subway zone, so it will be hard to go and look for work. So I spoke out and said, "No, I'm opposed to this."

When I got back to the office, I'm inundated by telephone calls from friends who were mad as hell. I'm called by Stanley Geller, one of my oldest supporters who's been involved in all my campaigns. He's a good lawyer, a super lawyer, who defended me when Carmine DeSapio tried to get me off the ballot in 1963, and he calls and says, "Ed, I just heard you say on the radio that you're against low-income housing." "I didn't say that," I reply. "I said I'm against the Forest HIlls low-income housing project." He said, "You can't be against *any* low-income housing project." I said, "Stanley, if that project goes up, it will destroy the neighborhood. The people there will move out." "I don't care if they move out," he said, "the Jews in Forest Hills have to pay their dues." So I replied, "Stanley, you're an old friend, you're a very rich man, and you've helped me throughout the years. I'm very appreciative of your support. And you have this wonderful brownstone on Twelfth Street; I really wish I owned one like that. And you also have this marvelous home in the Hamptons, this near-Olympic-size pool, and you've been kind and invited me there, and I wish I owned that, too.

And the day your kids were born, Stanley, you registered them in private schools. You're telling me that the Jews in Forest Hills have to pay their dues? I'm telling you they are willing to pay their dues, only they're not willing to pay *yours!*" And my good friend Stanley Geller hung up on me. We didn't speak for a year.

PLAYBOY: So you feel you've been given a bum rap on the racial question? It's as simple as that?

KOCH: No, it's not as simple as that. But the black and Hispanic communities, not the middle class, have been the ones given favored treatment by my administration, and quite correctly so. My defense, if it requires a defense, is that you should put the money where the need is, so fifty-six percent of our total operating budget over the past four years has gone to serve the twenty-six percent of the city's population that falls below the poverty line. How has their actual day-to-day lot been improved? The single most important thing, I think, is education. Kids are reading above norms for the first time. There's also been greater black representation in government. I've been accused of not doing enough, but compared with previous administrations, I think I've been terrific.

PLAYBOY: Yet the charge of insensitivity to minorities persists.

KOCH: Of course it persists! But it isn't borne out by the recent election. If I'd been guilty of this charge of discrimination, wouldn't it have been reflected in the vote? It wasn't. I'm more strongly supported in the black and Hispanic communities than either the media or, worse still, some of the black leadership will acknowledge. I got sixty percent of the black vote and there have been figures as high as seventy percent for the Hispanics.

PLAYBOY: But doesn't this overlook—

KOCH: It's a lot of baloney. I mean, people just repeat this crap.

PLAYBOY: So, once and for all, if you've been as evenhanded toward minorities as you claim, why does the perception that you're racially insensitive persist?

KOCH: I think it's intentional, frankly.

PLAYBOY: You think there's a conspiracy to get Ed Koch?

KOCH: No, not a conspiracy. I don't believe in conspiracy theories; I really believe that Oswald killed Kennedy. What I'm saying is that I believe there are opinion-makers and that the opinion-makers are largely on the left.

PLAYBOY: You don't get criticized as much as most politicians. You get along great with the press, don't you?

KOCH: I happen to have very good relationships with the editors of the three major papers, correct. I see them regularly, and three or four times a year, I will ask for an editorial luncheon.

PLAYBOY: Reportedly, you speak quite often with Rupert Murdoch, the conservative press baron who recently bought *The New York Post* and was an ardent supporter of Reagan.

KOCH: I know how that rumor got started, and it's nonsense. The journalist who started it is a schmuck. As for Murdoch himself, I've found *The New York Post's* editorial positions to be extraordinarily supportive of what's good for the city or, if you will, of *my* vision of the city.

PLAYBOY: Even though the *Post* is seen by its detractors as the most sensational and vulgar tabloid in the city?

KOCH: What? Its headlines? "KILLER BEES COMING TO NEW YORK CITY"? I believe bees *are* coming, ultimately. They're working their way up an inch at a time from the Yucatan. But why should people call *The New York Post* vulgar unless they want to call one million readers vulgar? The real rag that Murdoch owns is *The Village Voice.*

PLAYBOY: Ah, yes, your favorite. How do you feel about New York's major black newspaper, *The Amsterdam News?*

KOCH: An anti-Semitic rag. They constantly refer to [Manhattan borough president] Andy Stein as "Finkel"—not Finkelstein but *Finkel.* What are they trying to convey? Obviously, that he's a Jew. He changed his name from Finkelstein to Stein—he didn't change it from Stein to Brown—so there's no question it's a slur. If you look at *The Amsterdam News,* you'll find that not only are they anti-Semitic, they've become radical as well. They've come out against every black and Hispanic council member.

PLAYBOY: Thus their attacks on you can't be construed as reflecting the views of the black community?

KOCH: Oh, God, you're starting this again? No, they can't. How can *The Amsterdam News* represent the black community if the black community doesn't even read it? Their circulation has fallen to nothing.

PLAYBOY: You are on record speaking of black anti-Semitism in general, not just at that newspaper. We quote from some tapes you made for an oral-history project, but which were recently published in a profile of you by journalist Ken Auletta: "I find the black community very anti-Semitic. I don't care what the American Jewish Congress or B'nai B'rith will issue by way of polls showing that the black community is not. . . . My experience with blacks is that they're basically anti-Semitic. Now, I want to be fair about it. I think whites are basically antiblack. . . . But the difference is: It is recognized as morally reprehensible. . . ."

KOCH: You got the quote a little screwed up.

PLAYBOY: It appeared verbatim in *The New Yorker.*

KOCH: It's not exactly that way. When I said, "Let's be fair about it, whites are . . ." I meant that the same kind of discriminatory practices exist on both sides. The quote was from a tape made in 1974 or 1975. It was uneditd, and it didn't express my complete thought. Had I been given the opportunity, I would have expanded upon it.

PLAYBOY: Fine. Why not take the opportunity now?

KOCH: There are two thoughts there that need clarification. One is, it wasn't a symmetrical statement. I said that blacks are basically anti-Semitic. If I were to define it, I was talking principally about black leaders, those I know. Obviously, I don't know the whole black community. Substantively, I *still* believe that there are lots of blacks in leadership positions who are anti-Semitic. I don't withdraw the comment at all.

But I also want it understood *why* I think the leaders are anti-Semitic. They're frustrated with their own unsuccessful efforts to alleviate the conditions of poverty and black suffering. It's nice to have a scapegoat. And traditionally, Jews have always been the scapegoats of Western society. It may also be simple envy. They say, "Well, the Jews came up through the system; why is it that they've been able to escape poverty in such large numbers?"

PLAYBOY: Do you think, then, that Jews ought to feel a *special* obligation toward blacks? That because of their own experience of oppression, they ought to be better, more sacrificing, than gentiles?

KOCH: I have no guilt complex. My father didn't own slaves. He came here from Poland when he was fifteen, so I am not guilty of that, nor do I believe I have to pay reparations for it. I spent time in 1964 defending blacks against the KKK in Missis-

sippi. I may *still* have an obligation today, yes, but no more than I do to the Chinese or to any other group being discriminated against.
PLAYBOY: That's what's intriguing about you—all that time spent on liberal causes during the Sixties, a period you now denounce as excessive. Besides civil rights, you also opposed the Vietnam War, didn't you?
KOCH: Yes, by voting against military-appropriation bills in Congress. And by demonstrating. I marched, both in Washington and here in the city. But it wasn't as simple as it may seem. On one occasion, there was a Communist-operated anti-Vietnam War creation, the Fifth Avenue Parade Committee—
PLAYBOY: "Communist?"
KOCH: I don't want to say they were all Communists; I don't want this to sound like Koch's fear of the Communists. [Laughs] But in my judgment, the major movement at that time *was* Communist-dominated—
PLAYBOY: You're talking about leadership? Funding from Moscow?
KOCH: No, I'm not talking about spies and I have no idea how they were funded. I'm talking about ideological alliances with Moscow, about people who perceived North Vietnam as an idealistic country and South Vietnam as fascist. Myself, I believed that North and South Vietnam were both dictatorships, one by the left, the other by the right, and that they deserved each other. At the time, though, there were lots of people who idealized North Vietnam.
PLAYBOY: Jane Fonda, for example?
KOCH: I don't want to call Jane Fonda a Communist because I don't know that she is. But she was certainly far left and idealized North Vietnam. Cora Weiss, too. With their recordings from Hanoi—despicable! My feelings came to a head at a meeting at Hunter College. Bella Abzug had called in all of the seventeen members of the New York City Congressional delegation. There was a huge crowd, a lot of red flags and Hanoi partisans, and she asked us to lend our names to sponsor this Fifth Avenue Parade Committee. Almost everybody said, yes, they were going to sign up [laughs], but I refused. They began to yell and scream at me. I said, "Listen, I will walk with Communists and Black Panthers, but I will never let them lead me." Then you know what happened? The crowd began yelling, screaming that I was another Joe McCarthy.
PLAYBOY: Where was Abzug in relation to all of this?
KOCH: I don't remember precisely what she said when I refused, but she certainly concurred with the majority.
PLAYBOY: Is that when you called her "a savage"?
KOCH: I don't remember saying that, but I wouldn't retract it if I did. It's not a word I'd normally apply to her, but it's OK.
PLAYBOY: How would you describe her today?
KOCH: Bigmouth. [Laughs] I found her to be very pushy, counterproductive in a whole list of areas. I hold her responsible for ERA's defeat in New York state. People forget that the Equal Rights Amendment *lost* in New York. I was for ERA—I still am—but Bella was perceived as *the* ERA spokeswoman and was so strident and aggressive that her attitudes frightened people.
PLAYBOY: A further irony that's tied into your feelings about the excesses and license of the Sixties is the often-repeated comment that many of the radicals came from spoiled, upper-middle-class families.
KOCH: Sure, I know some of them; the kids went to the best schools and ultimately decided that what they wanted to do was destroy society. I don't know what happened

to the kids' brains, whether it's a screw loose or a question of education. In a way, it's like what my mother used to tell my brother: "You should have a kid like you. God will punish you!" [Laughs] What can I say? As children, they heard all about the injustices and the need for revolution, how wonderful the Soviet Union is, how U.S. society is fascist, and—unknowingly in many cases, I'm sure—the children become so enraged that they did things that today horrify their parents.

PLAYBOY: What's come across surprisingly strongly in this interview is an abiding suspicion of the Soviets and of Communism. Just how deep does this run? Are the Russians out to bury us, as the saying goes?

KOCH: Ultimately, yes, if by bury you mean take over. I think their goal is to make the Soviet Union the center around which all other countries orbit as satellites, including the United States and the countries of Western Europe. There are people in the United States who could be called their counterparts, of course, but fortunately, they don't represent the vast majority of the leadership or of the voting public.

PLAYBOY: You don't see elements of this analogous attitude—call it a Cold War mentality—in the present Republican push for a big defense budget?

KOCH: I've always believed we should be ahead of the Soviet Union in our ability to defend ourselves. I was one of the few "liberals" in Congress who voted for defense-spending bills when others from New York City did not. That distinguished me. But I'm disturbed by Reagan's defense budget as well. The administration's current analysis assumes that only the social programs are filled with fraud and waste, while military spending has been honest and necessary. I'm not so sure about that. The same acid test has to be applied to both, because both have been filled with sloth, waste and inefficiency.

PLAYBOY: It's been said that the mayor of New York City has to have a fully formulated foreign policy. Do you ever envy any of your fellow mayors who don't have to articulate such positions?

KOCH: No, I enjoy it, frankly. New York is special that way. We have more Puerto Ricans than in San Juan, more blacks than in Nairobi, more Italians than in Naples and, as we said before, more Jews than in Tel Aviv. . . . Shall we stop for lunch?

[Over lunch, at Koch's suggestion, a network TV show featuring an extremely friendly interview with Koch was turned on.]

PLAYBOY: We're suspending one interview to watch another. Why are we watching it now? Why not tape it and replay the program for yourself later?

KOCH: First of all, I won't get home till late. And second, we're having lunch.

[The TV commentator makes some favorable remarks about Koch's policies.]

This is tremendous! [Referring to the show]

PLAYBOY: [As the program ends] OK? We're back on. Would you test the mike?

KOCH: This is Ed Koch with his lox and bagels!

PLAYBOY: Fine. It was unusual, watching you watch yourself on television. The frequent comment that Ed Koch is a little narcissistic—

KOCH: Sure I am, a little bit. Not overmuch. I was thinking about that when we put the set on—I was sure you were thinking, Gee, he wanted to watch himself while we were here. The answer to that is, it's not true. Yesterday, when we taped over lunch, you ate; I didn't. I decided that wasn't going to happen again. Second, time is a very precious commodity to me and I wanted to see that show. But, yes, I do watch interviews of myself. I think it's helpful to learn how I'm coming across, especially since you can rarely fool the tube. What you see is generally more accurate than when you're with the person face to face.

PLAYBOY: We've talked to some people active in New York politics, and one of the more common theories of Ed Koch is that the mayoralty has transformed him from a shy, wallflowerish politician—

KOCH: Shy, absolutely. A totally retiring personality! [Laughs]

PLAYBOY: With all the media attention, isn't there a part of you that says, "Me? How did I do it, how did I get here?"

KOCH: I *am* a retiring person. But at the same time, I'm able to do quite well in public, and this isn't phony. What you see is what you get.

PLAYBOY: One of your oldest political associates claims that if power corrupts, your only corruption is that as mayor, you've become vastly animated as a personality. Really, aren't you getting off on the show business of all of this?

KOCH: Oh, sure, I enjoy the attention. Sometimes what I do will be faulted, but I know I present New York City's case in the best light and, yes, I enjoy it. As for my personality's changing, that's inaccurate. I'm no different from when I was a congressman, just more proficient.

PLAYBOY: The same *chutzpah?* You're claiming you were always "Eddie the Lip," as one of the New York dailies recently put it?

KOCH: Yes, sir. The difference is that before, you weren't listening. It's all in the eye of the beholder.

PLAYBOY: Do you think you've changed the way you look?

KOCH: No. I dress the same way, although it's strange that people think I dress better. I buy the same Brooks Brothers suits—on sale—as I did in 1952.

PLAYBOY: That far back? Why Brooks Brothers?

KOCH: Oh, it was part of my feeling that three-button suits were the thing to wear. [Laughs] I'm a very conservative person in my likes and dislikes. I don't go to fancy restaurants, either.

PLAYBOY: No? Supposedly, your great passion in life, aside from politics, is food.

KOCH: Vastly overstated.

PLAYBOY: We've heard otherwise. What is this, your fourth cook this year? How is he working out?

KOCH: Fine. Altogether, there were five cooks in four years. [Arches his eyebrows] Doesn't *everybody* have five cooks in four years?

PLAYBOY: Don't you go out to New York's great restaurants? Lutèce, for instance?

KOCH: Are you kidding? Once, I went to Lutèce and I was very upset. I almost always pay for my own meals, but that time I was invited. I had a wonderful-sounding dish and it turned out to be Swedish meatballs. I said to myself, "Jesus Christ, I come to Lutèce, I end up with Swedish meatballs?" It's a very good restaurant, but it's too expensive for me. I can give you six restaurants where for fifteen dollars or less, you can get what I consider an excellent meal.

PLAYBOY: In keeping with the same motif—you as everyman—you've also ridden the subway, so you know what the problems are, right?

KOCH: Of course, any number of times.

PLAYBOY: And your mission is to present New York City's case in the best light. Now, how can you possibly find a positive way of talking about the subway when it's so symbolic of the city's problems—its dirt, inefficiency and crime? Be creative, convince us it really isn't the nightmare everyone thinks it is.

KOCH: You tell me whether or not we have a problem. On that TV show we just watched, I gave the figure of 350 felonies a week committed on the subway system, a subway system that carries three and a half million people daily. It's fractional, but people are afraid, granted. So you have to deal with that and put on more cops—ten percent of our total police force is assigned to the subway system, while only two percent of the city's crimes are committed there.

PLAYBOY: That's going to make the subway better?

KOCH: Look, it's improving on a week-to-week basis now, but the truly large difference will occur when the new subway cars come on the line. The major complaint about the subway is the long delays due to mechanical breakdowns. Better maintenance is one answer—getting the Municipal Transit Authority people to work more than the three or four hours a day they do in some shops now. [Laughs] So either we'll get them to work the full day—which is only six and three-quarters hours to begin with—or we'll contract out our maintenance. Up to now, I've been getting plenty of courtesy but little action.

PLAYBOY: And graffiti? Wasn't it fashionable some time back to talk about subway graffiti as an indigenous art form?

KOCH: Bullshit. Bullshit twice! Part of the problem started in 1966 with *The New York Times* piece, but they now recognize how much they were in error. One of the things I'm proudest of, though, was getting the transit authority to put up a fence around one of the subway yards to do something about graffiti. Initially, I urged the MTA to build a fence around the subway yard and put a dog in the yard to keep these vandals out. The response was, "No, the dog would step on the third rail." I said. "That's ridiculous; dogs don't step on the third rail. Why is it that vandals don't step on the third rail? But if you're so upset about a dog's stepping on the third rail, then build two fences and have the dog run between them." The head of the MTA replied, "But somebody might fall between the two fences and the dog might bite them." "I thought that's what dogs were for," I said, "but if you're worried, why not put a wolf in?" Because, I explained, there is no recorded incident of a wolf's ever having attacked a human being, except if the wolf was rabid. Wolves have had a bad rep through history, see. Then a *New York Times* reporter told me I was only partially right. He'd gone to the zoological library—something that the city of New York undoubtedly pays for—and found that while no wild wolf has ever bitten a human unless it was rabid, there are cases of domesticated wolves' having attacked people. So right away, I said that of course I'd meant wild wolves—you put a wild wolf between those two fences, and if the wolf becomes tame, you replace him. Now, I told that ridiculous story all around town in order to shame the MTA into getting something done. They were livid. It so happens that the head of the MTA has a lot of friends in high places, on editorial boards and the like, and naturally, it got back to him. It was the only way I could get them to do anything. So now they've built fences around the yard and put in a dog, and it works.

PLAYBOY: But the subways are still covered with graffiti.

KOCH: They've done it with only one yard out of the twenty-one yards in the city! At the end of each month, they used to pick up three thousand empty spray cans out there. After they put up the fence, there were only five! That's gotta tell you something.

PLAYBOY: What? That you can bring some pressure publicly? Using the press or anything else that comes to hand?

KOCH: Yeah, like ridicule. The wolf story. But what I really want is the power to hire and fire the president of the transit authority, John Simpson. Not that I would fire him right off, but it would change the relationship so that he would relate to me as a commissioner, not as an independent authority.

PLAYBOY: Is it possible that you're not talking about this at a great-enough remove? That you really don't see what we're driving at? For most people who don't live in New York, the whole transit problem is a staple for Johnny Carson jokes, jokes that hit home, but only your home, not Atlanta or any other city. Why? Why is New York's transit system such a shambles of inefficiency?

KOCH: How would these people like to live in Boston, where the subway closed down from lack of funding? We've *never* closed our subway. But people publicize our problems more because New York is the place of major interest. I'm not saying we don't have problems; only that compared with the delivery of services elsewhere, we don't do too badly.

PLAYBOY: The other form of urban blight we touched on earlier was crime. What changes do you think we need to make a dent in that problem?

KOCH: What we need is to make the protection of society itself more paramount in those areas where protection has traditionally been for the defendant.

PLAYBOY: Like what, specifically?

KOCH: Restoring the death penalty, as I've said. I've always been in favor of it because I think it works as a deterrent. Even if it did not, however, society should express its moral outrage at horrendous crimes. Also, with crimes of violence, we should impose mandatory sentences. The best illustration is New York's new gun-control law. Prior to this, very few people who were apprehended and convicted for illegal possession of guns ever went to jail. As a result of the campaign that I initiated and that had enormous support in the newspapers, more than seventy percent of the people convicted of gun violations now go to jail for a mandatory minimum sentence of one year.

PLAYBOY: Mandatory is mandatory, right? Why do thirty percent get off? There are still two million illegal handguns in New York.

KOCH: Notwithstanding my opposition, the law has a loophole. If a judge finds extenuating circumstances, he or she can, at his or her discretion, dismiss the charge or, in the interest of justice, reduce the sentence.

PLAYBOY: Capital punishment, mandatory sentencing, what else?

KOCH: I want to release the names of juvenile or adolescent felons. The law prohibits it now, but I think society should have a sense of public disdain. People should have to live with their criminal past. Records of juvenile offenders that are sealed should be made available to the courts so if someone's on trial as an adult, his earlier record should bear upon sentencing.

Look, crime *is* getting worse in New York City as well as in the rest of the country, and unless we deal with it far more strictly, the trend is going to continue—no question. The solutions are age-old: speedy trials, pretrial detention, more cops and stricter sentencing. There's also another route, and I hope this won't be characterized as "Koch's concentration camps": There's no reason to build massive prison complexes costing a hundred thousand dollars per cell. You can set up compounds in our state forest or national parks, prisons with tents and barbed wire and dogs, if necessary. Whatever it takes—

PLAYBOY: Wolves?
KOCH: Wolves, sure. Not to torture people but to separate them from society to keep them from committing more crimes. I'm all for that; I'm for it on a *large* scale. The greatest impact on a person who snatches a necklace or who writes graffiti on a subway car or on public buildings is to be put away and be put away abruptly, even if the sentence itself is minor or brief.
PLAYBOY: Speaking of criminals who don't get put away, do you find any irony in the fact that Little Italy, New York's traditional Mafia neighborhood—
KOCH: Is safe? [Laughs]
PLAYBOY: Yes.
KOCH: I don't think it has so much to do with the Mafia as with the fact that people will run out into the street to help if there's trouble. The same thing can be found in the Hasidic areas, like Williamsburg and Borough Park. It's like they're small-town; everyone knows their neighbors.
PLAYBOY: And the Mafia in New York City?
KOCH: Yes, Virginia, there *is* a Mafia. And it is engaged, so I understand, in drugs, gambling, prostitution, extortion as it relates to linens and also, I guess, pickles. [Laughs]
PLAYBOY: You mentioned prostitution. You're also famous for "the john hour": airing on local radio the names of those arrested for soliciting prostitutes. Why not just make prostitution legal and let cops do more important work elsewhere?
KOCH: I don't think the public wants a city like Amsterdam, where you have women with whips in shopwindows. [Laughs] Moreover, it doesn't work. They tried it in France and dropped it. In Boston, the so-called Combat Zone, it didn't work, either. It's the same response I have to legalizing heroin. The public doesn't want it, I don't want it.
PLAYBOY: What's the answer, then? Just hiring more cops?
KOCH: Frankly, I don't think that would necessarily solve our problem, because [laughs] thirty-two thousand people were arrested for felonies in 1980 just in the borough of Manhattan. Out of this thirty-two thousand only six thousand were indicted! There's more than just simple apprehension of the criminal. The system is made up of the cops, the DA's office, the courts, the probation service, and the prisons. They all have problems. We could use more cops and we've added to the number of cops, but it's quite expensive.
PLAYBOY: One of the most common pressures applied to a politician is the lure of easy money. But a theme you've underscored in this interview is the honesty of this administration. *Is* it possible—is it conceivable—that some scandal could erupt?
KOCH: It's simply not possible that five years from now, someone is going to find that this administration was crooked. It isn't. I can't say there aren't any crooks in the city government, since with 250,000 people working for us, both in city and in state jobs, there've gotta be *some* crooks. But I do not tolerate it. If I find out you're a crook, I won't move you out without anybody knowing about it because it might be an embarrassment. No, I'll call the DA personally and say, "*Get* this guy!"
PLAYBOY: That sounds like a real hard-ass style. On the other hand, you're quoted as saying, "I run the city like a large Jewish family." What does that mean, that you're everybody's mother?
KOCH: I didn't say it, Bob Wagner said it. I suppose he means that I delegate authority and listen to their opinions. Few other administrations have allowed commissioners to do what they want to do within the boundaries of policy as set by the mayor.

Wherever possible, I like to come to a decision on a consensus basis. But I don't wait for a consensus. I discuss the matter with all the people involved. I hear them out. I see if there's a common thread. When the positions have been unanimous or near-unanimous, I can't recall ever saying, "Well, I'm opposed." More likely than not, however, there isn't consensus, and then I'll say, "This is what we're going to do. This is the policy." The Jewish-family aspect of it is that during meetings, you can say anything you want, be as tough or as critical as you feel you have to be. You can take different positions, as though it were a family sitting down at dinner.

PLAYBOY: Once again, the hell with decorum?

KOCH: Of course. Only, when I've made a decision, then you gotta go and carry it out. In private with me, you can continue to try to persuade me that I've made a mistake, but you cannot shoot my policies down in public.

PLAYBOY: For many politicians, it would be a liability to grant an interview, especially an interview as extensive as this one, unless the risks were worth it. If you're not campaigning for reelection, why are you doing this? Why bother?

KOCH: I don't want to be ridiculously modest, but when people talk about New York City, they talk about me. Ergo, I believe I help the city by being up front and visible. But there are other aspects of it. I enjoy the jousting. I like the battle of wits.

PLAYBOY: The confrontation?

KOCH: The intellectual discussion. *You* call it confrontation. But it has nothing to do with furthering my political ambitions. I know, I've heard the rumors about myself: that I might run for New York state governor; that or as the Democratic Vice-Presidential nominee in 1984. But anyone who suggests I run for governor is no friend of mine. [Laughs] It's a terrible position, and besides, it requires living in Albany, which is small-town life at its worst. I wouldn't even consider it. As for the Vice-Presidency, well, everybody says that next to the President, I have the most exciting job in the country. Not to denigrate senators or anyone else, I think they're right. My job might even be better than the President's.

PLAYBOY: You're grinning again.

KOCH: [Laughs] I know. My job *is* better than the President's. I don't want to say that New York's mayor is as powerful as the President, but in terms of direct involvement in the daily lives of people, I may have more impact. I have lots of authority and I think I use it.

PLAYBOY: While you're still grinning, are you entirely ruling out, say, a Mondale-Koch draft in 1984?

KOCH: It will not happen. There *are* no drafts in this country. Take my word for it, you're a candidate or you're not. I'm *not* a candidate.

PLAYBOY: Not even if people whose judgment you respect were to say, "Ed, think beyond yourself. It's important for the country?" So?

KOCH: The answer is, I'm not a candidate, *so*. It has nothing to do with shyness, coyness or reticence. Either I will run for reelection for a third term or I will go into the private sector. I used to say that at the age of sixty-five I'd ask for a position on the editorial board of *The New York Times*. [Laughs] I happen to have a great sense of inner security about my abilities, so I don't have to be jollied up or stroked about how effective I am. I know it. I also know that there are a myriad of people out there just as able and effective as I am. But right now, I'm not worried about reelection.

PLAYBOY: All right. As we wind up, we'd like to try, one last time, to challenge this cheery assessment of life in the city, to get you to admit that dirt and crime can take their toll—

KOCH: Look, I've said that crime is escalating everywhere, and we're getting our share of the escalation in New York. But if you live here and are affected by crime, what are your options? Escape? Escape to where? You can't escape. Crime follows you to the suburbs, because, unquestionably, suburban crime is rising faster than our own. It's ridiculous to talk about fleeing to the suburbs as a refuge.

PLAYBOY: America is more than big cities and overcrowded suburbs. For many, there's still a more pastoral existence—life in the country.

KOCH: The country? Rural America? This is a joke! [Laughs]

PLAYBOY: Come on, Ed. Of course it exists, and there are lots of people who've become fed up with city life—college-educated people who have taken pay cuts to live better lives out in the country.

KOCH: It may be that there are hordes of people who've moved to rural America, but I'm not aware of them. Also, this is an elitist approach, and I don't include too many elitists among my friends.

PLAYBOY: Then at least respond to the *urge* many people have to get away from urban life—

KOCH: What do you want me to say?

PLAYBOY: Just that you can't keep applying this relentless logic of yours to the reality that many people are scared shitless of living in New York City.

KOCH: You're raising a red herring.

PLAYBOY: A red herring? By trying to get you off your hobbyhorse?

KOCH: By showing the infirmities of New York City.

PLAYBOY: Not the infirmities. By acknowledging that New York City has *enormous* problems—real ones, not illusions. If you admit to the problems, then it becomes more credible when you speak of New York's advantages.

KOCH: Correct. But let's leave out rural America, with the cows.

PLAYBOY: Cows? God, Ed Koch really *is* a snob!

KOCH: Well, choosing between living with people and living with animals. . . . [Laughs] But look, there's no question: Living in New York City means paying a price, obviously. There's a lack of privacy. The crowds; the hugeness of the city. There's also the anonymity, because nobody gives a damn—but this can be nice in a way, since it means you can lead your own life; nobody interferes. You also pay a price in the environment: air pollution. The cost of living is generally higher—but so are the salaries, and there are always sales where you can shop cheaply if you take the time.

PLAYBOY: What about the loss of time because of lousy city services, late subways?

KOCH: As opposed to wasting time in a car? Or out in the country, wasting time in a pickup truck? [Laughs] When you have to drive twenty miles to buy a gingham dress or [laughs louder] a Sears Roebuck suit? [Cracks up] This rural-America thing—I'm telling you, it's a joke.

PLAYBOY: But the fact that people are moving to the Sun Belt is no joke.

KOCH: I don't deny the phenomenon of the Sun Belt, but that operates on fantasy, too. People are told that there's no unemployment in Houston, and there probably isn't—but that's because the federal government has discriminated against the Northeast and the older cities. But moving to the Sun Belt isn't the answer. It's a fad. Ultimately, a lot of people will be coming back. Despite our transportation problem, despite our crime, they *are* coming back. Obviously, many people prefer New York's more hurried pace. And nothing prevents you from slowing down by relaxing in a theater or strolling in the park. We happen to have *great* parks, and the truth of the matter is that the safest police precinct in New York City happens to be Central Park.

PLAYBOY: Because people don't go to Central Park! At least not at night.

KOCH: That's not entirely true—

PLAYBOY: No? Then shall we take a stroll together this evening? Let's cross Central Park, from east to west, just after dusk, OK?

KOCH: Not me! [Laughs] That's just tempting fate. Nothing would happen, but that's just tempting fate!

PLAYBOY: OK, one last question—and it's the one you always ask: How're you doin', Ed?

KOCH: During the last campaign, I used to say to voters, "It may be that as a result of everything I've done, a lot of you will get together and throw me out. That's OK. I'll get a better job, but you won't get a better mayor." Now, what I was honestly trying to convey was that I'd like to be recalled as one of the great mayors of the city of New York, and I'm going to do everything to accomplish that. Not the greatest mayor, mind you, but as one of the great mayors. I know that life is ephemeral, particularly in politics. Nothing you do will last forever; it just doesn't work that way. But what I want to do is put things into place that will last for a long time before they go back the old way. And that, I think I've done.